HOW TO 2000

How To 2000

Raytheon E-Systems

IDG BOOKS WORLDWIDE™

IDG Books Worldwide, Inc.
An International Data Group Company
Foster City, CA • Chicago, IL • Indianapolis, IN • Southlake, TX

How To 2000 ™
Published by
IDG Books Worldwide, Inc.
An International Data Group Company
919 E. Hillsdale Blvd., Suite 400
Foster City, CA 94404
www.idgbooks.com (IDG Books Worldwide Web site)

Library of Congress Catalog Card No.: 97-74336

ISBN: 0-7645-3101-8

Printed in the United States of America

10 9 8 7 6 5 4 3 2 1

1DD/QR/RS/ZX/FC

Distributed in the United States by IDG Books Worldwide, Inc.

Distributed by Macmillan Canada for Canada; by Transworld Publishers Limited in the United Kingdom; by IDG Norge Books for Norway; by IDG Sweden Books for Sweden; by Woodslane Pty. Ltd. for Australia; by Woodslane Enterprises Ltd. for New Zealand; by Longman Singapore Publishers Ltd. for Singapore, Malaysia, Thailand and Indonesia; by Simron Pty. Ltd. for South Africa; by Toppan Company Ltd. for Japan; by Distribuidora Cuspide for Argentina; by Livraria Cultura for Brazil; by Ediciencia S.A. for Ecuador; by Addison-Wesley Publishing Company for Korea; by Ediciones ZETA S.C.R. Ltda. for Peru; by WS Computer Publishing Corporation, Inc for the Philippines; by Unalis Corporation for Taiwan; by Contemporanea de Ediciones for Venezuela; by Computer Book & Magazine Store for Puerto Rico; by Express Computer Distributors for the Caribbean and West Indies. Authorized Sales Agent: Anthony Rudkin Associates for the Middle East and North Africa.

For general information on IDG Books Worldwide's books in the U.S., please call our Consumer Customer Service department at 800-762-2974. For reseller information, including discounts and premium sales, please call our Reseller Customer Service department at 800-434-3422.

For information on where to purchase IDG Books Worldwide's books outside the U.S., please contact our International Sales department at 415-655-3200 or fax 415-655-3295.

For information on foreign language translations, please contact our Foreign & Subsidiary Rights department at 415-655-3021 or fax 415-655-3281.

For sales inquiries and special prices for bulk quantities, please contact our Sales department at 415-655-3200 or write to the address above.

For information on using IDG Books Worldwide's books in the classroom or for ordering examination copies, please contact our Educational Sales department at 800-434-2086 or fax 817-251-8174.

For press review copies, author interviews, or other publicity information, please contact our Public Relations department at 415-655-3000 or fax 415-655-329

For authorization to photocopy items for corporate, personal, or educational use, please contact Copyright Clearance Center, 222 Rosewood Drive, Danvers, MA 01923, or fax 508-750-4470.

ABOUT IDG BOOKS WORLDWIDE

Welcome to the world of IDG Books Worldwide.

IDG Books Worldwide, Inc., is a subsidiary of International Data Group, the world's largest publisher of computer-related information and the leading global provider of information services on information technology. IDG was founded more than 25 years ago and now employs more than 8,500 people worldwide. IDG publishes more than 275 computer publications in over 75 countries (see listing below). More than 60 million people read one or more IDG publications each month.

Launched in 1990, IDG Books Worldwide is today the #1 publisher of best-selling computer books in the United States. We are proud to have received eight awards from the Computer Press Association in recognition of editorial excellence and three from *Computer Currents'* First Annual Readers' Choice Awards. Our best-selling *...For Dummies®* series has more than 30 million copies in print with translations in 30 languages. IDG Books Worldwide, through a joint venture with IDG's Hi-Tech Beijing, became the first U.S. publisher to publish a computer book in the People's Republic of China. In record time, IDG Books Worldwide has become the first choice for millions of readers around the world who want to learn how to better manage their businesses.

Our mission is simple: Every one of our books is designed to bring extra value and skill-building instructions to the reader. Our books are written by experts who understand and care about our readers. The knowledge base of our editorial staff comes from years of experience in publishing, education, and journalism — experience we use to produce books for the '90s. In short, we care about books, so we attract the best people. We devote special attention to details such as audience, interior design, use of icons, and illustrations. And because we use an efficient process of authoring, editing, and desktop publishing our books electronically, we can spend more time ensuring superior content and spend less time on the technicalities of making books.

You can count on our commitment to deliver high-quality books at competitive prices on topics you want to read about. At IDG Books Worldwide, we continue in the IDG tradition of delivering quality for more than 25 years. You'll find no better book on a subject than one from IDG Books Worldwide.

John Kilcullen
CEO
IDG Books Worldwide, Inc.

Steven Berkowitz
President and Publisher
IDG Books Worldwide, Inc.

Eighth Annual Computer Press Awards 1992

Ninth Annual Computer Press Awards 1993

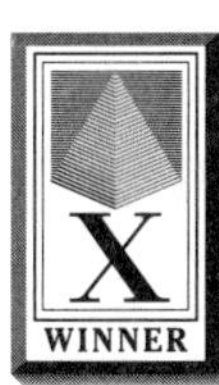

Tenth Annual Computer Press Awards 1994

Eleventh Annual Computer Press Awards 1995

IDG Books Worldwide, Inc., is a subsidiary of International Data Group, the world's largest publisher of computer-related information and the leading global provider of information services on information technology. International Data Group publishes over 275 computer publications in over 75 countries. Sixty million people read one or more International Data Group publications each month. International Data Group's publications include: **ARGENTINA:** Buyer's Guide, Computerworld Argentina, PC World Argentina; **AUSTRALIA:** Australian Macworld, Australian PC World, Australian Reseller News, Computerworld, IT Casebook, Network World, Publish, Webmaster; **AUSTRIA:** Computerwelt Osterreich, Networks Austria, PC Tip Austria; **BANGLADESH:** PC World Bangladesh; **BELARUS:** PC World Belarus; **BELGIUM:** Data News; **BRAZIL:** Annuário de Informática, Computerworld, Connections, Macworld, PC Player, PC World, Publish, Reseller News, Supergamepower; **BULGARIA:** Computerworld Bulgaria, Network World Bulgaria, PC & MacWorld Bulgaria; **CANADA:** CIO Canada, Client/Server World, ComputerWorld Canada, InfoWorld Canada, NetworkWorld Canada, WebWorld; **CHILE:** Computerworld Chile, PC World Chile; **COLOMBIA:** Computerworld Colombia, PC World Colombia; **COSTA RICA:** PC World Centro America; **THE CZECH AND SLOVAK REPUBLICS:** Computerworld Czechoslovakia, Macworld Czech Republic, PC World Czechoslovakia; **DENMARK:** Communications World Danmark, Computerworld Danmark, Macworld Danmark, PC World Danmark, Techworld Denmark; **DOMINICAN REPUBLIC:** PC World Republica Dominicana; **ECUADOR:** PC World Ecuador; **EGYPT:** Computerworld Middle East, PC World Middle East; **EL SALVADOR:** PC World Centro America; **FINLAND:** MikroPC, Tietoverkko, Tietoviikko; **FRANCE:** Distributique, Hebdo, Info PC, Le Monde Informatique, Macworld, Reseaux & Telecoms, WebMaster France; **GERMANY:** Computer Partner, Computerwoche, Computerwoche Extra, Computerwoche FOCUS, Global Online, Macwelt, PC Welt; **GREECE:** Amiga Computing, GamePro Greece, Multimedia World; **GUATEMALA:** PC World Centro America; **HONDURAS:** PC World Centro America; **HONG KONG:** Computerworld Hong Kong, PC World Hong Kong, Publish in Asia; **HUNGARY:** ABCD CD-ROM, Computerworld Szamitastechnika, Internetto online Magazine, PC World Hungary, PC-X Magazin Hungary; **ICELAND:** Tolvuheimur PC World Island; **INDIA:** Information Communications World, Information Systems Computerworld, PC World India, Publish in Asia; **INDONESIA:** InfoKomputer PC World, Komputek Computerworld, Publish in Asia; **IRELAND:** ComputerScope, PC Live!; **ISRAEL:** Macworld Israel, People & Computers/Computerworld; **ITALY:** Computerworld Italia, Macworld Italia, Networking Italia, PC World Italia; **JAPAN:** DTP World, Macworld Japan, Nikkei Personal Computing, OS/2 World Japan, SunWorld Japan, Windows NT World, Windows World Japan; **KENYA:** PC World East African; **KOREA:** Hi-Tech Information, Macworld Korea, PC World Korea; **MACEDONIA:** PC World Macedonia; **MALAYSIA:** Computerworld Malaysia, PC World Malaysia, Publish in Asia; **MALTA:** PC World Malta; **MEXICO:** Computerworld Mexico, PC World Mexico; **MYANMAR:** PC World Myanmar; **NETHERLANDS:** Computer! Totaal, LAN Internetworking Magazine, LAN World Buyers Guide, Macworld Netherlands, Net, WebWereld; **NEW ZEALAND:** Absolute Beginners Guide and Plain & Simple Series, Computer Buyer, Computer Industry Directory, Computerworld New Zealand, MTB, Network World, PC World New Zealand; **NICARAGUA:** PC World Centro America; **NORWAY:** Computerworld Norge, CW Rapport, Datamagasinet, Financial Rapport, Kursguide Norge, Macworld Norge, Multimediaworld Norge, PC World Ekspress Norge, PC World Nettverk, PC World Norge, PC World ProduktGuide Norge; **PAKISTAN:** Computerworld Pakistan; **PANAMA:** PC World Panama; **PEOPLE'S REPUBLIC OF CHINA:** China Computer Users, China Computerworld, China InfoWorld, China Telecom World Weekly, Computer & Communication, Electronic Design China, Electronics Today, Electronics Weekly, Game Software, PC World China, Popular Computer Week, Software Weekly, Software World, Telecom World; **PERU:** Computerworld Peru, PC World Profesional Peru, PC World SoHo Peru; **PHILIPPINES:** Click!, Computerworld Philippines, PC World Philippines, Publish in Asia; **POLAND:** Computerworld Poland, Computerworld Special Report Poland, Cyber, Macworld Poland, Networld Poland, PC World Komputer; **PORTUGAL:** Cerebro/PC World, Computerworld/Correio Informático, Dealer World Portugal, Mac*In/PC*In Portugal, Multimedia World; **PUERTO RICO:** PC World Puerto Rico; **ROMANIA:** Computerworld Romania, PC World Romania, Telecom Romania; **RUSSIA:** Computerworld Russia, Mir PK, Publish, Seti; **SINGAPORE:** Computerworld Singapore, PC World Singapore, Publish in Asia; **SLOVENIA:** Monitor; **SOUTH AFRICA:** Computing SA, Network World SA, Software World SA; **SPAIN:** Communicaciones World España, Computerworld España, Dealer World España, Macworld España, PC World España; **SRI LANKA:** Infolink PC World; **SWEDEN:** CAP&Design, Computer Sweden, Corporate Computing Sweden, Internetworld Sweden, it.branschen, Macworld Sweden, MaxiData Sweden, MikroDatorn, Nätverk & Kommunikation, PC World Sweden, PCaktiv, Windows World Sweden; **SWITZERLAND:** Computerworld Schweiz, Macworld Schweiz, PCtip; **TAIWAN:** Computerworld Taiwan, Macworld Taiwan, NEW ViSiON/Publish, PC World Taiwan, Windows World Taiwan; **THAILAND:** Publish in Asia, Thai Computerworld; **TURKEY:** Computerworld Turkiye, Macworld Turkiye, Network World Turkiye, PC World Turkiye; **UKRAINE:** Computerworld Kiev, Multimedia World Ukraine, PC World Ukraine; **UNITED KINGDOM:** Acorn User UK, Amiga Action UK, Amiga Computing UK, Apple Talk UK, Computing, Macworld, Parents and Computers UK, PC Advisor, PC Home, PSX Pro, The WEB; **UNITED STATES:** Cable in the Classroom, CIO Magazine, Computerworld, DOS World, Federal Computer Week, GamePro Magazine, InfoWorld, I-Way, Macworld, Network World, PC Games, PC World, Publish, Video Event, THE WEB Magazine, and WebMaster; online webzines: JavaWorld, NetscapeWorld, and SunWorld Online; **URUGUAY:** InfoWorld Uruguay; **VENEZUELA:** Computerworld Venezuela, PC World Venezuela; and **VIETNAM:** PC World Vietnam. 3/24/97

CREDITS

ACQUISITIONS EDITOR
Michael Roney

DEVELOPMENT EDITORS
Deborah Craig
Kenyon Brown

TECHNICAL EDITOR
Michael Collis

COPY EDITORS
Deborah Craig
Ami Knox

PRODUCTION COORDINATOR
Susan Parini

BOOK DESIGNER
Kurt Krames

GRAPHICS AND PRODUCTION SPECIALIST
Ed Penslien

QUALITY CONTROL SPECIALIST
Mark Schumann

ILLUSTRATOR
Greg Maxson

PROOFREADER
Mary C. Barnack

INDEXER
Sherry Massey

About the Authors

Dean Sims is Raytheon's Senior Program Manager of Year 2000 Services, author, and the development manager of the How To 2000 process. He based his contributions to this work on 15 years of experience supporting enterprise-level system conversions and large scale implementations. Dean's broad technical and business background began as systems engineer developing systems in assembler, COBOL, and later 4th GLs for EDS. He managed systems implementations on IBM, HP, Unisys, and distributed PC platforms for banks, credit unions, savings and loans, and an international conversion for Budget Rent-A-Car. Dean's work at Raytheon includes service to the U.S. Departments of Education, Defense, and Transportation. He was the driving force to have *How To 2000* adopted as a Raytheon standard. Dean holds a B.B.A. and B.A. from Baylor University and been blissfully married for 15 years. He spends his free time serving his church, his wife Elizabeth, and two favorite children Jacob and Sarah. Dean's approach to life is founded on Phil 4:13, "omnia possum in eo qui me confortat."

Jeanne Minahan Robinson is a principle software engineer with Raytheon E-Systems and an assistant professor of systems engineering with George Mason University. Her primary field of interest is software requirements engineering, although she also pursues research in the areas of software metrics and software cost estimation. Growing up as an Army brat throughout the United States, Dr. Robinson graduated from the University of Notre Dame with a B.A. in Liberal Arts in 1977. She attained an M.S. in Information Systems in 1992, and a Ph.D. in Information Technology in 1995 from George Mason University. She developed software systems for a number of commercial and government agencies, including the U.S. Department of Defense, the U.S. Department of Transportation, the Federal Bureau of Investigation, the Environmental Protection Agency, the Internal Revenue Service, and the Department of Education. Dr. Robinson's most enthusiastic supporters are her husband, George Pinckney Robinson, Jr., and her sons, Andrew and Timothy.

Christopher McConnell is Raytheon E-Systems' manager and technical lead for the Year 2000 project. He has worked in the computer industry for the past 19 years. Chris has constructed various manufacturing support systems and lead conversions including DOS to MVS to UNIX, and third-to-fourth generation technologies. These re-engineering projects and conversions serve as the foundation for his understanding of handling complex computer projects and his broad-based technical knowledge. Chris started in Arizona with his first major project in 1980, developing a network operating system for Apple II computers in 6502 assembly language. Later he re-engineered several mainframe and minicomputer software systems. Chris served as a PC consultant throughout the early 1980s. A sudden move in 1983 migrated Chris and his family to Virginia and his current employer. He has been happily married for over 20 years and has three children. He is active in his church's choir, plays the piano, enjoys strategic computer games, and volunteers time with his children's swim team.

Eileen Silo is a systems/test engineer at Raytheon E-Systems Falls Church. She is experienced in a wide range of computer platforms and applications, applying simulation and workload emulators to performance analysis and system testing. Her diverse background has required her to take the "big picture" view of systems. Eileen demonstrates a knowledge of how system components work as separate entities and as part of an overall operation. With an undergraduate degree in math she was first exposed to information technology at the National Security Agency. Eileen later went to work as an independent consultant in Washington, D.C., primarily performing design and analysis. Consulting provided her with a wide variety of experiences, ranging from system tuning to credit union consulting for ATM placement, transaction charging, and IT procurement. Eileen enjoys her home and travel, and hopes to eventually spend several months a year gazing at the green hills and stone walls of Yorkshire, England.

Jay Shapiro is a Raytheon E-Systems program manager, currently applying *How To 2000* for several clients. He programmed professionally in BASIC, several assembly languages, FORTRAN, PL/1, and Ada, and managed Ada, C, COBOL, and fourth-generation language projects. Jay has worked for the federal government and commercial firms on image processing, graphic, device control, and data storage technologies for stroke graphic, nuclear power plant simulation, the Hubble Space Telescope, air traffic control system, antisubmarine warfare, and student loan management applications. He received a computer science degree in 1980 from the University of Maryland, and started in the profession by writing games for unremembered PC brands before Apple and IBM wiped them out. Jay and his wife Lou live in Annapolis, Maryland with their two Renaissance children, Rachael and Madeline.

Chad Wilbanks was *How To 2000*'s Principal Research Consultant. Chad's hard work, positive attitude, and sound business insights contributed greatly to this work. He captured the essence of the team's spirit when he stated, " I was fortunate to have worked closely with some astounding individuals and am honored to have contributed to this work. However, I am even prouder to call these fine people my friends." "He that walketh with wise men shall be wise...." Proverbs 13:20.

"An ounce of action is worth a ton of theory." —Friedrich Engels

This book is dedicated to the team of individuals that took the action to address this century's most insidious business problem. —Dean Sims

Preface

The Year 2000 problem is said to be the most insidious business problem of our century, far beyond a software issue. Simply defined, it is the risk of costly interruptions or liabilities to your business arising from product or service failures that stem from the mishandling of dates on or before the end of this century.

How To 2000 is a risk management tool. It is a unique and detailed Year 2000 resource applicable to any size business or government operation. It is a cost-and time-saving utility that offers definition to your Year 2000 compliance efforts—a structured and systematic approach to Year 2000 analysis, risk management, project tracking, quality assurance, and change control. This book offers clear and easy-to-understand instructions to bring your systems into Year 2000 compliance. It helps you address questions such as:

- How will the Year 2000 problem affect your business?
- What methods can you use to assess your Year 2000 situation?
- How can you correctly scope and budget your Year 2000 efforts?
- What level of automation can you apply to this process?
- What pitfalls will you encounter in the selection of candidate solutions?
- How do you plan a successful technical effort and ensure that testing is complete?
- What will you monitor to control this effort?
- How will you manage change control and quality in this process?
- How will you define criteria to retire, re-engineer, and replace systems and data?
- What happens after your systems become compliant?
- Where should you look for resources?

Who Should Read This Book

Many people, in all facets of business, will find *How To 2000* invaluable:

- Business leaders can use it to manage risk and change.

- Managers can use it as a project handbook, to facilitate communication and monitor progress.
- Contracts and legal staff will find valuable considerations, deliverables, and preventive legal risk scenarios.
- Project and technical team members can benefit from detailed task descriptions, technical appendixes, and CD-ROM-based tools. (The CD-ROM contains project planning templates, a working Year 2000 repository, draft presentations, and more.)
- Auditors and consultants can use it to ensure completeness and quality.

How This Book Is Organized

The key to this book is that it provides a "deliverable-based" methodology. Project phases are clearly described, and discrete deliverables or work products are defined as measures of success within each project phase. Th1rocess is organized into nine interrelated project phases, each covered in a chapter of this book:

- **Chapter 1: Phase 1: Planning and Awareness**: During this phase you institutionalize Year 2000 awareness, dispel myths, define compliance, scope your project, and gain management support.
- **Chapter 2: Phase 2: Inventory**: During this phase you create a Year 2000 repository; coordinate tool requirements; inventory systems, software, facilities, equipment, and contracts; and determine your technical risk.
- **Chapter 3: Phase 3: Triage**: During this phase you assess technical, business, and legal risks; and prioritize what needs to be fixed first and what may not need fixing at all.
- **Chapter 4: Phase 4: Detailed Assessment**: During this phase you identify where each Year 2000 failure may occur; determine the most effective solution to apply; and plan and estimate the time and cost to repair, re-engineer, retire, or replace your systems.
- **Chapter 5: Phase 5: Resolution**: During this phase you repair, re-engineer, retire, or replace your systems; create bridges and patches to interface with

other systems; create data conversions when necessary; and begin testing your changes.

- **Chapter 6: Phase 6: Test Planning**: During this phase you define test plans, identify and prepare test resources, and negotiate third-party support.
- **Chapter 7: Phase 7: Test Execution**: During this phase you dry run test plans, verify and validate system functions and Year 2000 changes, test third-party integration, report test results, repair test anomalies, and prepare to deploy compliant systems.
- **Chapter 8: Phase 8: Deployment**: During this phase you notify affected parties; plan for system rollbacks; conduct data conversions, system deployments, and conduct install verifications; and rollback if necessary.
- **Chapter 9: Phase 9: Fallout**: During this phase you manage the removal of bridges and patches; recertify standards (EDI, EFT, and so on); control configurations and quality; and reinstitute lessons learned.

These chapters are supported by a detailed set of appendixes, a glossary, an index, and a CD-ROM:

- **Appendix A: Problem Definition Catalog**: Defines and categorizes Year 2000 technical problems.
- **Appendix B: Solution Sets**: Correlates to the Problem Definition Catalog, offering technical solutions for each problem, and weighing the pros and cons of each solution.
- **Appendix C: Legal and Contract Considerations**: Discusses Year 2000 legal concerns for both the public and private sectors.
- **Appendix D: Sample Presentations**: Describes multiple presentation templates provided on the CD-ROM.
- **Appendix E: Applicability of Tools**: Indicates the degree of automation you can apply to your Year 2000 project, defines the types of tools available, and describes the pros and cons of each.
- **Appendix F: Key Tasks Outline**: Defines the roles for often missed project management, configuration management, and quality control activities.
- **Appendix G: Year 2000 Repository**: Defines a working Year 2000 repository available on the CD-ROM, offers direction as to when and what Year 2000 information you should capture and update.

- **Appendix H: Integrated Project Plan**: Explains how to access an integrated Year 2000 project plan template on the CD-ROM.
- **Appendix I: How To 2000 Risk Management**: Describes *How To 2000*'s approach to risk management, addressing business risk, technical risk, and project risk.
- **Appendix J: Steps To Prepare Your PC for the Year 2000**: Provides clear instructions that you can follow to assure that your PC and some popular software are in Year 2000 compliance.
- **Appendix K: What's on the CD-ROM?**: Describes the contents of the CD-ROM that accompanies this book.
- **Glossary:** Clarifies technical and business terms used throughout the document. The glossary also includes Year 2000 compliance definitions for the private and public sectors, to help you save time.

CD-ROM Contents

The accompanying CD-ROM offers your Year 2000 project team valuable tools and resources that you can immediately apply to your project. These tools will enable your team to get a head start on project control and will help with day-to-day project direction. The CD-ROM contains

- Adobe Acrobat Reader and an electronic version of this book for easy reference
- A Microsoft Project Plan Template that is a mirror image of the How To 2000 process
- A Microsoft Access compatible database provides a working Year 2000 repository
- Microsoft PowerPoint presentation templates for management customer awareness, trade show support, and Triage briefing
- World Wide Web bookmarks page to over 300 Year 2000 sites

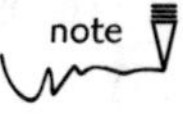

Please note that some of the templates provided on the CD-ROM require users to support Microsoft application software. See

Appendix K for a description of the contents of the CD-ROM. See the section "CD-ROM Installation Instructions" at the end of the book for details on installing the CD-ROM.

Due to its modular construction the CD-ROM resources can easily be separated and assigned to working groups to be adapted to the needs of your business.

Book Conventions

The body of this document describes the management, technical, and legal deliverables required to assure your Year 2000 compliance. Accompanying each deliverable are details describing "Year 2000 unique" task considerations, required inputs, outputs, and individual task sequencing.

Each chapter contains:

- **A phase table of contents**: Each chapter of *How To 2000* opens with a table of contents to provide readers with a quick reference to the material in that phase.
- **A list of objectives for the chapter:** Each chapter opens with a list of objectives that corresponds to the objectives outlined in the introduction.

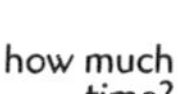

- **A phase overview**: Each chapter begins with brief comments about the purpose of the phase, the types of activities that may occur during the phase, and its value to the project as a whole. The phase benchmarks for cost and time spent are also included. These benchmarks are provided as broad guidelines to judge your progress against *How To 2000* averages.
- **Summary of Deliverables**: This section summarizes the deliverables for the phase to provide an overview of the phase.
- **Deliverables, Tasks, and Dependencies**: These detailed sections are the heart of the How To 2000 process. Deliverables are clearly defined "work products" that are developed as part of your compliance efforts. *How To 2000* uses deliverable production to measure compliance progress. Each deliverable is broken down into the related tasks required to produce it. Tasks are first summarized, and then discussed in detail. The detailed discussions describe tasks and often present guidelines that address key Year 2000 considerations. Tasks are numbered corresponding to the task

numbers found in the accompanying Integrated Project Plan (Appendix H). As shown in the following example, resources, inputs, outputs, and sequencing information are provided graphically to speed understanding.

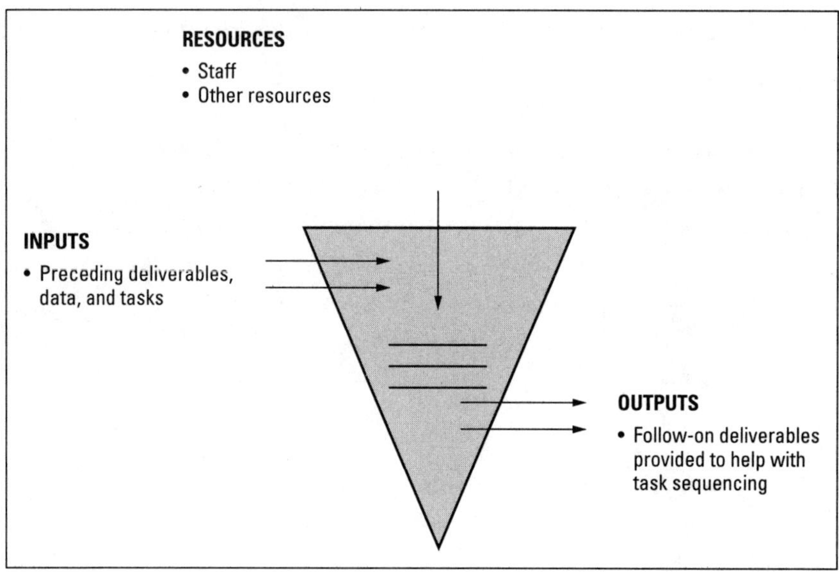

- **Business Impacts**: These sections describe how your business may be affected by the implementation of this project, business considerations, other compliance efforts, and the effects of noncompliance.
- **Phase Risks**: These sections provide you with a list of expected risks relevant to each phase and then suggest ways you can mitigate these risks. Business risk, technical risk, and project or phase risk are examined in relevant phases.
- **Success Factors**: Each phase description ends with a checklist of essential project success factors. Use this checklist to ensure that you have considered all critical project components and phase elements.
- **Reference Material**: This section refers you to pertinent *How To 2000* support material and quick-start elements found in the appendixes and on the CD-ROM.

What's Next?

The How To 2000 methodology does not rely on one tool or one technical approach. The right approach, the right tool, and the right technique will, of course, vary depending on your business needs. What is "right" for you will be defined by the requirements of your individual Year 2000 dilemma and your business resources. By following this methodology, you can implement the right compliance approach for your organization while incorporating advances in technology. *How To 2000* shows you how to implement Year 2000 compliance. The methods you use, the tools you employ, and the solutions, you choose may determine whether you stay in business.

Acknowledgments

Special thanks to:

Technical editors and support: Mike Collis, Roberta Brown, Brian Collins, Gary Forbus, Maria Sachlis, Dan Kennedy, Carl O'Riley, Max Mansur, Andre Tarro, Bruce Dautrich.

Graphics: Ed Comitz, Lucy Murphey, Mary Wolhford, Clarence Abicrombe, Frank Lambdia, George McGregor.

Editing and production: Brian Wagner, Wade Gunn, Barbara Weaver, Doug Dreibelbis, Kevin Droney, Mark Zeender.

Contents at a Glance

Contents

Introduction

The Year 2000 is fast approaching, and along with it comes the specter of the Year 2000 computer date problem. What is the Year 2000 problem and what can you do to protect your business against it? This introduction outlines the origins and the scope of the problem, and provides an overview of this book's detailed, nine-phase approach to reaching Year 2000 compliance.

How To Approach the Year 2000

The chapters of this book explain a nine-phase Year 2000 compliance process in great detail, supplying guidelines on risk management, project tracking, configuration management, and quality control. Carrying out these processes will help your business survive the Year 2000 date problem.

The Year 2000 Dilemma

"[The Year 2000 is the] first century change ever faced by an automated society"

—Caper Jones, SPC Inc.

The Year 2000 computer date problem is a business problem of staggering magnitude, simultaneously affecting most major computer systems around the world. Failures stemming from this dilemma will cause pervasive business problems on or before January 1, 2000. Whether you are a manufacturing concern, a bank, a defense contractor, a public utility, or a multinational corporation, you will be affected.

Our economy depends on the use of computers. Enterprises and their partners are intricately linked with computer-related technologies. Most computer systems rely on the accurate use of dates, which among other things are used for account openings, expirations, sorting and organization, arithmetic operations, and event triggers and controls. Many processes that store or calculate dates have been tailored to fit the twentieth century only, and cannot handle years that begin with 20 instead of 19. When required to use the Year 2000 date, these processes will fail, and these failures may cause entire computer systems to fail. Worse yet, the computer system may not fail but may produce inaccurate information or controls.

The Year 2000 century date problem affects software, hardware (embedded systems), and databases from literally every source. Understanding the root cause of the problem is not difficult. Over the past 30 years, most computer systems have been designed to represent century dates with two digits rather than four (for example, 1999 is represented as 99, as in 12/31/99). Today's technology assumes the first two century digits to be 19. If computers interpret the Year 2000 as solely 00, errors in date representation and date calculations can occur. In the worst case scenario, computer systems will fail. (And remember, when dealing with dates, that a 1 percent margin of error can yield a 100 percent failure.) Systems fail for several reasons, some of the most common of which are listed here:

- Misinterpreting 00 as 1900 rather than 2000
- Sharing system information erroneously
- Malfunction due to missing programs and information
- Sorting data incorrectly
- Treating dates as flags
- Leap year problems
- Shutdown because the date was used in an arithmetic calculation (divide by 0)
- Password and software license expiration

When a computer system fails, a rapid chain reaction of events follows, translating system anomalies into real business problems. As the millennium approaches, century date malfunctions could cause businesses to experience payroll system failures, forecast and invoicing inaccuracies, manufacturing line shutdowns, navigational system malfunctions, erroneous forecasting, or inaccurate accruals. Other business utilities are also affected, including electrical, fire alarms, security systems, elevators, telephones, credit cards, copy machines, check processors, stop lights, and even air traffic control systems.

Fixing Year 2000 problems can be a business competitive issue. If you fix your Year 2000 problems, you have services and compatibility to offer customers that another business may not have. If you do not fix your Year 2000 problems, customer service and productivity problems could result in lost business.

The Year 2000 problem is complicated because dates are used in subtle and unpredictable places, including those that may be embedded in obscure computer system logic. The first challenge is to find the problems. The task then is to fix *all* problems without affecting business functions.

In short, you are in a race against time. With the Year 2000 approaching, you should ask yourself these questions:

- How will Year 2000 issues manifest themselves in my business?
- What about my suppliers and partners?
- Are there legal ramifications?
- How much will it really cost to fix?
- Who has the tools to fix the problem?
- What about quality, change control, and standards?
- Can we handle this problem alone?
- How much risk is there for my business?
- Where do we start and how?

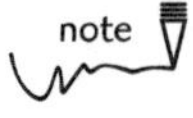

There is no "silver bullet" for the Year 2000 problem. There's no solution or toolset that can be universally applied to the Year 2000 problem (see Appendix B, "Solution Sets").

Because the use of dates is so pervasive, the Year 2000 issue is compounded by the factors summarized in the following table.

COMPOUNDING FACTORS	DESCRIPTION
A variety of software, hardware, and operating systems	Multiple vendors, versions, and releases of software, hardware, and operating systems are now embedded with noncompliant date logic. The proliferation of technologies, languages, and computer platforms creates an environment that is difficult to manage.
Vendor support	Technology vendors are faced with costly support challenges that will affect your compliance efforts: • Some vendors will go out of business rather than support an expensive Year 2000 upgrade, requiring you to identify alternative solutions.

Compounding Factors	*Description*
	• Others will offset their costs by forcing you to "upgrade" by purchasing new releases. Some of these releases may bundle features that you do not want or need. • Vendor Year 2000 compliance will not occur at the same time, requiring you to manage the testing and implementation of vendor technologies.
Supply chain impacts	If your supply chain does not adequately address the Year 2000 problem, your ability to deliver goods and services may be affected. Adopt an approach that assures you are in your partner's Year 2000 plans.
Proliferation of electronic interfaces	Today's systems do not stand alone. They are interlaced with other systems and networks with electronic interfaces. Many of the interfaces that affect you may not be within your span of control. Note that some businesses will do nothing to prepare for the Year 2000. These enterprises may affect your ability to conduct your core operations.
Testing	All of your problems may not be repaired simultaneously. Bridges (see the Glossary) and patches that replicate systems and interfaces must be created to fully test functions as they are brought into compliance. Verification of compliant systems includes development, integration, production, use, and removal of bridges. Managing this dynamic environment will be a challenge.
Scarcity of system resources	You will need "production level" resources to perform comprehensive systems testing. These resources may not be available to you in-house. As many enterprises prepare to test, there may be a shortage of computing facilities and resources.
Insufficient staff resources	As we near the millennium, computer professionals become increasingly difficult to retain. The demand for computer professionals may triple the cost of obtaining and retaining them.
Variety of date representations	Dates are represented in literally thousands of forms. Many forms are subtle, so it will be a challenge to identify all forms, in all languages, on all computer systems, before the Year 2000.

continued

COMPOUNDING FACTORS	DESCRIPTION
Emergence of legal, insurance, and procurement considerations	There may be legal issues concerning product warranty, contaminated third-party data, export restrictions, financial statement disclosure, SEC mandated officer and director liability, and business interruption insurance.
Projected project costs	The Federal Accounting Standards Board (FASB) defined Year 2000 repairs as a maintenance activity. The cost of compliance must be treated as an expense in the year it is incurred rather than as a capital improvement. Large organizations are estimating tens of millions of dollars to assure compliance. (If a company adopts a "replace or upgrade" strategy whereby business functionality is also improved as a result, this rule may not apply.)
Variety of technical permutations	The problem affects data files, screens, utility programs, packaged applications, reports, interfaces, operating systems, control languages, parameter libraries, naming standards, hardware, and more. In addition, the problem affects utilities such as phones, elevators, security, and lighting systems not commonly suspected of being a problem.
IS track record inefficient	Many Information System departments have a history of overruns and late deliveries. But be warned: The Year 2000 project due date *will not slip*.
Continued proliferation of the problem	The Year 2000 problem persists as enhancements and fixes may introduce problems into software. In fact, the issue can be more difficult to identify in newer technologies where computer code is embedded in objects, icons, and models.

Because every Year 2000 compliance project will be unique, your project calls for a structured and disciplined management approach, a plan that makes use of proven processes. *How To 2000* offers you both guidance and experience in this critical area.

A Walk Through Year 2000 Compliance

How To 2000 is organized into nine chapters—each one describing a specific phase in the Year 2000 compliance process. (The nine phases involved in Year 2000 compliance are also described briefly in the sections that follow.) Every chapter includes clearly defined deliverables and provides detailed instructions for how to manage your compliance effort—helping assure that your project is completed *on schedule* at the lowest possible cost.

How To 2000 presents a "deliverable based" methodology. The phases and deliverables are designed to build on their predecessors. The deliverables evolve to ensure that your requirements are met. As phases progress, *How To 2000* shows you how to generate the right level of detail while clarifying your Year 2000 problem at the earliest possible point. *How To 2000* provides a clear road map to Year 2000 compliance, as shown in the following graphic.

How To 2000™ Road Map

Detection

PLANNING AND AWARENESS

- Ensure Management Awareness
- Obtain Management Commitment
- Approve Inventory and Triage Plan
- Create Year 2000 Enterprise Schematic

- Compliance Definition
- Policy and Notifications
- Enterprise Schematic

- Identify Inventory Elements
- Establish Basis for Triage
- Validate Software

- Systems Inventory
- Electronic Partnership Catalog
- Applications by Platform
- In-house Tool List
- Technical Risks
- Year 2000 Repository

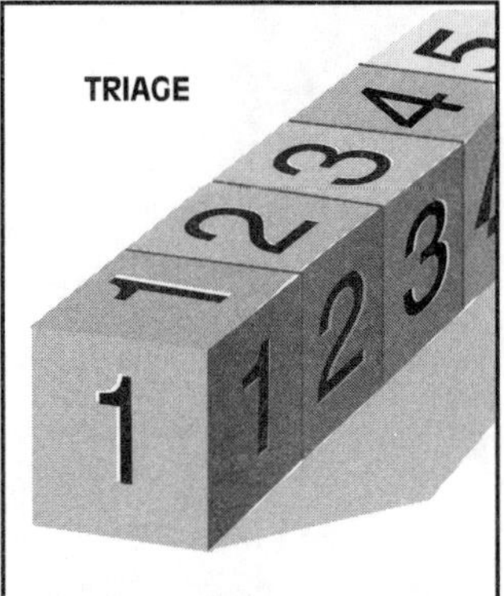

- Assign Year 2000 Project Priorities
- Create Assessment Plan Approval

- Tools
- Business Risks
- Inventory Elements To Be Assessed

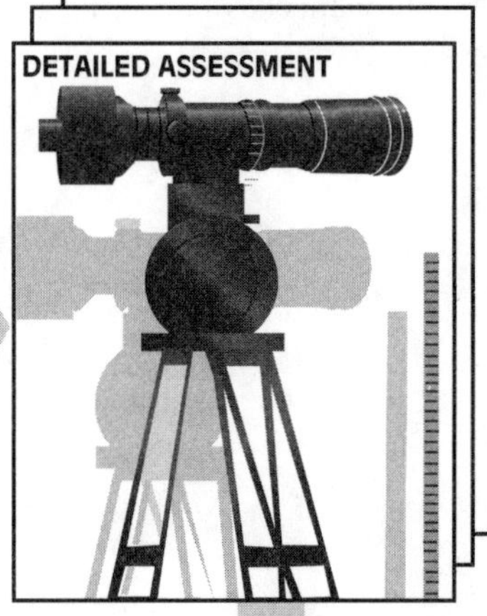

- Locate Year 2000 Anomalies
- Classify Problems
- Define Solutions
- Approve Correction Plan

- Resources, Tools
- Solution Sets
- Partition Definitions

- Partition Definitions
- Solution Sets
- Integration Schedule

Correction

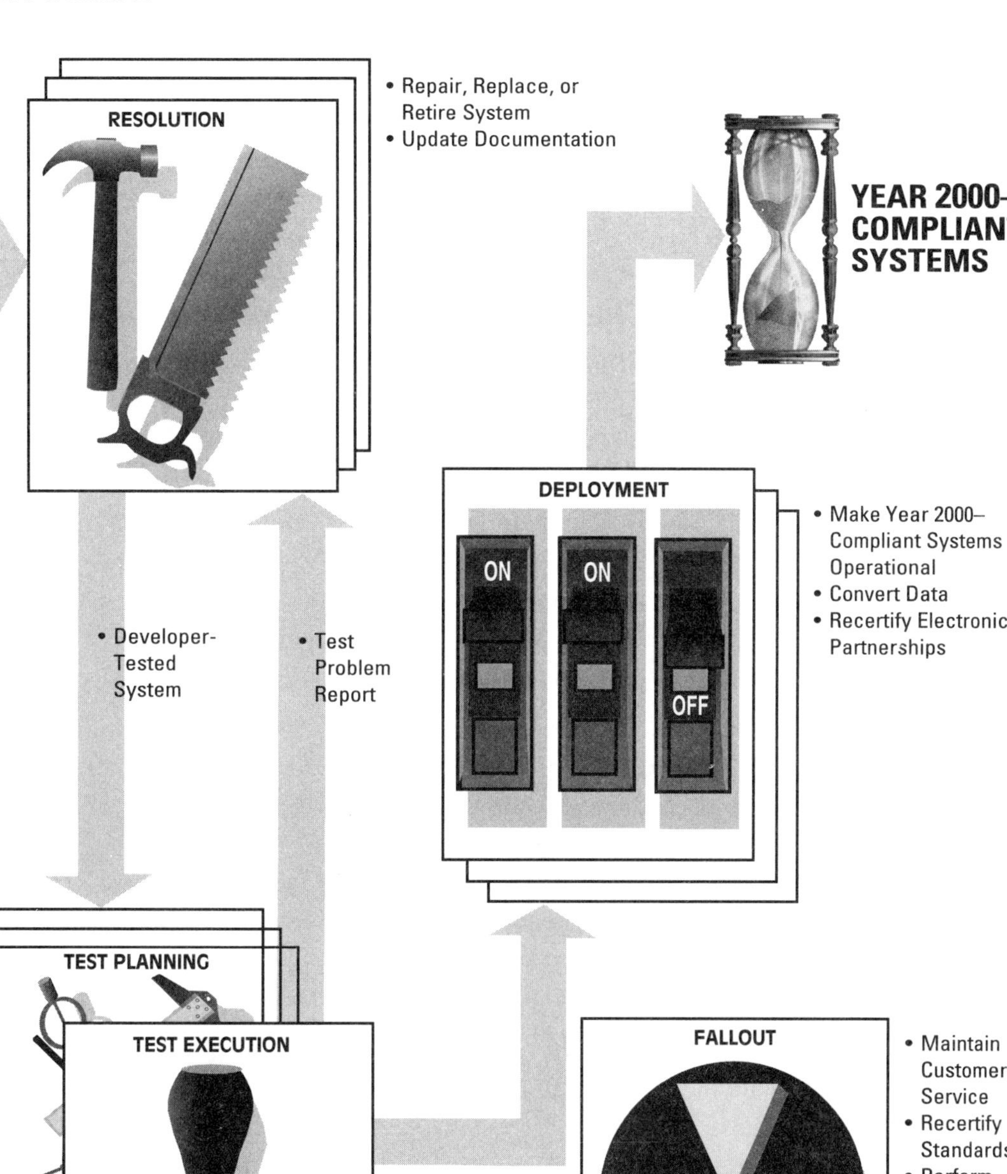

RESOLUTION
• Repair, Replace, or Retire System
• Update Documentation
YEAR 2000–COMPLIANT SYSTEMS
• Developer-Tested System
• Test Problem Report
DEPLOYMENT
ON
ON
OFF
• Make Year 2000–Compliant Systems Operational
• Convert Data
• Recertify Electronic Partnerships
TEST PLANNING
TEST EXECUTION
APPROVED
APPROVED
FALLOUT
• Maintain Customer Service
• Recertify Standards
• Perform Configuration Management
• User-Accepted Systems
• Deployment Plan
• Contingency Plan
• Third Party Bridges

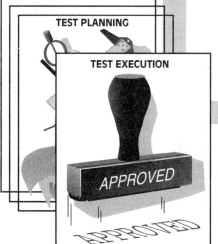

Predefined project milestones help you measure your progress. Using the step-by-step process definitions will speed up your compliance efforts.

How To 2000 helps you to:

- Bring your systems into Year 2000 century date compliance
- Manage your Year 2000 risk
- Reduce your Year 2000 project costs
- Provide visibility to project progress with detailed tracking techniques
- Assure that your business is in your partner and vendor Year 2000 plans
- Ensure quality while controlling changes to your systems
- Identify key resources to speed up your Year 2000 project completion
- Communicate strategic Year 2000 decisions and positions
- Acquire the right tools, make the right plans, and get the right support personnel
- Stay in business

Detection and Correction

The nine phases of compliance are divided into two logical stages: detection and correction. During the initial detection stage you define compliance, locate individual problems, and assess the scope of your correction efforts. This detection process is described in depth in Chapter 1, "Planning and Awareness," Chapter 2, "Inventory," Chapter 3, "Triage," and Chapter 4, "Detailed Assessment."

During the correction stage, you retire, repair, replace or re-engineer system components and data. You create bridges and patches to manage third-party interfaces, and then integrate, test, and deploy corrected systems into production business operations. The correction process is explained in detail in Chapter 5, "Resolution," Chapter 6, "Test Planning," Chapter 7, "Test Execution," and Chapter 8, "Deployment."

Once the first corrected function is deployed, that function is considered compliant. Customer service and Year 2000 bridge configuration management begin. This period is entitled "Fallout" because so many unpredictable variables occur. Fallout is covered in Chapter 9. Business as usual cannot resume until the effects of your compliance efforts are resolved. The amount of time Fallout lasts varies based on the quality of your compliance efforts and your dependence on third-party compliance efforts.

Project Funding

You should break down your Year 2000 project funding into four distinct budgets:

Budget Grouping	Rationale
Planning and Awareness	Relatively small budget. Used to finance compliance definition, corporate awareness, and initial planning.
Inventory and Triage	Large enough budget to create an inventory of potentially affected systems and to prioritize the assessment of those systems.
Detailed Assessment	A budget large enough to locate each Year 2000 anomaly and plan its repair, replacement, or retirement.
The Correction Stage	A budget large enough to fund resolution, testing, and deployment of compliant systems. Do not forget to include resources required for contingency planning here.

If you need to use outside resources, you should contract in parallel with the detection and correction stages. There should be two separate sets of contracts, with each contract corresponding to the goals of each phase.

The compliance phases in *How To 2000* are described in a logical, step-by-step order to make them easier to understand. However, whenever possible, you should conduct tasks from multiple project phases at the same time to reduce costs and save time.

The Planning and Awareness Phase

Objectives:

- Define compliance for your organization.
- Communicate the complexity and depth of the Year 2000 problem to senior management.

- Develop an "Enterprise Schematic" showing relationships for all computer systems and networks.
- Identify the business impact of noncompliance and communicate to your organization.
- Obtain senior management Year 2000 project commitment.
- Gain senior management approval for Inventory and Triage costs and resources.

Planning and Awareness (Chapter 1) is the first step in the detection stage and the kickoff of your Year 2000 compliance effort. Key tasks include defining compliance for your organization, an initial project plan and budget, senior management commitment, organizational awareness of the Year 2000 compliance and its potential impact, and resource and funding approval for Year 2000 Inventory and Triage (the next two phases in the compliance process).

During this phase, your Year 2000 team will also construct an Enterprise Schematic that details each major automated system and network in your organization (see the sample Enterprise Schematic in Chapter 1). The Enterprise Schematic is a graphic representation of your system environment. The completed schematic will note those systems in the span of your organization's control, those systems in the span of your organization's influence, and those systems over which you have no control.

While constructing the Enterprise Schematic, conduct a legal audit or "contract inventory" of your contractual commitments and supplier obligations. Understand how or whether you will have legal obligations in warranties and support contracts. You will use this information in later phases to help prioritize system repair and prepare necessary contractual actions.

The Enterprise Schematic and the contract inventory will help you determine the boundaries of your project and consider the potential Year 2000 impact to your business objectives. The deliverables prepared and presented in this phase are intended to bring visibility to the problem and the project throughout your organization. Institutionalizing your Year 2000 program is key to your success.

The Inventory Phase

Objectives:

- Establish your Year 2000 repository.
- Identify all automated systems or Inventory elements in your organization.

- Catalog electronic partners and interfaces.
- Ascertain which systems will be affected by the Year 2000 date.
- Identify and catalog internal tools that could assist with Year 2000 detection and correction.
- Assess technical risks associated with each system.

After the initial planning is complete and your organization is on the way to understanding the problem, you need to take an inventory of the automated systems that support your business (see Chapter 2). Using the Enterprise Schematic as a starting point, examine each system to identify applications and systems. Note that automated systems do not just consist of mainframe, mid-level, and desktop systems. They also include embedded systems in manufacturing equipment, elevators, telephone switches, security and lighting systems, and more. In addition, electronic interfaces are identified as part of the Enterprise Schematic.

Establish a data store, or Year 2000 repository. You will use this repository throughout your compliance efforts to collect data for tracking and reviewing project accomplishments. This repository will benefit your organization long after the year 2000. You can use it to control the costs of future system modifications and to manage technological change in your organization. Inventory information logged into the Year 2000 repository becomes your configuration baseline. You should use your current configuration management system to log repository data (see Appendix G, "Year 2000 Repository"). Once the baseline is complete, make a qualitative Year 2000 impact assessment on the individual "system components." Also create a "system configuration status report" that identifies configuration items (see the Glossary) that are incompatible, missing, unused or archived. (Some organizations develop this report as part of the Detailed Assessment phase. Others use system configuration status information as part of Triage decisions.)

Balance the correct level of inventory by determining how much information your organization requires to make Triage decisions (Triage is discussed next). Identifying and classifying specific problems *is not* the purpose of the inventory. However, be careful not to skim over the inventory step. Failure to identify a noncompliant inventory element may have serious repercussions. During later testing phases, entire systems could be listed as noncompliant due to the missed inventory element. Moreover, failing to conduct the initial inventory phase in conjunction with a legal audit may lead to problems in preserving the organization's legal rights against software vendors.

The Triage Phase

Objectives:

- Assess business risks associated with each system.
- Assign a business priority to each system or Inventory element.
- Define scope by determining which systems will receive Year 2000 detection and correction efforts.
- Develop plans, costs, and schedules for Detailed Assessment, and obtain senior management approval for these items.

The purpose of Triage (see Chapter 3) is to examine your core business operations and prioritize your Year 2000 work in preparation for the Detailed Assessment phase to come. You should assign a priority to each system component based on business impact, contractual commitment, cost, and expected time to repair. Some system components will not be affected at all, and you can eliminate these elements from further Year 2000 assessment to reduce project scope and cost. Next, identify expected technical and business risks and create the initial risk mitigation plan. Update the Year 2000 repository to reflect priority and risk mitigation decisions.

This book explains how to create a Detailed Assessment plan in which you identify specific Year 2000 problems and establish correction plans. Senior management must be involved in Triage decisions. Triage should detail expected business operation impacts and costs. At the completion of this phase you should have a funded and staffed Detailed Assessment team.

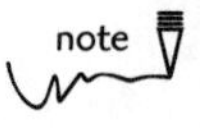

Large enterprises will need to run Inventory and Triage on a cyclical basis to assure that new procurements or system developments are Year 2000 compliant.

The Detailed Assessment Phase

Objectives:

- Complete Detailed Assessment for each system (detailed problem identification and classification).
- Group systems into logical partitions for movement through the correction cycle (resolution, test, and deployment).

- Determine to repair, replace, or retire specific affected systems.
- Develop detailed plans, schedules, and costs for correction cycle.
- Communicate the explicit size and boundaries of your Year 2000 problem to senior management and obtain approvals for the correction cycle.

Detailed Assessment (see Chapter 4), the final detection phase, is concerned with the details of your Year 2000 problem. During this phase, you identify the location of each Year 2000 anomaly; categorize the problem (see Appendix A, "Problem Definition Catalog"); determine the appropriate solution sets (see Appendix B, "Solution Sets"); and develop comprehensive plans, schedules, and expected costs to correct your problem. You also update and use the Year 2000 repository that you compiled in Inventory and refined in Triage. You group computer systems into logical units or partitions. Partition groupings are repaired, tested, and deployed as a group. Partitioning is based on identifying the large groups of related system components. These groups of systems can be repaired and moved into production without interrupting business and with minimal bridging and patching.

You should perform Triage again near the end of the Detailed Assessment phase. It is imperative that you first correct the systems that have the biggest impact on your business. These systems may be either the ones that you think may fail first or the ones your business relies on the most. Large, diversified organizations may not have the time or resources to correct all of their problems. So, planning what to fix now, what to fix later, and what not to fix at all will greatly affect your operations. In the Detailed Assessment phase, you will plan your technical effort. This plan will provide the basis for controlling, costing, and scheduling the nature and scope of your correction cycle. At the conclusion of this phase, you should know how large your Year 2000 problem is and have a handle on the expected impact it will have on your business. You must obtain resolution cost and schedule approvals from senior management. Decisions made here will affect systems and policy concerning acquisitions, partners, subcontracts, contracts, and investors.

note **There are many tools to help you with the Detailed Assessment phase. It's important to define and apply the right tool set. Keep in mind, however, that a large portion of your Year 2000 work cannot be automated.**

The Resolution Phase

Objectives:

- Implement resolution decisions (repair, replace, or retire system).
- Define system level go/no-go decision criteria.
- Obtain and apply commercial off the shelf (COTS) Year 2000 resolution products.
- Develop and execute required customized solutions.
- Complete initial unit testing of applied solutions.
- Provide documentation and training to users affected by Year 2000 solutions.
- Identify expected fallout and impact(s) of solution application.

Resolution (see Chapter 5) is the first phase in the correction cycle. During Resolution, you resolve specific Year 2000 problems. Resolution criteria are based on your organization's definition of compliance (see the Glossary for sample compliance wording). This phase includes engineering efforts to repair, replace, re-engineer, or retire both system data and converted data. In addition, you create technical bridges and patches to assure that your systems can continue to interface with third parties during and after your correction efforts. Partition groups, defined in the Detailed Assessment phase, should move through correction, testing, and deployment in batches. You may apply several different solutions to a single partition. Appendix B, "Solution Sets," contains a list of possible solutions, along with their pros and cons. Specifications for the Resolution phase should include the criteria for a deployment go/no-go decision. Go/no-go decisions are based on the degree of compliance reached by each partition in relation to your organization's definition of compliance. The compliance definitions become criteria for completion that help the technical staff maintain scope.

Defining and controlling interfaces is an important part of the Resolution phase. Each partition may need customized bridges to interface with noncompliant partners and systems. Bridges should be prepared while program engineering occurs. Preliminary unit testing and data conversion programming also occur during Resolution.

Retired systems are phased out and user notification begins in this stage. This forms part of the overall plan. Systems due to be retired may be kept in a 1999 state for access to historical data.

This phase begins a cycle of multithreaded parallel project tasking. Several partition groups will cycle through correction, testing, and deployment simultaneously. As systems undergo changes, the Year 2000 repository becomes an indispensable configuration management tool that helps you manage version, release, and change data for each affected module. Your overall cross-project communication and coordination become imperative at this stage of the Year 2000 project.

The Test Planning Phase

Objectives:

- Develop comprehensive test plans to prevent noncompliant solutions from reaching production operations.
- Coordinate with third parties and electronic partner interfaces.
- Formulate contingency plans, including fallout and fallback plans.
- Obtain and construct mirror test environments and data.
- Acquire test tools and train users in their operation.

Year 2000 test challenges for most organizations are enormous. You must consider operating system dependencies, third-party interfaces, vendor dependencies, compiler upgrades, user acceptance, test system resources, and the potential need for regression testing. Conventional testing may prove to be inadequate.

Testing should occur in two distinct phases: Test Planning (Chapter 6) and Test Execution (Chapter 7). Test Planning activities begin during Detailed Assessment to capture deliverable requirements. However, most of the Test Planning runs parallel to the Resolution phase.

The purpose of Test Planning is to help you develop test plans for verifying and validating "partition level" Year 2000 compliance. You develop a test plan for each partition moving through the correction cycle. During Test Planning, you communicate and coordinate with third-party systems and interfaces not within your control. If possible, make sure that your Year 2000 needs are reflected in the compliance plans of these third-party interfaces.

You should also develop contingency plans during the Test Planning phase, including a "rollback" plan. Rollback occurs when a newly deployed partition creates an unanticipated and unacceptable business problem. Systems "roll back" to their original state prior to Year 2000 correction and deployment.

Partition test plans should include data conversion as well as testing of multiple production cycles (daily, end of week, end of month, end of quarter, and so forth). If your systems trigger special business cycles (such as compounding accruals, testing of "prime" dates affected by Year 2000, inventory aging or adjustment, and so on), make sure to include these triggers in your test plans.

The Test Execution Phase

Objectives:

- Verify that all related development and test preparations are complete.
- Fully test each partition or "deployment entity," including bridges and data conversions.
- Involve end users in test execution.
- Negotiate final third-party compliance agreements and/or bridge definitions.
- Obtain end user acceptance for each compliant partition.

The purpose of the Test Execution (Chapter 7) phase is to verify and validate Year 2000 compliance of systems that have undergone modification and unit testing. Test Execution begins as the first partition grouping completes the Resolution phase. Test Execution follows explicit test plans.

The identified test team and end user management make the final judgment to deploy repaired or replaced partitions. Test anomalies should be logged into the Year 2000 repository and flawed modules sent back to Resolution for correction.

The Deployment Phase

Objectives:

- Ensure that contingency plans are in place.
- Conduct final coordination with third parties and electronic partners.
- Stage appropriate bridges and data conversions for deployment.
- Deploy systems into production operations.
- Execute final system validation.
- Make go/no-go decisions.
- Prepare for Fallout.

Deployment (Chapter 8) is the final phase in the correction cycle. Once deployed, your system is considered Year 2000 compliant. Nonetheless, some of your systems still maintain Year 2000 bridges and patches that support interface communications.

During Deployment, corrected and tested systems are released into production operation. As soon as a tested partition is deployed, final system validation occurs and the go/no-go decision is made.

A no-go decision will result in the execution of the rollback plan that restores systems to their predeployment state. A go decision signals the release of a Year 2000 compliant system to production operations. However, because all compliant systems are not deployed simultaneously, you will need temporary bridges. You should revise the Year 2000 repository to reflect a partition version release. You should also log and track specific third-party interface bridges in the Year 2000 repository.

Bridges and converted data are deployed with compliant partitions. Deployment can seriously affect third parties and electronic partners. It is imperative that you coordinate deployment with third parties and interfacing system owners.

The Fallout Phase

Objectives:

- Regulate continued Year 2000 compliance.
- Minimize impact of compliance efforts on business operations.
- Assure continuous customer service.
- Reimplement third-party certifications (EDI, EFT, and so on).
- Maintain Year 2000 bridge and interface modification control.

The purpose of the Fallout phase (Chapter 9) is to ensure long-term Year 2000 success. Included in Fallout are tasks that must be completed following the implementation of compliant system—customer service, bridge control, anomaly repair, quality assurance, and configuration management, to name a few. Also included in Fallout are tasks that must be completed after January 1, 2000.

To minimize the impact on business, customer service should be supplied through a reliable infrastructure. Year 2000 bridges will expire as interfacing systems become compliant and problems created in the correction stage need to be addressed. As this occurs, consider retesting and deployment. Some organizations also revisit triage decisions upon the release of each compliant partition.

During fallout, the Year 2000 repository should be merged with your regular production change management database. System configuration management can return to regular operations. Finally, during the Fallout phase, lessons learned are reincorporated into your compliance process. Remember, you are releasing your systems to production in partition groups.

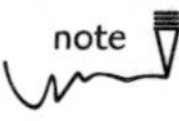

Fallout does not mark the return to regular production operations. The Fallout phase is completed when:

- There are no Year 2000 patches or bridges.
- New system anomalies have been corrected.
- Regular production business operations have begun.

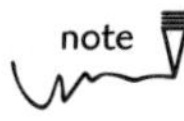

***How To 2000* makes no attempt to determine the size of your Fallout effort.**

The nine phases described in *How To 2000* are unique. There are currently many approaches that offer Year 2000 solutions. Most of these approaches define only five phases to compliance, consequently offering less definition. The following table provides a functional comparison between How To 2000 phases and other plans.

How To 2000 Phases	Five-Phase Processes	Key Elements in How To 2000
Planning and Awareness	Awareness	• The enterprise schematic
		• Legal contract inventory
		• Prepared presentations and memos
		• Ready to tailor project plan
Inventory		• Enterprise systems inventory and schematics, including software, hardware, embedded systems; third-party interfaces
		• Year 2000 repository
		• Year 2000 tool inventory and assessment
		• Technical risk assessment

How To 2000 Phases	Five-Phase Processes	Key Elements in How To 2000
		• Software preparation and validation
Triage		• Business risk assessment
		• Business, legal, technical system prioritization and planning
		• Detailed assessment planning
Detailed Assessment	Assessment	• System assessment
		• Partition development
		• Resolution and correction cycle plans
Resolution	Renovation	• Retire, repair, replace or re-engineer
		• Bridge development
		• Data conversion development
		• Unit testing
Test Planning		• Test environment/Tool preparation
		• Partition level test plans
		• Integration and regression test plans
		• Electronic partnership coordination
Test Execution	Validation	• Formal dry run
		• Test plan execution
		• Electronic partner and third-party reconciliation
Deployment	Implementation	• Deployment and data conversion planning
Deployment and data conversion		• Strategy for retention of historical data
		• Bridge and patch verification
		• Contingency (roll back) plan
Fallout (Unique to *How To 2000*)	N/A	• Post deployment customer service
		• Resolution anomaly repair
		• Bridge and patch management
		• CM, QA
		• Lessons learned

How To 2000 Guidelines

Very few projects cross business areas, chains of command, span of control, technical systems, and budgets the way the Year 2000 project does. There will be significant technical and business challenges associated with your Year 2000 project. Applying sound management practices is critical to your success. *How To 2000* offers guidance in the following four principal management areas throughout the compliance process.

- **Risk Management**: This book is in large part a risk management tool. Appendix I, "How To 2000 Risk Management," describes the How To 2000 risk mitigation approach and defines key types of risk associated with your compliance efforts. Business Risk, Technical Risk, and Project Risk are discussed in the appropriate phases, and *How To 2000* offers techniques for risk mitigation and management.
- **Project Tracking**: The Year 2000 compliance effort is a project demanding careful planning, management, and control. *How To 2000* offers specific directions and tasks to review the project's evolving deliverables, accomplishments, risks, estimates, commitments, and plans. The purpose of these tasks is to determine whether real progress is being made and to implement corrective actions when performance deviates from approved plans. See the Project Tracking section of Appendix F, "Key Task Outlines," for an overview of How To 2000 Project Tracking tasks.
- **Configuration Management:** Year 2000 compliance initiatives require a strong configuration management discipline. If you follow the detailed instructions in *How To 2000,* you will maintain the appropriate data on system components (software, hardware, and data) to analyze and control changes to systems. You will share relevant change data with both developers and users. How To 2000 deliverables are also subject to configuration management and control. Configuration data will be logged, analyzed, and maintained in the Year 2000 repository (see Appendix G). See the Configuration Management section of Appendix F, "Key Task Outlines," for an overview of How To 2000 Configuration Management tasks.
- **Quality Control**: Evolving deliverables must meet stated and planned objectives. *How To 2000* has built Quality Control tasks throughout the compliance process to address system and deliverable quality control. See

the Quality Control section of Appendix F, "Key Task Outlines," for an overview of How To 2000 Quality Control tasks.

This book offers several standards by which to measure your Year 2000 project progress. (See the Year 2000 Phase Benchmarks graphic that follows. The percentages reflect several Raytheon software compliance projects, using a combined windowing and 4-digit techniques.) This data represents averages and guidelines that you can use as benchmarks to assess your Year 2000 progress. The following *How To 2000* Benchmark graphic displays these five criteria:

- **Cost**: Relative cost of each phase represented as a percentage of the total expected cost.
- **Time**: Relative time spent on each phase, represented as a percentage of the total expected project time. Note that Fallout is not included as a percentage of the entire project. Fallout occurs during the resumption of normal business.
- **Risk**: *How To 2000* recommended risk assessment points. You should assess different types of risks at different phases of the project.
- **Budget**: Getting and keeping senior management involved in the project is critical. *How To 2000* has established recommended budget approval and project review points as a tracking and visibility mechanism.
- **Vendor Tools**: There are hundreds of tools to help you in your compliance efforts (Many are listed on the *How To 2000* CD-ROM in HTML or Web-page format). Different tools are used during the different compliance phases. *How To 2000* compares the effectiveness of vendor tools applied against each phase. These effectiveness measures indicate the degree of automation that you can expect to apply to each phase.

Here are some general guidelines for your project:

- Get senior management support.
- Century date compliance is different for every business.
- The best people to run your project are the ones who know your systems.
- Recognize Year 2000 as an enterprise problem.
  - Product lines (liabilities, embarrassment, lost business)
  - Internal systems
  - User desktops

- Institutionalize your project. Get everybody involved!
- Check contracts for potential liabilities.
    - Do not limit research to Year 2000 language. Consider also warranties against defects and failures.
- Carry out the Year 2000 as a discrete and measurable project.
- Run as many phases in parallel as possible.
- The person responsible for the project should report to senior management.
- Stop the problem from growing by involving procurement and contracts.
- Get help to supplement your staff.
- Screen all new COTS products.
- Do not be fooled by tool vendors' claims. Remember, tools are good, but they only address a portion of the problem.
- Try to deploy by early in last quarter 1998. Leave enough time to thoroughly test.
- Do not expect a quick fix.
- Have a contingency plan.
- If you have not already started, start *now*.

History

No Year 2000 discussion would be complete without considering who is at fault for this mess. In reality, economics and sound tactical business decisions are to blame. The following table lists some of the causes that have been introduced during the past 30 years.

Cause	*Description*
Computing resource restraints	Until recently, space in both computer memory and storage were expensive. Managers were encouraged to use less space. Programmers used two-digit instead of four-digit dates to save money.
Lack of applied standards	There are no universally applied standards for representing data of any sort; programmers represent dates in a form convenient to their purpose without the benefit of data naming or field definition conventions.
Long-living applications	Few expected programs written in the 1960s and 70s to be around today. They thought that these programs would be replaced. Even with new languages, this problem can still exist.
Backward compatibility	Users demand that new releases of software be compatible with old releases—that is, because the old release has two-digit years the new release has to accommodate two-digit years. Users do not want to convert data and files (cost and convenience).
Code reuse of historical data	Economies demand code reuse. Programmers are directed not to reinvent the wheel, so they write new systems that incorporate existing data rather than use new techniques to avoid propagating the problem.
User demand	Labor time in data entry—that is, users wanted to fill in two digits instead of four.
Creative programming	Engineers have used dates for a myriad of technical reasons (end of file, expiration dates, pointers, and so on). These factors contribute to the magnitude and subtleties of the Year 2000 problem.
Human habit	This generation has spent their lives writing and thinking in terms of a two-digit century (checks, contracts, bills, programs, and more). Engineers simply use what they are used to and the problem continues.

How To 200

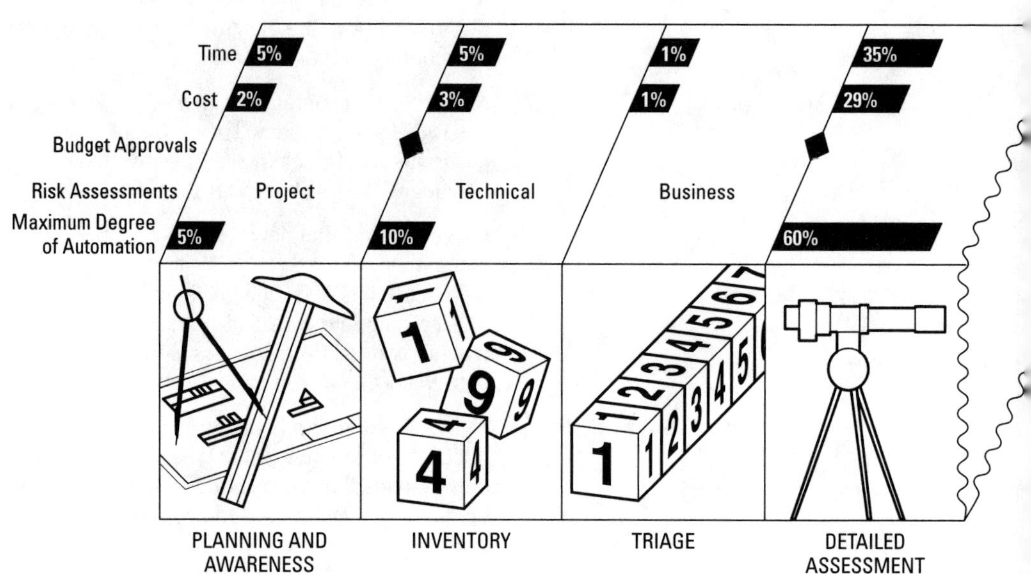

Time
5%
5%
1%
35%
Cost
2%
3%
1%
29%
Budget Approvals
Risk Assessments
Project
Technical
Business
Maximum Degree
of Automation
5%
10%
60%
PLANNING AND
AWARENESS
INVENTORY
TRIAGE
DETAILED
ASSESSMENT

hase Benchmarks

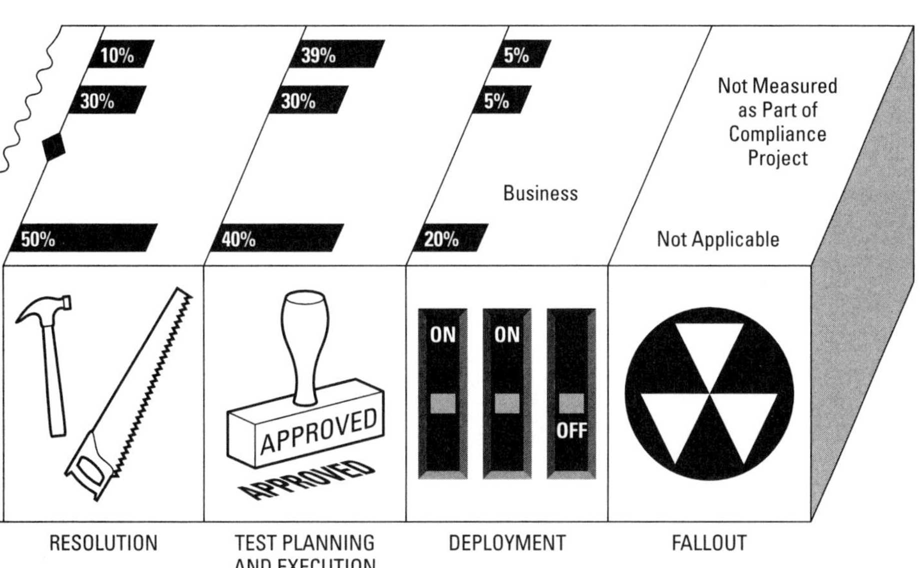

Element	Description
Time	Relative time spent on each phase represented as a percentage of the total expected time
Cost	Relative cost of each phase represented as a percentage of the total expected cost
Budget Approvals	Recommended budget approval points for *How To 2000*
Risk Assessments	Recommended risk assessments by phase for *How To 2000*
Maximum Degree of Automation	Relative effectiveness of vendor tools applied against each phase

CHAPTER 1

Phase 1: Planning and Awareness

PLANNING AND
AWARENESS

Objectives

- Define compliance for your organization.
- Communicate the complexity and depth of the Year 2000 problem to senior management.
- Develop an "Enterprise Schematic" showing relationships for all computer systems and networks.
- Identify the business impact of noncompliance and communicate to your organization.
- Obtain senior management Year 2000 project commitment.
- Gain senior management approval for Inventory and Triage costs and resources.

The first phase of the detection stage, Planning and Awareness, is when you get your compliance project off the ground. It's crucial to the future success of your project to get started on the right foot.

Building Awareness

During the Planning and Awareness phase, you foster an awareness of the potential seriousness of your organization's Year 2000 problems. and convey the scope of the effort required to find and address those problems. You will also initiate a Year 2000 project, providing a systematic framework within which these problems will be solved.

It is difficult to exaggerate the extent of the Year 2000 problem. You'll find operating systems, password and security codes, data, hardware, embedded, and software systems (both commercially available and customized), and many other types of automated systems that are not Year 2000 compliant. For this reason, you need to make managers at all levels and in all business areas and departments aware of the Year 2000 problem. They must understand what resources they will need to manage the impact that Year 2000 will have on your organization.

You need senior managers to commit to providing necessary Year 2000 project resources, including the management support required to accomplish Year 2000 tasks. There must be communication and support, not only between all

departments within your organization, but also with customers and business partners. It's crucial to balance Year 2000 project needs against those of the various companies, departments, existing programs, and development endeavors.

How To 2000 provides powerful tools for gaining the management support you need: Appendix A, "Problem Definition Catalog," and Appendix B, "Solution Sets," define various categories of Year 2000 problems most organizations will encounter, and provide guidance for their resolution. You should tailor this material to your needs and use it in conjunction with other management briefing materials.

Your management briefings must also address the concerns of executives, managers, and staff who think the Year 2000 problem has been exaggerated. You should place Year 2000 in the proper context: It's not a complex technical problem, but a series of difficult management and business problems that can have a very real impact on your organization's profitability, customer service, and production.

At the conclusion of the Planning and Awareness phase, you should have written approval to initiate the Inventory and Triage phases of your Year 2000 project, along with the necessary budget for the completion of those phases.

The cost for completing the Planning and Awareness phase should not exceed 2 percent of your Year 2000 project cost.

The time devoted to Planning and Awareness tasks should correspond to approximately 5 percent of the Year 2000 project schedule.

Summary of Deliverables

This section summarizes the deliverables for this phase of the Year 2000 compliance project. The section "Deliverables, Tasks, and Dependencies" later in this chapter includes detailed descriptions of each deliverable and the associated supporting tasks.

Management Awareness Briefings

This series of briefings should provide senior managers with a broad understanding of the potential impact of the Year 2000 problem on the organization's operations. Presenting this material helps you secure authorization to initiate Year 2000 project publicity efforts. You also need approval to proceed with cost and schedule estimates for Inventory and Triage.

Compliance Definition

The definition of "Year 2000 compliance" often differs from one organization to the next. Here you devise a definition of compliance that accommodates your business environment and your anticipated Year 2000 problems. Your Compliance Definition is a critical measure of success and completion of compliance efforts. Your definition of compliance should identify possible sources of Year 2000 problems and should describe the functionality of a Year 2000 compliant system. The Glossary contains sample definitions of compliance.

Enterprise Schematic

An "Enterprise Schematic" depicts your organization's primary automated systems and the interfaces between them. It includes hardware systems, major software applications, interfaces, and firewalls that directly support your organization. Your organization may already have a "top level" schematic, as well as several "lower level" schematics that describe the automated systems of particular business units or departments. There's a sample Enterprise Schematic in the Enterprise Schematic deliverable (1.3) discussed later in this chapter.

Organization Awareness Campaign

The Organization Awareness Campaign consists of a set of notifications that inform the various departments in your organization about the Year 2000 program. These communications alert general staff, middle management, and executive management that your Year 2000 effort has begun. Institutionalizing your Year 2000 effort ensures that no single department has to shoulder the whole responsibility. Each department-specific notification should define the role of the department in assisting the program, and describe what the department can do to minimize perpetuation of the problem. In addition, outside contractors and business partners should be aware of your organization's plans to resolve potential Year 2000 problems that may affect them.

Year 2000 Project Communications Plan

The Year 2000 Project Communications Plan identifies the communication channels your Year 2000 project will use—both within your organization, and when dealing with contractors and business suppliers. Although you should use established communication channels whenever possible, these may frequently prove inadequate. This is because Year 2000 issues often cross systems, management chains of command, and budgets much more than do typical business activities. It is therefore essential that you develop robust and efficient communication channels to support the distribution of Year 2000 project information.

Policy and Public Relations Plan

The Policy and Public Relations Plan describes how to address the legal ramifications of Year 2000 noncompliance, and the public relations efforts you may need to take to mitigate possible Year 2000 anxieties on the part of customers, shareholders, auditors, regulators, or outside media. The plan explains how to ensure that your organization's existing contractual and legal language is Year 2000 compliant, and outlines how to avoid Year 2000 compliance problems in future agreements or procurements. This plan may also incorporate methods to enlist the support of your organization's public relations mechanism.

Initial Project Plan

The Initial Project Plan provides a rough-order-of-magnitude estimate of the funding, resource, and schedule requirements for your Year 2000 project. It should also estimate the cost, time, and staff requirements for each phase, expressed as a percentage of overall project cost, time, and staff.

Note that presenting your initial Year 2000 plan to senior management may engender support for the job, but not the priority to set aside other less critical projects. Make sure that senior management supports both the plan and the priority. Be careful not to spend an inordinate amount of time rationalizing your initial plan. Assure management that clarifications to your plan and precise cost estimates will follow your detailed assessment work.

Inventory and Triage Plans

The Inventory and Triage Plans deliverable describes specific tasks that will be performed while developing detailed plans for Inventory and Triage. The plans should include schedules and budgets for these phases.

DELIVERABLES, TASKS, AND DEPENDENCIES

The deliverables prepared and presented in this phase make the Year 2000 problem and project visible throughout the organization. All levels of management must understand that the continued success of the organization depends upon the success of the Year 2000 project. How you handle this first phase sets the tone for the project and can determine whether it is successfully completed.

You may need to modify the sequencing of deliverables, or individual task inputs and outputs, to conform to your particular business environment or organizational culture.

1.1 Management Awareness Briefings

The Management Awareness Briefings are intended to make management aware of the serious consequences of a failure to address your organization's Year 2000 problems. You will solicit senior management approval to establish a Year 2000 project.

The tasks associated with this deliverable should not take long to complete, but they are critical to the success of the project.

Task Overview

- Investigate Year 2000 Problem
- Identify Isolated Business Units
- Develop Management Awareness Briefings
- Present Management Awareness Briefings

1.1.1 Task: Investigate Year 2000 Problem

The key to obtaining management commitment is to communicate how your organization's ability to stay in business may be directly related to the Year 2000 issue: An understanding of the various ways in which the century change can affect manual and automated data processing activities is not in itself sufficient.

In this task you:

- Use the *How To 2000* appendixes and CD-ROM to get background information about the Year 2000 problem and then begin to relate that to your organization.
- Use other resources (Internet, newspapers, magazines) to deepen your understanding of the Year 2000 problem and its urgency. The *How To 2000* CD-ROM provides a Web page with links to major Year 2000 Web sites and Year 2000 vendors.
- Identify the level of awareness of Year 2000 issues within your organization and among management levels.
- Talk to project managers and IS managers to learn what they have heard from their contacts:
  - Vendors offering Year 2000 compliant releases
  - Electronic partners
  - Auditors and regulators
  - Users who may already be experiencing problems (for example, contract expirations, budget projections)
  - Year 2000 related terms and conditions appearing in procurement specifications or guidelines
- Identify the business risks associated with failing to address the Year 2000 problems within your organization.

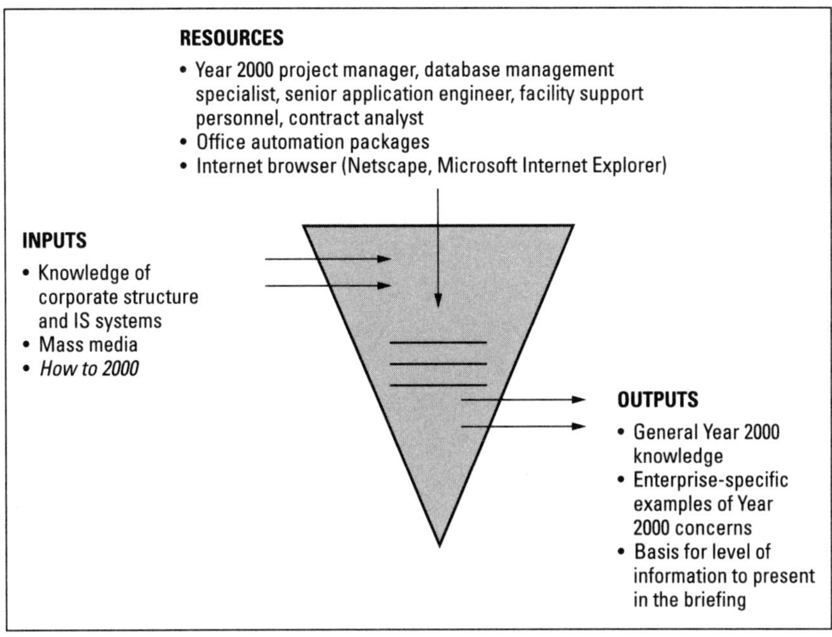

1.1.2 Task: Identify Isolated Business Units

Your organization may contain business units that maintain their own IS personnel or operate on separate budgets. These "isolated business units" often operate in secure areas using classified systems and data. Clearly identifying these units will help you create your Enterprise Schematic later and will ensure Year 2000 project completeness. In this task you:

- Identify the isolated business units within your organization.
- Outline their IS structure in your Management Awareness Briefings insofar as they present special management, funding, and coordination problems.
- Invite isolated business unit managers to your Management Awareness Briefings.

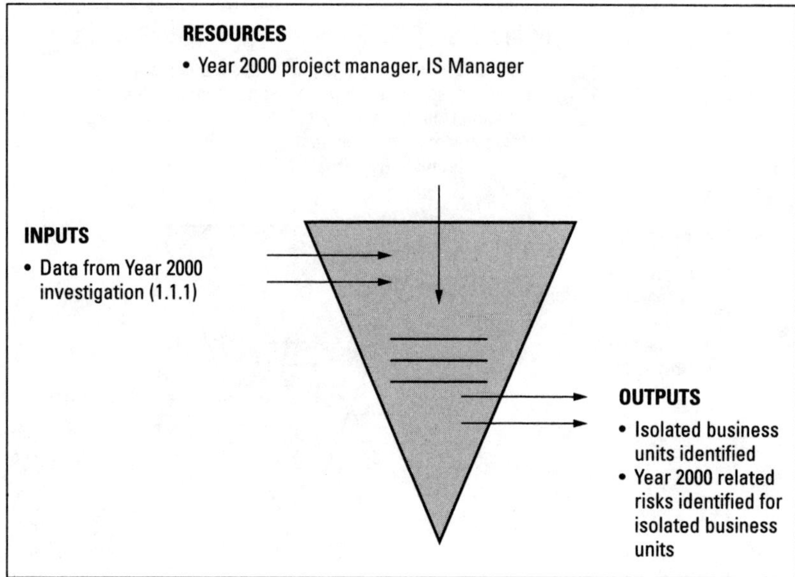

1.1.3 Task: Develop Management Awareness Briefings

This task develops a series of briefings designed to provide senior management with information allowing them to:

- Formally establish a Year 2000 project.
- Authorize notification of the Year 2000 project to all related business areas, including guidelines to reduce the introduction of new Year 2000 problems.
- Approve staff and funding needed to complete the deliverables that define the general scope of the project in this phase.
- Authorize notification of the Year 2000 project to contractors, business partners, and electronic partners.
- Approve Year 2000 project progress tracking plan.

Appendix D includes a sample outline of a management briefing. This detailed outline includes all of the elements required to communicate the scope of the Year 2000 problem. You can divide it into several mini-briefings to suit your project needs. You can also add elements suited to your organization.

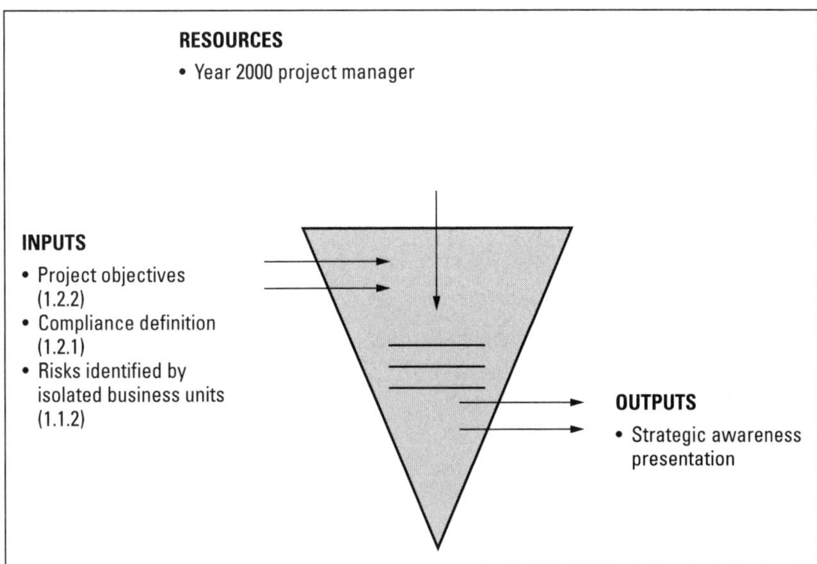
RESOURCES
• Year 2000 project manager
INPUTS
• Project objectives (1.2.2)
• Compliance definition (1.2.1)
• Risks identified by isolated business units (1.1.2)
OUTPUTS
• Strategic awareness presentation

1.1.4 Task: Present Management Awareness Briefings

Once you have gathered the necessary information about Year 2000 problems and analyzed the possible Year 2000 consequences for your organization, you are ready to brief management. In this task, you present the Year 2000 awareness material to at least the following management levels:

- Senior management with preliminary budget authorization approval
- Key data processing managers who understand what can happen if the Year 2000 problem is not addressed
- Managers (for example, program managers or product line managers) whose approval is needed to obtain required sign-off for budget and resources, to communicate with external partners, client contacts, and so on

The briefings will include:

- A general description of the Year 2000 problem and its potential effect on your organization
- The risks of delaying Year 2000 solutions
- An overview of the Year 2000 solution options
- The potential operational impacts of the Year 2000 solution process

- An overview of plan milestones and management reviews (this assures management that future clarifications and details can be provided with additional information)

Your briefings should be the culmination of informal attempts to make management aware of the Year 2000 problem. Your briefings are successful if you:

- Gain senior management commitment to the project
- Obtain approvals to develop the remaining deliverables in this phase

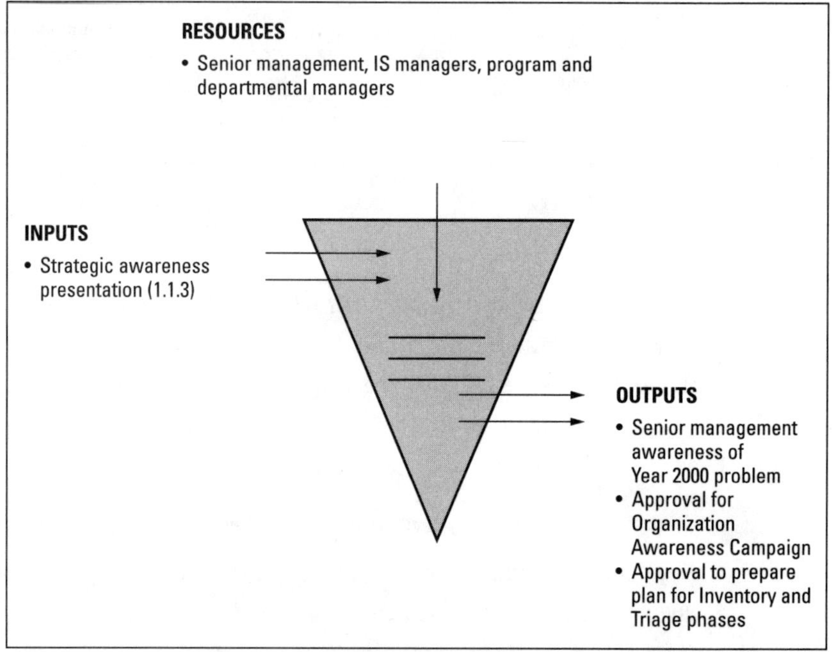
RESOURCES
• Senior management, IS managers, program and departmental managers
INPUTS
• Strategic awareness presentation (1.1.3)
OUTPUTS
• Senior management awareness of Year 2000 problem
• Approval for Organization Awareness Campaign
• Approval to prepare plan for Inventory and Triage phases

milestone

Management Awareness Briefings completed. Quality assurance verifies that the deliverable conforms to its intended goal. Project control baselines the deliverable and updates tracking metrics.

1.2 Compliance Definition

During or immediately after the Management Awareness Briefing, explicitly state the goal of your Year 2000 project, and the objectives that will help you achieve that goal. Both the goal—compliance—and the supporting objectives must be defined clearly and concisely.

There are some sample definitions of "compliance" in the Glossary. You can use these definitions to develop a definition of compliance that makes sense for your organization.

Task Overview

- Define Compliance for Your Organization
- Define Year 2000 Project Objectives for Your Organization

1.2.1 Task: Define Compliance for Your Organization

Define compliance to accommodate your organization and its anticipated Year 2000 problems. It may be useful to define "levels" of compliance, with specific criteria for compliance with each level. Your Compliance Definition should identify possible sources of Year 2000 problems and should describe the functionality of a Year 2000 compliant system.

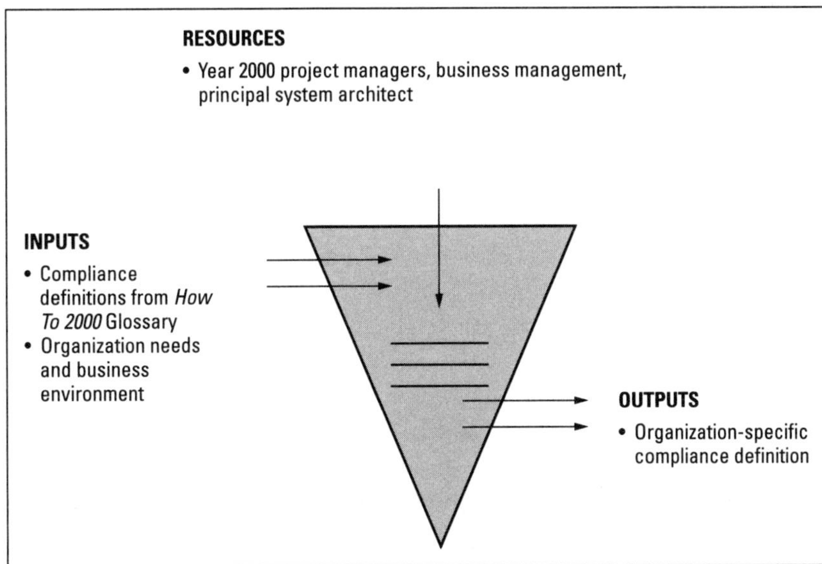
RESOURCES
• Year 2000 project managers, business management, principal system architect
INPUTS
• Compliance definitions from *How To 2000* Glossary
• Organization needs and business environment
OUTPUTS
• Organization-specific compliance definition

1.2.2 Task: Define Year 2000 Project Objectives for Your Organization

After you develop an organization-specific definition of compliance, you need to develop the Year 2000 project objectives that will help you achieve compliance. These objectives should include schedules and functionality specific to each organization. You will communicate these objectives to managers, employees, contractors, business partners, and electronic partners as part of your Organization Awareness Campaign. If you have business systems with an annual cycle (like Accounting), you should deploy them before the end of 1998.

Here are examples of Year 2000 project objectives:

- Ensure compliance of all critical business systems by December 1998.
- Ensure compliance of all electronic partners by December 1999.
- Ensure that annual production cycles that end on or before the end of 1998 can span the century change.

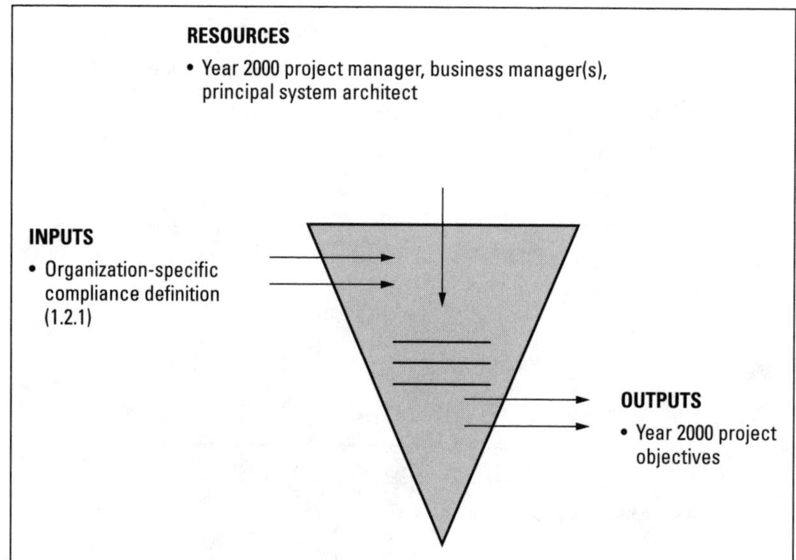

milestone  **Compliance Definition completed. Quality assurance verifies that the deliverable conforms to its intended goal. Project control baselines the deliverable and updates tracking metrics.**

1.3 Enterprise Schematic

A Year 2000 Enterprise Schematic is an illustration showing all the computer and automated systems, applications, data and control interfaces (including those with electronic partners), connections, firewalls, and so on within an organization. The schematic also depicts large embedded systems such as security and environmental systems. There's a sample Enterprise Schematic in the following graphic.

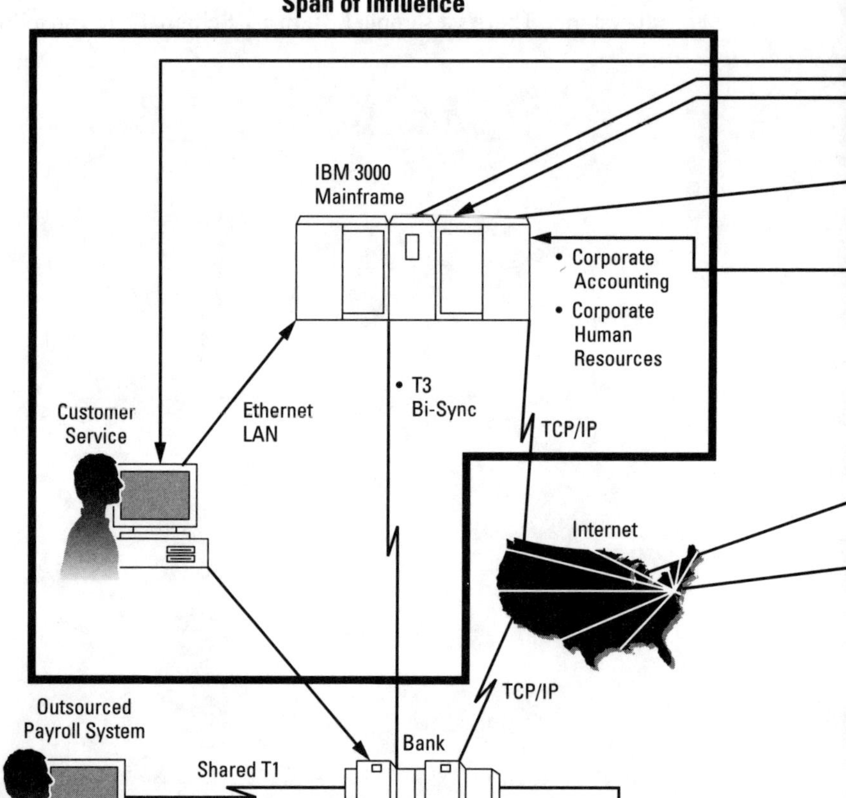

Span of Influence
IBM 3000
Mainframe
• Corporate
Accounting
• Corporate
Human
Resources
Customer
Service
Ethernet
LAN
• T3
Bi-Sync
TCP/IP
Internet
TCP/IP
Outsourced
Payroll System
Bank
Shared T1
Data Entry
AS400 Material Supply

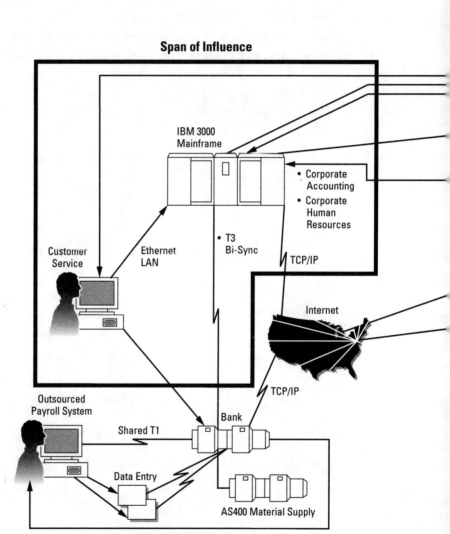

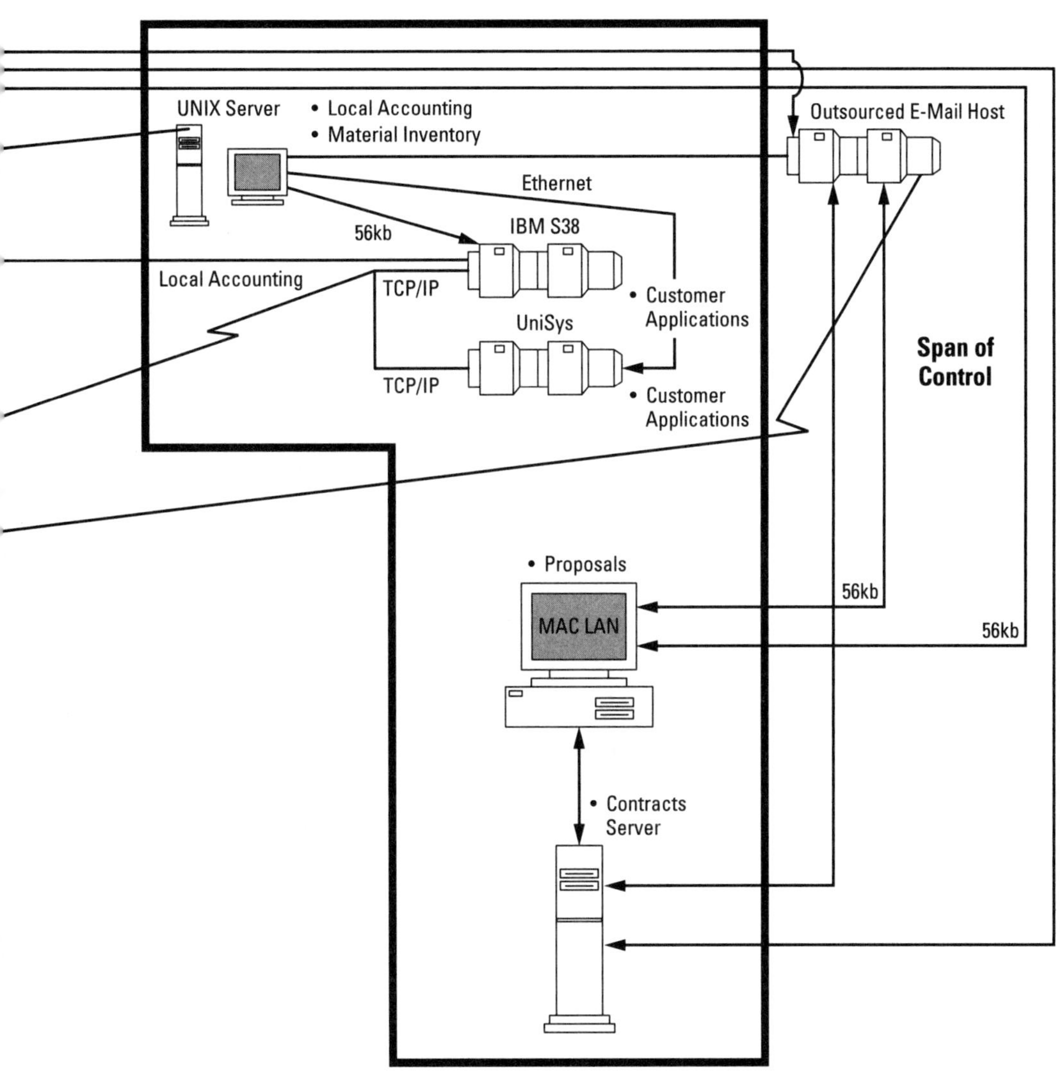
UNIX Server
• Local Accounting
• Material Inventory
Outsourced E-Mail Host
Ethernet
56kb
IBM S38
Local Accounting
TCP/IP
• Customer Applications
UniSys
TCP/IP
• Customer Applications
Span of Control
• Proposals
56kb
MAC LAN
56kb
• Contracts Server

The Enterprise Schematic provides several vital functions:

- It clearly communicates the scope of your anticipated Year 2000 effort.
- It depicts those systems that:
  - You control.
  - You influence.
  - You neither control or influence but affect you (examples are the Internet, major commercial software, and so on).
- It provides a basis for your inventory effort.

Task Overview

- Develop a Draft Enterprise Schematic
- Conduct a Review of Enterprise Schematic

1.3.1 Task: Develop a Draft Enterprise Schematic

Your Information Technology group may already possess a draft Enterprise Schematic. If so, you can update it and ensure that it covers all organization-wide systems. In addition, consider requesting records from your procurement organization to identify newly purchased items that may not show up otherwise.

Depending on your corporate organization and physical locations, you may need to develop or update several "local" Enterprise Schematics, each covering one or more business areas. Isolated business units will need to develop or update schematics as they plan their Year 2000 activities.

This schematic, or set of schematics, is the basis for budgeting and executing the Inventory phase; it identifies the areas that have to be investigated and should therefore be as complete as possible. Creating a master Enterprise Schematic depicting the interrelationships between organizations will help ensure this completeness.

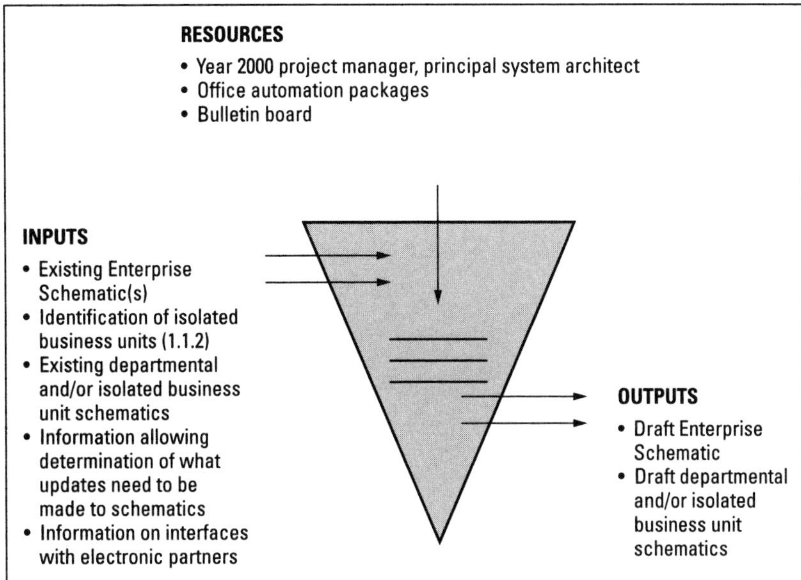
RESOURCES
• Year 2000 project manager, principal system architect
• Office automation packages
• Bulletin board
INPUTS
• Existing Enterprise Schematic(s)
• Identification of isolated business units (1.1.2)
• Existing departmental and/or isolated business unit schematics
• Information allowing determination of what updates need to be made to schematics
• Information on interfaces with electronic partners
OUTPUTS
• Draft Enterprise Schematic
• Draft departmental and/or isolated business unit schematics

1.3.2 Task: Conduct a Review of Enterprise Schematic

The draft Enterprise Schematic and any local Enterprise Schematics should be reviewed by appropriate business and program managers and revised, if necessary. Business managers must accept responsibility for the accuracy and completeness of the portion of the Enterprise Schematic that corresponds to their areas. A mechanism for controlling changes to the schematic must be put in place for the life of the Year 2000 project.

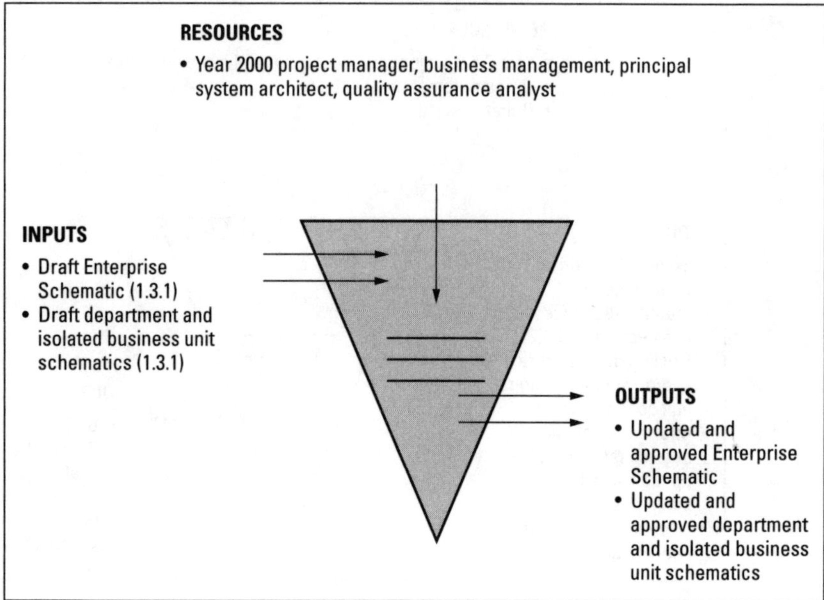

RESOURCES
• Year 2000 project manager, business management, principal system architect, quality assurance analyst
INPUTS
• Draft Enterprise Schematic (1.3.1)
• Draft department and isolated business unit schematics (1.3.1)
OUTPUTS
• Updated and approved Enterprise Schematic
• Updated and approved department and isolated business unit schematics

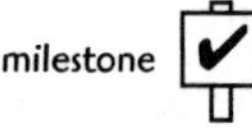

Enterprise Schematic and local Enterprise Schematics completed and approved by cognizant managers and placed under configuration control. Quality assurance verifies that the deliverable conforms to its intended goal. Project control baselines the deliverable and updates tracking metrics.

1.4 Organization Awareness Campaign

The Organization Awareness Campaign is implemented in two stages. The first stage involves formally notifying your organization's various departments and business units of an established Year 2000 project. The second stage consists of more detailed notifications requiring specific action.

The first formal notification should come from senior management. This general communication should inform the heads of departments and business units that a Year 2000 project has been established, and solicit their cooperation in the process.

The second set of notifications will come from the Year 2000 project team. These notifications are tailored to each recipient. Their purpose is to clarify the role each department or group will play in the Year 2000 effort, to request their active assistance and feedback, and to provide guidance for their activities. These notifications should also describe how to prevent the Year 2000 problem from growing because you continue to develop and procure noncompliant software and hardware.

Each task associated with this phase addresses a distinct audience, and covers the preparation, approval, and distribution of tailored notifications concerning the Year 2000 project.

Awareness briefings should be offered to your entire organizational staff. To complete the compliance efforts on time, organizations are enlisting support from the general staff. (Workstation validation is an example of this support; see Appendix J for the details.) Consider offering "lunch time" awareness briefings to clarify the specific issues facing your organization.

Consider institutionalizing your Year 2000 program as part of new hire training. You can even make rollouts of new or rebuilt PCs include your Year 2000 compliance fixes (again, see Appendix J).

Task Overview

- Distribute Year 2000 Project Establishment Notification
- Distribute Year 2000 Notification to IS Staff
- Distribute Year 2000 Notification to Contracts and Procurement
- Distribute Year 2000 Notification to Legal Counsel
- Distribute Year 2000 Notification to Organization's Public Relations
- Distribute Year 2000 Notification to Isolated Business Units
- Distribute Year 2000 Notification to Contractors, Business Partners, and Electronic Partners
- Distribute Year 2000 Notification to Employees

1.4.1 Task: Distribute Year 2000 Project Establishment Notification

The project establishment notification comes from senior management. It notifies key managers that a formal Year 2000 project has been established, and identifies the key members of the Year 2000 project staff. This notification gives the Year 2000 project team authority to contact managers. Their cooperation will be

needed not only to inform their staff, but also to access staff resources for the Year 2000 project.

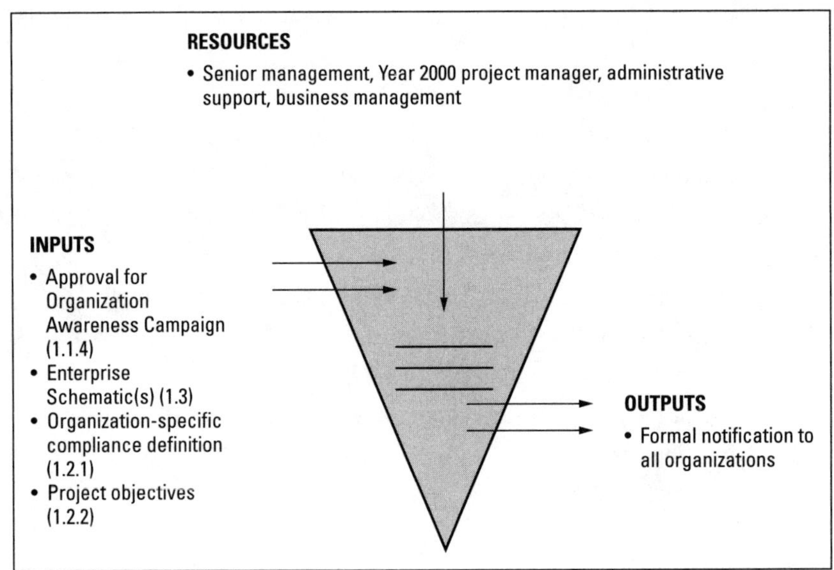
RESOURCES
• Senior management, Year 2000 project manager, administrative support, business management
INPUTS
• Approval for Organization Awareness Campaign (1.1.4)
• Enterprise Schematic(s) (1.3)
• Organization-specific compliance definition (1.2.1)
• Project objectives (1.2.2)
OUTPUTS
• Formal notification to all organizations

1.4.2 Task: Distribute Year 2000 Notification to IS Staff

The cooperation of your organization's IS staff is crucial to the success of your Year 2000 project. Notification will consist of several types of memos and briefings:

- IS management notification. If senior IS management did not attend one of your Management Awareness Briefings, you should brief them on the overall project and solicit their participation.
- IS staff notifications. Work with IS management to develop notifications:
  - Informing IS staff of the project, including a description of its phases
  - Describing how they can prevent the introduction of new Year 2000 problems
  - Explaining what activities will occur during Inventory
  - Describing the types of records they should keep as potential problems are encountered, along with progress assessment and reporting requirements

- You may wish to specifically request IS staff and managers to develop guidelines for ensuring that any new hardware or software purchased or developed is Year 2000 compliant.

Encourage IS staff to provide as much feedback as possible on the Year 2000 problem or solutions for your organization. You can even set up an e-mail box or Web page for information exchange.

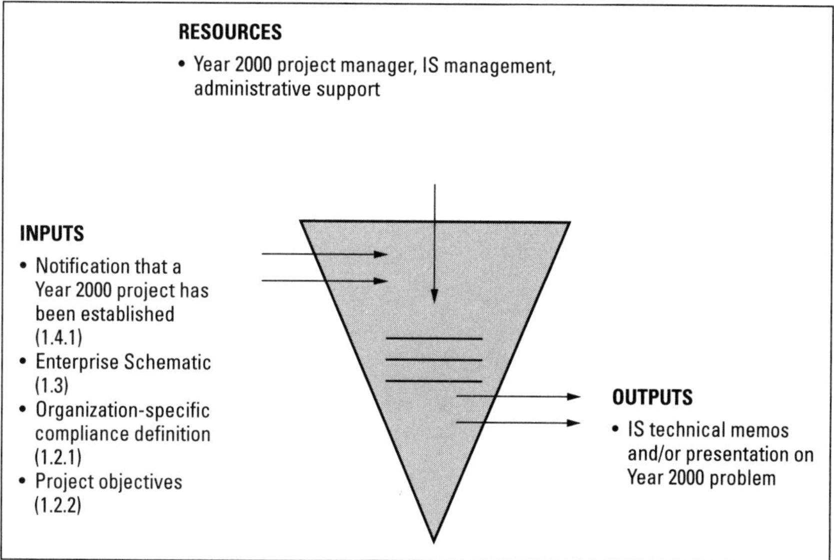
RESOURCES
• Year 2000 project manager, IS management, administrative support
INPUTS
• Notification that a Year 2000 project has been established (1.4.1)
• Enterprise Schematic (1.3)
• Organization-specific compliance definition (1.2.1)
• Project objectives (1.2.2)
OUTPUTS
• IS technical memos and/or presentation on Year 2000 problem

1.4.3 Task: Distribute Year 2000 Notification to Contracts and Procurement

In this series of notifications, you inform contracts, subcontracts, and procurement staffs of the Year 2000 project of the necessity for:

- Providing protection to your organization for systems, hardware, and software developed or being developed for external customers
- Ensuring that any new systems, software, or hardware purchased are Year 2000 compliant
- Ensuring that any systems, hardware, or software developed by or on behalf of your organization are Year 2000 compliant

- Notifying business areas or isolated business units of specific Year 2000 contract and procurement issues
- Updating procedures for selecting vendors and contractors to include Year 2000 compliance requirements

Your contracts and procurement staffs should work closely with your legal counsel as your organization pursues Year 2000 compliance. You may need to develop contractual indemnification, departmental position, or language with the help of legal counsel to protect the organization, its employees, and its products. Appendix C is a white paper on Year 2000 legal and contractual issues. You can find sample compliance agreements and other sample contractual documents on the Internet. Here is a sample memo.

Organization Classification Unclassified

Job Number

Date: NOV. 8, 1996 File Number

To: Chief, Procurement

From: Year 2000 Project Manager Distribution

Subject: Year 2000 Compliant Procurements and Subcontracts

As you are aware, a Year 2000 task group has been formed within our organization. We are currently using ***How To 2000*** to help us assess and resolve Year 2000 issues. You are invited to participate in our efforts as part of the Year 2000 Task Group. In fact, there are several meetings where your participation will be vital to the success of our mission. Specific issues requiring your expertise are

1. Ensuring that any new commercial hardware or software products purchased or released by our organization are Year 2000 compliant.
2. Ensuring that software and/or hardware developed for our organization is Year 2000 compliant.
3. Ensuring that subcontracted maintenance of hardware or software products does not create or reinforce noncompliant products and that noncompliant problems identified by subcontracted maintenance and support organizations are properly reported to our organization.

Also, our organization must soon be prepared to warrant our products as Year 2000 compliant to meet potential new government contracting requirements. This issue will require significant effort on the part of your division.

As a first step in meeting the goals noted above, I am providing the attached information to be used in developing appropriate "Terms & Conditions" (T&C) for procurement and contracting vehicles. You are requested to attend a meeting on 8 November to review these inputs with the goal of developing a draft set of "T&C guidelines" for our organization. We hope to have this draft completed by 22 November. A final draft will be prepared sometime in the first quarter of 1997. We must complete the draft and the final version within this time frame to meet our internal and external Year 2000 obligations. Of course, each division within our organization may wish to develop appropriate variations of the T&C wording.

If you would like more comprehensive information, please feel free to contact my office.

Your assistance in this effort is greatly appreciated.

Attachment 1 - Compliance Definition

Year 2000 Compliance Agreement

Year 2000 Warranty

Recommended Year 2000 Contract Language

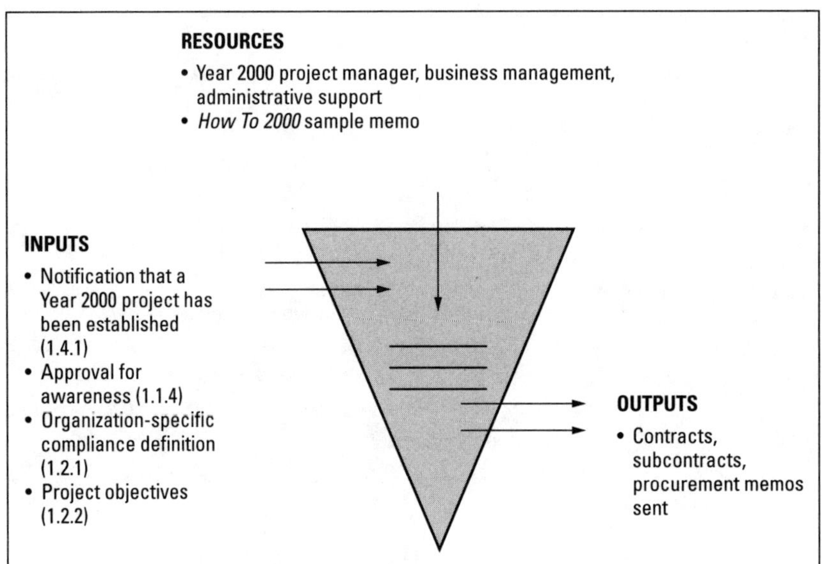
RESOURCES
• Year 2000 project manager, business management, administrative support
• How To 2000 sample memo
INPUTS
• Notification that a Year 2000 project has been established (1.4.1)
• Approval for awareness (1.1.4)
• Organization-specific compliance definition (1.2.1)
• Project objectives (1.2.2)
OUTPUTS
• Contracts, subcontracts, procurement memos sent

1.4.4 Task: Distribute Year 2000 Notification to Legal Counsel

This notification explains the Year 2000 project, its purpose, and its objectives. It also outlines the possible legal issues concerning Year 2000 noncompliance and requests legal counsel's active involvement in:

- Defining (together with public relations) organization policy on communications with clients, auditors, regulators, shareholders, and outside media on Year 2000 compliance
- Working with contracts, subcontracts, and procurement staffs to generate appropriate Year 2000 compliance language
- Building an understanding of potential company and personal liability for Year 2000 noncompliance
- Tracking disclosure requirements from auditors and regulators
- Tracking Directors and Officers (D&O) insurance, limitations of liability, and corporate indemnification to ensure protection to programmers for Year 2000 noncompliance

You may wish to include Appendix C as an attachment to this notification.

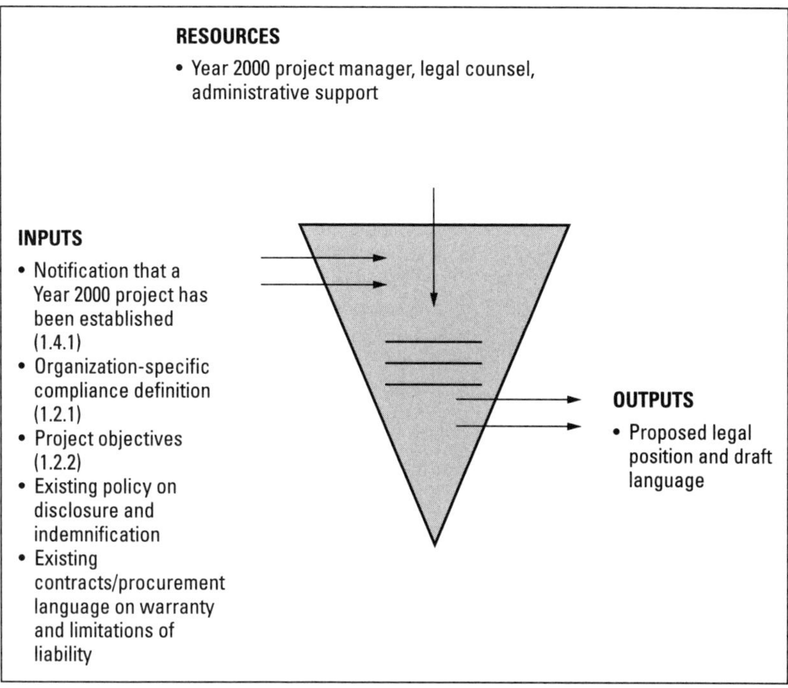

RESOURCES
• Year 2000 project manager, legal counsel, administrative support
INPUTS
• Notification that a Year 2000 project has been established (1.4.1)
• Organization-specific compliance definition (1.2.1)
• Project objectives (1.2.2)
• Existing policy on disclosure and indemnification
• Existing contracts/procurement language on warranty and limitations of liability
OUTPUTS
• Proposed legal position and draft language

1.4.5 Task: Distribute Year 2000 Notification to Organization's Public Relations

If you have a centralized coordinator for external requests (for example, customers, auditors, shareholders, outside media), prepare and send a memo about the Year 2000 project, its purpose, and its objectives. You should solicit comments and questions, and ask for participation in developing the Year 2000 Project Policy and Public Relations Plan. Attach a copy of the Year 2000 authorization memo if the coordinator was not on the original distribution list.

If your organization has contracts or isolated business units that handle their own public relations, copy this notification to those managers for their public relations contact. These contacts need to know that an overall Year 2000 Policy and Public Relations Plan will be developed. Ask for input from these project managers or their assigned project public relations coordinators for the plan. Tell them about the probability of inquiries from outside media, shareholders, regulators, auditors, and clients. Offer to help coordinate responses to these inquiries, and

provide prepared information for press releases; shareholder mailings; and auditor, regulator, and client inquiries.

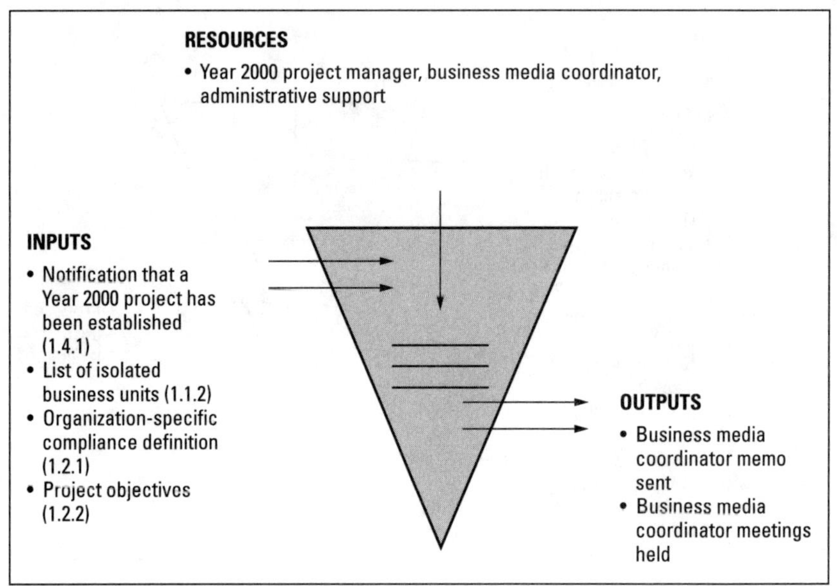
RESOURCES
• Year 2000 project manager, business media coordinator, administrative support
INPUTS
• Notification that a Year 2000 project has been established (1.4.1)
• List of isolated business units (1.1.2)
• Organization-specific compliance definition (1.2.1)
• Project objectives (1.2.2)
OUTPUTS
• Business media coordinator memo sent
• Business media coordinator meetings held

1.4.6 Task: Distribute Year 2000 Notification to Isolated Business Units

You must notify all business units—including isolated business units—of the Year 2000 project, its purpose, and its objectives. Although these unit managers should have attended at least one of your management briefings, the notifications should include any information specific to each unit, including:

- The need for staff training in the conduct of Year 2000 project activities.
- The need to inform you of existing security measures (for example, clearances) for this business unit. This may be only be relevant for isolated business units.
- The need to provide and maintain a current Enterprise Schematic for their units.
- The need to plan for the resources they will need to address and resolve their Year 2000 problems in accordance with approved methodology.

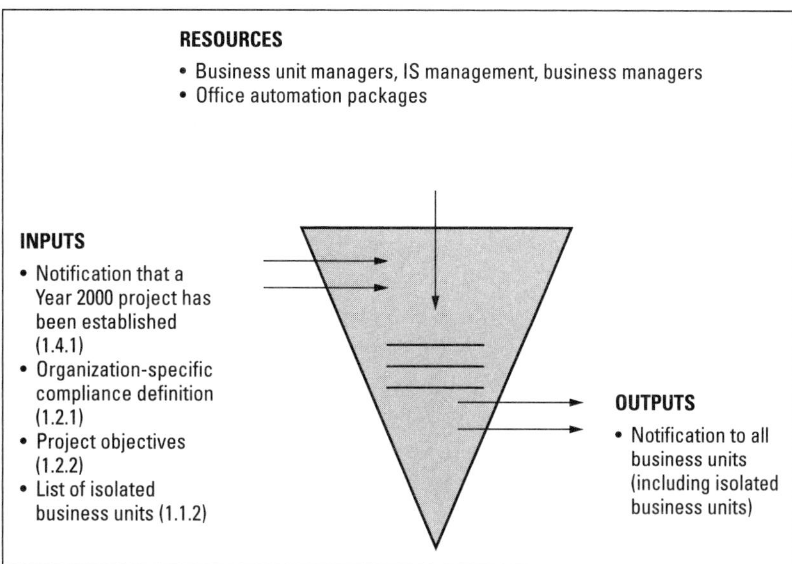
RESOURCES
• Business unit managers, IS management, business managers
• Office automation packages
INPUTS
• Notification that a Year 2000 project has been established (1.4.1)
• Organization-specific compliance definition (1.2.1)
• Project objectives (1.2.2)
• List of isolated business units (1.1.2)
OUTPUTS
• Notification to all business units (including isolated business units)

1.4.7 Task: Distribute Year 2000 Notification to Contractors, Business Partners, and Electronic Partners

This notification explains the Year 2000 project, its purpose, and its objectives. It invites feedback and active participation from contractors, business partners, and electronic partners. The notification to electronic partners should request:

- Status of Year 2000 compliance of their interfaces with your organization
- Information about any re-certification requirements or standards
- The vendor definition of compliance

Depending upon your business environment, this notification may need to be sent by the business units themselves.

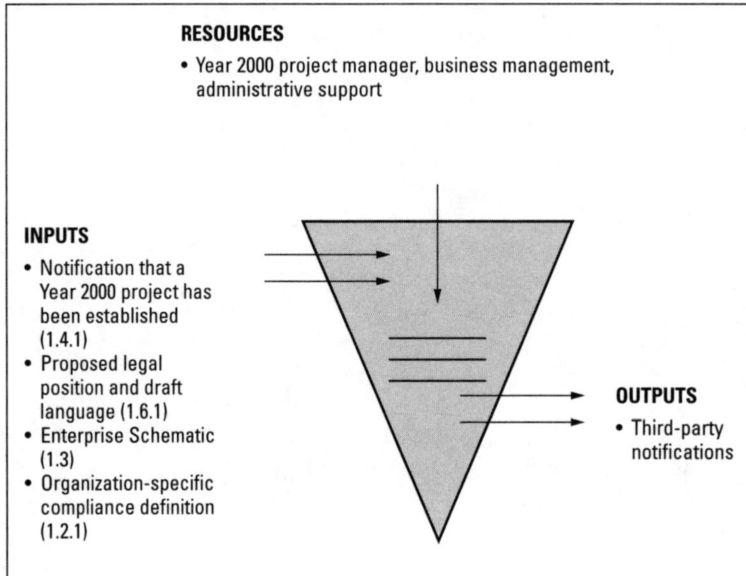

RESOURCES
• Year 2000 project manager, business management, administrative support
INPUTS
• Notification that a Year 2000 project has been established (1.4.1)
• Proposed legal position and draft language (1.6.1)
• Enterprise Schematic (1.3)
• Organization-specific compliance definition (1.2.1)
OUTPUTS
• Third-party notifications

1.4.8 Task: Distribute Year 2000 Notification to Employees

This notification may take several forms: memos, e-mails, general briefings, or bulletin board announcements informing staff of the purpose and objectives of the compliance project. Individual notifications, which may actually be generated and signed by department managers to their staff, should also:

- Explain how the century date change might affect their work.
- Identify broad areas where employee PC software, databases, and/or other routines may need to be revised.
- Explain that employees will be notified when changes made to systems will affect them (for instance, system downtime, training).
- Mention the critical importance that the current staff has on the Year 2000 project. Note that retaining selected staff is a major factor in your success. Some companies will continue to downsize while executing their Year 2000 projects. You must monitor and manage the perceptions system changes will have on key staff (for example, selecting to replace your current systems may send a message that your current staff is not needed).

In the Year 2000 Project Communications Plan (section 1.5), you will set up mechanisms for ongoing employee communication and employee feedback.

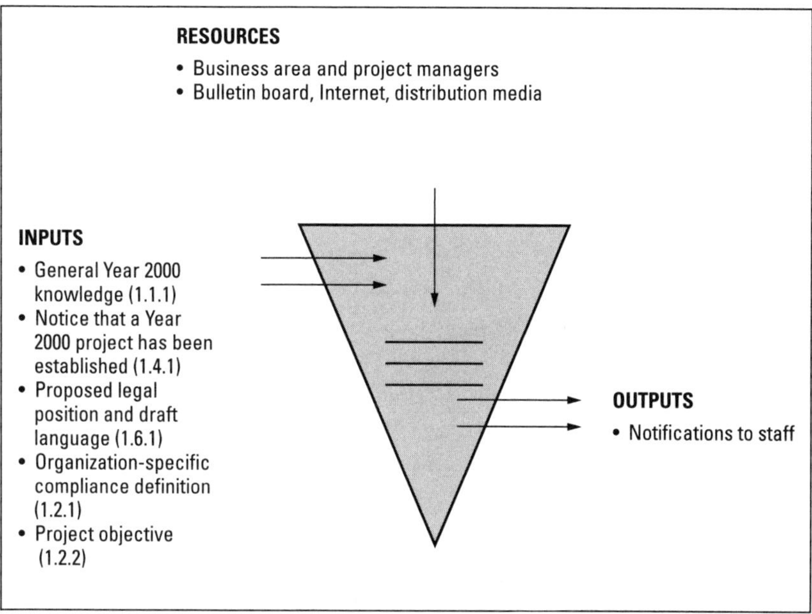

RESOURCES
• Business area and project managers
• Bulletin board, Internet, distribution media
INPUTS
• General Year 2000 knowledge (1.1.1)
• Notice that a Year 2000 project has been established (1.4.1)
• Proposed legal position and draft language (1.6.1)
• Organization-specific compliance definition (1.2.1)
• Project objective (1.2.2)
OUTPUTS
• Notifications to staff

Initial Organization Awareness Campaign completed. Quality assurance verifies that the deliverable conforms to its intended goal. Project control baselines the deliverable and updates tracking metrics.

1.5 Year 2000 Project Communications Plan

In this task, you identify how—and to whom—you are going to distribute project information and updates. You also identify how you are going to receive comments, suggestions, and information. It is of primary importance to determine communication channels with contractors, business partners, and electronic partners.

Task Overview

- Establish Communications to and from All Management Levels

- Establish Communications to and from Contractors, Business Partners, and Electronic Partners
- Update Employees
- Present and Approve Year 2000 Project Communications Plan

1.5.1 Task: Establish Communications to and from All Management Levels

You must establish management communication channels for the project. These channels must support frequent contact on project needs and progress. Contacts may be made via conference calls, meetings, briefings, memos, or e-mail. Each phase may require some adaptation in communication methods.

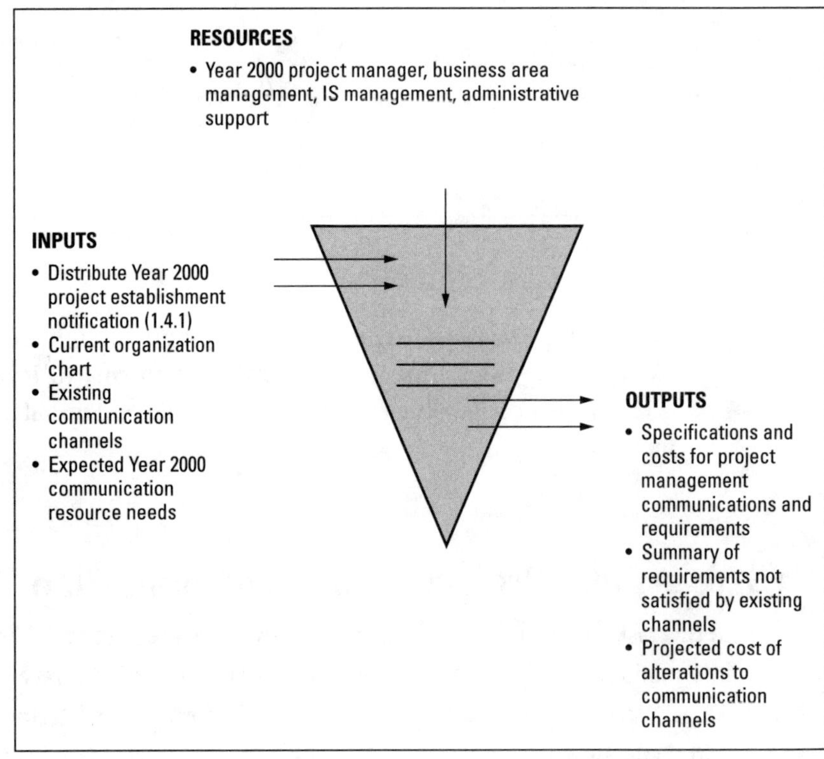

RESOURCES
• Year 2000 project manager, business area management, IS management, administrative support
INPUTS
• Distribute Year 2000 project establishment notification (1.4.1)
• Current organization chart
• Existing communication channels
• Expected Year 2000 communication resource needs
OUTPUTS
• Specifications and costs for project management communications and requirements
• Summary of requirements not satisfied by existing channels
• Projected cost of alterations to communication channels

1.5.2 Task: Establish Communications to and from Contractors, Business Partners, and Electronic Partners

The importance of effective communications to and from contractors, business partners, and electronic partners cannot be overemphasized. You have no control over external schedules and budgets, yet you must meet your own Year 2000 compliance criteria while maintaining external interoperability and existing business agreements. You need to determine, not just the schedules of relevant external Year 2000 compliance efforts, but also whether those schedules are consistent with the needs of your various business areas and overall Year 2000 project. If they are not, make plans to develop, control, and ultimately maintain interface bridges —all within the Year 2000 deadline.

Use the Enterprise Schematic to help identify those systems that you control, that you have influence over, or that you cannot influence but that affect your operations.

To accomplish this, you must establish clear methods of communication: teleconferences or in-person meetings backed up with written minutes, letters, or e-mail. Whether formal or informal, communications must be frequent, cooperative, and informative.

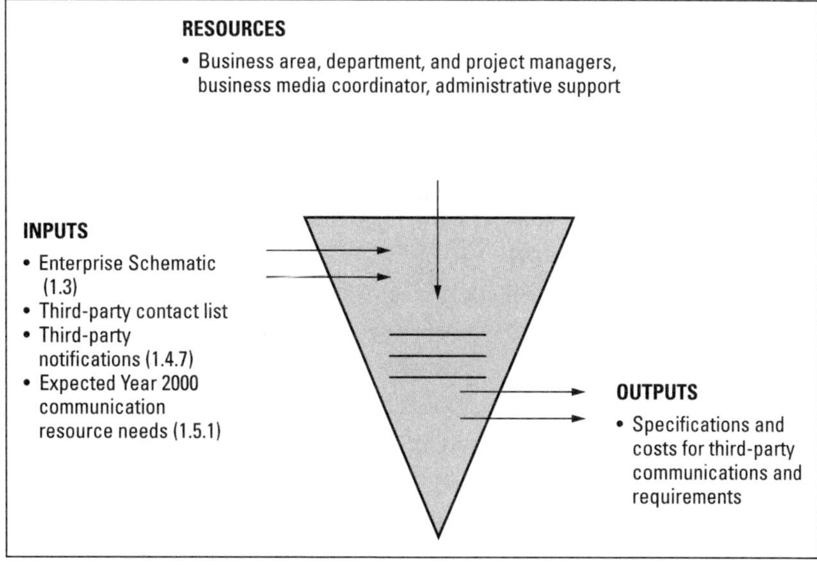
RESOURCES
• Business area, department, and project managers, business media coordinator, administrative support
INPUTS
• Enterprise Schematic (1.3)
• Third-party contact list
• Third-party notifications (1.4.7)
• Expected Year 2000 communication resource needs (1.5.1)
OUTPUTS
• Specifications and costs for third-party communications and requirements

1.5.3 Task: Update Employees

Establish methods for keeping employees updated on compliance policy and project progress. You can do this through periodic meetings, e-mail, a Web site, memos, or bulletin board notices. If you use bulletin board notices or a Web site, keep them updated and *establish how frequently updates will appear*; otherwise, employees tend to pass them up.

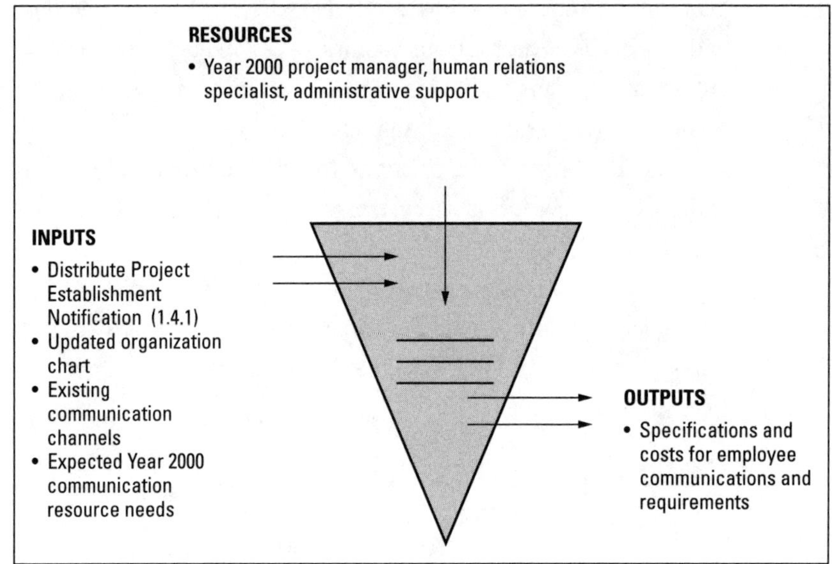
RESOURCES
• Year 2000 project manager, human relations specialist, administrative support
INPUTS
• Distribute Project Establishment Notification (1.4.1)
• Updated organization chart
• Existing communication channels
• Expected Year 2000 communication resource needs
OUTPUTS
• Specifications and costs for employee communications and requirements

1.5.4 Task: Present and Approve Year 2000 Project Communications Plan

Submit your Year 2000 Project Communications Plan for approval. Obtain the resources and/or budget necessary to activate it.

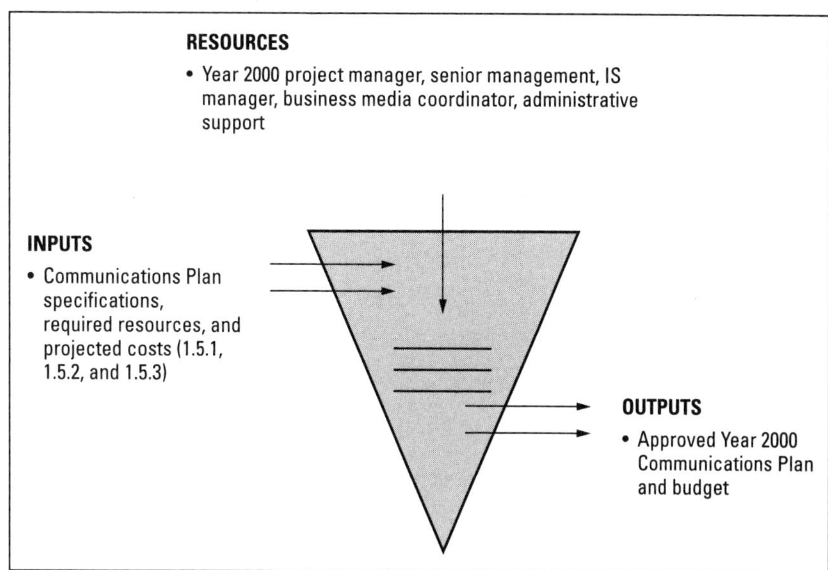
RESOURCES
• Year 2000 project manager, senior management, IS manager, business media coordinator, administrative support
INPUTS
• Communications Plan specifications, required resources, and projected costs (1.5.1, 1.5.2, and 1.5.3)
OUTPUTS
• Approved Year 2000 Communications Plan and budget

milestone

Year 2000 Project Communications Plan completed and approved. Quality assurance verifies that the deliverable conforms to its intended goal. Project control baselines the deliverable and updates tracking metrics.

1.6 Policy and Public Relations Plan

This plan includes tasks for addressing the legal ramifications of Year 2000 non-compliance and for establishing public relations coordination to answer inquiries about your organization's Year 2000 compliance status.

Task Overview

- Identify Project Responsibilities for Legal Counsel
- Identify Project Public Relations Coordination

1.6.1 Task: Identify Project Responsibilities for Legal Counsel

Your organization's legal counsel, contracts, and procurement staffs will work with a knowledgeable Year 2000 person to update vendor and contractor selection

criteria to include Year 2000 compliance. You'll also need legal counsel to provide guidance in the areas of:

- Defining organization policy (together with public relations) covering communications with clients, auditors, regulators, shareholders, and outside media on Year 2000 compliance
- Working with contracts and procurement staffs to generate appropriate Year 2000 compliance language
- Developing an understanding of potential company, officer, and employee responsibility and liability relative to Year 2000 noncompliance
- Tracking disclosure requirements from auditors and regulators
- Tracking D&O insurance, limitations of liability, and corporate indemnification to ensure employee protection for Year 2000 noncompliance

The plan should establish methods for distributing pertinent information as the project progresses. It should contain tasks to create a legal inventory of systems and contracts that may be affected by Year 2000 anomalies. The legal inventory is an important part of establishing "due diligence" (as opposed to gross negligence). It should provide requirements and a timetable for developing suggested Year 2000 compliance language, guidelines for answering inquiries concerning your organization's Year 2000 compliance status, and screening criteria to select vendors and contractors that meet Year 2000 compliance requirements. Developing the screening criteria will most likely be the responsibility of the contracts and procurement staffs, but will require legal input. These criteria may also need to be communicated to project managers or isolated business unit managers who may be involved in vendor, contractor, or product selection.

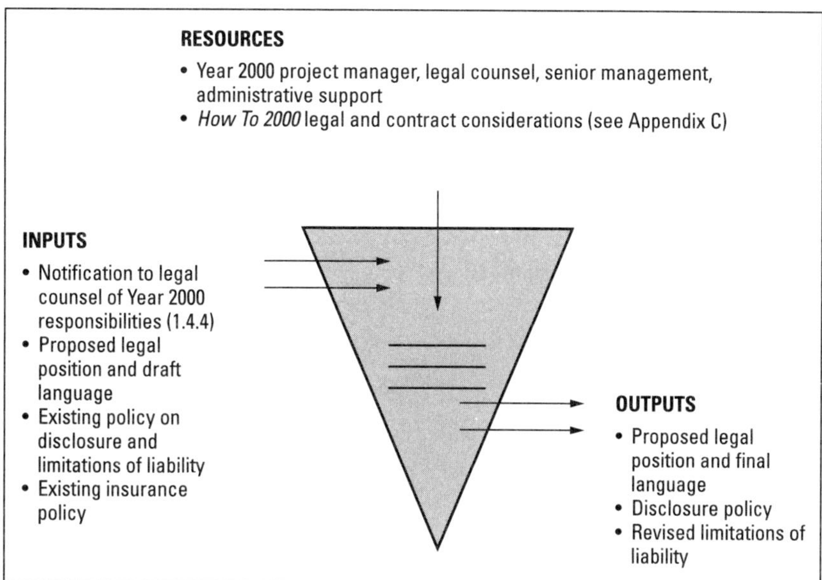

RESOURCES
• Year 2000 project manager, legal counsel, senior management, administrative support
• How To 2000 legal and contract considerations (see Appendix C)
INPUTS
• Notification to legal counsel of Year 2000 responsibilities (1.4.4)
• Proposed legal position and draft language
• Existing policy on disclosure and limitations of liability
• Existing insurance policy
OUTPUTS
• Proposed legal position and final language
• Disclosure policy
• Revised limitations of liability

1.6.2 Task: Identify Project Public Relations Coordination

Although your organization may not solicit inquiries on Year 2000 compliance, you are likely to get them. There is one primary reason for shareholders, customers, outside media, regulators, and auditors to be interested in your organization's Year 2000 compliance: It can have a huge impact upon your profitability, even upon whether you stay in business.

The Policy and Public Relations Plan must both establish methods of communicating project goals and progress to external parties, and clearly define the persons or offices who will answer inquiries from specific sources. You also need to establish methods for internal reporting to ensure that updated information on project progress is always available.

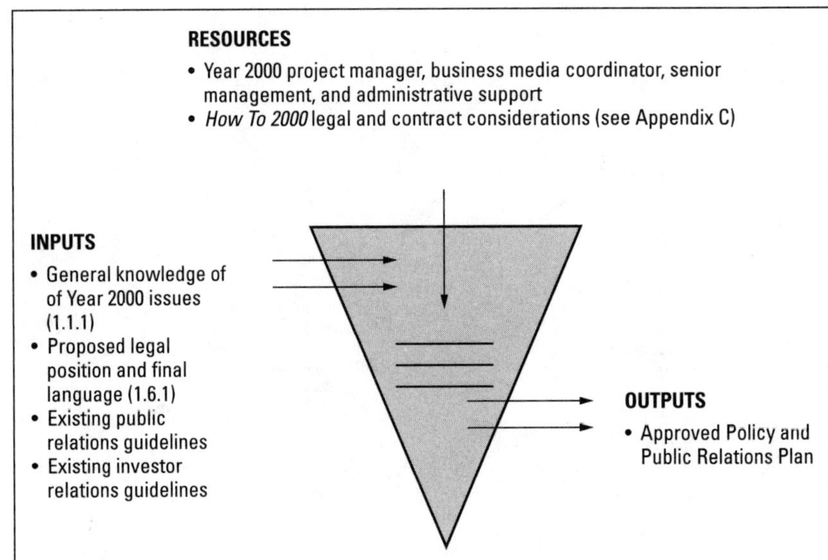

milestone  **Policy and Public Relations Plan completed and approved. Quality assurance verifies that the deliverable conforms to its intended goal. Project control baselines the deliverable and updates tracking metrics.**

1.7 Initial Project Plan

Your Year 2000 Project Plan must include

- A description of the method for gaining authorizations on schedules, budgets, and resources throughout the project.
- A description of the authority of Year 2000 managers to access required resources. You need a clear delineation of this authority because of the sheer volume of the effort, the level of concurrent activity, and the short deadline.
- An outline of how phase or deliverable managers are to work with external partners. (For example, clarify how much authority they have to make time and schedule commitments to external entities, or tell them to describe to what extent they are working around external schedules.)

Task Overview

- Identify Key Project Team Members
- Assess Overall Project Risk
- Review Existing Configuration Management Plan and Apply to Year 2000 Project
- Review Existing Quality Assurance Plan and Apply to Year 2000 Project
- Develop Project Schedule/Budget and Progress Tracking Plan
- Present and Approve Initial Project Plan

1.7.1 Task: Identify Key Project Team Members

Identify key project team members, their responsibilities, the limits of their authority, and their reporting channels. These people will be responsible for conducting the Year 2000 project phases, managing some deliverables, developing budgets, acquiring resources (staff and equipment), working out schedules, and communicating project progress. The following positions should be identified:

- The Year 2000 deputy project manager will help the Year 2000 project manager with data reviews; meetings; coordination; internal and external communications and notifications; and tracking actual project schedule, budget, and resources against planned schedule, budget, and resources.
- The Year 2000 phase managers will conduct the individual phases or portions of phases under the direction of the Year 2000 project manager and deputy project manager. These managers will oversee the accomplishment of phase deliverables and ensure that personnel assigned to conduct the phases have the tools and resources to finish each deliverable on schedule.
- Your organizational Enterprise Schematic, plus any smaller schematics of complex business areas, will give you some idea of how widespread and complex your Year 2000 project may become. Use these schematics to identify key technical staff: senior-level programmers, subject matter experts, principal system architects, and other high-level staff that are likely to be required for the entire project. This estimate will change and grow in detail as each phase is conducted. However, management will require a rough-order-of-magnitude estimate to determine whether it will

use consultants, contractors, and temporaries to conduct the project, or hire the resources into the organization.

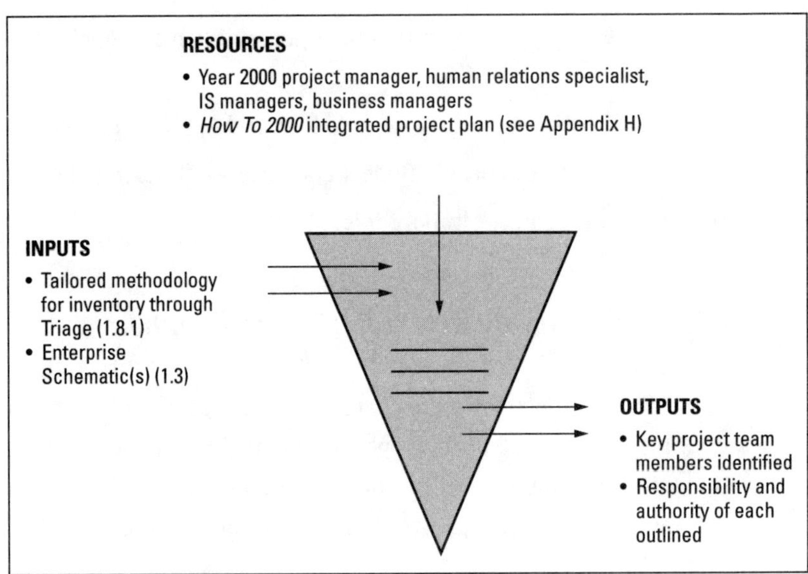
RESOURCES
• Year 2000 project manager, human relations specialist, IS managers, business managers
• How To 2000 integrated project plan (see Appendix H)
INPUTS
• Tailored methodology for inventory through Triage (1.8.1)
• Enterprise Schematic(s) (1.3)
OUTPUTS
• Key project team members identified
• Responsibility and authority of each outlined

1.7.2 Task: Assess Overall Project Risk

Appendix I discusses risk management. Review this appendix and then identify and assess the risks that you expect to face throughout your Year 2000 project. That assessment will lay the foundation for the phase-specific determinations of project risk that begin each Year 2000 project phase. The following table identifies risks that you may face in more than one Year 2000 project phase. These are "potential risks." You must modify and supplement this list as appropriate to your organization and your Year 2000 project.

Potential Risk	*Probability*	*Impact*	*Risk Severity*
Inadequate human resources	Medium	High	High
Schedule shortfall	High	High	High

Two risks that will most likely apply to all organizations are

- Inadequate human resources. One risk probably faced by every Year 2000 project manager is the potential failure to obtain the resources needed to complete this project. Staff is the critical resource in any Year 2000 endeavor, and inadequate staffing is a risk that you should consider at every stage of the Year 2000 project. Staff retention is an important component of inadequate human resources risk. Identify those who are critical to your success, determine how to keep them, and then consider the development and initiation of a "staff shortage contingency plan," especially as a means of replacing mission-critical personnel, if necessary. In addition, senior managers must be aware of the critical need for person-hours if the Year 2000 project is to be successful.
- Schedule shortfall. Obviously, the Year 2000 deadline cannot slip. January 1, 2000, will arrive on schedule. Unfortunately, you will probably be short on time, so your Year 2000 project cannot tolerate large-scale schedule slippage. Consider your company's history of late or canceled software projects. Because schedule shortfalls can spell disaster for a Year 2000 manager, they should be considered an important risk. You can use standard schedule-tracking mechanisms to track this risk. You may want to develop a contingency plan that addresses possible schedule slippage.

  Because the end date of the schedule will not slip, the Initial Project should include schedule monitor and recovery plans. Monitor and recovery plans may include efforts such as periodic and progress-based internal reviews to assess progress and identify corrective actions, reallocation of human and computing resources, addition of staff through hiring or contracting, procurement of turnkey solution providers, inclusion of additional tools, re-prioritization of required systems, and so on.

Once you have listed and assessed the possible overall project risks for your organization, highlight these risks in your briefing, along with the mitigation options and the estimated time and cost of each option. Once you identify isolated business units in your organization, you also need to identify the Year 2000 risks unique to those units because of their structure.

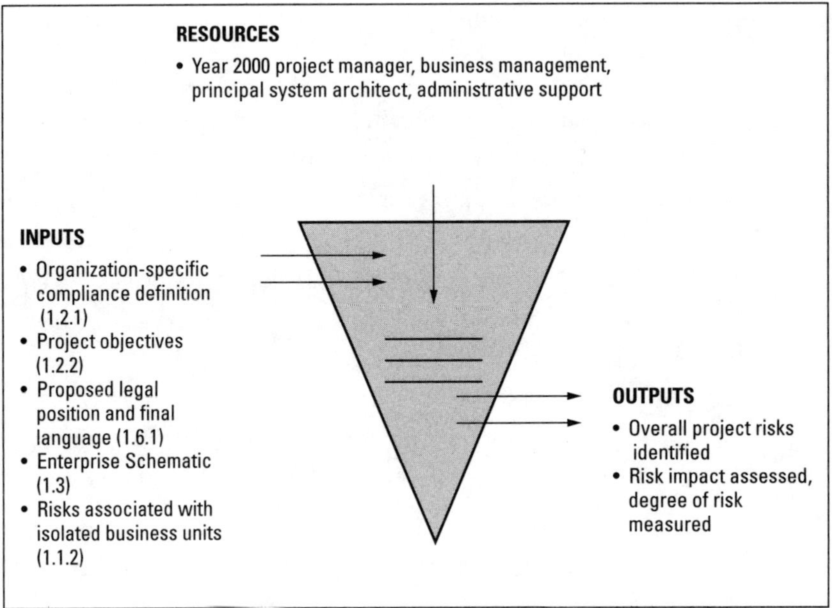
RESOURCES
• Year 2000 project manager, business management, principal system architect, administrative support
INPUTS
• Organization-specific compliance definition (1.2.1)
• Project objectives (1.2.2)
• Proposed legal position and final language (1.6.1)
• Enterprise Schematic (1.3)
• Risks associated with isolated business units (1.1.2)
OUTPUTS
• Overall project risks identified
• Risk impact assessed, degree of risk measured

1.7.3 Task: Review Existing Configuration Management Plan and Apply to Year 2000 Project

In this task, examine your organization's Configuration Management Plan and ensure that procedures will cover Year 2000 project tasks. Add the appropriate procedures to the plan to cover unique Year 2000 activities. For example, different systems may use different CM processes or products; or different processes may be in place for in-house, contractor, or electronic partner use. If so, determine what CM controls you absolutely need for each phase and make sure there is a CM process to meet these requirements. If you have no CM procedures, *do not consider* implementing an entire CM process as part of your Year 2000 plans; there is not enough time. Implement only those controls that you need to get through the Year 2000 compliance process (for example, vendor tracking, anomaly identification, testing, version control, and so on).

Establish a CM repository for the Year 2000 project.

Make the CM plan available to all parties working on the project and note any changes you made to standard plans.

Issue a memo requesting adherence to the CM plan. This memo should outline the project risks if CM is not followed. Everyone must understand these risks.

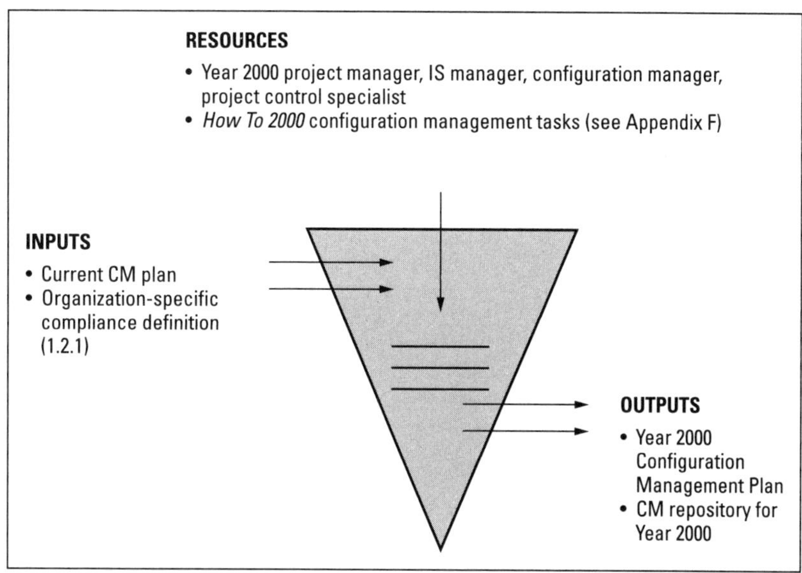
RESOURCES
• Year 2000 project manager, IS manager, configuration manager, project control specialist
• How To 2000 configuration management tasks (see Appendix F)
INPUTS
• Current CM plan
• Organization-specific compliance definition (1.2.1)
OUTPUTS
• Year 2000 Configuration Management Plan
• CM repository for Year 2000

1.7.4 Task: Review Existing Quality Assurance Plan and Apply to Year 2000 Project

Assure quality for both Year 2000 deliverables and the systems you are repairing. You'll probably have to modify or develop your organization's Quality Assurance/Quality Control Plan to cover the tasks unique to the Year 2000 project. Quality assurance (QA) for the Year 2000 project should be conducted at a level at least equal to that specified in the current plan, and you may want to apply additional rigor to the QA role. For projects governed by customer specifications or standards, the QA plan modifications have to be consistent with those specifications. Items to consider in enhancing the QA plan include:

- Additional or different metrics
- Quality and completeness of the Year 2000 repository
- Adherence to modified development procedures and standards for hardware, software, and systems
- Adherence to Year 2000 project plan
- Tracking to closure, and reporting to management deviations from the Year 2000 plan, procedures, and standards
- Compliance with existing and modified quality requirements

Distribute the revised QA plan to all personnel working on the project, highlighting the changes from the original plan. In the cover memo for the new QA plan, be sure to remind the recipients about the crucial nature of adhering to the QA requirements as well as the risks of noncompliance. Due to the compressed and inflexible schedule of the Year 2000 project, failure to conform to sound QA guidelines will jeopardize the success of the project. On projects requiring customer approval of the QA plan, obtain that approval from the customer.

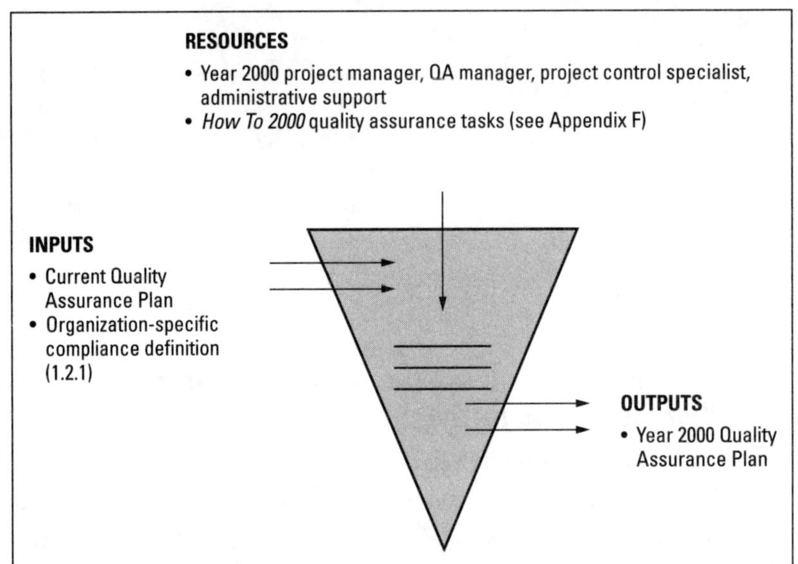
RESOURCES
• Year 2000 project manager, QA manager, project control specialist, administrative support
• How To 2000 quality assurance tasks (see Appendix F)
INPUTS
• Current Quality Assurance Plan
• Organization-specific compliance definition (1.2.1)
OUTPUTS
• Year 2000 Quality Assurance Plan

1.7.5 Task: Develop Project Schedule/Budget and Progress Tracking Plan

In this task, you use any information you have to build a rough-order-of-magnitude schedule and budget for the Year 2000 project. This schedule should outline the timetable for conducting each project phase. It's important to show management how the Year 2000 project activities must dovetail with, or in some cases supercede, those of other departments and ongoing projects. The schedule should show each phase and the associated deliverables and tasks, along with equipment usage over the same calendar period. The projected resource requirements, in conjunction with the schedule, will allow you to create a rough-order-of-magnitude budget for the overall project. The first refinement of this budget after approval of the Initial Project Plan will take place as part of the task in which detailed plans are developed for the Inventory and Triage phases.

This book identifies potential risks that could occur during each phase of the project. Build enough "slack" into the time estimates for each Year 2000 project phase to deal with problems that occur.

The Initial Project Plan should also include the formal plan for tracking progress throughout the Year 2000 effort. The tracking plan should provide for periodic and event-driven reviews to determine the level of conformance with the planned technical effort, schedule, budget, and resource utilization. The tracking plan should also address feedback mechanisms to management to support resource allocation decisions and to update other Year 2000 schedules based on lessons learned.

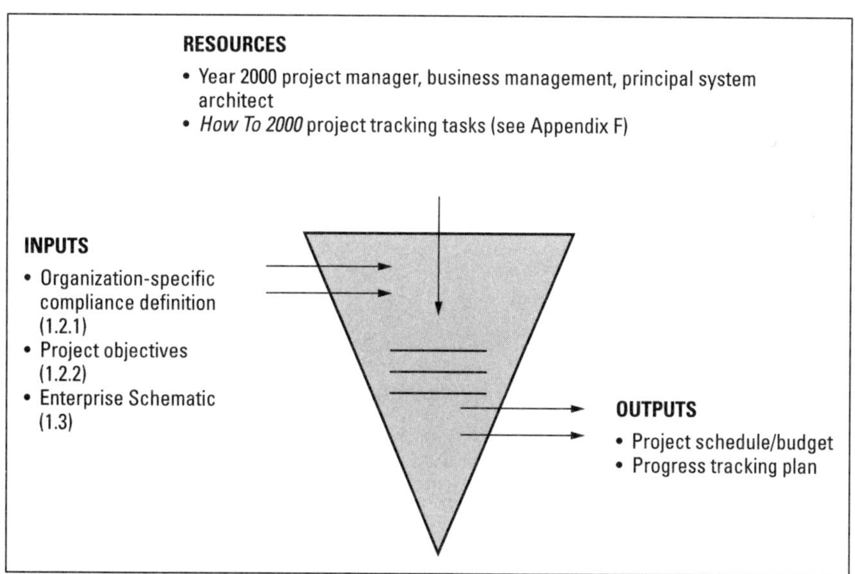

RESOURCES
• Year 2000 project manager, business management, principal system architect
• How To 2000 project tracking tasks (see Appendix F)
INPUTS
• Organization-specific compliance definition (1.2.1)
• Project objectives (1.2.2)
• Enterprise Schematic (1.3)
OUTPUTS
• Project schedule/budget
• Progress tracking plan

1.7.6 Task: Present and Approve Initial Project Plan

This is a major approval point for your Year 2000 project. You will gain approval for more detailed phase schedules and budgets as you proceed, but this is the point at which you are given the "go ahead" to ensure that your organization will attain Year 2000 compliance. The importance of this task in relation to your overall compliance goal cannot be overemphasized.

Management will be particularly interested in your scheduling and cost estimates. Budget and resource projections will be critical factors that management must consider before approving your key project team member positions and initial plan. Note that this may take more than one iteration.

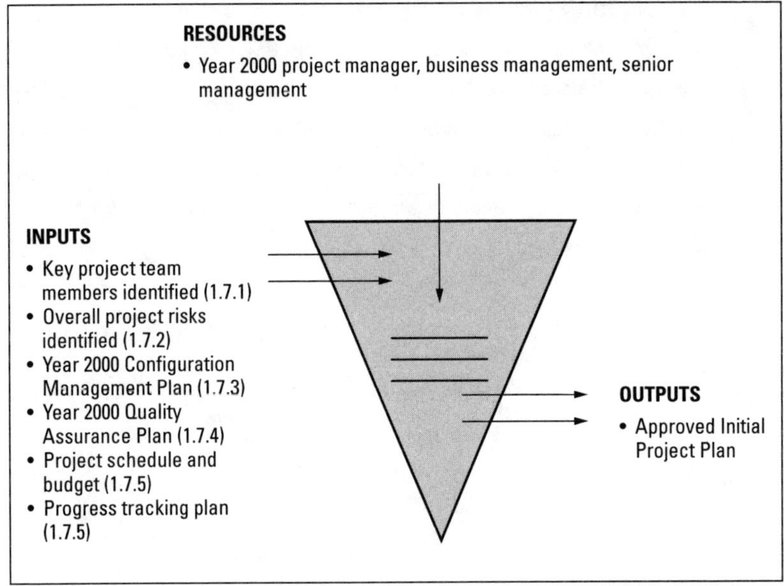
RESOURCES
• Year 2000 project manager, business management, senior management
INPUTS
• Key project team members identified (1.7.1)
• Overall project risks identified (1.7.2)
• Year 2000 Configuration Management Plan (1.7.3)
• Year 2000 Quality Assurance Plan (1.7.4)
• Project schedule and budget (1.7.5)
• Progress tracking plan (1.7.5)
OUTPUTS
• Approved Initial Project Plan

milestone

Initial Project Plan completed and approved. Quality assurance verifies that the deliverable conforms to its intended goal. Project control baselines the deliverable and updates tracking metrics.

1.8 Inventory and Triage Phase Plans

Following approval of the Initial Project Plan, you must develop some detailed plans for the Inventory and Triage phases of your Year 2000 project. You must complete Triage activities before you can develop detailed plans for the subsequent compliance phases.

Task Overview

- Tailor Methodology for Inventory and Triage

- Identify Inventory and Triage Resource Requirements
- Develop Schedule/Budget for Inventory and Triage
- Present and Approve Inventory and Triage Schedule/Budget

1.8.1 Task: Tailor Methodology for Inventory and Triage

Use the Inventory and Triage sections as a base from which to list the deliverables and objectives for conducting Inventory and Triage within your organization. Consider how you could best conduct these phases within the processes, structure, and culture of your organization. Different business areas, especially isolated business units, may require individualized approaches. Outline these decisions in the plan. This information is also used as input to the Initial Project Plan.

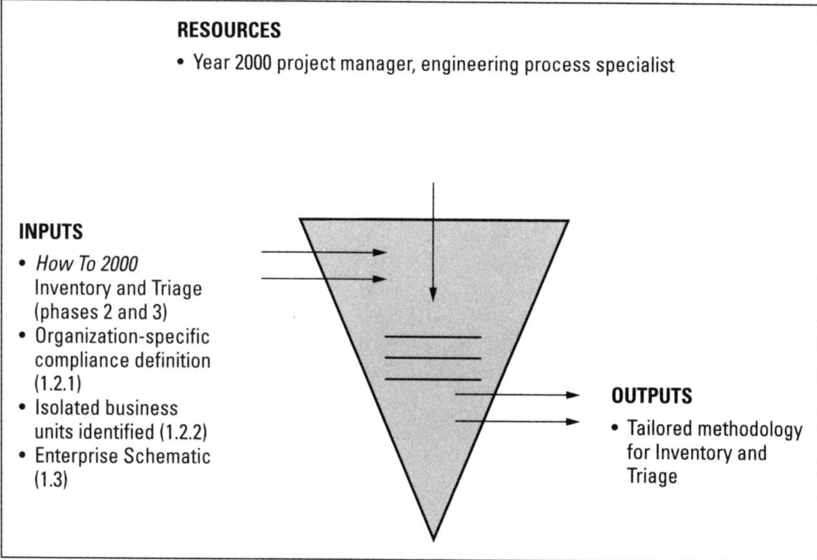
RESOURCES
• Year 2000 project manager, engineering process specialist
INPUTS
• How To 2000 Inventory and Triage (phases 2 and 3)
• Organization-specific compliance definition (1.2.1)
• Isolated business units identified (1.2.2)
• Enterprise Schematic (1.3)
OUTPUTS
• Tailored methodology for Inventory and Triage

1.8.2 Task: Identify Inventory and Triage Resource Requirements

In this task, you list the resources needed to conduct Inventory and Triage activities. These resources include not only personnel, but tools needed for Inventory, including word processing tools for general administration, and tools for collect-

ing, building, and maintaining the data repository. See Appendix E for a more complete definition of tools.

Depending upon the size of your organization and the diversity of your environment, you may need to have multiple Inventory teams. This can allow you to keep the Inventory time short, expenses down, and the project moving. A team should include at least one senior-level programmer, a senior analyst, and two junior-level programmers.

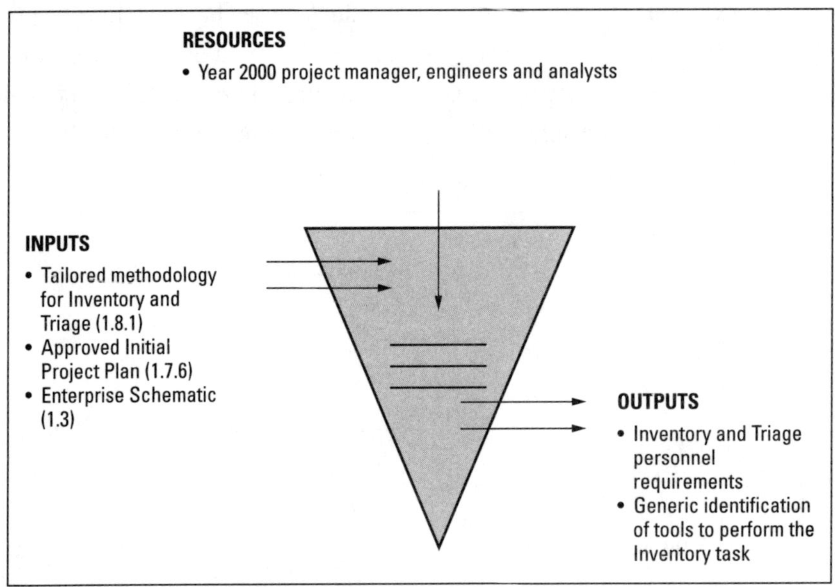
RESOURCES
• Year 2000 project manager, engineers and analysts
INPUTS
• Tailored methodology for Inventory and Triage (1.8.1)
• Approved Initial Project Plan (1.7.6)
• Enterprise Schematic (1.3)
OUTPUTS
• Inventory and Triage personnel requirements
• Generic identification of tools to perform the Inventory task

1.8.3 Task: Develop Schedule/Budget for Inventory and Triage

To develop the schedule, you must consider where your Inventory phase will start. If your Inventory practices are spotty, you will need to plan additional time. If configuration management will be loosely implemented, you may encounter inaccurate or nonexistent records of upgrades, maintenance performed, and source code used. You may even encounter pieces of systems that were password-protected by someone who is no longer with your organization. You may have systems that were developed or acquired before your organization adopted a consistent CM process.

When determining how much of the effort can be conducted in parallel, and what the costs may be, you can use the following:

- The rough-order-of-magnitude schedule and budget included in the Initial Project Plan
- The decision on whether in-house or contracted labor will be used to conduct the Inventory phase
- Your starting point for Inventory—solid information or sketchy

The schedule should include easily measured progress points or milestones that will be used to track progress. Examples might include

- Inventory of XYZ Division complete
- Audit of XYZ Division Inventory complete and Inventory updated
- Inventory complete
- Triage complete

You should undertake a review when Inventory is completed, and then Triage is completed, to determine conformance of actual technical effort, schedule, budget, and resource utilization with what was planned. You should request and obtain specific feedback to allow Year 2000 planners to more accurately plan remaining efforts.

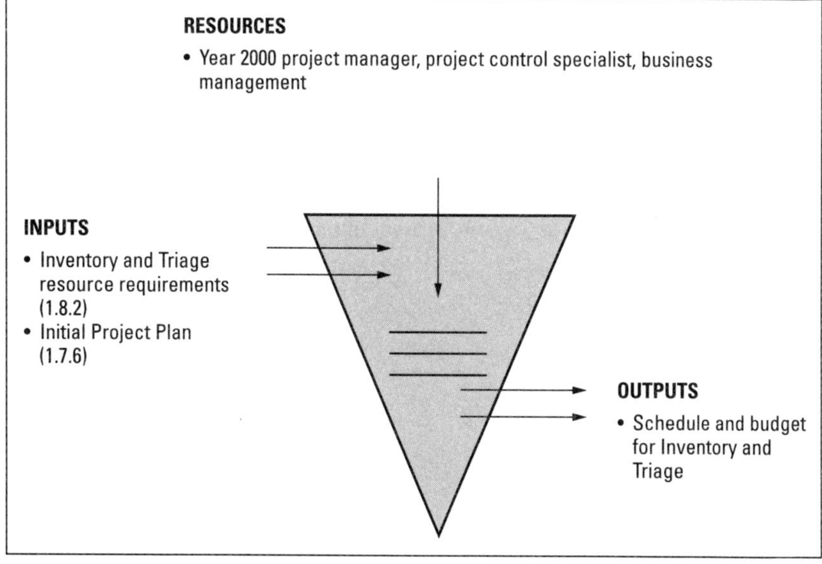
RESOURCES
• Year 2000 project manager, project control specialist, business management
INPUTS
• Inventory and Triage resource requirements (1.8.2)
• Initial Project Plan (1.7.6)
OUTPUTS
• Schedule and budget for Inventory and Triage

1.8.4 Task: Present and Approve Inventory and Triage Schedule/Budget

Management is most interested in your budget, followed by your staffing requirements and scheduling. These are important because of the way they may affect ongoing, revenue-producing projects, or planned departmental upgrades. Get approval for your plan (including the budget, schedule, and staff acquisitions) and move to Inventory and Triage.

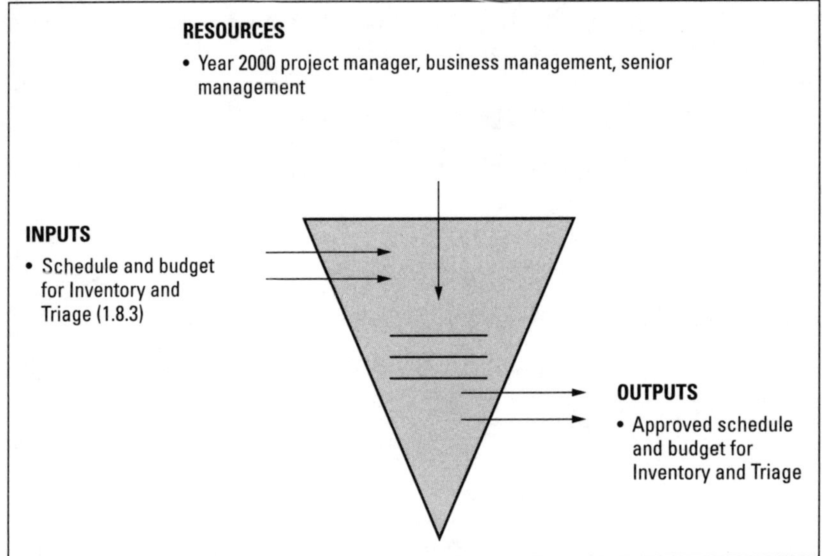
RESOURCES
• Year 2000 project manager, business management, senior management
INPUTS
• Schedule and budget for Inventory and Triage (1.8.3)
OUTPUTS
• Approved schedule and budget for Inventory and Triage

milestone

Inventory and Triage Phase Plan completed and approved. Quality assurance verifies that the deliverable conforms to its intended goal. Project control baselines the deliverable and updates tracking metrics.

Business Impacts

The tasks undertaken during the Planning and Awareness phase will not significantly affect your business processes. Relatively few resources are expended during this phase since it primarily involves Year 2000 staff and senior managers.

However, the long-range impact of Planning and Awareness activities will be significant. Business managers must initiate plans to modify their operations to accommodate anticipated Year 2000 project activities. These modifications must address the following concerns:

- **The proliferation of the Year 2000 problem must be halted.** In addition to solving existing Year 2000 compliance problems, you must prevent new instances of noncompliance. Procurement personnel, contracting officers, designers, and developers must ensure that newly developed systems and newly purchased COTS products are Year 2000 compliant.
- **System and environment capacity must be sufficient to incorporate Year 2000 solutions.** To incorporate Year 2000 solutions, existing systems and environments may require additional memory, processing capability, and disk space.
- **Resolution of Year 2000 problems may require significant allocation of labor and equipment resources.** You must decide how to handle the anticipated demand for personnel and equipment to implement Year 2000 solutions. You have to choose between using either in-house or contract personnel to review essentially 100 percent of your active systems and code, and potentially to rewrite a substantial portion of it—while continuing with normal operations. You can make this decision fairly early in the Year 2000 project, or delay it until late in the Detailed Assessment phase. Because the demand for Year 2000 programmers is expected to increase as the Year 2000 approaches, you must also develop a plan to retain newly hired programmers. You may need to institute a Year 2000 personnel incentive program.
- **You must consider Year 2000 rules on cost capitalization.** The Emerging Issues Task Force (EITF) of the Financial Accounting Standards Board (that is, the rule-making body for certified public accountants) issued a ruling on

July 18, 1996, that prohibits all U.S. companies from capitalizing costs for Year 2000 modifications. This ruling was upheld by the Board in March 1997. Although it included instances where such upgrades could be capitalized, you must consider this ruling when budget planning is underway.

- **Existing budgets may require modification.** Investigation and implementation of Year 2000 solutions will affect personnel, budgets, and in-house hardware resources. Completed budgets for the current year and for future years will require modification to accommodate Year 2000 project tasks.
- **It may be wise to halt concurrent development.** New development projects and procurements may need to be reevaluated or postponed. Because of the organizational breadth of infrastructure development projects, you should carefully evaluate IS-sponsored projects before authorizing continued development. In the case of development projects, it may be safer to postpone them rather than to risk the emergence of interface incompatibilities between Year 2000 compliant and noncompliant systems.

Phase Risks

Potential Event	*Probability*	*Impact*	*Risk*
Enterprise Schematic inaccurate	Medium	High	High
Initial Project Plan underestimates necessary Year 2000 resources	Medium	High	High

Planning and Awareness Phase Risks

There are two primary risks associated with the Planning and Awareness phase: The Enterprise Schematic may be inaccurate and the Initial Project Plan may underestimate the necessary resources for the Year 2000 project.

Enterprise Schematic Inaccurate

The Enterprise Schematic is the basis for the overall vision of your organization's systems. If this vision is flawed, your Year 2000 endeavors will also be flawed. In the worst-case scenario, you could fail to ensure Year 2000 compliance of critical systems because of a flawed Enterprise Schematic. Inaccurate or incomplete Enterprise Schematics can also result in gross inaccuracies in planning and budgeting, with the attendant loss of credibility for the program and shortfall of funds and resources. In other words, an inaccurate Enterprise Schematic is an important Planning and Awareness risk.

There are a couple of ways of mitigating this risk:

- Institute a mechanism for verifying Enterprise Schematics. Initial versions should be carefully reviewed and verified by as many knowledgeable people as possible. If possible, the Enterprise Schematics should be verified by personnel from every business area or department.
- Make business managers responsible for reviewing and approving portions of the schematics that apply to their departments or business areas. This way they will be far more likely to help develop the schematic. In addition, ensure that these managers are aware of the long-range impact of this schematic.

Project Plan Underestimates Necessary Year 2000 Resources

Most system developers recognize how hard it is to accurately estimate project resources. For the Year 2000 project, this task may be particularly troublesome. Most likely, you have never participated in a project that affects so many systems, and so many of your organization's business processes. You will have no points of reference, and for this reason your estimations of Year 2000 resource requirements may be extremely inaccurate. Make sure management knows that additional acquisition of resources may be necessary.

There are a couple of ways of mitigating this risk:

- Strive for accuracy in your estimates, but not for high precision. Present your estimates as a numeric range rather than as an individual number. (For example, "Staff resources for Inventory are estimated at 8,000 to 10,000 man-hours.") Document your assumptions, as well as any uncertainties.

Don't forget that testing will be iterative; all systems will not come into compliance at the same time. This may affect the sizing of your plan.

- Develop a contingency plan for acquiring additional project resources. Reevaluate project resource allocation at several different times as the project progresses. Acquire additional resources according to the contingency plan. Make management realize that additional resources may be requested at later stages of the Year 2000 project.

Success Factors

In successfully completing the Planning and Awareness Phase, you carried out the following steps:

Success Factor	*Deliverable*
Investigated the Year 2000 problem and its potential impact on your organization	Management Awareness Briefings
Identified isolated business units	Management Awareness Briefings
Briefed senior management on the importance of the Year 2000 project	Management Awareness Briefings
Obtained approval to initialize a Year 2000 project	Management Awareness Briefings
Defined Year 2000 compliance for your organization	Compliance Definition
Defined your Year 2000 objectives	Compliance Definition
Developed Enterprise Schematics for your organization and business areas	Enterprise Schematic
Made all related departments aware of their Year 2000 project roles and responsibilities. These departments included IS, procurement, legal counsel, public relations, isolated business units, contractors, and business and electronic partners.	Organization Awareness Campaign

SUCCESS FACTOR	DELIVERABLE
Developed a plan to establish communication channels and processes in support of the Year 2000 project	Year 2000 Project Communications Plan
Developed a Year 2000 legal policy plan	Policy and Public Relations Plan
Developed a Year 2000 public relations plan	Policy and Public Relations Plan
Defined scope and size estimates for the entire project, including underlying assumptions	Initial Project Plan
Assessed overall project risk	Initial Project Plan
Reviewed existing Configuration Management Plan and tailored it to the needs of the Year 2000 project	Initial Project Plan
Reviewed existing Quality Assurance Plan and tailored it to the needs of the Year 2000 project	Initial Project Plan
Considered the entire Year 2000 project schedule through final deployment	Initial Project Plan
Identified progress milestones for the Year 2000 project	Initial Project Plan
Identified critical resources needed for Year 2000 project success in project plan	Initial Project Plan
Developed technical resource cost estimates, based on scope and size, for the entire project	Initial Project Plan
Obtained approval for Year 2000 initial budget, schedule, and plan	Initial Project Plan
Developed a plan for Inventory and Triage staff, schedule, and budget	Inventory and Triage Phase Plans
Obtained approved budget for Inventory and Triage	Inventory and Triage Phase Plans
Identified phase risks and potential mitigation approaches	All deliverables
Identified deliverables that would be developed during this phase	All deliverables
Used adequate communication interfaces throughout your organization to support the tasks associated with this phase	All deliverables
Assigned phase tasks to various groups in your organization and ensured management approval for those tasks	All deliverables

continued

SUCCESS FACTOR	DELIVERABLE
Identified the deliverables for which each group was responsible and ensured that each group accepted responsibility for those deliverables	All deliverable
Identified key milestones for the accomplishment of tasks for this phase	All deliverables
Identified milestone thresholds beyond which some corrective action will be taken	All deliverables
Used metrics to track and measure progress with respect to these milestones	All deliverables
Ensured that each responsible group accepted and adhered to the schedule for completion of this phase	All deliverables

REFERENCE MATERIAL

This list mentions reference material you can turn to for additional information on your Year 2000 compliance project:

- Appendix A, Problem Definition Catalog
- Appendix B, Solution Sets
- Appendix C, Legal and Contract Considerations
- Appendix D, Sample Presentations
- Appendix E, Applicability of Tools
- Appendix F, Key Tasks Outline
- Appendix H, Integrated Project Plan
- Appendix I, How To 2000 Risk Management
- Appendix J, Steps to Make Your PC Year 2000 Prepared
- Glossary
- *How To 2000* CD-ROM

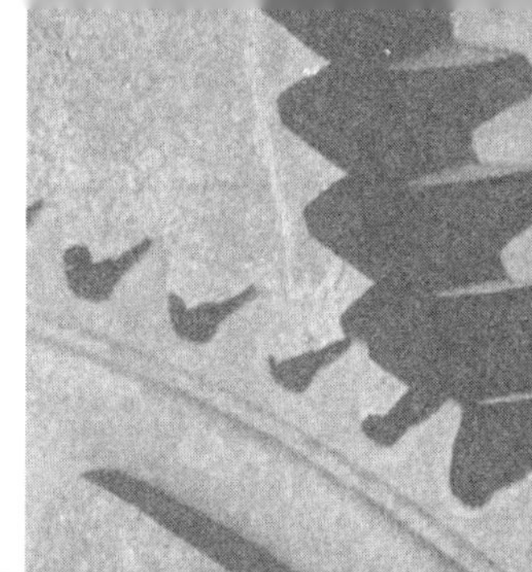

CHAPTER

Phase 2: Inventory

2

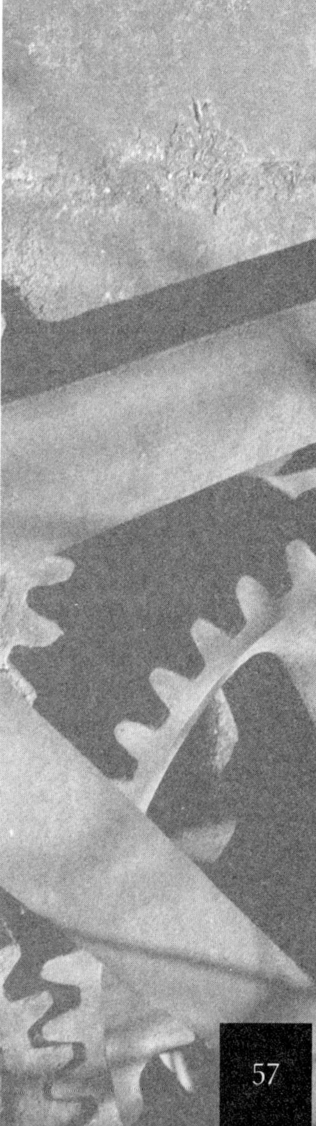

INVENTORY

Objectives:

- Establish your Year 2000 repository.
- Identify all automated systems in your organization.
- Catalog electronic partners and interfaces.
- Ascertain those systems that will be affected by the Year 2000 date.
- Identify and catalog internal tools that could assist with Year 2000 detection and correction.
- Assess technical risks associated with each system.

Phase 2, Inventory, you take stock of your current systems so you can determine the best method for bringing them into Year 2000 compliance.

TAKING INVENTORY

Before you can decide how to tackle the Year 2000 problem, you must grasp the size and boundaries of the problem. How many of your organization's systems will be affected by Year 2000 problems? To what extent are those problems and systems interdependent? Which of these systems were developed within your organization and which are COTS (commercial off the shelf) systems? Which of these systems are actively used in your organization and which are used only occasionally?

To answer these questions, you must carry out the dual tasks of identification and discovery: Identify every system in your organization, and discover how many of those systems are likely to be affected by Year 2000 problems. During the Inventory phase, you do just that.

The primary goal of this phase is to complete an inventory of all automated systems (or Inventory Elements) within your organization. Your organization's systems will include software applications, operating systems, commercial off the shelf (COTS) software, computing hardware, communications hardware, third-party interfaces, and embedded systems (for example, E-PROMS, microcontroller chips, PC BIOS, and so on). Inventory participants must do two things: Identify systems they believe will be affected by a Year 2000 problem, and assess the extent

to which these systems will be affected. A secondary goal is to identify automated tools that can support your Year 2000 project.

Because your organization will continue to acquire and/or develop new systems throughout the life of your Year 2000 Project, new Year 2000 problems may enter your organizational environment even as you are fixing existing problems. Consequently, you may be required to repeat Inventory phase activities. Indeed, due to the dynamic nature of the environment in which most organizations operate, several iterations of both Inventory and Triage tasks may be necessary.

Quality assurance has a minor auditing role during Inventory. Because of the novelty of the tasks undertaken during this phase, your organization may not have applicable standards or quality directives. However, QA should monitor the activities to ensure that any relevant plans are followed. Any deviations from these plans should be reported and tracked.

The information collected during Inventory will be captured in the Year 2000 repository. This repository will provide managers with the information resources they need to make sound decisions during future Year 2000 endeavors.

The costs for the completion of Inventory should not exceed 3 percent of your Year 2000 project cost.

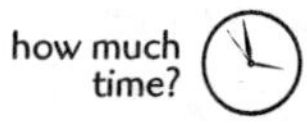

The time devoted to Inventory tasks should comprise 5 percent of the Year 2000 project schedule.

Summary of Deliverables

This section summarizes the deliverables for this phase of your Year 2000 compliance project. The section "Deliverables, Tasks, and Dependencies" later in this chapter includes detailed descriptions of each deliverable and the associated supporting tasks.

Inventory Phase Startup

The Inventory Phase Startup deliverable provides the requisite Inventory work environment.

Internal Tool Inventory

The Internal Tool Inventory deliverable provides a list of your organization's automated tools that may support Year 2000 endeavors.

Tool Analysis and Vendor Tool Identification

The Tool Analysis and Vendor Tool Identification deliverable provides an assessment of the specific types of automated tools necessary to complete the Year 2000 project. This assessment is compared with the Internal Tool Inventory, and organizational tool deficiencies are identified. This deliverable also provides a listing of vendor tools that can support tasks for which tool deficiencies have been identified.

Staffing Estimate and Vendor Services Inventory

The Staffing Estimate and Vendor Services Inventory deliverable provides an estimate of the personnel necessary to complete the Year 2000 project. Based on this estimate, internal shortfalls of Year 2000 staff are identified. This deliverable also provides a listing of vendor services that can support tasks for which staff shortfalls have been identified.

System Inventory

The System Inventory deliverable provides a comprehensive inventory of all systems in your organization. Information obtained via the System Inventory will be stored within the Year 2000 repository.

Inventory Schematic

The Inventory Schematic depicts the systems and system relationships currently functioning within your organization. This schematic is based upon the information contained within the Year 2000 repository and serves as a top-level summary of that information.

System Configuration Status Report

The System Configuration Status Report deliverable describes any existing configuration problems associated with your organization's systems, including instances of mismatched object and source code, instances in which source code does not compile, and instances in which certain system components no longer exist. This information may influence critical decisions made during the Triage phase. In

addition, this information will facilitate the reduction of time and resources devoted to Detailed Assessment phase tasks.

Inventory Element Dependencies

The Inventory Element Dependencies deliverable provides a listing of the technical dependencies among the various systems, or Inventory Elements, currently operating in your organization. An example technical dependency might be "Word processor *X* requires operating system *Z* to function successfully."

Technical Risk Inventory

The Technical Risk Inventory deliverable provides a list of the technical risks associated with each system in your organization. An example of a technical risk is "If operating system *Z* fails to function properly, software applications *W*, *X*, and *Y* will not be able to operate." Technical risk, which concerns a system's ability to function, should not be confused with Business risk, which concerns a system's impact upon organizational objectives.

Deliverables, Tasks, and Dependencies

The deliverables completed in the Inventory phase will allow you to obtain detailed information about the systems in your organization and the tools and services you will need to support your Year 2000 effort.

2.1 Inventory Phase Startup

The Inventory Phase Startup provides the resources that must be available to ensure the efficient completion of all Inventory phase tasks. Upon completion of this deliverable, the environment needed to successfully execute the Inventory phase will be in place.

Task Overview

- Acquire Human Resources for Inventory
- Establish Inventory Tracking

- Brief Staff Members on Inventory Plan
- Define Detailed Requirements for Inventory Tools
- Acquire Tools for Inventory
- Establish Inventory Work Environment
- Establish Repository and CM Environment

2.1.1 Task: Acquire Human Resources for Inventory

You will identify the specific staff members who will participate in Inventory activities. You will ensure these staff members are contacted and given preliminary instructions for task initiation. These staff members will receive detailed instructions about this task later.

The details of the personnel acquisition process will depend upon the structure of your organization, the processes it uses to assign people to tasks, the overall staffing situation, and the priority that senior management has established for your Year 2000 project.

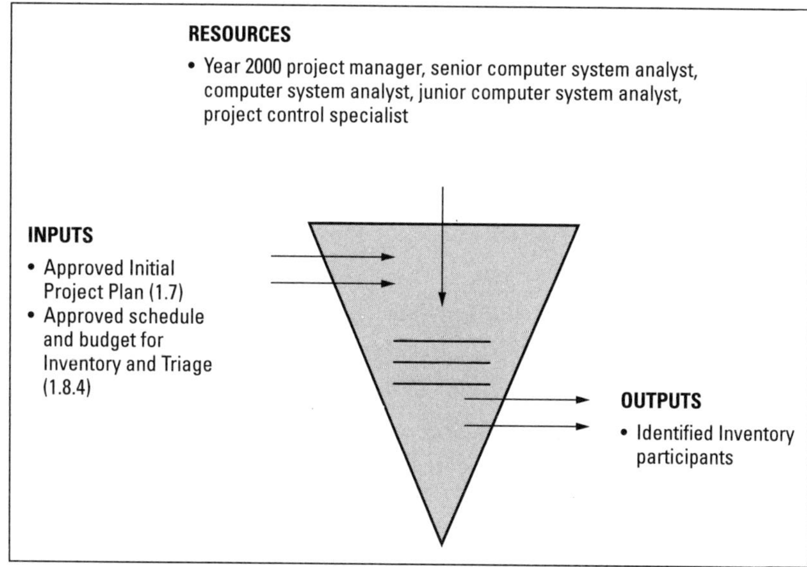
RESOURCES
• Year 2000 project manager, senior computer system analyst, computer system analyst, junior computer system analyst, project control specialist
INPUTS
• Approved Initial Project Plan (1.7)
• Approved schedule and budget for Inventory and Triage (1.8.4)
OUTPUTS
• Identified Inventory participants

Task Guidelines

- You may want to initiate interactive sessions to review and make selections from the personnel roster.
- You should use a communication method of choice (memo, phone, fax, e-mail) to convey messages to affected staff.

2.1.2 Task: Establish Inventory Tracking

Using the schedule and progress measurement requirements set forth in the Progress Tracking Plan (1.7.5), define specific phase milestones, measurement points, and progress review meetings that will let you accurately assess your actual progress against the overall schedule for this phase.

When evaluating progress against your Inventory phase schedule, consider the status of the work products, as well as the resources expended in developing these products. You should continually evaluate the status of risk mitigation activities. If you find discrepancies between planned and actual task completions, you should reallocate appropriate resources. In addition, you should use the feedback mechanisms established in the Progress Tracking Plan to allow knowledge gained in this phase to influence future tracking and schedule decisions.

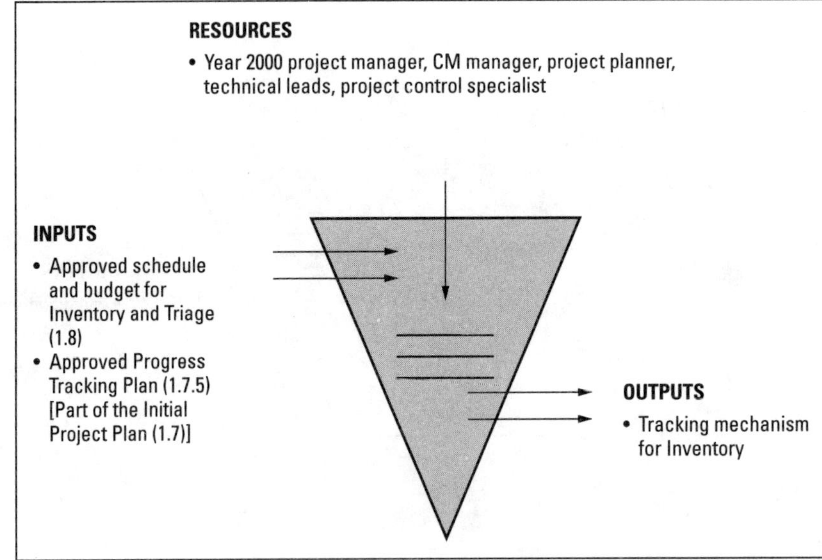
RESOURCES
• Year 2000 project manager, CM manager, project planner, technical leads, project control specialist
INPUTS
• Approved schedule and budget for Inventory and Triage (1.8)
• Approved Progress Tracking Plan (1.7.5) [Part of the Initial Project Plan (1.7)]
OUTPUTS
• Tracking mechanism for Inventory

2.1.3 Task: Brief Staff Members on Inventory Plan

Provide a comprehensive Inventory phase briefing to staff members who will be participating in Inventory activities. Topics should include individual responsibilities within this phase, recognition of key players, the Inventory phase schedule, and appropriate information concerning the Inventory phase work environment.

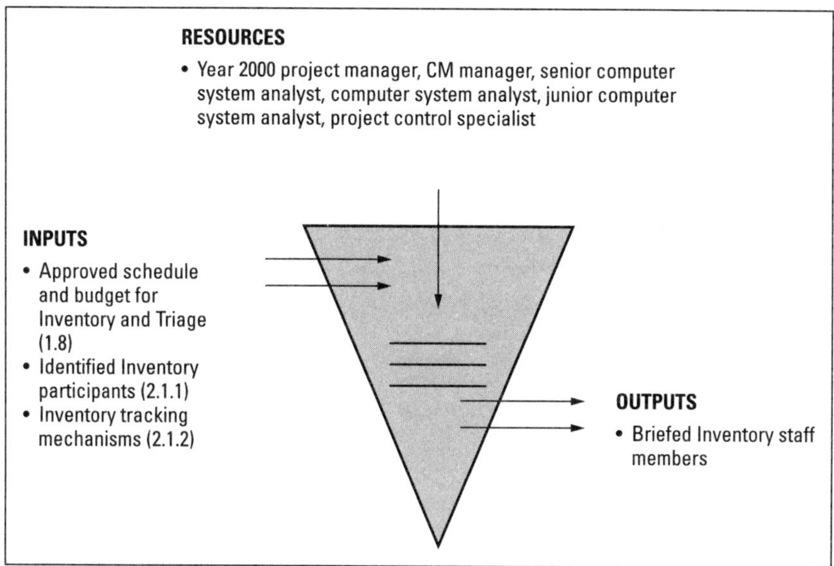
RESOURCES
• Year 2000 project manager, CM manager, senior computer system analyst, computer system analyst, junior computer system analyst, project control specialist
INPUTS
• Approved schedule and budget for Inventory and Triage (1.8)
• Identified Inventory participants (2.1.1)
• Inventory tracking mechanisms (2.1.2)
OUTPUTS
• Briefed Inventory staff members

Task Guideline

- This briefing will be the initial "all hands" gathering. As such, the person or persons who conduct the briefing have a unique opportunity to set the tone for the entire Year 2000 endeavor. The enthusiasm you bring to this briefing will influence the level of enthusiasm that each staff member will bring to Inventory activities.

2.1.4 Task: Define Detailed Requirements for Inventory Tools

Prior planning for Inventory (see Planning and Awareness phase, Inventory and Triage Phase Plans deliverable) included the identification of tools that would be used during Inventory. These tools included

- General administration (word processing tools)

- A data repository to receive and maintain the information collected during this phase

During this task, you specify the detailed requirements for these tools.

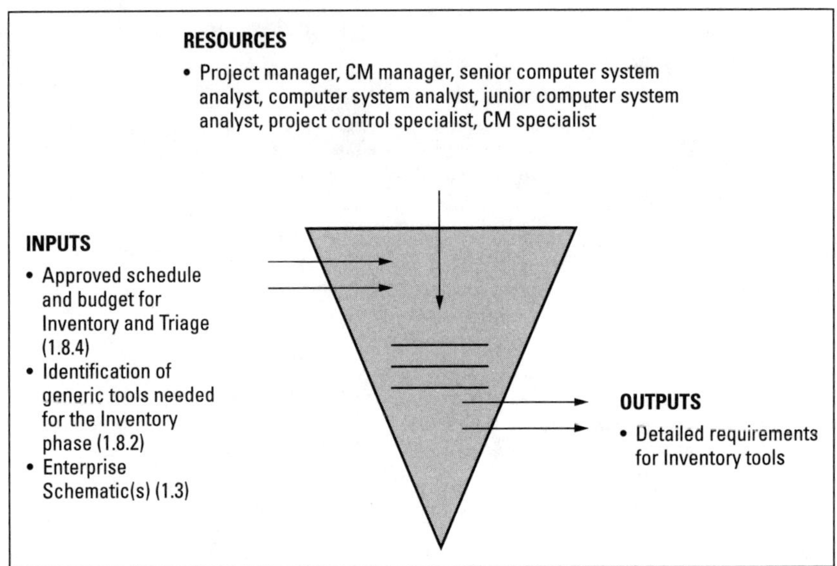
RESOURCES
• Project manager, CM manager, senior computer system analyst, computer system analyst, junior computer system analyst, project control specialist, CM specialist
INPUTS
• Approved schedule and budget for Inventory and Triage (1.8.4)
• Identification of generic tools needed for the Inventory phase (1.8.2)
• Enterprise Schematic(s) (1.3)
OUTPUTS
• Detailed requirements for Inventory tools

Task Guidelines

- The importance of the data repository tool cannot be overemphasized. Information about all the systems considered in your Year 2000 project will be maintained in the repository. This information will be used to support critical thinking and decision-making throughout the Year 2000 conversion process. You must estimate the quantity and format of incoming information and ensure that this estimate is clearly reflected in your repository requirements. In addition, the repository will be used to record and track the changes made to each system as the project progresses. Consequently, the Year 2000 repository will serve as your primary Configuration Management support tool.
- You may want to initiate one or more interactive sessions to estimate tool demands and specify tool requirements.

2.1.5 Task: Acquire Tools for Inventory

The detailed requirements for Inventory tools will be used to identify specific tools for use during this phase. Once you have generated a list of candidate tools, you must determine which ones you will acquire to support the Inventory activities. You probably will not need all the tools on your candidate list; only a toolset sufficient to support your planned Inventory activities and schedule. Create a written rationale for accepting or rejecting individual tools or suites before you begin the acquisition process. Once your justifications have been documented, acquire the tools you need to support Inventory.

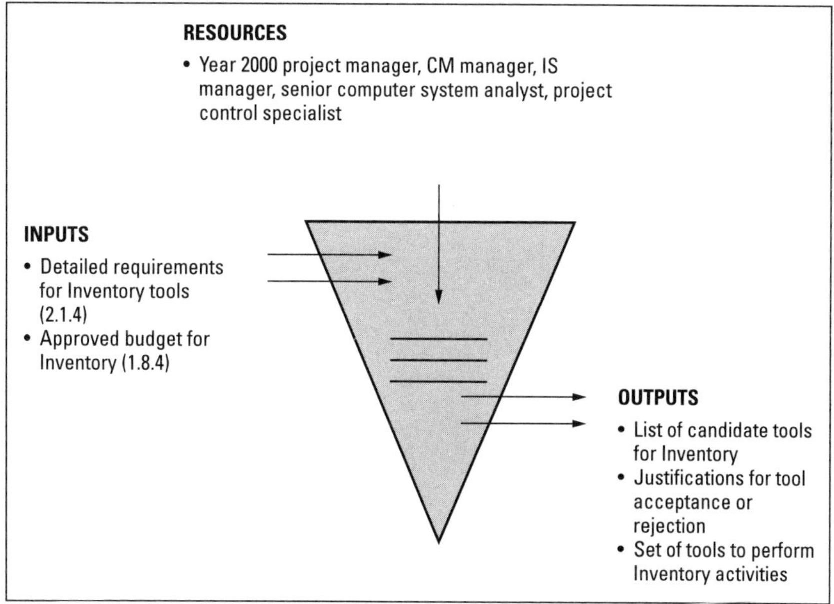
RESOURCES
• Year 2000 project manager, CM manager, IS manager, senior computer system analyst, project control specialist
INPUTS
• Detailed requirements for Inventory tools (2.1.4)
• Approved budget for Inventory (1.8.4)
OUTPUTS
• List of candidate tools for Inventory
• Justifications for tool acceptance or rejection
• Set of tools to perform Inventory activities

Task Guidelines

- Your management may have established one or more tools or suites as organizational standards. In addition, special license agreements may currently exist with various tool vendors. Be sure to evaluate the suitability of any such suites or individual tools during the candidate identification process.
- Your organization's policies will define the appropriate method of acquiring tools.

2.1.6 Task: Establish Inventory Work Environment

Set up the office environment in which Inventory staff will operate throughout this phase.

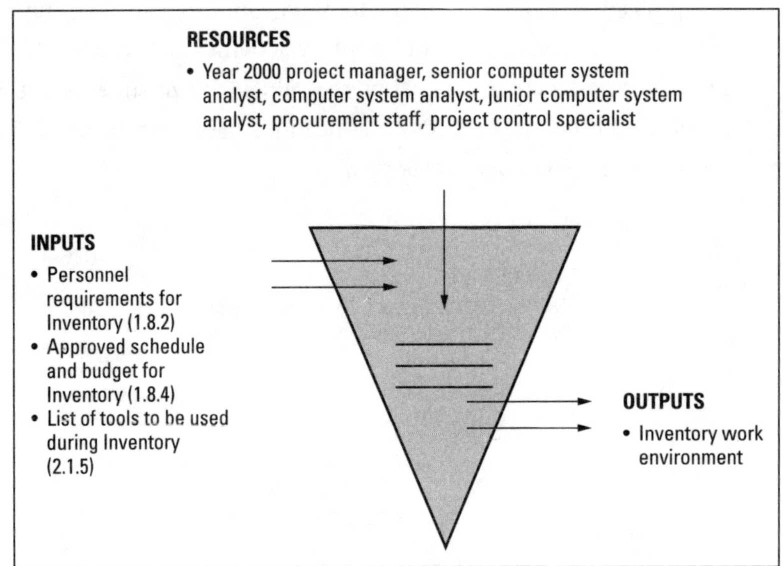
RESOURCES
• Year 2000 project manager, senior computer system analyst, computer system analyst, junior computer system analyst, procurement staff, project control specialist
INPUTS
• Personnel requirements for Inventory (1.8.2)
• Approved schedule and budget for Inventory (1.8.4)
• List of tools to be used during Inventory (2.1.5)
OUTPUTS
• Inventory work environment

Task Guidelines

- The more robust your rationale for resources (personnel requirements, tasking descriptions, tool requirements), the more straightforward this task will be.
- An approved schedule for Inventory activities will expedite the procurement process.

2.1.7 Task: Establish Repository and CM Environment

During this task you configure and ensure the sound operation of the Year 2000 data repository. The data repository will contain all information gathered throughout the Year 2000 project, and must be continually accessed and updated. Upon initiation, the Year 2000 repository should be placed under formal Configuration Management.

Appendix G contains a sample data schematic for a Year 2000 repository. You can use this schematic as the foundation for your repository definition efforts.

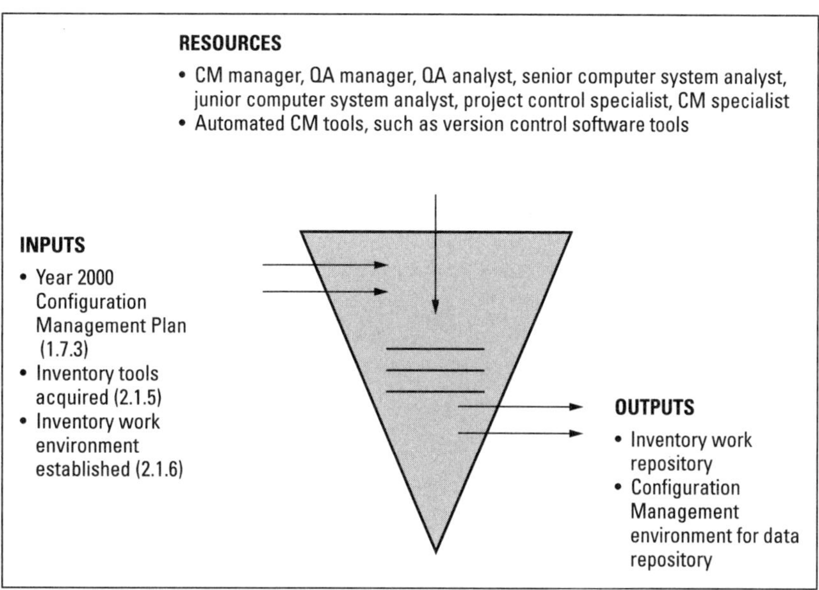
RESOURCES
• CM manager, QA manager, QA analyst, senior computer system analyst, junior computer system analyst, project control specialist, CM specialist
• Automated CM tools, such as version control software tools
INPUTS
• Year 2000 Configuration Management Plan (1.7.3)
• Inventory tools acquired (2.1.5)
• Inventory work environment established (2.1.6)
OUTPUTS
• Inventory work repository
• Configuration Management environment for data repository

Task Guidelines

- You tailored your organization's CM procedures to suit the needs of your Year 2000 project (1.7.3) when creating the Initial Program Plan. CM considerations should include, but are not limited to:
  - The designation of a specific staff member as the database administrator
  - The initiation of a mechanism to control changes to the repository, including the designation of a Configuration Control Board, or a person or persons to act in this capacity
  - The initiation of the mechanism to enforce version control within the repository, ideally using an automated tool
  - The initiation of a configuration auditing mechanism

milestone

Inventory Phase Startup completed. Quality assurance verifies that the deliverable conforms to its intended goal. Project control baselines the deliverable and updates tracking metrics.

2.2 Internal Tool Inventory

The Internal Tool Inventory provides describes existing tools within your organization that can be used to support your Year 2000 project.

Task Overview

- Define Functional Tool Requirements
- Create and Circulate Internal Tool Questionnaire
- Analyze Questionnaires
- Capture Internal Tool List

2.2.1 Task: Define Functional Tool Requirements

Based on your current knowledge of the activities that will be undertaken throughout the Year 2000 project, you define the functional attributes of the tools used to support Year 2000 project activities.

As your Year 2000 project progresses, you will use various tools to:

- Develop and maintain your Year 2000 repository.
- Identify storage structures that contain dates.
- Identify process elements that compare dates, compute dates, store dates, and present dates.
- Identify date storage structures that are not Year 2000 compliant.
- Identify process elements that are not Year 2000 compliant.
- Convert noncompliant date storage structures to Year 2000 compliant.
- Convert noncompliant process elements to Year 2000 compliant elements.
- Ensure that data structures are Year 2000 compliant.
- Ensure that process elements function successfully.

The types of tools that will perform these functions include:

- Standard maintenance tools (both hardware and software).
- Code editors.
- Compilers.
- Database utilities, including data dictionaries, data search mechanisms, and testing tools.

You may want to derive requirements from existing tools that you know would be useful in a Year 2000 project. Some of these tools could be used in a variety of system development projects. Some are specifically targeted at a Year 2000 project audience. Although the complexity of any Year 2000 endeavor precludes the use of a single tool to support all of your Year 2000 tasks, many of these tools could prove useful. These tools include:

- **Software Inventory Tools**: Tools in this category identify all programs in a system and their components (modules, copybooks, subroutines, commands, screens, and report generators).
- **Date Reference Identification Tools**: Tools of this type can identify two-digit date references. Dates are tracked in a number of ways, including via browsers for basic text scanning and code inspection. Context searching identifies how a date is referenced.
- **Configuration Management Tools**: Many IS groups possess standard CM tools. These should be reviewed for possible application to Year 2000 tasks.
- **Impact Analysis Tools**: Tools of this type can help your organization understand the effect of system changes by tracing relationships within and among programs and systems. These tools often provide statistics concerning system cross-referencing, program size (in lines of code), total number of programs affected by a certain event, the number of lines of code that must be altered to achieve a certain standard, and so on. Although some of these tools are aimed specifically at the Year 2000 market, generic versions often support system maintenance tasks. Many of these tools use complex graphics to clarify the relationships among system components. Others may insert colors or flags directly into lines of code.

Your tool requirements should expand upon these general functions and should be tailored to the needs of your organization. Although some tools you decide to use may be Year 2000 specific, others could also be used in a variety of system development projects, and may continue to be useful outside the context of the Year 2000 project.

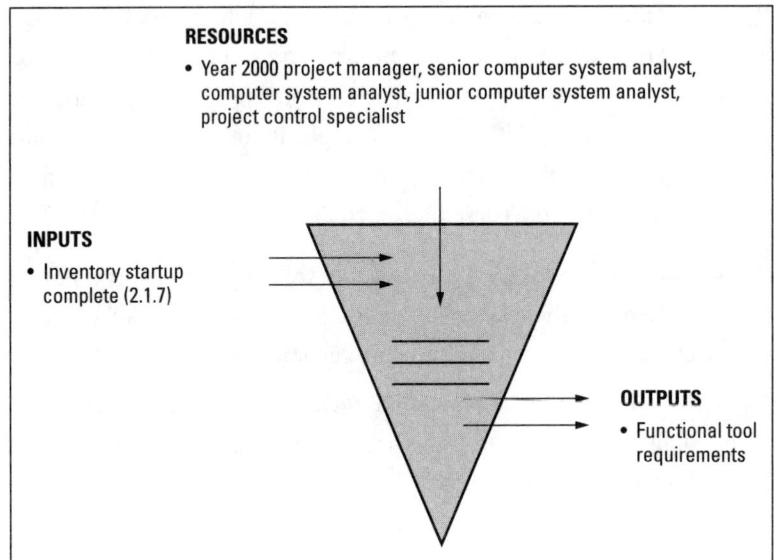
RESOURCES
• Year 2000 project manager, senior computer system analyst, computer system analyst, junior computer system analyst, project control specialist
INPUTS
• Inventory startup complete (2.1.7)
OUTPUTS
• Functional tool requirements

Task Guidelines

- You may want to initiate an interactive requirements engineering session to review each anticipated Year 2000 task and define tool requirements.
- These functional requirements should include various levels of detail. For example, a top-level requirement may state, "The system shall be able to match patterns," while a more detailed requirement may state that, "The system shall be able to identify code which matches the following pattern: [*pattern.*]." This hierarchy of functional requirements will allow you to identify tools that provide various levels of support for the Year 2000 project. The more general requirements may be fulfilled by tools that have uses other than supporting the Year 2000 project, while more detailed requirements may be fulfilled only by Year 2000-specific tools. For most Year 2000 projects, both generic and Year 2000-specific tools will prove useful.

2.2.2 Task: Create and Circulate Internal Tool Questionnaire

Develop a questionnaire based upon the functional requirements defined in the previous task. Circulate this questionnaire throughout your organization.

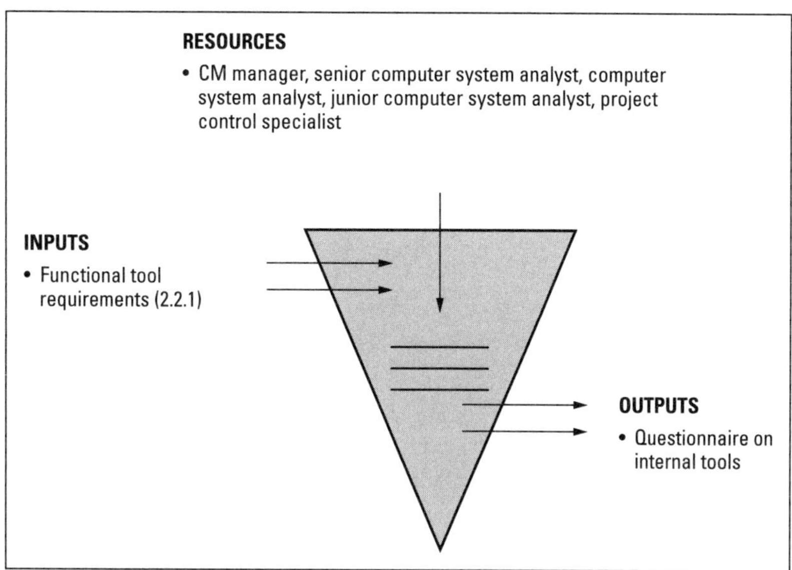
RESOURCES
• CM manager, senior computer system analyst, computer system analyst, junior computer system analyst, project control specialist
INPUTS
• Functional tool requirements (2.2.1)
OUTPUTS
• Questionnaire on internal tools

Task Guidelines

- Keep the questionnaire simple and straightforward. If it is too long or complex, you will not receive enough responses to be useful.
- The questionnaire should solicit the following information regarding tools that fulfill one or more of the functional requirements: tool name, tool ID, tool location, point of contact, summary of tool functionality, and availability constraints on tools, if any.

2.2.3 Task: Analyze Questionnaires

Evaluating the information in the returned questionnaires lets you identify tools that could be used to support the Year 2000 project.

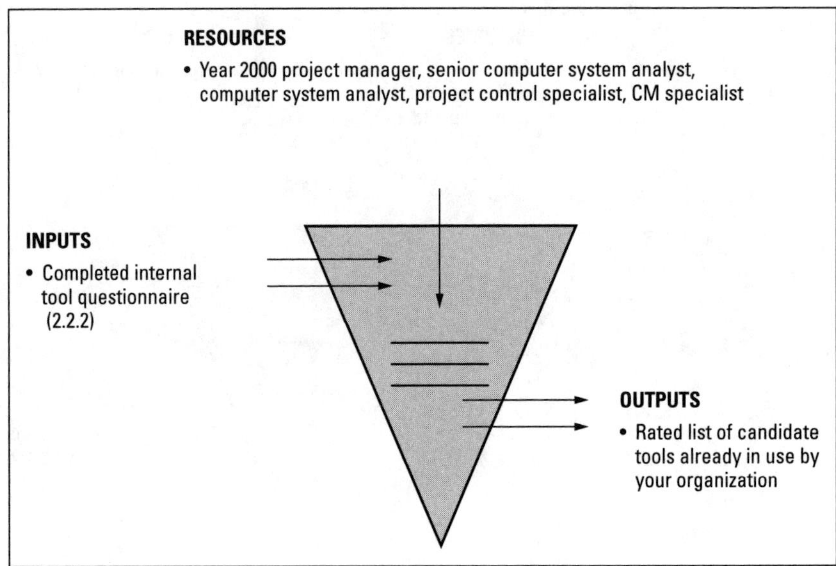
RESOURCES
• Year 2000 project manager, senior computer system analyst, computer system analyst, project control specialist, CM specialist
INPUTS
• Completed internal tool questionnaire (2.2.2)
OUTPUTS
• Rated list of candidate tools already in use by your organization

Task Guidelines

- You may wish to initiate interactive sessions to review and evaluate questionnaires.

Tools identified in the questionnaire will be rated according to:

- **Functionality**: What functions they can provide
- **Availability**: Whether they will be available for the entire Year 2000 project, or only for a portion it
- **Workload**: How much of the project workload they can handle
- **Cost of operation**: Whether it will be cost effective to use the tool
- **Alternatives**: Whether other tools could fulfill the functions provided by this tool

2.2.4 Task: Capture Internal Tool List

Based on your analysis of the questionnaires, decide which of your organization's tools can support the Year 2000 project. Capture this information in the Year 2000 repository. Make sure to adhere to standard CM practices as this information is captured and maintained. This list—tool existence, tool attributes, tool availability—will certainly change over time.

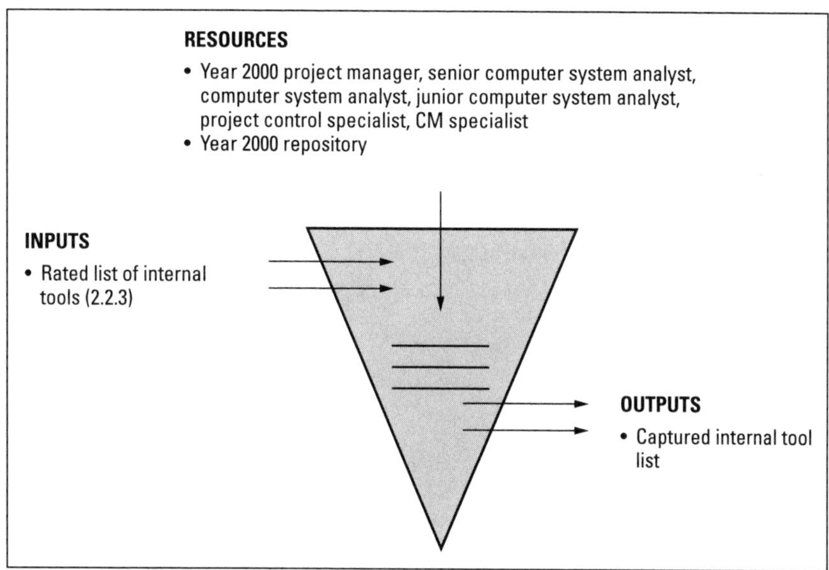
RESOURCES
• Year 2000 project manager, senior computer system analyst, computer system analyst, junior computer system analyst, project control specialist, CM specialist
• Year 2000 repository
INPUTS
• Rated list of internal tools (2.2.3)
OUTPUTS
• Captured internal tool list

Task Guideline

- Information describing the functional requirements satisfied by the tools you have chosen should be included in the data repository.

milestone

Internal Tool Inventory completed. Quality assurance verifies that the deliverable conforms to its intended goal. Project control baselines the deliverable and updates tracking metrics.

2.3 Tool Analysis and Vendor Tool Identification

This deliverable provides a summary of Year 2000 project tool requirements that cannot be fulfilled by tools identified in your Internal Tool Inventory. In addition, you identify Year 2000 project tools that may fulfill these requirements and could be developed within your organization or purchased from a vendor.

Task Overview

- Identify Deficiencies of Internal Tools
- Review/Evaluate Available Vendor Tools
- Recommend Buy/Build Decision
- Identify Vendor Tools for Acquisition

2.3.1 Task: Identify Deficiencies of Internal Tools

Compare the functional tool requirements with the requirements satisfied by tools contained in the Internal Tool Inventory. The requirements that cannot be fulfilled by existing tools become the list of tool deficiencies for the Year 2000 project.

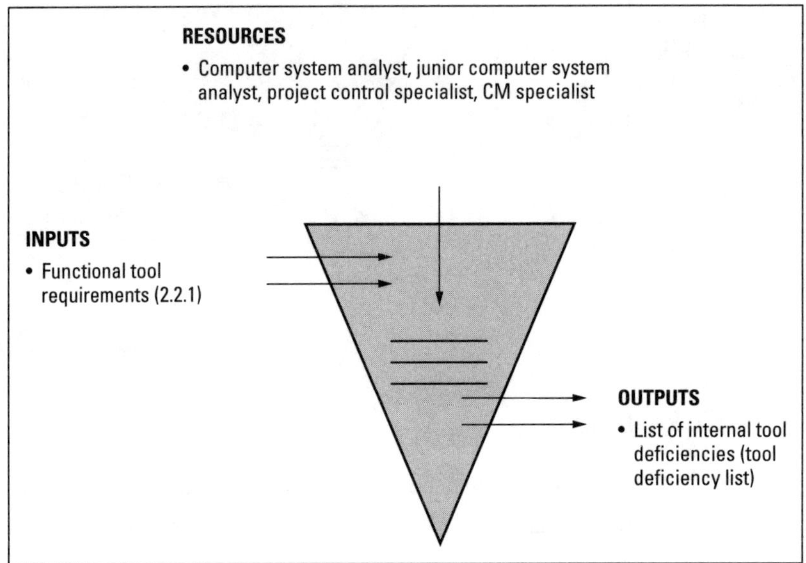
RESOURCES
• Computer system analyst, junior computer system analyst, project control specialist, CM specialist
INPUTS
• Functional tool requirements (2.2.1)
OUTPUTS
• List of internal tool deficiencies (tool deficiency list)

Task Guidelines

- Because the functional tool requirements and the Internal Tool Inventory are captured within the Year 2000 repository, you can identify discrepancies between the two by using a standard database utility that identifies records not shared by two tables.
- You can use available pattern matching methods for the comparison.

2.3.2 Task: Review/Evaluate Available Vendor Tools

You can obtain a comprehensive list of Year 2000 vendor tools from the *How To 2000* CD-ROM. Using this list, identify those tools that provide the functionality summarized in the tool deficiencies list, which you created in the previous task. Ideally, you will be able to identify several tools that address each deficiency. The selected tools will be incorporated within a list of vendor tool candidates. Items on this list become candidates for acquisition at later stages of the Year 2000 project.

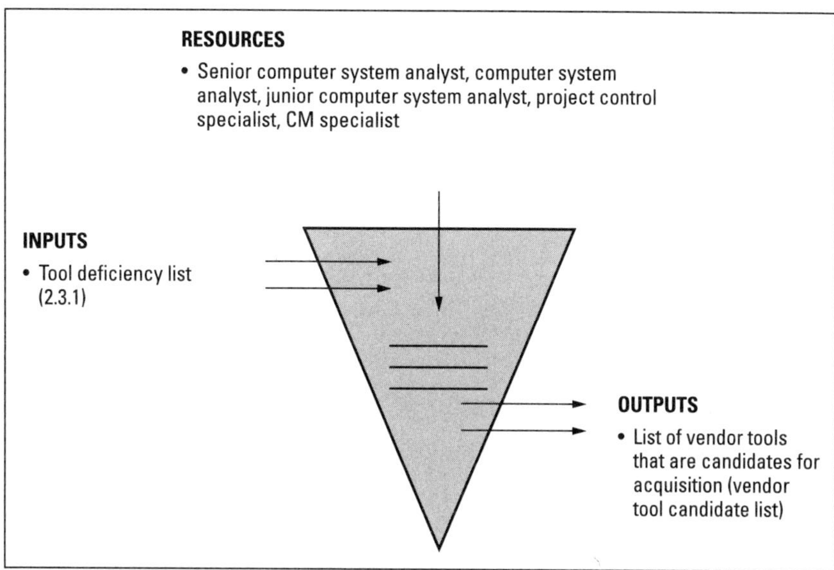
RESOURCES
• Senior computer system analyst, computer system analyst, junior computer system analyst, project control specialist, CM specialist
INPUTS
• Tool deficiency list (2.3.1)
OUTPUTS
• List of vendor tools that are candidates for acquisition (vendor tool candidate list)

Task Guidelines

- Pattern matching methods may help you identify vendor tools that match the functionality captured in Tool Analysis and Vendor Tool Identification.
- Organizational considerations may influence your choice of vendor tool candidates. For example, if your organization has experienced poor performance from, or support for, tools developed by a particular vendor, you may want to omit that vendor's tools from this list.
- Questions to ask about Year 2000 tools under consideration:

  Inventory and Assessment Tools:

  - Does the tool automatically create an inventory?
  - What repository tools (DBMS tools) are compatible with this tool?
  - What programming languages are supported?
  - How is missing source code handled?
  - Is the code scanned (faster) or parsed (more complete)?
  - What is the throughput of the assessment process?
  - Can the user modify search criteria used for assessment?
  - Does the tool assess code, data, or both?
  - Does the tool provide solution suggestions?

Resolution Tools:

- How much of the correction process is automated?
- What languages are supported?
- Does this tool use the products generated by an Inventory and Assessment tool?
- Are modifications made to data, data structures, code, or all three?
- Is the code restructured?

2.3.3 Task: Recommend Buy/Build Decision

Based on the vendor tool candidate list produced in the previous task, identify the vendor tools that you wish to acquire and those whose functions you can develop within your organization.

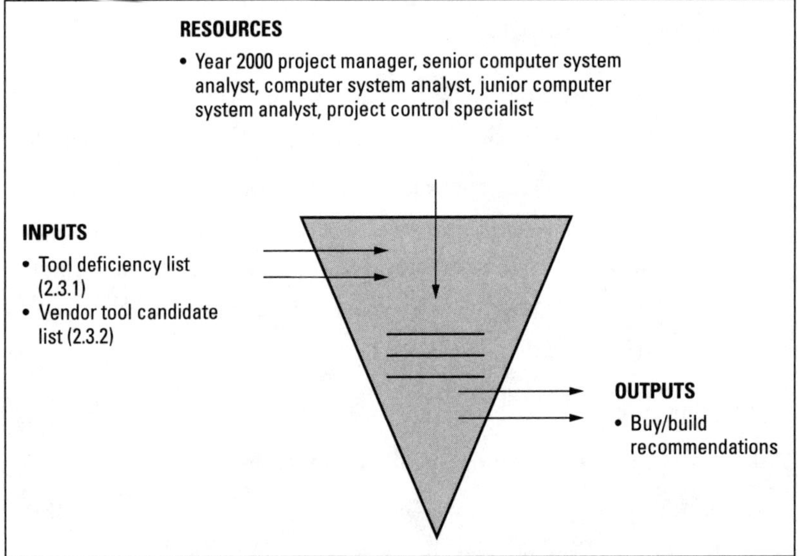
RESOURCES
• Year 2000 project manager, senior computer system analyst, computer system analyst, junior computer system analyst, project control specialist
INPUTS
• Tool deficiency list (2.3.1)
• Vendor tool candidate list (2.3.2)
OUTPUTS
• Buy/build recommendations

Task Guidelines

- You may wish to initiate interactive sessions to review input information and formulate decisions.
- These buy/build recommendations will depend upon the resources available within your organization. Primary considerations will include

acquisition funding, development resources (environment, personnel), time to develop versus time to acquire.

2.3.4 Task: Identify Vendor Tools for Acquisition

Based on the buy/build recommendations made in the previous task, create a list of the specific Year 2000 tools to acquire from vendors. If possible, also specify the approximate time period target for the acquisition. You must obtain the appropriate management approval for this list. Acquisition will occur, as necessary, during the Detailed Assessment phase and the Resolution phase.

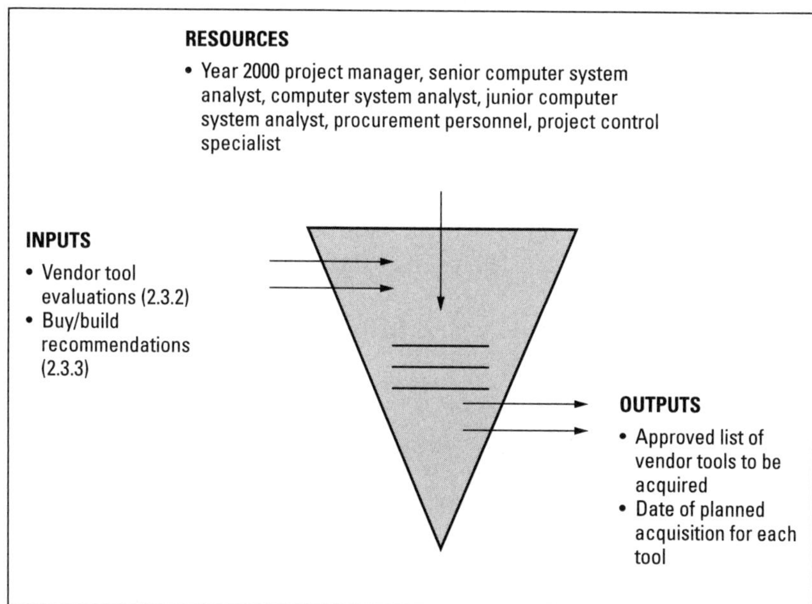
RESOURCES
• Year 2000 project manager, senior computer system analyst, computer system analyst, junior computer system analyst, procurement personnel, project control specialist
INPUTS
• Vendor tool evaluations (2.3.2)
• Buy/build recommendations (2.3.3)
OUTPUTS
• Approved list of vendor tools to be acquired
• Date of planned acquisition for each tool

Task Guideline

- You may wish to initiate interactive sessions to review input information and formulate decisions.

milestone

Tool Analysis and Vendor Tool Identification completed. Quality assurance verifies that the deliverable conforms to its intended goal. Project control baselines the deliverable and updates tracking metrics.

2.4 Staffing Estimate and Vendor Services Inventory

This deliverable provides a rough-order-of-magnitude estimate of the Year 2000 project staffing requirements. It also provides an inventory of the vendor, or subcontractor, services available to support Year 2000 endeavors. The staffing requirements will allow you to estimate staffing needs that can be fulfilled within your organization as well as those that must be fulfilled through vendor services. Detailed personnel planning, including assignment of individual staff members to specific Year 2000 project tasks, occurs later in the project.

Task Overview

- Identify Rough-Order-of-Magnitude Staffing Requirements
- Identify Possible Organizational Staffing Shortfalls
- Review/Evaluate Vendor Services
- Determine Vendor Services Available for Acquisition

2.4.1 Task: Identify Rough-Order-of-Magnitude Staffing Requirements

Provide senior management with a rough-order-of-magnitude estimate of staffing requirements that identifies the categories and approximate number of staff needed to complete the Year 2000 project. At this stage, your estimate will be imprecise. For example, you cannot determine specific staffing needs for the Resolution phase before finishing the Detailed Assessment phase. However, because it is important to anticipate the scope of the vendor services that you may need, you must formulate a general idea of the needed staff and the percentage of those needs that will be fulfilled in-house.

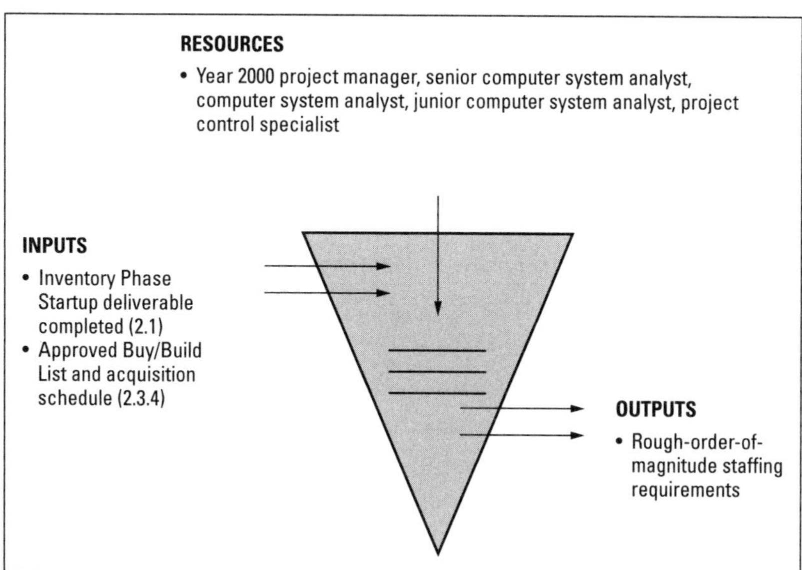
RESOURCES
• Year 2000 project manager, senior computer system analyst, computer system analyst, junior computer system analyst, project control specialist
INPUTS
• Inventory Phase Startup deliverable completed (2.1)
• Approved Buy/Build List and acquisition schedule (2.3.4)
OUTPUTS
• Rough-order-of-magnitude staffing requirements

Task Guidelines

- You may want to initiate interactive sessions to identify personnel categories and estimate staffing numbers.
- You must ensure that any staffing estimate formulated at this stage is clearly identified as "rough order of magnitude." It is especially important that no one in senior management presumes this estimate to be the final determination of Year 2000 project personnel needs. To maintain credibility, you should also clearly document the reasons for the uncertainty. Access to this staffing estimate should be limited to those with a true need to know. The fewer people who see this estimate, the smaller the chance that it can come back to haunt you.
- The following table lists the types of personnel you should consider when formulating your estimate. You may need additional technicians during testing if you must test on systems separate from those in operational use, or if you must schedule test time outside normal operating hours. As you can see, the number of people shown for most categories is given in general terms. You'll only need one project manager, and probably only one database administrator and technical writer. However, many factors determine actual requirements for the other categories. The possible ranges for relative terms such as "low," "medium," and "high" will depend

upon the size of your organization. Even within a particular organization, the actual staffing numbers for these categories will depend upon the number of systems you must inventory, the decisions you make during the Triage phase, and the results of the Detailed Assessment phase.

PERSONNEL CATEGORY	PHASES WHEN NEEDED	NUMBER
Programmers	Resolution	Many
Test technicians	Test Execution	Many
Test engineers	Test Planning, Test Execution	Many
Software engineers	Detailed Assessment, Resolution	Many
Hardware engineers	Detailed Assessment, Resolution	Many
Quality assurance	All phases	A few
Configuration management	All phases	A few
Clerical support	All phases	A few
Database administrator	All phases	One
Technical writer	All phases	A few
Project manager	All phases	One

2.4.2 Task: Identify Possible Organizational Staffing Shortfalls

Based on the personnel needs determined in the preceding task, you will identify possible shortfalls within your organization for fulfilling these needs. The shortfall estimates will necessarily be imprecise. Make sure that management understands the imprecision associated with these estimates.

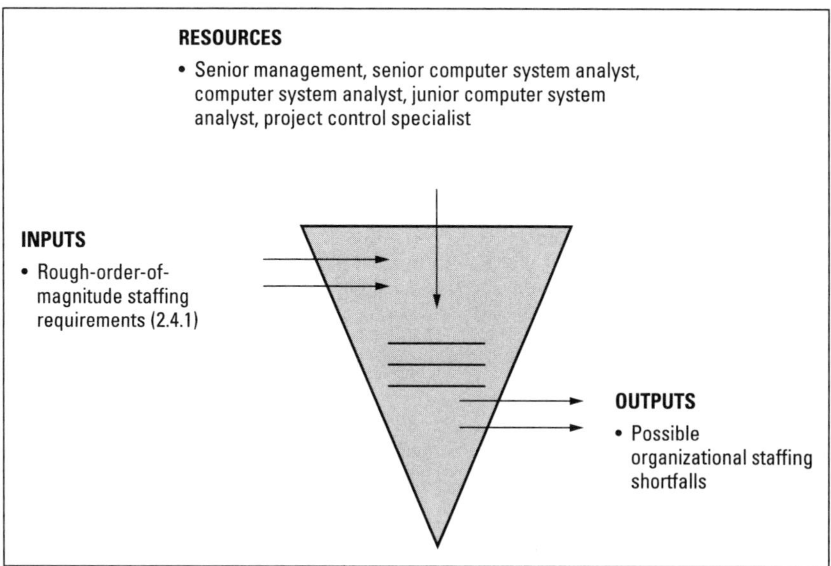
RESOURCES
• Senior management, senior computer system analyst, computer system analyst, junior computer system analyst, project control specialist
INPUTS
• Rough-order-of-magnitude staffing requirements (2.4.1)
OUTPUTS
• Possible organizational staffing shortfalls

Task Guideline

- You can use the following table to systematically identify personnel shortfalls.

Personnel Category	Phases When Needed	Number	Available In-House
Programmers	Resolution	Many	Some
Software engineers	Detailed Assessment, Resolution	Many	Some
Clerical support	All phases	A few	All
Database administrator	All phases	One	No
Technical writer	All phases	One	Yes
Project manager	All phases	One	Yes

2.4.3 Task: Review/Evaluate Vendor Services

You can obtain a comprehensive list of Year 2000 vendor services from the *How To 2000* CD-ROM. Using this list, identify services that could fulfill the staffing shortfalls identified in the previous task. Hopefully, you can identify several services

that address a particular staffing shortfall. The selected services will be incorporated in a list of vendor service candidates. Services on this list become candidates for acquisition late in the Year 2000 project.

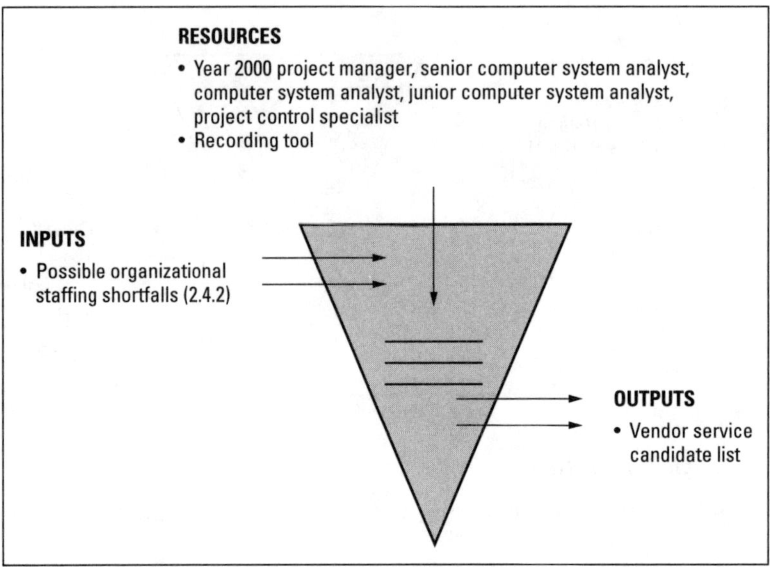
RESOURCES
• Year 2000 project manager, senior computer system analyst, computer system analyst, junior computer system analyst, project control specialist
• Recording tool
INPUTS
• Possible organizational staffing shortfalls (2.4.2)
OUTPUTS
• Vendor service candidate list

Task Guidelines

- Acquire more information about the scope and cost of these services from individual vendors, as necessary.
- Evaluate each candidate vendor service according to the following criteria:
  - How long has this vendor been in business?
  - What is the vendor's overall business reputation?
  - What services and/or products does the vendor offer?
  - Does the vendor's experience with other products and services enhance its ability to successfully complete your Year 2000 tasks?
  - How did the vendor get into the Year 2000 business?

- Has the vendor proven through previous experience that it can successfully handle a Year 2000 project of this scope and size?
- What other organizations have purchased Year 2000 services from this vendor?
- Does the vendor have adequate resources to successfully complete your Year 2000 project?
- Who will actually work on the project?
- Will project personnel include subcontractors acquired by the vendor?
- What will be the turnover of personnel assigned to your Year 2000 project?
- What method will be used to monitor vendor work?
- What methods will be used to communicate with the vendor?
- By what mechanism will the vendor address your concerns/complaints?
- Does the vendor offer a warranty?
- What are the conditions of the warranty?
- Where will the work be performed?
- What computing systems will be used?
- What type of office or administrative support, if any, must you provide to the vendor?
- What deliverables will the vendor provide to you?

2.4.4 Task: Determine Vendor Services Available for Acquisition

Based on your identification of vendor services that could fulfill your Year 2000 project staffing shortfalls, create a list of the vendor services that you plan to acquire to complete the Year 2000 project. Your list should also include the projected schedule for acquisition of these services. Actual acquisition of these services will take place during later phases of the Year 2000 project.

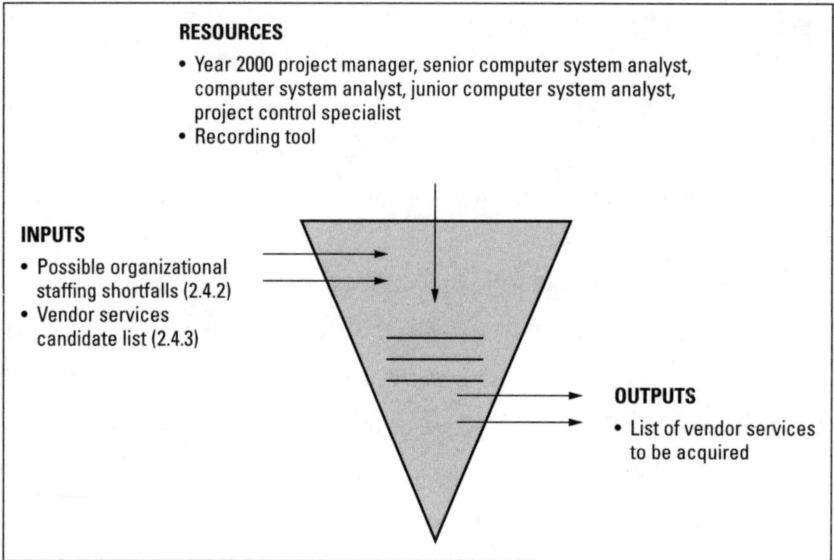
RESOURCES
• Year 2000 project manager, senior computer system analyst, computer system analyst, junior computer system analyst, project control specialist
• Recording tool
INPUTS
• Possible organizational staffing shortfalls (2.4.2)
• Vendor services candidate list (2.4.3)
OUTPUTS
• List of vendor services to be acquired

Task Guidelines

- When creating this list, you must weigh project resources, particularly time and funds. You may want to disregard the more time-consuming or more expensive vendor services.
- Recognize attributes of your organization that may restrict the type of vendor services you want to acquire. For example, your organization may have established a relationship with one of these vendors and may anticipate a price reduction based on "old friend" status.
- The list of available vendor services should be approved by management, as appropriate to your organization.
- You may wish to establish preliminary agreements with one or more vendors once the vendor services list is approved. The price of Year 2000 vendor services may dramatically increase as the perceived deadline draws nearer, or the availability of such services may become severely limited.

milestone

Staffing Estimate and Vendor Services Inventory completed. Quality assurance verifies that the deliverable conforms to its intended goal. Project control baselines the deliverable and updates tracking metrics.

2.5 System Inventory

The System Inventory provides a complete inventory of the systems in your organization. The inventory will include a wealth of information concerning each system: its location, number of users, importance to the organization, primary functionality, age, current licensing agreement, risk elements, and more. This inventory will also include information about systems that are likely to incorporate Year 2000 problems. Upon completion of this deliverable, you will be able to update your previous rough-order-of-magnitude assessment of the size of your organization's Year 2000 problem. The information contained in this deliverable will also pave the way for Detailed Assessment phase tasks.

This inventory information is significantly more detailed than the Enterprise Schematic developed during the Planning and Awareness phase of the project (1.3.2). The Enterprise Schematic was intended to support rough-order-of-magnitude planning. It also revealed the extent to which automated systems permeate not only the revenue-producing areas of your organization, but vital operational and infrastructure areas as well. The System Inventory, however, is intended to be an exhaustive identification of all systems in your organization. It is not an awareness or motivational tool; it is a definitive compilation of all systems that are candidates for assessment and correction.

Task Overview

- Develop System Survey
- Perform System Survey
- Capture System Inventory
- Verify System Inventory
- Baseline System Inventory
- Establish Change Control

2.5.1 Task: Develop System Survey

During this task, you will develop a survey that will facilitate the identification of each and every system in your organization. You will also ensure the capture of this basic system information in the Year 2000 repository. The survey should solicit the minimum amount of system information needed to support Triage phase activities. By keeping the Inventory survey short and focused, you increase

2
HOW TO
000

your chances of obtaining complete and timely responses. You should not be concerned about the lack of comprehensive information about each system. You'll gather significantly more system-specific information during the Detailed Assessment phase.

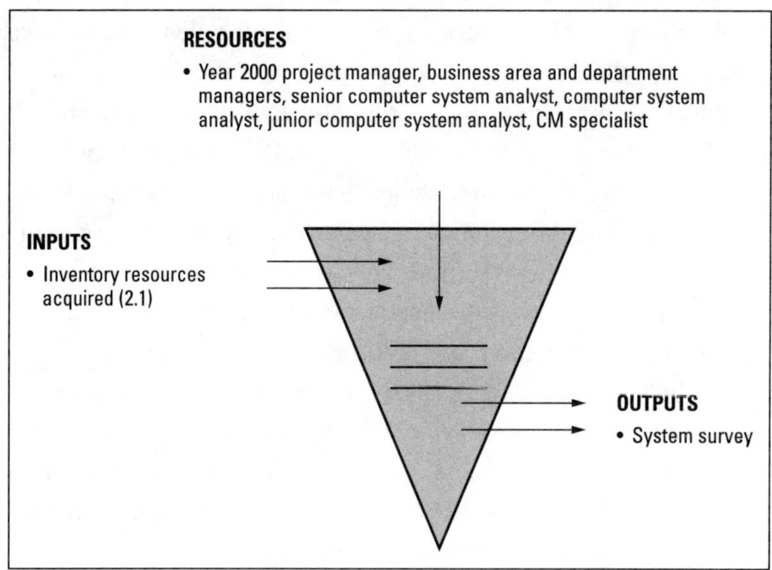
RESOURCES
• Year 2000 project manager, business area and department managers, senior computer system analyst, computer system analyst, junior computer system analyst, CM specialist
INPUTS
• Inventory resources acquired (2.1)
OUTPUTS
• System survey

Task Guidelines

- A typical system survey should solicit the following information:
  - Inventory element name
  - Inventory element ID number
  - Inventory element acronym
  - Person completing survey (contact information)
  - Person to contact for inventory element (contact information)
  - Inventory element version number
  - Number/identification of duplicate inventory elements
  - Controlled by which organizational entity?
  - Access (security) information/limitations
  - Supports which areas of business?
  - Importance to business objectives

  - Effect on business of inventory element failure
  - Available replacement functionality in the event of inventory element failure
  - Number of system users (past, present, future)
  - Location
  - Plans for projected retirement/replacement
  - Purpose of inventory element
  - Functionality summary
  - Year 2000 compliance status
  - Probability of Year 2000 impact
  - Magnitude of Year 2000 impact
  - Internally developed, contractor developed, or COTS?
- You should follow your organization's procedures for surveys and questionnaires.
- This survey must solicit information on both custom-developed systems (internally or contractor developed) and COTS systems. Among the different types of systems included in this inventory will be:
  - Hardware
  - Software
  - Operating systems
  - Firmware
  - Control languages
  - Databases
  - Networks
  - Embedded systems

2.5.2 Task: Perform System Survey

After identifying specific survey recipients, distribute the survey and retrieve completed copies. Survey instruments should be directed to system managers or principal users, if possible.

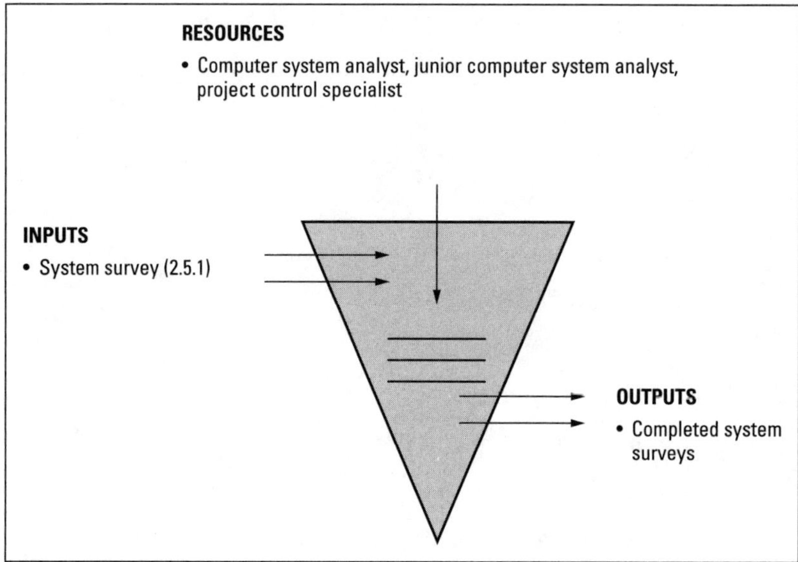
RESOURCES
• Computer system analyst, junior computer system analyst, project control specialist
INPUTS
• System survey (2.5.1)
OUTPUTS
• Completed system surveys

Task Guidelines

- You can usually get a list of system managers and users from your organization's IS department or procurement department.
- Survey media will be determined by the logistics of your organization, although electronic surveys will reduce the data entry chores for your survey staff.
- The success of the entire Year 2000 effort is directly related to the quantity and quality of the system information that you receive in response to this survey. You need broad-based management support to ensure the success of your survey. Completion of the surveys will take time and effort on the part of a potentially large number of employees, and you must ensure that these employees are sufficiently motivated.
- Initiate a document tracking system that ensures the retrieval of all survey instruments. You may need to issue reminders to some system managers. Via the document tracking system, you should be able to determine the status of a specific survey instrument at any time during the survey endeavor.

2.5.3 Task: Capture System Inventory

As survey retrieval is underway, capture system information in the Year 2000 repository, which should be configured to receive information in all fields defined in the initial task of this deliverable.

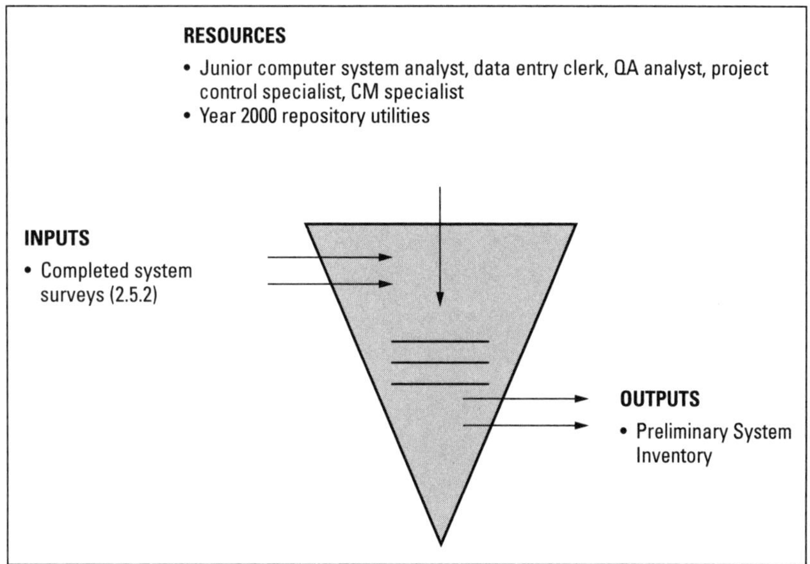
RESOURCES
• Junior computer system analyst, data entry clerk, QA analyst, project control specialist, CM specialist
• Year 2000 repository utilities
INPUTS
• Completed system surveys (2.5.2)
OUTPUTS
• Preliminary System Inventory

Task Guidelines

- If you retrieve more than one survey instrument regarding the same system, enter a separate record for the information contained in each instrument.
- Reconciliation of potentially conflicting information regarding a specific system should be deferred until all system information has been captured in the repository.

2.5.4 Task: Verify System Inventory

To ensure the integrity of system information captured in the repository, you need a way of verifying this information. The most efficient method of verification is an organized cross-check of system information by staff members who possess broad-based knowledge concerning your organization's systems.

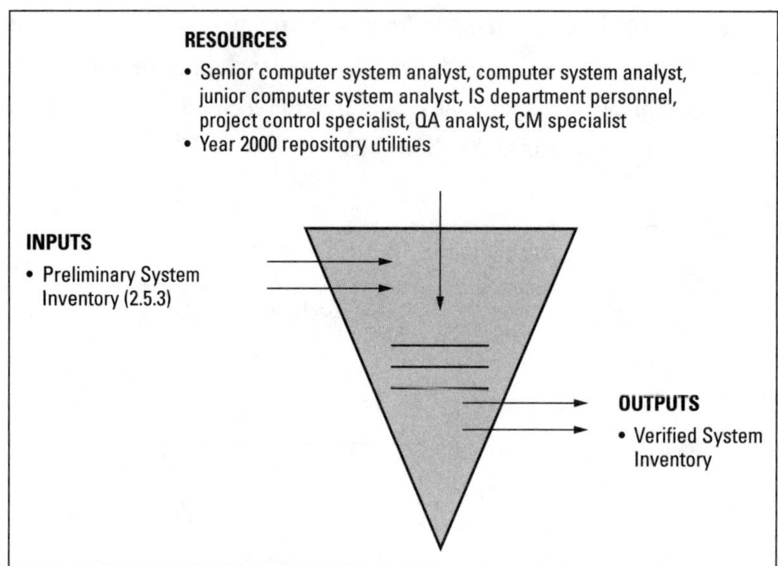
RESOURCES
• Senior computer system analyst, computer system analyst, junior computer system analyst, IS department personnel, project control specialist, QA analyst, CM specialist
• Year 2000 repository utilities
INPUTS
• Preliminary System Inventory (2.5.3)
OUTPUTS
• Verified System Inventory

Task Guidelines

- IS department staff members and QA staff members are ideal candidates for verification activities.
- After incoming survey information has been entered into the repository, verification staff can review and verify this information on an individual basis or as a group.
- System information problems identified by the verification staff should be resolved jointly by the verification staff and the staff members who authored the survey instrument in question.
- If system information is altered due to verification activities, you must ensure that repository change control mechanisms are used to preserve the originally submitted information as well as the updated information.
- Any changes to system information should be communicated to appropriate system managers and users.

2.5.5 Task: Baseline System Inventory

When all system information has been received, captured in the repository, and verified, you must baseline the System Inventory.

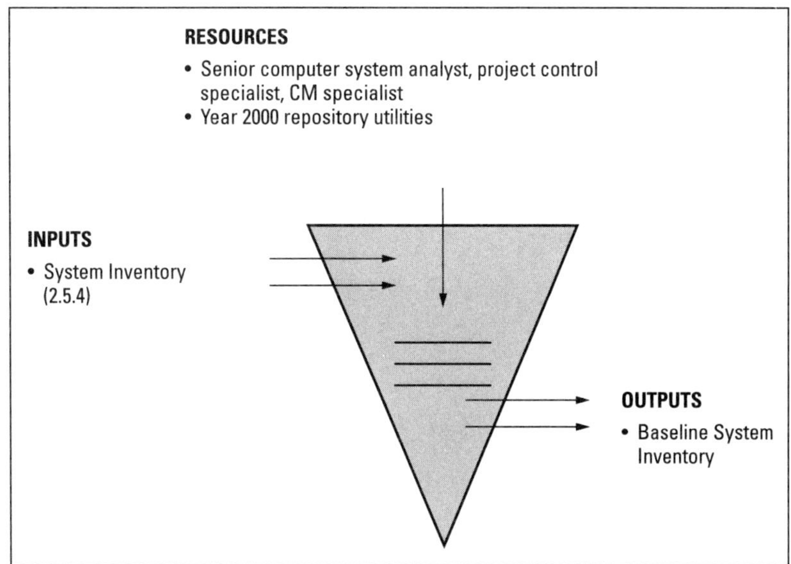
RESOURCES
• Senior computer system analyst, project control specialist, CM specialist
• Year 2000 repository utilities
INPUTS
• System Inventory (2.5.4)
OUTPUTS
• Baseline System Inventory

Task Guidelines

- You may want to publish a system inventory document at this point. Both this document and the corresponding repository records must be baselined.
- The points of contact for each system (2.5.1) must understand that any changes to their systems that relate to information in the system inventory baseline must be conveyed to the Year 2000 project staff.

2.5.6 Task: Establish Change Control

After establishing a baseline, you must control change for all artifacts that relate to system information, including:

- Repository records
- Published documents that incorporate system information
- Hard copies of survey instruments, if held

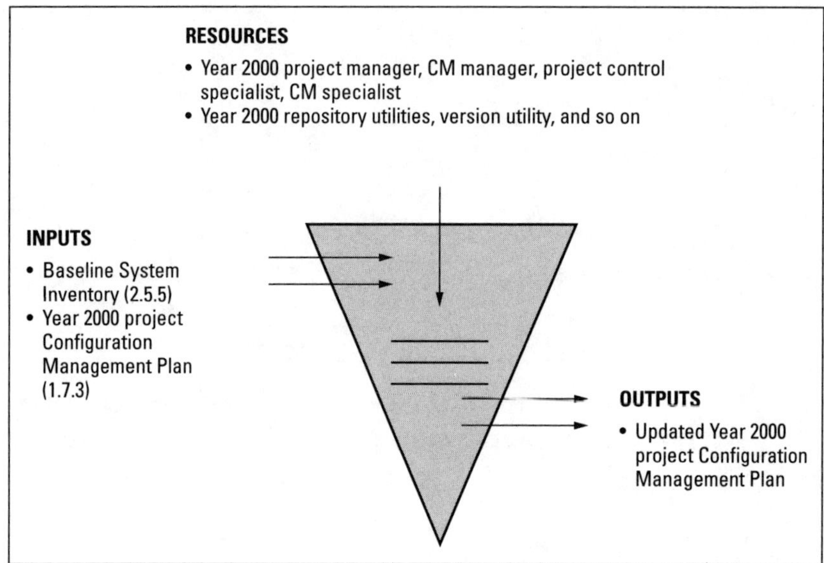
RESOURCES
• Year 2000 project manager, CM manager, project control specialist, CM specialist
• Year 2000 repository utilities, version utility, and so on
INPUTS
• Baseline System Inventory (2.5.5)
• Year 2000 project Configuration Management Plan (1.7.3)
OUTPUTS
• Updated Year 2000 project Configuration Management Plan

Task Guidelines

- Use change control procedures that have been defined within your Year 2000 project CM plan. If necessary, update the plan to include additional procedures, or changes to established procedures.
- Select someone to perform the duties of a configuration control manager (CCM).
- If you deem it appropriate, select personnel to serve on a configuration control board (CCB).
- Specify the types of repository changes that can be made routinely and those that must be referred to the CCM and/or the CCB. All changes, regardless of size and importance, should be captured within the change control mechanism.
- The change control mechanism should capture the following information, at the very least:
  - Person suggesting change
  - Person authorizing the change
  - Date of change proposal
  - Date of change

- Reason for change
- Impact of change on other records (change dependencies)

milestone  **System Inventory completed. Quality assurance verifies that the deliverable conforms to its intended goal. Project control baselines the deliverable and updates tracking metrics. Configuration management verifies that Year 2000 repository updates adhere to CM procedures.**

2.6 Inventory Schematic

The Inventory Schematic provides a schematic drawing of all systems included in the system inventory and identifies the relationships and dependencies among them. It allows you to assess the technical impact of a specific system upon related systems.

The Inventory Schematic expands and revises the Enterprise Schematic developed during the Planning and Awareness phase. By doing so, the Inventory Schematic enhances your top-level understanding of the operation of the information systems within your organization.

Task Overview

- Develop Inventory Schematic

2.6.1 Task: Develop Inventory Schematic

Develop a comprehensive schematic that portrays the existing systems in your organization and the relationships among these systems. All systems in the system inventory should be included in this schematic.

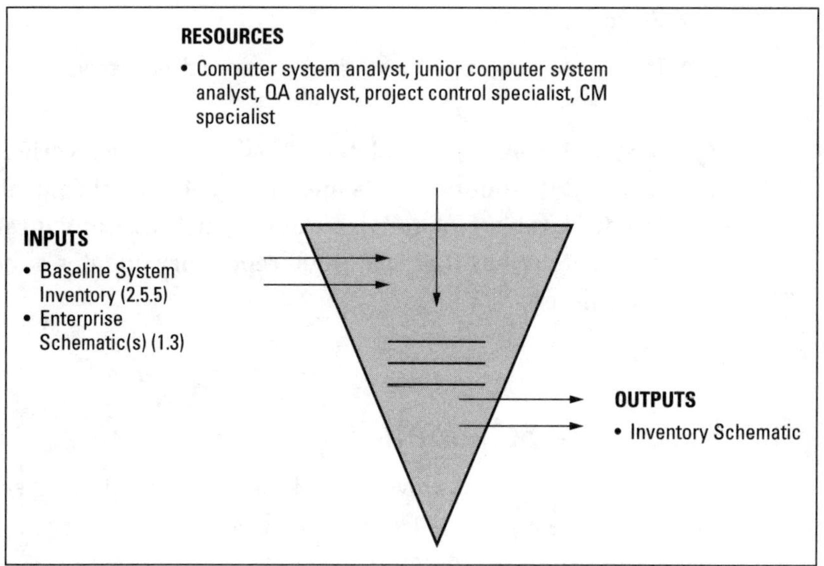
RESOURCES
• Computer system analyst, junior computer system analyst, QA analyst, project control specialist, CM specialist
INPUTS
• Baseline System Inventory (2.5.5)
• Enterprise Schematic(s) (1.3)
OUTPUTS
• Inventory Schematic

Task Guidelines

- This schematic will include many different types of system hardware, software, operating systems, firmware, control languages, databases, networks, and embedded systems.
- A schematic is typically a drawing, or graphic, in the form of a directed graph. Some people utilize a predefined method of information system portrayal, such as Yourdon's Data Flow Diagram method, when developing a schematic. Others simply use the basic constructs of a directed graph—nodes and arcs—to portray individual systems and the relationships among them. You might want to develop your own constructs for your schematic drawing, constructs that make sense within your organizational environment.
- Whatever drawing conventions you decide to use, remember to keep it simple. The most important attribute of any schematic is clarity. Your schematic should provide a clear and concise depiction of your systems and the relationships among them.
- The exact nature of the schematic drawing depends upon the size and complexity of your organization's information systems. Some organizations may be able to depict their entire System Inventory and the system relationships in one drawing. However, most organizations will need a

series of drawings. Each drawing will portray a subset of the System Inventory and the relationships among the systems in that subset. You need to explicitly define the relationships among the individual drawings that comprise the entire schematic. How you divide systems into subsets for schematic representation depends on your organization: Only you can determine which subsets make sense for your schematic task.

- When you make decisions regarding the drawing conventions to use during this task, keep in mind that you are attempting to pinpoint your organization's "linchpin" systems. What are the systems upon which many other systems are dependent? Which systems will have a significant impact on other systems should they be impaired by Year 2000 problems? You may want to find a method of designating some systems as technically "critical" to your total information system structure.
- Define a process whereby each system in the inventory is captured within the schematic. You may want to go through each system, one by one, and add it to the appropriate area of the schematic. Alternatively, you may want to organize systems by logical subsets, define a schematic for each subset, and then add each subset to the general schematic. Possible subset divisions can include
  - Division of systems by the eight system types stated above. For example, you may want to group and depict all network systems before grouping and depicting hardware or software.
  - Division of systems by organizational entity. For example, you can organize system subsets according to the business divisions in your organization.
  - Division of systems by the number of system dependencies assigned to each system. For example, based on Inventory information, you can identify the "linchpin" systems within your organization and use these as the basis for schematic development.
- As a guide to your Inventory Schematic effort, you should use the Enterprise Schematic created or updated during the Planning and Awareness phase.

milestone **Inventory Schematic completed. Quality assurance verifies that the deliverable conforms to its intended goal. Project control baselines the deliverable and updates tracking metrics. Configuration management verifies that Year 2000 repository updates adhere to CM procedures.**

2.7 System Configuration Status Report

The System Configuration Status Report identifies systems that have configuration problems: systems for which configuration items are either missing, outdated, or cannot be assessed for compliance. Configuration items include operational software or hardware modules, system requirements artifacts, system design artifacts, software source code modules, system object code modules, and any other object that supports the development or operation of an existing system. A particular system's configuration items are used during the Detailed Assessment phase to support the determination of that system's Year 2000 compliance status. If configuration items are missing, outdated, or cannot be accessed, assessment activities could be hampered or, in the worst case, halted altogether.

Because of the potential impact of configuration problems on assessment tasks, you must recognize these problems prior to making critical Triage phase decisions. In addition, information concerning the status of various configuration items can be very useful for planning Detailed Assessment phase activities.

Operational system modules that have been archived or retired can be considered to be outdated configuration items. Software source code modules or hardware schematics that do not correspond to the operational system can be considered "nonaccessible" configuration items. An operational software or hardware system for which no source code or schematics exist can be considered to have missing configuration items.

Task Overview

- Identify Configuration Problems

2.7.1 Identify Configuration Problems

This task involves three key activities: Identify Retired or Archived Configuration Items, Identify Missing Configuration Items, and Identify Noncompatible Configuration Items.

Identify Retired or Archived Configuration Items

Identify the operational components of systems that have been removed from active use or archived. Make sure that these operational components are not intended for future use. Carefully coordinate with system users before making this determination.

Identify Missing Configuration Items

Identify systems for which configuration items are missing. Recruit system users to help you search for the following:

- Software object code
- Software source code
- Hardware schematics
- System development artifacts, including system requirements and design documentation

Identify Noncompatible Configuration Items

Ensure the compatibility of configuration items that relate to the same system. System requirements, system designs, system source code, or system schematics must all mirror the system's operational components. You may need to recompile software code to identify noncompatible configuration items for software systems.

2
HOW TO
000

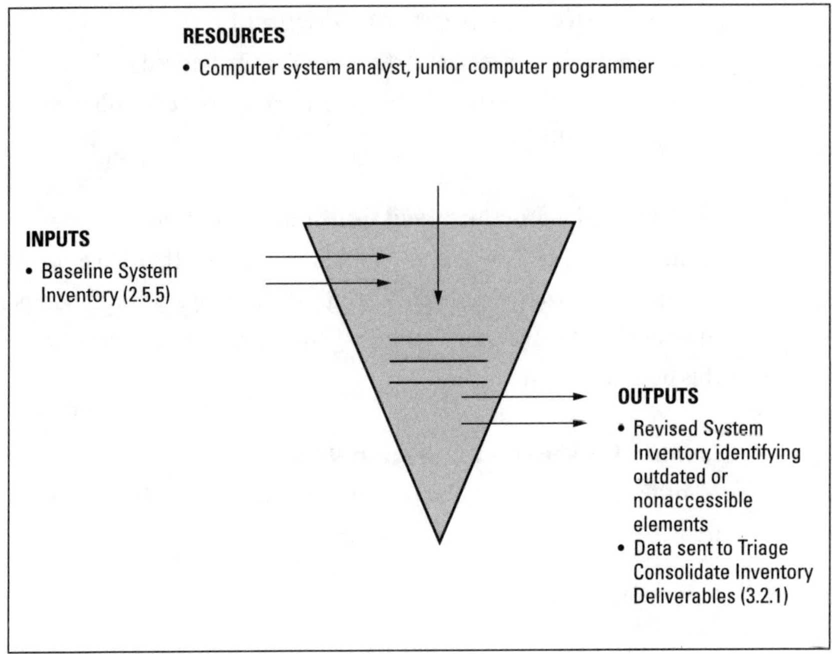
RESOURCES
• Computer system analyst, junior computer programmer
INPUTS
• Baseline System Inventory (2.5.5)
OUTPUTS
• Revised System Inventory identifying outdated or nonaccessible elements
• Data sent to Triage Consolidate Inventory Deliverables (3.2.1)

Task Guidelines

- Information concerning possible configuration problems can be acquired in conjunction with tasks undertaken during the completion of the System Inventory.
- You may choose to execute software compiles only during the Detailed Assessment phase. However, you could gain valuable knowledge concerning the compatibility of a system's configuration items if you execute these compiles during the Inventory phase. In deciding when to execute compiles, realize that information about the compatibility or noncompatibility of configuration items could heavily influence Triage phase decisions.
- Results from this task should be summarized and reviewed with senior management during the Triage phase.
- Information concerning configuration problems should be captured in the Year 2000 repository.

System Configuration Status Report completed. Quality assurance verifies that the deliverable conforms to its intended goal. Project control baselines the deliverable and updates tracking metrics. Configuration management verifies that Year 2000 repository updates adhere to CM procedures.

2.8 Inventory Element Dependencies

This technical prioritization of the systems in your organization will guide the development of schedules and resource allocation plans for the Detailed Assessment phase and the correction stage.

Do not confuse technical priorities with business priorities. A technical prioritization indicates the importance of each system in relation to the technical operation of the systems in your organization. In contrast, a business prioritization indicates the importance of each system in relation to the business goals of your organization. For example, because so many software applications are dependent upon its continued operation, a certain operating system may be technically critical to your organization. However, because this operating system is not directly related to the business goals of the organization, it would not be considered important from a business point of view. In contrast, an EDI translation application may be minimally dependent upon other systems in your organization and, consequently, would be low on the technical prioritization list. However, if no business can be transacted with external partners without this EDI application in place, it would be high on the business prioritization list.

The business prioritization of your organization's systems will take place during the Triage phase.

Task Overview

- Identify System Dependencies
- Develop Technical Priority List

2.8.1 Task: Identify System Dependencies

Develop a list of dependencies for each system in your organization. For each system, you should list

- The systems that are dependent upon its operation.
- The systems upon which its operation depends.

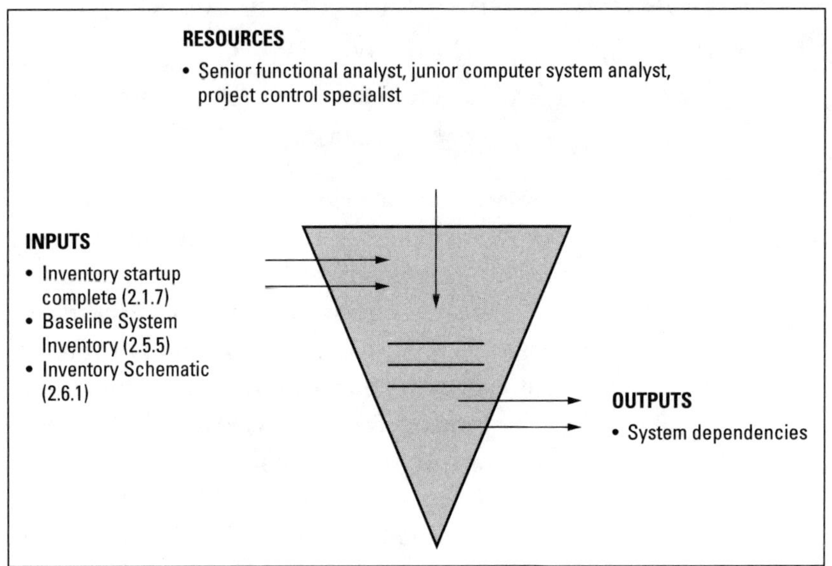
RESOURCES
• Senior functional analyst, junior computer system analyst, project control specialist
INPUTS
• Inventory startup complete (2.1.7)
• Baseline System Inventory (2.5.5)
• Inventory Schematic (2.6.1)
OUTPUTS
• System dependencies

Task Guidelines

- You may want to capture the degree of dependency between two systems (that is, record whether one system is completely, or only partially, dependent upon the other system).
- You can obtain dependent information from the Year 2000 repository and from the Inventory Schematic.

2.8.2 Task: Develop Technical Priority List

Based on the list of system dependencies, assess the technical importance of each system in your organization and assign a priority accordingly.

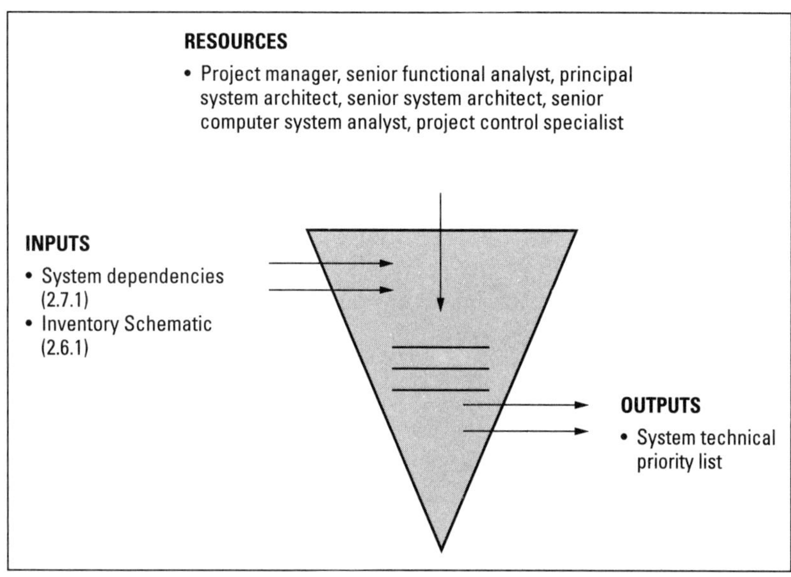
RESOURCES
• Project manager, senior functional analyst, principal system architect, senior system architect, senior computer system analyst, project control specialist
INPUTS
• System dependencies (2.7.1)
• Inventory Schematic (2.6.1)
OUTPUTS
• System technical priority list

Task Guidelines

- The format for this priority list is shown in the following table.

System ID	*Number It Is Dependent Upon*	*Number Dependent Upon It*	*Comments*	*Priority*
Op System 1	2	34	Supports a wide variety of applications	Critical
Hardware 3A	2	1	Runs a single application	Low
Network 2Z	2	47	Backbone	Critical
Network 3F	4	1	Router	Low

- Each system is assigned a priority based on predefined priority categories: Critical, High, Medium, and Low.
- You can adjust the variation within these Likert Scale priority categories, if you wish. It is up to you to define the criteria by which systems are

assigned to these priority categories. For example, you may rate as "Critical" those systems that will cause organization-wide information system shutdown if they fail. If such an organization-wide shutdown is simply not possible in your organization, you may rate as "Critical" those systems whose failure will result in the shutdown of more than 20 other systems. Alternatively, you may assign a "Critical" priority to those systems upon which many other systems are dependent and which would require a substantial investment of time and effort for repair in the event of failure. Ultimately, the definition of "Critical" must be derived from your understanding of your organization.

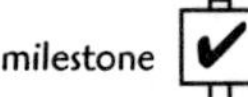

Inventory Element Dependencies completed. Quality assurance verifies that the deliverable conforms to its intended goal. Project control baselines the deliverable and updates tracking metrics. Configuration management verifies that Year 2000 repository updates adhere to CM procedures.

2.9 Technical Risk Inventory

The Technical Risk Inventory is an inventory of the technical risk associated with each of your organization's systems. This summary of technical risk will be a valuable input to the management decisions required in the later phases of the Year 2000 project.

To address this task properly, you should review Appendix I, "*How To 2000* Risk Management." This appendix defines "technical risk" and elaborates on this book's approach to risk management.

Task Overview

- Extract Risk Information from System Inventory
- Calculate Technical Risk by System

2.9.1 Task: Extract Risk Information from System Inventory

You will find system risk information in the Year 2000 repository. The person who completed the survey instrument for a specific system was asked to assess the following two risk factors concerning that system:

- Probability that the system will be impacted by one or more Year 2000 problems
- Technical magnitude of that impact

Survey respondents were asked to rate each of these factors on a 0-1 scale.

For example, a survey respondent may think it's very likely that a particular software application contains a number of date-based calculations. He or she may also know that the system developers regularly used two-digit year fields within dates. Consequently, this respondent indicates that the probability that this system will be impacted by Year 2000 problems is very high, say .9. Because no other systems are dependent upon this application, and the failure of this application will have a rather minimal effect on the operation of your organization's information systems, the impact of this failure is rated as .2.

Extract these system risk factors from the Year 2000 repository and assemble this information into a list or table.

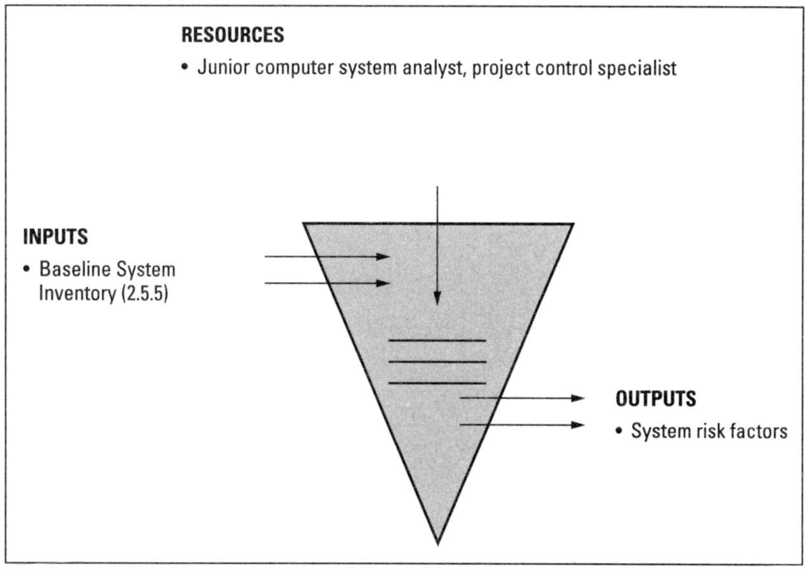
RESOURCES
• Junior computer system analyst, project control specialist
INPUTS
• Baseline System Inventory (2.5.5)
OUTPUTS
• System risk factors

Task Guideline

- If you did not include guidelines for assigning risk factors as part of your System Inventory survey instructions, risk factor values will not have been consistently assigned for all systems. Some respondents may have determined that a software application that probably incorporates a few two-digit year fields has a .9 probability of being impacted by a Year 2000 problem, while others may have determined that this same risk factor should be assigned a value of .8. You must remain cognizant of this type of inconsistency when gauging the validity of the risk factor values contained in the Year 2000 repository.

2.9.2 Task: Calculate Technical Risk by System

Use the risk factor information extracted in the previous task to calculate the technical risk associated with each system. To calculate technical risk, simply multiply the risk factors.

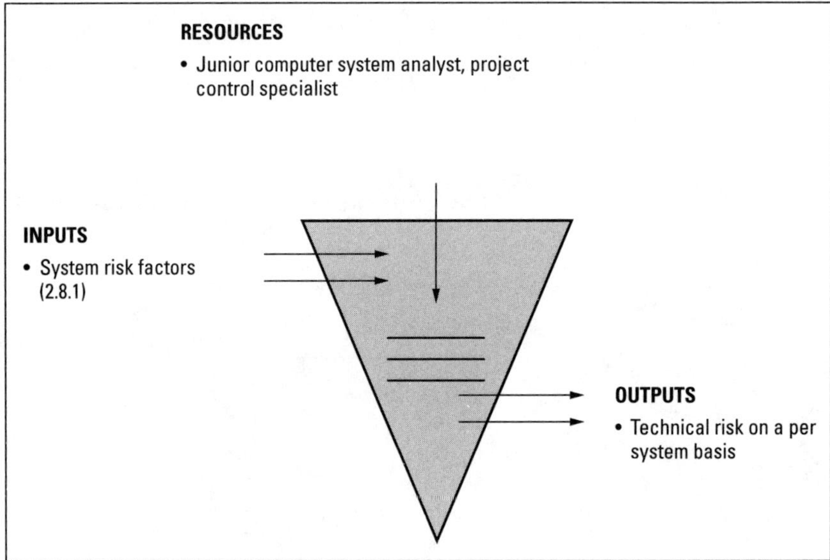
RESOURCES
• Junior computer system analyst, project control specialist
INPUTS
• System risk factors (2.8.1)
OUTPUTS
• Technical risk on a per system basis

Task Guidelines

- Because of the lack of uniformity in the determination of risk factor values, you may wish to express system technical risk using Likert Scale values associated with a range of numerical values. Expressing technical risk in broad terms will soften the impact of questionable values that may be incorporated in risk calculations. After completing the numerical calculations of technical risk, convert the resultant numerical values to the corresponding Likert Scale values.

- Numerical values of technical risk correspond to the following Likert Scale values:
  - Very high: .8 and above
  - High: .6 to .8
  - Medium: .4 to .6
  - Low: .2 to .4
  - Very low: .2 and below
- The technical risk value associated with each system should be captured in the Year 2000 repository. A system listing sorted by technical risk can be created, if desired.

Technical Risk Inventory completed. Quality assurance verifies that the deliverable conforms to its intended goal. Project control baselines the deliverable and updates tracking metrics. Configuration management verifies that Year 2000 repository updates adhere to CM procedures.

Business Impacts

The tasks undertaken during the Inventory phase will not greatly affect your business processes. Though it will certainly take time to complete the system survey, you shouldn't need to allocate substantial time and effort to Inventory tasks. Detailed Assessment phase and Resolution phase activities will have a far more profound effect upon your business processes.

Many people in your organization will be participating in this Inventory. Most of those participants will be the system users who will respond to your requests for information about their systems.

To ensure that you receive all this system information in a timely manner, make sure that system users and their managers are supportive of the Inventory effort. To achieve the level of organization-wide cooperation that you need, ensure that:

- System users and their managers are aware of the intent and objectives of Inventory.
- The resources needed to accomplish Inventory tasks (time, support tools, facilities) are available to these system users.
- Senior management understands and supports the workload that will be imposed upon these managers and technical personnel.

Phase Risks

Potential Event	*Probability*	*Impact*	*Risk*
System Inventory incomplete	High	High	High
Survey information inaccurate	High	Low	Low

Inventory Phase Risks

The primary risk associated with the Inventory phase is that your System Inventory might be incomplete. An additional risk is that the survey information might be inaccurate.

System Inventory Incomplete

By far your most serious concern is that the System Inventory might be incomplete. The one system that you fail to capture within your survey can come back to haunt you when the Year 2000 time bomb strikes. The chance that this might happen is, most likely, high. It is hard to uncover every last system in a large organization. The impact is also high. One missed system could spell disaster.

Methods of Risk Mitigation:

- Institute a "call back" or "nag" mechanism in conjunction with your Inventory tasks. If a survey recipient has not responded within the specified length of time, an information item will be generated for prompting you to recontact the recipient.
- Keep the Inventory survey short and to the point. System users will be far more likely to complete and return a survey that is simple and easily understood than one that is lengthy and complex. Solicit just enough information to establish the identity, basic functions, and potential Year 2000 entanglements of each system. Do not worry about collecting comprehensive information about each system at this point. You will obtain this information during the Detailed Assessment phase of your Year 2000 project.

Survey Information Inaccurate

Unfortunately, some of the overburdened people who complete these surveys may not provide complete and accurate information. Luckily, most of these inaccuracies will be found during the Inventory verification process or during the Detailed Assessment phase. In other words, although there's a good chance that at least some survey information will be inaccurate, the impact will most probably be low.

Methods of Risk Mitigation:

- Institute an "initial review and return" task within your Inventory endeavor. Following the receipt of survey information, the information should be reviewed. Missing or questionable information can be noted and the survey returned to the survey recipient for rework.
- Ensure that all survey recipients realize the importance of the Year 2000 project. You must stress the importance of their tasks to provide complete and accurate system information.

Success Factors

In successfully completing Inventory, you carried out the following steps:

Success Factor	*Deliverable*
Developed requirements for tools that will support Inventory	Inventory Phase Startup
Developed requirements for tools to support the Year 2000 project	Internal Tool Inventory
Identified tools internal to your organization that could be used to support the Year 2000 project	Internal Tool Inventory
Identified tool deficiencies within your organization	Tool Analysis and Vendor Tool Identification
Defined criteria for evaluating and selecting vendor tools that could be used to support the Year 2000 project	Tool Analysis and Vendor Tool Identification
Evaluated vendor tools that could be used to support the Year 2000 project	Tool Analysis and Vendor Tool Identification
Made buy/build decisions concerning Year 2000 support tools based on information on tools available within your organization and vendor tools	Tool Analysis and Vendor Tool Identification
Identified vendor tools that could be used to support the Year 2000 project	Tool Analysis and Vendor Tool Identification
Identified rough-order-of-magnitude staffing requirements for the Year 2000 project	Staffing Estimate and Vendor Services Inventory
Identified internal staff shortfalls	Staffing Estimate and Vendor Services Inventory
Defined criteria for evaluating potential subcontractors	Staffing Estimate and Vendor Services Inventory
Evaluated subcontractors based on these criteria	Staffing Estimate and Vendor Services Inventory
Identified potential subcontractor services that could be used during the Year 2000 project	Staffing Estimate and Vendor Services Inventory
Completed a comprehensive system survey	System Inventory
Ensured that the system survey included complete and clear guidelines defining Year 2000 compliance	System Inventory
Ensured that the system survey included guidance for directed system users to analyze system work products as a method of identifying systems that might be affected by the Year 2000 problem	System Inventory
Obtained an assessment of Year 2000 compliance or noncompliance for all of the systems in your organization	System Inventory

SUCCESS FACTOR	DELIVERABLE
Captured information gathered in the Inventory in the Year 2000 repository	System Inventory
Ensured that your Inventory repository includes information about known Year 2000 compliance problems	System Inventory
Verified the accuracy of the information collected during Inventory	System Inventory
Verified the completeness of the information collected during Inventory	System Inventory
Used change control procedures within that repository	System Inventory
Checked configuration items in and out of the repository in a manner that maintains the correctness and integrity of the baseline	System Inventory
Maintained audit trails of the changes to information in the repository	System Inventory
Defined configuration units for the information that was captured during Inventory	System Inventory
Ensured that baselines created during Inventory consist of these configuration units	System Inventory
Identified the system relationships that are internal to your organization	Inventory Schematic
Identified the relationships between systems and entities that are external to your organization	Inventory Schematic
Identified systems that are outdated or nonassessable	System Configuration Status Report
Identified the technical dependencies among systems in your organization	Inventory Element Dependencies
Obtained a technical prioritization of the systems in your organization	System Inventory
Identified technical risks with each system in your organization	Technical Risk Inventory
Identified phase risks and potential mitigation approaches	All deliverables
Identified deliverables that would be developed during Inventory	All deliverables

continued

Success Factor	*Deliverable*
Used adequate communication interfaces throughout your organization to support the tasks associated Inventory	All deliverables
Assigned phase tasks to various groups in your organization and ensured that management approved those tasks	All deliverables
Identified the deliverables for which each group was responsible and ensured acceptance of that deliverable responsibility by each group	All deliverables
Identified key milestones for the accomplishment of tasks for Inventory	All deliverables
Identified milestone thresholds beyond which some corrective action will be taken	All deliverables
Used metrics to track and measure progress with respect to these milestones	All deliverables
Ensured that each responsible group accepted and adhered to the schedule for completion of Inventory	All deliverables

Reference Materials

This list mentions reference material you can turn to for additional information on your Year 2000 compliance project:

- Appendix E, Sample Memos
- Appendix G, Year 2000 Repository
- Appendix H, Integrated Project Plan
- Appendix I, How To 2000 Risk Management
- *How To 2000* CD-ROM

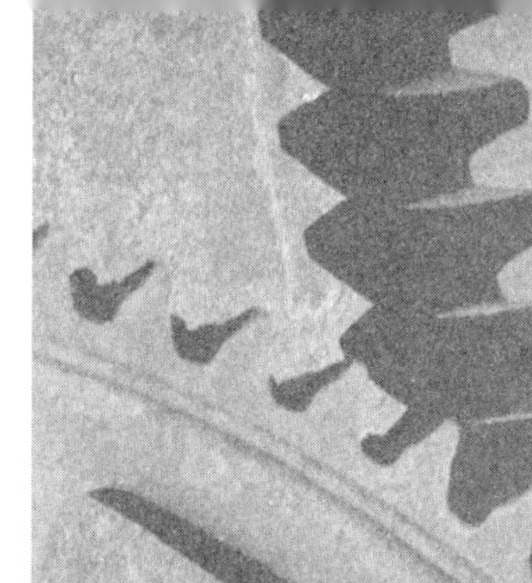

CHAPTER 3

Phase 3: Triage

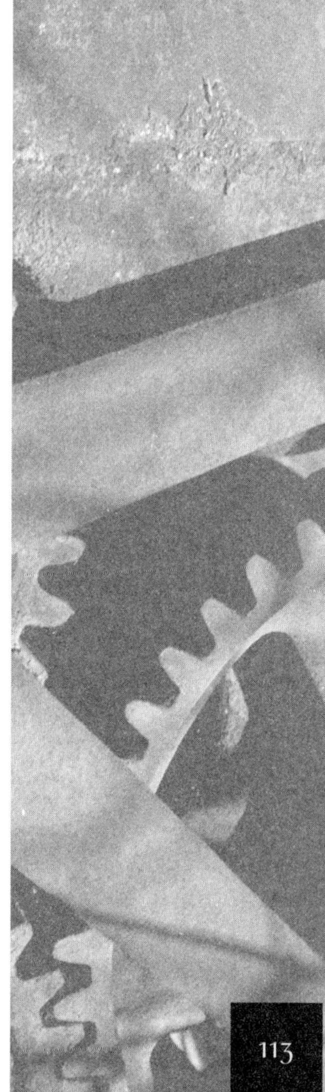

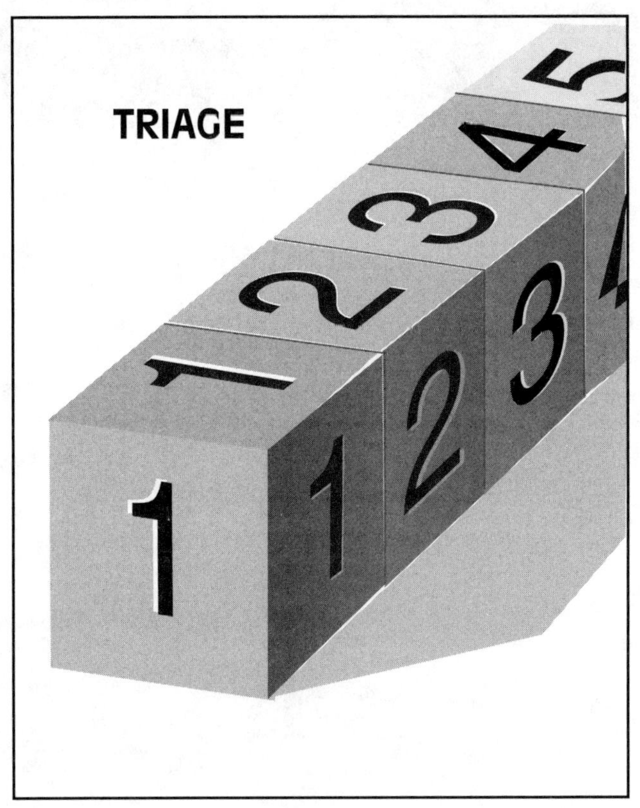
TRIAGE

Objectives:

- Assess business risks associated with each system.
- Assign a business priority to each system or Inventory element.
- Define scope by determining which systems will receive Year 2000 detection and correction efforts.
- Develop plans, costs, and schedules for Detailed Assessment, and obtain senior management approval for these items.

During Phase 3, Triage, you determine where you should concentrate your efforts as you proceed with your Year 2000 efforts. The decisions you make during this phase will help you create a detailed plan for the completion of system assessment tasks.

Strategic Decisions

During Inventory, you discovered the size and boundaries of your Year 2000 problem. You now have an estimate of how many systems within your organization will partially or completely fail when the millennium arrives. Do not be surprised if you are overwhelmed by the magnitude of the problem. Many organizations face the daunting prospect of modifying most of the systems in their organization.

Although you may face a seemingly enormous task, you must be realistic about what you can accomplish within the available time and with the available resources. You must decide what you can do now, what you will do in the future, and what you will not do at all. This decision-making process is the heart of the Triage phase.

During Triage, you will take a good look at the business objectives of your organization. You will decide which course of action will allow you to continue meeting those objectives while diffusing the Year 2000 time bomb. You will identify those systems that are the most important to your business objectives, those that are the least important, and those that are somewhere in the middle. This prioritization, tempered by technical and economic considerations, will allow you to formulate the schedule for the Detailed Assessment phase. You will also complete other planning activities for Detailed Assessment.

As in the Inventory phase, quality assurance has a minor auditing role during Triage. However, QA will monitor the activities to ensure that any plans that apply are followed, that any standards or guidelines established by the Year 2000 project management are followed, and that, if there are deviations, they are reported and tracked to completion.

Triage should be short and sweet, lean and mean. Like triage activities within the medical arena, speed is of the essence. You will decide which systems need immediate attention, which systems will be addressed at a later time, and which systems will not be addressed at all. You will analyze the information collected during Inventory, assign a priority to each system, and plan for the Detailed Assessment phase.

The decisions you make made during Triage will have a profound effect on all future Year 2000 endeavors. It may be necessary to review and revise these decisions during later phases of your Year 2000 project. Changes in your organization may necessitate several iterations of both Inventory phase and Triage phase activities.

The cost for completion of Triage should not exceed 1 percent of your Year 2000 project cost.

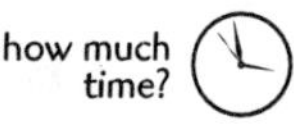

The time devoted to Triage tasks should comprise 1 percent of the Year 2000 project schedule.

Summary of Deliverables

This section summarizes the three deliverables for this phase of the Year 2000 compliance project. The section "Deliverables, Tasks, and Dependencies" later in this chapter includes detailed descriptions of each deliverable and the associated supporting tasks.

Triage Phase Startup

The Triage Phase Startup deliverable provides the requisite Triage work environment, ensuring that facilities, equipment, personnel, procedures, and nonproject participants are identified and in place.

Business Risks and Priorities

The Business Risks and Priorities deliverable summarizes the business risks associated with each system. It also provides a list of the business priorities associated with each system.

Detailed Assessment Plan

The Detailed Assessment Plan is a comprehensive plan for the successful completion of the Detailed Assessment phase, including a list of which systems are to be assessed and which are not.

Deliverables, Tasks, and Dependencies

The deliverables in Triage support the critical decision-making processes that will define the remaining activities of your Year 2000 project. You should complete Triage deliverables as quickly as possible to have more time for Assessment and Resolution tasks.

3.1 Triage Phase Startup

Triage Phase Startup provides the systems and resources that must be available to ensure the efficient completion of all tasks undertaken in Triage. Upon completion of this deliverable, the Triage environment will be in place.

Task Overview

- Ensure Adequacy of Triage Environment
- Establish Triage Tracking
- Identify Triage Participants

3.1.1 Task: Ensure Adequacy of Triage Environment

Make sure that resources required for Triage tasks are in place. Review your Inventory phase staff and environment in case you need to modify either. Because Triage is merely a short follow-up to Inventory, the support staff and environment

used for Triage will, in all likelihood, be identical to those used for Inventory. Make any necessary modifications.

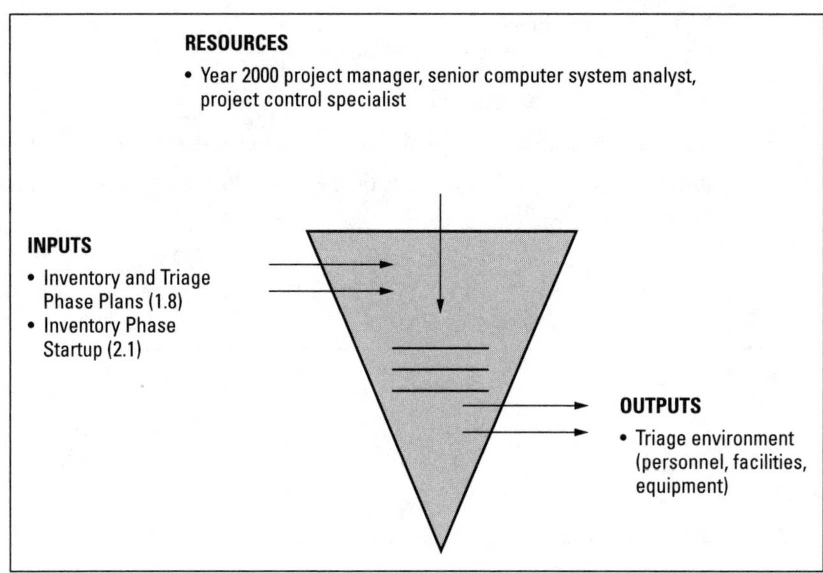
RESOURCES
• Year 2000 project manager, senior computer system analyst, project control specialist
INPUTS
• Inventory and Triage Phase Plans (1.8)
• Inventory Phase Startup (2.1)
OUTPUTS
• Triage environment (personnel, facilities, equipment)

3.1.2 Task: Establish Triage Tracking

Use the schedule and progress measurement requirements set forth in the Progress Tracking Plan to schedule specific milestones, measurement points, and progress review meetings within the approved overall Triage schedule (1.8.4). When evaluating progress against plan, consider the status of the work products themselves, the effort expended, and resources used. Also monitor the status of risk mitigation activities. You should use the feedback mechanisms established in the Progress Tracking Plan to make sure lessons learned during this phase are applied to the planning of future phases.

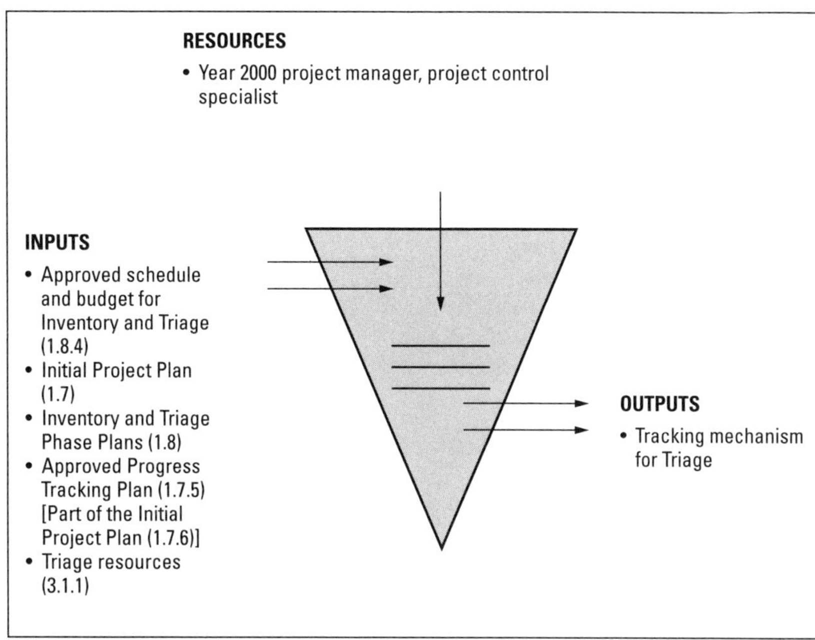
RESOURCES
• Year 2000 project manager, project control specialist
INPUTS
• Approved schedule and budget for Inventory and Triage (1.8.4)
• Initial Project Plan (1.7)
• Inventory and Triage Phase Plans (1.8)
• Approved Progress Tracking Plan (1.7.5) [Part of the Initial Project Plan (1.7.6)]
• Triage resources (3.1.1)
OUTPUTS
• Tracking mechanism for Triage

3.1.3 Task: Identify Triage Participants

As you identify senior managers, staff, and other key data management personnel who will make Triage decisions, be extremely careful that they have the authority to make decisions critical to your organization's future. You will need a fairly comprehensive group of decision makers to ensure the organization-wide acceptance of Triage decisions. The decisions this group makes must be binding to all areas of your organization. You must minimize any "second guessing" following these decisions.

The way you select these managers is highly dependent on the practices and politics within your organization. You may need to coordinate an enormous amount of input from a variety of sources to determine who will participate in Triage decision-making tasks. On the other hand, your organization's CIO or CEO may designate these managers. In any case, a very senior staff member will need to "bless" these selections.

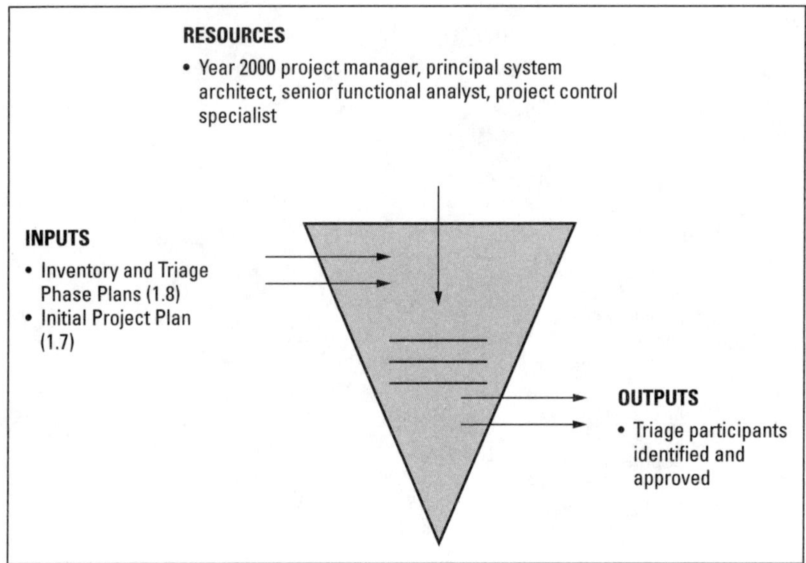
RESOURCES
• Year 2000 project manager, principal system architect, senior functional analyst, project control specialist
INPUTS
• Inventory and Triage Phase Plans (1.8)
• Initial Project Plan (1.7)
OUTPUTS
• Triage participants identified and approved

Task Guideline

- A clear distinction must be drawn between the Year 2000 project staff, who will support the Triage phase of the Year 2000 project, and the Triage participants, who will make the difficult Triage decisions. The identity and availability of the project staff were verified at the outset of the Triage phase (3.1.1).

milestone

Triage Phase Startup completed. Quality assurance verifies that the deliverable conforms to its intended goal. Project control baselines the deliverable and updates tracking metrics.

3.2 Business Risks and Priorities

The Business Risks and Priorities deliverable provides a prioritization of your organization's systems based on business-related, as opposed to technical, criteria. It also lists the business risks associated with each system. The determination of system priorities will be based, in part, on the information contained in this listing.

Task Overview

- Consolidate Inventory Deliverables
- Present Inventory Deliverables
- Assess Business Risk
- Assign Business Priorities
- Capture Business Risks and Priorities

3.2.1 Task: Consolidate Inventory Deliverables

During Inventory, you collected a massive quantity of system information. This information will support the analysis and decision tasks that occur during Triage, and it is your job to find an efficient method of utilizing this information. To avoid the common quandary of "information overload," you must consolidate this information, making it more accessible and easier to understand. You should also integrate System Inventory information with information about missing, out-of-use, and nonassessable configuration items.

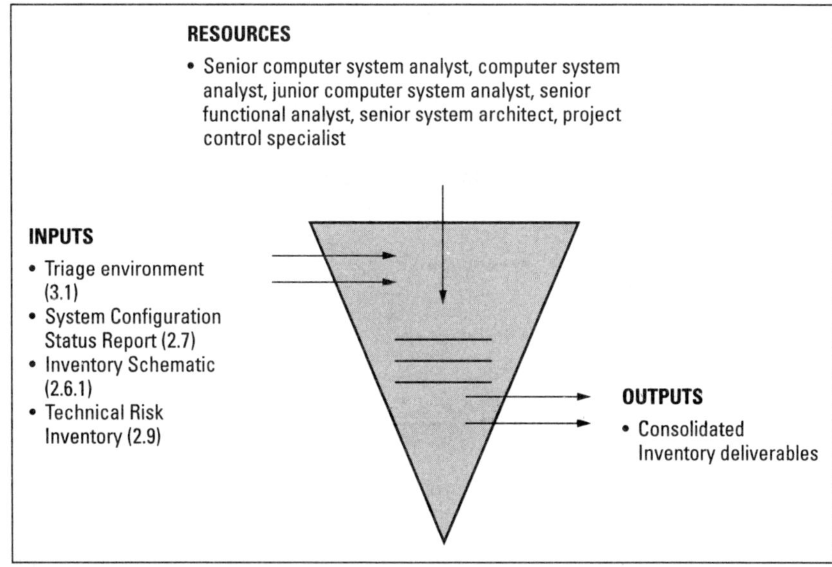
RESOURCES
• Senior computer system analyst, computer system analyst, junior computer system analyst, senior functional analyst, senior system architect, project control specialist
INPUTS
• Triage environment (3.1)
• System Configuration Status Report (2.7)
• Inventory Schematic (2.6.1)
• Technical Risk Inventory (2.9)
OUTPUTS
• Consolidated Inventory deliverables

Task Guidelines

- Develop a summary of Inventory information that facilitates a top-level understanding of the systems in your organization, the primary uses of those systems, and the technical risks associated with them. Using the records in the Year 2000 repository, you capture the following information about each system:
  - System ID
  - Primary function
  - Primary dependencies
  - Owner
  - Technical risk
- In all likelihood, you will be required to analyze and summarize existing information in order to define the "primary function" and the "primary dependencies" of each system.
- Following the capture of summary information concerning each system, you may wish to further summarize this information (by organizational unit, by technical risk category, by owner, and so on). For example, you may want to create a summary of all systems that have a designation of "Very High" technical risk. Alternatively, it may be helpful to prepare a summary of systems for each division or business area in your organization. You may find the Inventory Schematic (2.6.1) useful in developing these summaries. You should summarize information as necessary to facilitate an understanding of the Year 2000 problems in your organization. The specific attributes of your organization will define the type of summary most useful to you.

3.2.2 Task: Present Inventory Deliverables

Present the summary of system information developed in the preceding task (3.2.1) to the Triage participants. This presentation is intended to provide the Triage decision makers (not your project staff) with a general understanding of the systems in your organization and the Year 2000 problems associated with these systems. This presentation should set the stage for the upcoming Assess Business Risk and Assign Business Priorities tasks.

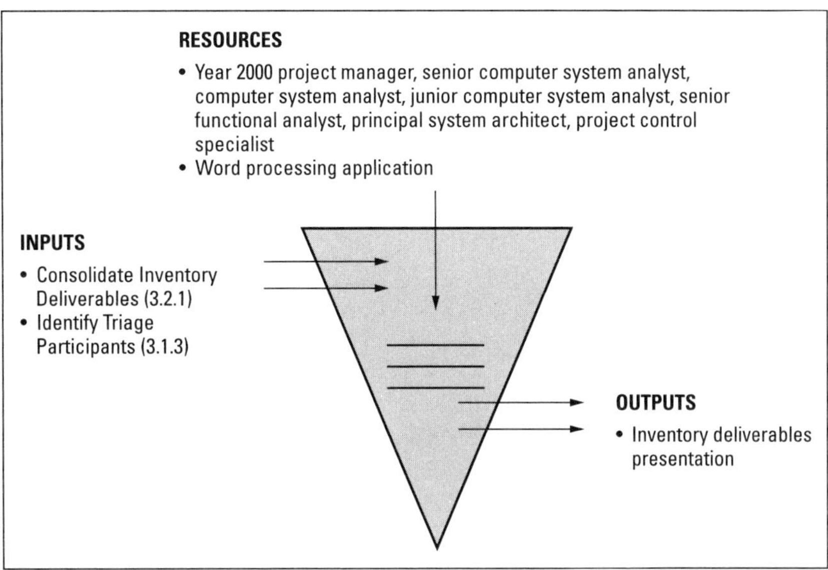
RESOURCES
• Year 2000 project manager, senior computer system analyst, computer system analyst, junior computer system analyst, senior functional analyst, principal system architect, project control specialist
• Word processing application
INPUTS
• Consolidate Inventory Deliverables (3.2.1)
• Identify Triage Participants (3.1.3)
OUTPUTS
• Inventory deliverables presentation

Task Guidelines

- This presentation should prepare the Triage participants (that is, the decision makers) to assess the business risks associated with each system, and to assign business priorities to those systems.
- Because the presentation is an overview of system information, you may want to develop handouts that incorporate detailed system information—participants can then study these handouts at their convenience.

3.2.3 Task: Assess Business Risk

During this task, the Triage decision makers assess the business risk associated with each system in your organization. You may want to review Appendix I, "*How To 2000* Risk Management," a discussion of risk as defined in this guide. To assess business risk, you need to assign values to two risk factors for each system:

- The probability that a Year 2000 problem associated with the system will have an adverse impact on business objectives
- The magnitude of that impact

As is traditional with risk calculations, make these assessments by assigning a value within a 0-1 scale. You calculate system business risk by multiplying the two factors.

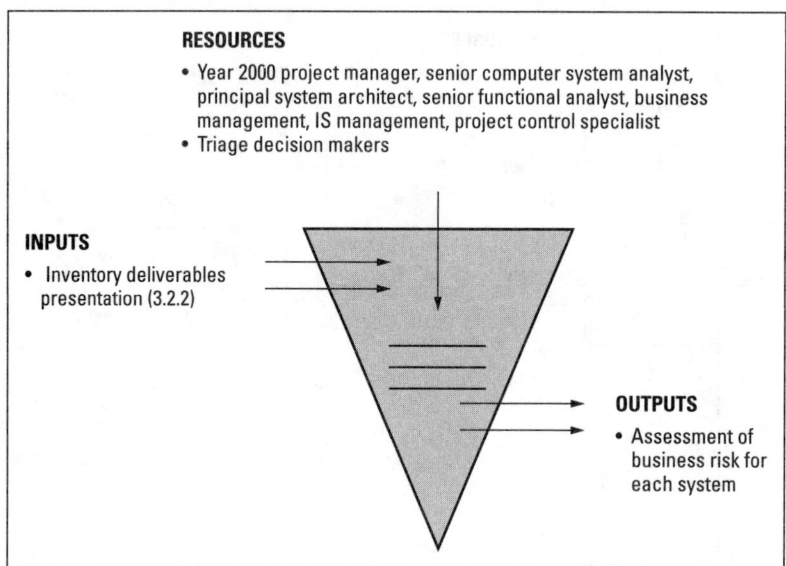
RESOURCES
• Year 2000 project manager, senior computer system analyst, principal system architect, senior functional analyst, business management, IS management, project control specialist
• Triage decision makers
INPUTS
• Inventory deliverables presentation (3.2.2)
OUTPUTS
• Assessment of business risk for each system

Task Guidelines

- You can use the following type of table to systematically assess system business risk.

System ID	Probability of Business Impact	Magnitude of Impact	Business Risk (Numeric)	Business Risk (Likert)
Hardware A	.8	.2	.16	Very low
Software	.9	.9	.81	Very high
Network K	.9	.3	.27	Low
Hardware X	.2	.2	.04	Very low

- As shown in the table, numeric risk values are converted to Likert Scale values. This conversion softens the impact of the definitely subjective and probably nonuniform assignment of risk factor values.
- Numerical values of business risk correspond to the following Likert Scale values:

- Very high: .8 and above
- High: .6 to .8
- Medium: .4 to .6
- Low: .2 to .4
- Very low: .2 and below

- Quality assurance reviews the business risk assessment, ensuring that all systems have been assessed and that management guidelines for performing the assessment were followed.

3.2.4 Task: Assign Business Priorities

Based on a variety of organizational considerations, including the business risk values assigned to each system, the Triage decision-making group assigns business priorities to each of your organization's systems. This task is the heart of the Triage phase, for these priorities, in concert with technical and economic considerations, will determine the order in which Year 2000 problems will be addressed.

Beware! This may be the most politically delicate task of your Year 2000 project. In all likelihood, business managers will come out of the woodwork to ensure that their systems are made Year 2000 compliant as speedily as possible.

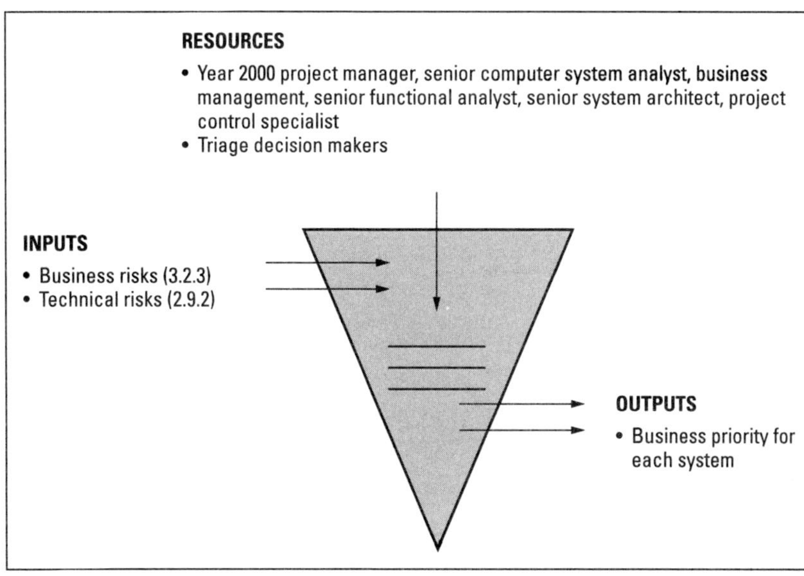
RESOURCES
• Year 2000 project manager, senior computer system analyst, business management, senior functional analyst, senior system architect, project control specialist
• Triage decision makers
INPUTS
• Business risks (3.2.3)
• Technical risks (2.9.2)
OUTPUTS
• Business priority for each system

Task Guidelines

- This task will not result in an ordered list of numerically prioritized systems. Rather, decision makers will simply assign one of several predefined priority levels—Critical, High, Medium, and Low—to each system. By assigning priority levels, as opposed to assigning ordered priorities, you will enjoy greater freedom in the development of your schedules for future Year 2000 project phases.
- You may wish to initiate an internal review mechanism to allow business managers to review and, if necessary, provide input to the priority assignment process.

3.2.5 Task: Capture Business Risks and Priorities

Capture the assigned system business risks and priorities within the Year 2000 repository. As always, you should ensure that standard configuration management practices are followed in the entry and maintenance of this information.

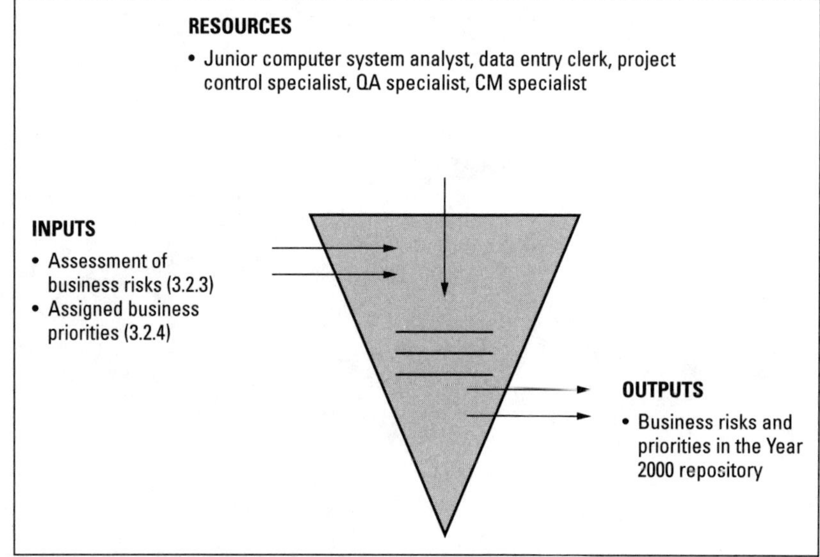
RESOURCES
• Junior computer system analyst, data entry clerk, project control specialist, QA specialist, CM specialist
INPUTS
• Assessment of business risks (3.2.3)
• Assigned business priorities (3.2.4)
OUTPUTS
• Business risks and priorities in the Year 2000 repository

Task Guideline

- Quality assurance will ensure that each system has been assigned a business priority and that these priorities have been captured in the Year 2000 repository.

milestone  **Business Risks and Priorities completed. Quality assurance verifies that the deliverable conforms to its intended goal. Project control baselines the deliverable and updates tracking metrics. Configuration management verifies that Year 2000 repository updates adhere to CM procedures.**

3.3 Detailed Assessment Plan

This deliverable provides the plan for executing the Detailed Assessment phase.

At this point in the project, you have completed an inventory of your systems and prioritized the systems based on your organization's business objectives. You know what you've got and where your priorities lie. You are ready to decide which systems will undergo detailed assessment, and then to refine your high-level staffing, schedule, and budget needs for the Detailed Assessment phase. The tasks in this deliverable let you create a detailed plan ensuring that assessment activities occur efficiently.

Task Overview

- Tailor the Methodology for Detailed Assessment
- Estimate Assessment Resources by System
- Select Systems To Be Assessed
- Identify Detailed Assessment Tools
- Identify Staff Requirements for Detailed Assessment
- Develop Schedule and Budget for Detailed Assessment
- Present and Approve Detailed Assessment Schedule/Budget

3.3.1 Task: Tailor the Methodology for Detailed Assessment

As mentioned previously, the Year 2000 methodology should be tailored to fit the needs of your organization. Before you begin planning for the Detailed Assessment phase, familiarize yourself with the tasks described in the Detailed Assessment phase section of this document and modify them according to the needs of your organization.

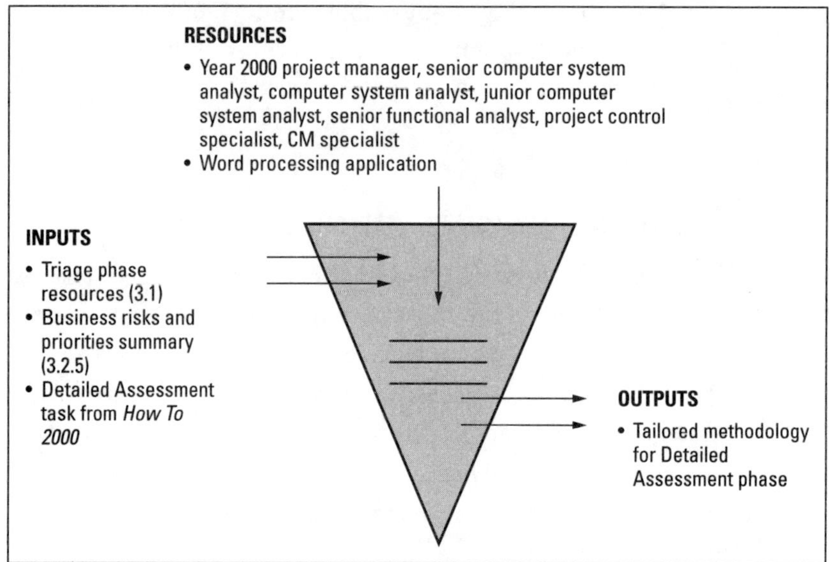

RESOURCES
• Year 2000 project manager, senior computer system analyst, computer system analyst, junior computer system analyst, senior functional analyst, project control specialist, CM specialist
• Word processing application
INPUTS
• Triage phase resources (3.1)
• Business risks and priorities summary (3.2.5)
• Detailed Assessment task from How To 2000
OUTPUTS
• Tailored methodology for Detailed Assessment phase

Task Guidelines

- You may wish to change the resources assigned to a task or tasks, collapse or expand the time frame, or eliminate one or more tasks.
- This revision of Detailed Assessment activities will support the definition of both staff and schedule that follows the completion of this task.
- Quality assurance will ensure that the tailored methodology is consistent with the intent of the phase objectives and will meet the success criteria.
- The tailored methodology must be placed under configuration management.

3.3.2 Task: Estimate Assessment Resources by System

Identify the resources required to complete a detailed assessment of each system in your organization and estimate the cost of acquiring them.

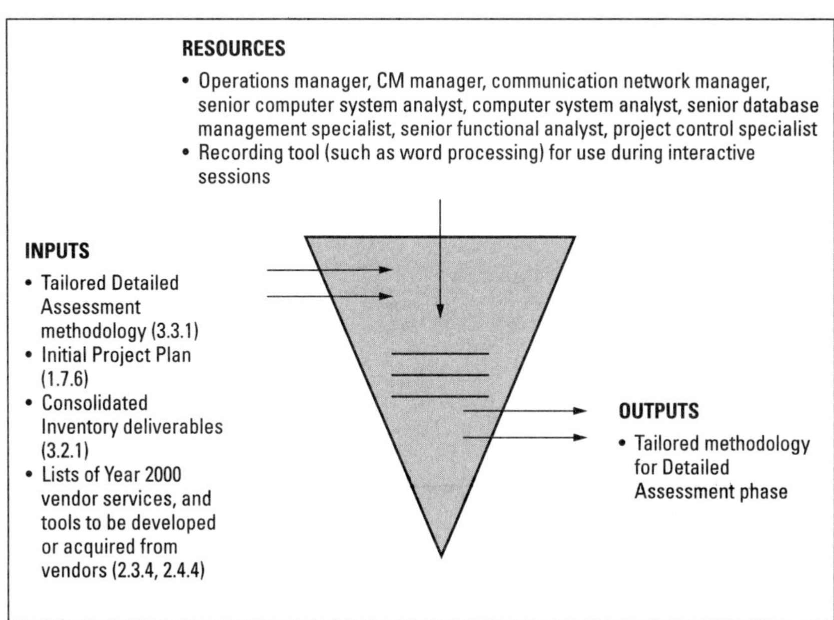
RESOURCES
• Operations manager, CM manager, communication network manager, senior computer system analyst, computer system analyst, senior database management specialist, senior functional analyst, project control specialist
• Recording tool (such as word processing) for use during interactive sessions
INPUTS
• Tailored Detailed Assessment methodology (3.3.1)
• Initial Project Plan (1.7.6)
• Consolidated Inventory deliverables (3.2.1)
• Lists of Year 2000 vendor services, and tools to be developed or acquired from vendors (2.3.4, 2.4.4)
OUTPUTS
• Tailored methodology for Detailed Assessment phase

Task Guidelines

Upon completion of this task, you will possess a list similar to the simplified example shown in the following table.

System ID	Staff	Tools	Other Resources	Total Resources
Software X	Programmer: 30 hours	Text editor: no cost	Office space: no cost	$750
Hardware Y	Electrical engineer: 80 hours	Vendor assessment tool: $100	Office space: no cost	$2500
Network Z	Network engineer: 10 hours	None	None	$300

- Resources needed for Detailed Assessment include the following:
  - **Personnel**: The staff members or contractors who will perform assessment tasks. Some examples are programmers who will review code; electrical engineers who must examine the schematics of, say, time code generators or readers; and system engineers who must search through interface specifications.
    Estimation metric: man-hours per personnel/labor category.
  - **Automated Tools**: Hardware, software, and other automated tools that you may need to perform or support assessment tasks. Included in this category would be the acquisition cost of Year 2000-specific assessment software applications, prorated among the number of systems to be assessed.
  - **Vendor Services**: You may have identified (via projected staffing shortfalls) vendor services required to support Detailed Assessment. If so, you also need to include them in your estimates.
  - **Other Resources**: Any other resources that you may need to support assessment activities. For example, you may need to allocate office space for assessment purposes if assessment will be conducted somewhere other than where the system normally resides.

  The complete listing of assessment resources by system may be quite lengthy.

- You may wish to consult personnel specialists for human resource cost information. In addition, these specialists may be able to help you create a "staff retention" strategy that is essential to any Year 2000 project. The retention of project personnel, especially key personnel, should be an ongoing concern for any Year 2000 project manager.
- You should consult procurement personnel about the cost of Year 2000-specific assessment tools.
- You may need to present this list of assessment resources to the Year 2000 project staff, members of senior management, or both. Presentation requirements are dependent upon the current situation in your organization.

3.3.3 Task: Select Systems to Be Assessed

Now that you possess a wealth of system information, you must decide which systems will be assessed and which will not. These decisions will be based on a variety of considerations: technical risk assessments, business risk assessments, business priorities, and available time and funds. Systems that are not assessed will no longer be included in Year 2000 project activities. There may be many reasons why you may not wish to assess a particular system: Perhaps that system is scheduled for retirement or replacement in the near future; perhaps the cost of assessment is simply too high; perhaps, considering the number of systems which must be assessed, the business priority of a system may simply be too low. The current situation in your organization will drive the selection of those systems that will come under consideration during the Detailed Assessment phase.

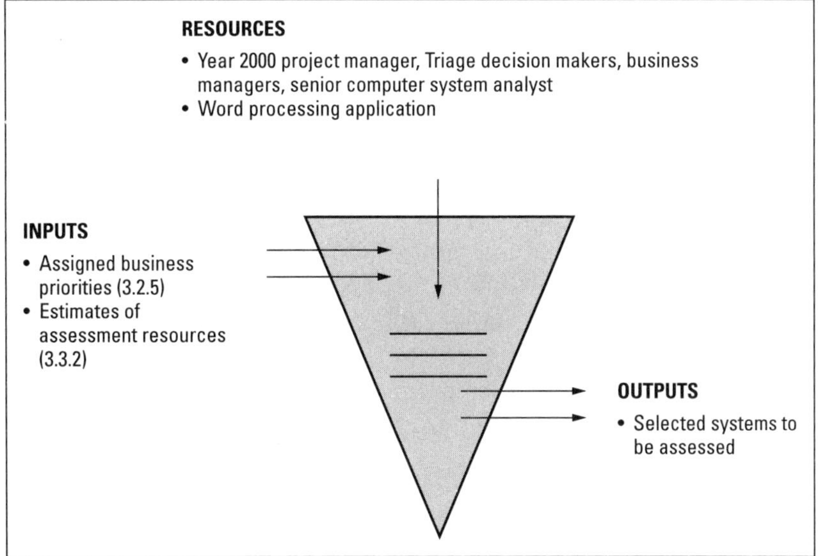
RESOURCES
• Year 2000 project manager, Triage decision makers, business managers, senior computer system analyst
• Word processing application
INPUTS
• Assigned business priorities (3.2.5)
• Estimates of assessment resources (3.3.2)
OUTPUTS
• Selected systems to be assessed

Task Guidelines

- Selection criteria will vary from one organization to the next, but will almost certainly be heavily influenced by the business priority and the estimation of assessment resources associated with each system. There are many ways of simplifying your selection process:
  - Stipulate that all systems designated Very High, High, or Medium priority are to be assessed.

- Rule out the assessment of systems that will incur assessment costs in excess of a certain amount.
- Assess all systems assigned a particular business priority first, starting with the highest priority, and proceed down the priority scale until your budget is exhausted.
- If you feel that "slow but sure" is the best approach, you can consider each system in turn, and make individual decisions regarding each one.

- Selection decisions may have profound political repercussions within your organization. As previously stated when discussing the assignment of business priorities, managers may expend inordinate efforts to ensure the assessment of the systems under their control—or to avoid it. It is up to you to balance the needs, the resources, and the personalities in your organization in your efforts to complete this task. From a practical standpoint, however, you may occasionally reach an impasse that requires senior management to intercede. The larger your organization, or the greater the number of isolated business units, the greater the likelihood that some selection decisions will require such intercession.
- Selection decisions can be made by a few individuals or by a group. Regardless of the number of people who participate in the selection process, these selections must be formally approved by a manager who has signoff authority for the results of this task.

3.3.4 Task: Identify Detailed Assessment Tools

You must identify the tools you need to conduct Detailed Assessment. These tools may come from vendors or be developed in-house. Vendor tools include estimating devices designed to calculate labor hours and costs to fix embedded date fields, functional assessment tools that use multiple search strings against source code to find date routines that will be affected by the Year 2000, and parsing tools to identify date field occurrences.

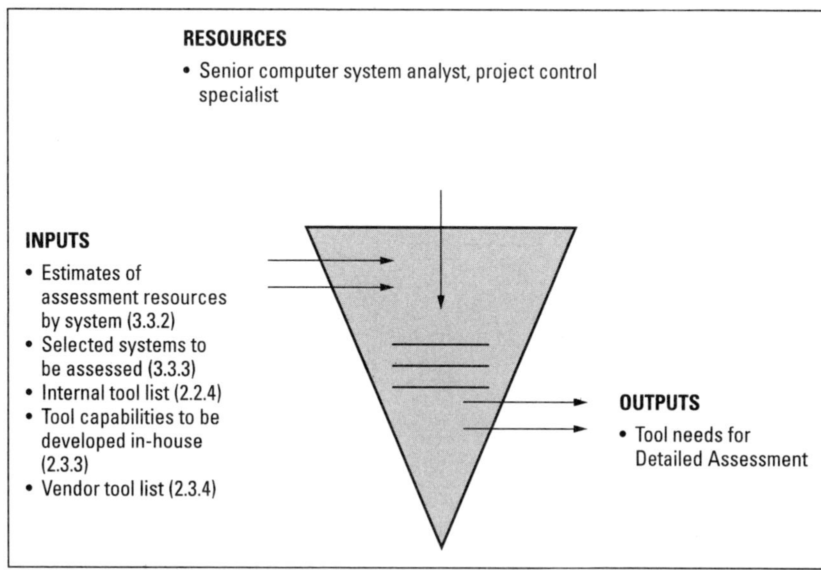
RESOURCES
• Senior computer system analyst, project control specialist
INPUTS
• Estimates of assessment resources by system (3.3.2)
• Selected systems to be assessed (3.3.3)
• Internal tool list (2.2.4)
• Tool capabilities to be developed in-house (2.3.3)
• Vendor tool list (2.3.4)
OUTPUTS
• Tool needs for Detailed Assessment

Task Guideline

- This task updates the initial list of tools developed during the Inventory phase. That earlier list identified tools needed in future phases, categorized according to whether they were already available in-house, would be developed in-house, or would be acquired from a vendor.

3.3.5 Task: Identify Staff Requirements for Detailed Assessment

After selecting the systems to be assessed, you must identify the specific staff members who will assess these systems. You must identify staff members internal to your organization, as well as contractors who will be hired to undertake Year 2000 assessment activities.

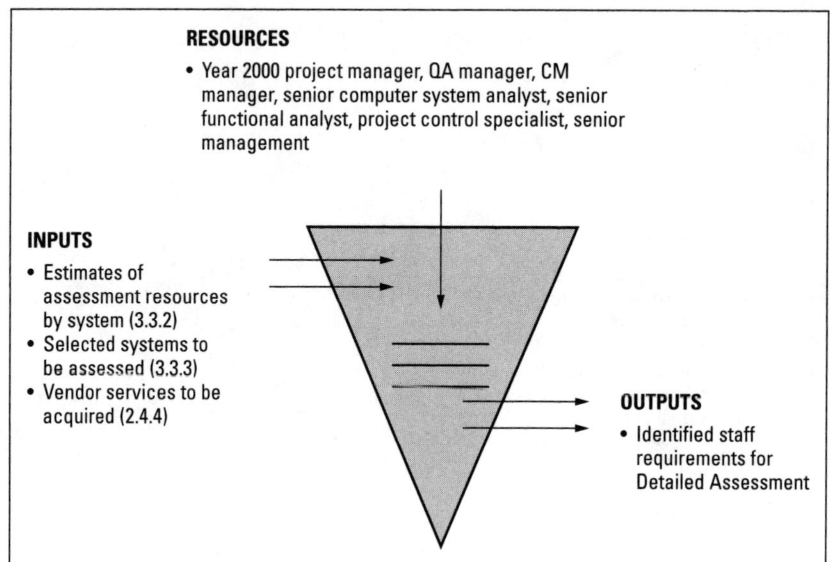
RESOURCES
• Year 2000 project manager, QA manager, CM manager, senior computer system analyst, senior functional analyst, project control specialist, senior management
INPUTS
• Estimates of assessment resources by system (3.3.2)
• Selected systems to be assessed (3.3.3)
• Vendor services to be acquired (2.4.4)
OUTPUTS
• Identified staff requirements for Detailed Assessment

Task Guidelines

- Coordinate your allocation efforts with human resources personnel and with the appropriate business managers.
- Introduce affected personnel to the assessment project as soon as possible.

3.3.6 Task: Develop Schedule and Budget for Detailed Assessment

Develop a detailed schedule for Detailed Assessment tasks.

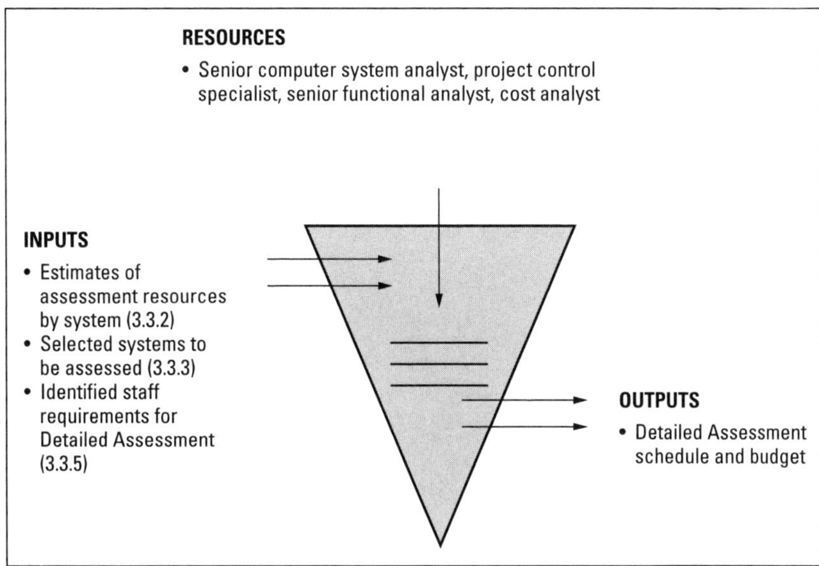
RESOURCES
• Senior computer system analyst, project control specialist, senior functional analyst, cost analyst
INPUTS
• Estimates of assessment resources by system (3.3.2)
• Selected systems to be assessed (3.3.3)
• Identified staff requirements for Detailed Assessment (3.3.5)
OUTPUTS
• Detailed Assessment schedule and budget

Task Guideline

- This schedule will probably reflect the parallel occurrence of many assessment tasks.

3.3.7 Task: Present and Approve Detailed Assessment Schedule/Budget

You are ready to submit your Detailed Assessment Plan for approval. You present your schedule and budget, as well as other significant information that senior management may need to approve budget and resources for conducting the Detailed Assessment phase.

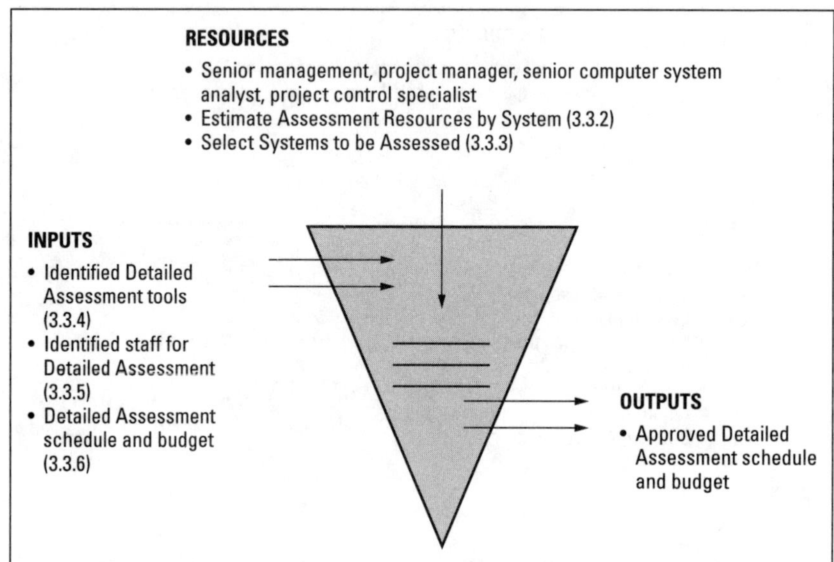

RESOURCES
• Senior management, project manager, senior computer system analyst, project control specialist
• Estimate Assessment Resources by System (3.3.2)
• Select Systems to be Assessed (3.3.3)
INPUTS
• Identified Detailed Assessment tools (3.3.4)
• Identified staff for Detailed Assessment (3.3.5)
• Detailed Assessment schedule and budget (3.3.6)
OUTPUTS
• Approved Detailed Assessment schedule and budget

Task Guideline

- Obtain an explicit management directive before initiating assessment activities.

Detailed Assessment Plan completed and approved.

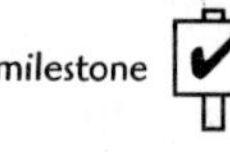

Triage Phase complete. Quality assurance verifies that the deliverable conforms to its intended goal. Project control baselines the deliverable and updates tracking metrics. Configuration management verifies that Year 2000 repository updates adhere to CM procedures.

Business Impacts

The tasks undertaken during Triage will not initially impact your business processes to any great extent. The allocation of time and effort to actual Triage tasks should be minimal.

However, Triage activities may cause quite a commotion within your organization. The main Triage task (the assignment of business priorities to systems) will engender swift action on the part of many managers, who may go to great lengths to ensure that the importance of their work and systems is recognized. Unfortunately, you may become involved in a certain amount of organizational infighting.

Triage tasks will have a profound, if indirect, effect upon your business processes in the future. During Triage, you decide what systems are to be assessed. You also decide what systems will be omitted from the assessment process and, consequently, dropped from consideration in the Year 2000 project. These decisions will be the starting point for potentially massive changes in the way your organization operates.

Triage decisions will reverberate throughout your organization for years to come. Managers will begin to reorganize the way they work based on Triage decisions. They will make plans for accomplishing their objectives without the support of the systems that will be taken out of operation during the Detailed Assessment and Resolution phases. They will revise their budgets to fund the replacement of systems that will not be repaired, and the training of users on the new systems. They will revise their schedules and budgets to accommodate the repair of systems that will be retained. They will plan their future department or project activities based upon the schedule you have developed for Detailed Assessment.

Phase Risks

Potential Event	*Probability*	*Impact*	*Risk*
Triage incomplete	Low	High	Low
Inaccurate business prioritizations	Low	High	Low

Triage Phase Risks

There are two primary risks associated with the Triage phase: One, Triage may be incomplete, and two, you may wind up with inaccurate business prioritizations.

Triage Incomplete

In the worst-case scenario, you would fail to complete Triage. In reality, it is unlikely that this will occur. By now, senior management should be fully supportive of the Year 2000 effort. You should have the backing and funding that you need to fulfill the relatively light resource requirements of Triage activities. In all likelihood, Triage will be completed swiftly and without major mishaps.

Methods of Risk Mitigation:

- Keep senior management informed of the importance of the Year 2000 process and the critical nature of Triage tasks.
- If you reach an impasse, do not hesitate to go to senior management to get it resolved. You cannot afford to lose time from your Triage schedule.

Inaccurate Business Prioritizations

The heart of Triage is assigning business priorities to your organization's systems. What if these assignments failed to mirror the true business objectives of your organization? For example, it would be detrimental to your organization to assign a low priority to a system that is critical to the daily operation of your business. In reality, the probability of making such a mistake in priority assignment is low. Hopefully, you will assemble knowledgeable and influential personnel to participate in Triage decisions. These staff members should make informed and sensible decisions regarding the business prioritization of each system. These decisions may well be highly political, however, and ultimately your Year 2000 project manager is responsible for these decisions.

Methods of Risk Mitigation:

- Limit the number of managers who participate in the assignment of system business priorities. An overabundance of managers, all of whom wish to have their systems labeled "High Priority," may lead to a political slugfest that accomplishes nothing. Your decision-making group should consist of a limited number of knowledgeable senior managers who have the authority and the organization-wide focus to assign business priorities.

- Incorporate as much flexibility as possible in the Detailed Assessment Plan. If post-Triage events prove that business priorities have been incorrectly assigned, a flexible plan for Detailed Assessment should allow you to reassign system business priorities without significant negative effects. The Detailed Assessment Plan should be able to withstand some modifications to the order in which systems will be assessed.

Success Factors

In successfully completing Triage, you carried out the following steps:

Success Factor	*Deliverable*
Ascertained that all resources you needed for Triage phase tasks were in place	Triage Phase Startup
Established a detailed schedule for the Triage phase, including milestones, progress metrics, and progress review meetings	Triage Phase Startup
Ascertained that the Triage decision makers were qualified and authorized to make the types of assessment decisions required	Triage Phase Startup
Provided a comprehensive summary of Inventory deliverables to those who participated in Triage activities	Business Risks and Priorities
Assessed the business risk associated with each system in your organization	Business Risks and Priorities
Assigned business priorities to each system to support the development of a logical sequence for transitioning systems to Year 2000 compliance	Business Risks and Priorities
Captured these system business risks and priorities within the Year 2000 repository	Business Risks and Priorities
Tailored the Detailed Assessment methodology to suit the needs of your organization and program	Detailed Assessment Plan
Identified critical resources needed to successfully complete Detailed Assessment	Detailed Assessment Plan

continued

Success Factor	Deliverable
Planned for the support tools you will need during Detailed Assessment	Detailed Assessment Plan
Planned for vendor support services you will need during Detailed Assessment	Detailed Assessment Plan
Developed estimates for Detailed Assessment scope and size	Detailed Assessment Plan
Developed cost estimates for the technical resources required in Detailed Assessment	Detailed Assessment Plan
Identified which systems will be assessed and which will not	Detailed Assessment Plan
Developed a schedule for Detailed Assessment	Detailed Assessment Plan
Identified the key milestones within your schedule for Detailed Assessment	Detailed Assessment Plan
Planned to follow standard quality assurance and configuration management procedures throughout Detailed Assessment	Detailed Assessment Plan
Gained approval for the schedule/budget for Detailed Assessment	Detailed Assessment Plan
Identified phase risks and potential mitigation approaches	All deliverables
Identified which deliverables would be developed during Triage	All deliverables
Used adequate communication interfaces throughout your organization to support the tasks associated with Triage	All deliverables
Assigned phase tasks to various groups in your organization and ensured that management approved those tasks	All deliverables
Identified the deliverables for which each group was responsible and ensured acceptance of that deliverable responsibility by the group	All deliverables
Identified milestone thresholds beyond which some corrective action will be taken	All deliverables
Used metrics to track and measure progress with respect to these milestones	All deliverables
Ensured that each responsible group accepted and adhered to the schedule for completion of Triage	All deliverables

Reference Material

This list mentions reference material you can turn to for additional information on this phase of your Year 2000 compliance project:

- Appendix H, Integrated Project Plan
- Appendix I, How To 2000 Risk Management
- Glossary
- *How To 2000* CD-ROM

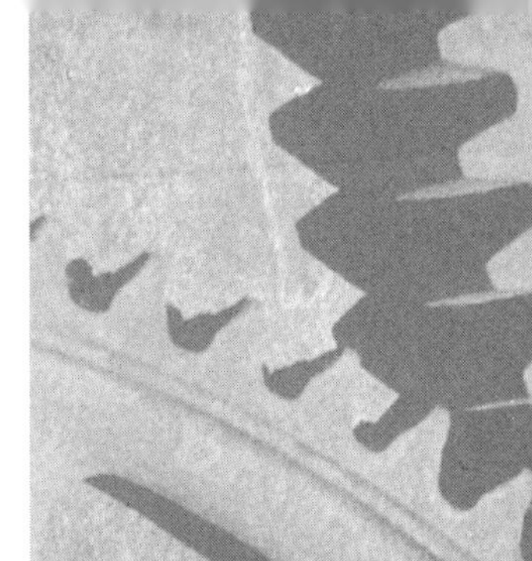

CHAPTER 4

Phase 4: Detailed Assessment

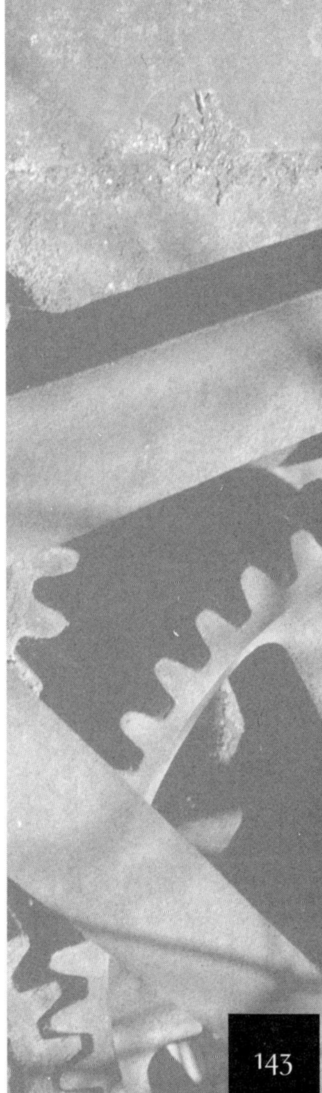

CHAPTER 4 **PHASE 4: DETAILED ASSESSMENT**

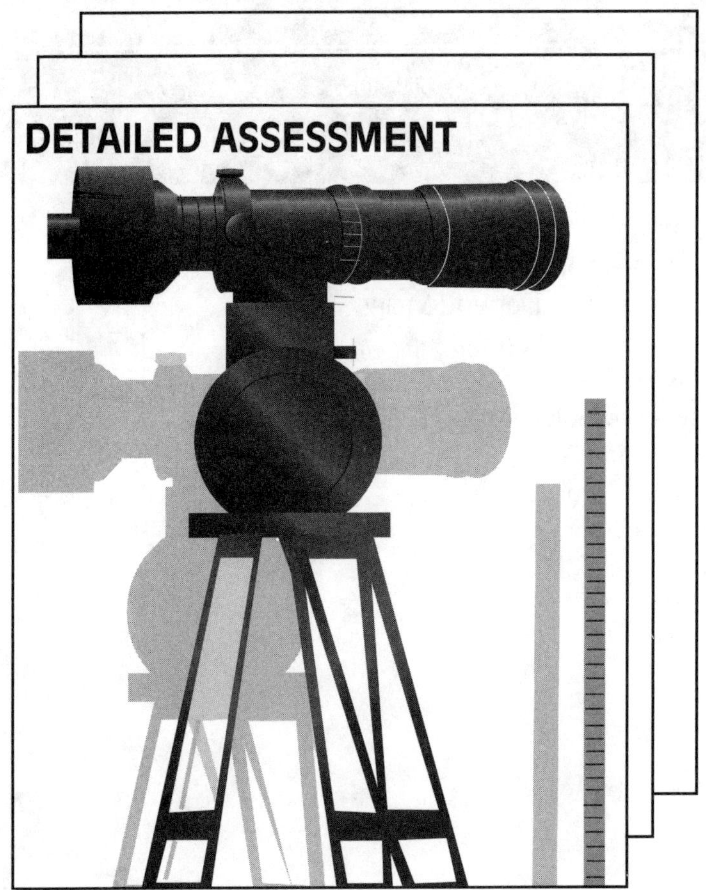

Objectives:

- Complete Detailed Assessment for each system (detailed problem identification and classification).
- Group systems into logical partitions for movement through the correction cycle (resolution, test, and deployment).
- Determine to repair, replace, or retire specific affected systems.
- Develop detailed plans, schedules, and costs for correction cycle.
- Communicate the explicit size and boundaries of your Year 2000 problem to senior management and obtain approvals for the correction cycle.

During Phase 4, Detailed Assessment, you take a careful look at all systems chosen during the Triage phase. Then you begin to plan how to bring these systems into Year 2000 compliance.

Assessing Systems

During this phase, you conduct a detailed assessment of each system selected in Triage. You need to familiarize yourself with every aspect of these systems, from the details of their maintenance agreements to the nuances of their code or circuitry. Based upon this explicit information, you choose an appropriate solution for each system's Year 2000 problems. These solutions will be implemented during the Resolution phase, which is described in the next chapter.

Information gathered during Detailed Assessment supplements the system information gathered during Inventory. During the Inventory phase, you determined the "black box" identity of each system (its name, location, basic functionality, and the possibility of Year 2000 impact). Assessment activities let you "open the box" and determine the complete nature of a given system. You examine the various components of each system and discover which components need to be modified to achieve Year 2000 compliance.

The cost for completion of Detailed Assessment should not exceed 29 percent of your Year 2000 project cost.

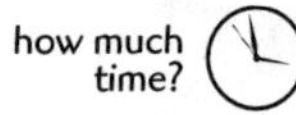

The time devoted to Detailed Assessment tasks should comprise 35 percent of the Year 2000 project schedule.

Summary of Deliverables

This section summarizes the deliverables for this phase of the Year 2000 compliance project. The section "Deliverables, Tasks, and Dependencies" later in this chapter includes detailed descriptions of each deliverable and the associated supporting tasks.

Detailed Assessment Phase Startup

The Detailed Assessment Phase Startup deliverable provides the resources (personnel, tools, and work environment) required to conduct Detailed Assessment activities.

System Assessment

The System Assessment deliverable provides a detailed assessment of your organization's systems and lists specific instances of Year 2000 noncompliance. It documents the source of Year 2000 problems and may include recommendations about solutions.

Draft Assessment Solutions

The Draft Assessment Solutions deliverable categorizes identified Year 2000 problems by problem type and lists an appropriate solution for each type. In addition, it identifies tools that will help you implement these solutions. The System Assessment and Draft Assessment Solutions deliverables are sometimes referred to as Impact Analysis.

System Resolution Plan

The System Resolution Plan deliverable provides a detailed plan and schedule for resolution (fix) of the Year 2000 problems identified during Detailed Assessment of each system. (That is, a detailed plan and schedule for the Resolution phase of the Year 2000 project.)

Correction Cycle Project Plan

The Correction Cycle Project Plan deliverable coordinates and meshes the System Resolution Plan with Testing and Deployment plans to provide a high-level plan for the completion of the next stage of Year 2000 activities, the correction cycle. This stage includes four phases: Resolution, Test Planning, Test Execution, and Deployment.

Deliverables, Tasks, and Dependencies

During the Detailed Assessment phase, you expand the information gathered during the Inventory phase, gaining a good picture of the makeup of systems selected during the Triage phase. From there, you devise solutions for each system's Year 2000 problems. You then coordinate each system's resolution plan into a master timeline plan encompassing all systems and resources necessary to accomplish your Year 2000 mission.

4.1 Detailed Assessment Phase Startup

The Detailed Assessment Phase Startup deliverable provides the resources needed to ensure that all Detailed Assessment tasks are completed efficiently. When you complete this deliverable, the Detailed Assessment environment will be in place.

Task Overview

- Acquire Tools for Detailed Assessment
- Develop Detailed Assessment Tools
- Acquire Human Resources for Detailed Assessment
- Brief Detailed Assessment Plan
- Develop and Execute Assessment Training
- Ensure Capture of Assessment Data in Year 2000 Repository
- Establish Detailed Assessment Tracking

4.1.1 Task: Acquire Tools for Detailed Assessment

During Triage you determined which tools you needed for your assessment activities. You will now acquire these tools. These tools must be installed properly and users must be trained how to use them.

A variety of assessment support tools are available from several vendors. These tools use several different approaches to identify system elements with Year 2000 problems. Some tools use multiple search routines to locate system components that will be affected by the Year 2000, while others use parsing technology to identify date field occurrences. Some assessment tools support the development of estimates of the hours and costs to fix embedded date fields.

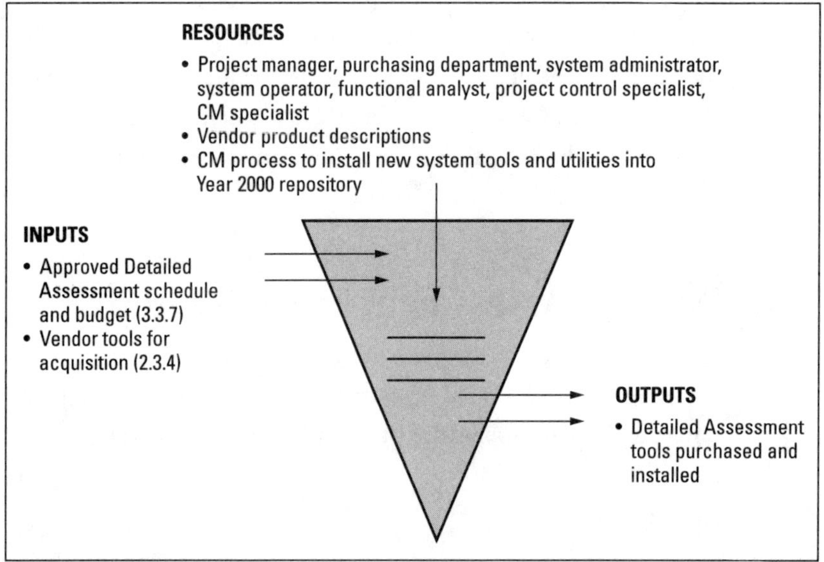
RESOURCES
• Project manager, purchasing department, system administrator, system operator, functional analyst, project control specialist, CM specialist
• Vendor product descriptions
• CM process to install new system tools and utilities into Year 2000 repository
INPUTS
• Approved Detailed Assessment schedule and budget (3.3.7)
• Vendor tools for acquisition (2.3.4)
OUTPUTS
• Detailed Assessment tools purchased and installed

4.1.2 Task: Develop Detailed Assessment Tools

Here you develop the assessment tools that you have chosen not to acquire. Development should proceed according to your organization's standard system development practices. You should ensure the inclusion of sound quality assurance tasks. Once a tool is developed, it should be tested and installed.

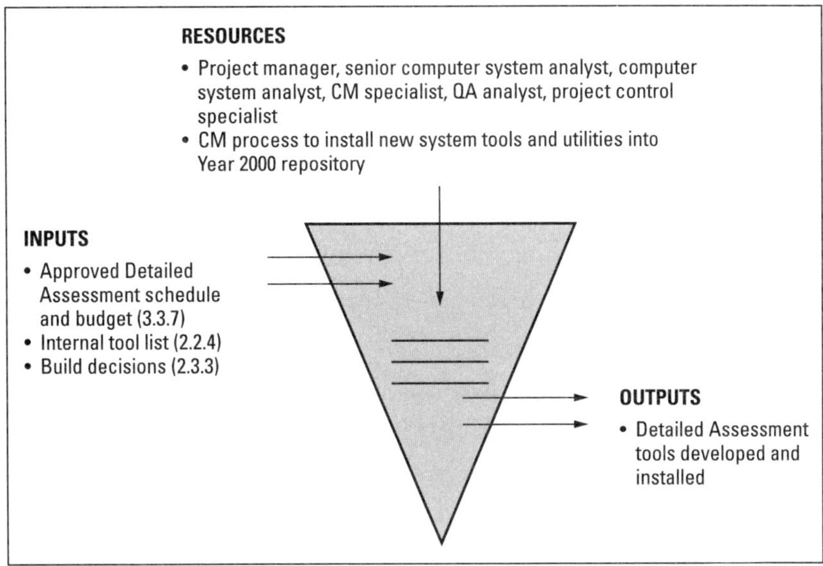
RESOURCES
• Project manager, senior computer system analyst, computer system analyst, CM specialist, QA analyst, project control specialist
• CM process to install new system tools and utilities into Year 2000 repository
INPUTS
• Approved Detailed Assessment schedule and budget (3.3.7)
• Internal tool list (2.2.4)
• Build decisions (2.3.3)
OUTPUTS
• Detailed Assessment tools developed and installed

4.1.3 Task: Acquire Human Resources for Detailed Assessment

You should acquire personnel to support assessment tasks according to the plans developed in Triage. You may acquire staff from both internal sources and external contractors.

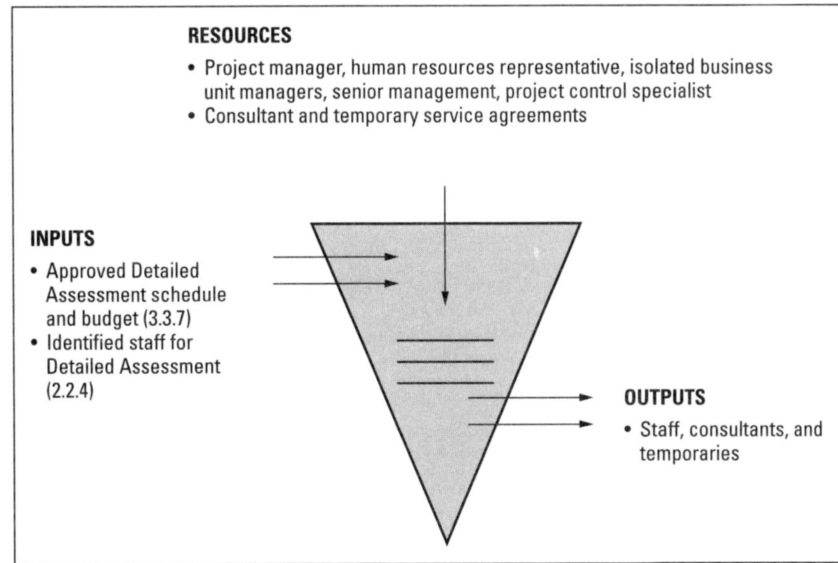
RESOURCES
• Project manager, human resources representative, isolated business unit managers, senior management, project control specialist
• Consultant and temporary service agreements
INPUTS
• Approved Detailed Assessment schedule and budget (3.3.7)
• Identified staff for Detailed Assessment (2.2.4)
OUTPUTS
• Staff, consultants, and temporaries

4.1.4 Task: Brief Detailed Assessment Plan

You will conduct a kickoff meeting with your Detailed Assessment staff. Topics covered should include:

- An overview of Detailed Assessment activities
- A summary of deliverables and their relationships
- An explanation of interface assessment and bridging concepts
- An explanation of assessment tool support, including in-house and vendor tools
- An overview of the Year 2000 repository and the importance of capturing comprehensive assessment information about each system
- A summary of staff assignments, responsibilities, and interactions
- The importance of Quality Assurance in ensuring that project standards and procedures are met
- A summary of available training opportunities

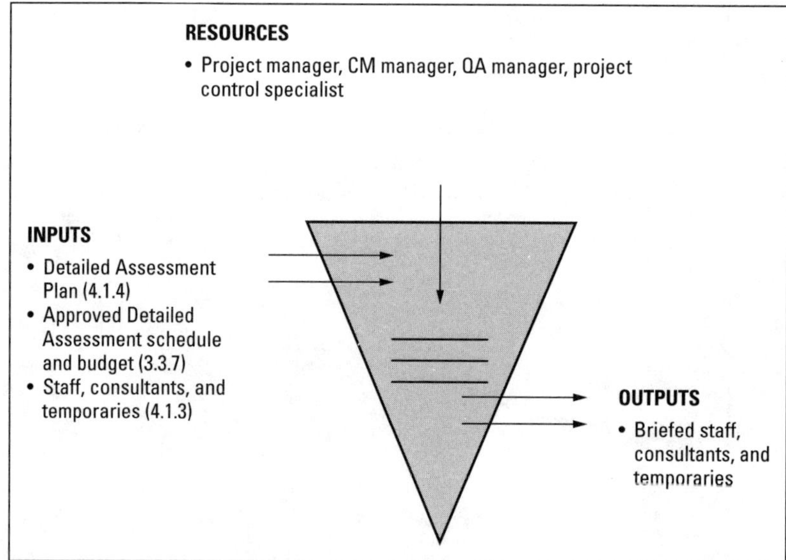
RESOURCES
• Project manager, CM manager, QA manager, project control specialist
INPUTS
• Detailed Assessment Plan (4.1.4)
• Approved Detailed Assessment schedule and budget (3.3.7)
• Staff, consultants, and temporaries (4.1.3)
OUTPUTS
• Briefed staff, consultants, and temporaries

4.1.5 Task: Develop and Execute Assessment Training

Assessment personnel need certain knowledge and skills to carefully and consistently assess your organization's systems. They must have opportunities to acquire this knowledge and these skills. Develop a training program that enables the assessment staff to become familiar with:

- The Year 2000 problems they are trying to identify
- Various ways these problems might be manifested in the systems being assessed
- The proper use of the tools for supporting their assessment activities
- The mechanisms they must use for communication, data capture, quality assurance, and other project support activities

You will probably need to develop a training session about general assessment tasks, as well as several system-specific training sessions.

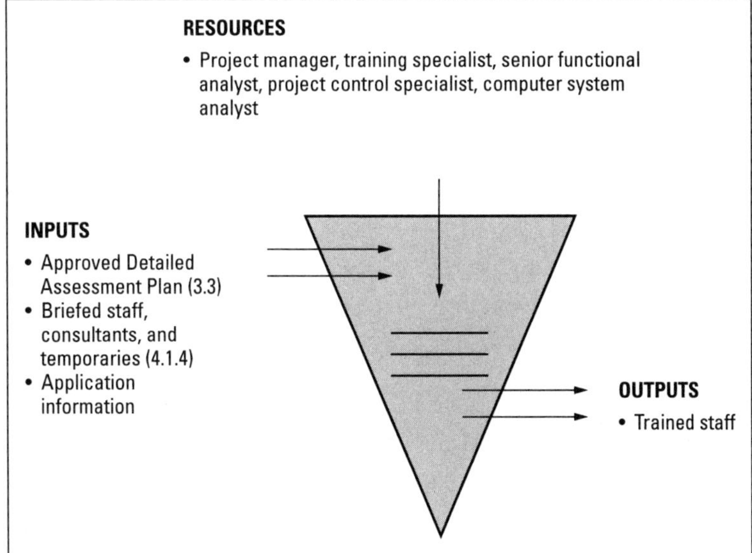
RESOURCES
• Project manager, training specialist, senior functional analyst, project control specialist, computer system analyst
INPUTS
• Approved Detailed Assessment Plan (3.3)
• Briefed staff, consultants, and temporaries (4.1.4)
• Application information
OUTPUTS
• Trained staff

4.1.6 Task: Ensure Capture of Assessment Data in Year 2000 Repository

The Year 2000 repository was established during Inventory. The repository must be ready to receive the information generated in Detailed Assessment. As the major system configuration management tool for this project, verify that the repository is continuing to successfully handle:

- Configuration units and baselines

- Changes to baselines
- Problem reports—the process of initiation, review, approval, tracking, and completion
- Configuration unit checkin and checkout, including concurrent checkouts.

All personnel engaged in assessment activities must recognize the critical importance of capturing all system information gathered in Detailed Assessment.

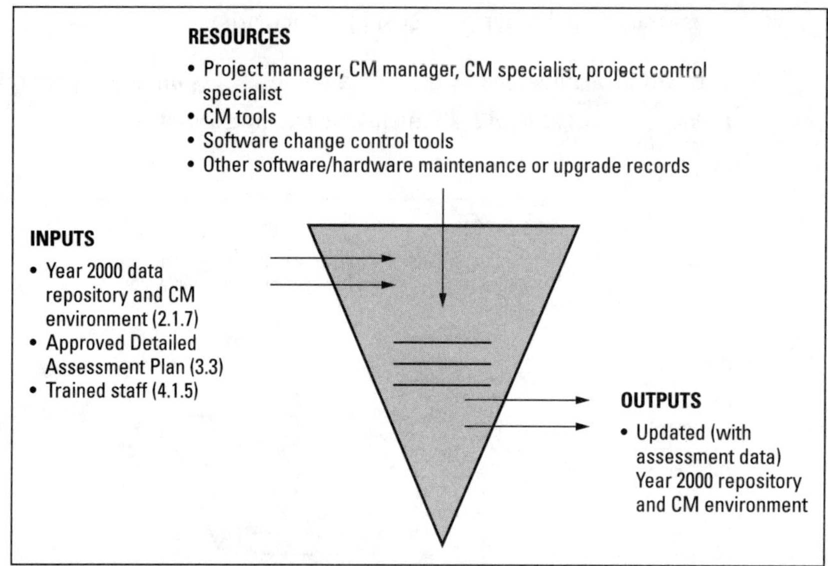

RESOURCES
• Project manager, CM manager, CM specialist, project control specialist
• CM tools
• Software change control tools
• Other software/hardware maintenance or upgrade records
INPUTS
• Year 2000 data repository and CM environment (2.1.7)
• Approved Detailed Assessment Plan (3.3)
• Trained staff (4.1.5)
OUTPUTS
• Updated (with assessment data) Year 2000 repository and CM environment

4.1.7 Task: Establish Detailed Assessment Tracking

It is imperative that you complete Detailed Assessment on schedule to allow as much time as possible to repair identified systems. Here you finalize the Detailed Assessment schedule, create tracking points or milestones, and define measurements of the tracking points to confirm conformance with the schedule. If your Detailed Assessment is large enough, schedule periodic internal and customer progress reviews to ensure conformance with the schedule, and to keep external clients informed of progress and accomplishments. If the actual schedule, budget, resources, or other tracked information are out of conformance with the plan, determine the proper corrective action and implement it if appropriate. Update the project plan to reflect the reallocation of resources and the adjustment of schedule, budget, or staffing.

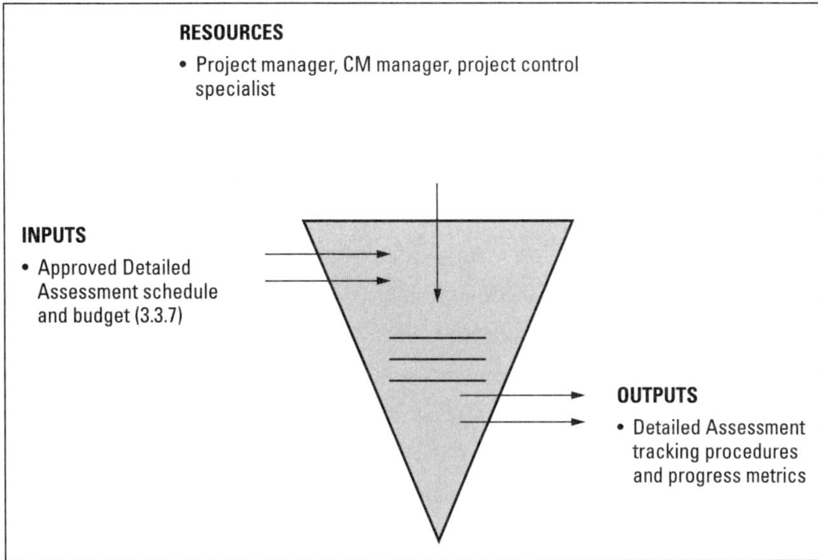

milestone  **Detailed Assessment Phase Startup complete. Quality assurance verifies that the deliverable conforms to its intended goal. Project control baselines the deliverable and updates tracking metrics.**

4.2 System Assessment

The System Assessment deliverable encompasses the actual Year 2000 assessment of your organization's systems. When this deliverable is complete, you will have detailed knowledge about the Year 2000 problems inherent in each of the assessed systems. You should assess individual systems concurrently, and should carry out the tasks in the deliverable in parallel. Carefully control and track the many activities that will take place during this deliverable.

Task Overview

- Assess Custom Software
- Assess Custom Hardware and Embedded Systems
- Assess COTS Systems
- Assess Electronic Partners

4.2.1 Task: Assess Custom Software

Custom software is software in your organization developed to perform a specific function or operation. It can be a stand-alone application; a small program that functions as part of, or in support of, a larger software package; or a large system consisting of many subsystems. The software may support the operational or infrastructure needs of your organization, or of an isolated business unit; or it may be for one of your customers. Custom software can be developed in-house, and can be developed specifically for your organization by contractors.

Appendix A includes a list of Year 2000 problems that you may encounter as you assess each system. You should read it and make sure you understand it. You may also find problems or deficiencies—some related to Year 2000 problems and others not—that are not included in Appendix A. All Year 2000-related problems should be captured. It may be worthwhile to separately document discovered problems that are not related to Year 2000 issues. However, you should not address them during the Resolution phase else you may lose Year 2000 project focus and valuable time.

Quality Assurance will audit assessment results to ensure that all custom software has been reviewed for potential problems.

To assess a custom software package, you will

- Assess source and object code:
  - Identify the location of each error by program or unit, and classify according to "problem type" as defined in Appendix A.
  - Identify and classify new types of Year 2000 errors.
  - Identify errors that affect data outside the program.
- Assess data dictionary:
  - Review the data dictionary, databases, data sets, and files.
    - Identify the location of each error by file or table name, including temporary work files if passed between programs.
    - Identify date fields not stored as date data elements.
    - Identify and classify new types of errors.
  - Identify file names that include the year.
- Assess copybooks and called objects:
  - Identify the location of source or data error.

- Assess stored code:
  - Check code found within data files.
  - Check code within databases (triggers, procedures, views, and so on).
  - Check code stored within CASE tools.
  - Custom code inside of query or report writing COTS packages.
- Assess control language:
  - Check whether some examples include JCL, shell scripts, PC. Bat files.
  - Review for date manipulation.
  - Identify file names that include the year.
- Assess parameter libraries:
  - Identify the location of any noncompliant dates in parameter files.
- Assess system documentation:
  - Review system requirements.
  - Review system designs.
- Assess system records:
  - Review testing records.
  - Review maintenance records.
  - Review configuration management logs.
- Interview system staff:
  - Interview system users.
  - Interview system developers, if available.
- Collect external originators (contractor) estimates:
  - Get cost and delivery dates from customized software contractors.

Task Guidelines

- To validate old systems with no source code, you might attempt "negative testing"—that is, running the application under Year 2000 conditions to see where it breaks. Be aware of possible side affects from such testing before you begin (for example, license premature expirations, interfaces, and so on).
- To reduce your assessment efforts, you might try "representative assessment." You can only use this technique if you have groups of similarly developed applications. You then extrapolate Detailed Assessment data on applications not reviewed from the Detailed Assessment data of applications you did assess. For example, your procurement and inventory systems were developed with the same language mixture, methods, techniques, and even the same development team. By assessing the inventory application, you can derive assessment estimates on your procurement application. There are inherit risks with this procedure. You might miss some of the unique Year 2000 problems found only within a specific application. Only staff with the necessary experience and seniority can adequately make this decision. The payoff is a much reduced Detailed Assessment cycle that saves both money and time.

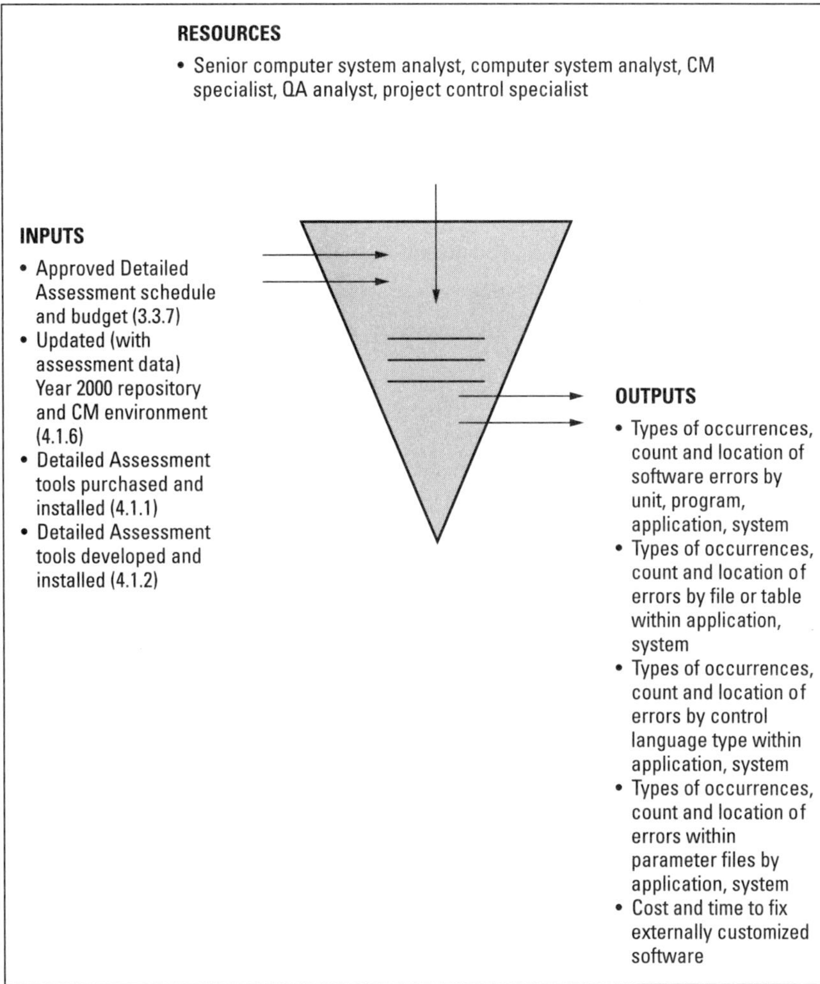

RESOURCES
• Senior computer system analyst, computer system analyst, CM specialist, QA analyst, project control specialist
INPUTS
• Approved Detailed Assessment schedule and budget (3.3.7)
• Updated (with assessment data) Year 2000 repository and CM environment (4.1.6)
• Detailed Assessment tools purchased and installed (4.1.1)
• Detailed Assessment tools developed and installed (4.1.2)
OUTPUTS
• Types of occurrences, count and location of software errors by unit, program, application, system
• Types of occurrences, count and location of errors by file or table within application, system
• Types of occurrences, count and location of errors by control language type within application, system
• Types of occurrences, count and location of errors within parameter files by application, system
• Cost and time to fix externally customized software

4.2.2 Task: Assess Custom Hardware and Embedded Systems

Custom hardware is hardware specifically developed either for use in your organization or as part of a project or product. Likewise, custom embedded systems are "black box" systems of hardware and/or software components developed for use in your organization or as a project or product. These systems may contain components that generate or manipulate dates.

Appendix A lists Year 2000 problems that you are trying to identify as you assess each system. The problem types discussed in Appendix A are equally applicable to traditional software and to embedded software, such as may be stored in ROM. Appendix A doesn't address hardware-specific problems. Some examples of

hardware-based Year 2000 problems include time code generators or readers that provide or receive the equivalent of two-digit year representations, or incompatible BIOS and physical clock combinations.

Because the actual components of hardware and embedded systems are often difficult to access, you must assess hardware and embedded systems by reviewing all applicable schematics and documentation, including interface specifications. Whenever possible, you should also interview system users and system developers.

Quality Assurance will audit assessment results to ensure that all hardware and embedded systems have been reviewed for potential problems.

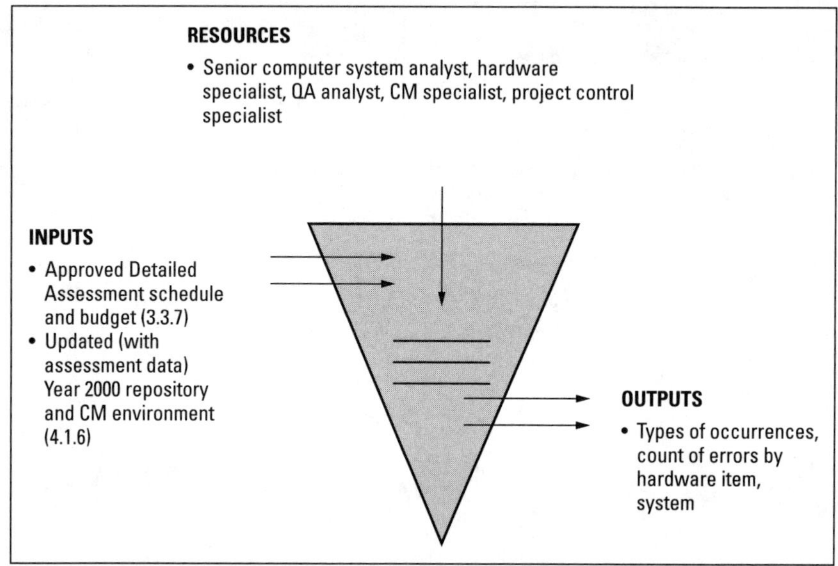
RESOURCES
• Senior computer system analyst, hardware specialist, QA analyst, CM specialist, project control specialist
INPUTS
• Approved Detailed Assessment schedule and budget (3.3.7)
• Updated (with assessment data) Year 2000 repository and CM environment (4.1.6)
OUTPUTS
• Types of occurrences, count of errors by hardware item, system

4.2.3 Task: Assess COTS Systems

A commercial off the shelf (COTS) system is any hardware or software system that was not developed specifically for your organization, but was a marketed product purchased for use in your organization, or for use in a product or project either currently in the field or under development. These systems are built by vendors to be used by many organizations, although some COTS products are tailored somewhat for use in a specific organization.

Because you have limited access to the components of a commercially developed system, you probably will not be able to completely assess many of your COTS products. You must interact with product vendors to assess the Year 2000 status of your COTS systems.

Your vendors should know that you have begun a Year 2000 project. You should request all information that you may need to determine Year 2000 compliance. Early in the project (1.6.1), your legal, contracts, and procurement departments were asked to develop a set of criteria for screening vendors to assess the Year 2000 compliance plans and status of their COTS products. Those departments should now be able to provide you with a standard questionnaire that you can use in interviews with vendors to make the necessary assessment. Try to develop and maintain a working relationship with your vendor. You might also want to contact user groups. Alternatively, you could ask the vendor to simply provide proof of Year 2000 compliance. Your legal department or counsel should review any such proof. If a vendor is making a system Year 2000 compliant, determine the date on which the compliant system will be available. Also determine whether the cost of the upgrade to a Year 2000 compliant version (and any customization) is covered under your maintenance contract. If not, capture and record the cost in your Year 2000 repository.

You must develop contingency plans to deal with vendors who do not plan to provide compliant systems, who will not be compliant in an acceptable time frame, or who simply do not cooperate with your inquiries.

Quality Assurance ensures that vendors have been surveyed regarding their Year 2000 compliance. The survey results must be incorporated into your Year 2000 data repository.

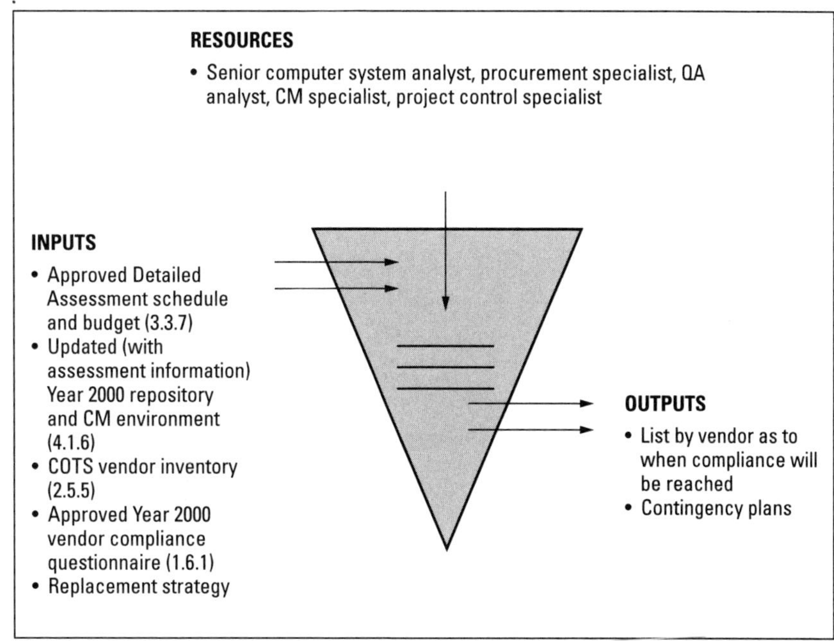

RESOURCES
• Senior computer system analyst, procurement specialist, QA analyst, CM specialist, project control specialist
INPUTS
• Approved Detailed Assessment schedule and budget (3.3.7)
• Updated (with assessment information) Year 2000 repository and CM environment (4.1.6)
• COTS vendor inventory (2.5.5)
• Approved Year 2000 vendor compliance questionnaire (1.6.1)
• Replacement strategy
OUTPUTS
• List by vendor as to when compliance will be reached
• Contingency plans

4.2.4 Task: Assess Electronic Partners

To assess electronic partners, you interact with them to find out their plans for making their systems Year 2000 compliant. You obtain the technical specifications for their Year 2000 compliant systems to ensure the successful interaction of your systems with theirs. These partners may also require the technical specifications of your Year 2000 compliant systems. There may also be regulatory tests or standards to which you must conform. After you verify successful system interaction, you will formally agree to continue the partnership. This agreement, or recertification, should be approved by the procurement and legal departments within your organization. You should develop contingency plans to deal with electronic partners who do not plan to achieve Year 2000 compliance within an acceptable time frame or have a history of falling behind schedule.

This process may occur at many different levels. Some electronic partners will interoperate with systems that are enterprise-wide within your organization. Examples of such systems include internal and external networks, EDI vendors, financial institutions, HR benefits administration, and organization-standard workstations or application packages. Other electronic partners will be specific to a particular project or department, or to individual isolated business units.

Quality Assurance ensures that every electronic partner has been surveyed about Year 2000 compliance as it applies to the interface to your organization or to ongoing projects within your organization.

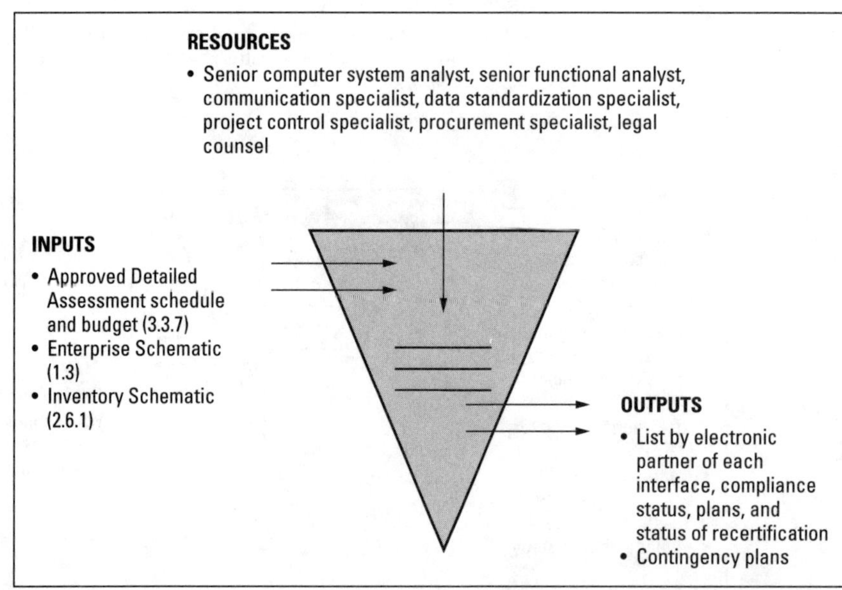
RESOURCES
• Senior computer system analyst, senior functional analyst, communication specialist, data standardization specialist, project control specialist, procurement specialist, legal counsel
INPUTS
• Approved Detailed Assessment schedule and budget (3.3.7)
• Enterprise Schematic (1.3)
• Inventory Schematic (2.6.1)
OUTPUTS
• List by electronic partner of each interface, compliance status, plans, and status of recertification
• Contingency plans

milestone  **System Assessment complete. Quality assurance verifies that the deliverable conforms to its intended goal. Project control baselines the deliverable and updates tracking metrics. Configuration management verifies that Year 2000 repository updates adhere to CM procedures.**

4.3 Draft Assessment Solutions

Now that you have detailed knowledge of the Year 2000 problems in your organization's systems, you can develop solutions to address these problems. The Draft Assessment Solutions deliverable supports the development of these solutions. When you complete this deliverable, you will have an approach to ensuring the Year 2000 compliance of each assessed system.

Task Overview

- Categorize Findings by Problem Type
- Define System Partitions
- Prepare Solution Sets by System
- Select Resolution Tools by System

4.3.1 Task: Categorize Findings by Problem Type

This task defines categories of Year 2000 problems, assigning each error detected during system assessment to one of the categories. To be certain your categories are meaningful and useful, you need a broad understanding of the types of Year 2000 problems identified in your organization's systems. The best approach is to conduct a high-level review of the information contained in the previous deliverable, System Assessment.

Quality Assurance will review the results to validate that all problems have been categorized.

RESOURCES
• Senior computer system analyst, QA analyst, project control specialist
INPUTS
• Appendix A, Problem Definition Catalog
• Types of occurrences, count of software errors by program, application, system (4.2.1)
• Types of occurrences, count of errors by hardware item, system (4.2.2)
• Types of occurrences, count of errors by system and electronic partner (4.2.4)
OUTPUTS
• Categorized Year 2000 errors by system

4.3.2 Task: Define System Partitions

The boundaries and components of each system must be clearly identified before you choose the Year 2000 solutions to apply to each system. Because many of your organization's systems share resources and interact with many other systems, you may have many alternatives when defining the scope of each system. Partition systems in the way that makes it easiest to resolve your organization's Year 2000 problems.

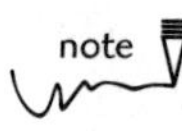

A good modeling technique is to reduce the number of interfaces between partitions.

You can define system partitions according to one or more of the following criteria:

- System size
- Types of Year 2000 problems
- Amount of effort required to resolve Year 2000 problems
- Numbers and kinds of interfaces
- Number and complexity of bridge programs that may be required

- Number of business units spanned (the fewer, the better)
- Timing of vendor compliance and recertification

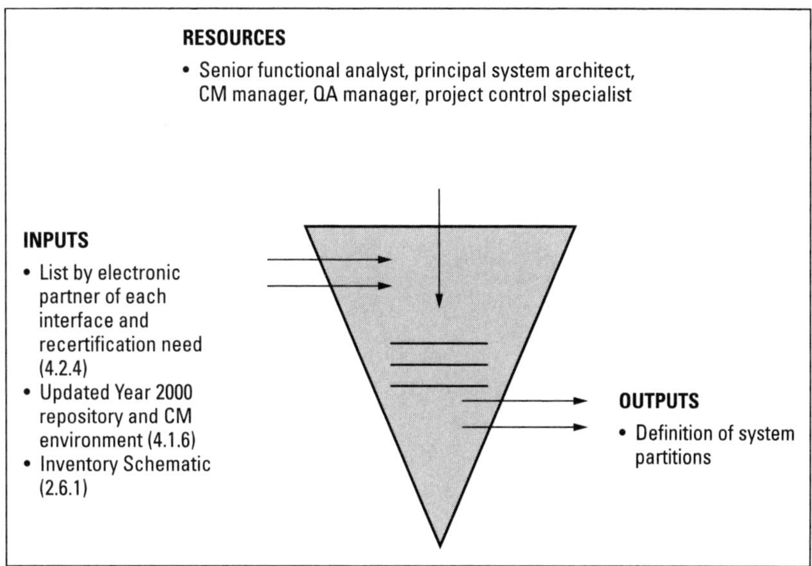
RESOURCES
• Senior functional analyst, principal system architect, CM manager, QA manager, project control specialist
INPUTS
• List by electronic partner of each interface and recertification need (4.2.4)
• Updated Year 2000 repository and CM environment (4.1.6)
• Inventory Schematic (2.6.1)
OUTPUTS
• Definition of system partitions

4.3.3 Task: Prepare Solution Sets by System

Appendix B, "Solution Sets," contains a summary of Year 2000 problems and solutions. Once you have identified which type of solution you are using for each category of Year 2000 problem, you can assign solutions on a system-by-system basis. (Systems are defined by the partitioning process described in the preceding task.) Then choose from the following approaches to resolving system noncompliance:

- **Repair the system**: Change the hardware, rewrite the software, write an interface bridge, or institute an operational procedure.
- **Replace the system**: Acquire a different system—one that is Year 2000 compliant.
- **Retire the system**: Simply "do without" the services or functionality the system provides, or implement the same service or functionality without automation.
- **Re-engineer the system**: Completely overhaul, rewrite, or redevelop the system.

- **Status quo**: Do nothing to the system in the hope that it will continue to function. You should prepare contingency plans for system failure or system erroneous results.

In determining solutions, you need to consider the following factors:

- Availability of automation tools
- Amount of effort expended for solution
- Future ease of maintenance
- Increased risk attached to more complex solutions
- Ability and availability of outsourcing companies or consultants
- Expected remaining life of the system
- Rate of return on investment (ROI)

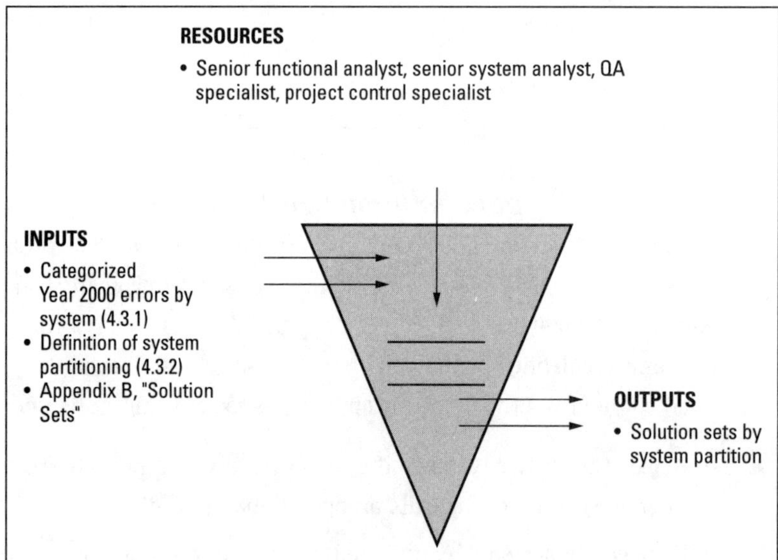
RESOURCES
• Senior functional analyst, senior system analyst, QA specialist, project control specialist
INPUTS
• Categorized Year 2000 errors by system (4.3.1)
• Definition of system partitioning (4.3.2)
• Appendix B, "Solution Sets"
OUTPUTS
• Solution sets by system partition

4.3.4 Task: Select Resolution Tools by System

Now you use the information obtained during Detailed Assessment to identify vendor tools to use during the Resolution phase. If these tools are not already available internally, you will develop them in-house, or purchase them from vendors. During the Inventory phase you developed lists of tools and requirements. You use these lists as a starting point—determining which tools are best suited to each system, or whether tools must be developed.

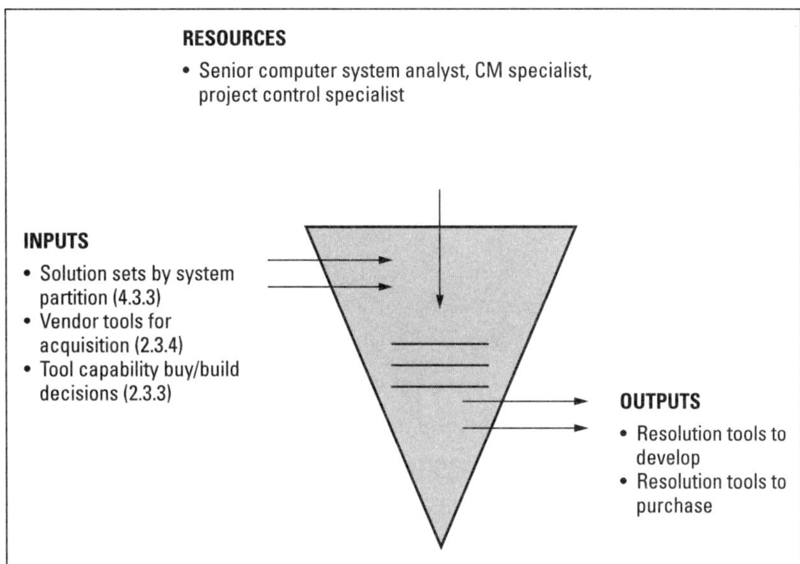

Draft Assessment Solutions completed. Quality assurance verifies that the deliverable conforms to its intended goal. Project control baselines the deliverable and updates tracking metrics. Configuration management verifies that Year 2000 repository updates adhere to CM procedures.

4.4 System Resolution Plan

The System Resolution Plan deliverable provides the many types of plans you will need to conduct Resolution activities in a comprehensive and efficient manner. In addition to developing Resolution plans for each system, you will develop plans for bridge construction, training, data conversion, procurement, and electronic partner compliance.

Task Overview

- Develop Electronic Partner Compliance Plan
- Develop Standard Practices for Resolution

- Develop System Resolution Plans by System
- Develop Interface/Bridge Plans
- Develop Data Conversion Plans
- Identify Business Process Impact Plan
- Develop Resolution Training Plan

4.4.1 Task: Develop Electronic Partner Compliance Plan

You have assessed the efforts of your electronic partners to solve their organization's Year 2000 problems. To maintain a successful electronic interface with each of these partners, you may have to modify these interfaces or build bridges to supplement them. You will now develop plans for modifying these interfaces and/or the construction of bridges. To develop these plans, you must obtain the technical specifications for interfaces and bridges used by each electronic partner.

Some of your electronic partners may have defined compliance for their organization and developed Year 2000 development standards. Make sure that your compliance definition and standards are compatible with theirs. You must agree on a standard for Year 2000 compliant data. A common Year 2000 data standard ensures that interfaces will be compatible once all Year 2000 solutions are implemented by both you and your partners. Any standards you devise should be reviewed by your IS staff, application owners, and electronic partners.

In some cases, an electronic partner may either ignore Year 2000 issues or not be able to solve Year 2000 problems in time. Either way, you must address this lack of action. You may want to help these partners with their Year 2000 problems (that is, developing both ends of a modified interface). Or you may want to locate another electronic partner that provides the same service and is willing to be Year 2000 compliant.

An electronic partner might also be implementing an interface that will be Year 2000 compliant, but their schedule may not dovetail with yours. In this case, you need to develop a bridge and bridge management plan, and both parties need to agree to the detailed schedule for interface changes.

Quality Assurance will review the plan to ensure that it complies with all known industry or recertification standards that apply.

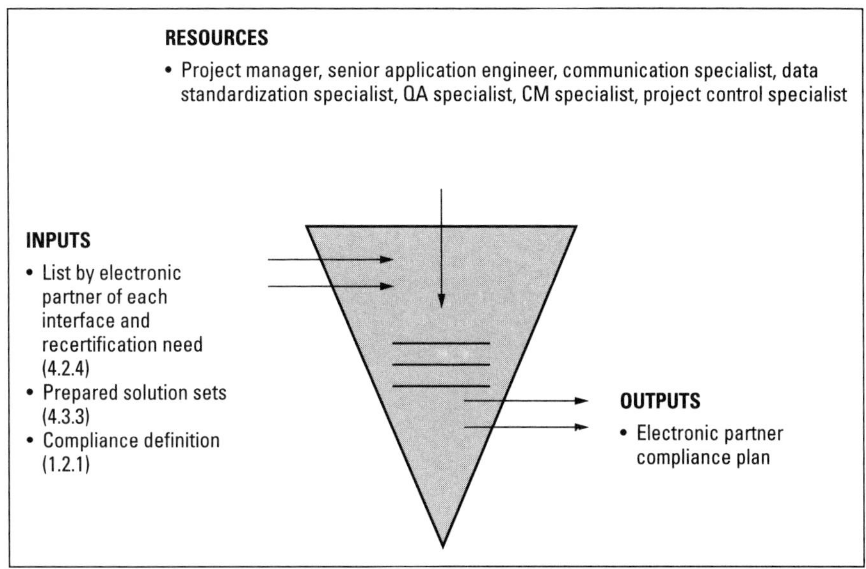

RESOURCES
• Project manager, senior application engineer, communication specialist, data standardization specialist, QA specialist, CM specialist, project control specialist
INPUTS
• List by electronic partner of each interface and recertification need (4.2.4)
• Prepared solution sets (4.3.3)
• Compliance definition (1.2.1)
OUTPUTS
• Electronic partner compliance plan

4.4.2 Task: Develop Standard Practices for Resolution

You must develop standard practices to ensure that your Resolution activities will be conducted in a disciplined and efficient manner and will result in a quality product. If possible, create standard practices that enable you to implement "assembly line" system modifications—identical modifications performed on one system after another. For example, if you define a standard method for applying a specific solution to a particular type of error, you may be able to apply that solution to several different systems. You can train several staff members in the application of that specific solution and have them concentrate their efforts only on the implementation of that solution. You can use a junior programmer or analyst for the job, releasing senior analysts and programmers for the more difficult and custom solution applications.

Using standard practices for Resolution tasks, as opposed to customizing solutions for every system, will provide consistency to your Resolution efforts. Also, using standard practices is generally less expensive and less time consuming than making customized system modifications. You can also record standardized system modification methods and use them for future system modifications. Using standard solutions may also simplify your testing process.

Earlier, you established a compliance definition for the project. Quality Assurance compares these standard practices with that compliance definition to ensure consistency.

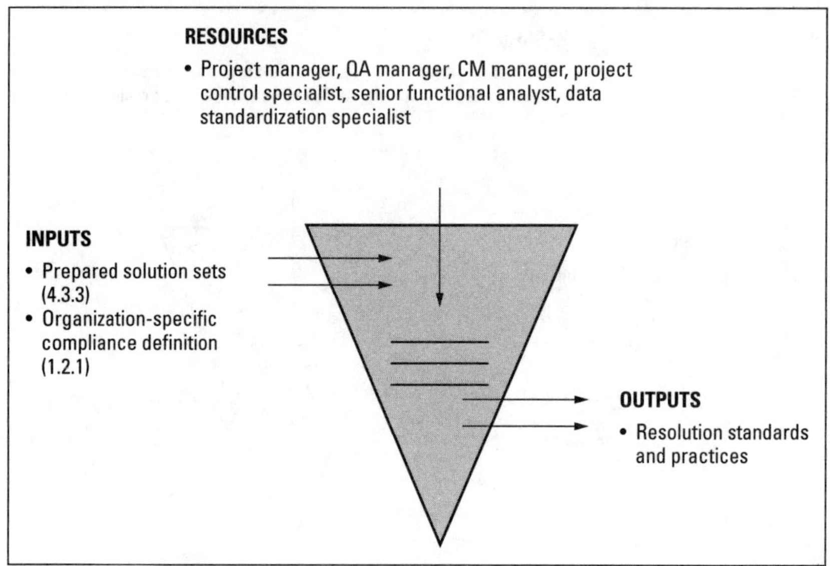

Task Guidelines

- Use junior programmers/analysts to apply standard solutions and free up senior programmers/analysts for more complex solution applications.
- Do an early test of possible solution prototype approaches to reduce risk of bad selection.
- Get early involvement from the test group to review testability of solutions.

4.4.3 Task: Develop System Resolution Plans by System

In the previous deliverable, Draft Assessment Solutions, you identified the solutions to be applied to specific systems. You will now develop plans to efficiently apply these solutions. Your plan for each system should include the following:

- The number and type of personnel needed to implement the solution.
- A time estimate for the application and testing of the solution.
- A list of tools—whether purchased or developed in-house—that will be used to support resolution tasks.
- A detailed specification for the system. The specification should describe the general purpose and functions of the system. It should also identify interface constraints, if any.

- A description of owner concerns, if any.

Your plan should define communication paths to ensure continued interaction with system users. The plan should be reviewed and approved by these owners.

Quality Assurance will review the plan to ensure compliance with the organization's and customer's document and application standards. Deviations will be corrected or approved by senior management.

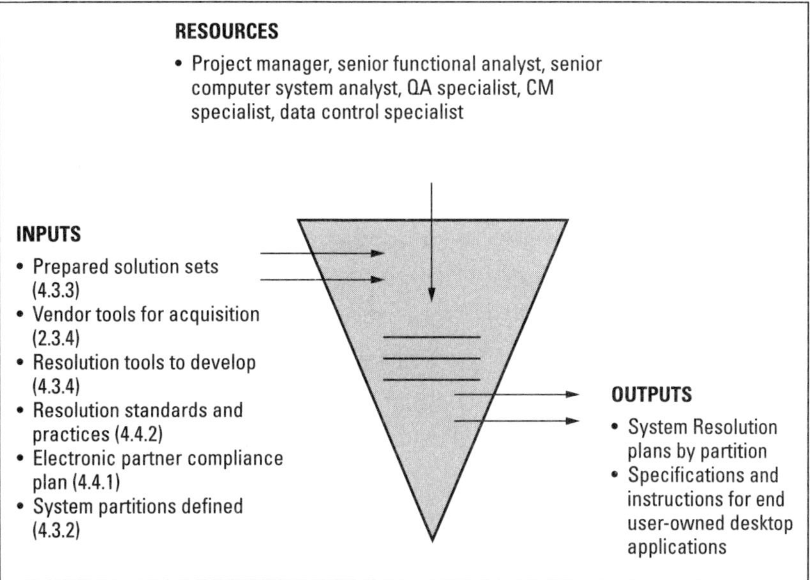

4.4.4 Task: Develop Interface/Bridge Plans

Ideally, you will concurrently resolve the Year 2000 problems of a given system and the systems with which it has an interface. But sometimes a Year 2000 compliant system must interface with a noncompliant system. In such cases, you could construct system "bridges" to maintain the viability of the systems on each side of the interface. You must develop plans for constructing and maintaining these bridges. (See Appendix B.)

Bridges serve two functions:

- They ensure that the data received by Year 2000 compliant systems from systems which are not Year 2000 compliant can be used by the compliant system to obtain correct results, and that files and databases are not corrupted.

- They ensure that data received by a noncompliant system from a compliant system can be used by the noncompliant system to obtain correct results, and can be stored by the noncompliant system without corrupting files or databases.

If compliance of one or both systems is to be achieved in stages, the bridges need to be updated in a manner consistent with the proposed changes and schedule to ensure continued interoperability of the systems. These bridges will remain in place until systems on both sides of the interface are compliant.

For example, your human resources department may transfer information with a bank to provide a direct deposit capability. The bank has already modified its system to ensure Year 2000 compliance; your organization has not. You must develop a bridge to translate the human resources data into a Year 2000 compliant format until the human resources system becomes Year 2000 compliant. Your organization and the bank must negotiate which side of the interface will provide which bridge services.

In each bridge plan, you must identify components of the bridge that will address each type of Year 2000 error encountered when interfacing a compliant system with a noncompliant system. The plan should include a time estimate for bridge construction and should identify the human resources required to complete construction. It should also include the schedule and human resources required to maintain the bridge as one or both systems move towards compliance. Do not overlook configuration management for the bridge. Be sure to consider the following factors:

- How important is it to your organization that the system in question continues to interface with another system or systems?
- Does the interface have multiple internal connections?
- Is the interface an electronic partnership?
- Do various system users pose operational constraints on the initiation of bridge construction?
- Will this affect recertification with one or more electronic partners?

Develop detailed specifications for any bridges to be developed. Each specification should describe the general purpose and function of the bridge or interface, identify the intended interface for which the bridge is constructed, and identify any interface constraints. Schedule a technical and peer review for each specification to prevent bridge design errors.

Quality Assurance will review the entire plan to ensure compliance with your organization's or customer's document and interface standards. Deviations will be corrected or approved by senior management.

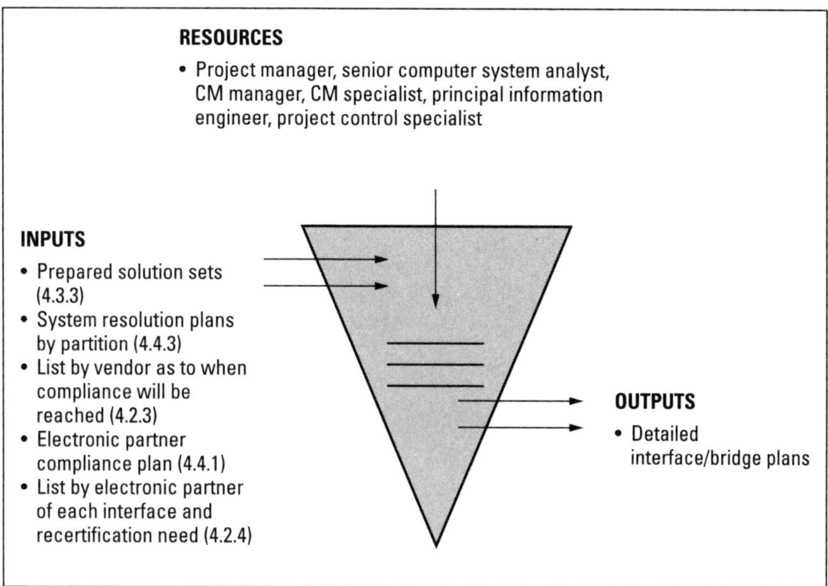

RESOURCES
• Project manager, senior computer system analyst, CM manager, CM specialist, principal information engineer, project control specialist
INPUTS
• Prepared solution sets (4.3.3)
• System resolution plans by partition (4.4.3)
• List by vendor as to when compliance will be reached (4.2.3)
• Electronic partner compliance plan (4.4.1)
• List by electronic partner of each interface and recertification need (4.2.4)
OUTPUTS
• Detailed interface/bridge plans

4.4.5 Task: Develop Data Conversion Plans

During this task, you identify data sets that must be converted to Year 2000 compliance.

You also prioritize these data sets to ensure prompt conversion of those critical to the operation of your organization. Develop detailed plans to implement these conversions. These plans should describe the cost, human resources, and tools to be used.

Data owners may choose to leave archived data unchanged until operational data is converted. In some cases, archived data may not be converted.

You may want to develop system-specific tools for data conversion. The specification for these tools should include a general description of the tool's purpose and function, interface constraints, system requirements, languages to be used, specific interfaces that would be affected, output generated, and so on. Do not forget to include plans to convert your test data sets.

You should schedule a peer review of each data conversion plan. In addition, you should review each plan with the appropriate users. Implementation of each plan should follow user approval of the plan.

Quality Assurance will review the plan to ensure compliance with your organization's and customer's document and data standards. Deviations will be corrected or approved by management.

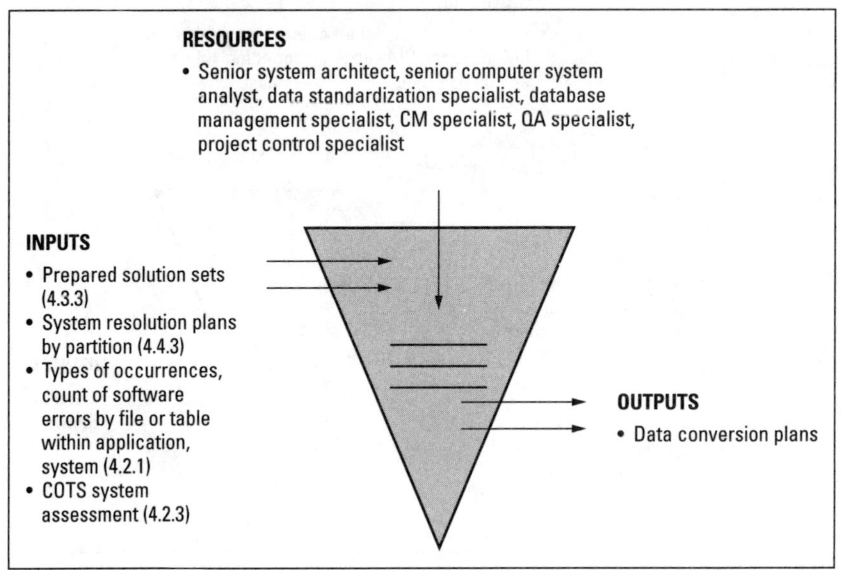

4.4.6 Task: Identify Business Process Impact Plan

While resolving Year 2000 errors, you may affect some standard business processes. For example, you may have preprinted forms with 19__ in the date field. These forms can no longer be processed through a system that now provides date information in four digits. You must decide whether to complete these forms manually, to get a new stock of these forms with a four-digit date field, or to develop an internal bridge to be used until the stock of forms is exhausted.

You need to identify these affected business processes, forms, and documents within your organization. Then you and the affected business managers need to decide what to do to ensure continued provision of the affected business operations.

If you decide to outsource a specific operation, you must identify the process to phase out the in-house operation (that is, schedule the turnover of data and labor in an orderly way, reuse or dispose of equipment, and reduce staff).

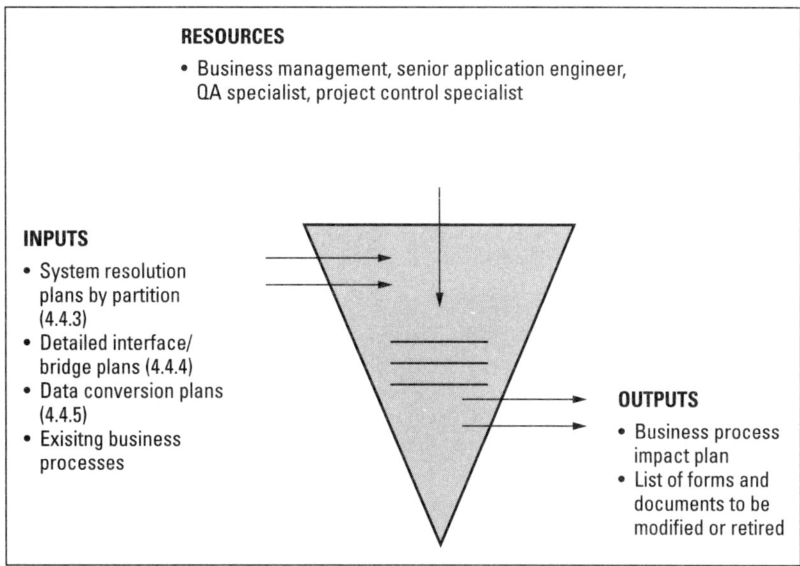

4.4.7 Task: Develop Resolution Training Plan

Personnel who participate in Resolution activities must have the necessary knowledge and skills to resolve Year 2000 problems carefully and consistently. They should have opportunities to acquire this knowledge and these skills. Develop a training program that allows staff to become familiar with:

- The standard practices developed for Resolution tasks
- The tools that will support Resolution activities
- The importance of adhering to your configuration management, quality assurance, and program tracking systems
- How they should interact with the system users

The plan should describe the method of conducting each training session: individual on-the-job training, group on-the-job training, classes external to your organization, and so forth. It should indicate who is responsible for conducting the training: in-house staff members, vendors, or an outside training specialist. Once the methods of training are identified, you should provide training cost estimates that include the number of training hours required per staff member, the costs for in-house trainers, and the costs of employing outside trainers.

Quality Assurance will review the plan to ensure compliance with your organization's and customer's document and training standards. Deviations will be corrected or approved by senior management.

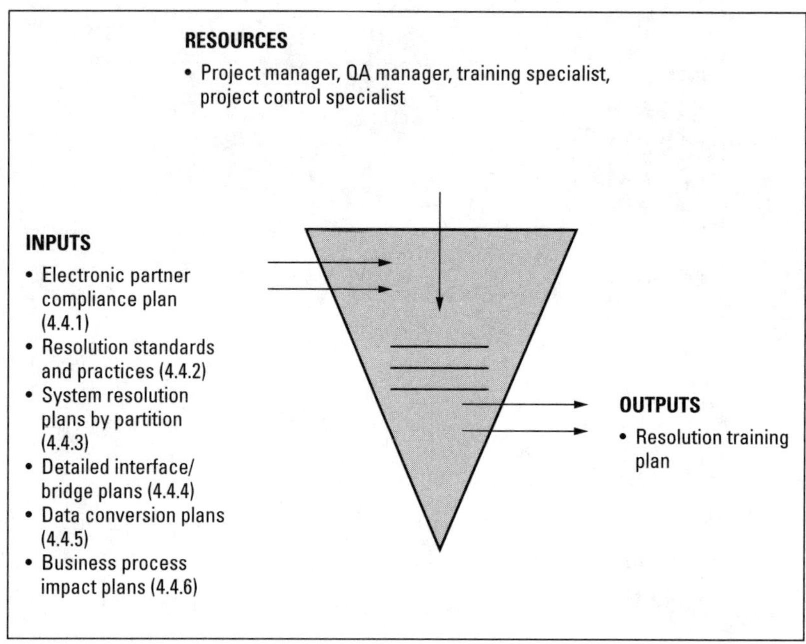

System Resolution Plan complete. Quality assurance verifies that the deliverable conforms to its intended goal. Project control baselines the deliverable and updates tracking metrics.

4.5 Correction Cycle Project Plan

The Correction Cycle Project Plan provides a plan for implementing all correction cycle tasks. The correction cycle includes four phases: Resolution, Test Planning, Test Execution, and Deployment. This plan should provide the foundation for your realization of Year 2000 compliance.

Task Overview

- Tailor Methodology for Correction Cycle
- Update System Technical and Business Risk Assessments

- Review and Revise Triage Decisions
- Consolidate System Resolution Plans
- Estimate Correction Cycle Resources by System
- Identify Staff Requirements for Correction Cycle
- Develop Procurement Plan for Correction Cycle
- Develop Schedule and Budget for Correction Cycle
- Present and Approve Plans, Schedule, and Budget for Correction Cycle

4.5.1 Task: Tailor Methodology for Correction Cycle

As mentioned, you should tailor all guidance provided in this book to your organization's needs. As you review and customize the tasks in the correction cycle, carefully evaluate the time allotted for the completion of each phase. The correction cycle takes up about 60 percent of the total Year 2000 project schedule. You may want to allow more time for testing or deployment to avoid deploying too close to the Year 2000 deadline.

Quality Assurance will review the tailored methodology to ensure consistency with the intent of the phase objectives and adherence to success criteria.

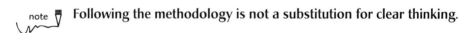

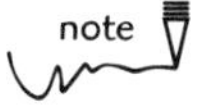

Following the methodology is not a substitution for clear thinking.

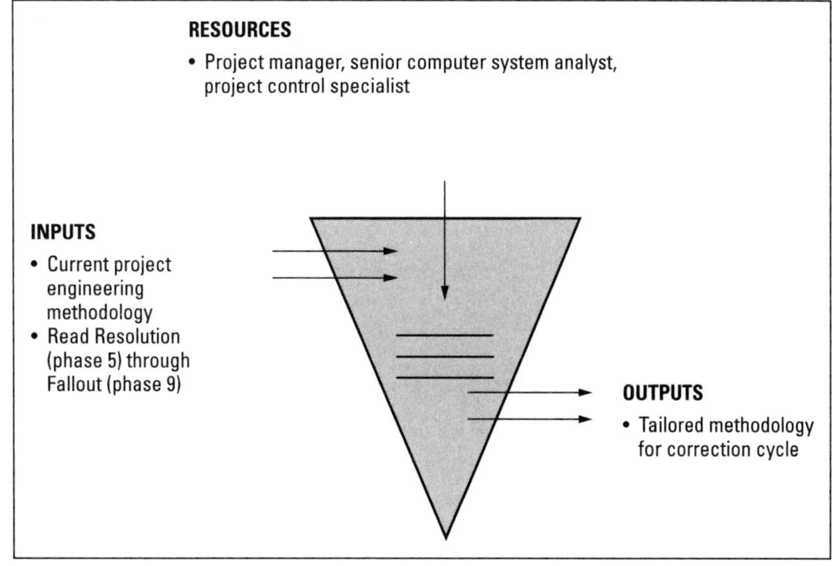

4.5.2 Task: Update System Technical and Business Risk Assessments

During Inventory, you gathered information about the technical risks associated with all systems in case they were not made Year 2000 compliant. Likewise, in Triage you assessed the business risks associated with these same systems. You should review and revise these risk estimates based on the knowledge you acquired during the Detailed Assessment of each system.

You should capture your updated estimates of technical and business risks in the Year 2000 repository. These updated risk estimates will help you schedule correction cycle tasks appropriately.

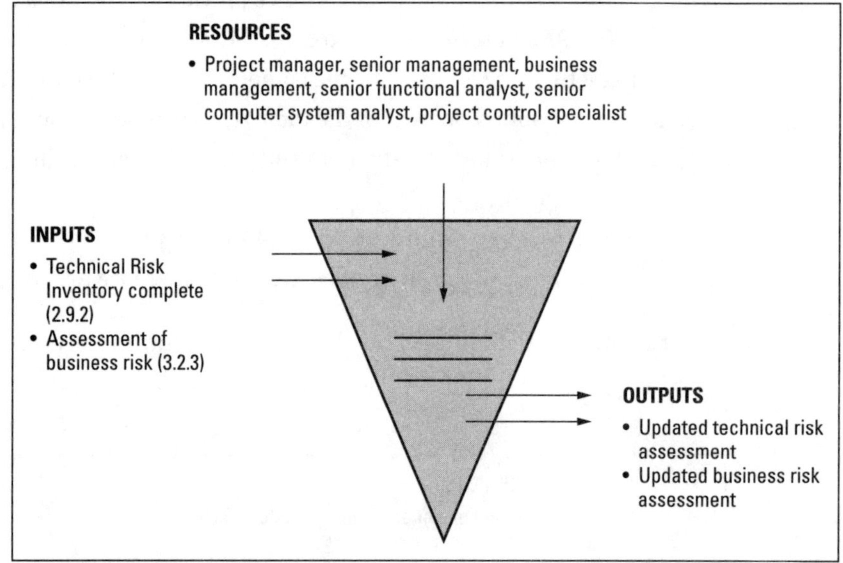

4.5.3 Task: Review and Revise Triage Decisions

After reviewing and revising technical and business risks, you must review and revise the Triage decisions that you made before conducting system assessments. In light of the knowledge gained during assessment activities, you may want to modify the business priorities assigned to certain systems. In addition, your overall business objectives may have changed somewhat as assessment tasks were underway. If possible, you should reassemble the people who participated in the original Triage decision-making process and ask them to review and revise their recommendations.

You should capture these revised business priorities in the Year 2000 repository; you will use them to guide your correction cycle schedule and budget planning tasks.

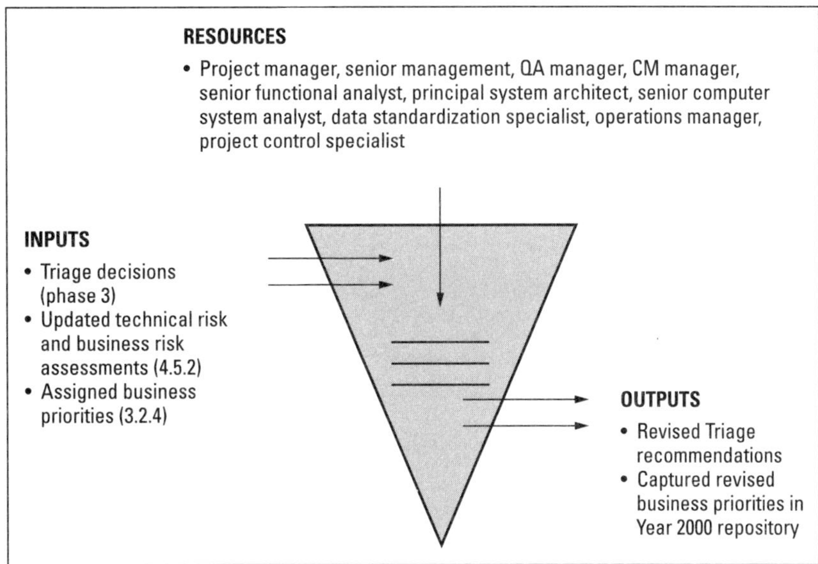

4.5.4 Task: Consolidate System Resolution Plans

Now you consolidate the many separate system resolution plans developed in the previous deliverable. These consolidated plans will help you create an overall schedule and budget for the correction cycle. As you perform this consolidation, you should try to identify common tasks to be performed for more than one system. You may be able to share resources in the implementation of these common tasks.

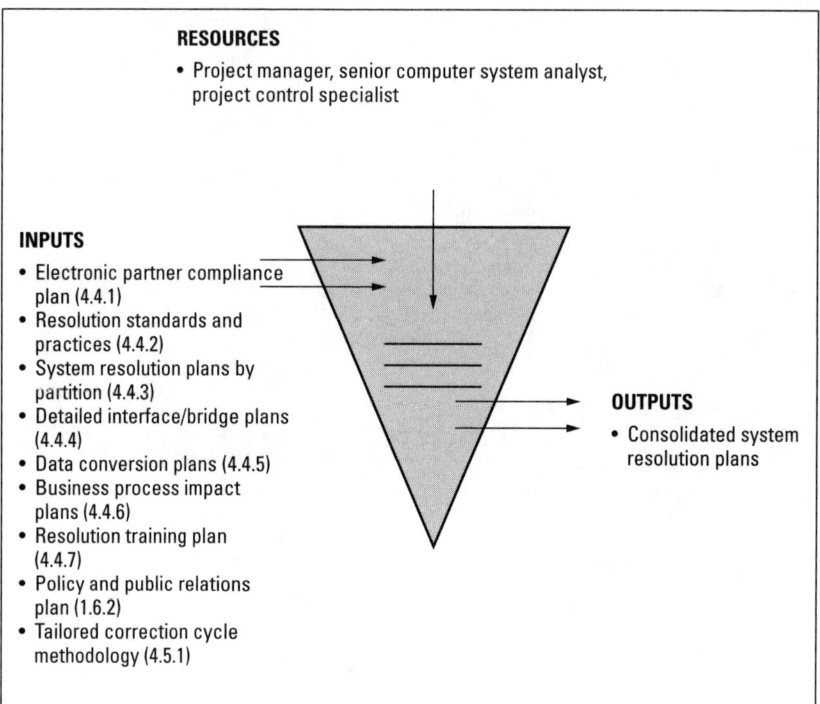

4.5.5 Task: Estimate Correction Cycle Resources by System

You must provide a cost estimate for making each system Year 2000 compliant. This estimate should consider labor, materials, equipment costs, and any costs of correction tools purchased from outside vendors. You should also include training costs. Use any cost benefits arising from additional business functionality to help offset your expenses.

Using your Triage priority list, you can create a list of system Resolution costs by business priority. In that way, you can calculate the cost of Resolution tasks for high-priority systems, medium-priority systems, and low-priority systems. This list will be invaluable for budget decision-makers who may need help about optimum ways to cut costs.

Throughout the correction cycle, you must capture actual costs incurred. You should track these actual costs against the system cost estimates developed within this task. You should recognize gross variations between estimated and actual costs and take corrective action, if necessary.

You may want to use a cost estimating and scheduling software program for this activity. See Appendix H, Integrated Project Plan.

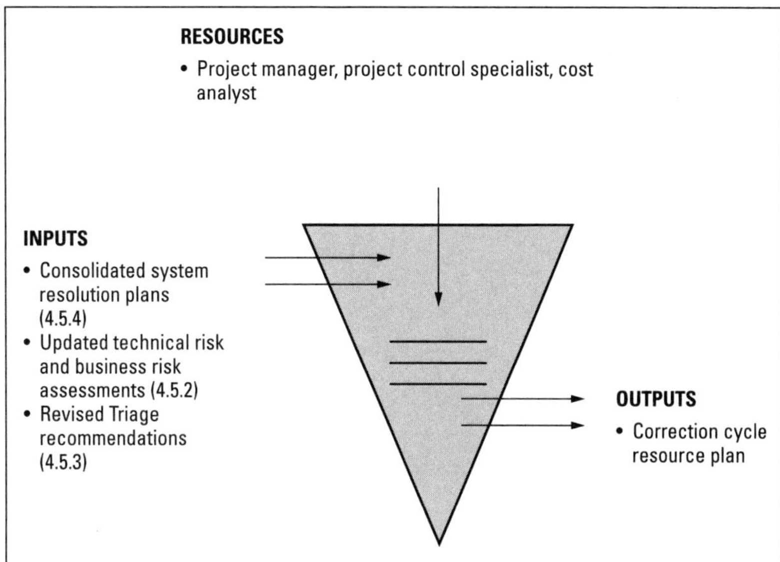

4.5.6 Task: Identify Staff Requirements for Correction Cycle

Identify the human resources necessary to successfully complete correction cycle tasks. You must identify personnel categories appropriate for correction tasks, the number of staff needed in each category, and the required level of experience of each staff position.

Once you have identified qualified and available staff for open positions in the correction cycle, you must determine staffing deficiencies by position and number. These deficiencies will help you acquire contractor services.

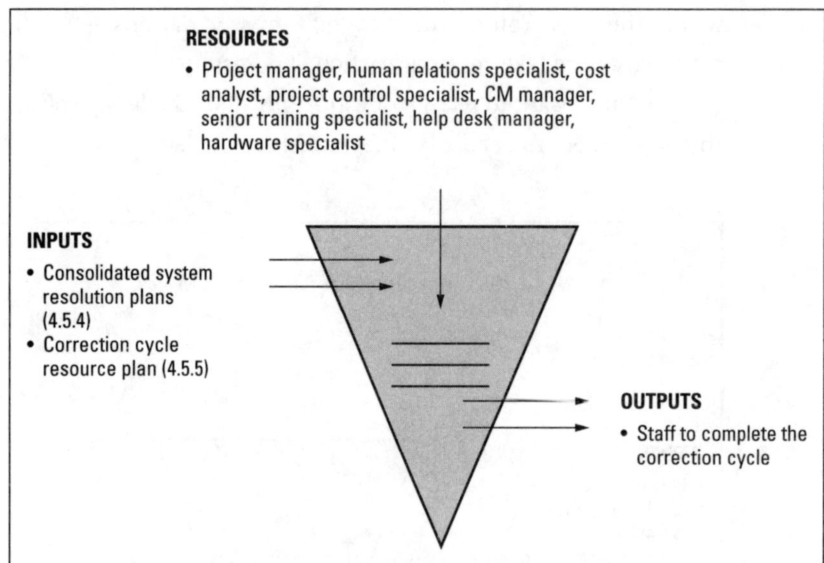

4.5.7 Task: Develop Procurement Plan for Correction Cycle

Throughout the correction cycle, you will forward many requests for material, tools, and labor to your procurement office. Work with your procurement staff to expedite the acquisition of these materials, tools, and labor. For example, you may want to consolidate requests that repeatedly use the same labor source or materials.

Also work with procurement officials to meet budget constraints. For example, the correction cycle schedule may show peak labor and equipment needs and product purchases concentrated in one quarter of the cycle. Most organizations do not wish to incur that type of concentrated expense. Enlist the support of your procurement staff to "level" acquisition costs.

Quality Assurance will review the plan to ensure your organization's and customer's document and procurement standards. Deviations will be corrected or approved by senior management.

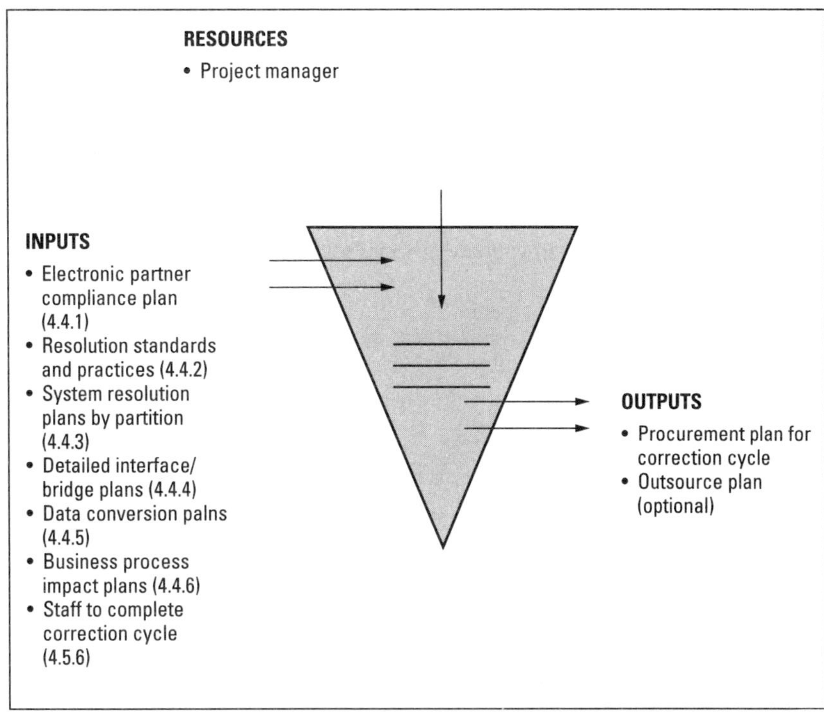

4.5.8 Task: Develop Schedule and Budget for Correction Cycle

Your correction cycle schedule should not reach beyond December 31, 1999. Preferably, the critical elements of your Year 2000 project should be completed before January 1999 so you have time to handle unanticipated problems and to complete at least one yearly cycle of your financial systems. The scheduling of each system will be dependent upon both its business priority and its technical dependency as well as the availability of necessary resources and the leveling of resources required.

Your detailed schedule should incorporate a certain amount of "slack time" to leave room for additional compliance tasks. Prepare a schedule that accounts for holidays, vacations, estimated sick leave, and personal days.

When you complete the correction cycle schedule, assign labor, materials, and equipment by schedule phase. You can then determine a budget based on

these assignments. Because this is the final Year 2000 scheduling and budgeting endeavor, you should proceed with care.

In this task you must identify:

- How the status of each correction cycle subproject will be tracked and reported
- How estimated costs to completion will be made, recorded, and summarized
- Who will approve cost to completion estimates

You must track the prepared schedule against actual project activity and report the results to appropriate management representatives overseeing the project. Where significant deviations occur, you need to take corrective actions. More scheduling and budget tasks are discussed in the sections on testing and deployment.

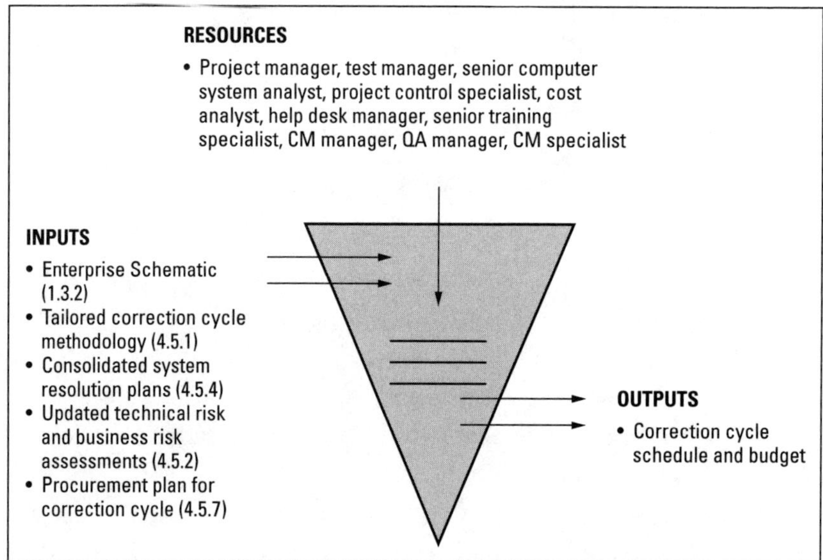

RESOURCES
• Project manager, test manager, senior computer system analyst, project control specialist, cost analyst, help desk manager, senior training specialist, CM manager, QA manager, CM specialist
INPUTS
• Enterprise Schematic (1.3.2)
• Tailored correction cycle methodology (4.5.1)
• Consolidated system resolution plans (4.5.4)
• Updated technical risk and business risk assessments (4.5.2)
• Procurement plan for correction cycle (4.5.7)
OUTPUTS
• Correction cycle schedule and budget

4.5.9 Task: Present and Approve Plans, Schedule, and Budget for Correction Cycle

Those who will approve your Year 2000 project must view your presentation. This group may be limited to senior management or their representatives. You may also want to include any courtesy participants—managers whose cooperation you need to finish the project or on whom the project will have a definite impact.

Your presentation should provide an overview of the information gathered during the Detailed Assessment phase, and should outline the risks and costs foreseen in the correction cycle. You should summarize Resolution, Testing, and Deployment activities and present a schedule for the completion of these activities. You should stress the concurrence of correction cycle tasks, and the interaction of these tasks with ongoing development and business operations. You should outline the tracking and reporting mechanisms that will be used throughout the correction cycle.

You may want to reinforce the need to complete your Year 2000 project as early as possible. Emphasize the need for cooperation throughout the entire organization in keeping required labor and equipment assigned to your project. Resources should not be reallocated to other "fires" or other projects. Make sure they understand that failure to complete the Year 2000 project on time can mean the demise of a contract, a department, or the entire organization.

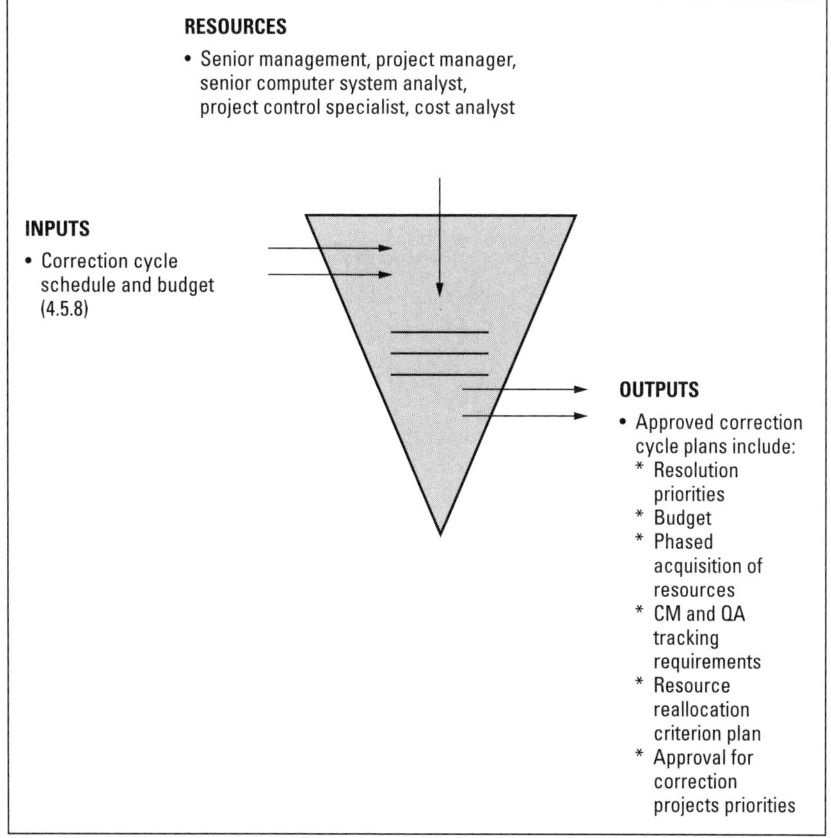

milestone  **Correction Cycle Project Plan complete. Quality assurance verifies that the deliverable conforms to its intended goal. Project control baselines the deliverable and updates tracking metrics.**

Business Impacts

During the Detailed Assessment phase, you will conduct system assessments, propose solutions to Year 2000 problems, and plan for the future. Although assessment activities may affect your business processes, most tasks undertaken during this phase will not affect the way you conduct business unless you conduct a high level of replacement and retirement decisions. Because of the short time available and scarce resources, you should keep these to a minimum.

Assessment activities involve the detailed examination of system artifacts (code, documentation, and so on). This examination will not usually require the suspension of systems from normal operation, although this may happen in some cases. System users will usually need to spend some time on the examination process, which may require that you reallocate some normal user tasks. However, assessment activities should have a minimal impact on the operation of most systems.

As Detailed Assessment progresses, you will identify solutions for specific Year 2000 problems. The implementation of these solutions, which takes place during Resolution, may have a dramatic effect on your normal business operations. Consequently, your plans for the next phase should consider the following:

- During Resolution, you must determine which business processes will be affected by the implementation of Year 2000 solutions.
- You must define how those business processes will be modified to accommodate solution implementation.
- You must include business managers in the planning process for business process modification.

Phase Risks

Potential Event	*Probability*	*Impact*	*Risk*
Incomplete identification of Year 2000 problems	High	High	High
Lack of system development artifacts	High	Medium	Medium
Identification of inappropriate system solutions	Medium	High	High
Inefficient scheduling of Resolution tasks	High	Medium	High

Detailed Assessment Phase Risks

There are four risks associated with the Detailed Assessment phase: You may not identify Year 2000 problems completely, you may lack system development artifacts, you may identify inappropriate system solutions, and you may schedule Resolution tasks inefficiently.

Incomplete Identification of Year 2000 Problems

As Detailed Assessment of a given system is underway, the person conducting the assessment may miss something. Some Year 2000 problems are harder to detect than others. In addition, the tedious nature of the assessment process can lead to a failure to detect a Year 2000 problem.

There are several ways of mitigating this risk:

- Ensure that the people undertaking assessment tasks are properly trained. They should have an explicit idea of what they are seeking as assessment progresses. Training should be thorough and iterative (that is, as assessment personnel gain knowledge, this knowledge should be shared with others engaged in assessment activities). You may want to institute a

"mentor" program that pairs experienced assessment staff with new assessment personnel.

- Use standard techniques to combat tedium (interleave assessment tasks with other duties, provide incentives for superior performance, ensure a pleasant work environment, after telecommuting).
- Institute an assessment verification system. If time allows, assessment personnel should review and revise each other's work, or a manual audit of your assessment tool results.

Lack of System Development Artifacts

Ideally, you will be able to procure a variety of system development artifacts to support the assessment of a given system. These artifacts will include such things as requirements and design documents, source and object code, test outputs, maintenance records, and so on. Unfortunately, some of these artifacts will not be available for some of your organization's systems.

Here is a way of mitigating this risk:

- Re-engineer critical system documents. You may need to partially or completely re-engineer some of the more important system artifacts. For example, you may need to capture a system's current requirements to select an appropriate Year 2000 solution for that system. Re-engineering activities, of course, can require a significant investment of time and ability. In many cases, however, these re-created artifacts will prove valuable well beyond the completion of Year 2000 activities.

Identification of Inappropriate System Solutions

Those who participate in Detailed Assessment endeavors will, fortunately, have many solutions to recommend for a given system. Unfortunately, they may choose the wrong solution. For example, someone may recommend the development of a windowing module to make a particular system Year 2000 compliant. However, it may turn out to have been better to completely modify all date fields to four digits. Unhappily, the unsuitability of a chosen solution may not be identified until Resolution activities are well underway.

Here is a way of mitigating this risk:

- Implement a proof of concept for a proposed solution. If you are unsure of the appropriateness of a given solution, consider testing that solution using a limited time frame and/or system scope. This type of proof of concept will not guarantee the suitability of a particular solution, but it will probably let you quickly identify unsuitable solutions.

Inefficient Scheduling of Resolution Tasks

During Detailed Assessment, you prepare the schedule for the next phase of the Year 2000 project, Resolution. This schedule will be heavily influenced by the business objectives of your organization and may not appropriately reflect technical concerns. For example, due to the organizational importance of the payroll system, you may wish to put it first on the "repair list." However, from a technical standpoint, it may not make sense to repair the payroll system before repairing other systems on which it is dependent.

There are a couple of ways of mitigating this risk:

- Ensure that technical information is available to those who participate in Resolution scheduling activity. Stress the importance of technical realities when business and technical priorities conflict.
- If business considerations obscure technical realities during Resolution, make sure that technical considerations are recognized during Deployment planning. Consider additional bridging development to allow system repair in a less technically efficient manner. If the progression of system repair, replacement, and retirement does not take place in a technically sensible manner, redouble your efforts to ensure that the deployment of these systems is technically efficient.

Success Factors

In successfully completing the Detailed Assessment phase, you carried out the following steps:

Success Factor	*Deliverable*
Acquired tools to support your assessment activities (for example, conversion tools and operational software)	Detailed Assessment Phase Startup
Briefed staff members about tasks to be accomplished during this phase	Detailed Assessment Phase Startup
Maintained a repository of known Year 2000 compliance problems and solutions	Detailed Assessment Phase Startup
Developed required tools for assessment	Detailed Assessment Phase Startup
Assessed custom software systems	System Assessment
Assessed hardware systems	System Assessment
Solicited recertification needs from electronic partners	System Assessment
Assessed vendor compliance of COTS systems	System Assessment
Assessed embedded systems	System Assessment
Categorized assessment problems by problem type	Draft Assessment Solutions
Defined system partitions based on Year 2000 problem categories	Draft Assessment Solutions
Identified candidate methods to attain Year 2000 compliance for each affected system or system-related component	Draft Assessment Solutions
Identified approaches for applying solutions (for example, repair, replace, retire, re-engineer, status quo, or outsource)	Draft Assessment Solutions
Evaluated candidate solutions against the established evaluation criteria for each system or system-related component	Draft Assessment Solutions
Reviewed with the appropriate managers or business owners the selected candidate solutions and incorporated input accordingly	Draft Assessment Solutions
Selected solutions that satisfied the established evaluation criteria for each system or system-related component	Draft Assessment Solutions
Communicated selected solutions to managers and business owners	Draft Assessment Solutions
Identified Resolution tools to be developed, modified, or acquired (for example, in-house, COTS)	Draft Assessment Solutions
Developed electronic partner compliance plan	System Resolution Plan

Success Factor	*Deliverable*
Included project managers and affected groups in negotiating changes to commitments that affect the project	System Resolution Plan
Reviewed with senior management project commitments made to either individuals or groups external to the organization	System Resolution Plan
Developed Resolution standards plan	System Resolution Plan
Developed Resolution plans by system	System Resolution Plan
Developed interface/bridge plan	System Resolution Plan
Developed data conversion plan	System Resolution Plan
Developed business process impact report	System Resolution Plan
Developed Resolution training plan	System Resolution Plan
Developed corporate legal plan	System Resolution Plan
Developed estimates for the scope and size of Resolution	Correction Cycle Project Plan
Identified the critical resources needed to successfully complete Resolution	Correction Cycle Project Plan
Estimated costs for Resolution technical resources	Correction Cycle Project Plan
Obtained agreement on Resolution estimates from all affected groups	Correction Cycle Project Plan
Developed schedule for Resolution activities, coordinating Resolution activities with other ongoing or planned system changes	Correction Cycle Project Plan
Obtained agreement on Resolution schedule from appropriate groups	Correction Cycle Project Plan
Reviewed Resolution plans with all affected groups	Correction Cycle Project Plan
Gained approval for Resolution activities from senior management	Correction Cycle Project Plan
Identified phase risks and potential mitigation approaches	All deliverables
Identified deliverables that would be developed during this phase	All deliverables
Used adequate communication interfaces throughout your organization to support the tasks associated with this phase	All deliverables

continued

SUCCESS FACTOR	DELIVERABLE
Assigned phase tasks to various groups in your organization and ensured senior management approval for those tasks	All deliverables
Identified the deliverables for which each group was responsible and ensured acceptance of that deliverable responsibility by each group	All deliverables
Identified key milestones for the accomplishment of tasks for this phase	All deliverables
Identified milestone thresholds beyond which some corrective action will be taken	All deliverables
Used metrics to track and measure progress with respect to these milestones	All deliverables
Ensured that each responsible group accepted and adhered to the schedule for completion of this phase	All deliverables

REFERENCE MATERIAL

This list mentions reference material you can turn to for additional information on this phase of your Year 2000 compliance project:

- Appendix A, Problem Definition Catalog
- Appendix B, Solution Sets
- Appendix C, Legal and Contract Considerations
- Appendix D, Sample Presentations
- Appendix E, Applicability of Tools
- Appendix F, Key Task Outlines
- Appendix H, Integrated Project Plan
- Appendix I, How To 2000 Risk Management
- Glossary
- *How To 2000* CD-ROM

CHAPTER 5

Phase 5: Resolution

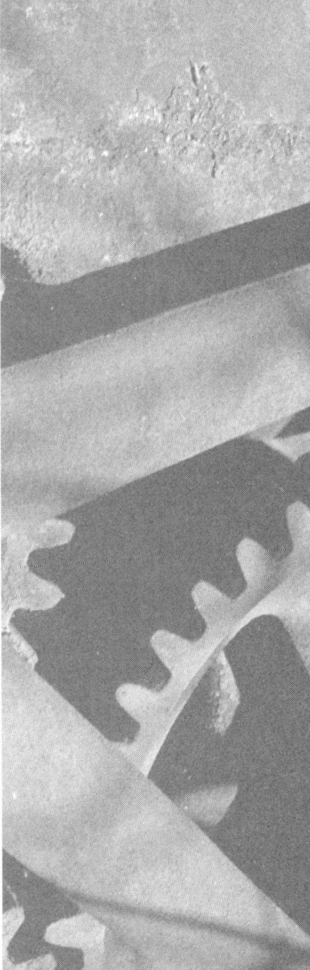

CHAPTER 5 **PHASE 5: RESOLUTION**

Objectives

- Implement resolution decisions (repair, replace, or retire system).
- Define system-level go/no-go decision criteria.
- Obtain and apply commercial off the shelf (COTS) Year 2000 resolution products.
- Develop and execute required customized solutions.
- Complete initial unit testing of applied solutions.
- Provide documentation and training to users affected by Year 2000 solutions.
- Identify expected fallout and impact(s) of solution application.

Resolution is the initial correction phase. At this time, you finally begin to put into place the solutions that you've devised after carefully carrying out all of the detection phases.

Resolving Year 2000 Problems

During Resolution, you apply the Year 2000 solutions you identified in the Detailed Assessment phase. You also conduct unit testing of modified systems. After unit testing is successfully completed, the modified system will undergo formal system testing. Formal system testing is described in the following two chapters on Test Planning and Test Execution.

Year 2000 problems will be resolved in one of four ways:

- **Repair**: Systems not Year 2000 compliant are manually modified, automatically modified, or both.
- **Replace**: Systems not Year 2000 compliant are replaced by Year 2000 compliant automated systems that incorporate similar functionality. Sometimes you need to keep the old system and data in a frozen or unaltered state for regulatory reasons. Auditors will ask for access to your old financial data from your previous accounting system.
- **Retire**: Systems not Year 2000 compliant are taken out of operation and not replaced by automated systems. In most cases, systems designated for retirement are of minimal importance to the accomplishment of business objectives. The data resources associated with retired systems may be

archived. In addition, you can use a manual system to duplicate some or all of the functionality of a retired system.

- **Re-engineer**: Systems not Year 2000 compliant are rewritten. Redevelopment of a system usually incorporates new system functionality and the infusion of new technology. The purpose of such a project extends beyond Year 2000 compliant issues and is usually *not* considered part of the project *or* its costs. Consider watching (not tracking) the progress of such projects within the Year 2000 project.

Resolution tasks (purchasing, code development, user training, documentation revision) associated with a specific partition will progress concurrently with similar tasks associated with other partitions. You may define subprojects to incorporate the Resolution tasks associated with individual systems or subsystems within a partition. A "subproject umbrella" may be a useful management tool to ensure the efficient accomplishment of many tasks associated with many systems. To maintain control of this complex set of Resolution activities, you should:

- Select a manager for each subproject who will be responsible and accountable for the successful completion of Resolution activities associated with a specific system.
- Carefully track the progress of each subproject against the Resolution schedule.
- Ensure that subproject managers coordinate their efforts with appropriate electronic partners.

When you finish the Resolution phase, you will have:

- Achieved Year 2000 compliance for those systems targeted for Resolution
- Successfully executed data conversion routines
- Constructed temporary interface bridges
- Defined go/no-go criteria for the planned deployment of each system

The cost for completion of Resolution should not exceed 30 percent of your Year 2000 project cost.

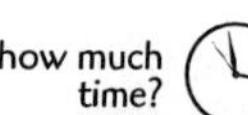

The time devoted to Resolution tasks should comprise approximately 10 percent of the Year 2000 project schedule.

Summary of Deliverables

This section summarizes the deliverables for this phase of the Year 2000 compliance project. The section "Deliverables, Tasks, and Dependencies" later in this chapter includes detailed descriptions of each deliverable and the associated supporting tasks.

Resolution Phase Startup

The Resolution Phase Startup deliverable provides the work environment needed to support Resolution activities. At this time, you acquire necessary labor and materials specified in the System Resolution Plan developed in the Detailed Assessment phase. These resources could include COTS products, contract labor, and internal labor needed to support Resolution tasks. In addition, you develop a plan to ensure the implementation of required training. You also implement cost and schedule tracking mechanisms.

System Retirement

The System Retirement deliverable provides a phase-out plan for any automated system selected for retirement. The plan includes guidelines for transferring valuable data to other systems and migrating users, customers, and other services from the old system to the new system. In addition, this deliverable ensures the cancellation of maintenance or warranty agreements associated with retired systems.

System Repair or Replacement

Th System Repair or Replacement deliverable describes Resolution activities undertaken on behalf of systems selected for repair or replacement.

Unit Testing

The Unit Testing deliverable describes the development of developer unit/system test plans and the execution of those plans. Test preparation is discussed in Chapter 6, Test Planning.

Documentation

The Documentation deliverable helps you update documentation relevant to systems or business processes that will be modified during the Year 2000 project.

Deliverables, Tasks, and Dependencies

The deliverables produced in the Resolution phase support the primary objective of your Year 2000 project: the implementation of changes to your organization's systems to ensure Year 2000 compliance. All of your planning and assessment activities culminate in the tasks you undertake in this phase.

5.1 Resolution Phase Startup

The Resolution Phase Startup deliverable provides the resources that must be available to ensure the efficient completion of all tasks undertaken in Resolution. When you complete this deliverable, the Resolution environment will be in place.

Task Overview

- Notify Impacted Parties of Resolution Plan Initiation
- Initiate Acquisition of Resolution Tools and Replacement Systems
- Acquire Contract Labor for Resolution
- Acquire Internal Human Resources for Resolution
- Set Up Resolution Environments
- Execute Resolution Training Plan
- Conduct Resolution Kickoff
- Ensure Capture of Resolution Data in Year 2000 Repository
- Ensure Implementation of Quality Assurance Process
- Establish Cost and Scheduling Tracking Mechanisms

5.1.1 Task: Notify Impacted Parties of Resolution Plan Initiation

You must notify internal departments, isolated business units, and electronic partners that Resolution activities will begin and may affect daily routines and operations. Distribute a general notification followed by other notifications to specific areas that will probably be affected by Resolution activities. Continue issuing notifications throughout testing and deployment activities to keep system users informed of potential impacts on their operations.

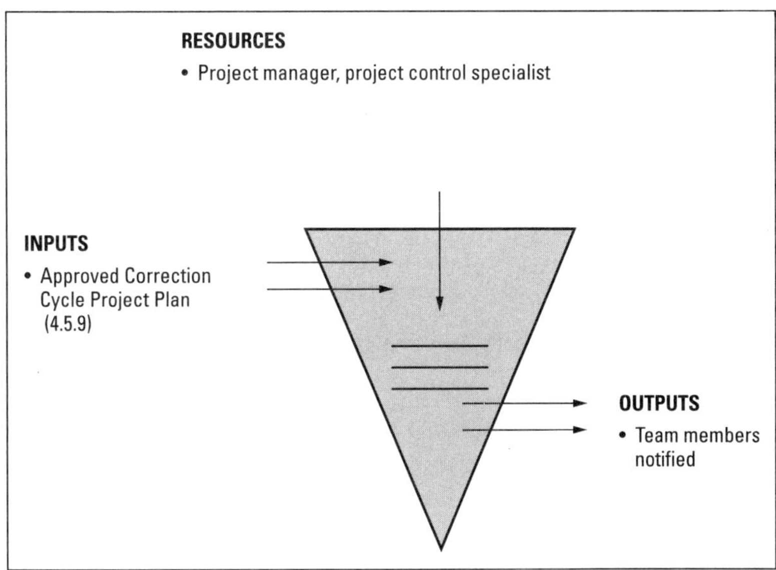

5.1.2 Task: Initiate Acquisition of Resolution Tools and Replacement Systems

You should acquire Resolution support tools as soon as possible after you complete the Correction Cycle Project Plan. In addition, you should start acquiring replacement systems. This may take a considerable amount of time, especially if you are ordering many replacement systems for several business areas. For this reason, you must plan and execute your replacement system acquisitions as early as possible in Resolution. Various internal budget and schedule constraints may require you to carefully plan your strategy for the acquisition of both Resolution tools and replacement systems.

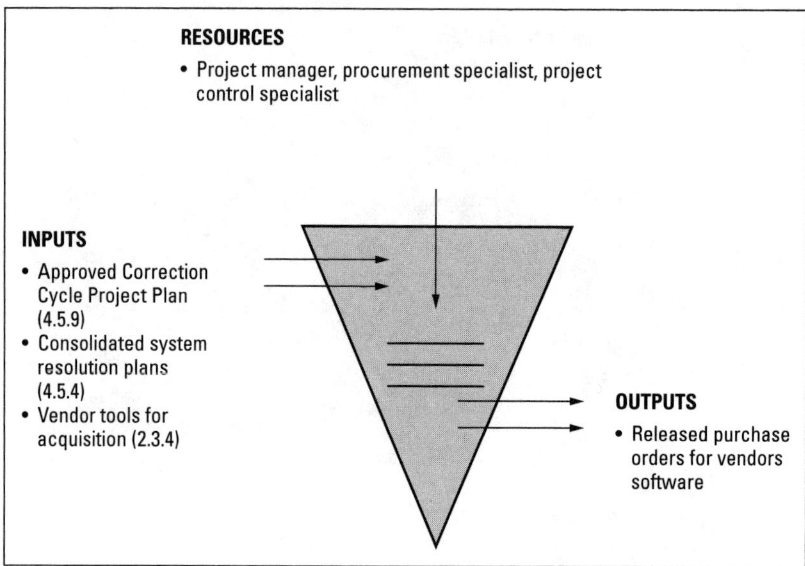

RESOURCES
• Project manager, procurement specialist, project control specialist
INPUTS
• Approved Correction Cycle Project Plan (4.5.9)
• Consolidated system resolution plans (4.5.4)
• Vendor tools for acquisition (2.3.4)
OUTPUTS
• Released purchase orders for vendors software

5.1.3 Task: Acquire Contract Labor for Resolution

Because of scheduling and budget constraints, you may have to start acquiring contract labor far before you need their services. Unless you are using a single outside consultant for all Resolution tasks, you will probably acquire contract services progressively according to a specific schedule. If you are using multiple contractors, make sure that your contracts include provisions for necessary reassignments.

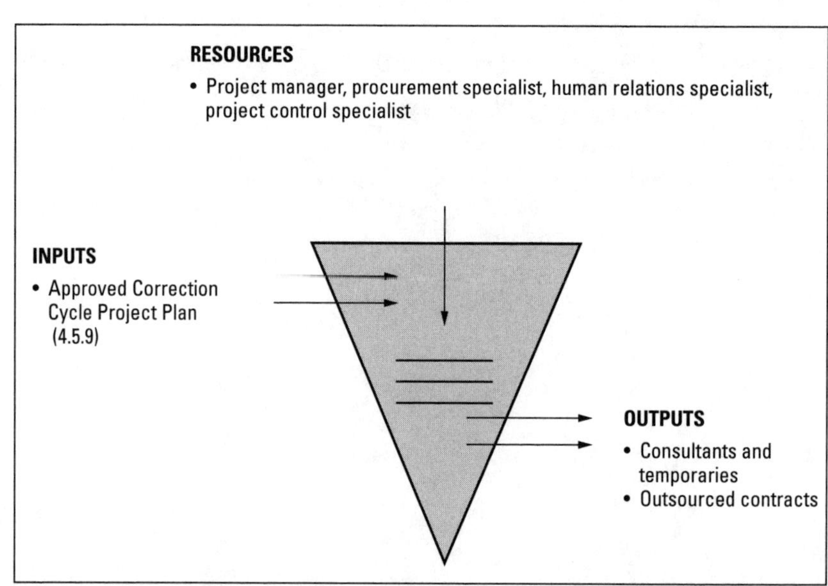

Task Guidelines

- You may need to outsource repair and replace actions, depending on your schedule and the number of in-house resources available and qualified to do the work. You need to have subcontract quality control mechanisms in place before acquiring any outside help and before beginning the repair and replace actions. When you look for consultants or vendors to help with the Resolution phase, be aware that some of their claims and costs may not be as they say due to the following factors:
  - Vendors and consultants expect to receive complete and clean inventories.
  - Vendors and consultants expect planning, triage, communication, and coordination to be done at your business.
  - Vendors and consultants expect validation and formal testing and deployment to be done at your business.
  - Vendors and consultants expect business processes and documents to be changed at your business.

5.1.4 Task: Acquire Internal Human Resources for Resolution

You have identified staff within your organization who will participate in Resolution activities. Before you begin these activities, you must verify the staff's availability. There may be possible difficulties in gathering your people together (political maneuvering, business changes, personnel changes, and so on.) You also need to determine when you expect people to begin work on Year 2000 subprojects, and when you expect to release them from the assigned duties.

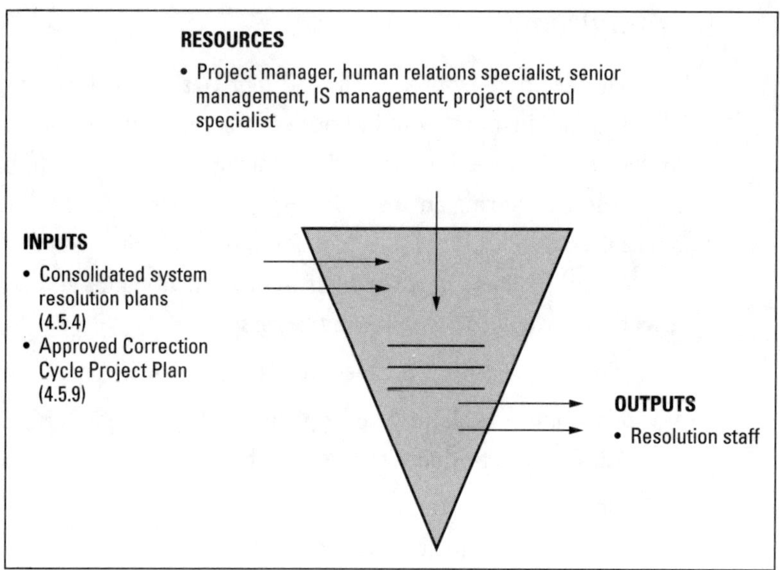

5.1.5 Task: Set Up Resolution Environments

Resolution activities will probably take place in several work areas. Each area must have the required software, hardware, networks, offices, desks, and phones. Configuration management will establish necessary mainframe connections and CM environments (that is, security, user libraries, and so on). Other logistical issues—such as badges, network logons, working hours, and safety equipment—may need to be addressed for new staff members or contract staff.

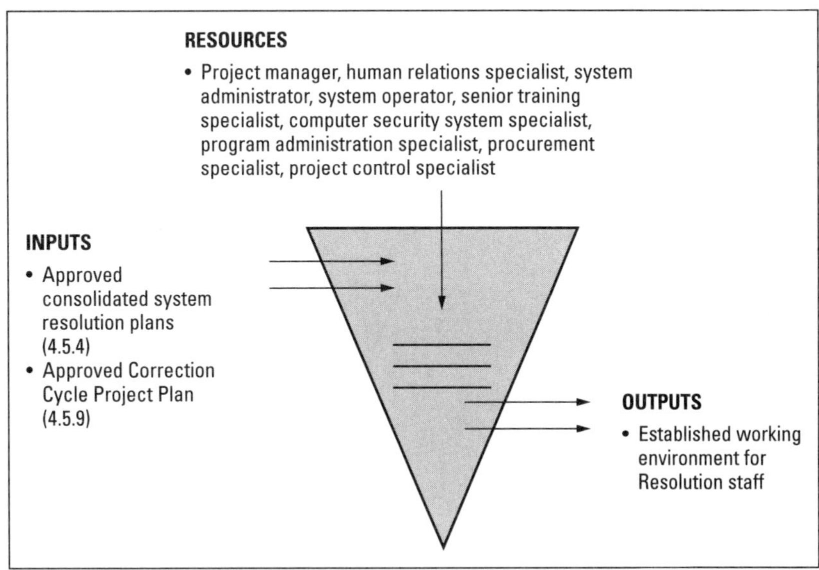

5.1.6 Task: Execute Resolution Training Plan

Resolution phase training can take a variety of forms. You can conduct some training in informal sessions that last a few hours. Other training may take place in week-long external classes that require registration two to three months in advance. You can employ an outside trainer whose services must be acquired through standard procurement procedures. You may need some lead time to obtain the necessary training at the appropriate time.

The acquisition of training will be an ongoing task for the remainder of the project. You may want to initiate an administrative mechanism to support continuous interaction with your organization's training and procurement offices.

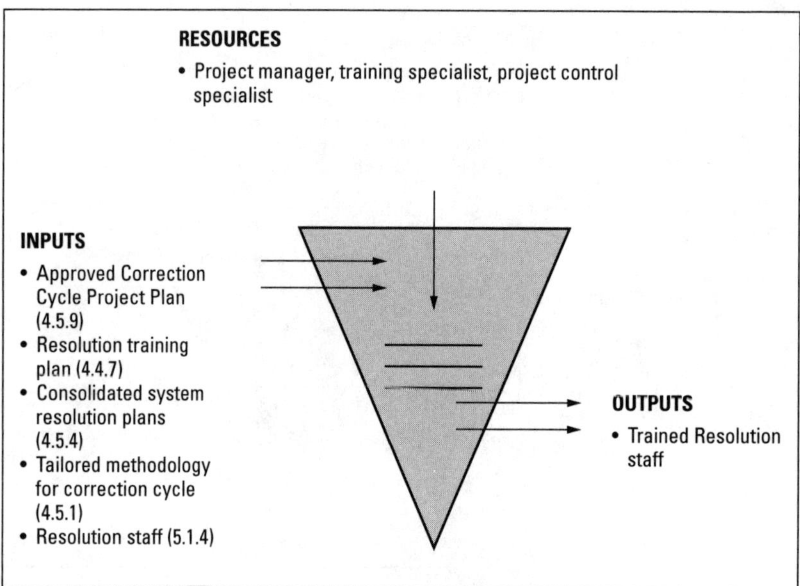

5.1.7 Task: Conduct Resolution Kickoff

You should organize a "kickoff" meeting with all staff involved in Resolution activities (that is, internal personnel, temporaries, and contract consultants). Provide an overview of Resolution tasks and summarize the undertakings of each partitional subproject.

You should cover the following topics:

- Year 2000 problems and solution sets
- System repair techniques
- Bridge development
- An overview of automated support tools
- Project and task assignments and responsibilities
- CM standards
- Quality Assurance role and responsibilities
- Project standards and procedures
- Communication and tracking of subproject status to central status collection
- Cost collection and estimated cost-to-completion process.

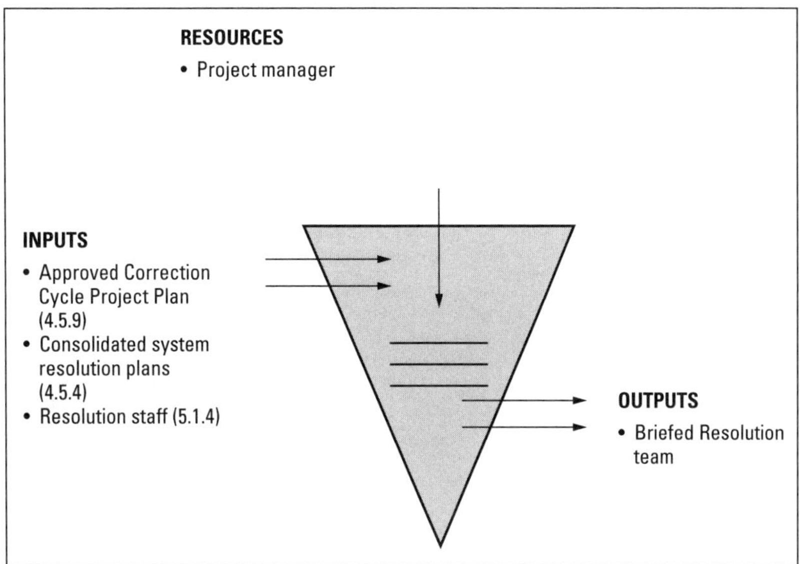

5.1.8 Task: Ensure Capture of Resolution Data in Year 2000 Repository

You established the Year 2000 repository during Inventory. The repository must be ready to receive the information generated during the Resolution phase. Because it's the major system configuration management tool for this project, the repository must continue to successfully handle:

- Configuration units and baselines
- Changes to baselines
- Problem reports—the process of initiation, review, approval, tracking, and completion
- Configuration unit checkin/checkout, including concurrent checkouts

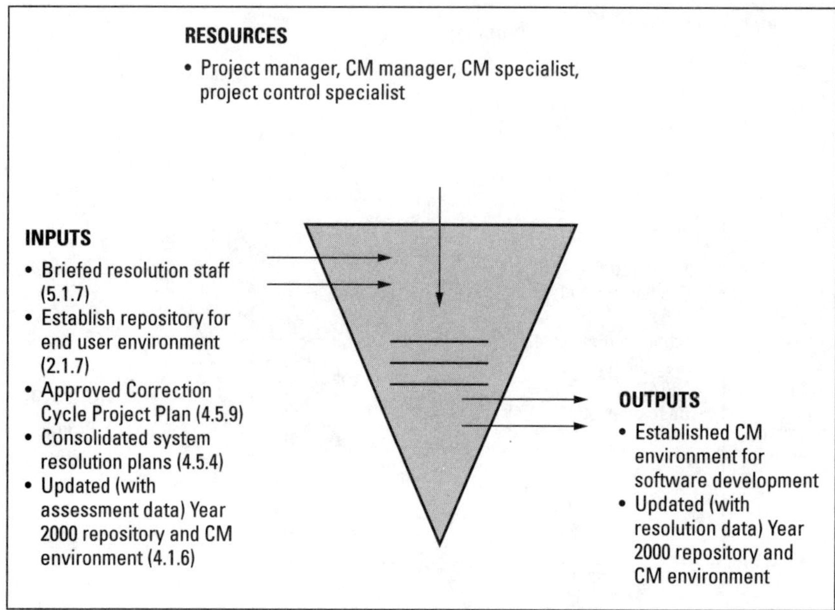

RESOURCES
• Project manager, CM manager, CM specialist, project control specialist
INPUTS
• Briefed resolution staff (5.1.7)
• Establish repository for end user environment (2.1.7)
• Approved Correction Cycle Project Plan (4.5.9)
• Consolidated system resolution plans (4.5.4)
• Updated (with assessment data) Year 2000 repository and CM environment (4.1.6)
OUTPUTS
• Established CM environment for software development
• Updated (with resolution data) Year 2000 repository and CM environment

5.1.9 Task: Ensure Implementation of Quality Assurance Process

During the early stages of your Year 2000 project, you implemented a quality assurance process.

This process verifies that development efforts will be executed in compliance with the organization's and project's defined plans, standards, and quality requirements. It also supports the tracking of quality deviations until they are resolved or approved by managers.

At this point, you review the provisions and practices of this process to ensure that Resolution activities do not negatively affect the quality of your systems. In addition, your organization's QA standards for system development should be reviewed and applied to Resolution tasks, as appropriate. You must also ensure that system modification tasks are closely monitored by a quality assurance specialist.

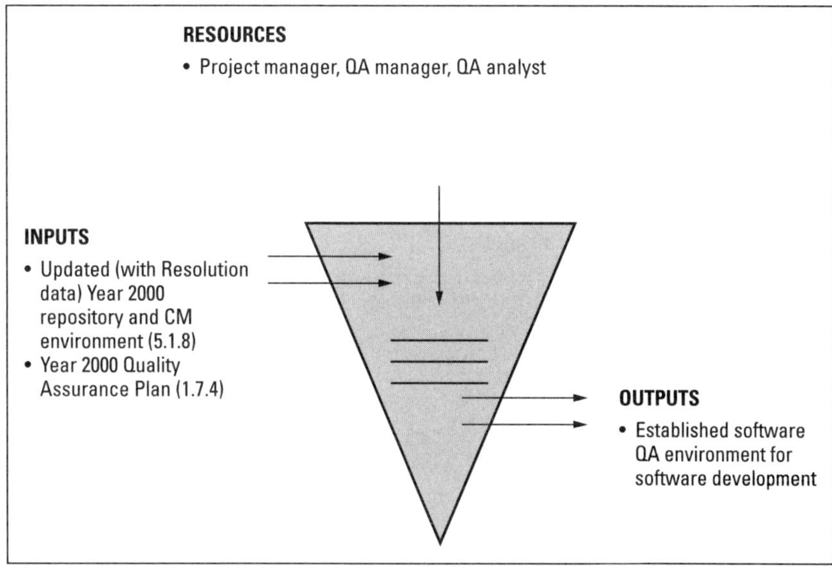

5.1.10 Task: Establish Cost and Scheduling Tracking Mechanism

You have used tracking mechanisms in earlier phases. It is particularly important to successfully establish and operate sound tracking devices during Resolution. Many system-specific Resolution activities will take place concurrently. You must carefully adhere to your established tracking procedures to avoid chaos. You will be tracking subproject activities as well as the resources and costs that support these activities. Make sure that your tracking mechanism can:

- Track a subproject's progress against schedule.
- Track solution application, testing, and deployment success against plans.
- Track business-critical functions against project deadlines.
- Track the progress of identified risk items against scheduled progress.
- Track resources used against resources planned.
- Track the size of deliverables.
- Track the subproject's software effort and costs.
- Track the project's critical computer resources.
- Track risks associated with resources (budget and staff). You should assess the success of your tracking methods at scheduled times during Resolution (that is, upon the completion of major milestones).

The tracking tool should support communication with system users concerning budget or schedule adjustments that affect specific systems. You should use internal progress reviews with customers to adjust resources, estimates, and schedules.

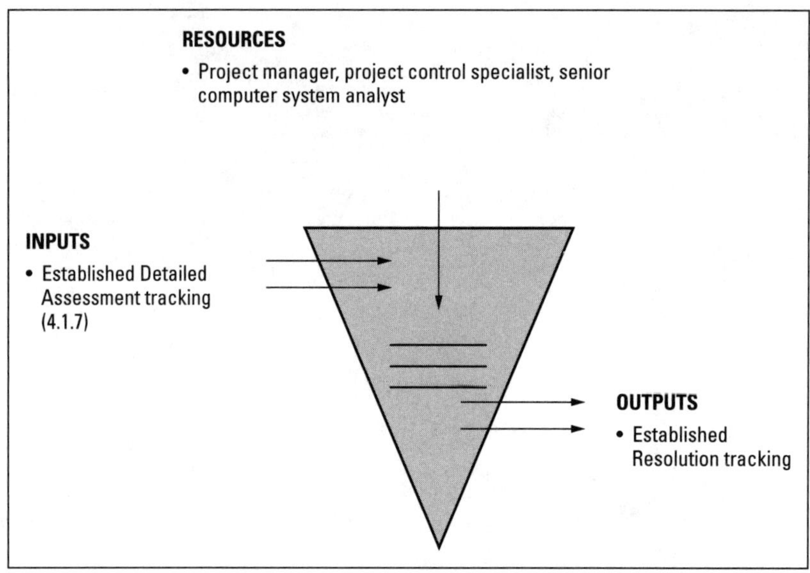

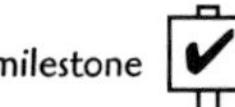

Resolution Phase Startup complete. Quality assurance verifies that the deliverable conforms to its intended goal. Project control baselines the deliverable and updates tracking metrics.

5.2 System Retirement

You apply the tasks in this deliverable to systems selected for retirement. Although retiring a system might seem easier than repairing it, you should handle retirements carefully to prevent a negative impact on the operations of system users. You must develop plans for the replacement of the functionality formerly provided by the retired system.

Task Overview

- Prepare Phase-out Plans
- Review and Approve Phase-out Plans

- Execute Phase-out Plans
- Notify Procurement of Obsolete Vendor Licenses

5.2.1 Task: Prepare Phase-out Plans

You must prepare system phase-out plans that incorporate both technical and business concerns. These plans must accommodate both users of the technical system and customers of the business process. The plans should outline detailed steps for shutting down operations. The plans should also describe how business processes will function to ensure functionality formerly provided by the retired system. Be sure to use sound CM procedures when phasing out data and systems.

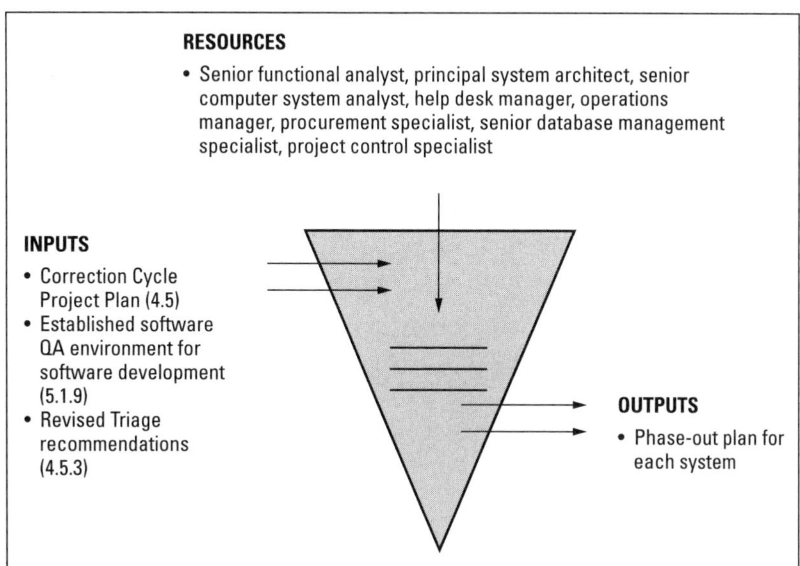

RESOURCES
• Senior functional analyst, principal system architect, senior computer system analyst, help desk manager, operations manager, procurement specialist, senior database management specialist, project control specialist
INPUTS
• Correction Cycle Project Plan (4.5)
• Established software QA environment for software development (5.1.9)
• Revised Triage recommendations (4.5.3)
OUTPUTS
• Phase-out plan for each system

5.2.2 Task: Review and Approve Phase-out Plans

Technical staff and system users must review phase-out plans. Only when a system's phase-out plan is approved should the plan be implemented.

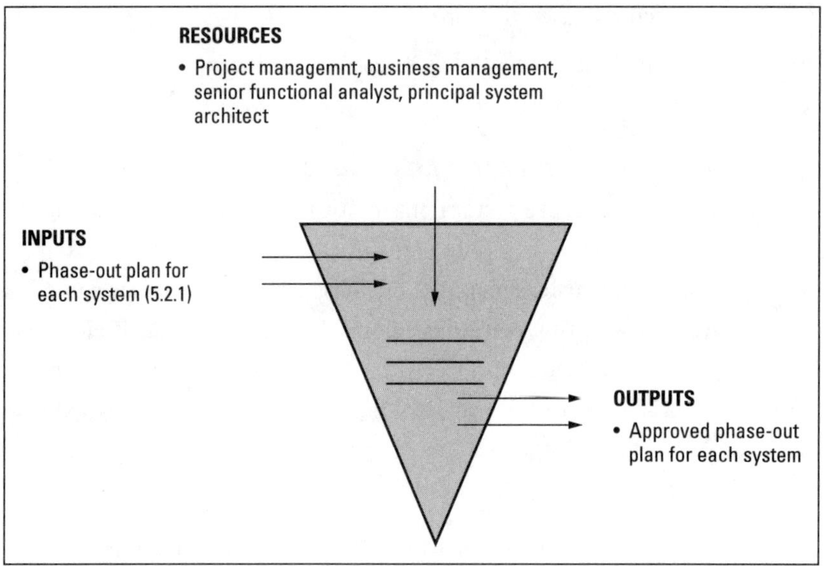

5.2.3 Task: Execute Phase-out Plans

You must carefully coordinate phase-out plans with system users. You should incorporate as much flexibility as possible into your execution schedule to avoid negative impacts on business operations. You should also phase out the old system after the replacement system has been deployed and successfully passed its production "keep" decision.

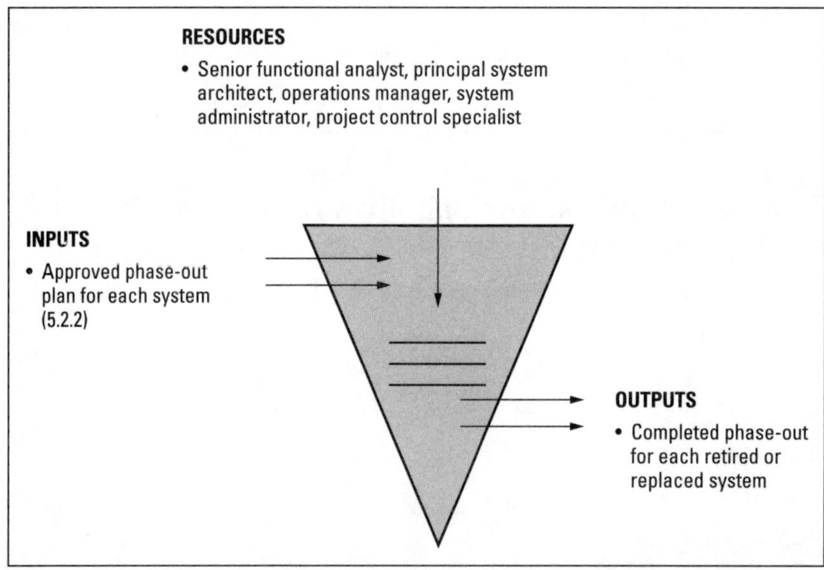

5.2.4 Task: Notify Procurement of Obsolete Vendor Licenses

You must notify your procurement office of the impending retirement of a given system. Provide them with appropriate information about license expiration and cost. They can then make arrangements to terminate maintenance or warranty contracts. In addition, they can ensure that system upgrades are not incorporated in future funding requests and budgets.

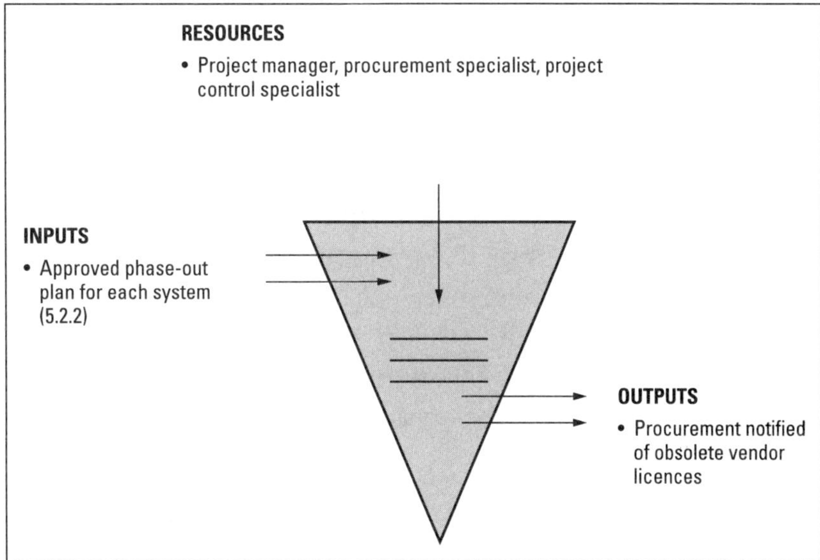

System Retirement complete. Quality assurance verifies that the deliverable conforms to its intended goal. Project control baselines the deliverable and updates tracking metrics. Configuration management verifies that the Year 2000 repository updates adhere to CM procedures.

5.3 System Repair or Replacement

The System Repair or Replacement deliverable supports Year 2000 Resolution tasks aimed at systems targeted for repair or replacement. Both of these approaches to instituting Year 2000 solutions have a significant impact on business operations, and continued interaction with system users is imperative. Because the repair or replacement of several systems will occur simultaneously, you must ensure adherence to sound task tracking methods.

Task Overview

- Notify Affected Parties of Repair/Replace Responsibilities
- Notify Procurement of Obsolete Vendor Licenses
- Replace Systems
- Develop Repair Tools
- Repair Systems
- Develop Bridge Code
- Develop Data Conversion Code

5.3.1 Task: Notify Affected Parties of Repair/Replace Responsibilities

Notify parties of repair or replace activities that will affect their business operations. Provide a list of system-related components either known or likely to be affected by the planned solution. Make arrangements to provide continued user support, as necessary. If the system directly affects production data sets, you must inform the configuration manager.

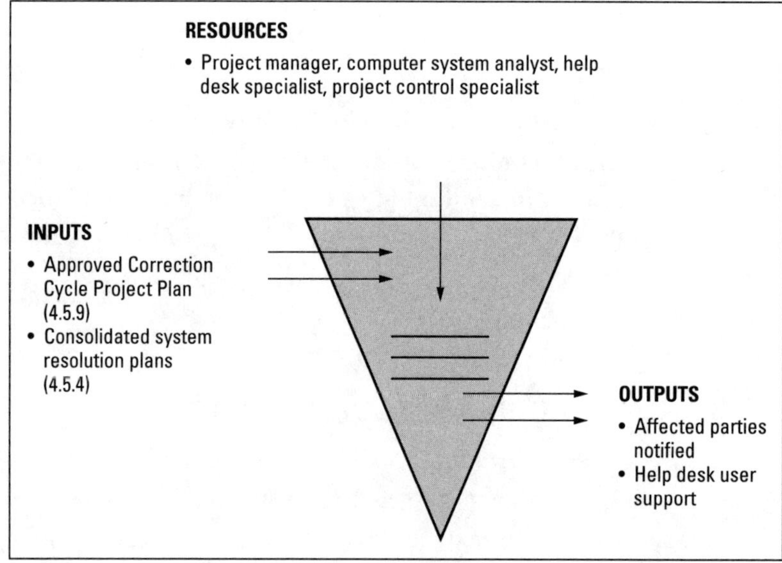

5.3.2 Task: Notify Procurement of Obsolete Vendor Licenses

In the previous deliverable, System Retirement, you notified procurement personnel of obsolete vendor licenses that affected retired systems. In this task, you issue similar notifications regarding replacing systems.

The maintenance agreements supporting some systems will also require termination.

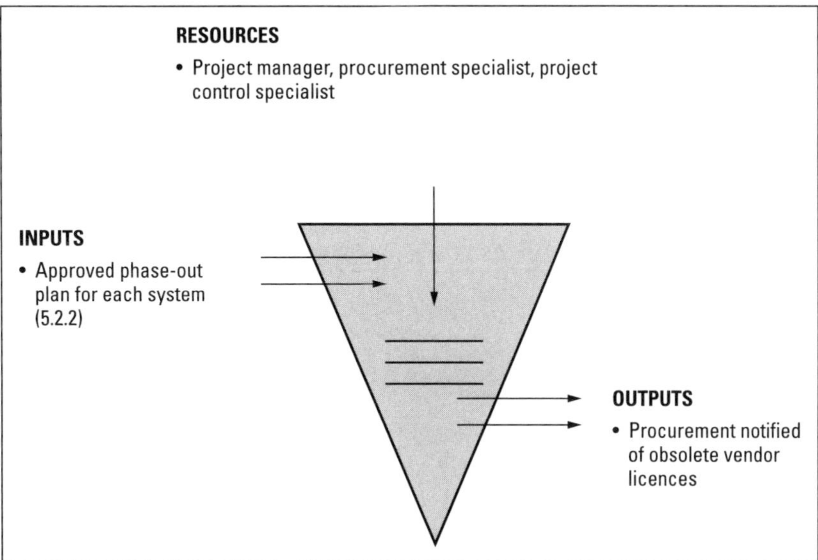

5.3.3 Task: Replace Systems

During this task, you acquire replacement systems. You interact closely with users to plan the deployment of these replacement systems. Carefully consider the impact of the replacement systems on existing systems and business operations.

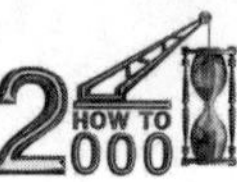

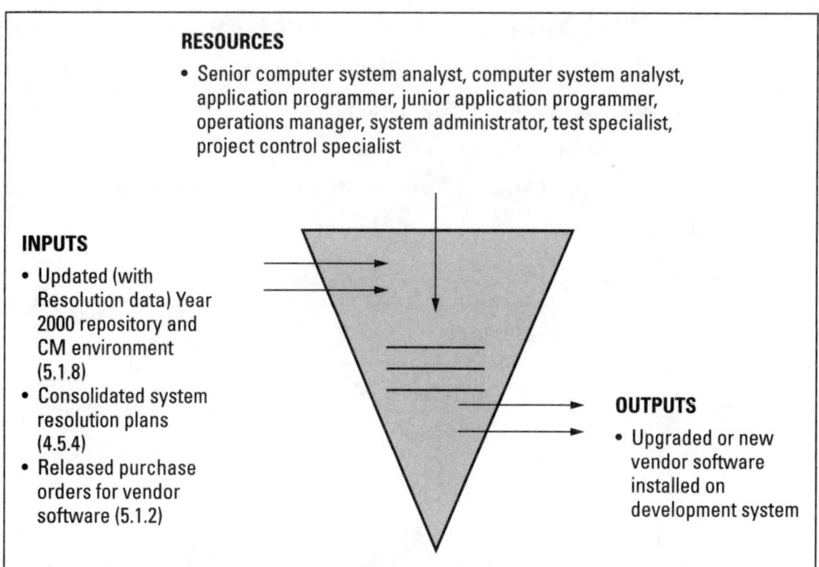

5.3.4 Task: Develop Repair Tools

During the Detailed Assessment phase, you decided to purchase some repair tools and to develop others. You should implement the development of repair tools as soon as possible after assessment activities are completed. Development should follow standard system development methodologies, including comprehensive testing.

Developed tools may include the following:

- Programs, scripts, or macros that locate and modify specific system components affected by a Year 2000 problem or problems
- Programs, scripts, or macros that support a particular vendor tool in locating or modifying system components affected by Year 2000 problems

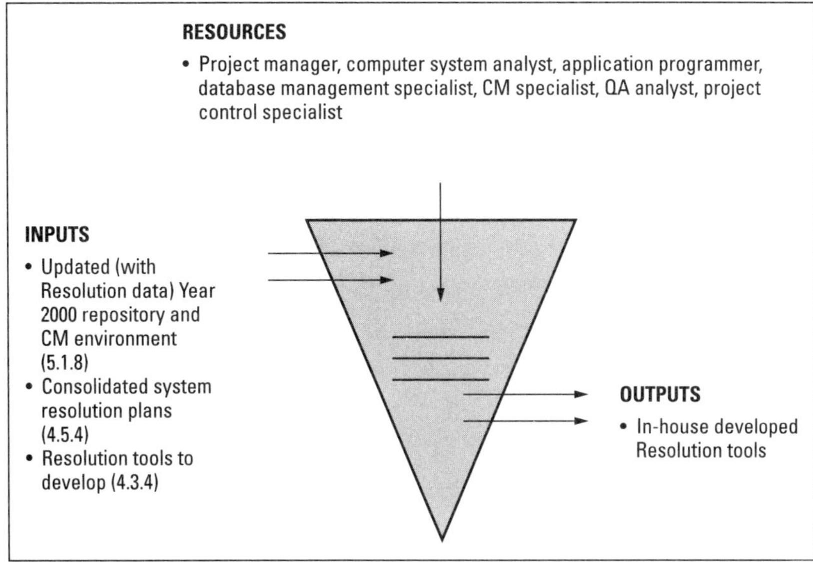

5.3.5 Task: Repair Systems

You will modify systems targeted for repair. Some of these modifications will be partially or completely implemented with automated tools. Ideally, these tools will be used in conjunction with an "assembly line" system modification process. Relatively junior personnel can execute these assembly line modifications under the supervision of more senior personnel.

For some systems, however, you will not be able to use automated tool support and/or assembly line processes for repair. Systems that incorporate an atypical Year 2000 problem, that are configured in an unusual manner, or that require a combination of Year 2000 modifications may need custom modifications. In these cases, experienced system developers must implement these modifications.

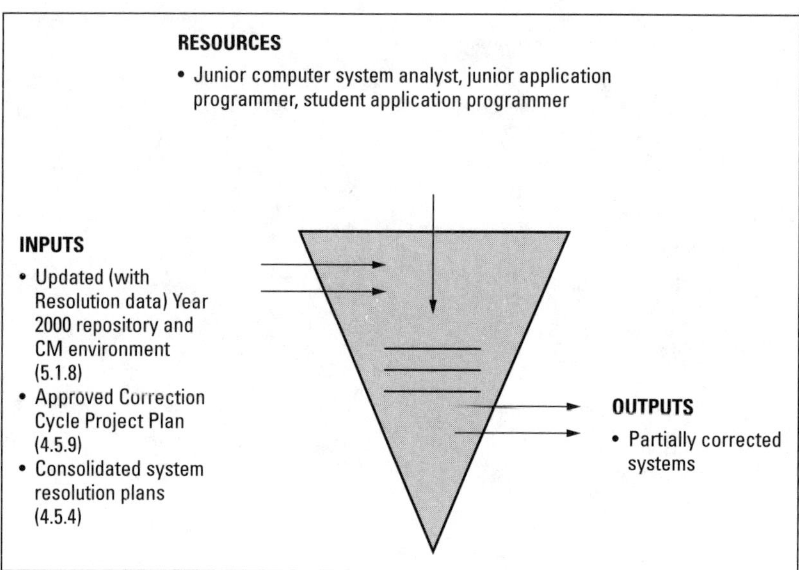

5.3.6 Task: Develop Bridge Code

Now you develop required system bridges according to the plans created in the Detailed Assessment phase. Develop bridges according to standard system development methodologies. When possible, try to "reuse" components of various bridges.

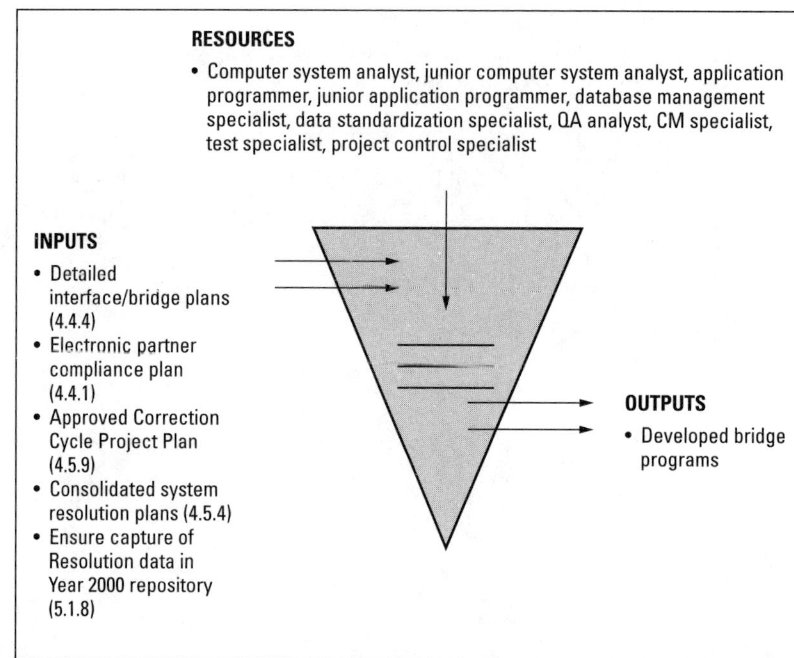

5.3.7 Task: Develop Data Conversion Code

Develop required data conversion routines according to the plans created in the Detailed Assessment phase. Develop routines according to standard system development methodologies. When possible, try to "reuse" components of various routines. These routines will be executed during Testing and Deployment.

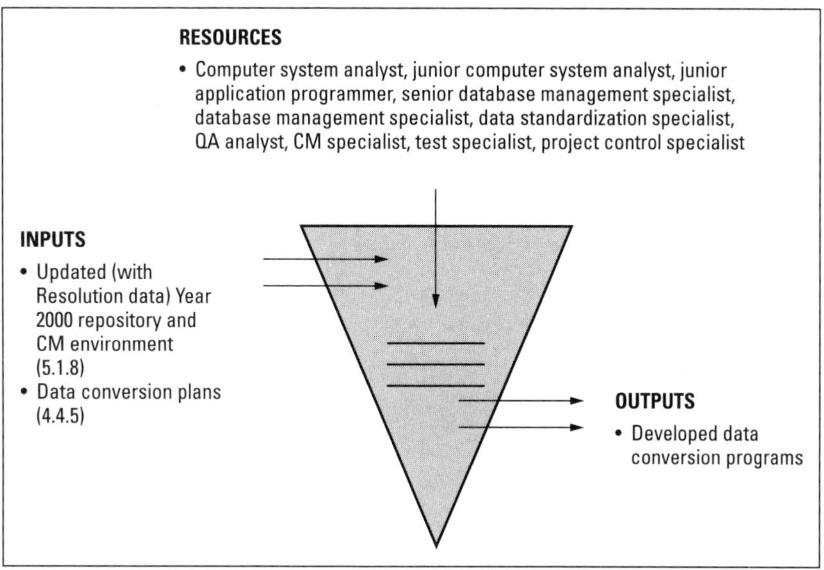

milestone  **System Repair or Replacement complete. Quality assurance verifies that the deliverable conforms to its intended goal. Project control baselines the deliverable and updates tracking metrics. Configuration management verifies that the Year 2000 repository updates adhere to CM procedures. This milestone will be accomplished multiple times throughout your project, once for each partition or subproject.**

5.4 Unit Testing

The Unit Testing deliverable supports developer testing of the repaired systems. This type of testing is informal in nature and allows the developers to ensure the accuracy of their system modifications. Errors found by these tests can be corrected as Resolution activities are underway. This type of testing is a necessary precursor to the formal testing that takes place during the next phase: Test Execution.

Task Overview

- Develop Developer Unit/System Test Plans
- Prepare Test Data
- Capture Development Test Baselines
- Execute Unit Tests
- Execute Developer System Tests

5.4.1 Task: Develop Developer Unit/System Test Plans

Develop plans for unit testing, the testing of system components that have been modified, and system testing. These plans will detail the procedures for each test. Tests are designed to discover errors related to Year 2000 modifications and should not test comprehensive system functionality. These tests evaluate system performance in the development environment and do not consider system performance in the targeted working environment. These plans should also include the testing of bridge programs and data conversion routines developed in the previous deliverables.

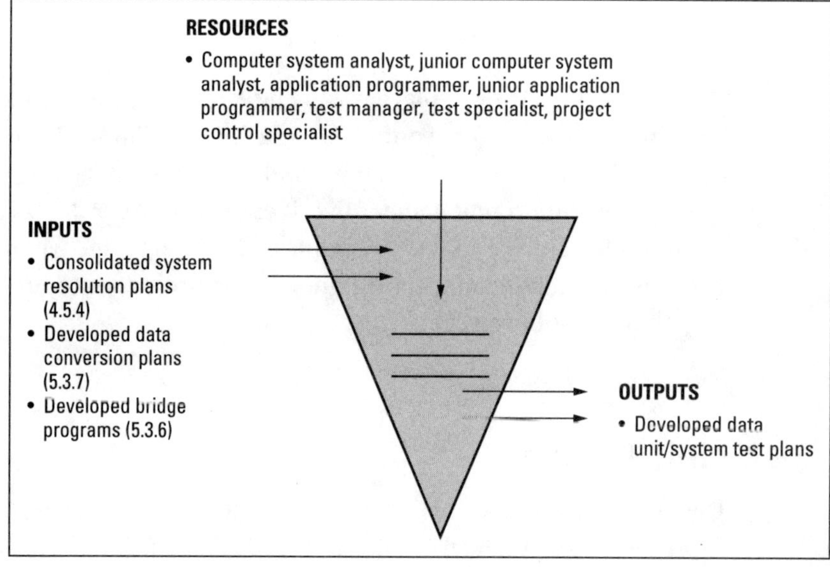

5.4.2 Task: Prepare Test Data

Prepare the test data sets that will be used for unit and system testing. Test data is commonly obtained by duplicating production data, by creating the data with testing support tools, or by creating the data set manually.

Make sure that test data is Year 2000 compliant where necessary. If you duplicate production data, you should use the data conversion tools previously developed.

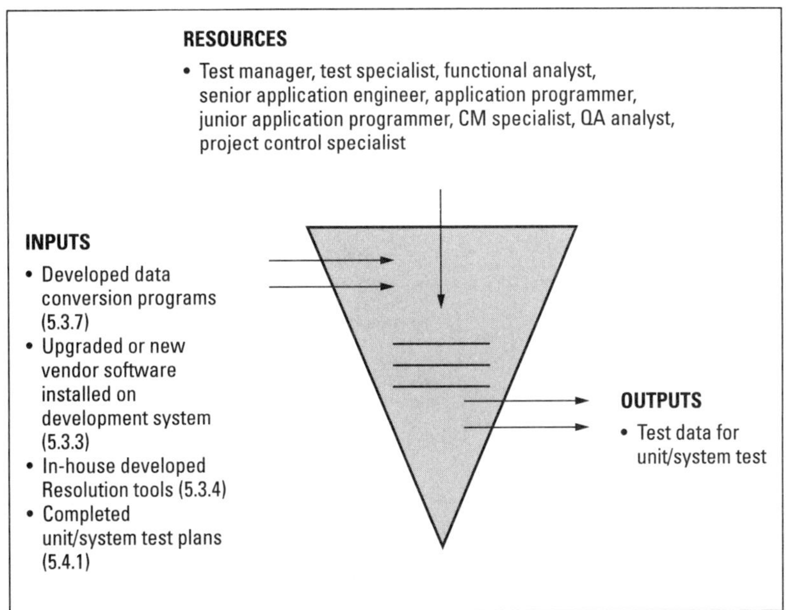

5.4.3 Task: Capture Development Test Baselines

Capture a test baseline from system output generated prior to system repair. You will compare this baseline to the output generated by the modified system to identify system errors. You can use comparison tools to determine the differences between the two sets of outputs.

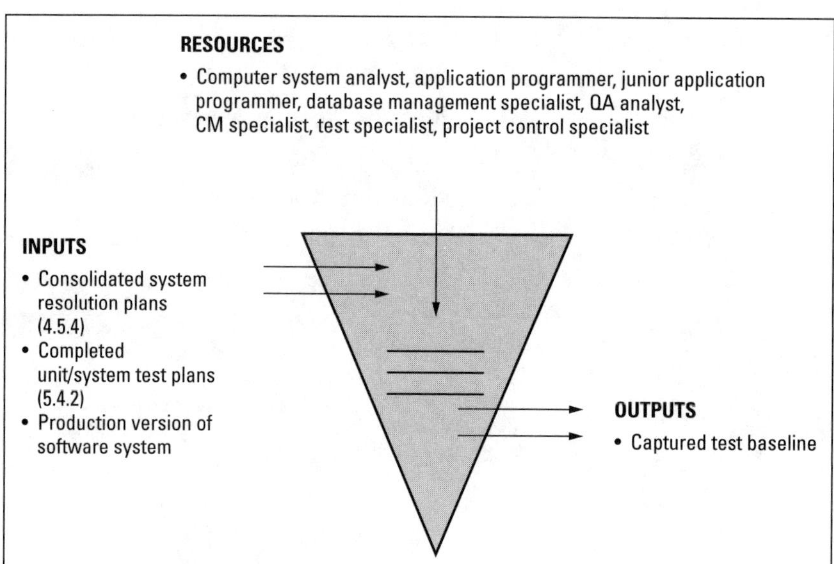
RESOURCES
• Computer system analyst, application programmer, junior application programmer, database management specialist, QA analyst, CM specialist, test specialist, project control specialist
INPUTS
• Consolidated system resolution plans (4.5.4)
• Completed unit/system test plans (5.4.2)
• Production version of software system
OUTPUTS
• Captured test baseline

5.4.4 Task: Execute Unit Tests

Here you execute unit tests (that is, tests of specific system components modified to be Year 2000 compliant) according to the unit test plans that you have developed.

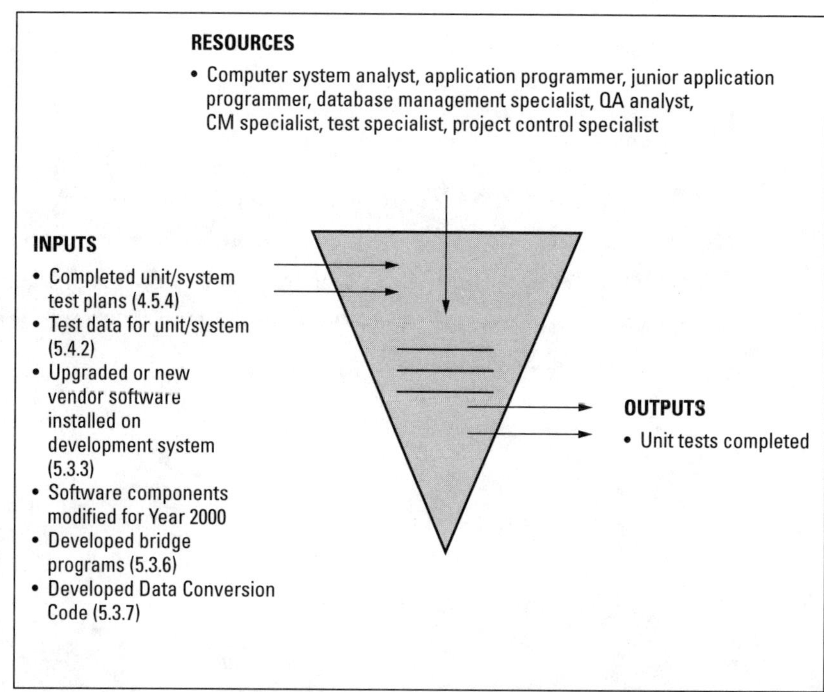
RESOURCES
• Computer system analyst, application programmer, junior application programmer, database management specialist, QA analyst, CM specialist, test specialist, project control specialist
INPUTS
• Completed unit/system test plans (4.5.4)
• Test data for unit/system (5.4.2)
• Upgraded or new vendor software installed on development system (5.3.3)
• Software components modified for Year 2000
• Developed bridge programs (5.3.6)
• Developed Data Conversion Code (5.3.7)
OUTPUTS
• Unit tests completed

5.4.5 Task: Execute Developer System Tests

After you complete unit testing, you execute tests of entire systems according to the system test plans you have developed.

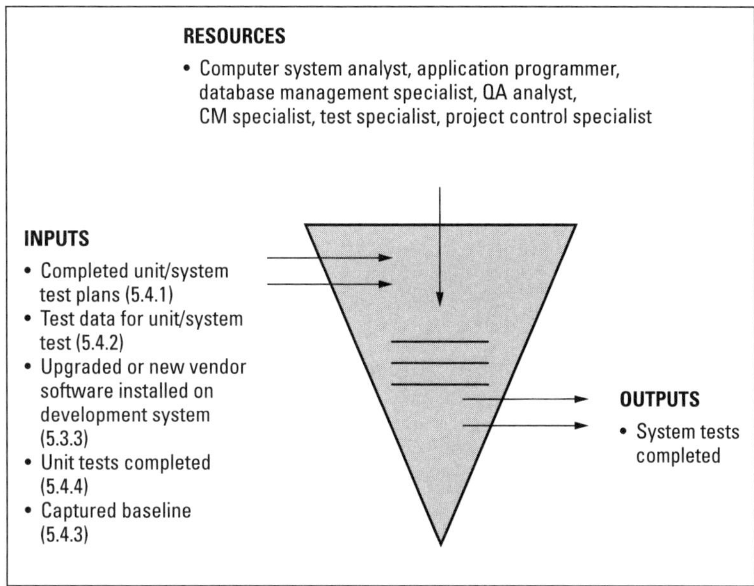
RESOURCES
• Computer system analyst, application programmer, database management specialist, QA analyst, CM specialist, test specialist, project control specialist
INPUTS
• Completed unit/system test plans (5.4.1)
• Test data for unit/system test (5.4.2)
• Upgraded or new vendor software installed on development system (5.3.3)
• Unit tests completed (5.4.4)
• Captured baseline (5.4.3)
OUTPUTS
• System tests completed

milestone

Unit Testing complete. Quality assurance verifies that the deliverable conforms to its intended goal. Project control baselines the deliverable and updates tracking metrics. Configuration management verifies that the Year 2000 repository updates adhere to CM procedures.

5.5 Documentation

The system modifications executed in the previous deliverables must be reflected in the documentation that supports the use of each system. The Documentation deliverable supports the review and revision of system documentation.

Task Overview

- Modify Business Process Documents
- Modify User/System Documentation
- Modify System Training Materials

5.5.1 Task: Modify Business Process Documents

Some of the business units in your organization may use manual business processes that are not compatible with Year 2000 compliance. For example, a particular business unit may require clerks to complete a certain type of form with two-digit dates. Now that the automated systems in these business units have been retired, replaced, or repaired to achieve Year 2000 compliance, you must ensure that the business processes supported by these systems are also Year 2000 compliant.

You must assist system users in the redesign of business processes that support Year 2000 compliant systems. These users should review their business processes, institute changes when necessary, and modify business process documentation to reflect these changes. The types of documents that may require modification include standard operating procedures and standard forms that support the transfer and storage of information.

You may need senior management approval for business process changes. In addition, you may need approval for the costs related to the modification of business process documents. Such modifications may result in costly document revision and reproduction tasks.

To be safe you should not publish modified documents until user acceptance testing is completed.

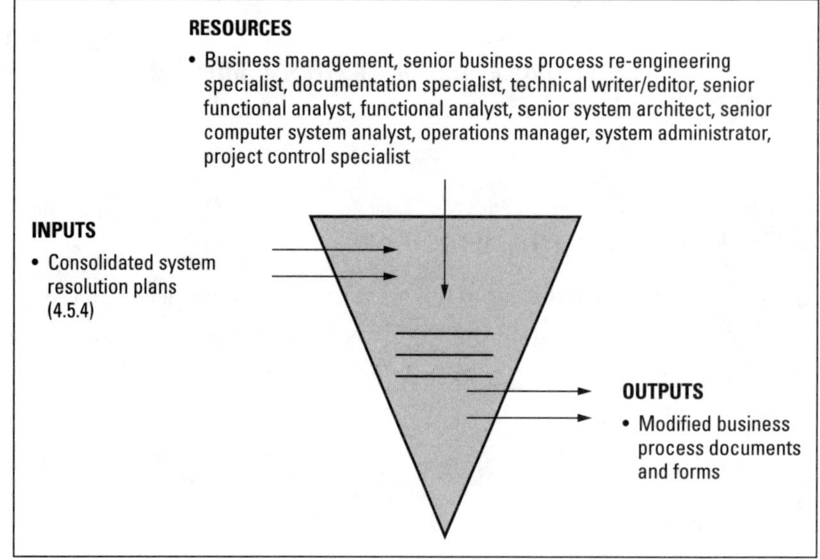
RESOURCES
• Business management, senior business process re-engineering specialist, documentation specialist, technical writer/editor, senior functional analyst, functional analyst, senior system architect, senior computer system analyst, operations manager, system administrator, project control specialist
INPUTS
• Consolidated system resolution plans (4.5.4)
OUTPUTS
• Modified business process documents and forms

5.5.2 Task: Modify User/System Documentation

You must ensure the accuracy of the technical documentation that accompanies your Year 2000 compliant systems. If a particular system will be modified, its technical documents may also require modification. For example, if you modify a software system that was developed within your organization, you should also modify the system's requirements and design documents. In addition, you may need to change operational support documents and user manuals.

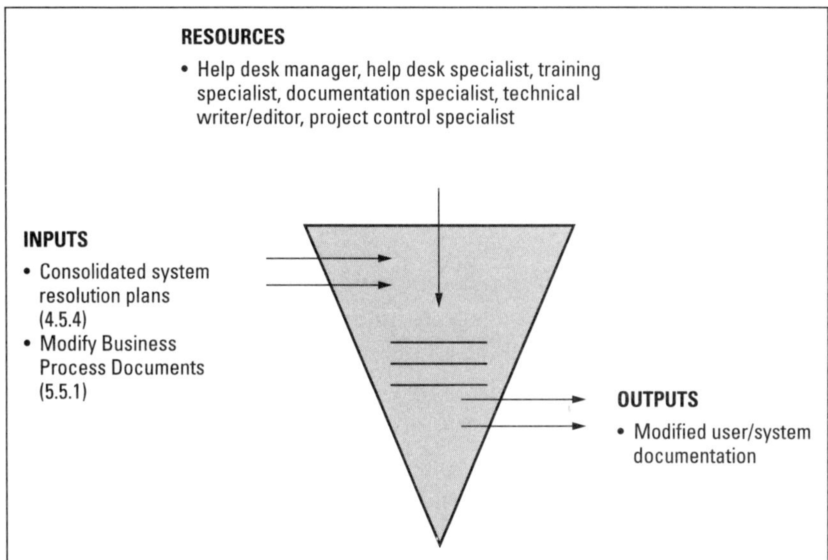
RESOURCES
• Help desk manager, help desk specialist, training specialist, documentation specialist, technical writer/editor, project control specialist
INPUTS
• Consolidated system resolution plans (4.5.4)
• Modify Business Process Documents (5.5.1)
OUTPUTS
• Modified user/system documentation

5.5.3 Task: Modify System Training Materials

You should modify any documentation or other materials that support system training to reflect the Year 2000 compliance of your systems. These materials may be used to retrain system users after these systems have been deployed.

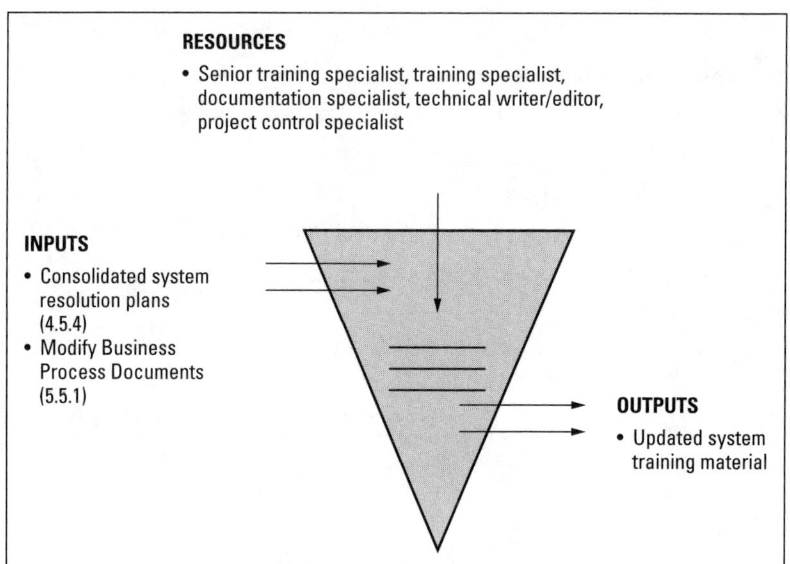
RESOURCES
• Senior training specialist, training specialist, documentation specialist, technical writer/editor, project control specialist
INPUTS
• Consolidated system resolution plans (4.5.4)
• Modify Business Process Documents (5.5.1)
OUTPUTS
• Updated system training material

milestone

Documentation complete. Quality assurance verifies that the deliverable conforms to its intended goal. Project control baselines the deliverable and updates tracking metrics. Configuration management verifies that the Year 2000 repository updates adhere to CM procedures.

Business Impacts

During this phase, you will fix your systems. Various subprojects will be in this phase at different times, others will be in testing, and still others deployed. Impacts to your business processes and documents begin to occur during this phase. Because systems are being changed, there is a tendency to shut down all business improvements to affected systems to ease configuration management problems. Some of the solutions set may result in changes that affect the documentation used to input data into the system, or the report outputs. Systems being retired or replaced can affect all aspects of how businesses perform their functions with customers and partnerships. For this reason, your plans should also consider the impacts described in the following sections.

Due to System Replacement

Managers who control replaced systems must cope with the following:

- The cost of purchasing and installing a new system
- Costs and time involved in training those who will use the new system
- Schedule delays caused by lack of familiarity with the new system
- Changes in business processes due to installation of a new system
- Migration of users, customers, and partnerships from old to new system

Due to System Repair

When a system undergoes repair, managers may have to modify business processes to accommodate the partial or total loss of that system's functionality. When system modification and testing is completed, the business environment in which the system exists should return to normal operation. However, maintenance costs for the modified system may rise or fall due to the completed repairs.

Due to System Retirement

Business units that control a retired system may be severely affected by the loss of the system. The business unit must continue to operate without the functionality previously supplied by the retired system, or it must somehow manually duplicate that functionality. In some instances, this functionality may be transferred to another automated system. If functionality is lost, the need for system support resources (labor, equipment, maintenance, warranties, budget) also disappears.

All managers who control systems targeted for inclusion in the Year 2000 project must cope with the impact of Year 2000 Resolution activities on ongoing development processes. Existing development projects may require modifications that consume time, labor, or other resources.

Phase Risks

Potential Event	*Probability*	*Impact*	*Risk*
Accomplishments are overstated	Medium	Medium	Medium
Lack of adherence to standard system development procedures	Medium	Medium	Medium
Mistakes due to monotony of task	High	High	High
Inefficient resolution due to outsourcing	High	Medium	Medium
Introduction of system side effects	High	High	High

Resolution Phase Risks

There are at least five risks associated with the Resolution phase: Accomplishments may be overstated; staff may neglect to adhere to standard system development procedures; there may be mistakes as a result of the monotony of the task; there may be an inefficient resolution because of outsourcing; and system side effects may be introduced.

Accomplishments Are Overstated

Systems developers tend to be overly optimistic about their work. Therefore, there is the risk of inaccurate reporting of accomplishments throughout Resolution. If the code development and testing groups are separate, you might witness code frequently changing status from fixing to testing and back again. This could leave the percentage complete at the same level for an extended period of time, despite a flurry of activity.

There are ways of mitigating these risks:

- Use incremental inspections and code walkthroughs. Formal code walkthroughs are a traditional way of monitoring system development progress. If system developers are asked to periodically present their work, they tend not to overstate their accomplishments. If there are many eyes reviewing the code, the code also tends to be debugged more thoroughly up front, resulting in less bug patching during the more formalized testing process.

Lack of Adherence to Standard System Development Procedures

Most organizations have comprehensive system development methodologies rooted in the notion that "haste makes waste" (that is, specific logical tasks must be accomplished in a systematic fashion to ensure a quality product). Unfortunately, when a project is behind schedule and/or over budget, developers often fail to complete all development tasks. These omitted tasks might mean that a product needs to be reworked substantially later in the development cycle. Because of the immovable Year 2000 deadline, you may be straining to accomplish your Resolution tasks, and might be tempted to abandon "good practice" procedures to accomplish Year 2000 repairs as soon as possible.

Here is one way of mitigating this risk:

- Ensure that Year 2000 developers receive clear and comprehensive guidance about the system development procedures required. Stress that the approach of the year 2000 should not scare them into abandoning standard development practices. Good development practices also include subcontract management with outside vendor programming "factories" or inside contract staff.

Mistakes Due to Monotony of Task

The repair tasks undertaken during Resolution will be repetitive and sometimes tedious. If a certain system incorporates a substantial number of date fields, all of which must be modified in the same way, programmers will soon grow bored with the task. Unfortunately, boredom breeds errors.

There are several ways of mitigating this risk:

- Make sure that standard morale support mechanisms are in place and functioning. Ensure a pleasant work environment. Reward diligence. Provide added incentives for successfully completing Year 2000 tasks.

Provide small morale-building "extras" to those participating in Resolution activities. For example, provide a free lunch every Friday.

- Rotate programmers among several tasks. Programmers may find their tasks more interesting if they work on several Resolution activities. In addition, it may increase productivity to allow programmers to interleave Year 2000 and non-Year 2000 tasks. Allowing programmers to "change the scenery" on a regular basis will help prevent the boredom associated with repeatedly performing similar activities.
- Compile a list of attributes common to staff who can tolerate a certain degree of monotony. Use this list to help you select personnel for Resolution tasks. Certain types of employees can tolerate tedious tasks better than others. Your management challenge is to track them down.

Inefficient Resolution Due to Outsourcing

Because of the tedium of Resolution tasks, you may want to outsource some of the repair activities. However, outsourcing may significantly increase the cost of accomplishing Resolution tasks. You will incur standard contractor-related costs related to dual overhead, increased learning curves, and inefficient communication. Unfortunately, your outsourcing costs may far outpace comparable internal costs.

Remember that you can outsource the work but you cannot outsource the responsibility. There are a lot of "get rich quick" vendors out there. Even well-intentioned vendors may find themselves overbooked with Year 2000 contracts. They also face many of the same Year 2000 difficulties—that is, turnover of key personnel.

There are several ways of mitigating this risk:

- Define explicit cost-control features within contractor procurement vehicles. Carefully define the level of effort expected and the level of overhead allowed.
- Develop and use efficient communication channels between your staff and contract staff. Contract staff will spend a certain amount of time becoming familiar with the systems they will repair or replace. Your staff must help the contract staff meet this challenge. In addition, your staff will need to help contractors as problems arise. To support contractors, you must ensure the continued function and use of explicitly defined methods of communication.

- Develop a specific contingency plan for dealing with contractor cost overruns. This contingency plan should help you if contractors need additional time or funds to accomplish Resolution tasks. You may want to switch contractors or complete these tasks with internal personnel.

Introduction of System Side Effects

All information system maintenance tasks can potentially insert new errors into a system being modified. The last thing you want to do is cause a system failure because of an error that has nothing to do with a Year 2000 problem.

There are several ways of mitigating this risk:

- Ensure the use of sound system development practices. As mentioned, you must stress the importance of adhering to standard development methods. Using a standard structured development approach often prevents coding "side effects."
- When developing a system test plan, make sure to include tests that are comprehensive in nature, as opposed to merely Year 2000 specific. Testing a system's broad-based functionality may uncover non-Year 2000 errors inadvertently introduced to a particular system.

Success Factors

In successfully completing the Resolution phase, you carried out the following steps:

Success Factors	*Deliverable*
Notified affected parties of Resolution plans that affect them	Resolution Phase Startup
Ordered new versions of COTS products being replaced	Resolution Phase Startup
Acquired adequate internal staff and contractors to conduct Resolution	Resolution Phase Startup

continued

Success Factors	*Deliverable*
Monitored performance of contractors on a regular basis with respect to agreed-to plans and deliverables	Resolution Phase Startup
Executed pertinent elements of the training plan	Resolution Phase Startup
Updated Year 2000 repository and CM procedures to capture and control Resolution information	Resolution Phase Startup
Ensured application of standardized system development methods to support quality products; maintained consistency and compatibility in plans, requirements, designs, code, tests, and documentation	Resolution Phase Startup
Ensured that concurrent development does not reintroduce Year 2000 problems	Resolution Phase Startup
Developed and reviewed phase-out plans for systems being retired	System Retirement
Notified procurement of obsolete vendor licenses	System Retirement
Developed tools to support Resolution tasks	System Repair or Replacement
Implemented system modifications with vendor tools, as appropriate	System Repair or Replacement
Implemented system modifications with internally developed tools, as appropriate	System Repair or Replacement
Isolated code and data changes from existing operational effort	System Repair or Replacement
Ensured continued operations when applying a solution	System Repair or Replacement
Developed code for system bridges, as necessary	System Repair or Replacement
Converted operational data according to established integration strategy	System Repair or Replacement
Developed developer unit/system test plans	Developer Testing
Executed unit test plans	Unit Testing
Modified business process documents to incorporate Year 2000 compliance system modifications	Documentation

Success Factors	Deliverable
Developed training plan to support preparation of personnel for use of Year 2000 compliant systems	Documentation
Updated documents used to operate and maintain the systems	Documentation
Identified risks and potential mitigation approaches	All deliverables
Identified deliverables developed during Resolution	All deliverables
Used adequate communication interfaces throughout your organization to support the tasks associated with Resolution	All deliverables
Assigned tasks to various groups in your organization and ensured that there was management approval for those tasks	All deliverables
Identified the deliverables for which each group was responsible and ensured acceptance of that deliverable responsibility by each group	All deliverables
Identified key milestones for the accomplishment of tasks for this phase	All deliverables
Identified milestone thresholds beyond which some corrective action will be taken	All deliverables
Used metrics to track and measure progress with respect to these milestones	All deliverables
Ensured that each responsible group accepted and adhered to the schedule for completion of Resolution	All deliverables

Reference Material

This list mentions reference material you can turn to for additional information on this phase of your Year 2000 compliance project:

- Appendix A, Problem Definition Catalog
- Appendix B, Solution Sets
- Appendix E, Applicability of Tools

- Appendix H, Integrated Project Plan
- Appendix I, How To 2000 Risk Management
- Glossary
- *How To 2000* CD-ROM

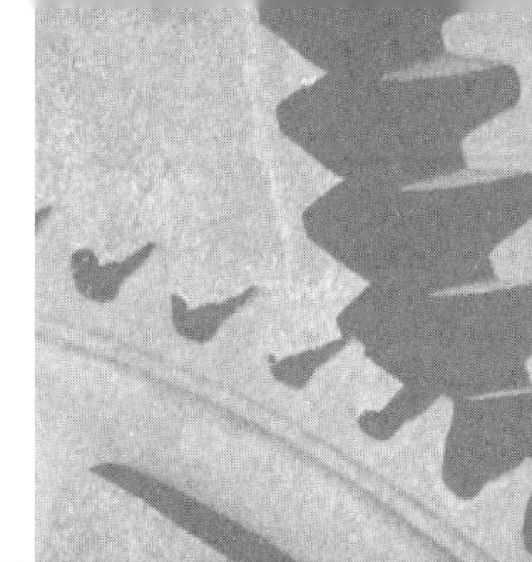

CHAPTER

Phase 6: Test Planning

6

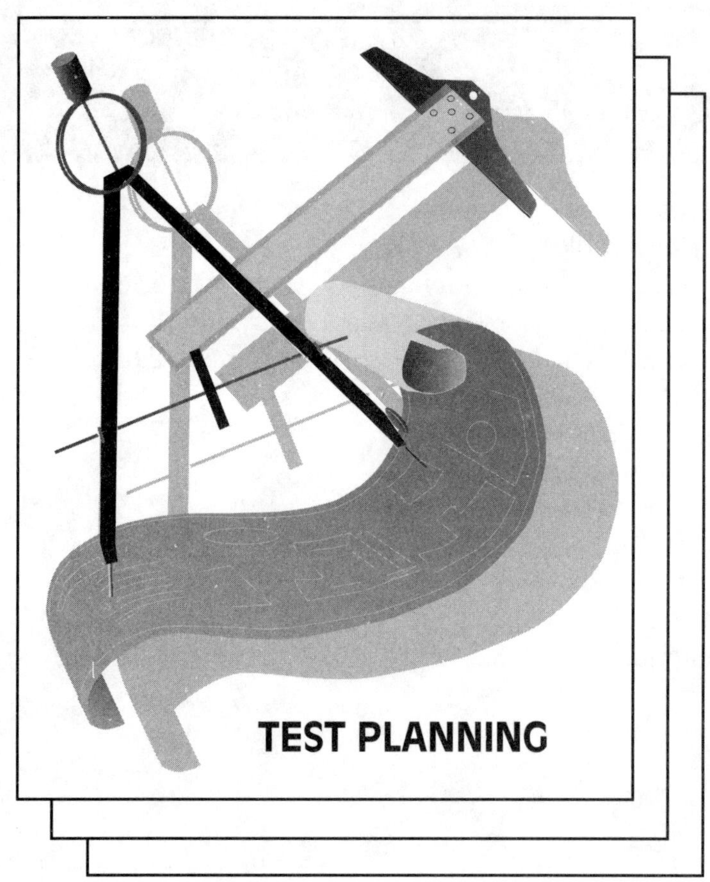
TEST PLANNING

Objectives

- Develop comprehensive test plans to prevent noncompliant solutions from reaching production operations.
- Coordinate with third parties and electronic partner interfaces.
- Formulate contingency plans, including fallout and rollback plans.
- Obtain and construct mirror test environments and data.
- Acquire test tools and train users in their operation.

During Phase 6, Test Planning, you prepare to conduct the testing described in the Test Execution phase. This phase helps you build careful plans for verifying and validating Year 2000 compliance of all relevant systems. It is critical that you begin Test Planning as early as possible, in parallel with Detailed Assessment, and that you consider the issues related to the Deployment and Fallout phases. Pay particular attention to your rollback requirements (see Chapter 8, Deployment). These tasks may affect your test acceptance criteria.

Preparing to Test

The Year 2000 Test Planning phase differs from Test Planning activities for typical systems development and implementation projects. Testing is a large part of any system development or system maintenance project. For the Year 2000 project, the test planning unit test/formal test/fix/retest cycle may require up to 40 percent of a typical system development budget. Your Year 2000 testing process is more complex and involves system interfaces outside the span of your control or influence. Each of these interfaces can lead to difficulties in coordination, bridging, and compliance timing. Year 2000 testing must assure that interfaces, bridges and patches, third parties, operating systems, hardware interfaces, and anomalies created in the Resolution are identified and resolved. Properly defined partitions and their associated test plans help to minimize the chance that systems will have to be recycled through resolution and test processes, thus saving time and money. Whereas most systems being developed and deployed go through a standard test cycle of unit, integration, system, acceptance, and finally deployment testing, the Year 2000 project must overlay many such concurrent cycles. This is one aspect

that makes Year 2000 test planning and execution unique. For Year 2000 testing, each partition, electronic partnership, and integration test is at the level of system/acceptance/deployment testing for standard projects.

Your Year 2000 test plan must include an approach to conducting a series of independent system tests, as well as a method of conducting organization-wide system testing. Because all automated systems within your organization are affected by the Year 2000 project, you must define a series of formal tests rather than a single formal acceptance test. These individual formal tests will build upon one another until you have achieved comprehensive, organization-wide testing. You should develop these independent test plans concurrently, while you're carrying out Resolution, Test Execution, and Deployment activities.

Begin your Year 2000 Test Planning process by developing an overall test plan that defines the time frames during which individual system tests will be planned and executed.

After you develop this overall plan, develop a plan for each test entity. (Usually a test entity will correspond to a partition.) Like most formal test plans, your test plans should include:

- The definitions of several test cases, as well as the definitions of test events for each test entity
- The identification of the test environments and test tools to be used
- The test scripts (that is, step-by-step instructions) for each test event, including definitions of acceptance criteria for each test event
- The description of required test data (databases, files, data characteristics)
- The definition of go/no-go user acceptance criteria related to the Deployment decision

You should solicit input from both system users and those participating in Year 2000 Resolution activities as you develop the overall test plan and the individual test plans.

The costs for completing Test Planning and Test Execution activities should not exceed 30 percent of your project cost.

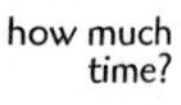

The time devoted to testing tasks in both Test Planning and Test Execution should not exceed 39 percent of the Year 2000 project schedule.

Summary of Deliverables

This section summarizes the deliverables for this phase of the Year 2000 compliance project. The section "Deliverables, Tasks, and Dependencies" later in this chapter includes detailed descriptions of each deliverable and the associated supporting tasks. Except for the Test Planning and Execution Phase Startup deliverable, all deliverables must consider the related needs of the individual partitions and their integration into the full system.

Test Planning and Execution Phase Startup

The Test Planning and Execution Phase Startup deliverable provides an overview of formal test tasks and the schedule for completing these tasks. You will integrate information gathered during Inventory and Detailed Assessment to understand what tests are needed, and you will create an overall schedule for testing.

Test Facility Environment Report

The Test Facility Environment Report deliverable describes the test environment. For this project, systems are not tested in the operational environment. A separate, controlled environment is outlined in this deliverable.

Test Support Tool Requirements

Depending on your environment, you may have to acquire specialized test tools (for example, activity generators, data collectors). The Test Support Tool Requirements deliverable documents your test tool requirements. In addition, it details which of these requirements can be met by existing tools, and which tools must be acquired.

Electronic Partnership Test Plan

When you complete Year 2000 Resolution activities, you may require recertification by some or all of your electronic partners. These partners may dictate the specific tasks that must be completed as part of a recertification effort, or you may define these tasks. In either case, you must coordinate a recertification test plan and schedule with each electronic partner. The Electronic Partnership Test Plan deliverable provides a summary of these plans and schedules.

Partition Test Description and Data

A partition is the basic entity for which a formal test is prepared and executed. A specific partition is first tested individually, and then tested in conjunction with other partitions with which it creates a larger entity. The Partition Test Description and Data deliverable describes each partition test. It also describes the data used for each test.

Integration Test Description and Data

The Integration Test Description and Data deliverable describes the formal system integration tests. These tests must address events that cross partition boundaries to ensure that the new integrated entity operates as required. This deliverable also describes the data used for each test.

Deliverables, Tasks, and Dependencies

The deliverables produced in the Test Planning phase are documents that will be used in the next phase: Test Execution.

6.1 Test Planning and Execution Phase Startup

The Test Planning and Execution Phase Startup deliverable defines the resources needed to ensure the efficient completion of all Test Planning and Test Execution tasks. When you complete this deliverable, the required testing environment will be authorized.

It also helps you develop an overall strategy for formal testing. This strategy provides:

- An overall schedule of Test Planning and Test Execution activities for all formal partition, integration, and deployment tests
- Identification of top-level test data and databases needed for testing
- Identification of top-level test cases

This strategy will incorporate information gathered during Inventory, as well as information about the partitions defined during the Detailed Assessment phase.

Task Overview

- Tailor Methodology for Testing
- Define Strategy for Formal Testing
- Acquire Human Resources for Testing
- Define Top-Level Test Cases
- Define Top-Level Test Data
- Establish Test Phases Tracking
- Present and Approve Formal Test Plan

6.1.1 Task: Tailor Methodology for Testing

Review the test deliverables and tasks suggested in this guide and tailor them to the needs of your organization. You must address the needs of both testing phases —Test Planning and Test Execution.

Your actual approach to Year 2000 test management will depend upon the scope and distribution of the systems to be tested. Your approach will also depend on the opinions and experience of the people responsible for the successful completion of these tests. You must decide how much of the testing process is to be completed in-house, how many systems are involved, how many IS organizations are involved, and whether there are separate test groups for each organization.

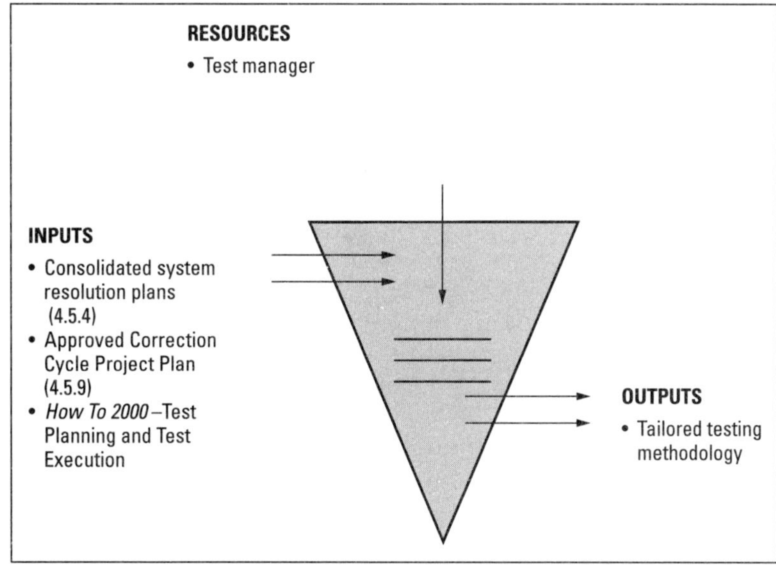
RESOURCES
• Test manager
INPUTS
• Consolidated system resolution plans (4.5.4)
• Approved Correction Cycle Project Plan (4.5.9)
• *How To 2000*–Test Planning and Test Execution
OUTPUTS
• Tailored testing methodology

Task Guidelines

- Compare your Year 2000 project's overall schedule with that of the methodology. Determine how much more or less time for the various phases is available for your actual activities and how to introduce parallelism.
- All of the test deliverables should be applicable to all Year 2000 conversions, but you may not always need to do them as formally as presented in the methodology. Also, you may need to adjust the review cycles/participants.
- Prepare a revised task, dependency, and schedule overview as a guide for Test Planning and Test Execution activities. This will be part of your checklist as you progress through the entire project.

6.1.2 Task: Define Strategy for Formal Testing

The test manager and the principal Detailed Assessment managers are the major contributors to this task, the goal of which is to get a general sense of the size of the overall test planning effort. It gives the test manager information necessary to select the needed staff. During this task, you use the Enterprise and Inventory Schematics, superimposing the system partitions defined as part of Detailed Assessment and incorporating Resolution plans to determine a testing and deployment order:

- Review the Inventory Schematic to identify applications that share resources (hardware, databases, interfaces). An overall testing, integration, and deployment strategy must take this into account.
- Know your overall time goals. Determine how many separate deployments are practical, given the size of your operations and the amount of time you have. Each separate deployment is potentially disruptive to operations and requires a lot of support. Because formal testing usually tracks deployments, you must work closely with system users to come up with an approach that makes sense to everyone.
- Verify the system partitions you defined during the Detailed Assessment phase. You must verify the scope and boundaries of each system when you initiate testing activities.
- Work out the integration/deployment sequence. Using the identified partitions, plan a sequence for testing and deploying them. Prepare this schedule knowing that it may change due to business, costs, or staffing reasons.

- System bridges were constructed during Resolution. Identify each bridge and its purpose in relation to each integration/deployment step. Also indicate as part of the integration when bridges are scheduled for removal.
- Record this information in a schedule, schematic, or interim report to which the testing team and others can refer.

You now have the preliminary information needed to size and staff Test Planning and to develop the Formal Test Plan.

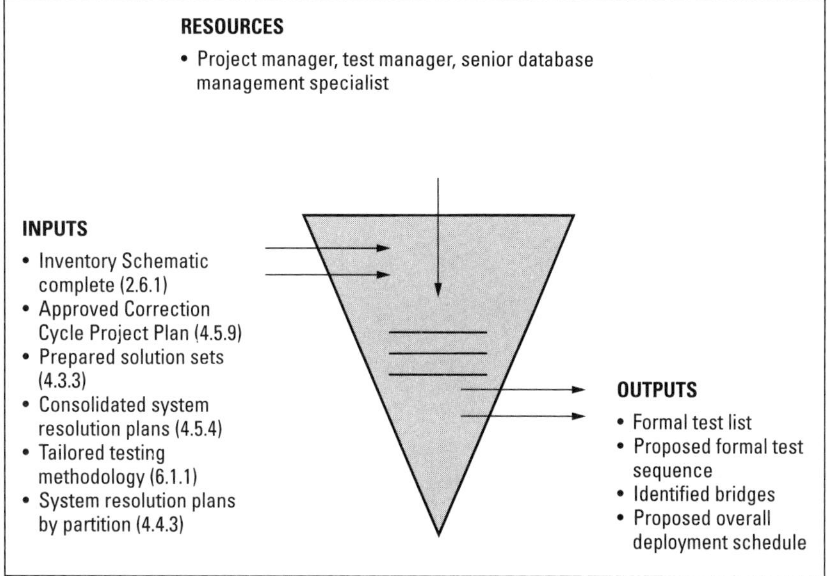
RESOURCES
• Project manager, test manager, senior database management specialist
INPUTS
• Inventory Schematic complete (2.6.1)
• Approved Correction Cycle Project Plan (4.5.9)
• Prepared solution sets (4.3.3)
• Consolidated system resolution plans (4.5.4)
• Tailored testing methodology (6.1.1)
• System resolution plans by partition (4.4.3)
OUTPUTS
• Formal test list
• Proposed formal test sequence
• Identified bridges
• Proposed overall deployment schedule

Task Guidelines

- Keep the users informed of test plans, since these will directly affect their operations.
- Look for opportunities to introduce parallel test preparation and execution across independent partitions. This will save overall time. You need to bring these events together, however, as part of integration planning.
- Raise any potential schedule conflicts and risks with project management as soon as you identify them. The test schedule is dependent on the Resolution tasks meeting their schedules. Identify where delays in Resolution results could cause the most impact.

6.1.3 Task: Acquire Human Resources for Testing

You have estimated the scope of the testing phases (planning and execution), and are now ready to identify the number and type of staff positions you need. You also need to identify the specific staff members who will fill these positions.

You do not need to use the same people, or even the same number of people, throughout test staffing activities. There are three primary test staffing phases you need to address: information gathering, test description writing, and test execution.

Information Gathering

You now know how many partitions, integration tests, bridges, and deployments you will be responsible for testing. You should also know what each test area addresses from a user point of view (for example, payroll, tax reporting, inventory). At this point, you need knowledgeable people with both test and applications background to:

- Identify specific test cases for each formal test
- Identify test data for each test
- Help define and plan test facility requirements
- Research and select test support tools

The staff for these activities must be self-starters who can be relied on to work with minimal direction and monitoring, and who know when to coordinate and report their findings. Depending on the schedule and number and complexity of the formal tests, this group can consist of as few as two or as many as six people. These people will also be contacting the developers and the users to better understand the functions and critical Year 2000 changes in each partition.

Test Description Writing

Each partition and integration test will have a corresponding Test Description and Data deliverable. These documents describe the overall execution and plan for the test, break down each test into a set of test cases (usually 10 to 20 of them), and include the step-by-step test procedures needed to address all required functionality covered by the test case. This activity takes a lot of effort and time, and you will probably need to add staff for it. Before they can write procedures, the writers have to work with the developers to determine what has been changed, use the system to understand how to test it, and/or review user documentation to determine all of the specifics to include in the procedures.

These people should have the following skills:

- They should write clearly.
- They should work well with both technical and nontechnical people (that is, developers and users).
- They should be able to take a detailed and orderly approach to a problem and break down activities into their individual steps.
- They should be able to work independently on relatively well-defined tasks.

The number of people needed for this effort depends on the size of the project. Also, the people who participated in information gathering may participate in these writing tasks. However, for a large project it is best for your initial test staff to oversee the test procedure writing and to act as coordinators as the overall project progresses. If you need new people, determine how many tests need to be written and whether the schedule permits the same people to complete work on one test procedure and then move on to another test. If there can be little or no overlap, you need to bring on more people. A manageable guideline is two to five writers per test.

Test Execution

At this point, planning for a specific test is complete and you are ready to see whether the applications meet the requirements. When a test is actually executed, you need more than just the person following the procedures. Each test should have the following participants:

- **Reader**: Someone should read the procedures and check that each step/activity has been completed. This person will also annotate the procedures to note any change in what was typed.
- **Workstation user**: This person actually does what the procedures say to do.
- **User representative**: This person indicates whether what happened meets the acceptance criteria—that is, whether things pass the test. The user representative signs off for each test and agrees to the wording of any problem description.
- **QA**: The QA representative certifies that the test was executed in compliance with the approved test plan. QA usually also keeps the official log of start/stop times, test deviations, and problems.

- **Test manager**: The test manager makes sure that everything is ready for the test, resolves any issues that arise during the test, and ensures that all participants do what is expected of them.

Most of these people are not part of the test staff, but you need to identify their participation as part of the costs for each formal test. Another staffing issue is how much concurrency is planned into the test. When this is required, each position needs a reader, workstation user, user representative, and QA person.

It is best that at least the reader is a member of the test team, and that this person has participated in writing the test procedures. This makes it easier to resolve any questions and/or problems that come up during testing. You can reduce staffing if the workstation user and user representative are the same person. Otherwise, the workstation user should also be a member of the test team. Quality assurance is independent.

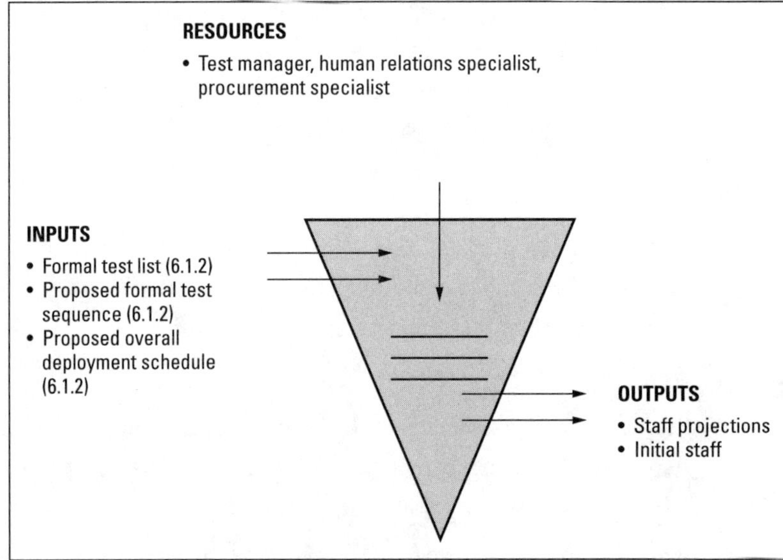
RESOURCES
• Test manager, human relations specialist, procurement specialist
INPUTS
• Formal test list (6.1.2)
• Proposed formal test sequence (6.1.2)
• Proposed overall deployment schedule (6.1.2)
OUTPUTS
• Staff projections
• Initial staff

Task Guidelines

- Take into account the overall schedule and availability of people when deciding how precise you need to be. Many test executions might be a year away, and the schedule and even sequence are likely to change by then. Place more emphasis on the short-term rather than the long-term estimates.

- Test Planning always takes more work than expected. Allow for changes in the overall Year 2000 project schedule.
- Expect to have to make staffing estimate and schedule changes, and thus look for ways to build flexibility into your plan.

6.1.4 Task: Define Top-Level Test Cases

This task applies to each formal test (partition, integration, deployment). Its purpose is to break down each test into its test cases. (A *test case* is a logical, functional portion of a test.) The scope of a test case depends on how big the overall function is, how much needs to be tested, and how many test cases it makes sense to manage. Test cases may also be based on functional areas which were changed. For example, if the system to be tested includes a main menu, you might define one or more test cases to each menu item.

Before you can define test cases, however, you need to make test assignments. Make these decisions based on staff members' backgrounds and familiarity with the areas covered in each partition and the overall schedule. Although you can prepare a draft of assignments, the final decision will involve group discussions.

Once tests are assigned, follow this approach to define their test cases:

- Do partition-level test case definitions first. Integration and deployment test cases will start with these.
- Work on the partitions that you need first. You will probably be doing this task either late in Detailed Assessment or early in the correction stage, so you should not be pressed for time yet. Unless you only have one or two partitions, you cannot do them all at once.
- Find out from the assessment team what is to be changed in the partition. Also, review the screens and other user-oriented information obtained during Inventory.
- Review user manuals and/or talk to the users to determine how the partition function breaks down into distinct areas.
- Come up with a draft set of 10 to 20 test cases. Each should have at least a few descriptive paragraphs describing what the function does and identifying what the test case will cover. Have an internal test group review the test case before showing it to users or the assessment team.
- Get comments from the users and assessment team and make necessary revisions.

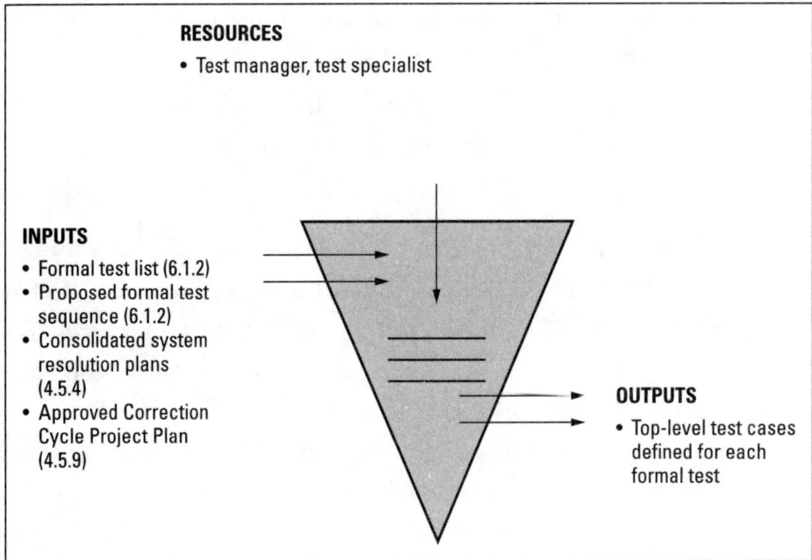
RESOURCES
• Test manager, test specialist
INPUTS
• Formal test list (6.1.2)
• Proposed formal test sequence (6.1.2)
• Consolidated system resolution plans (4.5.4)
• Approved Correction Cycle Project Plan (4.5.9)
OUTPUTS
• Top-level test cases defined for each formal test

Task Guidelines

- Ideally, the test team member who defines a test event's test cases will also write the formal test plan.
- This is a preliminary plan. Your objective at this point is to get approval for the overall formal testing sequence and content, and to get a handle on how much work needs to be done and in what time frame.

6.1.5 Task: Define Top-Level Test Data

Each formal test requires its own test data. Although this is identified as a separate task, it is done in conjunction with defining the test cases for a formal test. The two efforts will probably drive each other. They are separated because they are used differently and by different people as Test Planning progresses. Test cases are used by the test staff to help them write procedures. Test data is frequently prepared/gathered by development staff or users at the test team's direction.

The test data definition will include

- A list of the specific databases and files that will be read from, modified, and/or updated during the test.
- Specifics of the data characteristics in the databases and files.

- Identification of special test data (that is, data that does not normally exist in the partition being tested) that will need to be created. For example, such data may be needed because of a bridge that will be used in testing the partition.

Hopefully, there will be overlap between the data needed for different partitions, and there certainly will be overlap between data used for partition testing and data used for testing associated with integrating two partitions.

Keep in mind that this is really a top-level effort. Your main focus must be to look for any long lead time/custom data needs that have to be addressed early in the process.

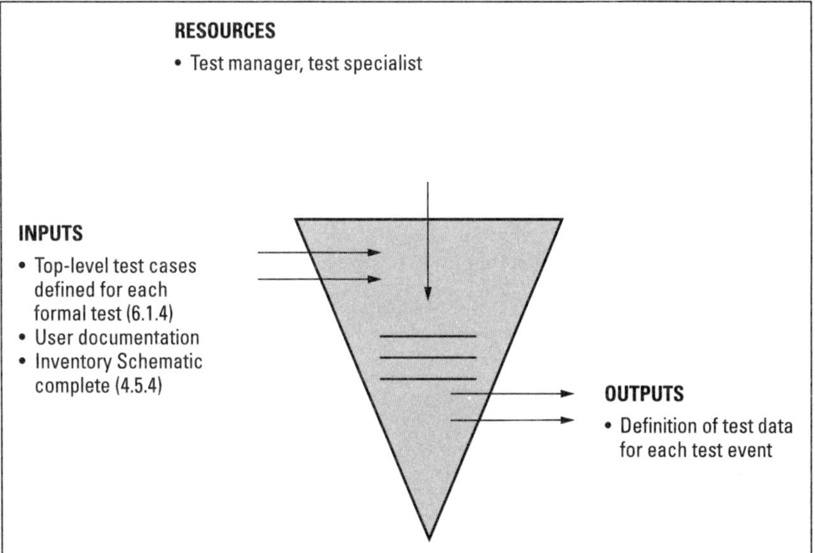
RESOURCES
• Test manager, test specialist
INPUTS
• Top-level test cases defined for each formal test (6.1.4)
• User documentation
• Inventory Schematic complete (4.5.4)
OUTPUTS
• Definition of test data for each test event

Task Guidelines

- The person who defines the test cases for a test should also do the data definition. However, when different people are defining test data for partitions that will be integrated, they should coordinate as they work on related data definitions.
- Make notes about required data while test cases are being defined.
- At this point, do not worry about a consistent level of detail. If you know more about some files or databases than others, write everything down. Eventually (that is, when you are writing the formal Test Description and Data deliverable) you will need to provide full, detailed data specifications.

6.1.6 Task: Establish Test Phases Tracking

Using the schedule and progress measurement requirements set forth in the Initial Project Plan, schedule specific phase milestones, measurement points, and progress review meetings. Use these meetings to compare actual work accomplished against planned work progress, effort, sizing, resource utilization, and risk reduction. If your organization has standard test preparation metrics, you may want to incorporate them into your tracking plans. Address discrepancies by reallocating appropriate resources. In addition, make sure to get feedback so planning for future phases accommodates the lessons learned.

The milestones and review requirements established here will be used during both Test Planning and Test Execution.

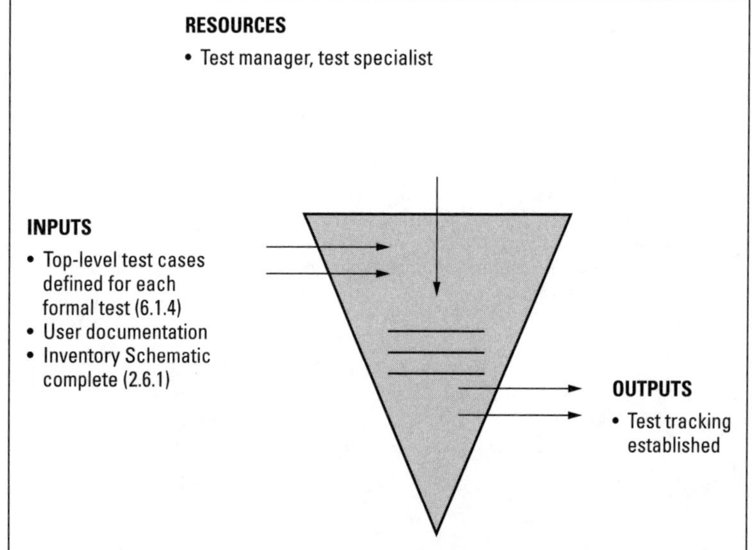
RESOURCES
• Test manager, test specialist
INPUTS
• Top-level test cases defined for each formal test (6.1.4)
• User documentation
• Inventory Schematic complete (2.6.1)
OUTPUTS
• Test tracking established

6.1.7 Task: Present and Approve Formal Test Plan

You now have all the information you need to prepare and present the Formal Test Plan and obtain approval for it.

This plan needs to include

- A schedule showing what will be tested (partitions, integration tests, deployments) and when.

- Test cases and data requirements for each test. For each test case, at least one paragraph should describe what is to be covered and what files and databases are to be used.
- Documentation of known requirements for each file and database.
- A list of assumptions associated with the plan. These assumptions should be tracked as the test cases and data are defined for each formal test.
- A list of risks associated with the plan. Like the assumptions, these risks should be tracked as the test cases and data are defined for each formal test.
- A list of contributors. If appropriate, you may want to identify the key organizations and/or people who were contacted for input to the document. This list could prove useful to the reviewers wondering whether something is correct. It indicates whom they should ask about the contents of your plan before they respond.
- Reviewers. Schedule a peer-level technical review of the plan, as well as a management review for budget and resource use approval.

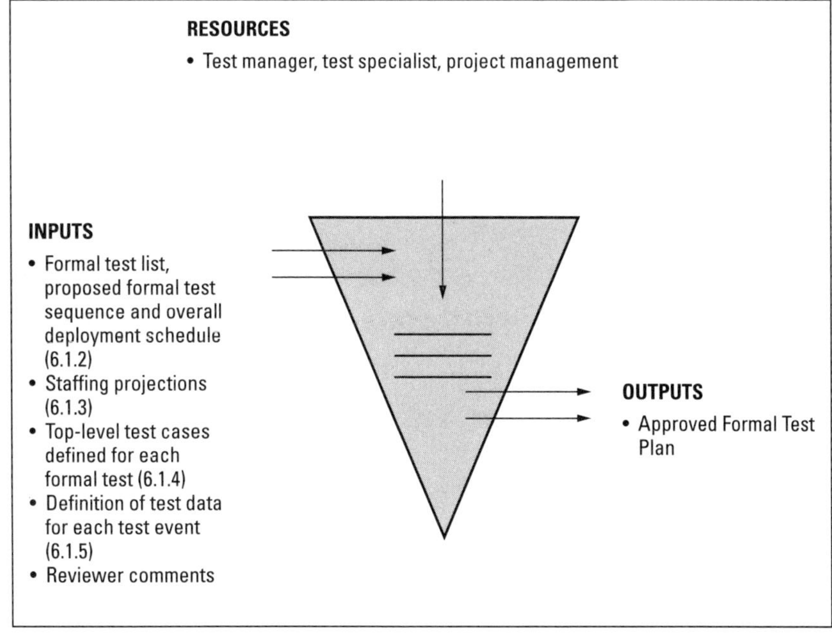
RESOURCES
• Test manager, test specialist, project management
INPUTS
• Formal test list, proposed formal test sequence and overall deployment schedule (6.1.2)
• Staffing projections (6.1.3)
• Top-level test cases defined for each formal test (6.1.4)
• Definition of test data for each test event (6.1.5)
• Reviewer comments
OUTPUTS
• Approved Formal Test Plan

Task Guidelines

- If possible, have the person with the most knowledge about an area respond to a question/comment about it. (For example, the person who defined the test cases should address any questions about how they are organized.) The test manager should officially respond to any issues in questions.
- Quality assurance will review the formal test plan for compliance to your organization's and project's plans, standards, and procedures, and will track deviations until closure or approval by project management.

Test Planning and Execution Phase Startup complete. Quality assurance verifies that the deliverable conforms to its intended goal. Project control baselines the deliverable and updates tracking metrics.

6.2 Test Facility Environment Report

Now that you have a general idea of your formal testing needs, you need to determine where you can execute these tests.

Both in-house and vendor Resolution staff have their own development environments for unit and system testing. These may or may not be where you should run your formal tests. The same applies to Deployment testing, which is accomplished in an operational environment.

Formal testing needs its own environment, and the test team is responsible for defining it and making sure it can be established. This deliverable supports the successful completion of these tasks.

Task Overview

- Identify Test Environment Requirements
- Identify Existing Test Environments
- Identify Alternative Test Locations
- Present and Approve Test Facility Environment Report

6.2.1 Task: Identify Test Environment Requirements

You need to devise a list of attributes that the test environment should have. You should determine the environment requirements of each formal test independently, since each test will be independent. Some requirements will be common to all test environments, but others will be needed only for a specific test or set of tests. For example, all the test environments may need user workstations and printers, but only some may need to exchange messages and/or files with a specific electronic partner. You will use these requirements to evaluate potential environments and select one for each test. In some cases, you can use the same system environment for several partition and integration tests. In other cases (for example, where systems are different), each partition may need its own environment.

Configuration management can help you define test environment requirements.

Some requirements are really "musts" (for example, you really need a specific UNIX system since that is what the software runs on), but some may be "would be nice." A "would be nice" might be an environment where only that partition, its data, and its bridges are resident. In most cases, you can get these by sharing the system with other software and data.

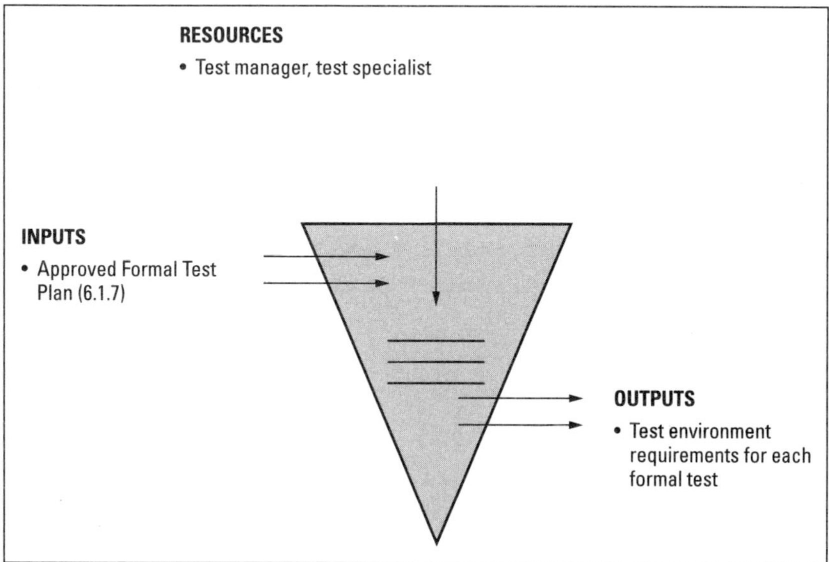
RESOURCES
• Test manager, test specialist
INPUTS
• Approved Formal Test Plan (6.1.7)
OUTPUTS
• Test environment requirements for each formal test

Task Guidelines

- Each member of the test team should define the environment requirements for the tests they worked on.
- The starting point for this specification is the operational environment of the partition. You can obtain this information by contacting operational support and the users.
- As information is gathered, team members working on requirements for similar systems should see what they have in common. If possible, it is better to reuse a given environment (maybe with minor changes) for multiple tests. Sharing information will also result in a more thorough list of requirements.
- All team members who worked on the partitions comprising integration tests should discuss the environment needs for such tests.
- After the environment requirements have been defined individually, the test team should perform a peer review, make revisions and clarifications, and prepare an internal document.

6.2.2 Task: Identify Existing Test Environments

The development groups (that is, the in-house staff who will be making Year 2000 changes) and any vendors (those responsible for updating systems in your organization to comply with Year 2000 standards) will test their areas before they turn a partition over to you. The environments they use could well satisfy your formal test requirements. This would be the ideal, but only if it meets the criteria. Often developers are not as formal in their testing as you will need to be.

Configuration management can help you identify successful testing environments.

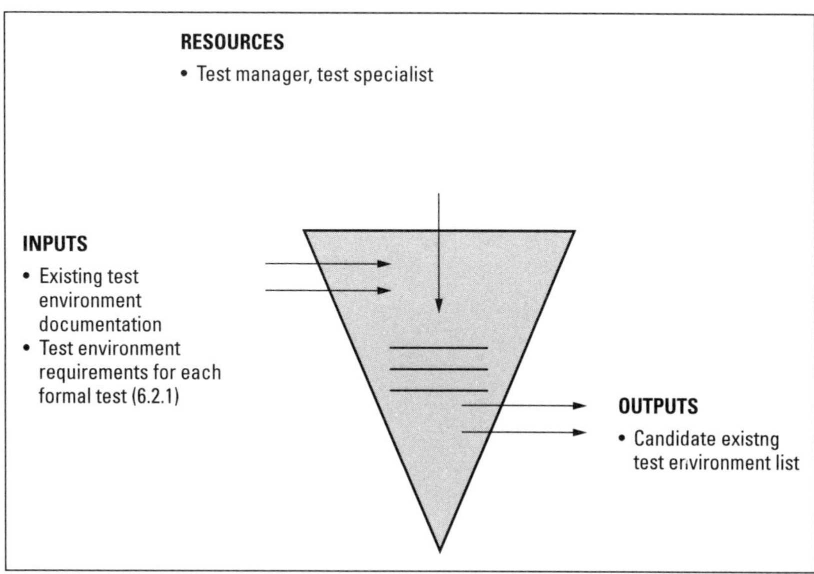
RESOURCES
• Test manager, test specialist
INPUTS
• Existing test environment documentation
• Test environment requirements for each formal test (6.2.1)
OUTPUTS
• Candidate existng test environment list

Task Guidelines

- These tasks can either be assigned to the same person who has been working on a test or assigned by system. This will depend on how similar the test environments are and what other things your staff is working on.
- Compare the formal test requirements with the test environments used by the developers, and evaluate the differences.
- For each test, determine whether an existing environment meets the requirements. If one does, document the assumptions for this determination. If not, pick the environment that comes closest to meeting the needs, and document what is not met and/or what would need to change to satisfy the requirements.
- Make sure that the environment is not needed for concurrent development work. Once a configuration is set up for formal testing, you do not want the developers using it until the test is completed.
- Again, share information among the team and perform peer review. For reviews, bring all team members together, even those not participating in this task directly.

6.2.3 Task: Identify Alternative Test Locations

You may not have found an existing test environment to satisfy each formal test. If so, you need to investigate where to obtain these other environments and estimate the cost and resources needed to make use of them.

If the existing test environments do not satisfy your needs, you will have to look elsewhere for solutions. Developers usually focus on a single system, maybe even a single application or language. Once you need to address integration tests, more than one system may be involved. Developers usually do not have a test environment that incorporates more than one system. Different organizations may even be involved.

There are three primary categories of alternative test locations, listed from most to least preferable:

- **Your disaster/recovery site**: This may or may not be viable. If it can be contracted for and configured to match your operational setup, it may work. However, if it belongs to another company that will let you use their system for a limited time in the event of a real disaster (as is frequently the case, usually as a mutual agreement to support them in a similar need), they may not want to disrupt their operations so you can do testing. It is worth investigating, however.
- **Your operational system**: If there are periods of time when the system is not used (for example, nights or weekends) and the tests can be scheduled for these times, you could load the test data and software, run the test, and then restore the operational environment. Of course, any time you need to offload/reload an operational environment, you run the risk of not getting things back in order on time. Each operation is different, however, and if this is your only practical option (for example, anything else costs lots of money), it may work.
- **Rental space**: Just as there are companies that provide disaster/recovery "warm sites" for customers, sometimes companies provide an environment that meets your needs and that you can rent to run your tests. This is the least desirable choice (it's costly and is least likely to really match operations).

Consult with configuration management to ensure that alternative test locations support CM standards.

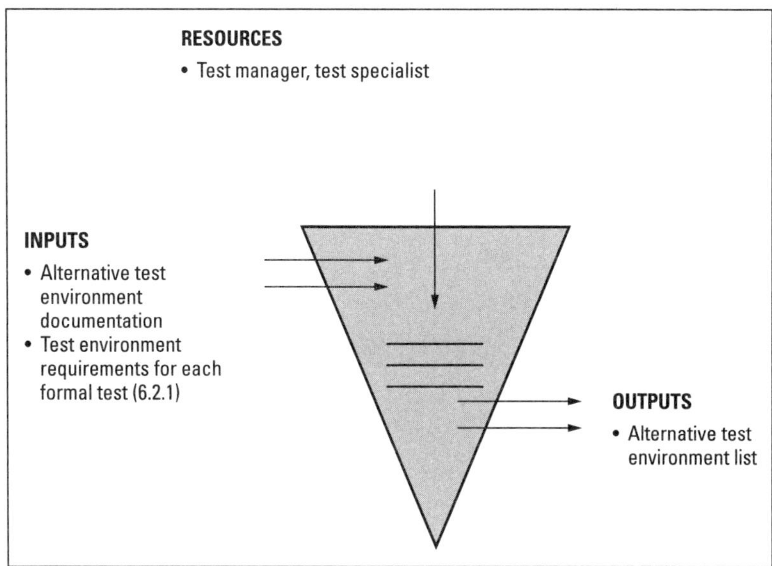
RESOURCES
• Test manager, test specialist
INPUTS
• Alternative test environment documentation
• Test environment requirements for each formal test (6.2.1)
OUTPUTS
• Alternative test environment list

Task Guideline

- There is no need to investigate all the options unless you believe the chosen solution may be withdrawn.

6.2.4 Task: Present and Approve Test Facility Environment Report

In this task, you create a report containing all of the information your team has collected. As test manager, you outline the report and assign your staff to write selected sections. You assign a reviewer to the report and obtain approval to proceed with related planning.

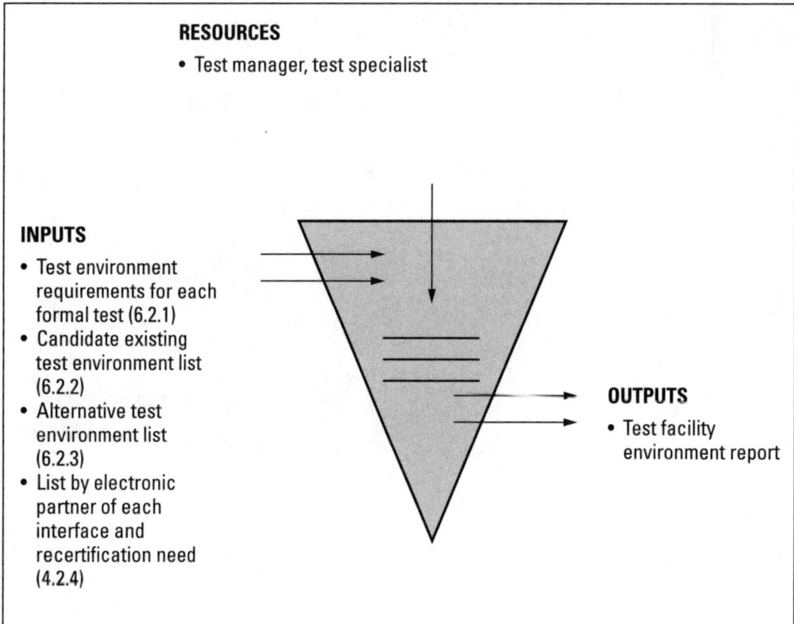

Task Guidelines

- After a given partition or integration environment has been defined (in-house or out of house), review it informally with the original contributors, the in-house contact for each electronic partnership, and a test team member who was not involved in gathering the information.
- Distribute the deliverable to the official list of reviewers, including quality assurance. Also distribute a copy to all other key people who provided information.
- Make appropriate revisions in response to comments. This becomes the working copy for detailed test planning.

Test Facility Environment Report complete. Quality assurance verifies that the deliverable conforms to its intended goal. Project control baselines the deliverable and updates tracking metrics.

6.3 Test Support Tool Requirements

You may need test support tools to initiate activity and/or to capture results.

Most of the tools you need for formal testing are the same as those required for development testing. For example, if an application is being changed to be compatible with an electronic partner, both the developers and formal testing need something to generate incoming (that is, from the partner) and accept outgoing (that is, to the partner) messages to test the interface. This kind of tool is a simulator, and it can be developed in-house.

Your analysis of test tools should try to take into account both developer testing and formal testing. If your formal testing needs a tool, development probably does too. However, although many tools used by the developers may be of use during formal testing, many will not. Developers have special needs that may not apply to formal testing (for example, for debugging, representing code not in place —that is, "stubs").

Task Overview

- Document Existing In-House Test Tools
- Identify Test Tool Requirements and Additional Tools Needed
- Identify Test Tool Sources
- Present and Approve Test Support Tool Requirements

6.3.1 Task: Document Existing In-House Test Tools

The software to be tested was previously tested and deployed. The Year 2000 effort is just correcting existing applications to make them Year 2000 compliant. Thus there is a reasonable chance that there are test tools in-house. You may not need all of them, but it's useful to identify them. They may even give you insight into what needs to be tested and how. These tools can help design the actual test procedures.

Tools will be test specific (partition or integration). For example, a tool that is needed to generate data from another partition will not be needed to test the integration of the partitions. Consider tools and their usefulness in terms of the overall project. This is part of what makes Year 2000 Test Planning different from other projects, even large ones, in which you have participated.

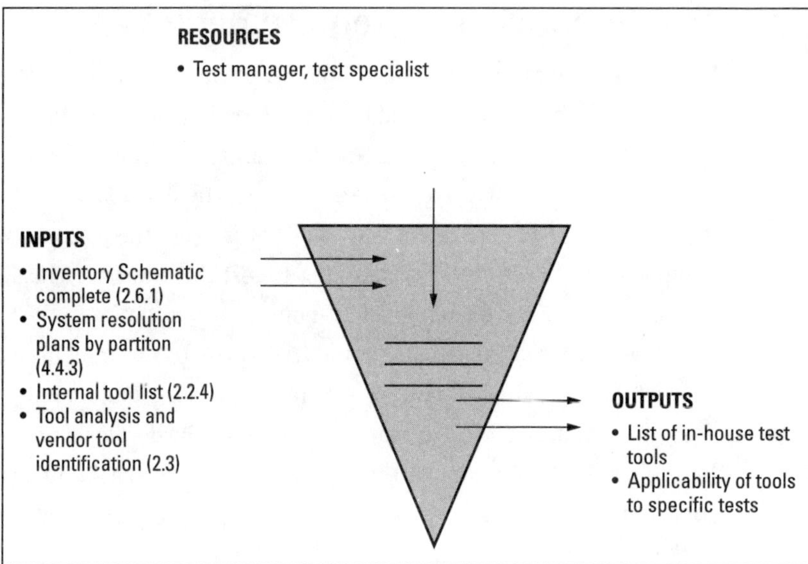

RESOURCES
• Test manager, test specialist
INPUTS
• Inventory Schematic complete (2.6.1)
• System resolution plans by partiton (4.4.3)
• Internal tool list (2.2.4)
• Tool analysis and vendor tool identification (2.3)
OUTPUTS
• List of in-house test tools
• Applicability of tools to specific tests

Task Guidelines

- You should organize tool documentation by system. Although some tools may be useful across systems, most will only apply to the system on which they operate.
- Distribute a questionnaire requesting information about in-house test tools that a development staff plans to use for its Year 2000 assignments. Solicit partition-specific information.
- Evaluate the test tools based on which specific tests each applies to. This mapping will be useful in preparing the test procedures.

6.3.2 Task: Identify Test Tool Requirements and Additional Tools Needed

Here you review the overall requirements of each test to identify where test tools are needed. Where an existing tool has not been identified for a specific requirement, describe the functions to be provided by the tool (for example, provide an interface with a specific application or electronic partner). Also describe what test benefits will be lost if the tool is not provided. This information gives you a basis for evaluating whether it is worth it to develop or purchase the tool.

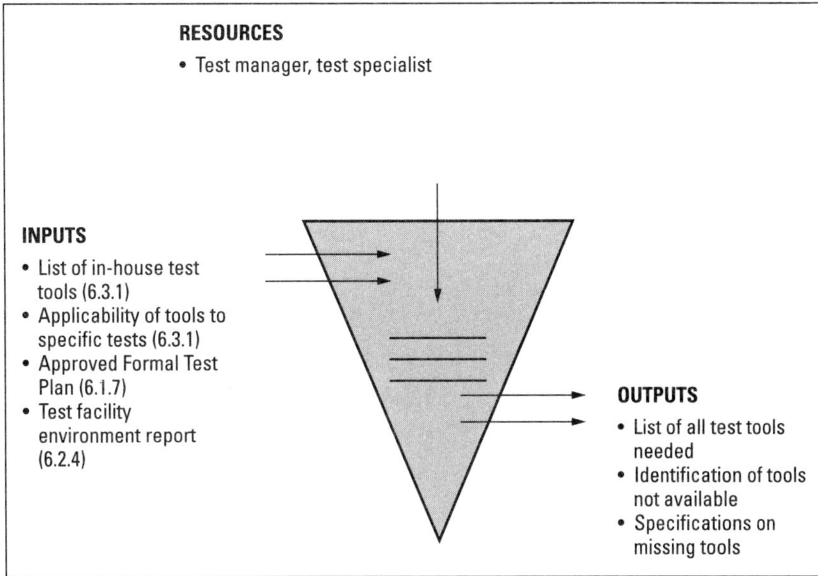

6.3.3 Task: Identify Test Tool Sources

You need to identify sources for tools that you have not been able to locate. There are two approaches to doing so:

- Distribute descriptions of additional test tools to the developers and solicit their comments. Some tools might exist or already be planned. Once a tool is identified, the developer may decide that it is needed for unit testing and is something that is easy (and necessary) to prepare in-house. In both these cases, the issue is resolved, and you do not need to do anything further except to document the resolution.
- For the remaining test tools with no in-house solution, you need to investigate available vendor tools. You can send for information on the applicable tools, including prices and availability. You may want to review the information with your developers. As mentioned, almost any tool that will be of use for formal testing should be of use for the developers.

Recommend a vendor test tool to fulfill testing tool needs where an in-house tool is not available or scheduled for development.

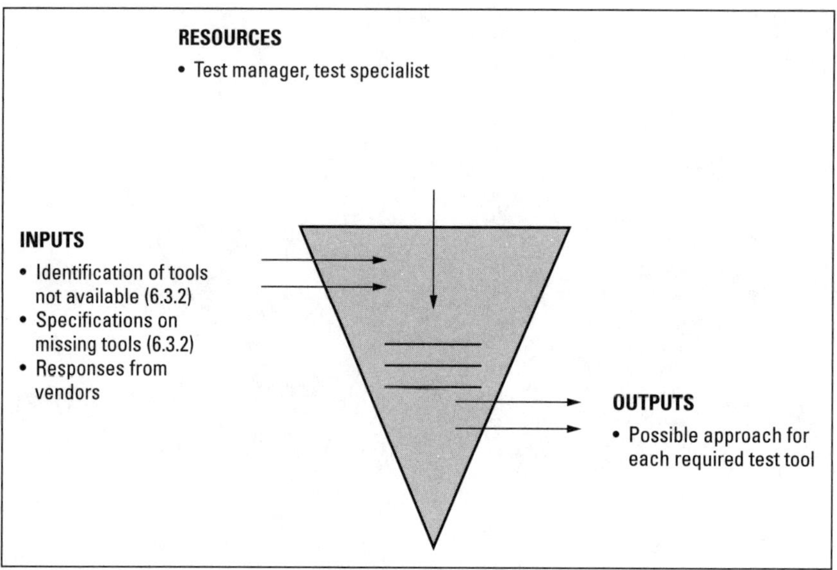

6.3.4 Task: Present and Approve Test Support Tool Requirements

This deliverable is primarily a matrix of each test (partition or integration), the test tools needed, a brief description of the purpose of the tool, and the source for the tool. Where the tool is not expected to be provided in-house (that is, it exists or is scheduled to be developed), you will provide further information, such as:

- The risk involved in not having the tool
- A recommended source for the tool
- Cost and lead time involved in procuring the tool

Quality assurance will review the requirements deliverable to verify that the matrix is complete and consistent with the requirements.

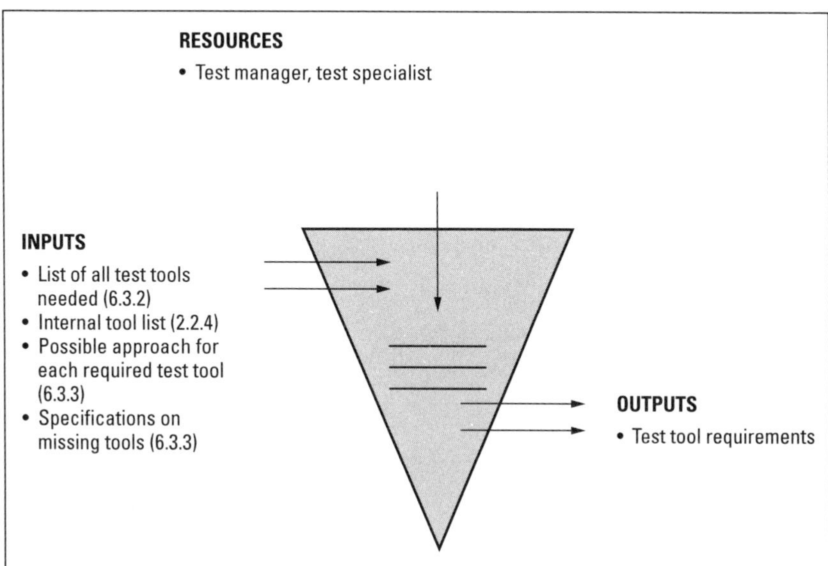

milestone 

Test Support Tool Requirements complete. Quality assurance verifies that the deliverable conforms to its intended goal. Project control baselines the deliverable and updates tracking metrics.

6.4 Electronic Partnership Test Plan

Earlier you defined all electronic partnership interfaces that must be tested and what is involved in each certification process. It is now time to determine exactly what happens during each certification test.

You need to prepare a separate Electronic Partnership Test Plan for each electronic partnership, and each is a stand-alone document. Each certification will be executed independently and possibly by different people.

Task Overview

- Prepare Electronic Partnership Test Plans
- Present and Approve Electronic Partnership Test Plans

6.4.1 Task: Prepare Electronic Partnership Test Plans

Each electronic partnership interface must be formally tested (that is, certified). In some cases, you will need to plan for two certifications for such an interface:

- Each partnership will require a certification test of the revised, in-house Year 2000 compatible software operating with the electronic partnership's Year 2000 compatible software. Both sides of the interface are thought to be Year 2000 certified going into the test.
- For some partnership interfaces, one end of the interface is upgraded and online before the other. In this case, you need a bridge to make data conversions on the fly so the two systems can continue operating together. Each sends and receives data in its current format. It doesn't matter whether your system or the partner has converted first. The bridge is always your responsibility to develop. As a safety factor, you should test that the bridge to an electronic partner operates as required; get it certified.

There is a unique aspect of electronic partnership certification planning: The detailed procedures are essentially the same, whether or not you do them as part of partition, integration, or deployment testing. The only differences to the plan have to do with test data and the environment used.

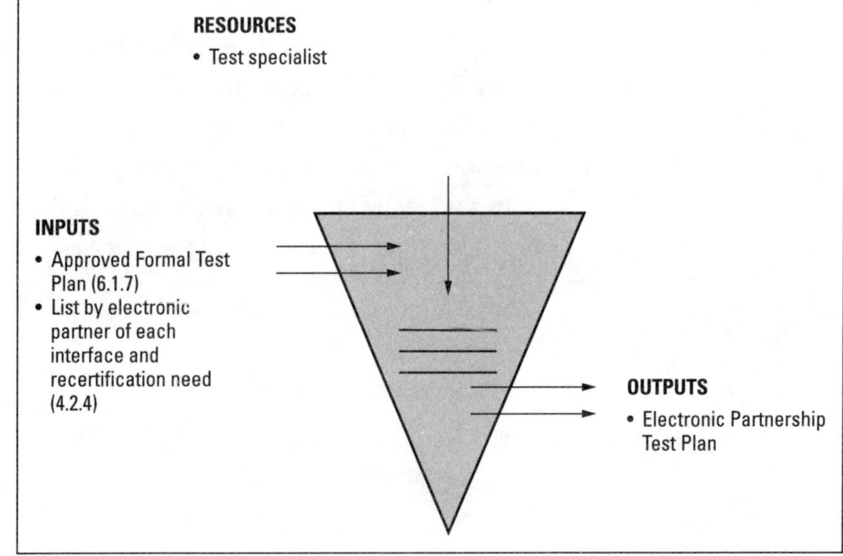

Task Guidelines

- To the extent possible, assign the team member who researched the interface's certification requirements to prepare the test plan. (See Test Facility Environments Report.)
- Review the previous certification plan and test report.
- Address all certification events (that is, partition, integration, deployment) for a given electronic partnership interface in the same test plan. Indicate the specifics for each event in the appropriate section.
- Base the plan on performing a separate partition/integration test before the actual certification test. As much as possible, all problems with your side of the electronic interface should be resolved before any online test with the electronic partner.
- Determine whether the plan to certify a bridge can be included in its comparable Electronic Partnership Test Plan. In general, this is a good thing to do, because the detailed procedures are the same; just the environment and test data are different. It keeps everything together, simplifies the review and correction cycle, and helps ensure that you use a consistent approach.
- Do an informal review of the test plan with the in-house contact person for the partnership. Also, if possible, go over what you have prepared with the partnership's representative, either informally by phone or by sending a draft.
- Perform a peer review before the formal review.
- Have quality assurance review the test plan for compliance to the organization's and project's plans, standards, and procedures; and track deviations until closure or approval by project management.

6.4.2 Task: Present and Approve Electronic Partnership Test Plans

After you prepare the individual Electronic Partnership Test Plans, you should present these plans to appropriate managers and gain approval for their implementation. Make sure the affected system users participate in these presentations.

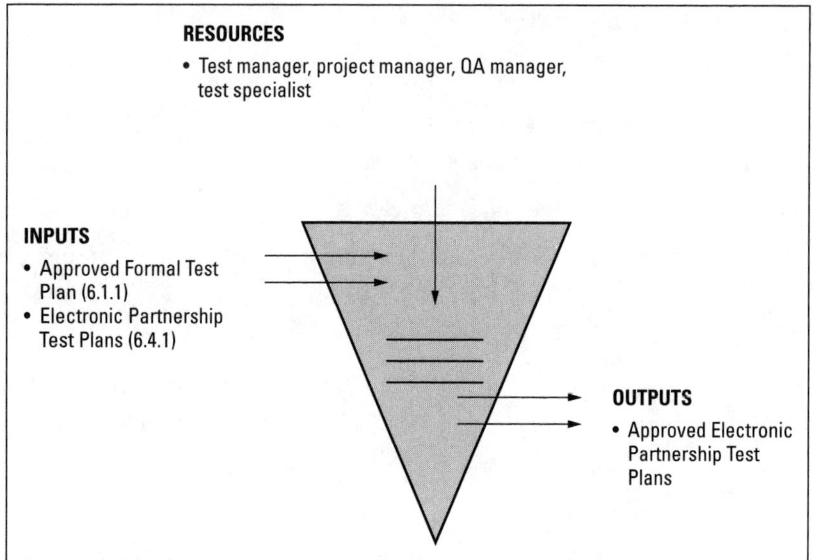

Electronic Partnership Test Plan complete. Quality assurance verifies that the deliverable conforms to its intended goal. Project control baselines the deliverable and updates tracking metrics.

6.5 Partition Test Description and Data

This deliverable provides all of the detailed information required to execute a formal partition test. You prepare a separate test plan for each partition. These plans are prepared in parallel with Year 2000 Resolution tasks. To a large extent, the success of the Year 2000 compliance effort depends upon the thoroughness of each partition test.

After they are drafted, these test plans are reviewed and approved by key managers (IS and user) to ensure that they fulfill their purpose of confirming Year 2000 compliance.

Each partition document includes:

- A brief description of the partition's function and system user community.
- A schematic of the test's hardware environment, including workstations, printers, and electronic partnership interfaces.
- A list of the application files, databases, and software (including COTS) that must be in place at the start of the test, indicating which ones have been

modified for Year 2000 compliance. The list should also indicate where each is to be installed.

- A list of all bridges, simulators, and other nonapplication hardware and software needed to support the test.
- A functional list of the people who will participate in the test (for example, QA, user, test engineers) and the role of each.
- The assumptions concerning the test.
- The format to be followed for test execution (for example, what to do if a problem occurs, how to change the procedures as appropriate).
- The actual detailed test procedures (that is, step-by-step instructions) for each test case. This is by far the largest part of the document and is the most critical in terms of a successful test and future successful deployment.
- User acceptance criteria for deciding to deploy the entity being tested, and corresponding test cases and procedures to test whether these criteria are met. (The comparable sections need placeholders, but would only be filled in if applicable.)

Task Overview

- Define Testing Staff Assignments
- Tailor Existing Test Procedures
- Brief Test Staff
- Prepare Partition Test and Data Descriptions
- Verify/Dry Run Test Cases
- Present and Approve Partition Test and Data Descriptions

6.5.1 Task: Define Testing Staff Assignments

Now that you have a better understanding of the testing environment and the testing tools, you must review and revise the staffing assignments you developed earlier. You may need a larger or smaller test team to accommodate the test environment or various test tools.

Determine whether your current staff is sufficient to write all of the necessary test plans and to support Deployment planning. As part of this process, come up with a preliminary document preparation schedule and work assignment matrix. This matrix should include

- A description of each test plan
- The schedule for the preparation of each test plan
- A description of the personnel who will prepare each test plan

Once you have completed this scheduling and revised your estimate of people needs, provide it to those preparing (or updating) the corrections cycle schedule/budget for inclusion in the Corrections Cycle Project Plan. (See the Detailed Assessment phase.)

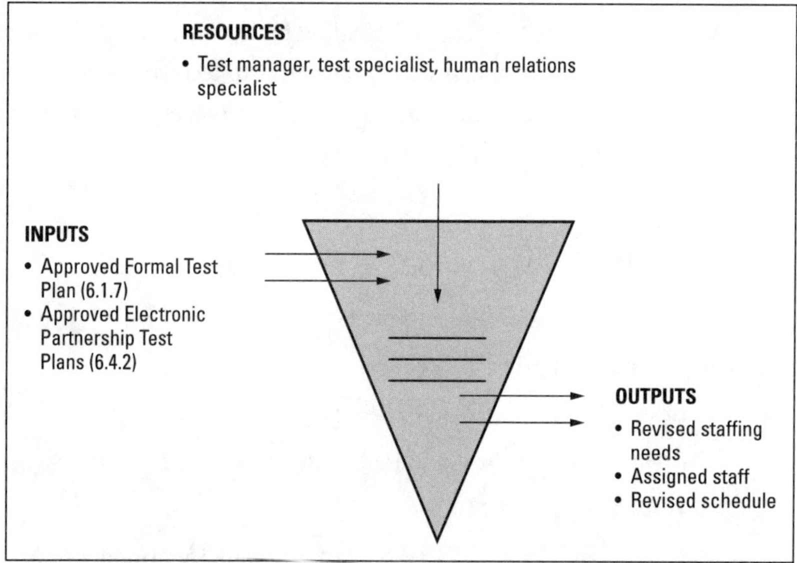

Task Guidelines

- Not all test plans need to be completed, or even worked on, simultaneously. Their preparation schedule should parallel the Resolution schedule, permitting more effective use of a smaller staff.
- Include the preparation of all test plans that you will need to prepare or participate in (partition, integration, deployment).

- Get input from your current staff as to how big an effort they think each plan will require.
- The people you request need good writing and people skills. They will work with the people doing the corrections and the users to determine what to test, and will then write up the steps required.
- Everyone (maybe with the exception of the test manager) should be involved in writing these test descriptions. The only exception is if the overall schedule is such that some people do Test Execution and no writing. However, this is not recommended.
- The responsibility for each test plan's completion (partition or integration) should be assigned to a specific person. Most likely, several people will work on it, but there should be one person doing reviews, making decisions, and answering questions if there are problems.

6.5.2 Task: Tailor Existing Test Procedures

Each organization has its own approved testing processes, and most likely an existing formal test document format. This is your starting point, and you need to tailor it to Year 2000 testing. If you do not have an existing format, make sure that the structure includes all the sections that need to be addressed and that they are presented in an orderly manner.

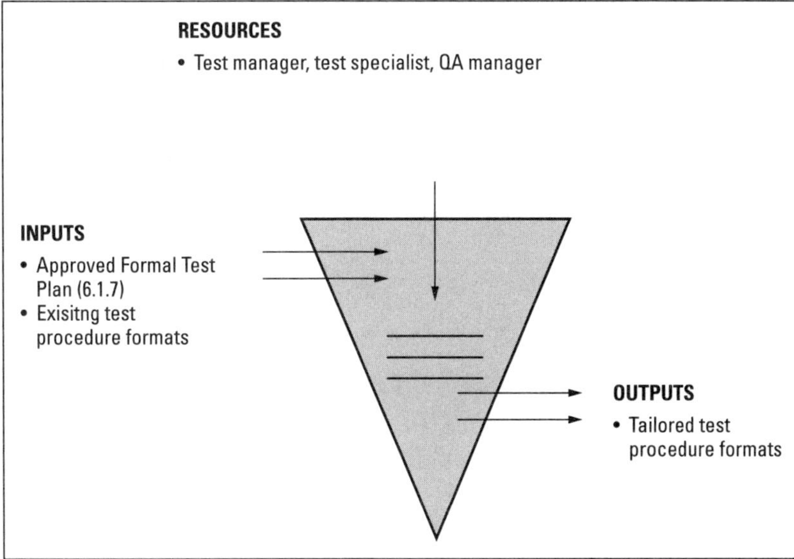

Task Guidelines

- Prepare a format for both partition and integration procedures. They do not have to be identical, but their overall structure and format should be the same.
- Check whether everything in the existing format is applicable.
- Determine what needs to be included but does not have a well-defined existing location (for example, specifying the use of bridges and electronic partnerships). Decide where to put these components.
- If you have made significant changes to an existing format, submit it for a peer, technical, or QA review to ensure that you are compliant with organization standards.
- Don't forget to include the specific Year 2000 Deployment and user acceptance criteria. Frequently, standard procedures will not require this, but each set of procedures must include these.

6.5.3 Task: Brief Test Staff

You are now ready to brief your test team about test details. You should hold a kickoff meeting for the entire test staff so that everyone can have the same understanding of:

- The Year 2000 problem
- The overall correction and test schedule
- The testing process to be followed
- The format of test documents
- The responsibilities of each person
- Appropriate guidelines and suggestions

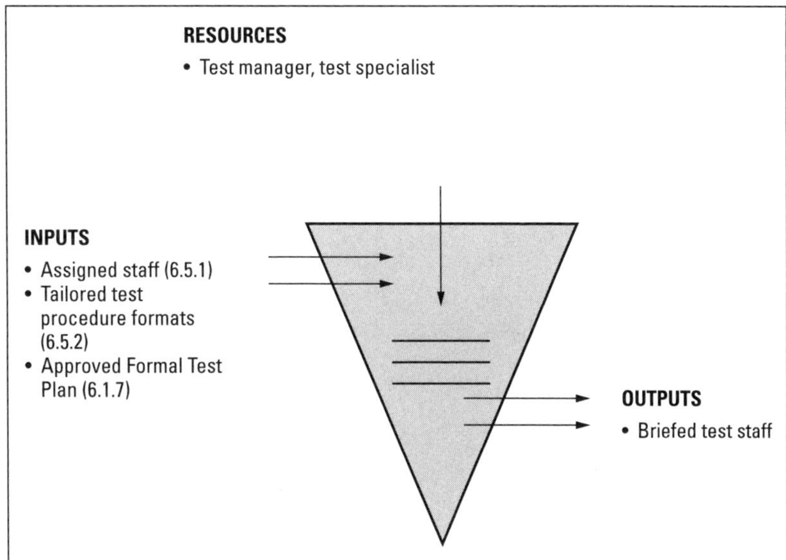

6.5.4 Task: Prepare Partition Test and Data Descriptions

Preparing partition test and data descriptions can be quite time-consuming. Year 2000 project testing differs considerably from development testing in that:

- Almost every software system, application, and interface will be changed over a relatively short time frame.
- The need for a timely deployment is more critical than usual. If a problem is not found until Deployment or, even worse, until the partition is operational, you may not be able to do a rollback. The earlier version may no longer be viable for the other partitions that are in place.
- The upgrading of this partition probably did not start with a stated set of functional requirements that had to be met. The requirements focused on the Year 2000 problem, not on what the partition does.

This task describes how to tailor your existing formal test planning processes to the Year 2000 problem.

Define Requirements

Derive a list of specific requirements/functions to be tested for each top-level test case. You should not and cannot write a test plan without knowing the requirements against which it is to be executed; this is the only way to know when you

are finished writing and have covered everything. More than likely it will be your responsibility to do this:

- Use lots of documents relating to your partition, all of which already exist: the Year 2000 compliance definition, the test cases, the Inventory Schematic, the correction plan (including a list of files/databases to be converted), and related user manuals.
- Starting with the test cases, write down functional areas that may involve dates. Use screens and batch jobs identified in the user manuals to help you.
- Make a list of test events (that is, specific things to try) for each functional area, making sure to cover all screens, reports, jobs, and interfaces that could involve dates (input, output, sorting, calculating, and so on). This comprises a first cut at what your test should address. Allocate each test event to a test case. If you cannot do this, you may need to add a test case.
- Make sure you consider a comprehensive range of dates in the partition test. This range includes dates falling before, during, and after the Year 2000 and leap year logic. Specific dates to be tested should include, but not be limited to: 31 December 1999; 01 January 2000; 28 February 2000 (leap year test); 1 March 2000 (leap year test); 31 December 2*xxx* (farthest date needed). In addition, test date range calculations and time/date roll-overs (both with the machine on and with it off). For some applications, day-of-the-week is also critical. If the Year 2000 solution approach involves using a base-date, you should also include high/low dates in the test cases.
- Have the key person responsible for your area's Year 2000 upgrades review what test events you have devised. This person should add any new fields and/or new functions, changed files/databases that your list does not address, and so on. The unit tests and lower-level integration tests may include events you should list but did not.
- Review unit test plans and code change documentation to help ensure that all modified code and data are tested.
- Have users also review your test event list. They know how it is really used. There may be special reports, database queries, scripts, and so on that support operations but that are not in the user manuals. If these items touch on Year 2000 changes, they should be considered.

- Work with the users to define major "threads" through the partition that relate to Year 2000 screens, files, databases, and reports. A *thread* is a logical sequence of actions that corresponds to an overall function. Very often formal tests make use of threads, since these correspond more closely to when and how a system is used. For example, if the partition includes contract support, a thread may start by recording a new contract, including its expiration date, making date-related modifications (for example, changing the expiration), and producing a report ordered by expiration date. These events are supported by different software modules, but all rely on the same information. Using threads tests if the system holds together.
- Make sure both the technical and user reviewers do not feel constrained by the defined test cases. You may end up changing them when you have gathered all of the requirements.

  After the reviews are completed, consolidate the events into a list of the requirements to be covered by the test plan. Provide this list to the people doing the upgrades. Their unit tests will, at a minimum, need to address these events.

Define Test Data

Once you know what you will be testing, you can define your test data. This includes the usual—files and databases to exist at the start; files created/deleted/changed; temporary files used (where appropriate); and the size, contents, and other required characteristics of the data. You have done this before, but there are several Year 2000-specific issues to consider:

- Data at the start of a test must include all appropriate dates to accommodate what you need to test.
- Your dates will be far in the future. Some partitions may only address relatively local dates, not years into the future (for example, payroll).
- Test data file dates as well as field content dates may not at all correspond to the system date. You will need lots of help from the developers.
- Some test events will require that the system date be set to 2000 or later (for example, when the system date is used to fill in a date field). *Do not try this on your own.* The operating system and/or other packages you need will probable expire and no longer work.

The partition's test plan should include the data required, who is responsible for developing it (that is, test team, implementers, users), and who will map the test cases or test events to the files. Test data may be one of your biggest problems for dry-running procedures. The developers will also have to set up test data for their unit tests. Coordinate your data requirements with the developers as you define these requirements. They may identify data you had not considered, in which case you will have to figure out where and how to include it and to add test events for it. The developers may also have left out data characteristics you included, and they will need to address them in their testing. This area requires a lot of cooperation.

Write the Test Steps

Although you have all written test steps before, there are special issues relating to this process. Each test event must explicitly state what Year 2000 related response to look for (for example, ascending-by-date lists should start with 00, not 99, and reports should have the correct century, based on entered data). Define your steps to make this clear.

Otherwise the writing process should seem familiar. You need to cover all requirements, make sure the steps are clear, and state success criteria.

Determine User Acceptance Criteria

If the partition is to be deployed without further integration with another partition, its formal test should include user signoff/acceptance activities. This can be similar to your standard process. However, because pervasive changes will have been made to an operational application and its data, you should obtain special user review and agreement of what is needed for acceptance.

If the users will not attend the entire formal test, you should add separate test cases that they will attend. These can repeat a subset of the other tests events, be entirely different, or substitute for test events that were planned for other test cases. The approach depends on your standard process, the schedule, and how critical the partition is. You do not need to follow the same approach for all partitions. In a large operation, different user groups prefer different involvement in the formal, predeployment testing.

The document should also include a section that addresses the criteria for the go/no-go decision regarding whether deployment should be initiated. In some cases, it is critical enough to get the partition into the operational environment that not all test events must be successful. For example, incorrect header information on printed reports might not stop deployment, but incorrect date-sort sequences might.

Write the Supporting Sections of the Document

Follow your standard format when you write the supporting sections of the document. Make sure to include all the remaining information identified at the start of this section someplace.

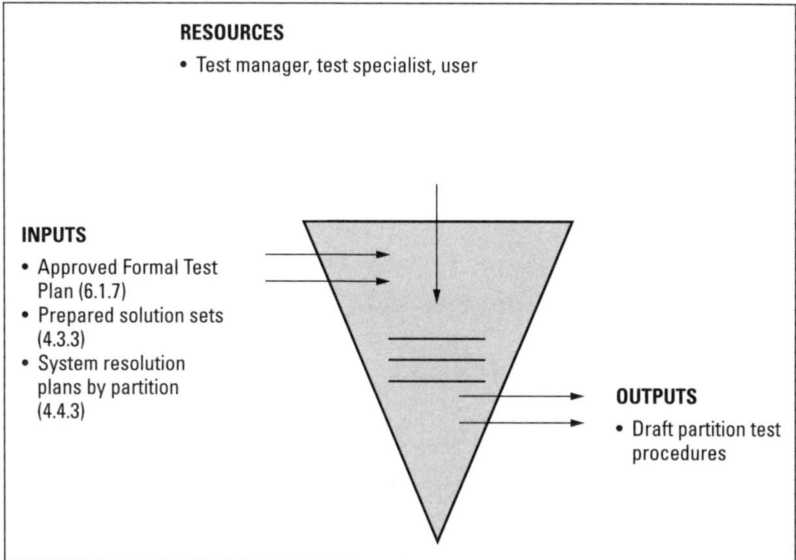

6.5.5 Task: Verify/Dry Run Test Cases

Test planners often use the system being developed/modified to ensure the completeness and accuracy of the test procedures. This validation will occur in Test Planning and will overlap system Resolution tasks. For this effort, you need an environment that includes updated Year 2000 software and files/databases and workstations, printers, or other devices.

At the early writing stages, there may not be many updated functions you can exercise, and whatever there is will probably be owned by the individual developers. You may be able to persuade them to let you try things out in their environment, or there may be a development partition where you can try out your procedures.

The best place to check out most of your steps is probably the operational system. The Year 2000 process should have minimal impact on the screens, functions, and reports of the existing application. Thus your test procedures should correspond to operational screens, data, and reports, and you should be able to use them to do most of your dry runs.

The important thing is to dry run in the development environment as soon as possible.

Of course, you must tailor how, and even if, this feedback effort can be accomplished, based on your internal processes and protocol. Also, if Resolution efforts are outsourced and the revised software is not readily available, these dry runs will have to be against the existing system, and procedures reflecting changes and/or additions will have to be based on change design documentation.

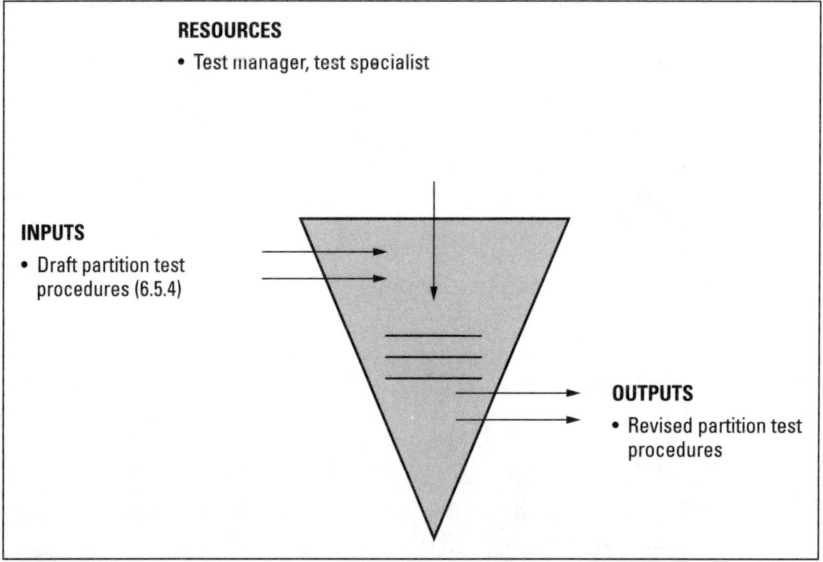

6.5.6 Task: Present and Approve Partition Test and Data Descriptions

This task covers the presentation and approval of the various partition test and data descriptions. These presentations should include any system users who may be affected by testing activities.

Test Execution for the partition can begin immediately after you complete this task.

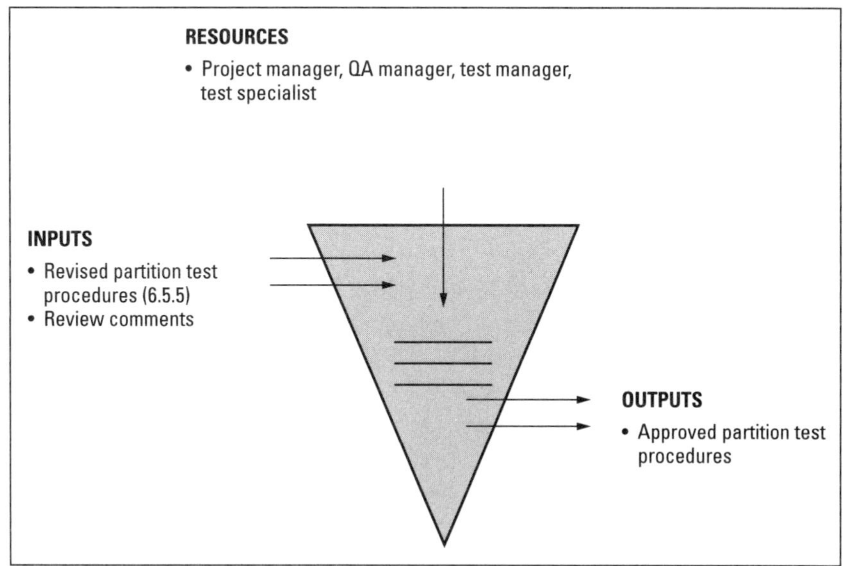

Task Guideline

- Perform peer and technical reviews before the formal presentation.

Partition Test Description and Data complete. Quality assurance verifies that the deliverable conforms to its intended goal. Project control baselines the deliverable and updates tracking metrics.

6.6 Integration Test Description and Data

This deliverable provides all of the information required to execute each formal integration test. Each integration test is based on the test plans for the partitions that are being integrated. There is a separate document for each test.

Refer to Prepare Partition Test and Data Descriptions (6.5.4) for help with the format and scope of this deliverable. Work on a particular integration test plan will usually not start until the test plans for the partitions it addresses have been drafted.

After a plan is drafted, it is reviewed and approved by key management (IS, user, and QA) to ensure that its execution confirms the Year 2000 compliance of the integrated entity.

Task Overview

- Prepare Integration Test and Data Descriptions
- Verify/Dry Run Test Cases
- Present and Approve Integration Test and Data Descriptions

6.6.1 Task: Prepare Integration Test and Data Descriptions

The methodology presented here is similar to that presented for individual partition test plans, but it includes specifics relating to integration testing. Review the material for partitions before reading what follows.

Define Requirements

The list of requirements to be covered in a specific integration test plan will include some from each partition being integrated and new ones that test date-related interfaces and functional threads across the partitions:

- Update the test cases previously defined for the test to reflect what finally was included in the related partition test plans. In general, there will be an integration test case for each test case in each of the partitions. There will also be integration-specific test cases to exercise functions that cross partitions. If previously integrated partitions are your starting point, start with their test plans. Build in what will have been tested and is now being integrated.
- Review the requirements allocated to each test case from the completed plans. Select a subset of these requirements touching on all or most functions supported by the partition (or previously integrated partitions). Make needed modifications to what the event is and/or what success the event is to include in the broader, integrated test entity.
- For the new test cases, define requirements for functions that operate across partitions. For example, if one partition produces reports that use data entered in another, a new requirement would be to update the database and see whether it is reflected correctly in the specific report.
- Have the key person responsible for your area's Year 2000 upgrades review what test events you have devised. This person should add items relating to the interface. The developer's own integration tests may include events you should have listed but did not.

- Have users also review your test events list. They know how it is really used. There may be special reports, database queries, scripts, and so on that support operations but that are not in the user manuals. If these items touch on Year 2000 changes, they should be considered.
- Work with the users to define major threads across the partitions that relate to Year 2000 screens, files, databases, and reports. Then test whether things have been integrated properly.
- As in the partition test plans, make sure that both the technical and user reviewers do not feel constrained by the defined test cases.

After the reviews are completed, consolidate the events into a list of the requirements to be covered by the test plan, grouped by test case. Provide this list to the people doing the upgrades. Their unit tests should address these events.

Define Test Data

Once you know what you will be testing, you can define your integration test data. For the most part, the files and databases will be the same as those defined for the individual partitions. The biggest change will be that one of the partitions may have been using nonconverted data, with a bridge between the software and database. This is frequently needed if the database is shared among many partitions and only one or a few have been Year 2000 updated. With the integration, the bridge to the database may be removed. You will account for this in your data. You may also need to include more extensive or new requirements to address this issue. This aspect of integration planning means that data and requirements definitions need to be closely coordinated.

Like the partition test plans, the integration plan should include what data is required, who is responsible for developing it (that is, test team, implementers, users), and who will map the test cases or test events to the files. Also, both a partition and an integration problem will be how to establish your test data environment for the required dry runs.

Write the Test Steps

Make sure that each test event explicitly states the Year 2000 related response for which you are looking. Define your steps to make this clear.

Determine User Acceptance Criteria

If the entity being integrated is to be deployed, its formal test should include user signoff/acceptance activities. This can be similar to your standard process. However, because pervasive changes will have been made to an operational application and its data, you should obtain special user review and agreement of what is needed for acceptance. Refer to the comparable discussion of this topic under Partition Test Description and Data.

Write the Supporting Sections of the Document

Follow your standard format when you write the supporting sections of the document, and include the remaining information identified at the start of this section.

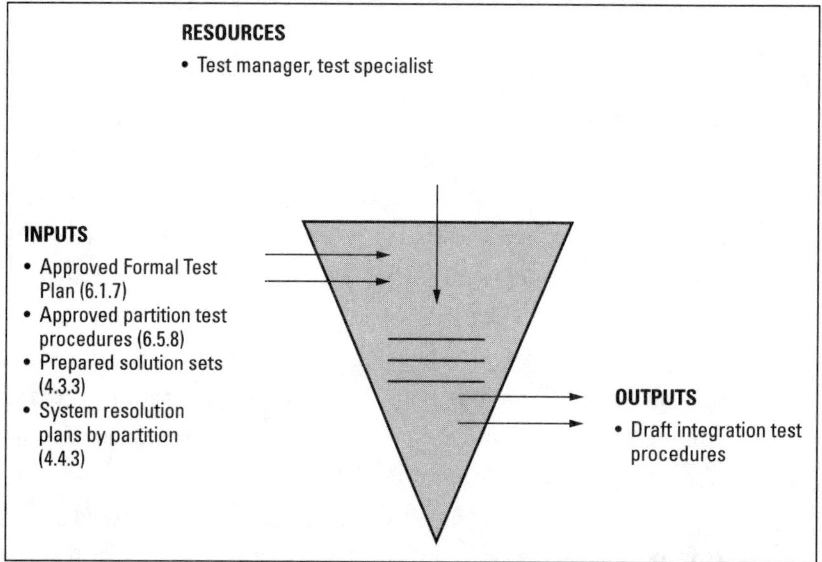

6.6.2 Task: Verify/Dry Run Test Cases

Many of the test steps will already have been dry run, since they were used in the previous partition tests. Identify whether anything has changed as a result of the integration. Only changes to the procedures need to be tested and verified. Most of the new test events probably use existing capabilities from the tested partitions, so you can use either deployed applications or existing test environments for this task.

Being able to verify procedures is much easier as integration progresses. However, it is just as important to dry run in the development environment as soon as possible. Look for problems and tell the developers as soon as you find them.

You will tailor how, and even if, this feedback effort can be done, based on your internal processes and protocol, and based on whether the Resolution effort is outsourced and/or the revised software is readily available.

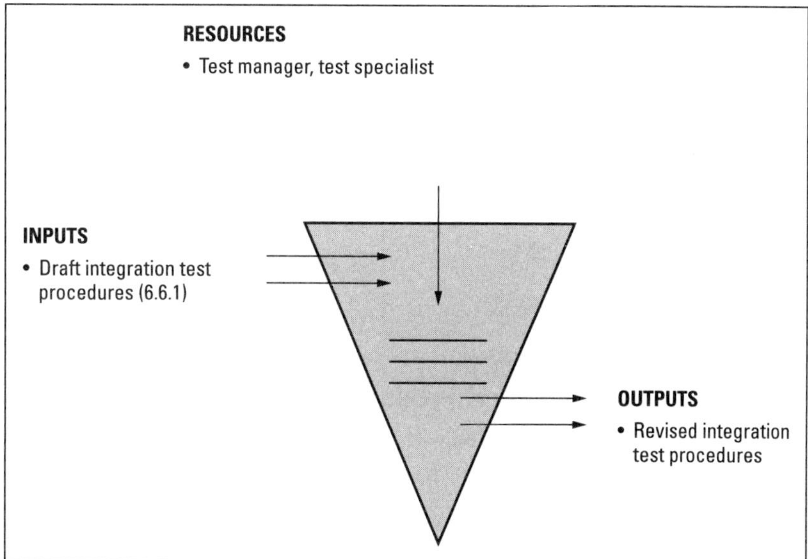

6.6.3 Task: Present and Approve Integration Test and Data Descriptions

This task covers the formal presentation and approval of Integration Test and Data Descriptions. You should conduct informal reviews so that the formal presentations result in minimal corrections.

The techniques for presenting integration test plans are similar to those for presenting partition test plans. The biggest difference is that the review group is larger and the presentation itself is more important.

Test Execution for the applications being integrated can begin anytime following the completion of this task.

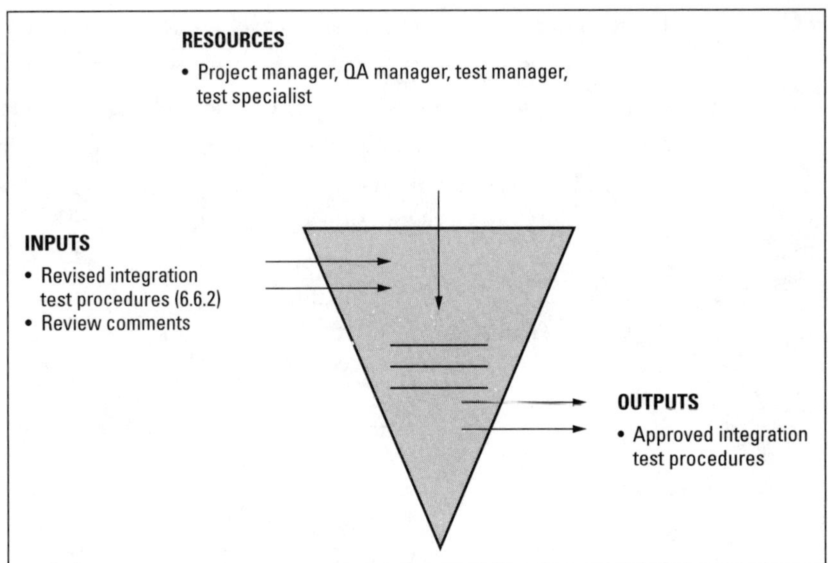

milestone **Integration Test Description and Data complete. Quality assurance verifies that the deliverable conforms to its intended goal. Project control baselines the deliverable and updates tracking metrics.**

Business Impacts

Test Planning tasks will not greatly affect your business processes. However, it will take time to complete this planning process; therefore, you should allocate substantial time and effort to these tasks. Test Execution activities will have a far more profound effect on your business processes.

Phase Risks

Potential Event	*Probability*	*Impact*	*Risk*
An existing Year 2000 problem is not identified in a specific test plan	High	High	High
Resolution slippage voids test plan	Medium	Medium	Medium

POTENTIAL EVENT	PROBABILITY	IMPACT	RISK
Nonavailability of test bed for test plan development	Low	Medium	Medium

Test Planning Phase Risks

There are three risks associated with the Test Planning phase: a Year 2000 problem may not be identified in a test plan, Resolution slippage may wind up voiding the test plan, and a test bed for test plan development may not be available.

An Existing Year 2000 Problem Is Not Identified in a Specific Test Plan

If an existing Year 2000 problem is not included in the corresponding test plan, there will not be a test to ensure the resolution of that problem. This omission may endanger the successful completion of your Year 2000 project. Should the problem remain unresolved, it may negatively affect your Deployment endeavors. Even worse, it may come to the attention of the users during operational use. If you have to "back out" the deployment or operation of a system because of an unresolved Year 2000 problem, the costs in resources and schedule will be significant, in fact far higher than the cost incurred had the problem been uncovered during Test Execution.

There are a couple of ways of mitigating this risk:

- Ensure close cooperation between those participating in Year 2000 Resolution activities and those involved in Test Planning. Resolution staff should realize that their input to Test Planning is critical. Test planners must be aware of every Year 2000 problem before the conclusion of Resolution tasks.
- Institute a careful tracking mechanism for Year 2000 problems. Your Year 2000 repository should support this mechanism.
- Include many threaded test cases, which follow a process and data across the entire partition, between partitions, and between a partition and systems that have not been changed.

Resolution Slippage Voids Test Plan

The completed test plan incorporates certain assumptions about the Resolution schedule. Activities defined in the test plan are highly dependent upon the order in which certain systems are repaired or replaced. If systems are not repaired or replaced according to the schedule, the test plan may not be valid. System testing may be delayed. The test plan may need to be modified or, in the worst case, totally replaced.

There are a couple of ways of mitigating this risk:

- Ensure ongoing communication between the Resolution team and those who develop the test plan. As mentioned, test planners and those participating in Resolution activities should maintain communication throughout both phases.
- The test plan should incorporate a certain degree of flexibility to accommodate Resolution slippage. As much as possible, try to delay the assignment of specific dates for the start of testing. If possible, the test plan should include relative dates only. Also, this plan should include a "Schedule Slippage Contingency" section.

Nonavailability of Test Bed for Test Plan Development

You need a functioning test bed to adequately develop the test plan. If this test bed is unavailable, the test plan may be incomplete or incorrect.

There is a way of mitigating this risk:

- Ensure the availability of a test bed before you initiate Test Planning. If a Test Planning test bed is unavailable, you should delay the initiation of this phase. If the test bed remains unavailable for an extended period of time, you may need to get help from senior management.

SUCCESS FACTORS

In successfully completing Test Planning, you carried out the following steps:

SUCCESS FACTOR	DELIVERABLE
Developed and obtained approval of top-level plan for testing modified systems, including top-level description of test cases and test data	Test Planning and Execution Phase Startup
Ensured that formal test events include all modified systems, including those modified by contractors	Test Planning and Execution Phase Startup
Ensured that integration testing of previously tested entities is planned and scheduled	Test Planning and Execution Phase Startup
Developed and executed plan for acquisition of human resources to support testing activities	Test Planning and Execution Phase Startup
Ensured that the top-level test plan included the validation of tests conducted by contractors	Test Planning and Execution Phase Startup
Developed requirements for test environments	Test Facility Environment Report
Identified existing and alternative test environments	Test Facility Environment Report
Identified electronic partner certification requirements	Test Facility Environment Report
Defined test tool requirements for test entities	Test Support Tool Requirements
Identified test tools that are available internally and those that must be acquired	Test Support Tool Requirements
Developed Electronic Partner Test Plans	Electronic Partnership Test Plans
Developed detailed test plans for each partition test event, including details on what to test and how to evaluate the results to ensure Year 2000 compliance and satisfaction of customer requirements	Partition Test Description and Data
Ensured that each partition test plan includes a statement of your Year 2000 objectives, a schedule that includes all formal test events, and a description of required facilities, human resources, and tools	Partition Test Description and Data
Defined test criteria for each partition test event	Partition Test Description and Data
Obtained user concurrence that partition test events and criteria are adequate	Partition Test Description and Data
Verified all partition test cases	Partition Test Description and Data

continued

SUCCESS FACTOR	DELIVERABLE
Defined a comprehensive integration strategy for testing, including all electronic partnerships, data conversions, and Year 2000 compliance issues	Integration Test Description and Data
Defined integration sequences in accordance with overall integration strategy	Integration Test Description and Data
Developed detailed test plans for each integration test event, including details on what to test and how to evaluate the results to ensure Year 2000 compliance and satisfaction of customer requirements	Integration Test Description and Data
Ensured that each integration test plan includes a statement of your Year 2000 objectives, a schedule that includes all formal test events, and a description of required facilities, human resources, and tools	Integration Test Description and Data
Defined test criteria for each integration test event	Integration Test Description and Data
Obtained user concurrence that integration test events and criteria are adequate	Integration Test Description and Data
Verified all integration test cases	Integration Test Description and Data
Identified phase risks and potential mitigation approaches	All deliverables
Identified which deliverables would be developed during this phase	All deliverables
Used adequate communication interfaces throughout your organization to support the tasks associated with this phase	All deliverables
Assigned phase tasks to various groups in your organization and ensured that there was management approval for those tasks	All deliverables
Identified the deliverables for which each group was responsible and ensured acceptance of that deliverable responsibility by each group	All deliverables
Identified key milestones for the accomplishment of tasks for this phase	All deliverables
Identified milestone thresholds beyond which some corrective action will be taken	All deliverables
Used metrics to track and measure progress with respect to these milestones	All deliverables

SUCCESS FACTOR	DELIVERABLE
Ensured that each responsible group accepted and adhered to the schedule for completion of this phase	All deliverables

REFERENCE MATERIAL

This list mentions reference material you can turn to for additional information on this phase of your Year 2000 compliance project:

- Appendix A, Problem Definition Catalog
- Appendix B, Solution Sets
- Appendix D, Sample Presentations
- Appendix F, Key Tasks Outline
- Appendix H, Integrated Project Plan
- Appendix I, How To 2000 Risk Management
- Glossary

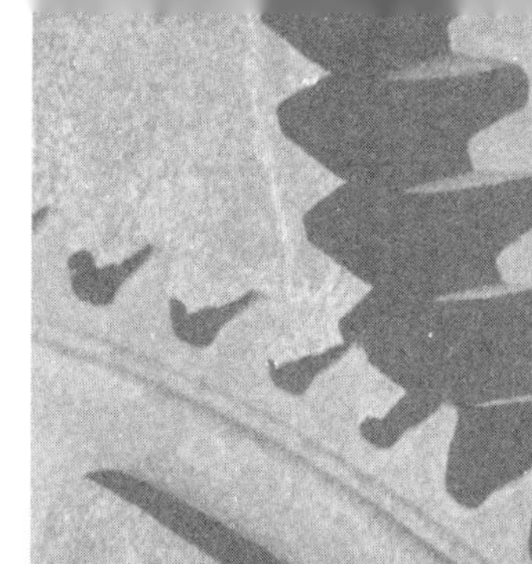

CHAPTER 7

Phase 7: Test Execution

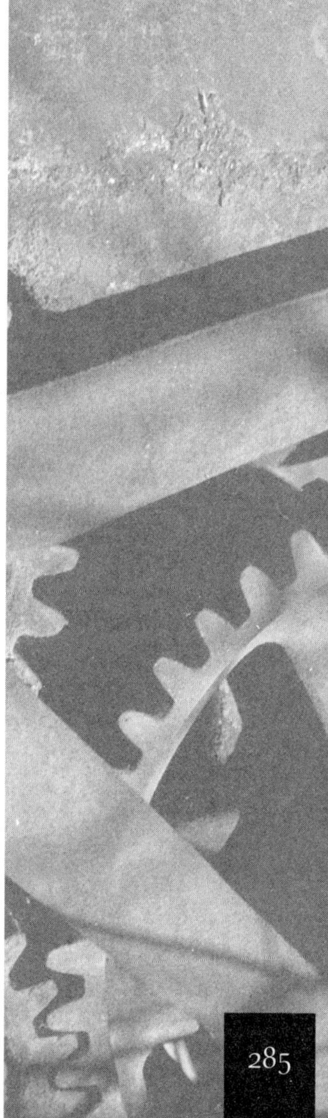

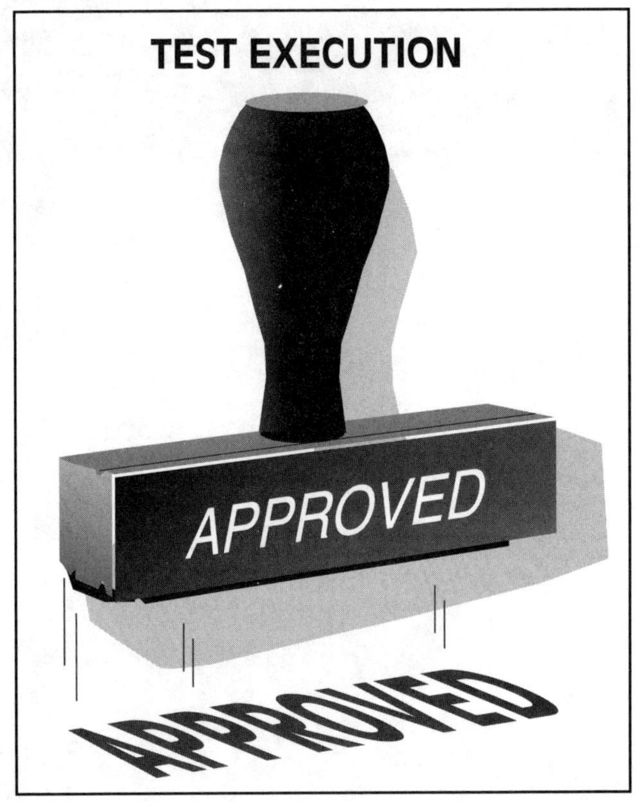
TEST EXECUTION
APPROVED
APPROVED

Objectives:

- Verify that all related development and test preparations are complete.
- Fully test each partition (that is, "deployment entity") including bridges and data conversions.
- Involve end users in test execution.
- Negotiate final third-party compliance agreements and/or bridge definitions.
- Obtain end user acceptance for each compliant partition.

Test Execution is when you actually carry out the tests that you have been preparing for so carefully throughout your Year 2000 project. Although this phase is demanding, it can also bring quite a bit of satisfaction.

Executing the Tests

Year 2000 Test Execution will be very different from typical testing endeavors. The key to Test Execution is to manage time by balancing risk and completeness. Reduce risk by managing third parties and items that fall on the fringe of your control. You will test each partition as a manageable and defined unit. You will test the many integration groups to which each partition belongs. You will test integration groups comprised of several smaller integration groups. Finally, you will conduct enterprise-level testing. You may end up testing every system and interface supporting your organization. However, do not be overwhelmed by the seemingly enormous scope of the testing endeavor. You can meet your testing goals if you proceed one step at a time and build each test upon the previous one.

For most system development and system maintenance projects, system creation or modification is followed by a small number of formal tests that demonstrate the fulfillment of all system requirements. After these tests are completed, the user verifies the success of the tests, accepts the system, and approves the system for deployment.

During Test Planning, you completed deliverables that incorporated all of the test plans to be used during the Year 2000 project. In contrast, each deliverable defined within Test Execution applies to an individual test plan. Indeed, you will

repeatedly create the deliverables defined in this phase, creating one set of Test Execution deliverables for each test plan defined in Test Planning. For example, if an enterprise's Year 2000 approach defines three partitions, you would have three separate test plans. You would also have integration test plans to verify that the partitions operate together as required. The test execution deliverables and tasks defined later in this chapter are needed for each of these partition and integration tests, since each had its own objectives, test cases, user signoffs, and so forth.

Each system test defined in a set of Test Execution deliverables is performed as a stand-alone event. The Year 2000 project manager and test manager must develop and monitor a comprehensive schedule that includes all of these formal tests. Many of these system tests will occur concurrently. Many will also parallel Resolution efforts.

The cost for completing all testing activities undertaken during both the Test Planning and Test Execution phases should not exceed 30 percent of your Year 2000 project cost.

The time devoted to testing tasks undertaken during both the Test Planning and Test Execution phases should comprise 39 percent of the Year 2000 project schedule.

Summary of Deliverables

This section summarizes the deliverables for this phase of the Year 2000 compliance project. The section "Deliverables, Tasks, and Dependencies" later in this chapter includes detailed descriptions of each deliverable and the associated supporting tasks.

Formal Dry Run Report

Ideally, every system test execution should initially go through a "dress rehearsal." This permits the test director to ensure the correctness and completeness of the test. This type of "dry run" also allows testers to avoid surprises during the formal, witnessed test. The Formal Dry Run Report details the results of the dry run. Because the primary purpose of the formal test is to verify that the partition is ready for deployment, you should always dry run the related test procedures in their entirety to ensure that the system, procedures, and testers are ready. This is true whether or not the formal test is witnessed. All such thorough dry runs should result in a report that documents any needed procedure changes and serves as a reference in case there are any problems during the actual test. Realistically, the Formal Dry Run Report helps protect the test team from criticism if problems occur at formal testing. It shows that you did everything possible to ensure that you and the system were ready for the test.

Test Kickoff Briefing

The Test Kickoff Briefing provides test participants with the following:

- An overview of the system attributes and/or functionality that will be addressed in the test.
- A description of the test environment.
- Clarification of the roles of the participants.
- A list of specific test procedures.
- A summary of the problems that you can expect during the test. These problems were identified during the dry run.

Test Execution Report

The Test Execution Report provides a record of events that take place during the formal, witnessed test. This deliverable includes

- A list of test attendees
- The schedule that was followed during the test
- A list of any problems encountered during the test
- User test verification in the form of "user signoffs"
- The results of the user go/no-go decision-making process

Electronic Partnership Recertification Report

The Electronic Partnership Recertification Report provides a Test Execution report that will be used to support the electronic partnership recertification process.

Deliverables, Tasks, and Dependencies

These deliverables provide a formal record of each Test Execution cycle. They may only cover the events of as little as a day, but they provide the critical signoff between Resolution and Deployment approval.

7.1 Formal Dry Run Report

A dry run test ensures that the developers have provided the correct versions of all data and software, that they work as expected, and that your test procedures as a whole are correct. Several Year 2000 issues may affect whether you do a dry run before a particular formal partition or integration test:

- There are so many tests (they have been going well) and this is a relatively simple one, so a desk check is considered sufficient. For some Year 2000 environments, this may be reasonable, especially if your standard process does not require a dry run in all cases.
- The test takes a long time to set up and execute, and the test environment cannot be allocated to doing this twice. Dry runs can be costly. When there are so many tests to be performed, these costs in time and personnel can be prohibitive.
- Management requests that you bypass it. If this happens, have a more thorough review of the pretest checklist to be followed to confirm that the test is ready to proceed. Although your test plan will have this defined to some extent (for example, the environment is as required, software and data are in place), if there is no dry run to fill in any gaps, you will need to pay more attention to this section of the plan and to its execution.

Although there are some reasons for not doing Year 2000 test dry runs, they are appropriate in most cases. Evaluate the risks associated with each test against the effort of doing the dry run. Because of the complexity of the overall project and the number of tests to be performed, dry runs should be performed whenever feasible, and at least for critical partition and integration tests performed during the early stages of Year 2000 deployment.

Task Overview

- Perform the Dry Run
- Present and Approve the Formal Dry Run Report

7.1.1 Task: Perform the Dry Run

This task involves these following activities:

- Decide who needs to attend. You probably have your own dry run processes defined, and you should follow them. Preferably, you should include a minimal set of people, but they should know what to look for and how to document and/or resolve problems.
- Have all required test setups performed (for example, installing software and data), including bridges and test tools.
- Confirm that the required start of test conditions are met.
- Run the test and record all problems.
- The go/no-go decision relative to the formal test will be based on the dry run results and the problems found. If you decide to go forward, the problems will be part of the Test Kickoff Briefing.

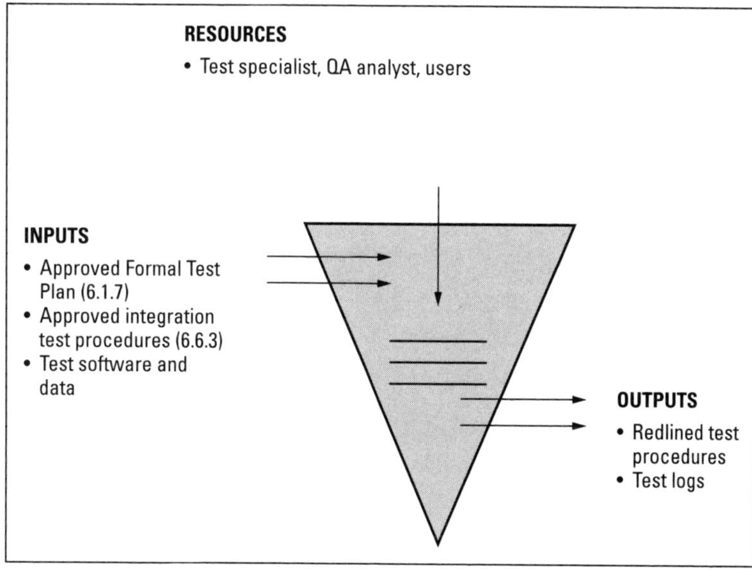

Task Guideline

- The person who wrote the test plan should direct the dry run.

7.1.2 Task: Present and Approve the Formal Dry Run Report

This task involves presenting the information gathered during the dry run and deciding whether conditions are ready for the formal test:

- Review the redlined procedures (setup and test) and make sure they are clear.
- Evaluate the problems found to make the go/no-go decision for the formal test. You should include the Year 2000 project manager in the decision if you are recommending a no-go, since this can have a significant impact on the overall project's schedule.
- If you decide to go forward, the problems need to be recorded and included as part of the Test Kickoff Briefing.
- If you decide to postpone the test (that is, because of setup, data conversion, or software problems), try to identify and estimate what you need for the test to be performed.

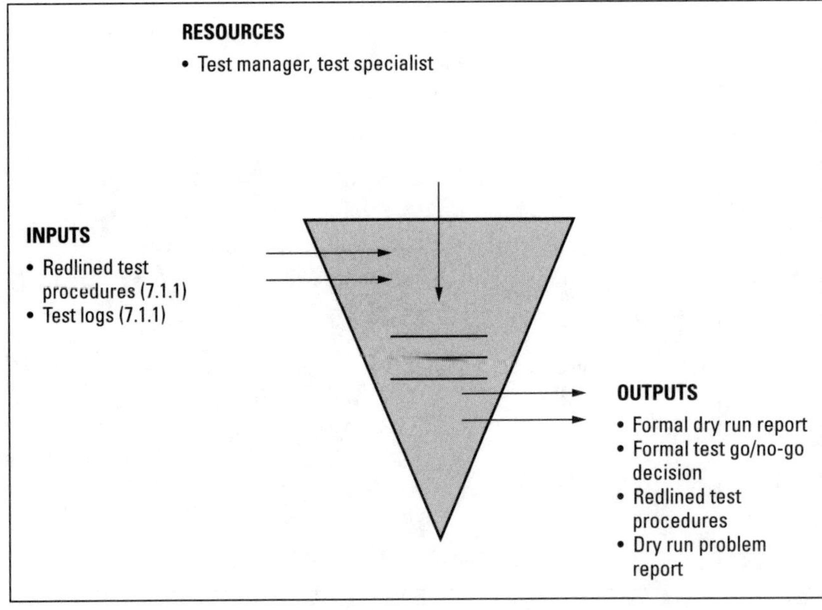

Task Guidelines

- Make sure all Year 2000-related problems and redlines are clearly described.
- Get resolution suggestions from the developers. They can help scope out how long it will take to fix things, if you decide to postpone the formal test.

milestone 

Formal Dry Run Report complete. Quality assurance verifies that the deliverable conforms to its intended goal. Project control baselines the deliverable and updates tracking metrics. Configuration management verifies that the Year 2000 repository updates adhere to CM procedures.

7.2 Test Kickoff Briefing

Before starting any formal test event, you should usually present a test readiness briefing. This briefing allows test personnel to gain an overall understanding of the activities to be undertaken during this phase.

Task Overview

- Prepare Formal Test Execution Briefing
- Prepare Electronic Partner Test Briefing

7.2.1 Task: Prepare Formal Test Execution Briefing

You should include specific Year 2000-related issues in the briefing:

- Identify what portions being tested were previously tested (applicable to integration tests). You need to do this to collect metrics characterizing problems encountered during formal testing.
- Identify known problems that will occur during the test. For example, if some report formats still say 19 rather than the correct century, this may not be important enough to postpone the test or even the deployment, but it should be known as the test starts.
- Identify whether this test is to result in a deploy/no-deploy decision and summarize what parts of the test are to be used to make that decision.

These issues are in addition to your usual pretest briefing items (for example, participants, schedule).

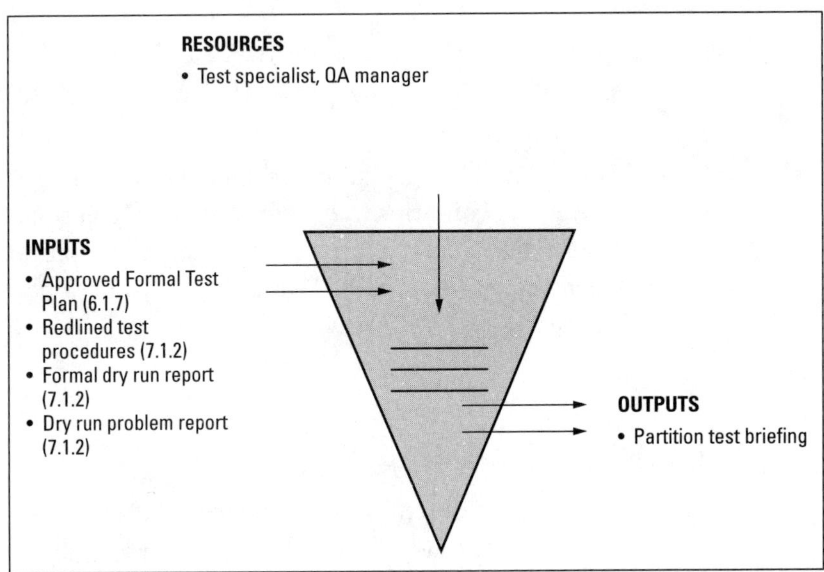

7.2.2 Task: Prepare Electronic Partner Test Briefing

You must prepare a briefing that summarizes your approach to testing the interfaces with your electronic partners. You should identify test participants, test schedule, and so on. It is important to clearly define the methods of communication you will use to maintain contact with your various electronic partners. You should discuss the types of problems that may be encountered and methods that will be used to resolve the problems.

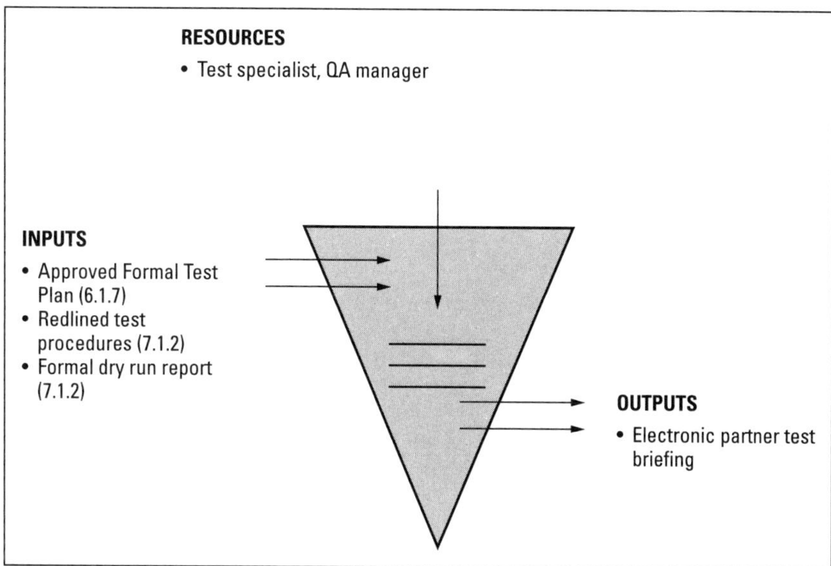

milestone  **Test Kickoff Briefing complete. Quality assurance verifies that the deliverable conforms to its intended goal. Project control baselines the deliverable and updates tracking metrics. Configuration management verifies that the Year 2000 repository updates adhere to CM procedures.**

7.3 Test Execution Report

The Test Execution Report supports all activities associated with the formal execution of a test plan.

Task Overview

- Set Up the Test Environment
- Deliver the Test Kickoff Briefing
- Execute the Test Procedures
- Prepare the Test Documentation and Report

7.3.1 Task: Set Up the Test Environment

The specifics of what happens during this task for a specific formal test are described in the test's Test Description and Data deliverable. If there was a dry run, this task should go relatively smoothly. If this is the first time these procedures are being followed, you should note any differences between what the plan says and what you did, and should indicate whether there is any change relating to data files or software installed.

Configuration management can help set up test environment components.

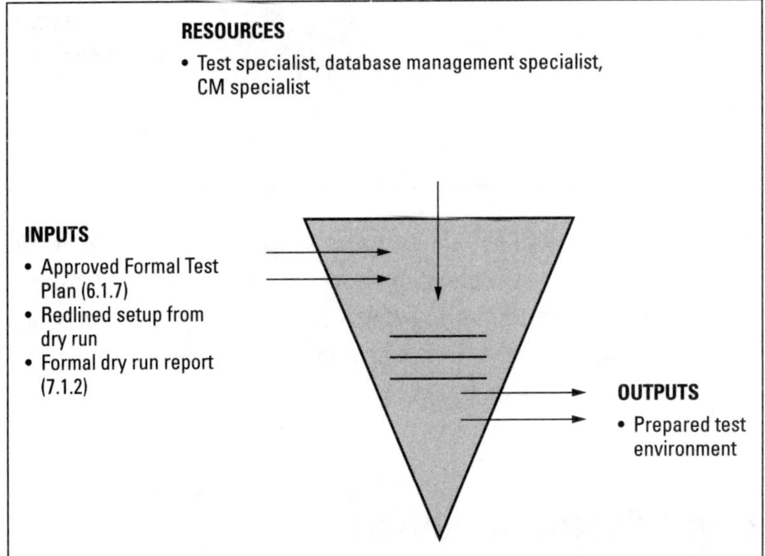

Task Guideline

- If you found setup redlines during a dry run, pay particular attention to these changes.

7.3.2 Task: Deliver the Test Kickoff Briefing

This is the formal gathering of all participants, including the users who may only observe that part of the test allocated to formal approval and signoff. It is important that everyone understands what is expected of the test. At the end of the briefing, there should be consensus to proceed with the test.

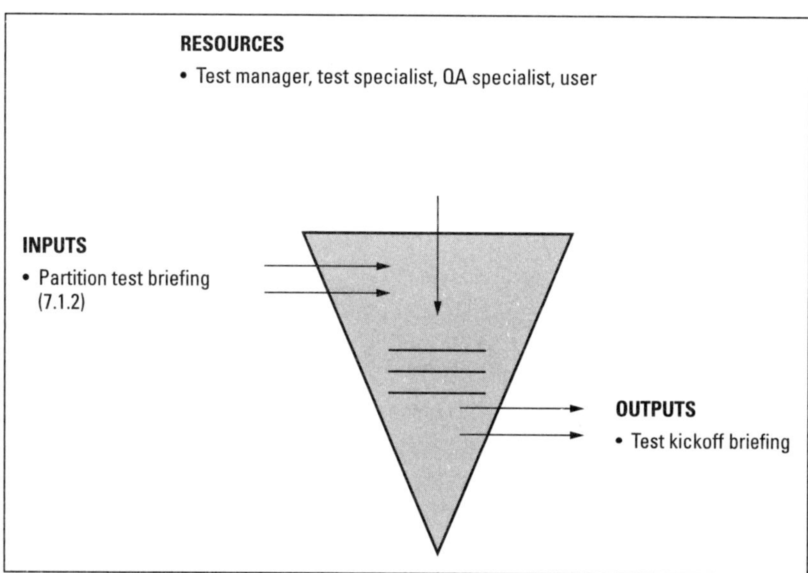

Task Guideline

- Even though you may be giving lots of these briefings, do not skip the actual briefing process. One purpose of the formal briefing is to emphasize individual responsibility for assigned tasks.

7.3.3 Task: Execute the Test Procedures

Follow the procedures, record all problems, and redline changes made during execution. If the test results are satisfactory, get appropriate signoffs and approvals to proceed to Deployment.

Anything that is Year 2000 specific about executing the test should have been noted in the test plan and procedures. Year 2000 test executions are the same as any other formal test, except that they may involve a larger set of applications, depending on where they occur in the overall Year 2000 implementation process.

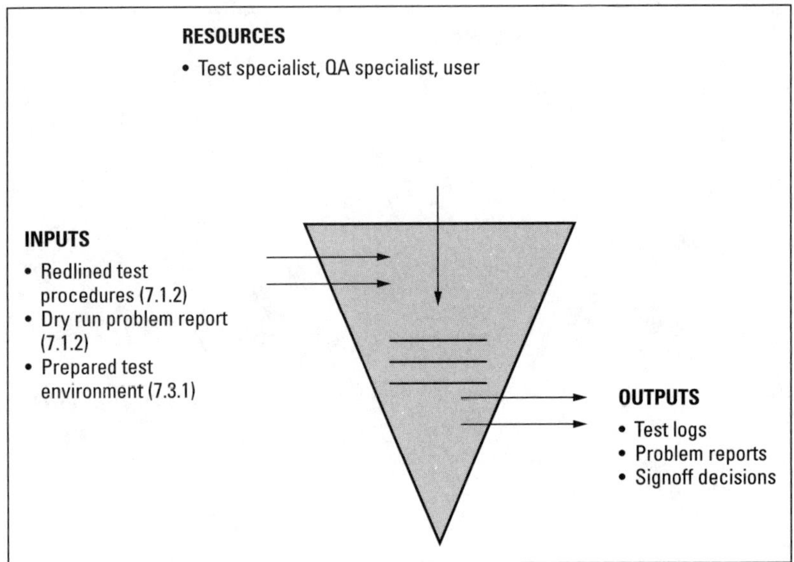

Task Guidelines

- If a dry run and this execution have unexpected differences, you should fully document the changes. There may be hidden date-related or database conversion problems.
- Record all discrepancies and/or problems. In addition, try to categorize Year 2000-related problems based on their impact on the deploy/no deploy decision. These criteria should have been identified when the test procedures were developed.
- Depending upon the quality assurance plan for this project, it is likely that a QA specialist will monitor the test execution.

7.3.4 Task: Prepare the Test Documentation and Report

All significant test results must be captured in the Year 2000 repository. Test result documentation will include:

- Logs
- Problem reports
- Signoff sheets
- Redlined procedures

- Hard copy output

In addition, you should write a formal test report that summarizes what was done, who participated, and the results. You probably have an existing format, but you should include the following Year 2000-specific test results:

- Categorize problems as Year 2000/non-Year 2000.
- Categorize problems as newly tested or from previously tested partitions.
- Report on deployment decisions, identifying workarounds for noncompliant problems.

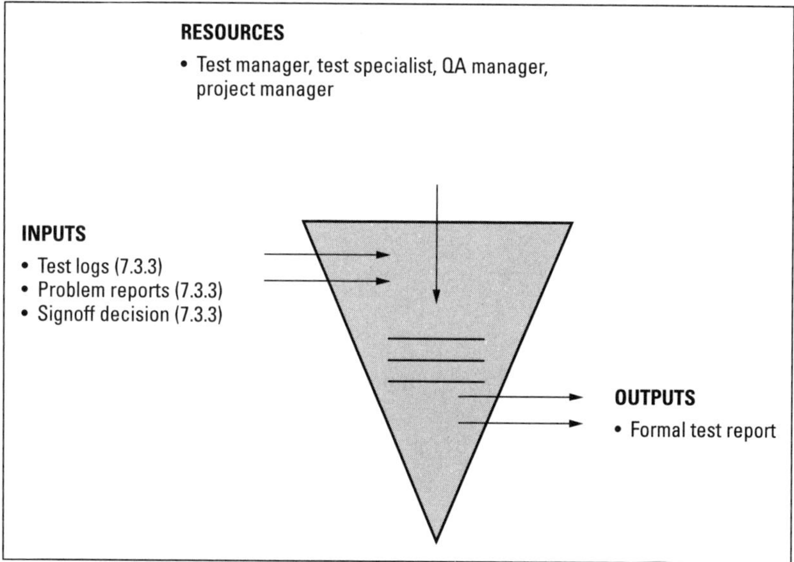

Task Guideline

- Make sure the Year 2000 project manager and quality assurance manager are aware of all Year 2000 problems, especially if they were detected in software that had passed a previous test.

Test Execution Report complete. Quality assurance verifies that the deliverable conforms to its intended goal. Project control baselines the deliverable and updates tracking metrics. Configuration management verifies that Year 2000 repository updates adhere to CM procedures.

7.4 Electronic Partnership Recertification Report

This deliverable supports tasks related to electronic partnership tests. You may choose to use the same test report format for recertifications as for the other tests. However, because planning, execution, and resolution are quite different, they are discussed in a separate section. The tasks associated with recertifications are the same as for other tests.

Task Overview

- Set Up the Test Environment
- Deliver the Test Kickoff Briefing
- Execute the Test Procedures
- Prepare the Test Documentation and Report

7.4.1 Task: Set Up the Test Environment

In addition to following normal test setup procedures (for example, installing required test software and data, and ensuring that the required configuration is in place), you should contact the coordinator for the electronic partner a few days before the test to reconfirm the schedule and plan, even if their process does not require such coordination. Identify any changes you may have made or require.

Configuration management can help set up test environment components.

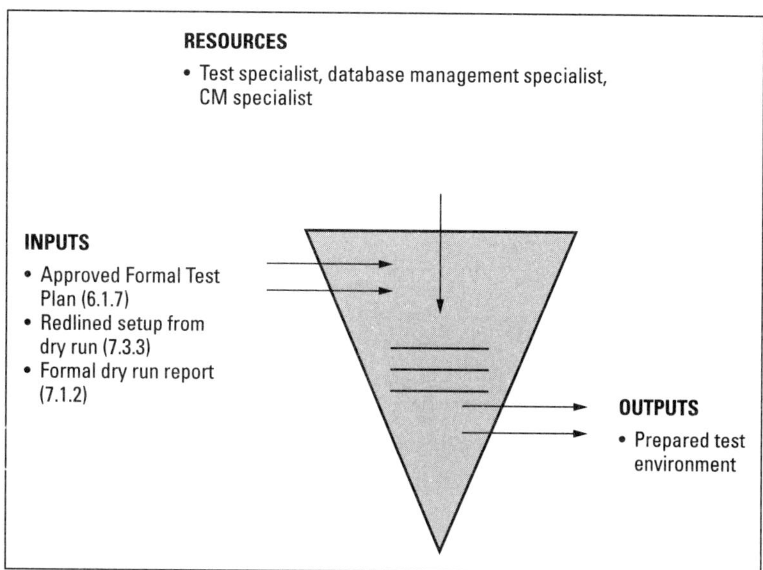

7.4.2 Task: Deliver the Test Kickoff Briefing

The Test Kickoff Briefing for the Electronic Partnership Recertification Report is much simpler than the one for the partition and integration tests; however, you will still brief all in-house participants before the test. This briefing may only take a few minutes, but at a minimum it should include a checklist of the setup, and a description of what will be included in the test and who does what.

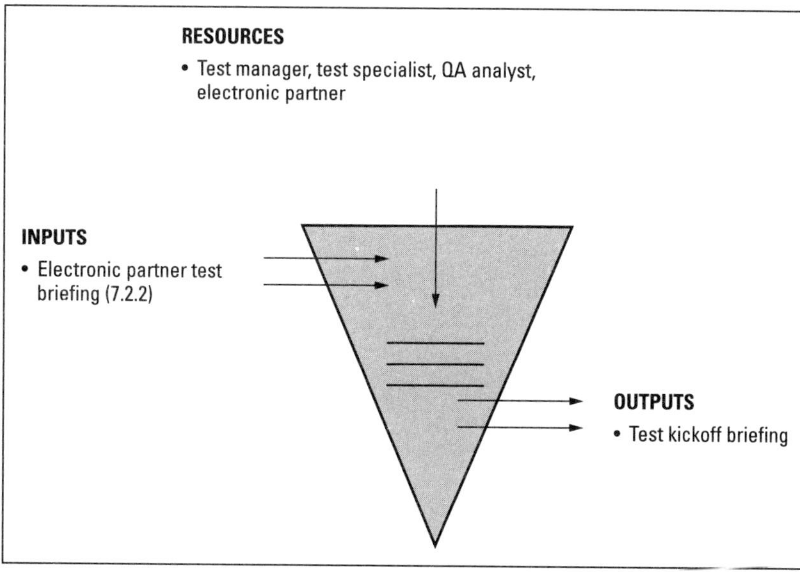

7.4.3 Task: Execute the Test Procedures

As with other formal tests, follow the procedures, record all problems, and redline changes made during execution. If all goes well, the software used during the test can be deployed to the operational system. Get confirmation (in writing) from the electronic partner that your new software has been certified. If there were problems, coordinate with your in-house people to determine when they can be fixed and then consult with the partner about when another test can be scheduled.

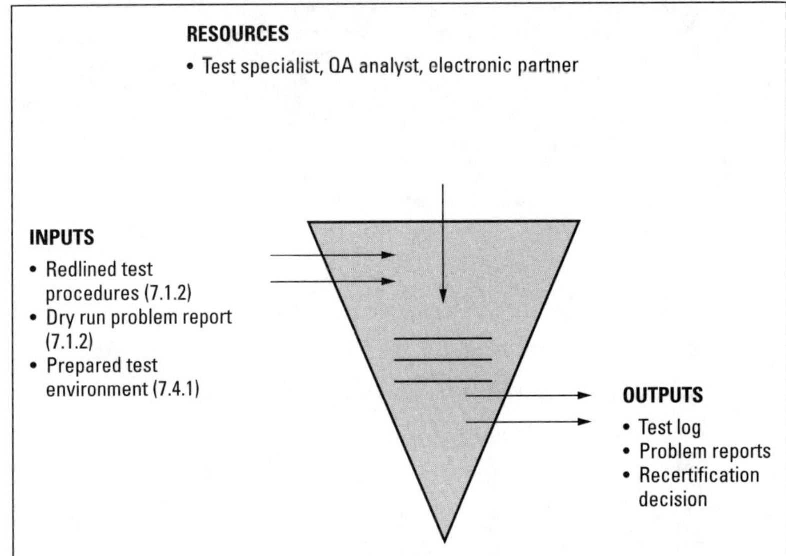

7.4.4 Task: Prepare the Test Documentation and Report

You must capture all significant test results in the Year 2000 repository. Categorize all problems based on whether they are Year 2000 related. Try to determine immediately what change may have caused non-Year 2000 problems. Since this is a recertification, the interface was operational.

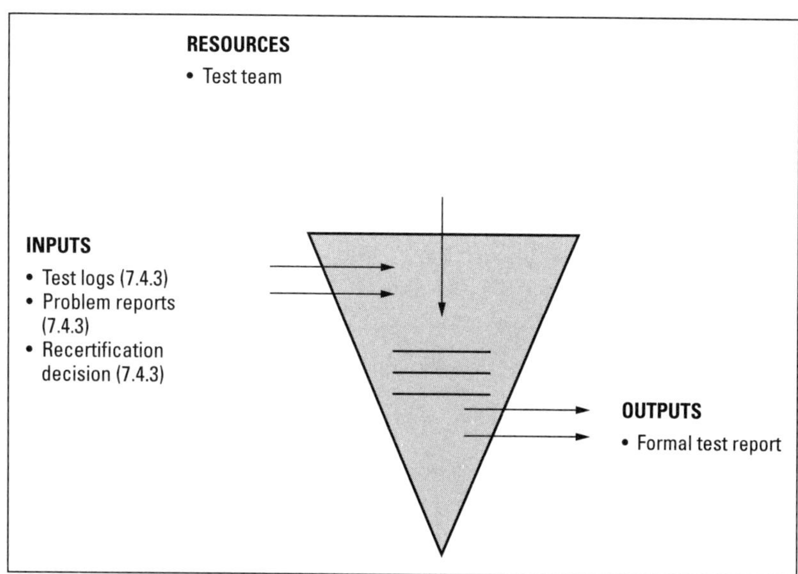

milestone

Electronic Partnership Recertification Report complete. Quality assurance verifies that the deliverable conforms to its intended goal. Project control baselines the deliverable and updates tracking metrics. Configuration management verifies that the Year 2000 repository updates adhere to CM procedures.

Business Impacts

Test Execution activities may have a substantial impact on your organization's normal operations. Like Resolution activities, Test Execution activities may hinder the normal operation of systems that are undergoing tests. A system may be partially or totally unable to function in its routine environment as testing proceeds.

Managers must create contingency plans that address this potentially serious loss of automated support. These managers may be required to duplicate system functionality with a manual process. Alternatively, tested systems may be temporarily replaced by automated systems with similar functionality. Managers must anticipate increased resource requirements that may accompany efforts to replace lost functionality.

Phase Risks

Potential Event	*Probability*	*Impact*	*Risk*
Test setup procedures are incorrect	High	Medium	Medium
Error-heavy test results	Medium	Medium	Medium
Interface recertification is delayed due to unsuccessful test results	Medium	Medium	Medium

Test Execution Phase Risks

There are three risks associated with the Test Execution phase: the test setup procedures may be incorrect, you may have error-heavy test results, and interface recertification may be delayed as a result of unsuccessful test results.

Test Setup Procedures Are Incorrect

During your Year 2000 project, you will assess, repair, and test a dauntingly large number of systems. Due to the magnitude of your testing inventory, it will be extremely difficult to estimate the proper test setup for every system. Therefore, you will almost certainly encounter flaws in the test setup procedures for one or more systems.

There are a couple of ways of mitigating this risk:

- Encourage informal testing on the part of system users or developers. These informal tests can be undertaken as Resolution activities come to a close. These tests will almost certainly provide invaluable guidance for your Test Planning activities.
- Compare/contrast system test plans. When completing a test plan for a specific system, ensure that the plan is compared to test plans aimed at similar systems. Test plan comparison may allow you to detect errors and/or omissions in one or both test plans.

Error-Heavy Test Results

System test personnel will always tell you that the ideal test yields no errors. If testing a given system identifies a significant number of errors, the system was prematurely tested. An error-rich system will be resubmitted for Resolution or, in the worst-case scenario, for Detailed Assessment. Needless to say, your Year 2000 project costs will increase significantly each time a system is recycled through previous Year 2000 phases.

There are a couple of ways of mitigating this risk:

- Emphasize the importance of unit testing on the part of those who participate in Resolution activities. If you conduct adequate unit testing, system testing should not engender many surprises.
- Encourage the use of traditional pretest system review methods, such as code walkthroughs (code walkthroughs are actually relatively low-cost "paper tests"). A thorough code walkthrough can often unearth errors faster and less expensively than a full operational test.
- A formal dry run will uncover a partition not ready for formal testing. If you find that formal testing must be rescheduled because of failed dry runs, allocate more time to unit test reviews to help catch problems earlier. If dry runs were cut out of your budget, put them back in.

Interface Recertification Is Delayed due to Unsuccessful Test Results

The successful completion of each electronic partner recertification will depend on the successful testing of an individual system. Because the continued operation of these electronic partner interfaces may be critical to your organization's operation, competitiveness, and/or ability to comply with regulatory rules, the efficient completion of recertification is extremely important.

There is a way of mitigating this risk:

- Emphasize the importance of unit testing on the part of those who participate in Resolution activities. It is difficult to overemphasize the importance of unit testing. Adequate unit testing is the best way of ensuring the success of formal system testing.

Success Factors

In successfully completing Test Execution, you carried out the following steps:

SUCCESS FACTOR	DELIVERABLE
Conducted a dry run of each test to verify the adequacy of the test environment, the test tools, and the test staff	Formal Dry Run Report
Prepared and delivered a comprehensive briefing concerning Test Execution activities	Test Kickoff Briefing, Test Execution Report
Executed the test plan for each partition test	Test Execution Report
Evaluated results of each partition test against evaluation criteria to determine degree of success	Test Execution Report
Reported results of each partition test	Test Execution Report
Tested all interfaces according to integration test plan	Test Execution Report
Evaluated results of each integration test against evaluation criteria to determine degree of success	Test Execution Report
Reported results of each integration test	Test Execution Report
Devised a strategy to correct and retest problems found during formal test	Test Execution Report
Conducted tests to ensure the recertification of electronic partners	Electronic Partner Recertification Report
Identified phase risks and potential mitigation approaches	All deliverables
Identified deliverables that would be developed during this phase	All deliverables
Used adequate communication interfaces throughout your organization to support the tasks associated with this phase	All deliverables
Assigned phase tasks to various groups in your organization and ensured that there was management approval for those tasks	All deliverables
Identified the deliverables for which each group was responsible and ensured acceptance of that deliverable responsibility by each group	All deliverables
Identified key milestones for the accomplishment of tasks for this phase	All deliverables
Identified milestone thresholds beyond which some corrective action will be taken	All deliverables
Used metrics to track and measure progress with respect to these milestones	All deliverables
Ensured that each responsible group accepted and adhered to the schedule for completion of this phase	All deliverables

Reference Material

This list mentions reference material you can turn to for additional information on this phase of your Year 2000 compliance project:

- Appendix A, Problem Definition Catalog
- Appendix B, Solution Sets
- Appendix D, Sample Presentations
- Appendix F, Key Tasks Outline
- Appendix H, Integrated Project Plan
- Appendix I, How To 2000 Risk Management
- Glossary

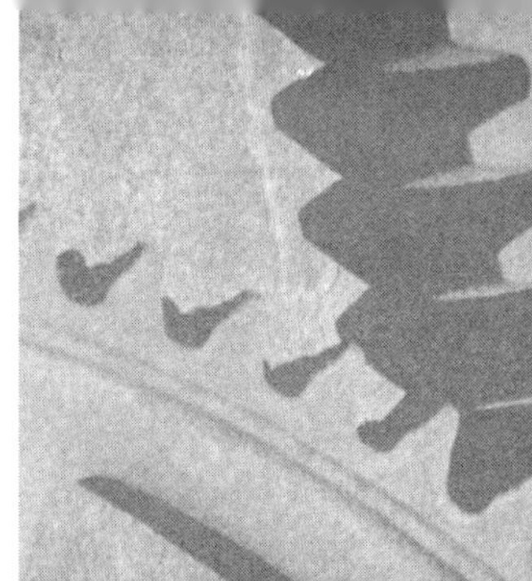

CHAPTER 8

Phase 8: Deployment

DEPLOYMENT
ON
ON
OFF

Objectives:

- Ensure that contingency plans are in place.
- Conduct final coordination with third parties and electronic partners.
- Stage appropriate bridges and data conversions for deployment.
- Deploy systems into production operations.
- Execute final system validation.
- Make go/no-go decisions.
- Prepare for Fallout.

Once you complete deployment, the final phase in the correction cycle, your system will be Year 2000 compliant.

Finishing the Correction Cycle

Deployment marks the final phase in the *How To 2000* correction cycle. The deliverables completed during this phase will support the successful transfer of Year 2000 compliant systems to your operational environment. These deliverables will support your efforts to deploy multiple systems simultaneously with minimal impact on users, interfaces, and customers. Like the deliverables described in Test Execution, each of these deliverables pertains to an individual system or partition. You will develop a separate set of these deliverables for each partition that you deploy. Although many of these deliverables are aimed at the Deployment of mainframes and other large systems in a full-scale production environment, you can tailor them for smaller application environments or hardware installations.

For most organizations, the activities and complicating factors involved in deploying a new or modified system are nothing new. However, Year 2000 Deployment activities will differ substantially from past system deployments. Year 2000 deployments have the following characteristics that make planning, scheduling, and execution unique:

- The sheer volume of Deployment efforts may be staggering. You may have to deploy most of the systems in your organization.
- Some partition groups may be deployed simultaneously, while others require sequential deployment.
- Your Deployment plans are subject to the availability of vendor and third-party compliance.
- Each partition requires tailored Deployment and rollback plans. Significant partition deployments may require additional customer service planning or other system support planning.
- The need to communicate with isolated business units, third-party interfaces, and technical and business groups becomes critical. Each of these groups requires potentially rapidly changing information.
- Coordinating Deployment efforts may be a challenge. Not all parties will become compliant at the same time. As you deploy new systems, you will need to negotiate responsibility for bridges and patches for each partition with affected parties.
- With the Year 2000 looming, you may have limited time to complete Deployment activities.
- You must complete the Deployment of critical systems. You simply cannot fail to deploy the systems that keep your organization in business.

The cost for completion of Deployment should not exceed 5 percent of your Year 2000 project cost.

The time devoted to Deployment tasks should comprise 5 percent of the Year 2000 project schedule.

Summary of Deliverables

This section summarizes the deliverables for this phase of the Year 2000 compliance project. The section "Deliverables, Tasks, and Dependencies" later in this chapter includes detailed descriptions of each deliverable and the associated supporting tasks.

Deployment Phase Startup

The Deployment Phase Startup deliverable provides the resources necessary to successfully complete Deployment tasks. Initial tasks include the orientation of the Deployment team, the verification of partition dependencies, and the maintenance of the Year 2000 repository.

Data Conversion Plan

The Data Conversion Plan provides a detailed description of the requirements, activities, schedule, and budget required to convert partition-related data. In addition, it defines "data accuracy metrics." The development of data update cycles is considered a key part of the conversion activity.

Deployment Plan

The Deployment Plan provides a detailed description of the requirements, activities, schedule, and budget required to deploy a partition. In addition, it defines "critical performance metrics." These metrics will be used to measure your success for newly deployed systems.

Deployment Preparation

The Deployment Preparation deliverable supports the execution of "pre-Deployment" tasks, which include the establishment of a notification network, the placement of vendor system components, the distribution of updated documentation, and the execution of user training. Once Deployment preparation is complete, you can begin the formal Deployment activity.

Data Conversion

The Data Conversion deliverable is the first step in the formal Deployment activity. This deliverable supports the backup, conversion, validation, and baselining of production data. It also supports the repair of inaccurate conversions.

Deployment Execution

The Deployment Execution deliverable supports the release of Year 2000 compliant systems into your operational production environment. Coordination, communications, and notifications are critical at this point in your project. You must consider the needs of isolated business units, third parties, and system users. Both systems and temporary bridges are deployed at this time.

Deployment Validation

The Deployment Validation deliverable supports the validation of successful system deployments. You will validate that the expected functions you are deploying are operating correctly and that your Year 2000 changes do not adversely affect your business. Successful validation procedures will vary drastically based on the solution sets you are deploying. A four-digit conversion may affect user displays whereby a windowing solution may impede user access to data. The key is to validate both expected system functionality and business operations. Baselines, success, and accuracy metrics are used to validate successful system Deployment and data conversion. The validation process results in a go/no-go decision. When you make a go decision, the system partition is considered Year 2000 compliant. If validation reveals errors that result in "gross" operational concerns, you make a no-go decision, and the system will "roll back" to a pre-Deployment state. Deployment Validation is also called validation "on install."

Rollback

The Rollback deliverable supports the execution of rollback procedures in the event of a no-go decision. You will use the baseline data and system backups to return the system to its pre-Deployment state.

Deliverables, Tasks, and Depfndencies

The deliverables in this phase support the reentry of your Year 2000 compliant systems into their operational environment. Although you may be pressured to deploy quickly, you must make sure that the tasks for these deliverables are accomplished carefully and completely.

8.1 Deployment Phase Startup

You begin Deployment by establishing your Deployment team and giving them an orientation to the project. This lets the Deployment team become acquainted with the project and the Deployment process.

Task Overview

- Establish and Brief Deployment Team
- Establish Deployment Tracking

8.1.1 Task: Establish and Brief Deployment Team

Establish a dedicated multidisciplinary team to conduct and manage cyclical Deployment efforts. This team will act as the point of convergence for multiple compliance initiatives. The Deployment team will interface with multiple parties involved with Deployment to assure completeness and continuity. The Deployment team will tailor each Deployment to meet the specific demands of partition users and interfaces. In addition, they will be responsible for incorporating and communicating "lessons learned" from each successive deployment. Note that the Deployment team mentioned here is a subset of the "support team" mentioned in earlier chapters.

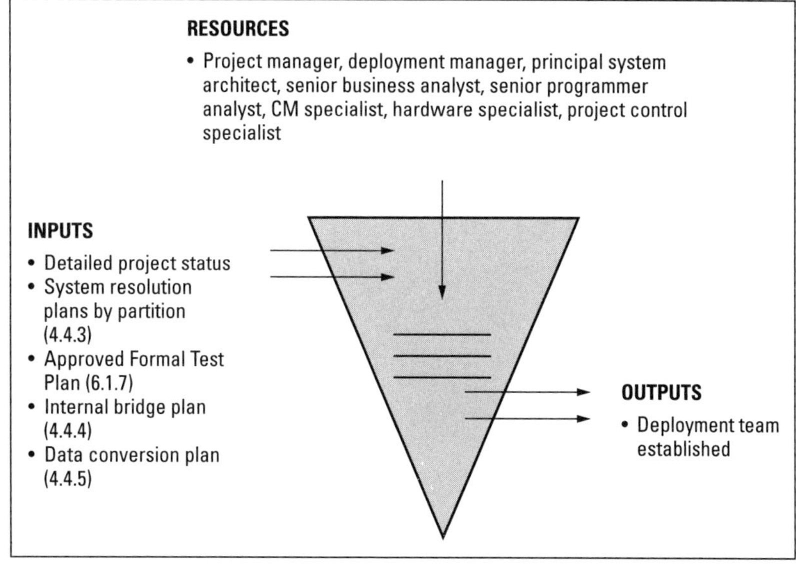

RESOURCES
• Project manager, deployment manager, principal system architect, senior business analyst, senior programmer analyst, CM specialist, hardware specialist, project control specialist
INPUTS
• Detailed project status
• System resolution plans by partition (4.4.3)
• Approved Formal Test Plan (6.1.7)
• Internal bridge plan (4.4.4)
• Data conversion plan (4.4.5)
OUTPUTS
• Deployment team established

Task Guidelines

- The deployment manager should have a technical background and a strong customer orientation and report directly to the Year 2000 project manager at an isolated business unit level.
- Use one Deployment team for each isolated business unit in your organization. Share best practices and lessons learned between Deployment teams.
- As much as possible, use members from your Detailed Assessment and Resolution team to form the Deployment team.

8.1.2 Task: Establish Deployment Tracking

Using the schedule and progress measurement requirements set forth in the Initial Project Plan, schedule specific Deployment milestones, measurement points, and progress review meetings. These meetings should be used to compare actual progress against planned work products for progress, effort, sizing, resource utilization, and risk reduction. You should address discrepancies by reallocating appropriate resources. Deployment tracking also includes the notification and coordination of third-party conversions, where a third party should be notified when your Year 2000 changes are deployed. In addition, you should establish a feedback loop to track third-party responses and integrate lessons learned into future phases.

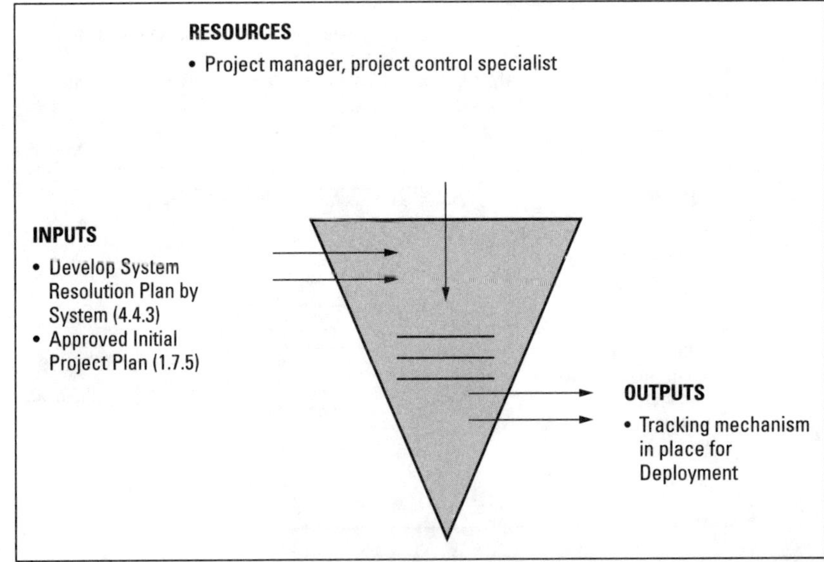

Deployment Startup Phase complete. Quality assurance verifies that the deliverable conforms to its intended goal. Project control baselines the deliverable and updates tracking metrics.

8.2 Data Conversion Plan

The Deployment team begins the formal Deployment process by understanding the data uses, cycles, and requirements. The team establishes data accuracy metrics that will be used in post-Deployment validation to confirm data conversion accuracy. Deployment combines this information to create a formal data conversion plan (later integrated with the Deployment plan).

Task Overview

- Reexamine Information Flow and Dependencies
- Define Data Validation Metrics
- Develop Conversion Plan

8.2.1 Task: Reexamine Information Flow and Dependencies

During this task your Deployment team reexamines the partition's natural information flow, business cycles, and data dependencies. Much of this information was used during the Testing phases to coordinate and execute partition tests and should be readily available. For example, when deploying an accounting system your Deployment team may need to consider state and federal reporting cycles, accrual basis, or financial third-parties readiness. Understanding the uses, the dependencies, and information flows of your partition will give the Deployment team critical insights into who needs to be notified and what sequence of events must take place during the partition deployment.

RESOURCES

- Principal system architect, senior business analyst, senior database administrator, project control specialist
- Year 2000 repository
- Access to business operations personnel

INPUTS

- System resolution plans by partition (4.4.3)
- Formal test report (7.3.4)
- Enterprise Schematic (1.3)
- Third-party interface requirements (4.4.4)
- List of partition data structures (4.4.5)

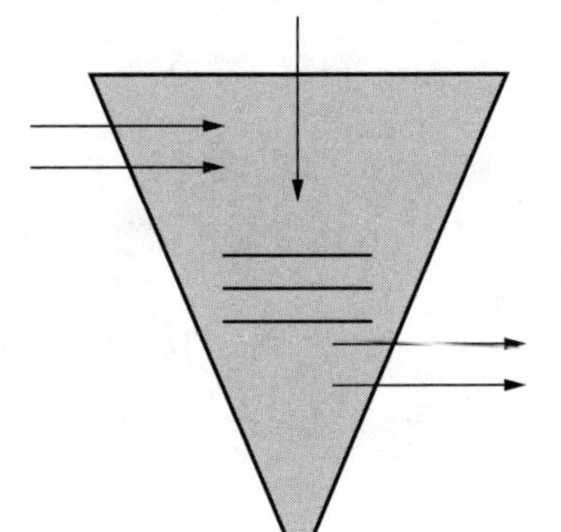

OUTPUTS

- Data cycle priorities report
- Draft data conversion schedule and sequence

Task Guidelines

- Consider the following when defining data cycle priorities:
  - Natural business cycles that create and use data
  - Third-party data requirements and cycles
  - Manual data entry
- Consider elapsed time to convert data, and to deploy systems and bridges.
- Access to support systems is necessarily restricted during the Deployment and conversion event.
- Knowing how long Deployment and data conversion will take will let business operations plan workarounds during times of restricted system access.
- Make note of the parties that will need to be involved with your Deployment. Customers, third parties, and other business operations are a few examples. You will use this list when you develop your notification network in Task 8.4.1.

8.2.2 Task: Define Data Validation Metrics

Business and technical Deployment team members will identify each data structure supporting the partition scheduled for Deployment. They will develop summary metrics to measure the accuracy of data conversion for each affected data structure. For example, an accounting system may use the number of account records before and after the conversion, or the sum balance of all accounts before and after the conversion. If your partition produces regular reports or measures, use these. However, be careful not to select more validation information than your team can review in a short period of time. Develop validation metrics for each critical component of your partition.

If the partition is comprised of mostly hardware or embedded systems, develop your validation metrics based on performance over time or number of different events.

You may choose to automate your validation metrics production. If so, deliver specifications for metric production to the Resolution teams for inclusion in their development efforts.

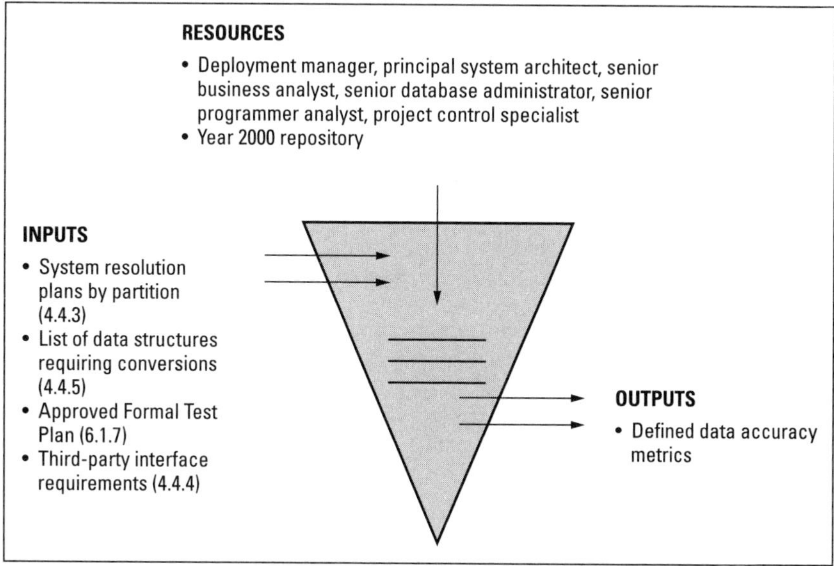

Task Guidelines

- Metrics should provide both summary validation information (number of records by type) and meaningful samples of detailed information (converted and nonconverted information).
- Interview test team members. They will have already thought through some of these metrics. However, remember that testing is focused on a functional level. This effort identifies metrics for each data structure.
- You must be able to produce and review metrics quickly. Validation of deployed systems and converted data occurs while system access has been restricted to users.
- You should take snapshots of data accuracy metrics before and after data conversion to determine unexpected changes.

8.2.3 Task: Develop Conversion Plan

For all partition data structures requiring conversion, create a Data Conversion Plan. Incorporate data cycle priorities and data validation metrics. Incorporate the conversion plan as part of the Deployment Plan in the next deliverable.

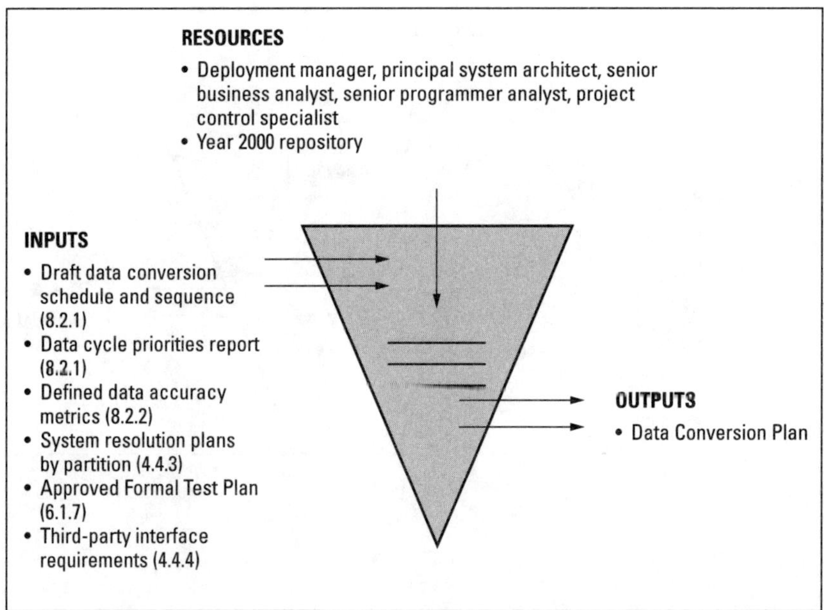

Data Conversion Plan complete. Quality assurance verifies that the deliverable conforms to its intended goal. Project control baselines the deliverable and updates tracking metrics.

8.3 Deployment Plan

The Deployment Plan addresses all the issues your team may run into involving the rollout of a partition of software, hardware, and data. It incorporates a contingency plan to roll back to a pre-Deployment state. This plan identifies the who, the how, and the when of deployment. It shows the sequence of merged compliance activities. The plan will be used during Deployment to keep all parties on the same track and aimed toward the same goal.

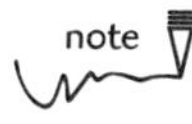

The successful Deployment of a partition occurs with minimal impact to the business operations, production systems, users, customers, and internal and external interfaces.

The Deployment manager is responsible for pulling together most of the information used to produce detailed requirements, activities, schedules, and budgets required to roll out the partition.

Task Overview

- Define Go/No-Go (Rollback) Criteria and Metrics
- Determine Critical Performance Indicators and Metrics
- Establish Deployment Sequence or Implementation Plan
- Determine Rollback Sequence
- Identify Impacted Business Processes
- Develop Customer Service Plan
- Develop User Training Plan
- Identify Notification Requirements
- Develop Deployment Plan
- Present and Approve Deployment Plan

8.3.1 Task: Define Go/No-Go (Rollback) Criteria and Metrics

The go/no-go (rollback) criteria are predefined measures you will use to accept or reject a deployed partition. Determine up front what parameters you will use to determine when Deployment is complete. You should complete this task in parallel with the initial Resolution tasks. Criteria affecting Resolution development should be communicated to and included in Resolution technical specifications. Develop a checklist, by partition, of the acceptable "go" criteria.

Elements of the go/no-go checklist include

- Data accuracy metrics
- Critical performance indicators
- Business impact of noncompliance in the scheduled time frame
- Current versus future impacts (that is, the new code works today, but still contains some bugs that need to be fixed before the year 2000)
- Impact to ensuing deployments

RESOURCES

- Deployment manager, CM specialist, development team, testing team, senior business analyst, business manager, administrative support
- Year 2000 repository

INPUTS

- Organization-specific compliance definition (1.2.1)
- System resolution plans by partition (4.4.3)
- Defined data accuracy metrics (8.2.2)
- Data Conversion Plan (8.2.3)
- Approved Formal Test Plan (6.1.7)
- Detailed Deployment requirements list
- Strawman criteria

OUTPUTS

- Go/no-go criteria

Task Guidelines

- Go/no-go criteria should be developed to a level of detail complementing the business priority of the partition. It should complement and be a mirror image of your compliance definition. The go/no-go criteria should be complete but not exhaustive. The key here is speed and accuracy. Deployments take place in hours and days, not weeks and months. The demands placed on these parameters can have a significant impact on the scope of your Deployment effort; take care to balance the completeness of your criteria with the time you require to execute Deployment.
- Members of the development team, the testing team, users, and the Deployment manager should determine the go/no-go criteria checklist. The development and testing teams can prepare a strawman criteria list, which should contain only critical items. The Deployment team ensures that staff is available to perform the go/no-go decision at Deployment time.

8.3.2 Task: Determine Critical Performance Indicators and Metrics

After the functions to be included in the partition are identified, a small group of development and test personnel should generate a list of critical performance indicators. This list will become part of the go/no-go criteria and will be a subset of the tests performed during partition testing.

You will use the critical performance indicators to baseline and validate partitions deployed to production.

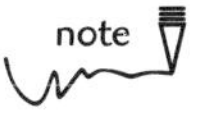

Do not confuse critical performance indicators with machine or system speed performance. The focus here is functional performance.

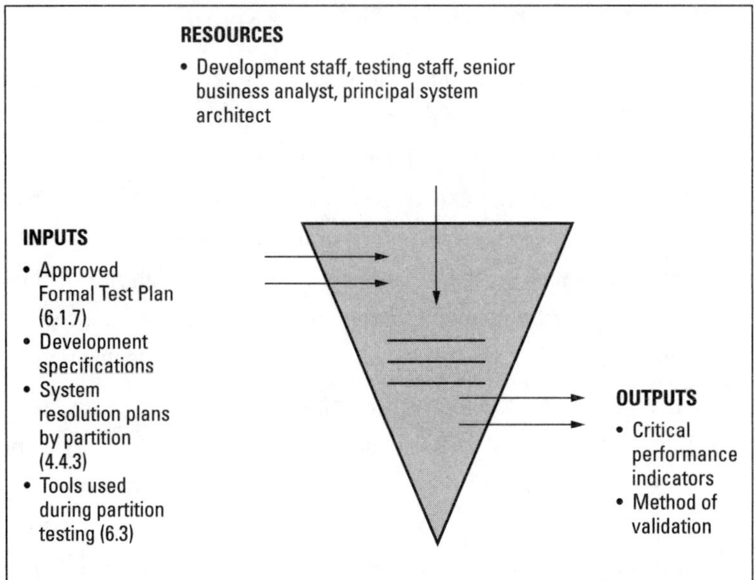

Task Guidelines

- When specifying the indicators, include specific functions; for example:
  - Perform accounts receivable query correctly within required response time.
  - Validate format of first 30 records on system *X*.
  - Confirm presence of four-digit year field on inventory check client GUI window.
  - Check reject rate on (function name) records transmitted to a third party.
  - Process 100 Parson's table updates per minute in CHRCH 108 program.
- You should also identify the tools and methods required to measure the specified performance indicators. If you need custom software, the development staff should have provided the needed tools to support integration and system tests, and they should be available from the configuration for the partition. In general, the tools for measuring the performance indicators should already be available, because the tests defined here are a subset of the tests performed during partition testing.

8.3.3 Task: Establish Deployment Sequence or Implementation Plan

This is when you investigate the deploying partition and determine the sequence of events that should occur to deploy your compliant system. This sequence will drive your Deployment schedule and potential rollback.

Use the data conversion sequence as a starting point and build into the schedule:

- Business operation requirements
- Hardware availability
- COTS availability and integration
- Data cycle sequence
- User readiness (training completion)
- System availability
- Expected Deployment elapsed time
- Conflicting Deployment schedules

RESOURCES

- Development manager, principal system architect, operations manager, hardware specialist, CM analyst, project control specialist, business manager
- Year 2000 repository

INPUTS

- Data Conversion Plan (8.2.3)
- System resolution plans by partition (4.4.3)
- Business operation requirements
- Integration status
- COTS availability and integration
- Training status
- Expected Deployment elapsed time
- Conflicting Deployment schedules

OUTPUTS

- Deployment sequence

8.3.4 Task: Determine Rollback Sequence

If the partition being inserted fails Deployment validation (no-go decision), you will need to determine in advance how to get back to your baseline pre-Deployment system.

Your CM manager may already provide a rollback procedure. If not, you should define one now.

You can define the rollback sequence by starting with the Deployment sequence. Production specialists can create a similar sequence chart specifying the steps that system operators should take to back out the updated partition and reinsert the baseline system into production.

There are often two types of rollback plans: One applies if you apply a no-go decision as part of your validation (that is, the system never really goes live), and one applies after you've installed, and then encounter unexpected problems, forcing you to "roll back." It's very important to avoid rollbacks due to unexpected problems. Unless the problems are catastrophic, you may create larger problems by moving partitions in and out of your production environment. In addition to the complexities surprise rollbacks present, you may have to contend with additional partitions that are scheduled for deployment next. If at all possible, do not consider rolling back deployed and accepted systems. Focus rollback plans on the partitions that fail validation, not deployed systems that present surprises.

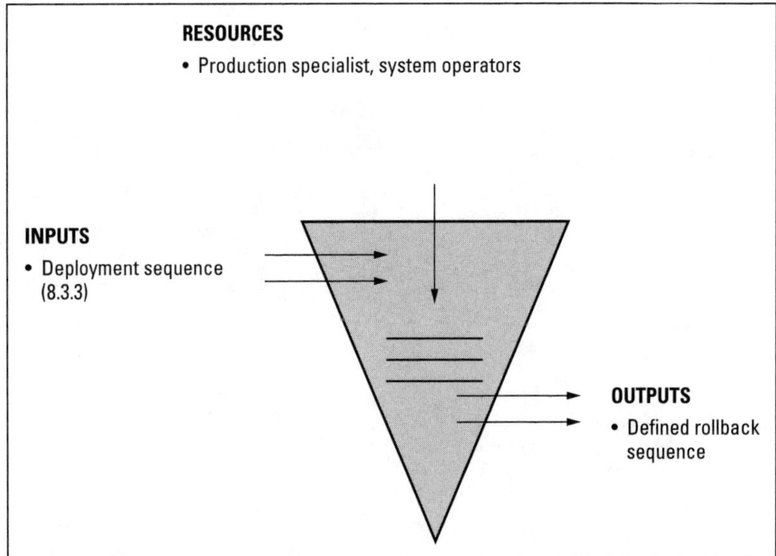

Task Guideline

- Production specialists who helped generate the Deployment sequence should be familiar with the steps required to get back to a properly operating system.

8.3.5 Task: Identify Impacted Business Processes

Review the processes being performed by users, customers, operators, and third parties in relation to your partition. Determine the impact of compliance updates on these business operations. The specific processes to be reviewed should be based on those updated in the partition.

Make recommendations to provide training or circumvent the impact on business operations.

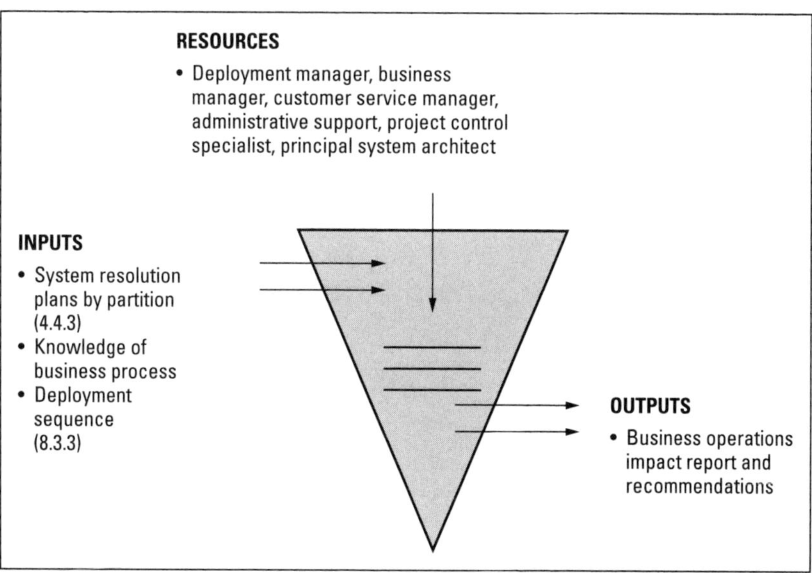

Task Guideline

- The deployment of a new COTS package may require a change in data entry procedures, new display and reporting formats, new system cycles and interfaces, and may even require specialized training. Ensure that customer service knows of the procedure change and/or data entry agents have been trained in the new process.

8.3.6 Task: Develop Customer Service Plan

Using the impacted business operations report generated in the preceding task, identify needed modifications to customer service and/or help desk operations.

Create and execute a plan to make these modifications. The requirements specified here will be implemented shortly before partition Deployment.

Deployment impact on customer service operations may include:

- Preparing customer service agents to be able to inform users of the source of the problem
- An increased workload due to potential user and customer problems with the updated system
- Prioritizing problem reporting to expedite problem resolution relating to partition Deployment

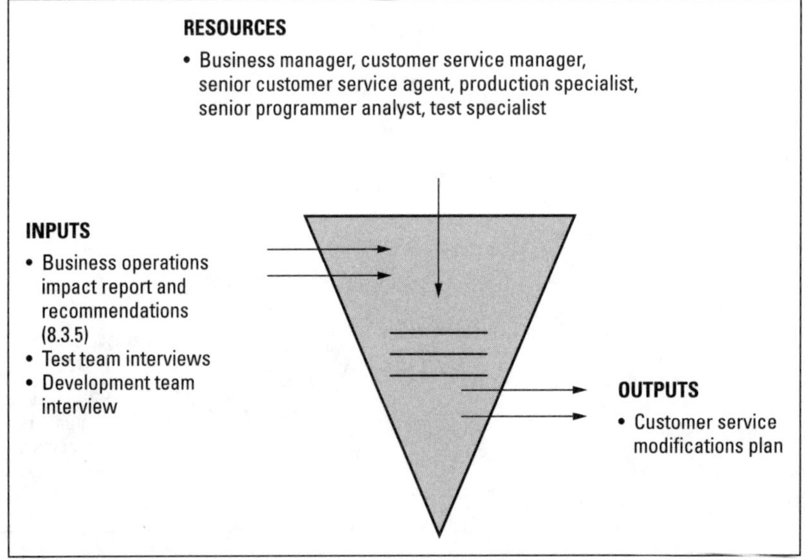

Task Guidelines

- The development team and Deployment team need to keep the customer service staff informed about changes to the partition being deployed. The customer service staff need to know how the deployed partition may affect the user.

- Determine the current capability to process calls and problems, and assess (and quantify) spare capacity within the existing organization.
- Incorporate lessons learned into the customer service staff's Deployment briefing.
- Estimate volume impacts to the customer service operation over time. (How many additional customer service calls can be expected immediately after Deployment? How many one week later? Will there be a change in the user interface that will cause the users some confusion?)
- Assign a senior customer service agent to attend Deployment coordination meetings.
- Use existing assessment techniques and metrics to assess and quantify the capabilities of the customer service operation. Supplement this effort by using any existing records. Updates to previous customer service capability assessments should include refinements as a result of actual capability measurements, and upgrades necessitated by previous Deployment cycles.
- Consider third-party interface coordination and the impacts on your customer service agents.
- COTS implementation may cause a spike in customer service calls due to the effectiveness of training.

8.3.7 Task: Develop User Training Plan

If the Deployment being planned modifies any user, customer, or operator interface, determine whether any training will be required.

Using the impacted business operations report, the customer service plan, the Deployment sequence, the data conversion plan, and the defined rollback sequence, determine your training requirements.

Develop a training plan/budget and schedule. Once the training requirements have been specified, the training manager or specialist creates a detailed plan for users, customers, and operators. The Deployment training plan includes a schedule by user operation, content and notification requirements, and the estimated costs of training sessions.

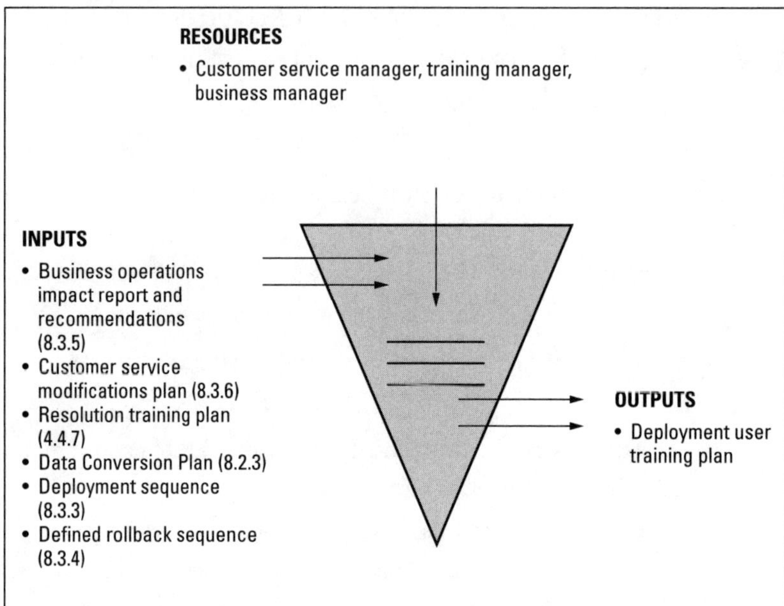

Task Guidelines

- Training may take the form of any of the following:
  - Broadcast notifications describing changes in user interfaces
  - Individual or group on-the-job training
  - Class training of users in the operation of new COTS software and of technical staff in its installation and maintenance
- Consider the circumstance where the system is going live with known operational workarounds as a result of errors that you have consciously agreed not to fix in this release/install.
- Appoint a training coordinator to develop the training plan and budget.
- The training effort will be directly proportional to the size of Deployment and user interface impact.
- Include this plan as part or your Deployment Plan.
- Expect modifications to the existing training budget due to changes in facility requirements, including additional space, employment, or supplies.

8.3.8 Task: Identify Notification Requirements

Deployment requires tight and frequent communications. The audience for these communications changes each time you deploy a different partition. Identify who and how you will keep all parties informed during Deployment and validation activity.

Estimate any additional costs you may incur or resources you may need to sustain these communications. If at all possible, identify these communications costs in Detailed Assessment. However, realize that many times these costs can not be estimated because third-party obligations have not yet been negotiated in Detailed Assessment.

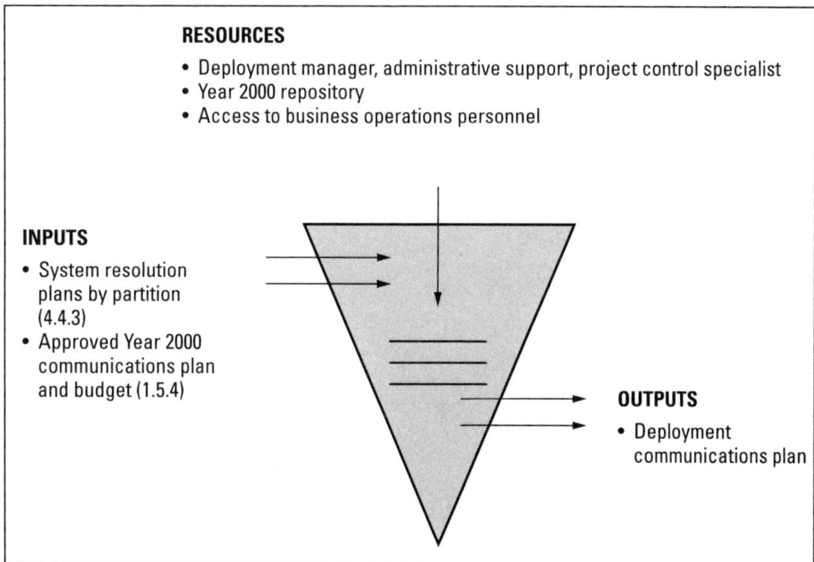

Task Guidelines

- Use the communication network established in Planning and Awareness. Modify the distribution list for each partition.
- If the partition being released adds significant user or customer capabilities (new COTS package), consider marketing advertisements, newsletters, or press releases as forms of notification.

8.3.9 Task: Develop Deployment Plan

Once all the impacts and issues regarding a Deployment have been examined, understood, and sized, consolidate the information from each of the preceding tasks and create a detailed Deployment Plan, including the schedule, Deployment sequence, and specific budget requirements.

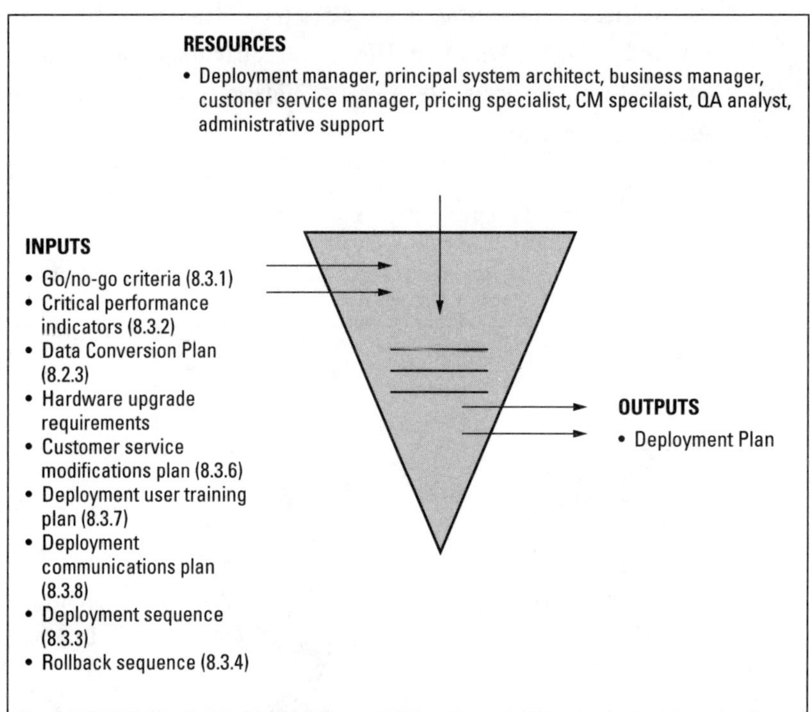

8.3.10 Task: Present and Approve Deployment Plan

Present the Deployment Plan to senior management or your customer for approval. Incorporate any requested management changes and issue the Deployment Plan to address management concerns and other issues.

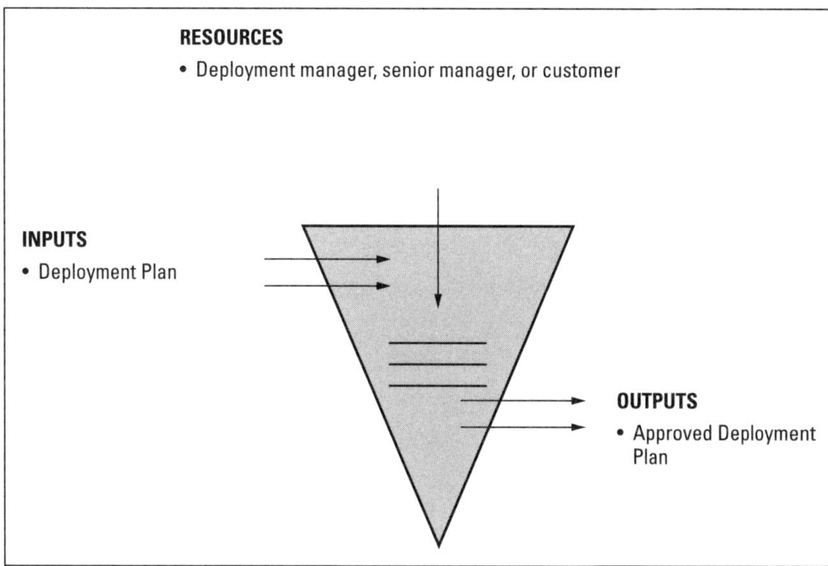

Deployment Plan complete. Quality assurance verifies that the deliverable conforms to its intended goal. Project control baselines the deliverable and updates tracking metrics.

8.4 Deployment Preparation

Before beginning the formal data conversion and Deployment activities, you must undertake several "housekeeping" tasks.

Task Overview

- Establish Notification Network
- Deliver Updated Documentation
- Conduct Deployment Training
- Prepare Customer Service
- Confirm and Capture System Deployment Information

8.4.1 Task: Establish Notification Network

Using the guidelines developed and approved in your Deployment Plan, establish your partition-level notification network. This notification network is the short

list of vendors, customers, and operations that may be affected by your partition Deployment.

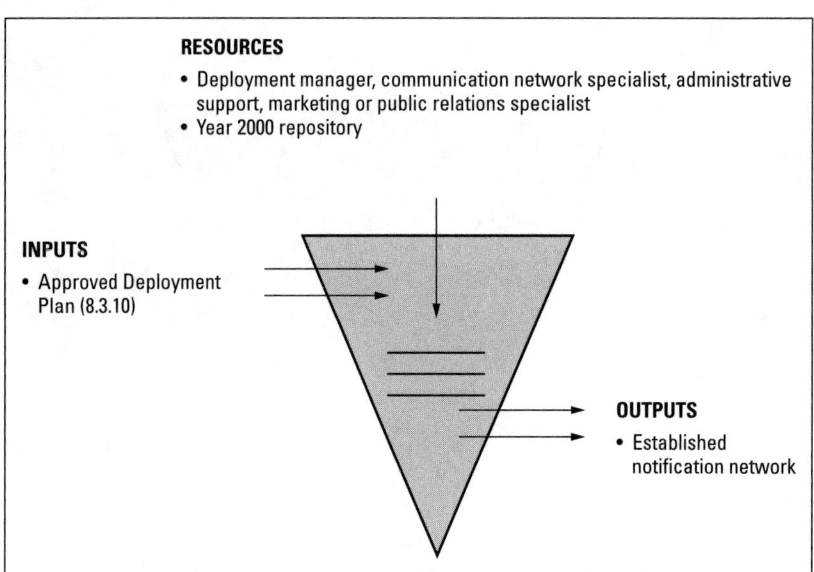

Task Guidelines

- Use your Year 2000 repository to identify the parties affected by your Deployment Plan.
- Use the lists created in Task 8.2.1.
- Consider using a contact manager utility (also called personal information manager, or PIM) to track which notifications went to each party and when they were sent.

8.4.2 Task: Deliver Updated Documentation

Release all appropriate documentation while you're doing user or customer training. You updated the updates to program, production, user, and customer documentation and forms during Resolution.

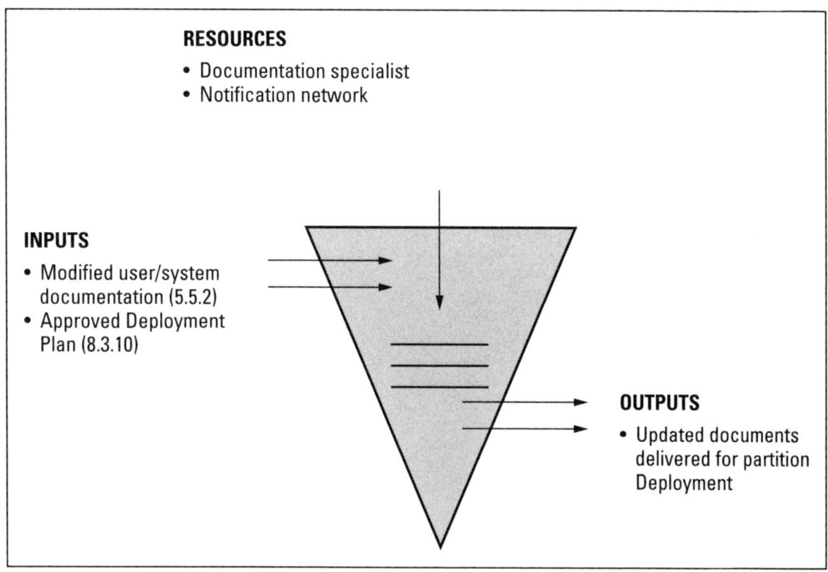

8.4.3 Task: Conduct Deployment Training

Conduct Deployment training in accordance with your Deployment training plan.

Use pre-Deployment versions of the partition to conduct training. Make sure that training finishes at the same time as the Deployment release.

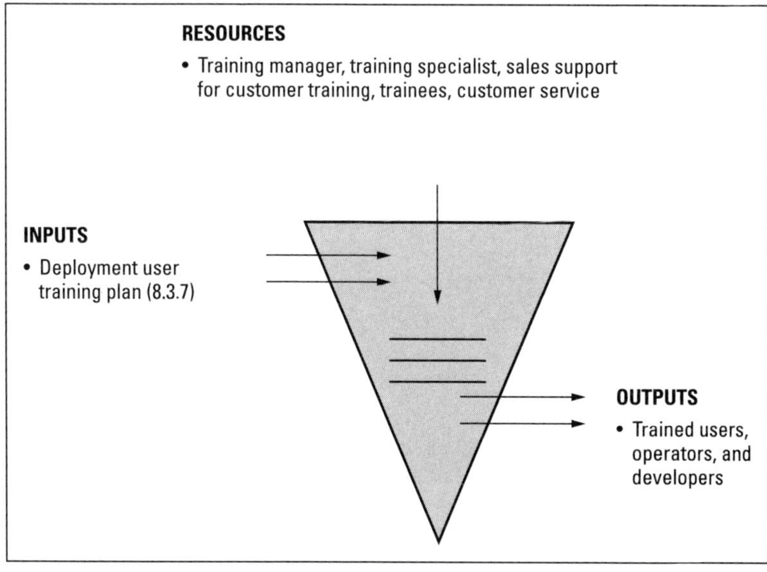

Task Guidelines

- You may need to modify training plans to reflect changes or delays in partition Deployment, or schedule additional training for the use and operation of the new partition.
- Determine a way of keeping training material current with actual Deployment. Depending on the size of Deployment and the impact on users, business owners, or operators, you may need several days to prepare and update training materials.

8.4.4 Task: Prepare Customer Service

Preparing your customer service organization is an ongoing task. You should prepare customer service agents in accordance with the Deployment Plan. In addition, you should require customer service agents to stay abreast of new issues arising from Deployment. Finally, incorporate lessons learned.

Establish a strong communications link between the Deployment team and customer service.

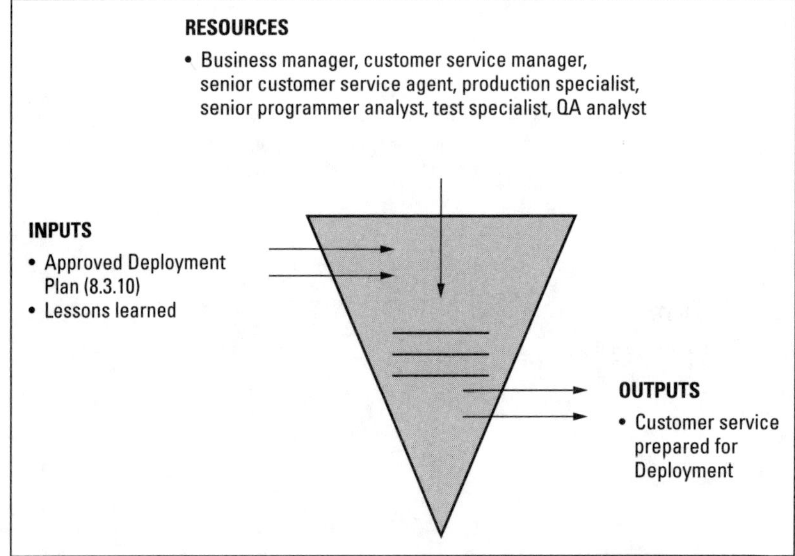

Task Guidelines

- Consider supporting the customer service staff with a senior member of the Deployment team for the days immediately following partition Deployment.
- Consider daily customer service briefings immediately following Deployment. Receive feedback from customer service and notify customer service of impending issues.

8.4.5 Task: Confirm and Capture System Deployment Information

Now you generate a confirmation list describing all the system components needed to deploy a partition. Log this list into the Year 2000 repository as your partition version/release list.

This detailed list defines the elements of partition Deployment. From this list, you will be taking baselines, verifying Deployment readiness, and controlling rollback, if required.

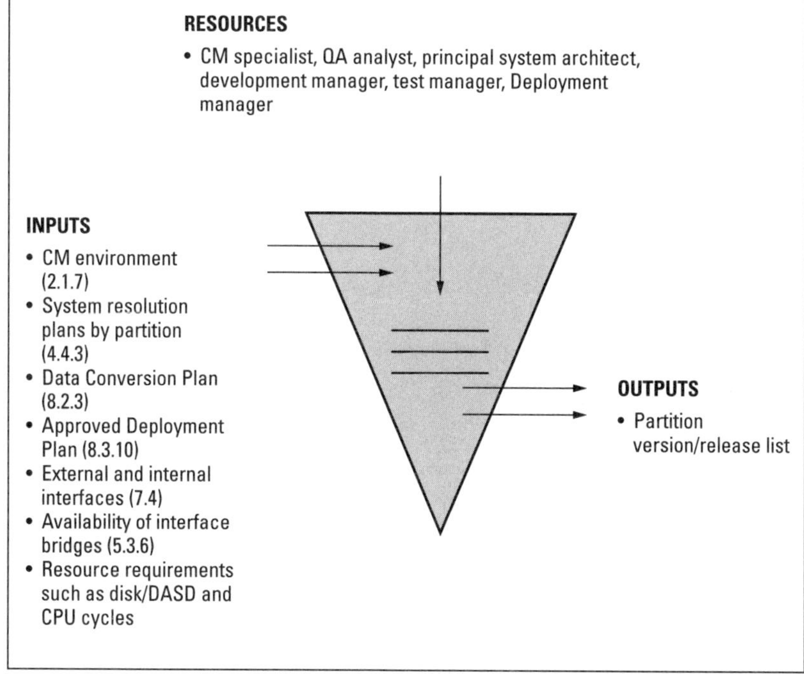

RESOURCES
• CM specialist, QA analyst, principal system architect, development manager, test manager, Deployment manager
INPUTS
• CM environment (2.1.7)
• System resolution plans by partition (4.4.3)
• Data Conversion Plan (8.2.3)
• Approved Deployment Plan (8.3.10)
• External and internal interfaces (7.4)
• Availability of interface bridges (5.3.6)
• Resource requirements such as disk/DASD and CPU cycles
OUTPUTS
• Partition version/release list

Task Guidelines

- The development, testing, and Deployment teams need to jointly verify the contents of the partition version/release list.
- Developers and testers should know about the contents of the partition to be deployed and should be able to work with the Deployment team to finalize Deployment requirements.
- Use the experience of the Deployment team in deploying other production work outside of Year 2000 to help avoid rollbacks.

Deployment Preparation complete. Quality assurance verifies that the deliverable conforms to its intended goal. Project control baselines the deliverable and updates tracking metrics. Configuration management verifies that Year 2000 repository updates adhere to CM procedures.

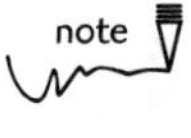

The next four How To 2000 deliverables are executed quickly while users are prohibited partition access. These are the tasks that move your Year 2000 compliant system into production.

8.5 Data Conversion

The first step in the formal Deployment activity is to prepare and convert the required partition data structures.

Task Overview

- Back Up Preconversion Data Structures
- Develop Configuration Management of Conversion Routines
- Convert Data
- Generate Post-Conversion Accuracy Metrics
- Validate Data Conversion
- Baseline and Back Up Converted Data Structures

8.5.1 Task: Back Up Preconversion Data Structures

Before converting data, make sure to take a backup copy of each data structure. Create "preconversion accuracy metrics" that baseline the data structures.

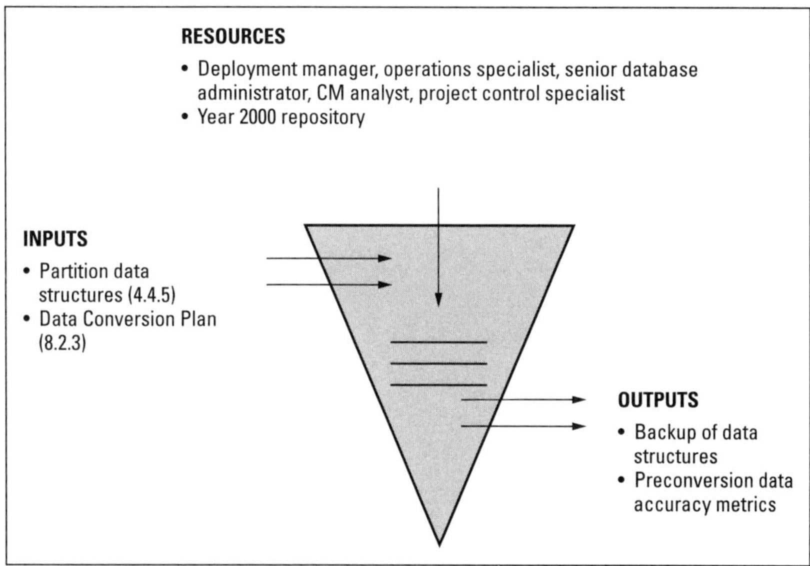

Task Guideline

- Prohibit user access to data structures before backing up.

8.5.2 Task: Develop Configuration Management of Conversion Routines

Before converting the data, make sure that any custom and/or COTS software used to convert the data is under configuration management and is part of the partition Deployment. This will ensure that the correct, tested versions of the conversion routines are used.

Normally, this task is a simple check-and-go operation. However, if you find a discrepancy, you must verify with the developers and development testers that the correct version is available and was used during testing.

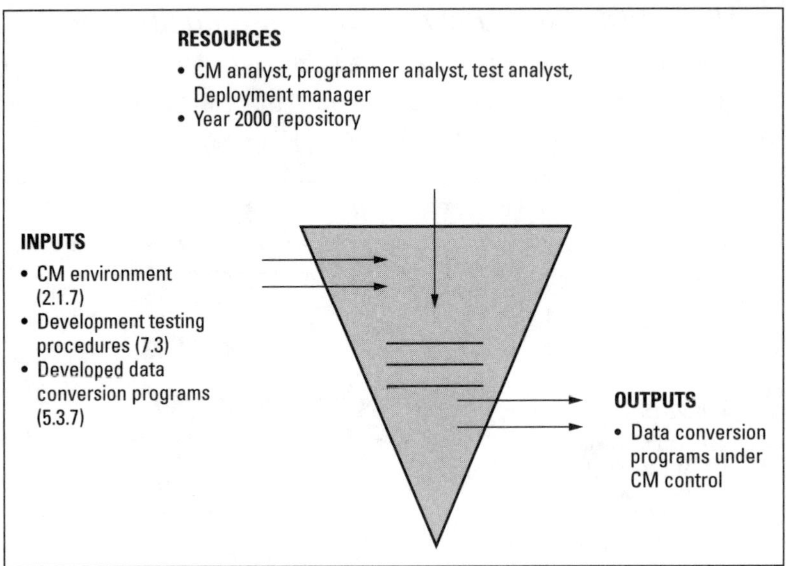

8.5.3 Task: Convert Data

Before Deployment to the new partition, you must convert the data being used to match the needs and requirements of the Deployment. During Detailed Assessment, you developed specifications for data conversion routines. During Resolution, the data conversion routines were written, unit tested, integration tested, and placed under configuration management. You must now convert the actual operational data.

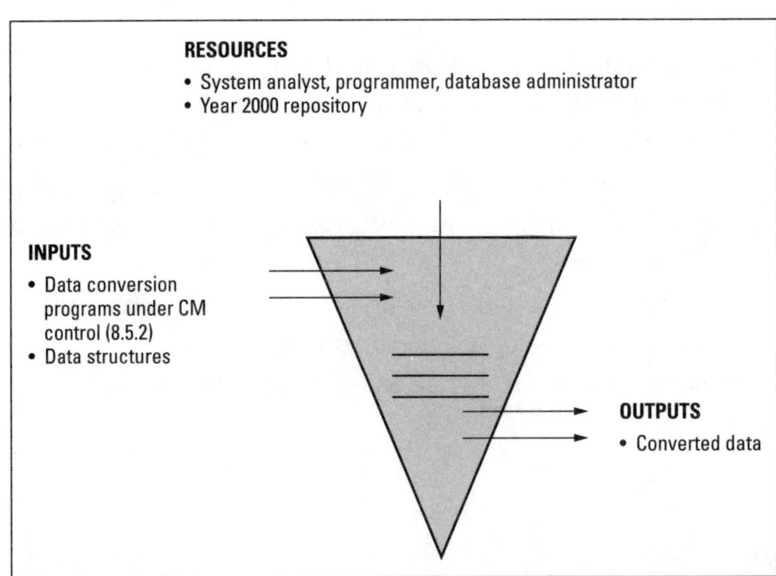

Task Guideline

- When you complete this task, all data required to run the new partition should meet the requirements of the partition, and allow production to continue.

8.5.4 Task: Generate Post-Conversion Accuracy Metrics

Create post-conversion accuracy metrics in accordance with your conversion plan.

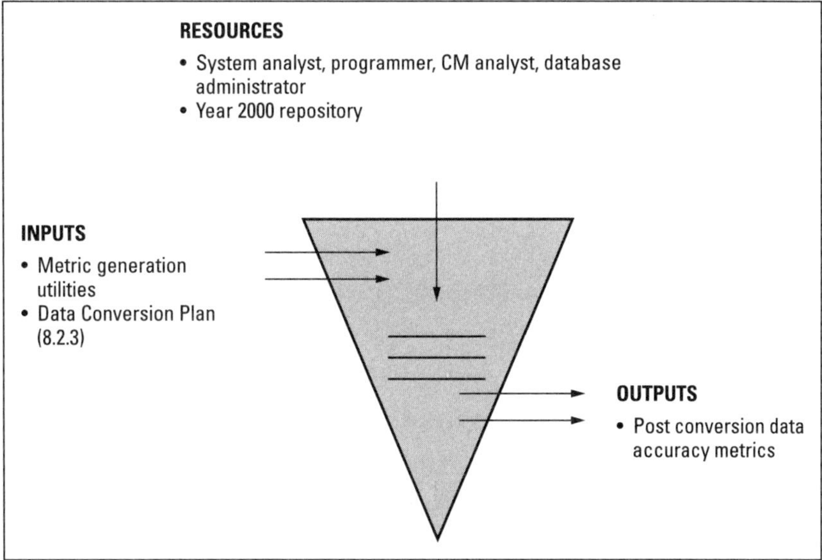

8.5.5 Task: Validate Data Conversion

Once the data has been converted and accuracy metrics generated, compare the pre- and post-accuracy metrics to determine the validity of the converted data.

Include some manual verification of data to visually inspect the quality of the converted data. Confirm that the appropriate files, data sets, and tapes were created, that the sizes were as expected, and that no errors were encountered during the conversion process. Note that some shops call this step "regression comparison." Create a quality assurance checkpoint here.

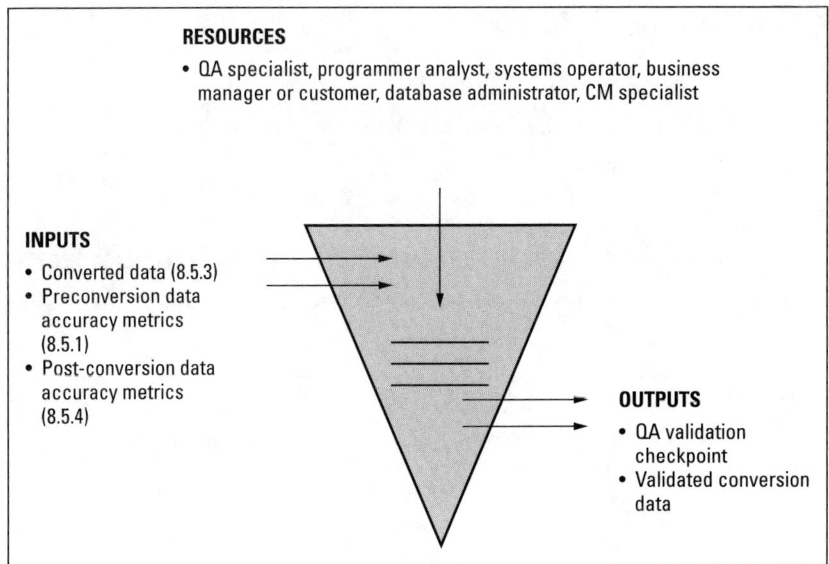

Task Guideline

- Involve end users or customers in these validation efforts as much as possible.

8.5.6 Task: Baseline and Back Up Converted Data Structures

Using full backup procedures (as modified for the new data), create a backup copy of validated data structures for archive, audit, and safety purposes. Depending on your environment, you may need to save the data to demonstrate how you got from "here" (preconverted data) to "there" (converted data).

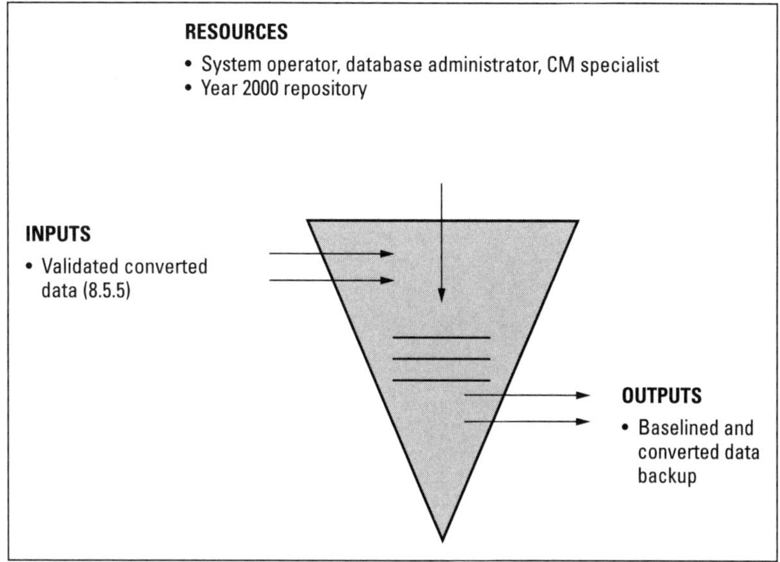

Task Guideline

- Allow enough time to fully create this backup. Backups can take time and resources, depending on the size of the data structure. You should allow around six hours per partition.

Data Conversion complete. Quality assurance verifies that the deliverable conforms to its intended goal. Project control baselines the deliverable and updates tracking metrics. Configuration management verifies that Year 2000 repository updates adhere to CM procedures.

8.6 Deployment Execution

The second step in Deployment is to release the prepared partition into the production environment. This set of tasks also takes place while users are restricted from system access.

Task Overview

- Distribute Deployment Notifications
- Determine Deployment Readiness
- Baseline and Back Up Pre-Deployment Environment
- Deploy Systems

8.6.1 Task: Distribute Deployment Notifications

Notify all parties of intended Deployment and time in accordance with your Deployment notification plans.

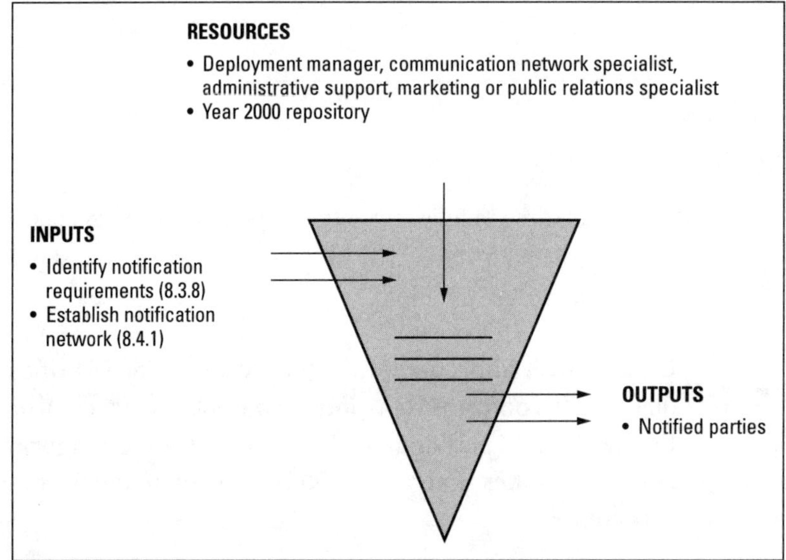

Task Guidelines

- Third-party notifications and bridge verification are critical actions at this point.
- If Deployment fails validation, immediately notify all parties again.

8.6.2 Task: Determine Deployment Readiness

Use the partition version/release and status reports list to perform a final verification that all required elements are in place and ready for Deployment (notifications prepared, customer service ready, partition and bridges tested, quality checked, data converted, user trained, and so on).

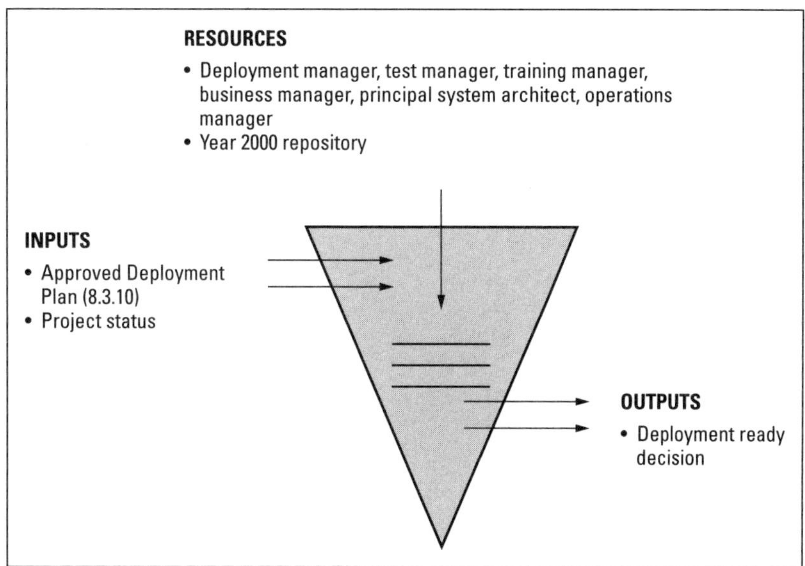

8.6.3 Task: Baseline and Back Up Pre-Deployment Environment

Before deploying the new partition, make sure to back up each partition element. Generate "pre-Deployment critical performance indicators" that baseline the existing partition's performance.

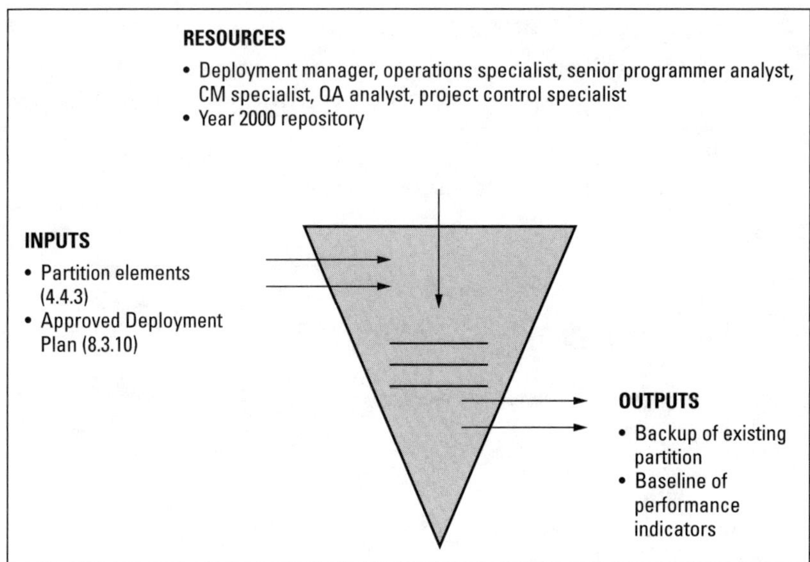

Task Guideline

- Prohibit user access to system partitions before backing up.

8.6.4 Task: Deploy Systems

Move your Year 2000 compliant partition into the production operational environment.

Catalog this change as a version/release in your Year 2000 repository.

Actually moving the updated partition should not take long. Move the identified elements in a batch as defined by your partition version/release list.

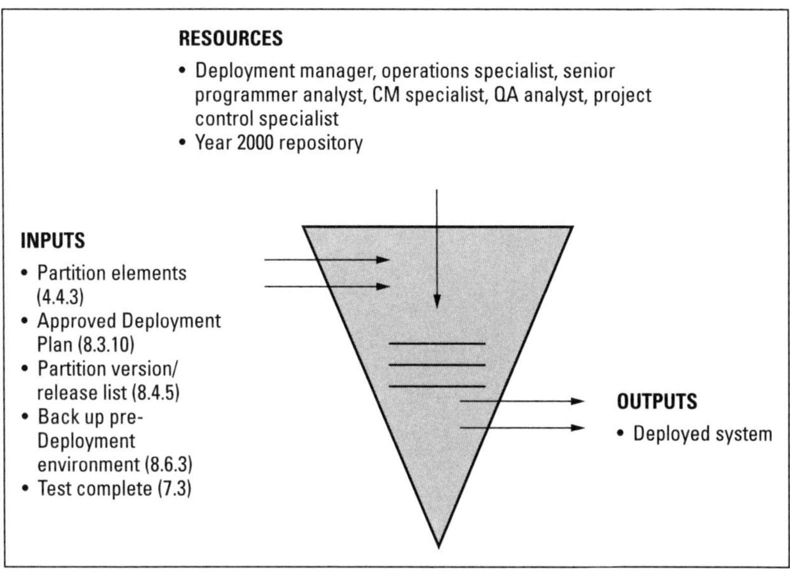

Task Guidelines

- Consider creating a temporary "release library" to house the Deployment elements during Deployment and validation. Once validation is complete, move the elements into their respective production libraries.
- Make sure that bridges and patches for all interface elements of your partition are properly deployed. These are elements that did not exist in your predeployed environment.
- Assign a post-Deployment team to monitor system performance and assist with customer service questions.

Deployment Execution complete. Quality assurance verifies that the deliverable conforms to its intended goal. Project control baselines the deliverable and updates tracking metrics. Configuration management verifies that Year 2000 repository updates adhere to CM procedures.

8.7 Deployment Validation

This is the third and possibly the final step in Deployment. You should execute these tasks while users are denied access to the deployed partitions. They occur quickly and in accordance with predefined Deployment Plans.

Once all the elements of a partition are deployed, use post-Deployment performance indicators to validate Deployment accuracy.

Make a go/no-go decision based on your validation assessment. If you make a go decision, the partition is considered Year 2000 compliant. If you make a no-go decision, execute the Rollback deliverable.

Task Overview

- Generate Post-Deployment Critical Performance Indicators
- Validate Deployment
- Make Go/No-Go Decision

8.7.1 Task: Generate Post-Deployment Critical Performance Indicators

Once the updated partition is deployed, generate post-Deployment critical performance indicators as defined in your Deployment Plan and in correlation with your compliance definition.

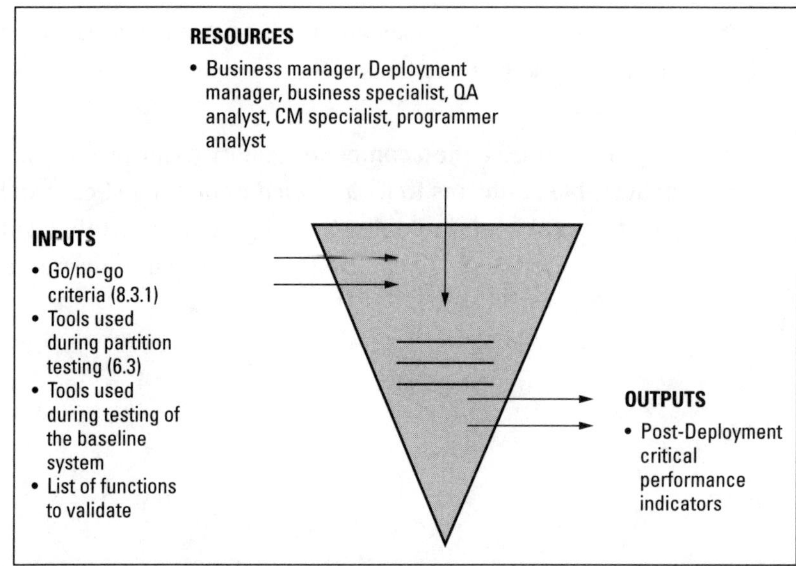

Task Guidelines

- Consider creating a brief chart listing each post-Deployment critical performance indicator and the associated metric. Use this chart to quickly assess the partition performance after Deployment.
- Use techniques similar to those used to test the baseline software.

8.7.2 Task: Validate Deployment

Once the post-Deployment critical performance indicators have been generated, compare them with the pre-Deployment critical performance metrics. Create a critical performance indicator report and log this information into the Year 2000 repository.

Include some manual verification of systems to visually inspect the quality of the deployed system.

Create a quality assurance checkpoint here.

Determine the impact on business operations of "coming live" with the Year 2000 compliant system.

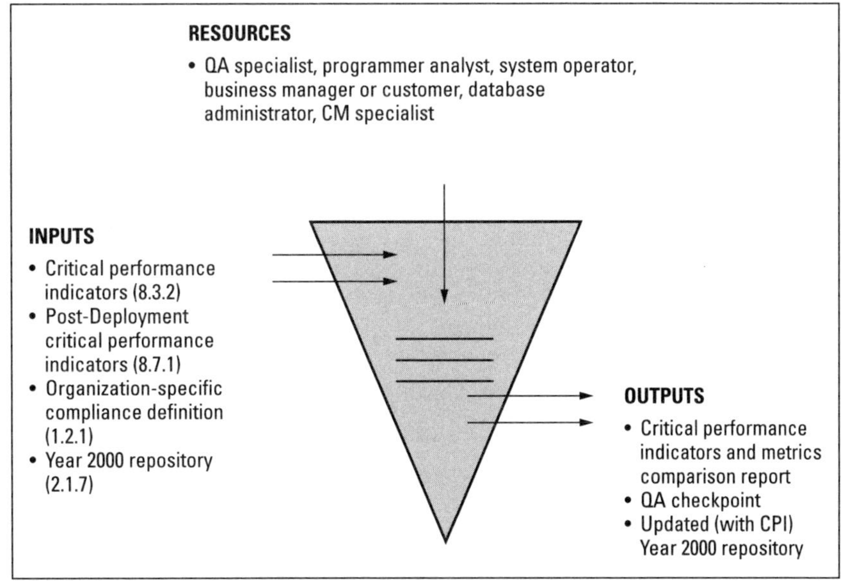

Task Guidelines

- Involve users or customers in the validation process as much as possible.
- Incorporate some statistically valid sampling of manual operations in the validation process.

8.7.3 Task: Make Go/No-Go Decision

Decide whether to open system access to end users or to roll back to the previous version of the partition. This is the go/no-go decision.

Base your decision on the partition go/no-go criteria and the findings of the critical performance indicator metric comparison report.

Update the Year 2000 repository with the appropriate version/release information.

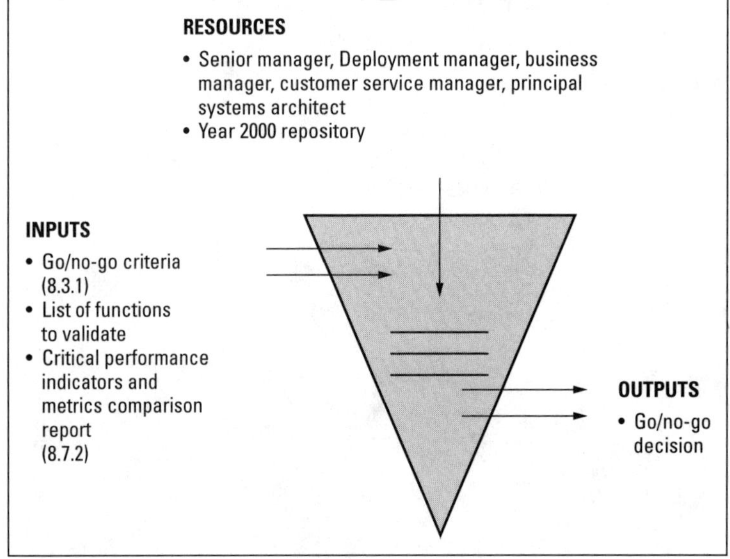

Task Guidelines

- Each failure to meet the criteria should be reevaluated carefully to ensure that the criteria were valid and truly critical. If a fix to the function could wait for the next maintenance cycle, the failure should not drive a no-go decision or rollback.

- Meet with each business owner or primary affected user. Recheck the requirements of the business owners and verify that each is in a position to deploy.
- Consider the pros and cons of a rollback and its impact on the user community before making a no-go decision. If there is a significant decision to be made (that is, there is some doubt about moving ahead), include senior management in the decision.
- Consider the impact to future deployments before finalizing a no-go decision or rolling back a partition.

Deployment Validation complete. Quality assurance verifies that the deliverable conforms to its intended goal. Project control baselines the deliverable and updates tracking metrics. Configuration management verifies that Year 2000 repository updates adhere to CM procedures.

8.8 Rollback

Rollback is a worst-case contingency plan. It is the last deliverable executed while users are prohibited system access.

Perform this deliverable if you make a no-go decision. Consider it only when you have business-critical problems with the partition being deployed. Except in the simplest cases, you should not make this decision lightly. Rollbacks involve retracting previous notices and reverting to old procedures, data, software, and interfaces. Rollbacks can send confusing messages and be detrimental to business relationships.

You should implement rollbacks with diligence and great care.

Task Overview

- Execute Rollback Plan
- Validate Restored Environment

8.8.1 Task: Execute Rollback Plan

Execute the rollback contingency portion of your Deployment Plan.

Some of the steps that should be considered in your Rollback Plan include:

- Send rollback notifications.
  - Advise customer service.
- Review and size customer service capabilities.
  - Retract isolated business units.
- Restore baseline data.
- Restore baseline procedures.
- Restore baseline software.
- Restore baseline version of bridges.
- Confirm functionality of baseline system.
- Coordinate rollback of supporting desktop software.
- Coordinate user data entry efforts to establish rollback.
  - Negotiate third-party agreements.

RESOURCES

- Deployment manager, operations manager, operations specialist, database administrator, principal system architect, customer service manager, business manager, programmer analyst, customer service agents, CM specialist, QA analyst, administrative support
- Year 2000 repository

INPUTS

- No-go criteria (8.3.1)
- Defined rollback sequence (8.3.4)
- Baseline system (Data, Procedures, Software, Bridges) (8.6.3)
- Baseline functionality metrics and measurement tools

OUTPUTS

- Restored functioning baseline system

Task Guidelines

- Rollback should occur before users are allowed to access deployed systems.
- Once end users access the updated partition and data is changed, this book strongly recommends not rolling back. Returning to your baseline system or data structures after data has changed implies the potential loss of information. At minimum, you will have to synchronize all affected data and interfaces. This is a potential timely and error-prone process. During the synchronization process, users will be banned from system use.

8.8.2 Task: Validate Restored Environments

Validate the partition rollback. Compare the restored system libraries and data structures with the backup baselines of both partitions and their associated data structures.

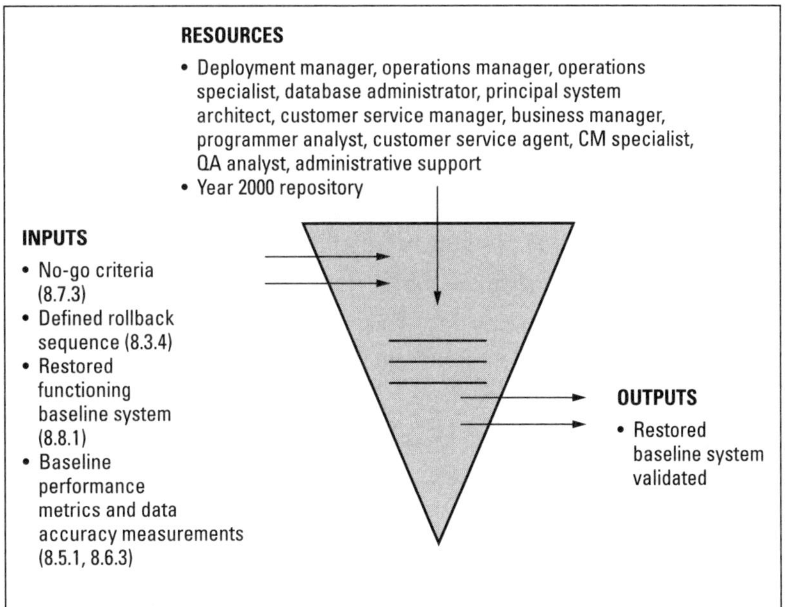

Rollback complete. Quality assurance verifies that the deliverable conforms to its intended goal. Project control baselines the deliverable and updates tracking metrics. Configuration management verifies that Year 2000 repository updates adhere to CM procedures.

Business Impacts

Your routine business processes may be significantly affected by Deployment activities. Systems that interface with newly deployed systems may need to be modified to accommodate the new systems. Some automated processes will be replaced, at least temporarily, by manual processes. A new version of a particular system may differ significantly from the former version, requiring that you retrain personnel. In some cases, you will also need to acquire new personnel.

Because you will deploy several systems simultaneously, the tasks related to the resolution, testing, and Deployment of one system may interfere with some tasks undertaken on behalf of another system. Fortunately, you may be able to consolidate tasks that apply to more than one system. In any case, you must carefully coordinate concurrent Deployment efforts.

As Deployment is underway, developers may periodically generate notices to keep users and customers informed of Deployment progress. These notices normally detail the changes made to the deployed system or related systems. You must carefully manage the volume of the notification process. If users receive too many change notices, or receive many change notices in a short period of time, they may become confused and/or annoyed.

Business managers may balk at the quantity of resources that they must allocate to Deployment tasks. You may be pressured to allow them to reallocate some of these resources, thus suspending or terminating some Deployment activities. Convince these managers that it is in their best interest to provide the resources for the complete, accurate Deployment of their systems. Also convince senior management of the need to fully fund Deployment.

Your business processes may be significantly affected by your Deployment activities, and they will also be affected by the Deployment activities of your electronic partners. External Deployment endeavors may cause the partial or total termination of services on the part of some electronic partners. You must carefully monitor the ongoing Year 2000 compliance efforts of your electronic partners. In addition, you must develop a plan to address potential Deployment failures on the part of these partners.

If you complete the Deployment of a specific system without a major mishap, Deployment tasks may not necessitate major adjustments to related business processes. However, if Deployment fails, this failure will certainly have a severe impact on these processes. If Deployment failure does occur, you must find a way to duplicate these business processes until the system's Year 2000 problems are addressed. Alternatively, you may have to live without these processes for an indefinite period of time.

Phase Risks

Potential Event	*Probability*	*Impact*	*Risk*
Technical considerations conflict with business priorities	Medium	Medium	Medium
Unrealistic concurrency in Deployment	Medium	High	High
Failure to coordinate vendor and third-party compliance	Medium	High	High
Failure to perform critical maintenance	Medium	Medium	Medium
Staff burnout	High	High	High

Deployment Phase Risks

There are five risks associated with the Deployment phase: Technical considerations may conflict with business priorities, there may be unrealistic concurrency in Deployment, you may fail to coordinate vendor and third-party compliance, you may fail to perform routine maintenance, and there may be staff burnout.

Technical Considerations Conflict with Business Priorities

The order in which you deploy your systems will be heavily influenced by technical considerations. For example, it would not make sense to deploy a given software application before deploying the operating system on which that application depends. Unfortunately, business considerations may conflict with the technical

realities of Deployment. For example, business objectives may drive the decision to put the payroll system first on the Deployment list, even though it may make more sense to initially deploy a particular support system on which many other systems depend.

There are a couple of ways of mitigating this risk:

- Develop one or more manual workarounds. If the Deployment of a technically critical system is delayed, a manual workaround can mimic the functionality of this system. Of course, developing these workarounds may drain precious resources.
- Ensure that Deployment decision-makers are aware of important technical information concerning each Deployment candidate. If these managers fully understand the technical ramifications associated with Deployment decisions, they will be less likely to allow business considerations to supersede technical realities.

Unrealistic Concurrency in Deployment

You may face organizational pressure to deploy all repaired systems as soon as possible, and may, as a result, attempt to deploy too many systems concurrently. However, you simply cannot deploy everything at the same time. You need to conduct Deployment incrementally to avoid potentially catastrophic general system failures.

There is one way of mitigating this risk:

- Acquaint managers with the benefits of incremental deployment. Make sure that the disadvantages of an overzealous Deployment schedule are widely known and accepted.

Failure to Coordinate Vendor and Third-Party Compliance

As indicated in the production of the Enterprise Schematic, some elements of your Year 2000 compliance efforts—such as vendor and third-party interfaces—are out of your direct control. Failure of a key vendor or interface may translate into failure in your business arena.

It is equally important to coordinate the timing of vendor and interface compliance. If vendor compliance plans cannot be meshed with your own, you are again at risk.

There are a couple of ways of mitigating this risk:

- Prioritize your vendor relationships and get senior management concurrence. Consciously decide when you will drop noncompliant vendors. Communicate these "drop-dead" dates to vendors and actively research alternatives. Drop vendors who refuse compliance.
- Dedicate staff and time to coordinate with vendors and third parties. This is a seasoned manager or system architect job. Do not rely on junior personnel to conduct these negotiations. Use contracts, subcontracts, and procurement support as resources to develop equitable solutions for your business.

Failure to Perform Critical Maintenance

While Year 2000 Resolution and Deployment continues, you may fail to implement other necessary system maintenance tasks. Of course, as the Year 2000 approaches, Year 2000 activities will tend to overtake all other tasks. However, neglecting standard maintenance may yield consequences that interfere with your ability to complete the Year 2000 project.

There are a couple of ways of mitigating this risk:

- Ensure the acquisition and scheduling of resources to continue routine maintenance activities. Do not allow these resources to be reallocated to Year 2000 tasks.
- Ensure that managers are aware of the importance of continuing routine maintenance activities. Be sure that explicit management decisions support the postponement or termination of maintenance activities.

Staff Burnout

Deployment activities often place heavy burdens on system development personnel. To prevent the disruption of business activities, Deployment tasks are often scheduled for odd hours (that is, nights and/or weekends). In addition, in case a Deployment task encounters problems, staff members are often pressured to speedily resolve these problems. Resolution efforts may, unfortunately, require many extra hours for system developers. Most staff will tolerate a certain amount of required extra effort. However, the time needed to deploy all Year 2000 project

systems may be substantial. Most staff members will begin to exhibit signs of burnout if asked to endure months of long, odd hours.

There is a way of mitigating this risk:

- Develop a "rolling staff" approach to Deployment. The Deployment tasks assigned to staff members can be intermingled with non-Deployment tasks. An occasional weekend off does a lot to ward off staff burnout!

Success Factors

In successfully completing Deployment, you carried out the following steps:

Success Factor	*Deliverables*
Briefed your Deployment staff concerning Deployment tasks and schedule	Deployment Phase Startup
Defined data cycle priorities	Data Conversion Plan
Defined post-conversion data accuracy metrics	Data Conversion Plan
Developed data conversion plans	Data Conversion Plan
Determined detailed Deployment and rollback criteria	Deployment Plan
Determined critical performance indicators and metrics	Deployment Plan
Defined schedule/sequence for Deployment and, if necessary, rollback	Deployment Plan
Identified impacted business processes	Deployment Plan
Developed post-Deployment customer service plan	Deployment Plan
Developed user training plan	Deployment Plan
Defined notification requirements	Deployment Plan
Developed and obtained approval for detailed Deployment Plan	Deployment Plan
Established notification network	Deployment Preparation
Delivered updated documentation	Deployment Preparation
Conducted user training	Deployment Preparation
Established customer services	Deployment Preparation

SUCCESS FACTOR	DELIVERABLES
Backed up preconversion data	Data Conversion
Converted data	Data Conversion
Validated data conversion	Data Conversion
Issued Deployment notifications	Deployment Execution
Determined Deployment readiness	Deployment Execution
Baselined and backed up pre-Deployment environment	Deployment Execution
Executed system Deployment using Deployment criteria	Deployment Execution
Validated Deployment	Deployment Validation
Executed and validated system rollbacks, if necessary	Rollback
Identified phase risks and potential mitigation approaches	All deliverables
Identified deliverables that would be developed during this phase	All deliverables
Used adequate communication interfaces throughout your organization to support the tasks associated with this phase	All deliverables
Assigned phase tasks to various groups in your organization and ensured that there was management approval for those tasks	All deliverables
Identified the deliverables for which each group was responsible and ensured acceptance of that deliverable responsibility by each group	All deliverables
Identified key milestones for the accomplishment of tasks for this phase	All deliverables
Identified milestone thresholds beyond which some corrective action will be taken	All deliverables
Used metrics to track and measure progress with respect to these milestones	All deliverables
Ensured that each responsible group accepted and adhered to the schedule for completion of this phase	All deliverables

Reference Material

This list mentions reference material you can turn to for additional information on this phase of your Year 2000 compliance project:

- Appendix A, Problem Definition Catalog
- Appendix B, Solution Sets
- Appendix F, Key Tasks Outline
- Appendix G, Year 2000 Repository
- Appendix H, Integrated Project Plan (CD-ROM)
- Appendix I, How To 2000 Risk Management
- Glossary

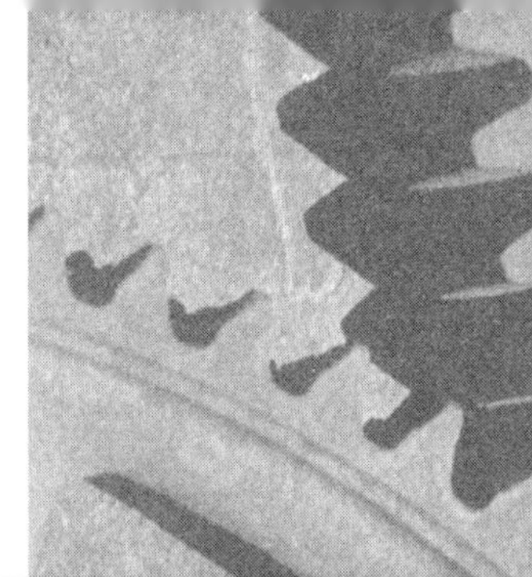

CHAPTER 9

Phase 9: Fallout

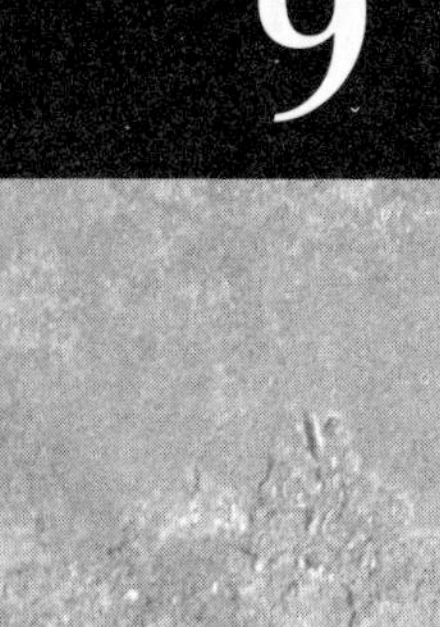

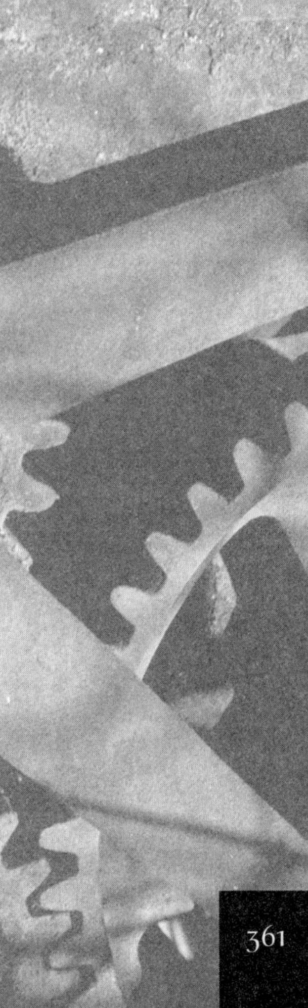

FALLOUT

Objectives:

- Regulate continued Year 2000 compliance.
- Minimize impact of compliance efforts on business operations.
- Assure continuous customer service.
- Reimplement third-party certifications (EDI, EFT, and so on).
- Maintain Year 2000 bridge and interface modification control.

The Fallout phase ensures long-term Year 2000 success. Fallout consists of tasks that you must complete after implementing a compliant system—including customer service, bridge control, anomaly repair, quality assurance, and configuration management—as well as tasks that you must complete after January 1, 2000.

Remaining Compliant

During the Year 2000 Fallout phase, you develop and initiate the administrative mechanisms that will support the continued operation of your Year 2000 compliant systems. This phase is also a period of administrative closure, a time to "tie up loose ends." Although a post-Deployment phase is typical of most systems development and systems maintenance projects, this phase is particularly vital to the successful completion of your Year 2000 project. The importance of Year 2000 Fallout stems from the fact that:

- Your Year 2000 efforts affected an enormous number of your organization's systems. If you neglect to support the continued operation of these systems, your entire organization may suffer.
- The problem of Year 2000 noncompliance will not disappear when you successfully deploy your Year 2000 compliant systems. You must take steps to ensure the compliance of newly developed or newly acquired systems. In addition, you must ensure the Year 2000 compliance of your electronic partners.
- Because of the scope of the Year 2000 project, not all Year 2000 compliance problems will be addressed. During Triage, you decided which systems

would be targeted for Year 2000 compliance and which would not. After each partition Deployment, you should reevaluate the earlier Triage decisions; reexamine the human, budget, and physical resources available; and conditionally include additional, previously triaged-out, systems into the resolution, test, deployment cycle.

Year 2000 Fallout begins when you successfully deploy a Year 2000 compliant system.

Fallout tasks will take place at the same time as tasks from earlier phases.

Because Fallout tasks will continue well beyond your Year 2000 project time frame, Fallout activities are not considered in the project cost.

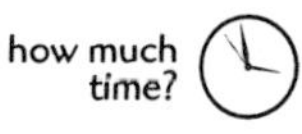

Because Fallout tasks will continue well beyond your Year 2000 project time frame, Fallout activities are not considered in the project schedule.

Summary of Deliverables

This section summarizes the deliverables for this phase of the Year 2000 compliance project. The section "Deliverables, Tasks, and Dependencies" later in this chapter includes detailed descriptions of each deliverable and the associated supporting tasks.

QA and CM Procedures Report

The QA and CM Procedures Report provides a summary of quality assurance and configuration management procedures that were used during the Year 2000 project. It also includes an assessment of the adequacy of each QA and CM procedure. Negative assessments are accompanied by recommendations for procedure improvement. Hopefully, the information in this document will prevent the future use of inadequate QA and CM procedures.

Customer Service Report

The Customer Service Report provides a detailed plan to support system users following system deployment. It helps you develop and implement a robust communication mechanism between users and members of the Year 2000 team. This communication system will operate during the months following Deployment to support the resolution of problems associated with the Deployment of Year 2000 compliant systems.

Bridge Control Report

The Bridge Control Report contains descriptions of the software "bridges" implemented during the Year 2000 project. This report is updated frequently to ensure the accuracy of information concerning the current status of each bridge. This report tracks the modifications, updates, and replacements associated with Year 2000 bridges.

Inventory Maintenance Report

During the Year 2000 project, you developed a detailed inventory of your organization's systems. The Inventory Maintenance Report records changes to that inventory. Like the Bridge Control Report, this deliverable is updated frequently to maintain an accurate depiction of your organization's systems.

Systems Reevaluation Report

During Triage, you identified the systems that would continue to be addressed in the Year 2000 project. You also identified those that would not be addressed. This deliverable reappraises these "forgotten" systems, evaluating each according to your organization's need for the system's future repair, replacement, or retirement. These systems are prioritized for future Year 2000 compliance efforts.

Lessons Learned

During your Year 2000 project, you had to constantly evaluate the tools and techniques you used to complete your tasks. You have certainly identified ways that you could have improved the execution of your Year 2000 tasks. This deliverable supports the collection of this evaluation information. In addition, it supports the use of this information for the improvement of your Year 2000 project practices. This improvement may result in future cost savings, schedule reductions, and system quality enhancements.

Deliverables, Tasks, and Dependencies

During Fallout, you can review the recently completed period of high-intensity activity, and determine whether the procedures that supported the development were adequate. In addition, now that the critical systems have been brought into compliance, you may want to reevaluate the systems that were not considered critical at that time and, possibly, bring them into compliance. Finally, you must plan to control the software bridges to noncompliant systems, and recertify your interface to external systems.

9.1 QA and CM Procedures Report

In the QA and CM Procedures Report, you review the QA and CM procedures used during Resolution, Test Planning, Test Execution, and Deployment, and determine what worked well and what needed improvement. You then generate a report suggesting changes to the QA and CM procedures and—after presentation, review, and approval—implement the changes to the procedures.

When you finish this deliverable, your QA and CM procedures should be tailored to your development methodology, be able to catch problems as early in the development cycle as possible, be able to avoid problems by functional review and tight configuration management, and not be overly onerous.

Task Overview

- Review QA Procedures
- Improve QA Procedures
- Review CM Procedures
- Improve CM Procedures

9.1.1 Task: Review QA Procedures

A review of the QA process should begin with a review of the measurements taken during development; you should evaluate the accuracy of those measurements in identifying problems as early as possible in the development cycle.

You should perform autopsies on both major and minor failures, and should identify measurements that could have helped avoid the failure earlier in the cycle. For example:

- Could a rollback have been avoided if the converted data had been thoroughly checked with automation rather than a manual spot check?
- Could a functional failure have been avoided if a peer review of the design of new software had been implemented?
- Could a performance failure have been identified before Deployment if timing performance requirements had been specified and tested?
- Are some QA procedures too onerous to the staff, and therefore not used?
- Do some QA procedures measure things that do not predict quality or failures?

The results of the review should be a report recommending specific changes to the QA processes in training, budget, schedule, processes, or procedures.

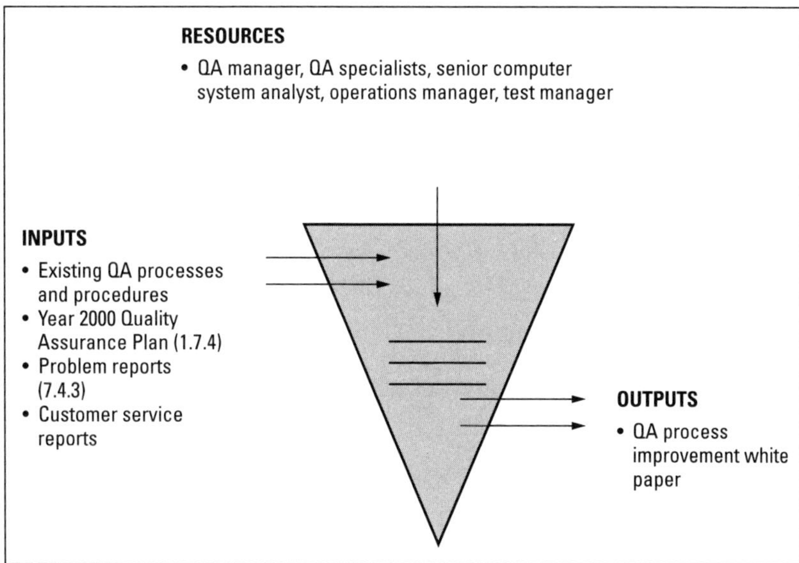

RESOURCES
• QA manager, QA specialists, senior computer system analyst, operations manager, test manager
INPUTS
• Existing QA processes and procedures
• Year 2000 Quality Assurance Plan (1.7.4)
• Problem reports (7.4.3)
• Customer service reports
OUTPUTS
• QA process improvement white paper

9.1.2 Task: Improve QA Procedures

Now that you know what you need to change to improve the QA processes, make the changes. Present the suggested modifications to the appropriate managers and technical specialists, adjust the improvements as specified by the consensus

obtained during the meeting, obtain the required approval to implement the improvements, and make the changes. Finally, provide separate training classes for your QA specialists and your development staff on changes to the QA processes and procedures. Be sure to let everybody know how the lessons learned during the Year 2000 effort have paid off with improved QA procedures.

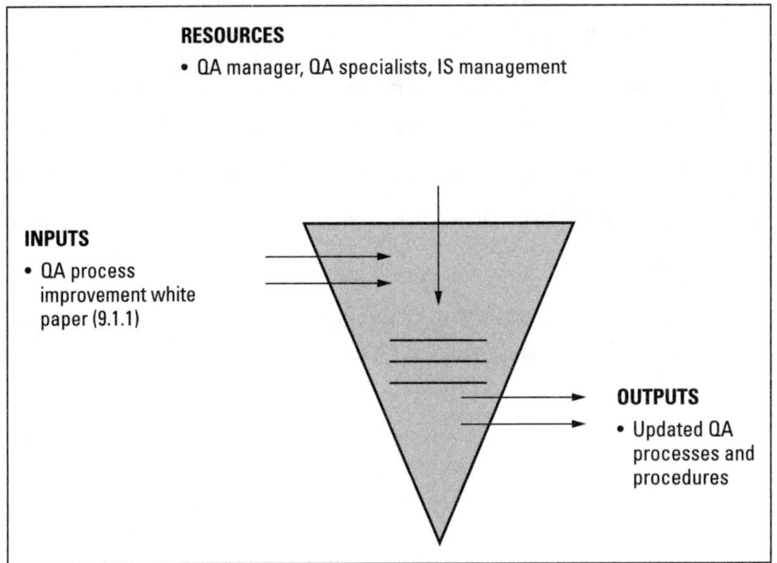

9.1.3 Task: Review CM Procedures

Besides reviewing QA procedures, as just described, you should review the configuration management procedures to determine whether you can improve the CM process. Here are some of the considerations:

- Do the CM procedures adequately control and track updates to system configuration?
- Do the CM procedures support reversion to a previously operating version of the system?
- Do the CM procedures adequately address desktop configurations?
- Is there a way to modify configurations without involving CM staff (upgrading COTS versions without upgrading the configuration)? If so, is this acceptable or desirable?

- Does the CM process adequately respond to the needs of the development and production staff?

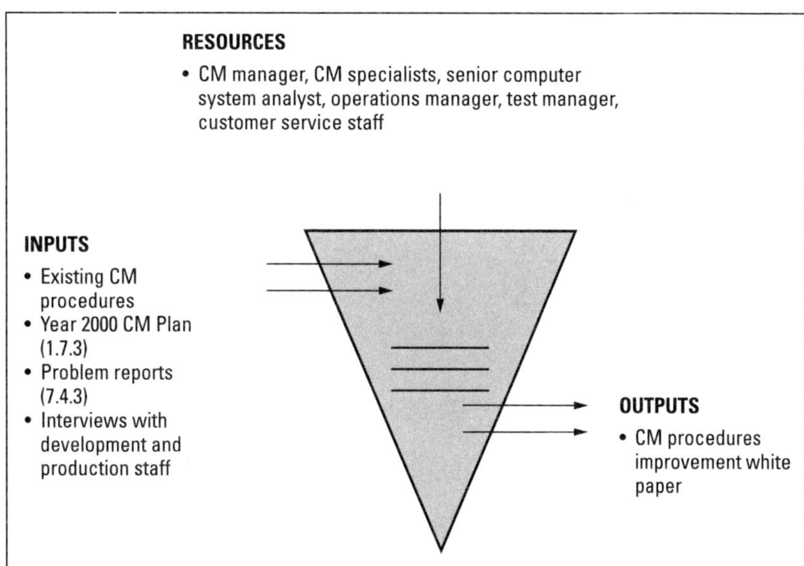

RESOURCES
• CM manager, CM specialists, senior computer system analyst, operations manager, test manager, customer service staff
INPUTS
• Existing CM procedures
• Year 2000 CM Plan (1.7.3)
• Problem reports (7.4.3)
• Interviews with development and production staff
OUTPUTS
• CM procedures improvement white paper

9.1.4 Task: Improve CM Procedures

Now that you know what you need to change to improve the CM procedures, make the changes. Present the suggested modifications to the appropriate managers and technical specialists, adjust the improvements as specified by the consensus obtained during the meetings, obtain the required approval to implement the improvements, and make the changes. Finally, provide separate training classes for your CM specialists and your development staff on changes to the CM processes and procedures. Be sure to let everybody know how the lessons learned during the Year 2000 effort have paid off with improved CM procedures.

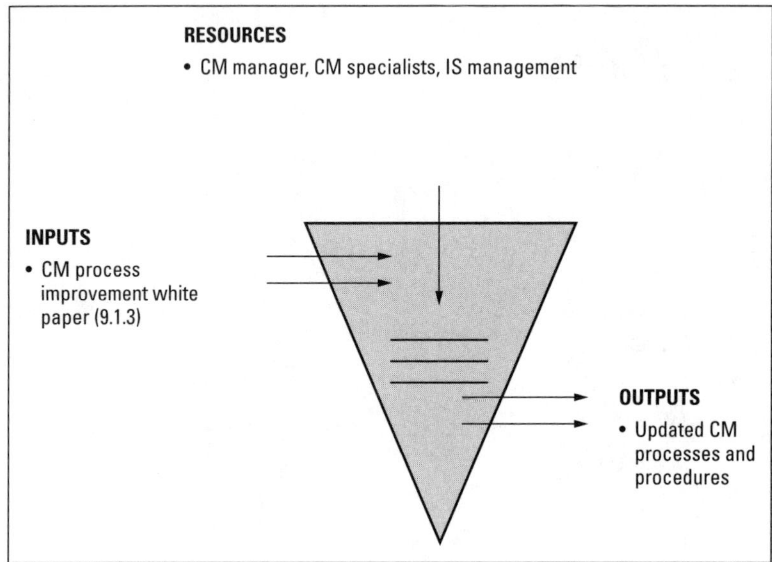

QA and CM Procedures Report complete. Quality assurance verifies that the deliverable conforms to its intended goal. Project control baselines the deliverable and updates tracking metrics. Configuration management verifies that Year 2000 updates adhere to configuration management procedures.

9.2 Customer Service Report

In anticipation of changing workloads, as analyzed and implemented during Deployment, the customer service capabilities are probably larger than required for normal post–Year 2000 operations. In addition, you may have modified customer service procedures to accommodate Year 2000 priorities.

Now that the critical Year 2000 work is complete, you implement the last task in the Customer Service Plan, adjusting the capacity of the customer service operation to reflect normal workloads. If your operation will continue to make Year 2000 deployments, the Customer Service Plan should reflect the anticipated long-term workload.

In addition, you should review problem reports received during the deployment of Year 2000 compliant systems to help you determine when valid customer problems were introduced into the deployed system. As part of your normal process improvement procedures, the problem source analysis should be fed back to the originating organization for corrective action.

Task Overview

- Execute Customer Service Plan
- Review Problem Reports
- Distribute Problem Reports

9.2.1 Task: Execute Customer Service Plan

Implement the changes specified in the Customer Service Plan created during Deployment. At this point, after the critical Year 2000 work has been completed, the Customer Service Plan probably specifies a reduction in the capacity of the customer service operation. Implement the required changes in staff, facilities, and procedures.

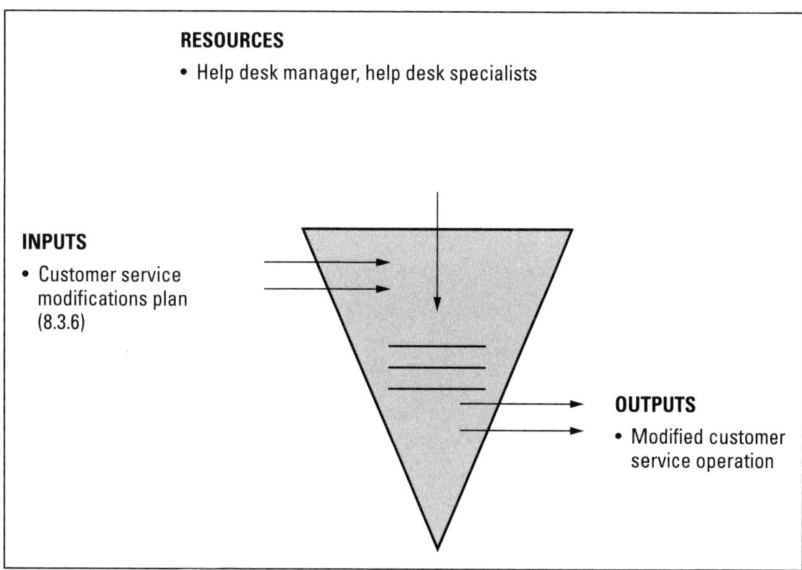

Task Guideline

- Migrating customers *off* of systems that you chose *not* to make Year 2000 compliant is also part of customer services. When implementing your customer service plan, you should integrate the needs for "retire systems" decisions.

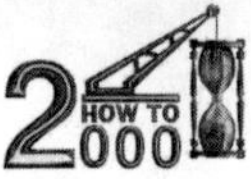

9.2.2 Task: Review Problem Reports

Problem reviews should take place monthly, and recommended improvements should be generated about once a quarter. The frequency that works best for your organization will depend upon the number of problem reports received, the complexity of the various organizations, the number of concurrent but separate development efforts, and other feedback mechanisms you have in place.

You need to understand the kinds of problems your users, customers, and operators are encountering. A quality assurance specialist or customer service analyst should review the reports for the period. The reviewer should classify the reports by the organization responsible and the priority of the problem. The point is not to assign blame, but to understand the source of the problems encountered.

The review should determine the source of the problems and determine whether a change to the QA procedures could have caught the problem earlier or prevented the problem. The cheapest problems to fix are those caught at the source.

If a change to the QA procedures is warranted, implement the appropriate change as soon as possible.

This review is not meant to replace the immediate review of a problem report that takes place when the complaint is received. Your customer service analysts will continue to review problem reports as they try to immediately resolve customer complaints. The review specified in this task will be a longer period review designed to improve the development, testing, deployment, and customer service process.

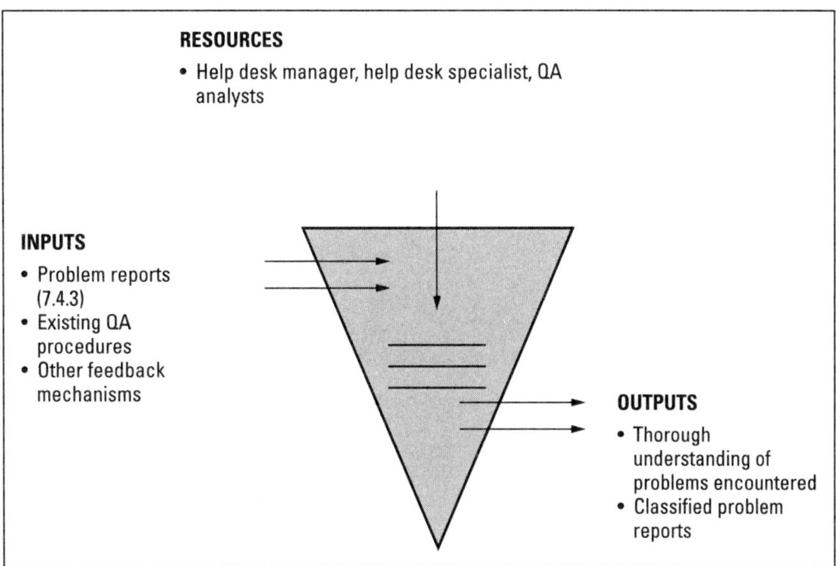

9.2.3 Task: Distribute Problem Reports

The problem reports and analyses should be passed back to the responsible organization. Assuming that high-priority fixes have already been implemented by the responsible organization, the point is not to make them feel guilty about all the problems they have, but to give them tools to help spot trends and localize problem sources.

The responsible organization should use this report to look at the set of problems they were responsible for over a long period and to try to improve their contribution to the development, testing, deployment, and customer service processes. The increased productivity of your development and maintenance staff supported by the process improvements made here will save your organization money long after all Year 2000 work is complete.

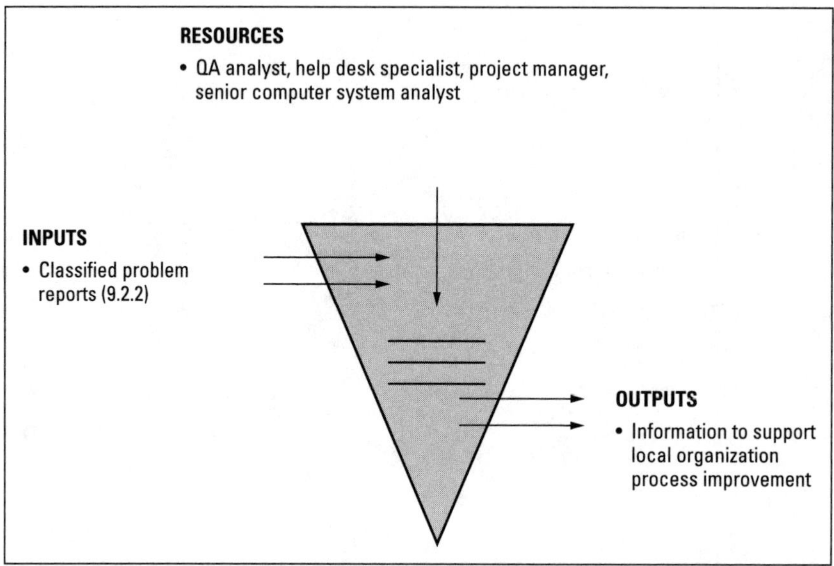

milestone **Customer Service Report completed. Quality assurance verifies that the deliverable conforms to its intended goal. Project control baselines the deliverable and updates tracking metrics. Configuration management verifies that Year 2000 repository updates adhere to CM procedures.**

9.3 Bridge Control Report

The Bridge Control Report is an ongoing effort to manage the interface bridges implemented during the previous correction cycle. The interface bridges are used by the system to "bridge" between two otherwise incompatible interfaces. For example, if a large customer has not yet updated its software to accept four-digit year fields in the tapes you send them, your interface bridge would accept the four-digit year field output by your updated software, and produce the customer tape conforming to the older interface.

A bridge may also be used in an internal interface between two packages, one that was updated due to the likelihood of critical failures and the other that was determined to have a low probability of failure. For example, an interface bridge was deployed with the first partition to interface to the second. At some later date the second package is updated, and the bridge is no longer needed.

As the interfaces "bridged" by this temporary software become Year 2000 compliant, the need for the bridges is removed or modified. The Bridge Control Report should identify each bridge between in-house systems, or between local and external interfaces, and specify the bridge requirements and the plan for updating the software so that the bridges are no longer needed. As these interfaces are updated, the bridges may be removed or modified.

Task Overview

- Review Changing Bridge Requirements
- Coordinate Interface Updates
- Recertify Electronic Interfaces

9.3.1 Task: Review Changing Bridge Requirements

As part of the analysis of updates to functionality, the interfaces were examined, and the requirements for bridges were specified. This paradigm still applies to noncritical updates after the primary Year 2000 work is completed. When you implement any changes to functionality that may affect an interface, you should examine the existing bridges—modifying or deleting them if necessary and appropriate.

The same review requirements apply to changes to external interfaces. When notified of an impending change to an external interface, or upon the implementation of updated software to accommodate an external interface already Year 2000 compliant, you should examine bridging requirements.

The result of this task, to be completed for each change in interfaces, is a bridge requirements specification identifying requirements to modify or delete existing bridges, or add new bridges.

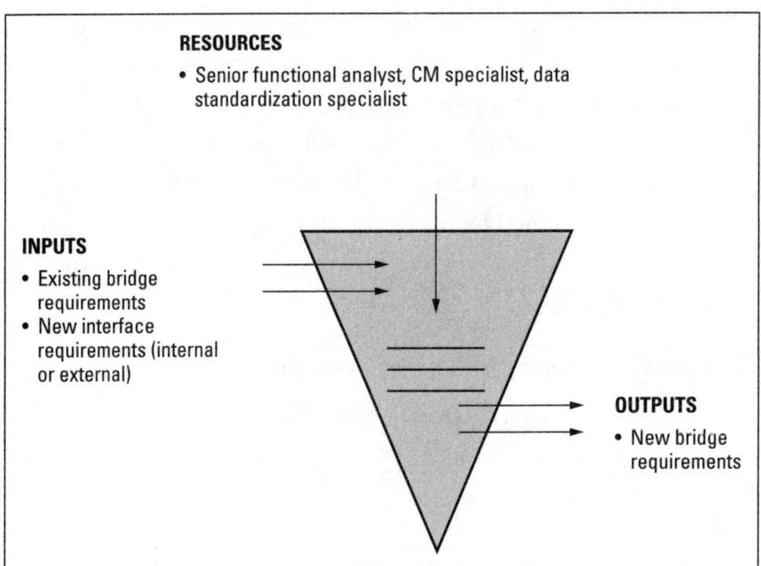

9.3.2 Task: Coordinate Interface Updates

Once you identify the requirements for the new interface bridges, the development staff creates or updates the bridges. This task is to coordinate insertion of the bridges into the production environment.

Coordinating internal bridges is a bit easier because the bridge software can tag along with the deployment of the software whose interface is changing. Coordinating external interfaces is a bit more difficult. In some cases the modified bridge may be the entire partition, and must be deployed, in a coordinated way, along with the update to the external interface. In addition, your organization must support coordinated testing of the interface, and be prepared to roll back the update if problems arise.

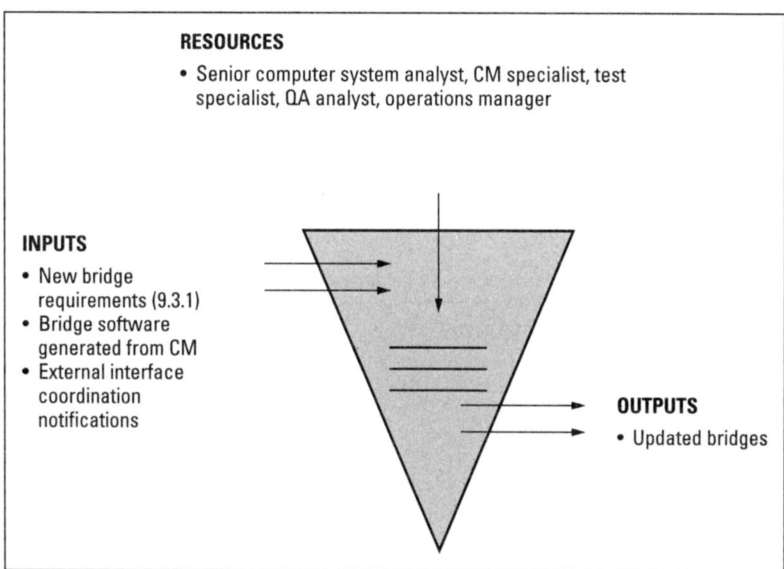

9.3.3 Task: Recertify Electronic Interfaces

Upon update of an interface governed by an external organization, your organization may have to complete a certification process defined by the external organization. Unfortunately, these certifications often involve paying the external organization to support testing, and to certify the accuracy of the data. The particular requirements are dictated by the external organization.

Suppose that your organization has completed all its critical Year 2000 updates and implemented a bridge to a paper vendor to whom you transmit transactions specifying your voluminous orders. The paper vendor has not yet updated its system to accommodate four-digit dates. Because the paper vendor accepts such transactions from hundreds of organizations, it has established a formal certification process to manage the effort of validating the format and content of transactions sent.

At some point, the paper vendor will update the interface so an organization doesn't order for delivery in 1900. When the interface update is made, you may be required to go through a formal certification. Because the vendor is critical to your business, you follow the procedures as closely as possible to avoid the electronic interface to the paper vendor.

The certification process begins with a payment of a $1,000 application fee to the vendor to receive a copy of the updated interface specification. Once you have completed and internally tested your interface, you must use the simulator pro-

vided by the paper vendor to simulate the interface and record the transactions. You must send a copy of the recorded transactions to the paper vendor for review, along with a $1,000 verification fee.

The paper vendor will notify you of acceptance and certify that your organization may continue to send electronic orders, switching the interface to a Year 2000 compliant one on a specified date.

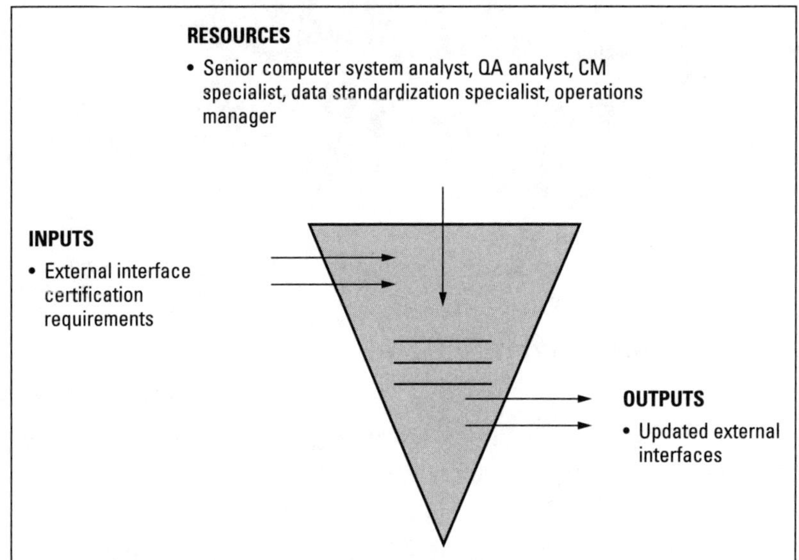

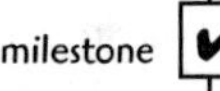

Bridge Control Report completed. Quality assurance verifies that the deliverable conforms to its intended goal. Project control baselines the deliverable and updates tracking metrics. Configuration management verifies that Year 2000 repository updates adhere to CM procedures.

9.4 Inventory Maintenance Report

In addition to a functioning Year 2000 compliant system, your organization now has a detailed inventory of all hardware, software, and interfaces in the enterprise. As you know from experience, an accurate inventory can be difficult to obtain. You can use the inventory to evaluate the environment, as well as to design upgrades, replacements, consolidations, and so on. Because the bulk of the expense was in generating the inventory, you should consider keeping the inventory current. The decision to maintain your detailed inventory should be based on the expectation of future need versus the increment in costs to perform inventory updates by including such a step in your CM procedures.

Task Overview

- Update Inventory Continuously

9.4.1 Task: Update Inventory Continuously

The existing CM procedures should be sufficiently tight to prevent the system configuration from being updated without an update to the enterprise inventory. The CM procedures should include the following provisions:

- Changes to hardware or software shall not be approved by the CM review unless reflected in an updated Enterprise Schematic and inventory list.
- No user-owned or user-written desktop software shall be installed on individual desktops. Access to such software must be through a common server.
- Insertion of desktop software onto a common server must go through the CM process.
- There should be periodic audits of user-controlled systems to ensure proper hardware and software configuration.

Maintenance of the enterprise inventory should not be significantly more expensive than letting the inventory become outdated.

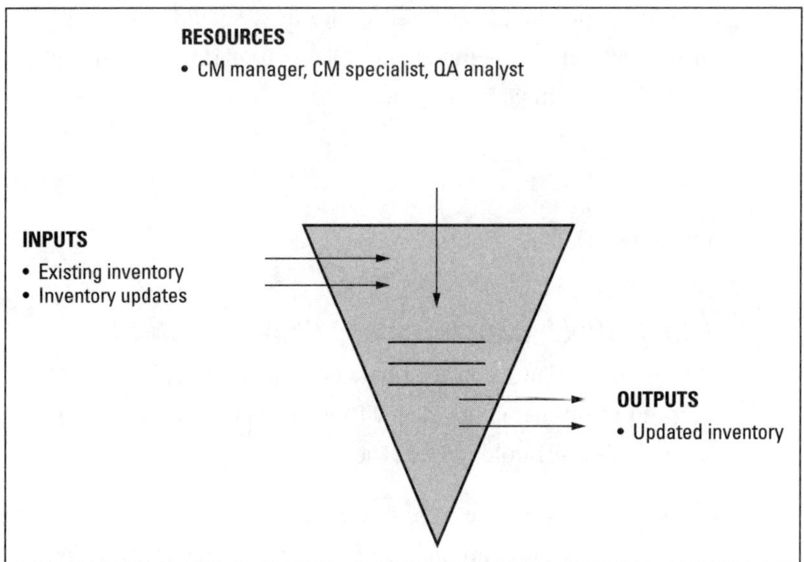

Inventory Maintenance Report completed. Quality assurance verifies that the deliverable conforms to its intended goal. Project control baselines the deliverable and updates tracking metrics. Configuration management verifies that Year 2000 repository updates adhere to CM procedures.

9.5 Systems Reevaluation Report

Now that the rush to update critical systems to achieve Year 2000 compliance is complete, you should review the completed Triage effort. The original Triage effort identified systems that were absolutely critical and had to be updated to keep from driving the company out of business. Now, you can evaluate and prioritize the remaining noncompliant systems, determining whether to update, replace, retire or ignore them.

Task Overview

- Conduct System Priority Survey
- Identify New Correction Cycle Candidates
- Present and Approve Correction Cycle Candidates
- Execute Correction Cycle Tasks

9.5.1 Task: Conduct System Priority Survey

In the original Triage evaluation, you conducted a survey of users to identify functionality that was not critical. For example, the payroll department may have had a program that printed paychecks in order by employee location. Because the program would fail after the beginning of Year 2000, and because it was deemed noncritical, it was removed from the production run and not included in the initial correction cycle. Now, the payroll clerks are complaining bitterly about having to sort the paychecks by hand. A brief discussion with the accounting manager may identify the desirability of this software that was retired during Triage.

Now that your critical systems are Year 2000 compliant, you should gather information about noncritical systems that should be made Year 2000 compliant. Ask users and managers to indicate which systems they believe should be included in a "second round" Year 2000 compliance endeavor. These users and managers will assign a business priority to each system that is not already Year 2000 compliant.

The scope and duration of this survey will be largely determined by your organizational environment.

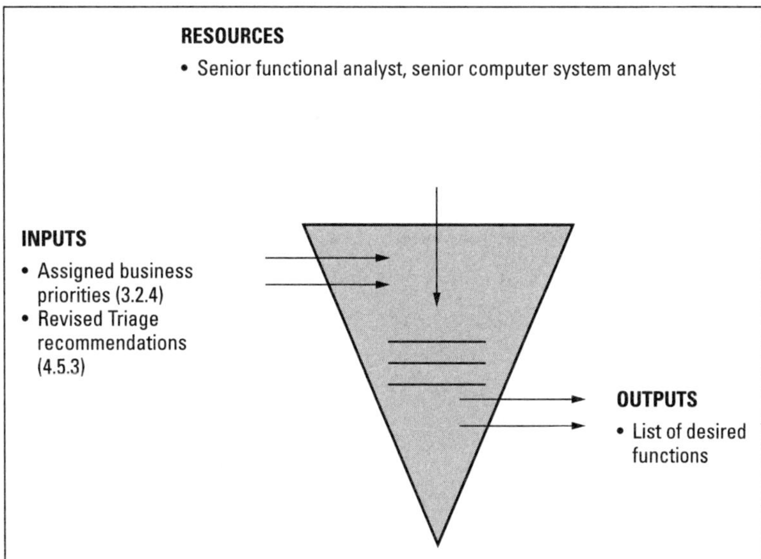

9.5.2 Task: Identify New Correction Cycle Candidates

You should evaluate information from two primary sources: the inventory of systems that are not already Year 2000 compliant, and the information gathered in

the system priority survey. This evaluation should support the identification of correction cycle candidates (that is, systems that will move through the correction cycle during the second round of the Year 2000 compliance project). Generate a list similar to the original list of systems to be assessed that was generated during Triage.

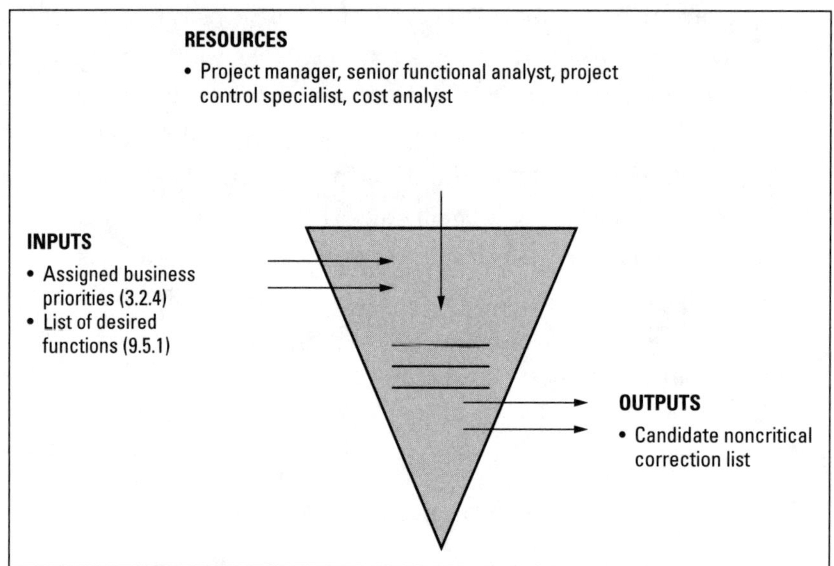

9.5.3 Task: Present and Approve Correction Cycle Candidates

As with all other Year 2000 project planning tasks, you must develop a budget and schedule for the Year 2000 compliance efforts to be undertaken on behalf of your correction cycle candidates. You must present a list of these candidates, with their corresponding budget and schedule, to the appropriate managers. Upon gaining approval of this list, budget, and schedule, you may execute correction cycle tasks.

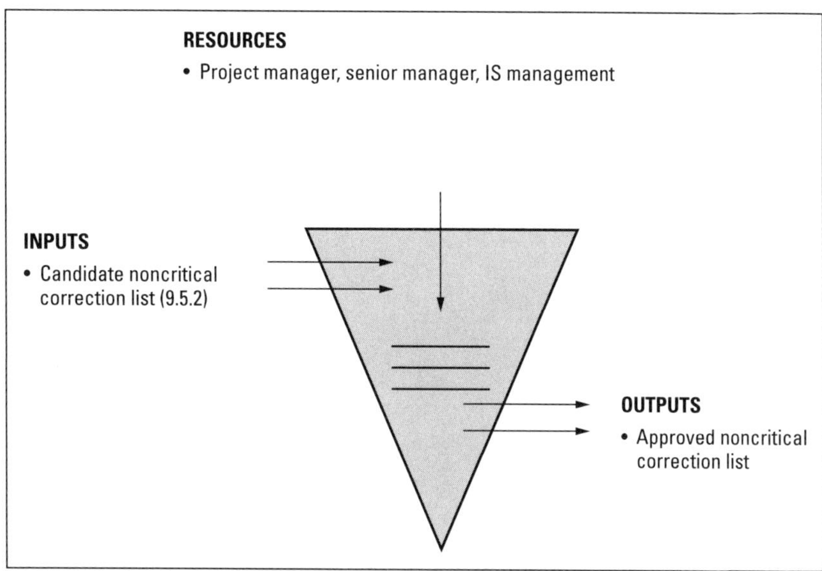

9.5.4 Task: Execute Correction Cycle Tasks

Although the systems you are addressing are not considered critical to your business objectives, you must still conduct comprehensive Resolution, Test Planning, Test Execution, and Deployment on behalf of each system. See Chapters 5 through 8 of this book for a full discussion of the tasks to be undertaken.

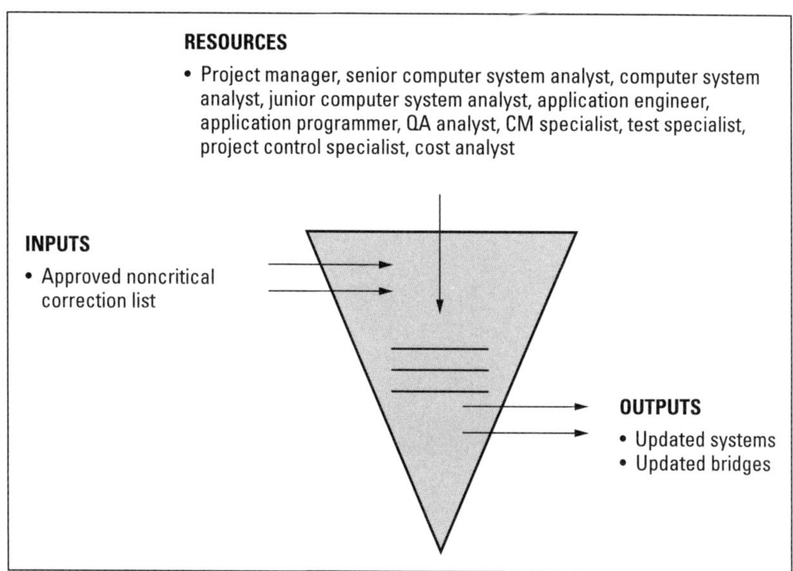

milestone 

System Reevaluation Report completed. Quality assurance verifies that the deliverable conforms to its intended goal. Project control baselines the deliverable and updates tracking metrics. Configuration management verifies that Year 2000 repository updates adhere to CM procedures.

9.6 Lessons Learned

As mentioned, groups of logical functions or partitions should move through the correction cycle in batches. Therefore, one group of systems will have achieved Year 2000 compliance while other groups are only beginning the correction cycle.

Each time a group of systems completes the correction cycle, you have the opportunity to collect information concerning what went right, what went wrong, and what you can do better next time. You can collect, evaluate, and use this information to improve your Year 2000 methodology.

You can also improve your Year 2000 methodology by using the "best commercial practices" from other organizations. As we approach the millennium, more and more organizations will devise methods to streamline Year 2000 compliance efforts. You should keep abreast of new Year 2000 methods and theories, and revise your Year 2000 efforts accordingly.

Fortunately, the Year 2000 issue is now well covered in both the popular and the technical press. In addition, many Web pages address Year 2000 problems and solutions. There are Web pages hosted by vendor and service organizations pushing their particular solution, and Web pages hosted by organizations who are publicly documenting their approach to solving problems or other helpful information. For example, the Federal government's Social Security Administration maintains a Web site that lists the compliance status of a large number of vendor products (`http://www.ssa.gov/year2000/y2klist.htm`). See the *How To 2000* CD-ROM for a guide to Year 2000 Web Pages.

The objectives of incorporating lessons learned are to:

- Enhance Deployment quality
- Reduce cost and time
- Reduce business, phase, or technical risk

Task Overview

- Analyze Process Evaluation Information
- Revise Year 2000 Methods

9.6.1 Task: Analyze Process Evaluation Information

As you complete Year 2000 compliance efforts on behalf of each system, make sure that correction cycle participants evaluate the tools and techniques they used. Carefully maintain this information. At appropriate intervals, consolidate and analyze this information for possible application to future Year 2000 efforts.

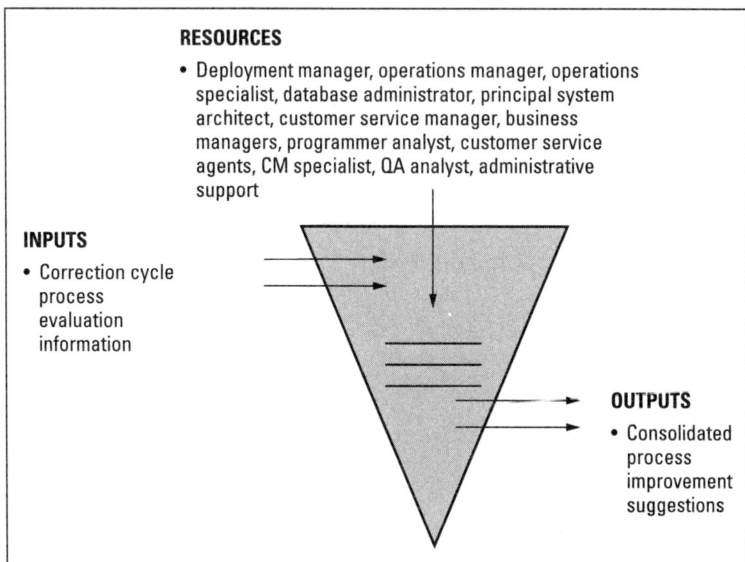

9.6.2 Task: Revise Year 2000 Methods

After capturing process evaluation and improvement suggestions, you should use these suggestions to revise your Year 2000 methods to be used in the future.

If necessary, modify your Year 2000 repository or project plans to accommodate these process improvements.

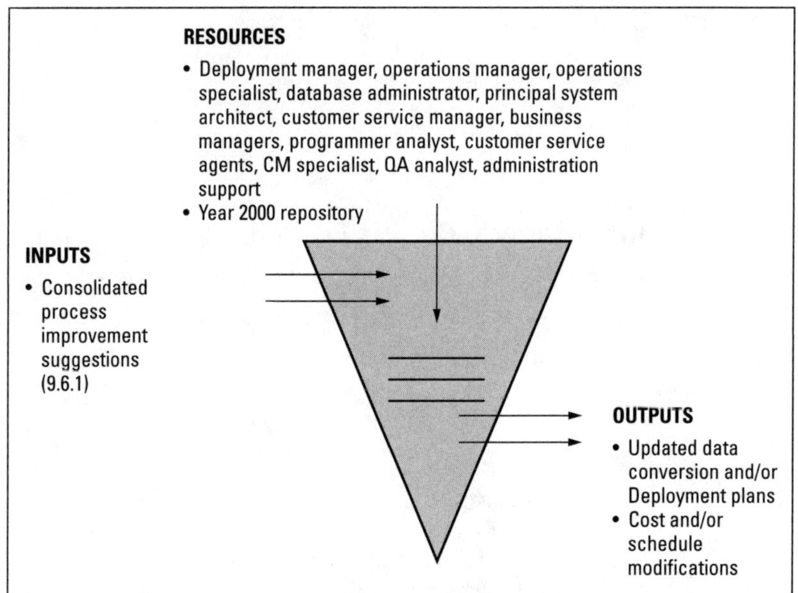

milestone **Lessons Learned completed. Quality assurance verifies that the deliverable conforms to its intended goal. Project control baselines the deliverable and updates tracking metrics. Configuration management verifies that Year 2000 repository updates adhere to CM procedures.**

Business Impacts

Hopefully, Fallout activities will affect your business processes in a positive manner. If system users encounter a problem related to a Year 2000 compliant system, they can seek help from the customer service center. Information about the Year 2000 inventory and Year 2000 bridges will be available when needed by managers or users. You have developed a plan for implementing Year 2000 compliance efforts for noncritical systems that remain Year 2000 noncompliant.

In addition, you have implemented an information feedback system that will allow your organization to avoid or minimize future problems by analyzing the problems encountered during the implementation of a Year 2000 compliant system.

Finishing the Year 2000 project will affect developer assumptions and standards for current and future development projects. Development standards will no longer allow developers to incorporate year-based obsolescence within newly developed systems. Hopefully, a requirement for Year 2000 compliance will be assumed for all of your organization's systems.

Phase Risks

Potential Event	*Probability*	*Impact*	*Risk*
Post Year 2000 problems will be worse than anticipated	Medium	High	High
New systems are acquired or developed that are not Year 2000 compliant	Low	High	Medium

Fallout Phase Risks

There are two risks associated with the Fallout phase: post Year 2000 problems may be worse than you expect, and you may acquire or develop new systems that are not Year 2000 compliant.

Post Year 2000 Problems Will Be Worse Than Anticipated

Although you have anticipated some of the problems that you will have to handle in the post Year 2000 time frame, it is impossible to anticipate every Year 2000 problem that may follow your organization into the new millennium.

There are a couple of ways of mitigating this risk:

- Develop a post–Year 2000 contingency plan. This plan will propose actions that you can take if you have failed to find and resolve every Year 2000 problem.
- Try to incorporate as much flexibility as possible in your post–Year 2000 development schedule. It may be wise to delay significant development

endeavors until you are confident that the Year 2000 has not brought unforeseen problems.

New Systems Are Acquired or Developed That Are Not Year 2000 Compliant

Unfortunately, your organization may inadvertently build or buy systems that are not Year 2000 compliant. Hopefully, the probability of this happening is low.

There are a couple of ways of mitigating this risk:

- Make sure to include Year 2000 compliance instructions in all organizational development and procurement directives. You must coordinate your efforts to ensure continued Year 2000 compliance with business managers and procurement officials.
- Form a Year 2000 review board. This board will review and ensure compliance of all newly developed or acquired systems. The need for this board may fade as the twenty-first century progresses, but it should maintain a high profile throughout the Year 2000.

Success Factors

In successfully completing the Fallout, you carried out the following steps:

Success Factor	*Deliverable*
Reviewed and evaluated QA measurements	QA and CM Procedures Report
Updated and improved QA measurements	QA and CM Procedures Report
Reviewed and evaluated CM procedures	QA and CM Procedures Report
Updated and improved CM procedures	QA and CM Procedures Report
Adjusted customer service capacity	Customer Service Report
Reviewed and evaluated problem reports	Customer Service Report
Communicated problem report analysis to originating organization	Customer Service Report
Documented changing bridge requirements	Bridge Control Report

SUCCESS FACTOR	DELIVERABLE
Coordinated interface updates	Bridge Control Report
Recertified electronic interfaces	Bridge Control Report
Updated Inventory and Enterprise Schematic diagram continuously	Inventory Maintenance Report
Surveyed users and managers for correction cycle candidates	Systems Reevaluation Report
Developed correction cycle candidates list	Systems Reevaluation Report
Gained approval to correct list of correction cycle	Systems Reevaluation Report
Executed correction of noncritical systems	Systems Reevaluation Report
Analyzed process evaluation information and developed process improvement suggestions	Lessons Learned
Identified phase risks and potential mitigation approaches	All deliverables
Identified deliverables that would be developed during this phase	All deliverables
Used adequate communication interfaces throughout your organization to support the tasks associated with this phase	All deliverables
Assigned phase tasks to various groups in your organization and ensured that there was management approval for those tasks	All deliverables
Identified the deliverables for which each group was responsible and ensured acceptance of that deliverable responsibility by each group	All deliverables
Identified key milestones for the accomplishment of tasks for this phase	All deliverables
Identified milestone thresholds beyond which some corrective action will be taken	All deliverables
Used metrics to track and measure progress with respect to these milestones	All deliverables
Ensured that each responsible group accepted and adhered to the schedule for completion of this phase	All deliverables

Reference Material

This list mentions reference material you can turn to for additional information on this phase of your Year 2000 compliance project:

- Chapter 3, Phase 3: Triage
- Appendix A, Problem Definition Catalog
- Appendix B, Solution Sets
- Appendix F, Key Tasks Outline
- Appendix H, Integrated Project Plan
- Appendix I, How To 2000 Risk Management
- Glossary
- *How To 2000* CD-ROM

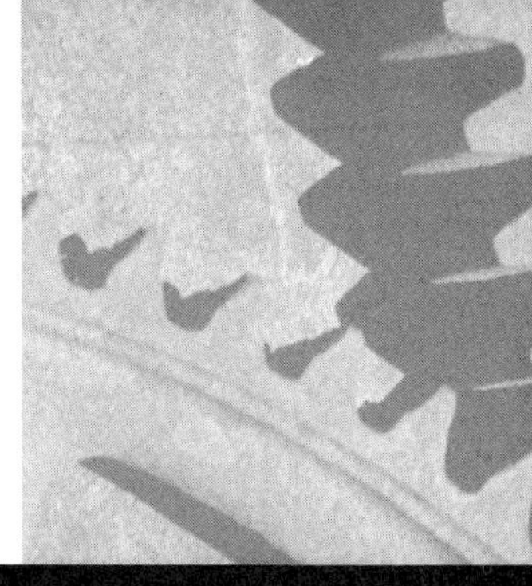

APPENDIX

A

Problem Definition Catalog

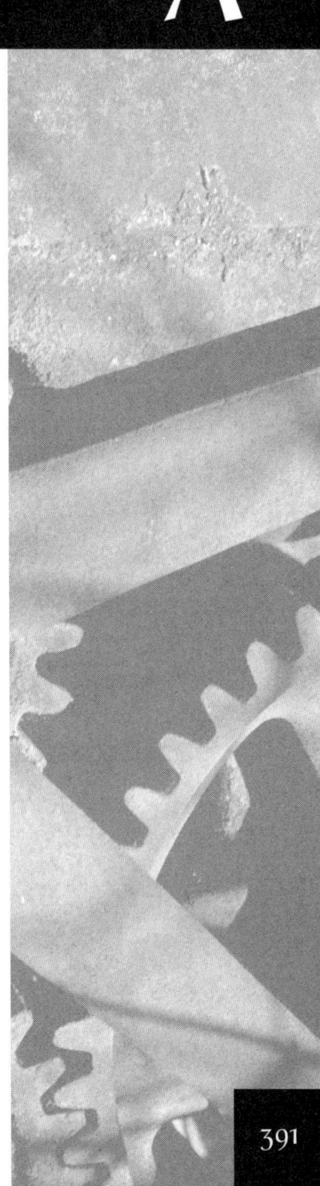

This Problem Definition Catalog is a powerful tool that you can use throughout your compliance efforts. It identifies the many ways the Year 2000 problem appears. Once you have fully understood the types of problems, their solutions—which are spelled out in Appendix B—will be easier to grasp. The following table describes how to use the Problem Definition Catalog throughout the nine How To 2000 phases. For more information, you can also consult definition of compliance in the glossary.

How To 2000 Phases	*Problem Definition Catalog Use*
Planning and Awareness	Use these definitions in your initial awareness, education, assessments, and planning to determine which problems may affect you.
Inventory	Facilitate tool evaluations to determine the strengths and weaknesses of tools you are evaluating during this phase.
Triage	Knowing the types of problems that affect you and the relative effort needed to correct these problems will help you prioritize your correction efforts.

continued

How To 2000 Phases	*Problem Definition Catalog Use*
Detailed Assessment	Problem definitions are critical during this phase. You will use them in developing the scope of your correction stage, determining partition groupings (see the glossary), supplementing assessment efforts provided by automated tools, and developing correction stage budgets.
Resolution	Technicians, quality assurance, and configuration management use these definitions.
Test Planning and Execution	Educate the test team. Use problem definitions to develop test plans and conduct formal testing.
Deployment	Use these definitions as input to system deployment go/no-go decision criteria.
Fallout	Define problem categories to customer support personnel who are responsible for addressing questions when failures occur.

Categorizing Year 2000 Software Errors

Use the problem categories outlined in the following tables as you identify potential Year 2000 risks while you execute deliverable 4.2, System Assessment, described in Chapter 4, Detailed Assessment. The problem categories are listed in descending order of their risk, the probability that each category will occur, and the magnitude of the consequences from failure (see Appendix I, How To 2000 Risk Management).

1. Ambiguous Century Representation

Ambiguous century representation is the best understood part of the Year 2000 problem. It is also the most prevalent problem.

PROBLEM TYPE	EXAMPLES
19*xx* assumed as year	Two-digit year instead of four-digit year. Only a 100-year range – 00 through 99 – is possible. Occurs with Julian, Gregorian, and other date formats. Some examples are *mm/dd/yy* and *yydddd*.
User interface does not allow four-digit years to clarify century	Users can only input two-digit years on screens. Batch parameter input limited in same fashion.
Year is part of file or tape name	Usually occurs in backup and archiving routines – for example, file0297.txt.
Sorting puts 20*xx* dates before 19*xx*	00, 01, 98, 99 instead of 1998, 1999, 2000, 2001.
Date within programs is truncated	If you input 1996, the program stores 96. If you input 2001, the program stores 01.
Century is hard coded	19 always displayed in front of two-digit years.
Assumption that the century is always derived from today's date	If you input 00 for 2000 during 1997, the program stores 1900. If you input 99 for 1999 during 2000, the program stores 2099.
Possible user misinterpretation	For example, 03/02/01 can be either March 2, 2001 (*mmddyy*, which is common in the U.S.); February 1, 2003 (*yymmdd*, which is a common sort order); or February 3, 2001 (*ddmmyy*, the International format). Another example is that 01/02/00 reports as 1/2/ because of zero suppression.

2. Interfaces

Dates are passed between programs, systems, platforms, enterprises, and companies. Dates are passed using files, memory, networks, documents, and other recording media. All interface problems could be derived from the other problem types. However, it takes a great deal of attention to solve interfaces correctly, and the solutions for these problems encompass different concepts than the other problem categories. Finally, most of the early Year 2000 project Deployment failures stem from interface problems.

PROBLEM TYPE	EXAMPLES
Dates truncated or misinterpreted	Read 010100 and assume Jan 01, 1900.
Modified date format misread	The date was numeric and is now stored as packed or encoded data.
Modified date format changes the locations of other data elements	The length of the interface can change. The data stream is 01011997XYZ. The system misreads the date as 010119 and the company as 97X or 97XYZ.
Cannot find file because file-name convention changes	As an example, file0297.txt became file021997.txt.

3. Date as a Special Flag or Data Element

This problem was created because dates were defined or used as something other than a strictly date data type. Some of the habits of reusing precious data or memory space carried forward with us today, even if the date was later defined correctly.

PROBLEM TYPE	EXAMPLES
Expiration dates	123199, 991231, 9/99/99, the Julian 99999, or 99365 (be careful of file expiration dates, security systems, and software license expirations).
Validation of date for invalid values	Commonly found as 00, 9/9/99, or 123199. Treated as invalid dates.
End-of-data list or end-of-file markers	Commonly found as 00 or 99. Year used as end of data stream. Could be 9/99/99.
Pointer abuse	Using a two-digit year as a pointer or index to memory, an array, or data structure.
Hard coded so that a specific year performs specialized logic	For example, if the year = 76, perform 76-calendar-print.
Date field is not always a date	For example, a flag or record indicator tells us that the field is not a date.
Algorithmic	For example, multiply by year, divide by year (divide by 0). Using the year in a mathematical formula.

PROBLEM TYPE	EXAMPLES
Text string contains date	Length of text can change. Data stream is 01011997XYZ. Misread date as 010119 and company as 97XYZ.
Intelligent keys or reconstruction	Date manipulated to form another field or key. For example, hashing and encryption algorithms. As another example, date used as part of account number, serial number, or order number.

4. Configuration Errors

Configuration errors are not Year 2000 specific. They are uncovered during any major project dealing with older code. Your Year 2000 project will deal with more older code than any other previous project. Hopefully, you will uncover only a few of these problems, but each occurrence can be very expensive or risky to resolve.

PROBLEM TYPE	EXAMPLES
Missing	Missing the correct version of compiler, operating system, database, or hardware necessary to recreate object.
	Missing source code.
	Missing object code and source code contains errors.
	Missing object code and available source code creates an object successfully. (Question whether this was the original source.)
	Missing object code and multiple source codes.
	Missing source code and multiple objects.
Multiples	Multiple source codes to object.
	Multiple objects and source codes.
	Multiple objects to source code.
Matching	Recompiling the source code creates an object that does not match the old object. (Be careful: It could be the result of new compiler version or operating system change.)

5. Rollover of Date Data Types

Problems with the rollover of date data types stored as an offset from a specified date—referred to as base dates or epochs—occur for the same reason that there are Year 2000 problems: not realizing the possible longevity of the software and its effect on dates. Surprisingly, many of these errors occur around the Year 2000. Now is the time to determine and capture this information.

PROBLEM TYPE	*EXAMPLES*
Date field represents number of days, seconds, or microseconds since a base date	Number field will roll back to 0 or result in undefined data.

6. Leap Year Problems

The failure to recognize the Year 2000 as a leap year is a minor and infrequent error for many, but has major consequences for some, especially financial institutions and applications.

PROBLEM TYPE	*EXAMPLES*
Incorrect logic in determining leap years	Centesimal year divisible by 400 (accounts for 1600, 2000, and 2400 as leap years; 1900 and 2100 are not leap years).

7. Programmer Bag of Tricks

Your favorite programming trick can be broken by the Year 2000 or your Year 2000 solutions. These problems can be the hardest errors to discover in your code.

PROBLEM TYPE	EXAMPLES
Change *mmddyy* to *yymmdd* (sometimes referred to casually as 9's complement or byte shifting)	Multiply date by 10,000.01. Works if the date element is defined as six-integer digits.
Change *yymmdd* to *mmddyy* (sometimes referred to casually as 9's complement or byte shifting)	Multiply date by 100.0001. Works if the date element is defined as six-integer digits.
Others	Realize programmers have used advanced algorithms and techniques to solve user problems for over thirty years. Make sure to test your systems thoroughly.

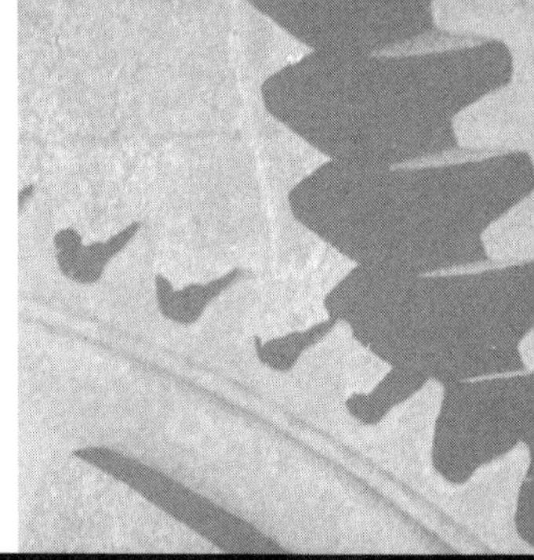

APPENDIX

B

Solution Sets

Selecting solution sets is one of the most critical steps of Detailed Assessment. We assume that you have completed "counting" the types of Year 2000 errors by item, application, and system. The table that follows lists various solutions and their effects on the project, both current and future costs. The solutions include both "data" approaches (you change the date data to include the century) and "procedural" approaches (you change the processing to determine the correct century). You must perform the cost-benefit trade-off in determining your solutions. Time is the key element in determining the optimal approaches. In addition you should consider

- The effort it will take
- Whether you will need one or many solutions
- Your project standards
- Maintenance

Time/Effort

- Consider the amount of total time/effort available for a solution.
- Consider the life expectancy of the system.
- Consider the number of date fields to convert.
- Consider the amount of data to convert.

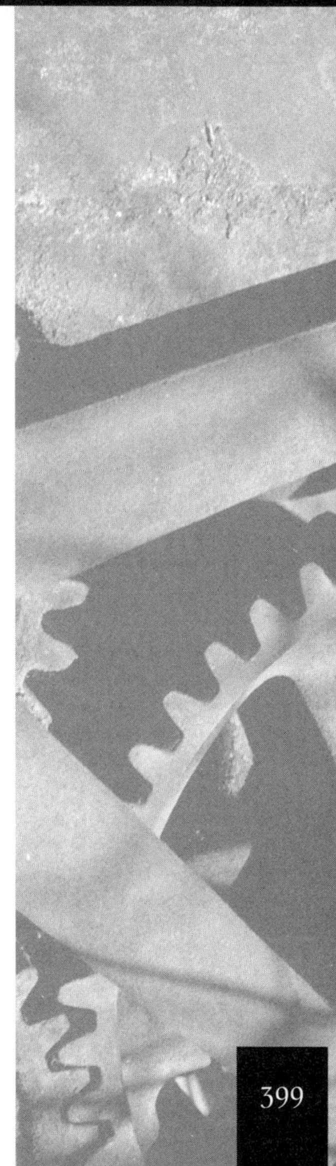

- Consider the availability of automation tools for a particular solution.
- Remember that more complex methods require more testing, more risk, and more maintenance cost.

One or Many Solutions

- Remember that different applications and systems may lead to different sets of solutions.
- Consider determining the most common problems and using them as a basis for solutions.
- If you have more than one problem category, you need more than one solution.
  Example problems: "Treating the date as a special flag" and "Magic number calculations"
  Example solutions: "Create new flag field" and "Adapt standard date manipulation routine"
- Consider that many different solutions can be confusing and expensive.
- Consider whether the operating system or interface returns four-digit years or whether century inference is needed.
- Be aware that the solution to one problem category can either help or hinder the solution to another problem category.
- Determine whether users have direct access to the data for *ad hoc* reports or downloads.
  - Consider the amount of work users will need to perform.
  - Consider that more complex solutions will require more technical support and have more risks.
- Consider combining complex conversion methods into a very complex solution only if forced to do so.
  Example of combined solution: convert to base date method and employ encoding at the same time.
- Devise a new solution that has not yet been considered.

Project Standards

- Consider creating standard common manipulation and conversion date programs for this project.
- Consider a combination of solutions or partial solutions for a specific problem.
  Example problem: User interface does not allow four-digit year to clarify century.
  Example solution: Convert to four-digit years, but leave some report outputs as two-digit years (report changes bypassed because the changes were considered cosmetic).
- Determine whether the method of fix will also become a project standard for the future.

Maintenance

- Consider the future ease and cost of maintenance after the Year 2000 project has been completed.

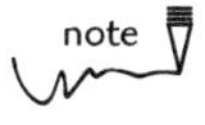

You must clearly state the project solution set so that programmers and users can quickly determine what has to be fixed and then fix it in a consistent manner. This will save time and money, reduce risks, and lower follow-on maintenance confusion. Make sure that your solution works before applying it in assembly-line fashion.

The following tables list the solution sets to the problems outlined in Appendix A. Read the text following the tables for a more complete description of solution sets.

1. Ambiguous Century Representation

Solution Set	*Examples*
1. Represent date with four digits.	*yymmdd* -> *ccyymmdd*
	yy -> *ccyy*
	MON/*dd*/*yy* -> MON/*dd*/*ccyy*
2. Represent date as offset from a specified date.	*yymmdd* -> ######
3. Encode compress/decompress.	*yymmdd* -> *c yymmdd*
4. Windowing (fixed).	29-99 = 1929-1999
	00-28 = 2000-2028
5. Windowing (sliding).	Dynamic version of solution 4.
6. Windowing (fixed or sliding) using program encapsulation.	Window shift the data before/after the program uses it.

2. Interfaces

Solution Set	*Examples*
1. Translate bridge.	Bridge module reads old or new format and translates to other format in either or both directions.
2. Pass multiple date formats.	Interface or bridge passes the date in both old and new formats simultaneously.
3. Pass multiple interfaces.	Interface or bridge constructs multiple interface formats.
4. Staged interface versions.	A complete cutover from one interface format to another format through one or more stages. You can achieve this by using different versions of the interface or different versions of the bridges.
5. Multiple combinations interface.	There are multiple versions to pass the data. You can use either multiple bridges or multiple interfaces to pass the other solutions.

3. Date as a Special Flag or Data Element

SOLUTION SET	EXAMPLES
1. Modify special handling to use a different date value.	Use different values; basic logic stays the same.
2. Modify special handling to use a different flag.	Change program logic; use new or different field as the flag. Remove the intelligence from keys.

4. Configuration Errors

SOLUTION SET	EXAMPLES
1. Fix the "best fit" source.	
2. Fix a disassembled version of source.	
3. Modify application system to bypass this program.	Re-engineer
4. Program encapsulation.	See "Ambiguous Century Representation" solution 6.
5. Patch the object.	

5. Rollover of Date Data Types

SOLUTION SET	EXAMPLES
1. Increase size of date data type.	##### -> #######
2. Change base date.	Old base date was 01-JAN-1600. New base date is 01-JAN-1800.

6. Leap Year Problems

Solution Set	*Examples*
1. Modify leap year calculations.	Centesimal year evenly divisible by 400.

7. Programmer Bag of Tricks

Solution Set	*Examples*
1. Determine new magic number.	Multiply by 10,000.0001 instead.
2. Replace with a more "standard" processing approach.	Program moves each subfield.
3. Others.	Depends on the trick.

Problem Category 1: Ambiguous Century Representation

Ambiguous century representation is the best understood part of the Year 2000 problem. It is also the most prevalent problem.

Solution 1: Represent Date with Four Digits

Expand all year or date fields by two digits or characters. In the following diagram, the existing two-digit year data is enlarged to include the century.

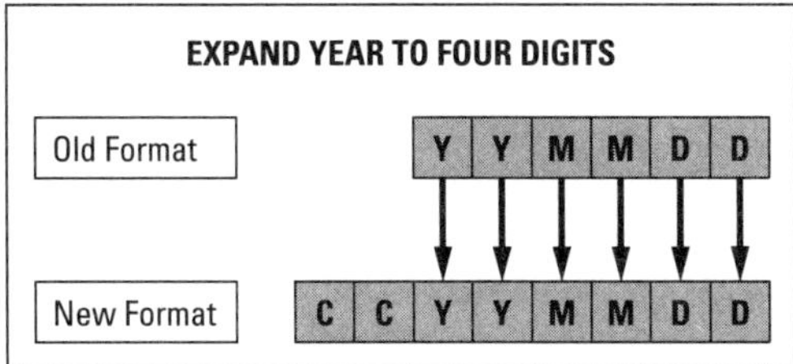

Steps

1. Change dates stored from *yymmdd* format to *ccyymmdd* format. The dates can expand
   - In front of the current field
   - At the end of records
   - In unused space
2. Change year from *yy* format to *ccyy* format.
3. Expand all date fields and temporary date fields to accommodate this.
4. Increase size of program variables that store the date.
5. Change sorts, expand user interfaces, and so on.

Pros

- Simple to understand, implement, test, and maintain.
- Works until 9999 AD. Done. Do not pay for this maintenance work again.
- Eliminates overhead of documenting complex date logic.
- Bridging requirements decrease as other interfaces pass four-digit years.
- Users understand this concept and can deal with it (desktop).
- Consistent approach with newly developed, future systems.

Cons

- More bridge programs may be required during deployments.
- Almost all data and program elements are affected.

- Recompiles necessary even if no direct date functionality.
- More disk space needed.
- May be more expensive, especially if the problem occurs with hard-to-modify file systems.

Solution 2: Represent Date As Offset from a Specified Date

Modify the current date field to a six-digit number representing the number of days since a base date. Many COTS database and operating systems use this method to store their dates internally. In the following diagram, the existing six-digit date is converted to the number of days since Jan 01, 1900. Instead of a 100-year range, the same six digits can now hold over 2,700 years.

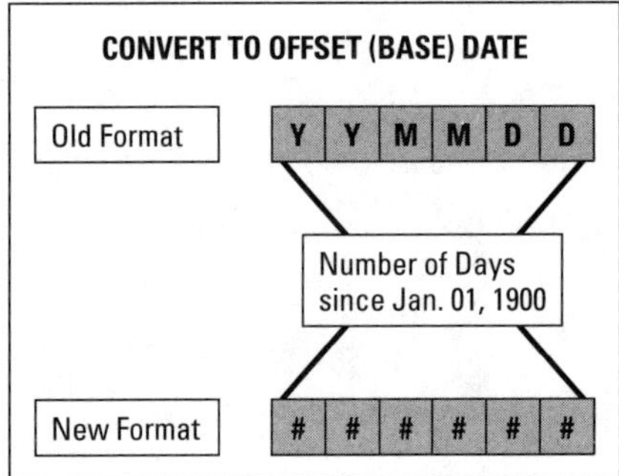

Steps

1. Change *yymmdd* to *dddddd* using standard data conversion routine. Select your base date. (For example, for a base date of Jan-01-1900, 000000 represents January 1, 1900; 000001 represents January 2, 1900; and so on.)
2. Dates read from files are converted to *ccyymmdd* and *yymmdd* using standard routine.
3. Dates written to file are converted to base number using standard routine.
4. Data conversion program uses these new standard routines.
5. Modify programs to handle enlarged date field only where required.
6. Modify user interface to handle enlarged date field only where required.

7. If date is part of file key, you may need different processing.

Pros

- Resolves problem with hard-to-expand file systems.
- Record length does not change, but field description may change.
- Date comparisons are easier to do in the future (subtract one from the other).
- Handles 999,999 days or more (about 2,737 years).
- Sorts will be correct; but field description changes.
- Consistent approach with newly developed, future systems.
- Bridging required only for external interfaces with electronic partnerships or COTS packages.

Cons

- Cannot change *yy* to *ccyy* without record expansion.
- User direct access to this data becomes very complicated (download, *ad hoc* queries).
- Requires standard routines in all affected languages.
- Maintenance and reading data dumps are more difficult.

Solution 3: Encode Compress/Decompress

Capture the century within the old confines of the date field using some encoding method. The following diagram demonstrates the conversion of a packed date to also include an encoded century byte.

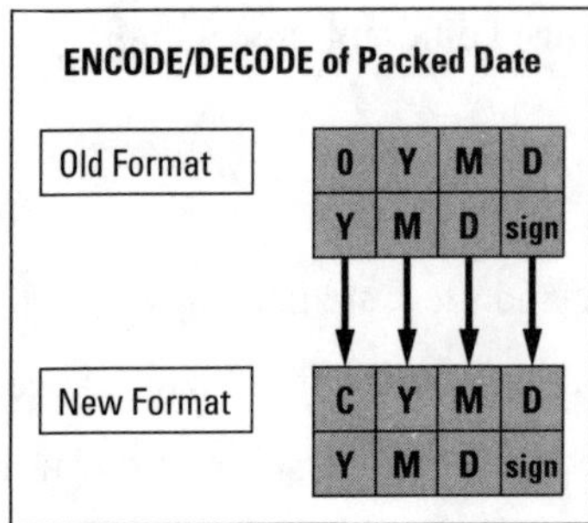

Steps

This solution has various alternatives. What follows is a generic version of a solution:

1. Change *yymmdd* character or digits to *cyymmdd* digits and store as compressed over top of old field. The century values (*c*) are 0 = 19, 1 = 20, 2 = 21, 3 = 22, and so on.
2. Change *yy* to *cyy* and store as compressed over top of old field.
3. Dates read from files are converted to *ccyymmdd* and *yymmdd* using standard routine.
4. Dates written to file are converted to *cyymmdd* using standard routine.
5. Data conversion program uses these new standard routines.
6. Some sorts need to be changed because the sorted field description changed.
7. If date is part of file key, different processing may be necessary.

Pros

- Record length does not change, but field description does change.
- Works until 2899 AD using century numbers 0 through 9. Works until 3499 AD with century characters 0 through F.
- Resolves problem with hard-to-expand file systems.
- Bridging requirements decrease as other interfaces pass four-digit years.

Cons

- More bridge programs may be required during deployments.
- User direct access to this data will be complicated (download, *ad hoc* queries).
- Requires standard routines in all affected languages.
- Maintenance and reading data dumps are more difficult.
- May not be consistent approach with newly developed, future systems.

Alternatives

- Encode year as hexadecimal. Instead of year 00 through 99 values, you have year containing 00-255 values. Good through year 2155.

Solution 4: Windowing (Fixed)

Move the 100-year window that the programs use (1900-1999) forward *x* years (for example, 1928-2027). You can do this by shifting the date inside the program (data encapsulation) during input/output routines. The following diagram demonstrates the range of years shifted by using this method.

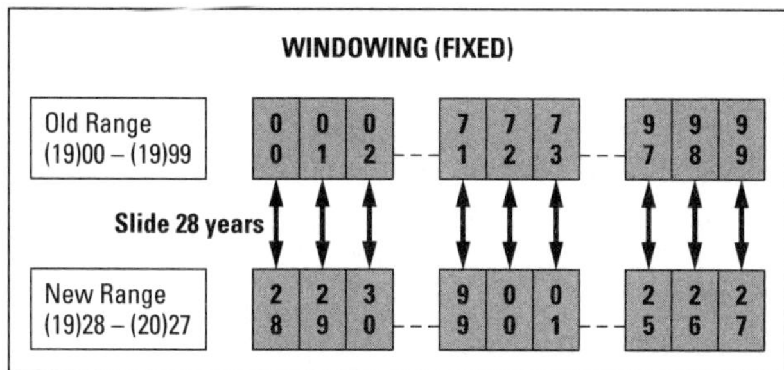

Steps

There are various alternatives with this form of data encapsulation. The most popular version is subtracting 28 from the year. It handles 2000 as a leap year and the days of the week match.

1. Dates read from files have 28 subtracted from the year. If year result is negative, add 100.
2. Dates written to file or output have 28 added to the year before they are written. If the year result is over 99, subtract 100.

Pros

- Record length does not change; field description stays the same.
- Reduced number of code changes to make.

Cons

- Works for only 28 years, which may not be long enough.
- Sorts will be incorrect without collating sequence changes.
- May incorrectly use date-specific logic (that is, 2004-28 = 76; if year = 76 perform 76-print-calendar for year 2004).
- May chop off earlier dates that are still needed (1900-1927).
- Requires standard routines in all affected languages.
- May not be consistent approach with newly developed, future systems.
- If date is part of file key, range selection may be incorrect.

Alternatives

- Put the number of years to slide (28) into a control file or files that can easily be changed (becomes a more dynamic sliding window solution).

Solution 5: Windowing (Sliding)

Move the 100-year window that the programs see (1900-1999) as though dynamically moved forward. The calculation to move the window can be control file-based (see alternative above). The calculation to move the window can be dynamically calculated as in the following example. We recommend that the windows be dynamically calculated by one or more control programs and the results stored in control files for the use of all affected programs.

This can be done by shifting the date inside the program (data encapsulation) during input/output operations.

Steps

This solution has various alternatives. What follows is a generic version of the solution using data encapsulation:

1. Determine the window range for each date scenario (for example, 'date lease starts' assumes no lease lasts more than 99 years).
2. Determine what value (fixed or variable) can control that date window (for example, assume that 5 is the youngest a mature active lease could be).

   Sample logic to determine century for mature active lease:

```
Max-Mature-CCYY = today - 5.
If Lease-Start-YY > max-Mature-YY.
  Then Lease-Start-CC = max-Mature-CC - 1.
Else Lease-Start-CC = max-Mature-CC.
```

Solving by substitution the preceding example using 2002 as today and Lease Start of 85:

```
1997 = 2002 -5
if 85 > 97
  then (not true)
else 19 = 19
```

Result is 19 for century.

Solving by substitution the preceding example using 2022 as today and Lease Start of 85:

```
2017 = 2022 -5
if 85 > 17
     then 19 = 20 - 1
else (not true)
```

Result is 19 for century.

Pros

- Record length does not change; field description stays the same.
- Reduced number of code changes to make.
- Works until about 9999 A.D.
- 100-year window should be wide enough; otherwise, you will always have a problem.

Cons

- Not all scenarios have a basis for value control. Use control file for these cases.
- It is risky to have too many assumptions concerning maximum and minimum values.
- The Detailed Assessment process may not have captured the scenarios. You need to determine the scenarios.
- Sorts will be incorrect without collating sequence changes.
- May incorrectly use date-specific logic (that is, 2004-28 = 76; if year = 76, perform 76-print calendar for year 2004).
- Can result in many solution sets; therefore, it is confusing and hard to maintain.
- May chop off earlier dates that are still needed.
- May not be consistent approach with newly developed, future systems.
- If date is part of file key, range selection may be incorrect.
- Requires standard routines in all affected languages for each scenario.

Solution 6: Windowing (Fixed or Sliding) Using Program Encapsulation

Shift the date data in the file prior to program execution, using either the fixed or the sliding window solution described earlier.

Step

1. A program, procedure, or script modifies the file as it is transferred between environments.

Pros

- Programs may not require any changes (covers up systems with poor integrity between source and object).
- Cheap method if there is a single interface file between two different systems (for example, mainframe download to PC).
- Record length does not change; field description stays the same.
- Sorts may be able to operate correctly without changes.

Cons

- Frequently converting large amounts of data may take too long.
- User access to program encapsulated (shifted) data is potentially confusing.
- May incorrectly use date-specific logic (that is, 2004-28 = 76; if year = 76, perform 76-print-calendar for year 2004).
- May not be consistent approach with newly developed, future systems.

Problem Category 2: Interfaces

Dates are passed between programs, systems, platforms, enterprises, and companies. Dates are passed using files, memory, networks, documents, and other recording media. All interface problems could be derived from the other problem types. However, it takes a great deal of attention to solve interfaces correctly, and the solutions for these problems encompass different concepts than the other problem categories. Finally, most of the early Year 2000 project Deployment failures stem from interface problems.

Solution 1: Translate Bridge

The bridge module or utility reads the old or new format interface data and translates it into the other format. If the bridge is installed on an interface that passes data from compliant to noncompliant partitions, it will read the new format and translate it into the old format. If the bridge is installed on an interface that passes data from noncompliant to compliant partitions, it will read the old format and translate it into the new format. The following diagram demonstrates a translation bridge installed to translate noncompliant data to compliant data. The translation of noncompliant data would probably use a windowing scheme to translate noncompliant dates to compliant dates. Bridge usefulness can extend beyond the Year 2000, but the translation scheme used redeposits all of the risks associated with the solution, including possible year misinterpretation. In addition, this process might change the name of the interface data.

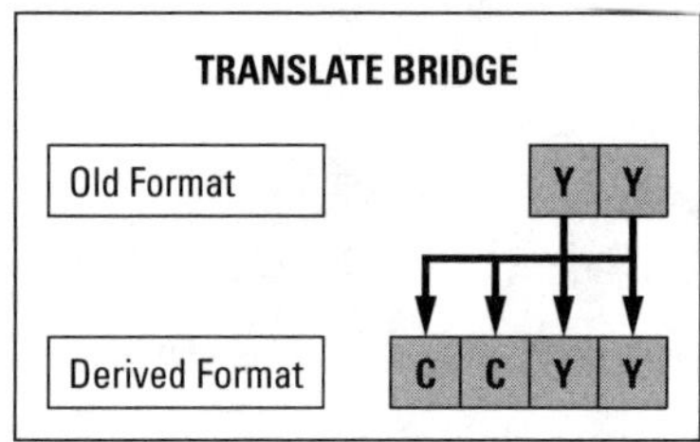

For changes within a single partition, this solution handles both passing and receiving interfaces.

Steps

1. Determine both old and new formats of the interface.
2. Select translation scheme.
3. Develop and test module.
4. Install bridge module and revised interface module during deployment of the partition involving the interface.
5. Deinstall bridge module when the other side of interface (partition) achieves compliant format.

Pros

- Easier to develop and maintain data translation as a single new module rather than a modification to an existing complex module.
- Easier to remove the bridge after both sides of the interface are compliant.
- Easier to troubleshoot problems when you have both before and after translation data available.

Cons

- Processing time will take longer when translation is a separate step (I/O).
- Disk space may not allow translation of the data.

Solution 2: Pass Multiple Date Formats

Modify existing interface module to pass one set of date data in multiple date formats. The following diagram demonstrates the translation of a single noncompliant year into both the noncompliant format and a compliant format. The creation of the new compliant format data would probably use a windowing scheme to translate noncompliant dates to compliant dates. For changes within a single partition, this solution handles passing interfaces.

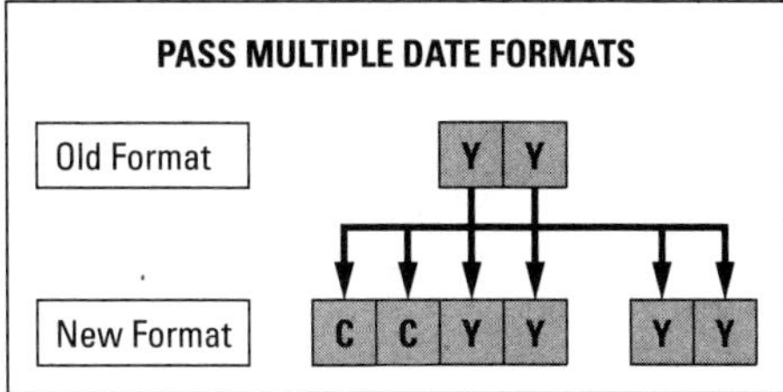

Steps

1. Determine both old and new formats of the interface and various date formats needed.
2. Determine date when both sides of the interface will change.

3. Develop and test module.
4. Install revised module or bridge during deployment of the partition involving the interface.
5. There is no planned deinstall.

Pros

- Handles multiple date formats for both now and the future.
- Faster processing time than translate bridge solution.
- Works best if you control the interface to multiple outside electronic partners and they are using different methods to handle year 2000 dates.

Cons

- Need for multiple formats may go away long before multiple format processing will be removed.
- All sides of interface must be deployed to accept interface data layout containing multiple formats.
- More disk space required if interface data is stored, especially if there are many dates and formats in the interface.

Solution 3: Pass Multiple Interfaces

The interface will contain two sets of data: both new and old interface formats. Recommend alternative; have bridge module construct other format (similar to Solution 1). For changes within a single partition, this solution handles passing interfaces.

Steps

1. Determine both old and new formats of the interface.
2. Select translation scheme.
3. Develop and test module.

4. Install revised interface module and bridge module during deployment of the partition.
5. Pass both sets of data.
6. Revise interface module or deinstall bridge module when the other side of interface (partition) achieves compliant format.

Pros

- Easier to develop and maintain data translation as a single new module rather than a modification to an existing complex module.
- Easier to remove bridge after both sides of interface are compliant.
- Easier to troubleshoot problems when you have both sets of translation data available on both sides of the interface.
- The other side of the interface can migrate towards compliancy or roll back a deployment without the need for close coordination.

Cons

- The interface must be able to handle and use only one of the multiple interfaces passed.
- Processing and passing the interface data requires the longest time of all of the solutions.
- Disk space may not allow both interface formats of the data.

Solution 4: Staged Interface Versions

The interface module or bridges will be modified to handle one or more versions of the interface. As the format of the interface is changed, newer versions of the interface modules or bridges are installed and the old version removed. For changes within a single partition, this solution handles both passing and receiving interfaces.

Steps

1. Determine both old and new formats of the interface.

2. Determine dates when either or both sides of the interface will change.
3. Decide on versions necessary.
4. Select translation scheme, if necessary.
5. Develop and test module(s).
6. Deinstall and install the various versions as the schedule dictates.

Pros

- This solution is the most processing efficient solution of all.
- This solution is also the most disk space efficient.

Cons

- Can require more testing and configuration management control than most solutions.
- This solution requires the closest coordination and timing on both sides of the interface.

Solution 5: Multiple Combinations Interface

There are multiple versions of the modules or bridges to pass the data. These versions can employ any or all of the other four solutions and more than one version of the interface can be active at one time. For changes within a single partition, this solution handles both passing and receiving interfaces.

Steps

1. Determine both old and new formats of the interface.
2. Determine dates when either or both sides of the interface will change.
3. Decide on solutions necessary and determine whether any bridges are part of the solution.
4. Select translation schemes, if necessary.
5. Develop and test module(s).

6. Install the versions of interface modules and bridge modules during deployment of the partition.
7. Deinstall or install additional versions as schedule dictates.

Pro

- This can be the most flexible solution set to solve tough requirements.

Cons

- This can be the most complex solution and the hardest to maintain configuration management.
- This can be the hardest to test, as all versions of the modules and bridges must be tested.
- Close coordination and timing is necessary on both sides of the interface.

Problem Category 3: Date as a Special Flag

This problem was created because dates were defined or used as something other than a strictly date data type. Some of the habits of reusing precious data or memory space carried forward with us today, even if the date was later defined correctly.

Solution 1: Modify Special Handling To Use a Different Date Value

Replace hard-coded value with a different hard-coded value. Similar to a fixed window solution.

Steps

1. Replace 123199 with, perhaps, 123150 (for 12/31/2050).

2. Replace 99 or 00 with, perhaps, 50 (for 2050) (for example, replace if year = 76 perform 76-print-calendar with if year = 1976 perform 1976-print-calendar).
3. Enlarge the length of text fields affected.
4. Modify algorithms that use dates.

Pro

- Simple fix to the programming code.

Cons

- Limited time before application logic needs to be fixed again.
- May not have available valid, new, hard-coded values to replace old values.
- May not be consistent approach with newly developed, future systems.
- May be confusing if date was shifted before the calculation takes place (see "Ambiguous Century Representation," Solutions 4 through 6).

Solution 2: Modify Special Handling To Use a Different Flag

Replace hard-coded value with a new or different variable. This separates date values from the procedural processing.

Steps

1. Replace 123199 with a date-based value, a count-down variable, or a different date value.
2. Replace 99 year with a new end-of-list variable for end-of-data list marker.
3. Replace year used as a memory or array pointer with a new field or pointer.
4. Move dates out of text strings.
5. Remove dates from algorithms that do not have to be date-dependent.
6. Remove the date intelligence from the keys.

Pros

- Fixes the problem until 9999 or later.
- Consistent approach with newly developed, future systems.

Cons

- Requires more programming logic changes, so it takes longer and costs more for the short term.
- Users may be dependent on intelligent keys and suffer withdrawal.

Alternatives

Define a new standard way to indicate

- Null date (for example, hexadecimal value 00 or a new variable)
- Never-expire date (for example, hexadecimal value FF or a new variable)

Problem Category 4: Configuration Errors

Configuration errors are not Year 2000 specific. They are uncovered during any major project dealing with older code. Your Year 2000 project will deal with more older code than any other previous project. Hopefully, you will uncover only a few of these problems, but each occurrence can be very expensive or risky to resolve.

Solution 1: Fix the "Best Fit" Source

Fix the "best fit" or "best educated guess" matching source code. Use the closest matching version of hardware, operating system, and database.

Steps

1. Determine the functions of the object being executed.

2. Determine the best fit-to-function source code.
3. Modify the best-fit source code to replicate old functions of old object.
4. Regression test for old functions existing within modified source.
5. Modify source code for Year 2000 changes and retest.
6. Remove or archive other old versions of source or object code.

Pro

- Source code will match for future maintenance.

Cons

- May be hard to determine functions of object.
- Risky because functions may be missed, allowing bugs or old features to be reintroduced.

Solution 2: Fix a Disassembled Version of Source

Create and fix a disassembled source code.

Steps

1. Use an automated tool to create a disassembly source from the object (backward engineered).
2. Modify source code for Year 2000 changes.

Pros

- Greater likelihood that all old functions are retained and captured into the source code.
- Source code will match for future maintenance.

Cons

- Understanding the disassembled source code will be much harder.
- Applying the Year 2000 fixes is more expensive.
- Future maintenance with this program will be more expensive.

Solution 3: Modify Application System To Bypass This Program

Remove offending program and patch the application system around it. Re-engineer.

Steps

1. Determine the functions of the object being executed.
2. Modify other programs to take over the functions.
3. Modify source code for Year 2000 changes.
4. Remove or archive the offending version of source or object.

Pros

- Source code will match for future maintenance.
- Solution if different versions of the object code are used by very few programs but need to be separated.
- May speed up processing if retired program was called frequently within a program.

Cons

- May move application environment from standardized version to multiple versions.
- May be hard to determine functions of object code.
- Risky because functions may be missed, allowing bugs or old features to be reintroduced.

Solution 4: Program Encapsulation

See "Ambiguous Century Representation," Solution 6.

Additional Cons

- Danger that the other Year 2000 problem categories will not be discovered in the object.
- Will not have source code for future maintenance.

Solution 5: Patch the Object

Directly patch object code.

Steps

1. Determine occurrences of code and logic to modify by scanning.
2. Patch object code directly.

Pro

- Works well if you use the fixed window solution and there are few areas to patch.

Cons

- Complex solutions will quickly increase the cost of patching.
- Danger that other Year 2000 problem categories will not be discovered in the object code.
- Will not have source code for future maintenance.

Problem Category 5: Rollover of Date Data Type

Problems with the rollover of date data types stored as an offset from a specified date—referred to as base dates or epochs—occur for the same reason that there are Year 2000 problems: not realizing the possible longevity of the software and its effect on dates. Surprisingly, many of these errors occur around the Year 2000. Now is the time to determine and capture this information.

Solution 1: Increase Size of Date Data Type

Enlarge the size of the field containing the base date number.

Steps

1. Increase date size: for example, from 5 digits to 7 digits.
2. Increase file lengths; increase size of program variable that stores the date.
3. Modify standard date conversion routines.

Pros

- Fairly easy program change to make.
- Simple to understand, implement, test, and maintain.
- Bridging requirements decrease as other interfaces pass four-digit years.
- Users understand this concept and can deal with it (desktop).
- Consistent approach with newly developed, future systems.

Cons

- More bridge programs required during deployments.
- Almost all data and program elements are affected.
- Recompiles necessary even if there is no direct date functionality.
- More disk space needed.

- May be more expensive, especially if the problem occurs with hard-to-modify file systems.

Solution 2: Change Base Date

Change the starting base date value.

Steps

1. Change base date from Jan 01, 1600 to Jan 01, 1700.
2. Write date conversion programs to modify existing data.
3. Modify standard date conversion routines that used old base date logic.

Pros

- Fairly easy change to make, especially if standard date conversion routines are solidly in place.
- Simple to understand, implement, test, and maintain.
- Bridging requirements decrease as other interfaces pass date using new base value.
- Consistent approach with newly developed, future systems.

Cons

- Not all programming units may have used the standard date conversion routines.
- More bridge programs may be required during deployments.
- May not be able to move base date value forward enough, so this is a limited solution.

Problem Category 6: Leap Year Problems

The failure to recognize the year 2000 as a leap year is a minor and infrequent error for many, but has major consequences for some, especially financial institutions and applications.

Solution 1: Modify Leap Year Calculations

Employ centesimal rule for calculating leap years.

Steps

1. There are four rules for calculating a leap year:
   - If the year is evenly divisible by 4, it is a leap year.
   - Unless the year ends in 00, it is *not* a leap year.
   - Unless the year is evenly divisible by 400, it is a leap year.
   - Unless the year is 3600, it is *not* a leap year.

Pros

- Fairly easy program change to make.
- May be able to delay deployment of this fix until February 29, 2000.
- Consistent approach with newly developed, future systems.

Con

- Cost may not justify the benefits of adding the extra day (February 29) in 2000 (depends on the event horizon for this problem).

Problem Category 7: Programmer Bag of Tricks

Your favorite programming trick can be broken by the Year 2000 or your Year 2000 solutions. These problems can be the hardest errors to discover in your code.

Solution 1: Determine New Magic Number

Replace old method and number with new method and number.

Steps

1. Old method: Modify date in format *MMDDYY* to *YYMMDD,* multiplying by 10,000.01. Modify date in format *YYMMDD* to *MMDDYY,* multiplying by 100.0001. Works if the date element is defined as six-integer digits.
2. New method: Modify *MMDDCCYY* to *CCYYMMDD,* multiplying by 10,000.0001. Modify *CCYYMMDD* to *MMDDCCYY,* multiplying by 10,000.0001. Works if the date element is defined as eight-integer digits.

Pro

- Fairly easy change to make.

Cons

- A different "ambiguous century representation" solution can make the new algorithm complex.
- The old method was perhaps nonstandard and undocumented.
- May not be consistent approach with newly developed, future systems.

Solution 2: Replace with a More "Standard" Processing Approach

Replace the old method with a more conventional method, as pictured in the following diagram.

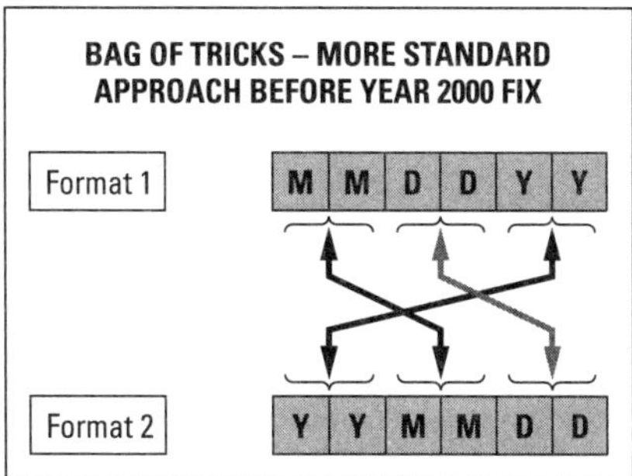

Steps

1. Replace *MMDDYY* with *YYMMDD,* multiplying by 10,000.01, throughout the program with move statements for each subfield (*MM, DD, YY*).

Pros

- Adheres to more standard and conventional methods of solving the problem.
- Future maintenance will be easier and less costly.
- Consistent approach with newly developed, future systems.

Cons

- Change requires more manual programming effort than Solution 1, "Determine New Magic Number."
- Costs more to make this change in the short term.

Solution 3: Others

Fixing and replacing other discovered programmer tricks will depend upon the trick. They will probably all have two common solutions available: Either determine the new trick to replace the old trick, or replace with a more standard programming approach.

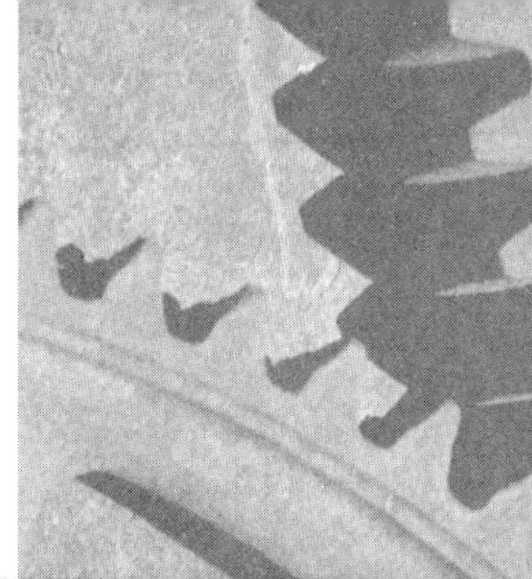

APPENDIX

C

Legal and Contract Considerations

The Year 2000 problem presents multiple challenges for legal, contract, auditing, and senior business staff. Appendix C offers you direction by providing several brief summaries of public domain resources that describe many of these risks in detail. Legal, contract, audit, and executive management challenges are faced by both the private and public sectors on an international scale.

Legal, contract, audit, and senior staff should realize that the Year 2000 problem is first and foremost a business problem. In the context of a "business issue" the Year 2000 problem is viewed as:

1. A potential delay in your ability to conduct business and/or
2. The creation of liabilities

Business delays and liabilities may be caused by one of the multiple sources of malfunctions discussed in this book or by a chain of events rooted in your downstream or upstream suppliers, services, products, or customers.

Organizations are realizing the need to include suppliers, services, products, and customers in their Year 2000 plans. Accordingly, the Federal Reserve Bank of New York, in its April 4, 1997 Year 2000 Alert, found: "Most institutions have focused their efforts to date on identifying the changes that must be made internally to address the Year 2000 issue. Most are well along in this process. Fewer institutions are as

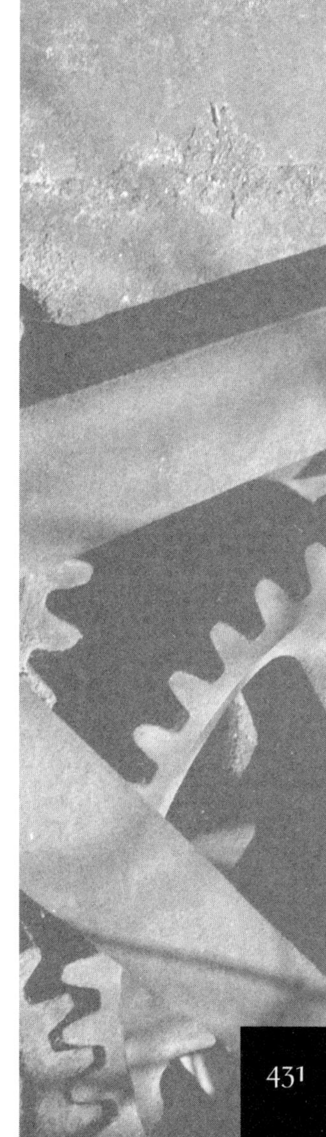

advanced in their thinking about how the Year 2000 may affect their dealings with customers, vendors, or service providers..."

The articles and references listed here are provided as considerations to support your Year 2000 efforts. They DO NOT represent a total or comprehensive review of the subject, but they do offer relevant information for your staff in hopes of facilitating your Year 2000 project.

Each of the articles referenced below can be easily accessed using the *How To 2000* CD-ROM World Wide Web bookmarks page included with this book.

For the Contract and Legal Staff

Legal Issues Concerning the Year 2000 "Millennium Bug"
Jeff Jinnett
Copyright © 1996 by Jeff Jinnett
(Jeff Jinnett is Of Counsel to the law firm of LeBoeuf, Lamb, Greene & MacRae, L.L.P., practicing in the area of computer law. He also serves as President of LeBoeuf Computing Technologies, L.L.C., a business subsidiary of LLG&M.)

`http://www.howto2000.com/article1.htm`

Mr. Jinnett presents a well-researched article that offers insights and considerations to counterbalance business problems caused by the Year 2000 conversion. This article will provide private sector organization's legal counsel, audit and senior management a good overview of the candidate legal issues. Generally, Mr. Jinnett presents a case for "preventative law." His article includes the following subheadings:

- Year 2000 Problem Corrective Costs In The Billions
- Modification Of Existing Computer System Versus Migration To New Systems
- No "Silver Bullet" Solution
- Many Companies Will Not Become Year 2000 Compliant In Time
- Technical/Legal Inventory
- Legal Audit
    - Potential Vendor Obligations

  - Product Switches
  - Contaminated Third Party Data
- General Contract Issues
  - Compliance Warranties
  - The Force Majeure Argument
  - Software License/Copyright Restrictions
  - Export Restrictions On Encryption Software
  - Due Diligence On Acquisitions
- Disclosure And Audit Issues
  - Accounting Standards Which May Mandate Disclosure
  - Statement Of Financial Auditing Standards
  - Statements On Auditing Standards
  - Pressure To Disclose Due To Potential Securities Law Liability Of Auditors
  - Disclosure In Auditors' Opinions
  - Securities Laws Which May Mandate Disclosure
  - Potential Liability Of Officers And Directors Of A Public Company Which Fails To Disclose A Year 2000 Problem And Then Fails To Become Year 2000 Compliant In Time
  - Standards Of Care Of A Director
  - Shareholder Suits
  - Documentation Of Year 2000 Compliance Program To Establish Due Diligence Defense And Protection Under The Business Judgment Rule
  - Statutory Limitations On Liability, Corporate Indemnification And D & O Insurance Coverage
  - Disclosure Due To Bank Examinations
- Statutory/Regulatory Compliance Mandates
- Insurance Issues
- Business Interruption Insurance
- Directors & Officers Liability Insurance
- Collateral Litigation Damage

Who Faces Financial Liability For The Year 2000 Problem?
Williams, Mullen, Christian & Dobbins, Attorneys at Law
Copyright © 1997

`http://www.howto2000.com/article2.htm`

This set of articles takes a focused look at who may be held responsible for Year 2000 compliance and why. The articles support three general target groups that will share the burden:

- Directors And Officer Liability (Fiduciary Care)
- Insurance ("Rescuer Or Co-victim?")
- Year 2000 Vendors And Computer Companies

Year 2000 "Millennium Bug" Litigation
Jeff Jinnett
Copyright © 1997 Jeff Jinnett

`http://www.howto2000.com/article3.htm`

In this article Mr. Jinnett examines why Year 2000 litigation may occur, its effects, damages and defenses. Again, in this article, Mr. Jinnett recommends "preventative law" measures. Sub-headings to the article include:

- Why Is Year 2000 Litigation Inevitable
- Cascade Effect Of Litigation
- Insurers Are Taking The Year 2000 Litigation Risk Seriously
- When Will The Litigation Begin
- Who Will Be The Parties To The Litigation
- What Are Some Potential Causes Of Action
- What Are Some Potential Defenses
- What Are Some Potential Damages
- What Is The Potential Collateral Impact Of The Litigation
- Litigation Arising Out Of Dependencies On Business Partners

Draft Year 2000 Warranty Language
Timothy J. Feathers
Hillix, Brewer, Hoffhaus, Whittaker & Wright, L.L.C.

http://www.howto2000.com/article4.htm

The Year 2000 warranty language in this article focuses solely on required "representations and warranties" that should be provided from a candidate software Licenser. Mr. Feathers offers a decent starting place and considerations for your own legal counsel.

However, Mr. Feathers does add this note: "NOBODY takes responsibility for how you use this document. You are strongly advised to consult with your own legal counsel in all legal matters. This is posted only to serve as an example of what might be included in a Year 2000 Warranty."

For the Audit and Accounting Staff

The **"Year 2000 Audit Guideline"**
Information Systems Audit and Control Association (ISACA)

http://www.howto2000.com/article5.htm

The ISACA provides a decent primer for your audit staff to build its own Year 2000 audit plan. The information in the article is presented in a generic fashion and should be carefully assessed and tailored to reflect the specific business needs of your operation.

Thinking Points For A Full Company Response To The Year 2000 Software Crisis
Jonathan E. Polonsky
Copyright ©1997 Thelen, Marrin, Johnson & Bridges LLP (forthcoming, *Year 2000 Journal Vol 1., No. 5*, 1997)

http://www.howto2000.com/article6.htm

This article offers a set of questions that probe the basic Year 2000 how-tos. The questions are accompanied by an easy-to-follow outline of considerations in Year 2000 project planning, auditing and risk management.

The Summary Article Outline includes:

- Initial Organizational Support
- Establishment Of Project Office And Project Committees

- External Corporate Communications And Disclosures
- Existing Licenses, Maintenance Agreements And Other Agreements
- Copyright Infringement Issues
- Insurance Risk Management
- Credit Risk Management
- M&A Activities
- Underwriting Activities
- Client Advisory And Investment Research Activities
- Year 2000 Compliance In Technology Products
- Vendors' Own Internal Year 2000 Compliance
- Technology Products Developed And Distributed By The Company
- Human Resources Issues
- Tax Strategy
- International Issues
- Regulatory Issues
- Documentation And Records

Year 2000 Tax Issues Preventing An Even Bigger Hit To The Bottom Line
Joan Paul
Copyright © 1997 Thelen, Marrin, Johnson & Bridges LLP. (Chapter 6 of *Drafting Licensing Agreements*, Third Edition, Aspen Law & Business, 1997)

`http://www.howto2000.com/article7.htm`

The costs of the Year 2000 fix may be significant. Tax treatment of these costs must be assessed. When this article was researched and written in January of 1997, "neither Congress, the courts, nor the I.R.S. had to date specifically addressed the tax treatment of Year 2000 fix costs." The author likens the Year 2000 problem to the S&L, environmental, and asbestos crises, then proceeds with some practical interpretations:

- Deductibility Of Year 2000 Costs
  - Repairs
  - Research And Development Costs

- Amortization Of Year 2000 Costs
- The Research Tax Credit

(Information contained in this article is current as of January 10, 1997.)

International Tax Consequences Of Year 2000 Fix Costs
Joan Paul
Copyright ©Joan Paul 1997 (June 1997)

`http://www.howto2000.com/article8.htm`

Ms. Paul summarizes this article best when she states "this article is intended to heighten the awareness of multinational user corporations undertaking an organization-wide Year 2000 compliance project to international tax issues created by project costs." Some of the more significant issues are discussed in her article, as outlined below:

- IRC section 482 and Related Issues - Transfer Pricing In Transactions Between Commonly-Controlled Corporations
  - Pricing Services Rendered To Affiliates
  - Pricing Property Transfers And Comparison With Pricing Services
  - Summary
  - Planning Opportunity Under Proposed Regulations And Recent Caselaw
- Foreign Tax Credits
- Operation Of Foreign Tax Credit Limitations
- Effect Of Year 2000 Costs On Foreign Tax Credit Availability
  - Foreign Affiliate Directly Incurs Year 2000 Fix Costs
  - Section 482 Allocation of Service Income From Foreign Affiliate
  - US Corporation Pays Year 2000 Fix Costs And Has Net Loss
- Foreign Tax Consequences

For the Executive Manager

The Year 2000 Software Crisis: Management And Legal Gauntlet Of The Millennium

Steven L. Hock

Copyright © Thelen, Marrin, Johnson & Bridges LLP 1996

`http://www.howto2000.com/article9.htm`

Mr. Hock provides an easy-to-read call to action for directors and executive management. This non-technical briefing focuses on some of the key Year 2000 issues affecting businesses. Mr. Hock's advice is offered in straightforward fashion, avoiding unnecessary scare tactics and myths often used ineffectively with senior executives. His article includes discussions on the following:

- Directors' And Officers' Liability And Securities Law Issues
- Tax Law Issues
- Legal Rights Under Existing Licensing, Maintenance, Outsourcing And Other Agreements
- Legal Issues Relating To Future Licenses And Agreements With Vendors Of Computer-Related Products And Services
- Legal Issues Regarding Mergers And Acquisitions
- Trade Secret And Intellectual Property Law Issues
- Legal Issues Relating To Non-Technology Contracts
- Labor And Employment Law Issues
- Legal Issues Relating To System Interfaces And Relationships With Non-Technology Suppliers
- Litigation Issues
- Legal And Non-Legal Issues Regarding Government
- The Problem As An Opportunity

For the Federal and State Government

Year 2000 Computer Problem Awareness Article For The Federal And State Government Entities
Jeff Jinnett
Copyright © 1996 Jeff Jinnett

http://www.howto2000.com/article10.htm

Again, Mr. Jinnett offers relevant support aimed at Federal and State agencies. This article should be considered a general governmental awareness briefing that provides the following instruction:

- A brief analysis of the history and background
- A determination of the costs of reviewing and rewriting computer codes for both the Federal government and the governments of states
- An analysis of the implications of the Year 2000 computer problem with respect to intergovernmental and integrated systems
- A determination of the period of time necessary to remedy the Year 2000 computer problem (including testing)
- The development of balanced and sound contracts to be used in necessary Federal procurement with respect to using private contractors in the computer industry
- An analysis of the effects and potential effects on the United States economy that would result if the Year 2000 computer problem is not resolved by June 1, 1999

CIO Counsel Subcommittee On Year 2000 & General Services Administration Office Of Government wide Policy (MK-Y2K)

http://www.itpolicy.gsa.gov/mks/yr2000/y201toc1.htm

This federal support information page provides a wealth of resources focused on the government's Year 2000 progress, definitions, and issues. On this web page you will find:

- Federal Progress Reports (Congress, OMB, GAO, CIO Counsel...)
- Updates To The Federal Acquisition Regulations (FAR)

- Acquisition Language Recommendations
- Year 2000 Related Conferences
- Federal Best Practices And Links To Agencies
- Compliance Status
- Standards And Time Related Data
- State Level Information
- Year 2000 Vendor Information
- Misc. Year 2000 Data

For Those Still Hard To Convince

The Computer Information Center(Compinfo) offers a wide variety of Year 2000 resources and links. If you are having a difficult time getting people on board with your Year 2000 project, navigate to `http://www.compinfo.co.uk/y2k.htm` and see:

How Year 2000 Date Problem Affects.....

- Governments
- Hardware And Software Suppliers
- Lawyers, Directors And Officers
- Auditors
- Investments
- Financial Services
- People And Communities
- Businesses
- Small Businesses

APPENDIX

Sample Presentations D

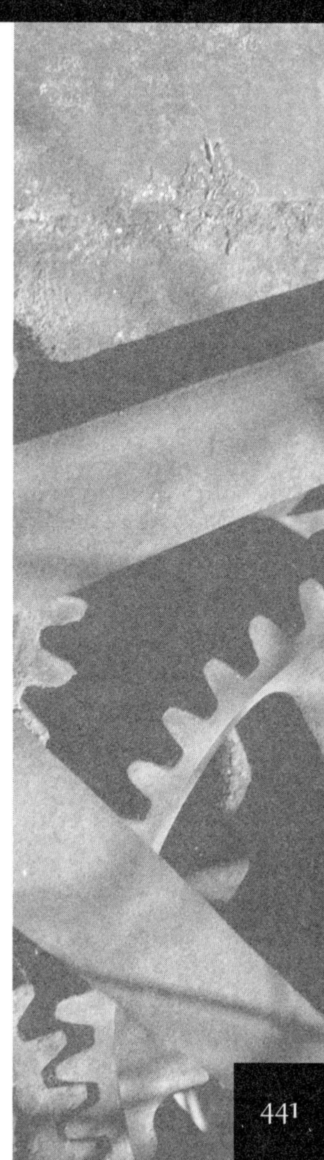

The CD-ROM that accompanies this book includes a set of sample presentations in Microsoft PowerPoint format. Your organization can use these briefings as the basis for general awareness and management briefings. The presentations are titled:

- A Brief Overview
- General Awareness
- Technical Problems and Solutions
- Detailed Management Briefing
- Trade Show
- Senior Management Briefing
- Triage Briefing

Microsoft PowerPoint

The presentations were generated using Microsoft PowerPoint, which requires your system to meet or exceed this configuration:

- Microsoft Windows 3.1 or later (Windows for Workgroups 3.11, 95, NT)
- 486/33

- 8MB memory
- 16MB disk space (to install PowerPoint)
- 35MB disk space (to install the How To 2000 presentations)

Although you can use PowerPoint to open the presentations directly from the CD, a preferable approach is to copy the files from the CD directly to your hard disk. The presentations require approximately 35MB of disk space. Use your preferred method to copy the files from the CD to the appropriate directory on your hard disk or network, start PowerPoint, and load the desired presentation.

The presentations are graphics intensive, and are stored in very large files. PowerPoint 97 manipulates these presentations much more efficiently than PowerPoint version 4.

Tailoring the Presentations

Each presentation contains material describing some aspect of *How To 2000* or the Year 2000 problem. If your project tailors the tasks, deliverables, and phases significantly, you may want to consider tailoring these presentations to match your plans.

The General Awareness, Technical Problems and Solutions, and Detailed Management Overview presentations contain placeholders for information specific to your Year 2000 project. For example, the Detailed Management Overview contains a section entitled "Our Year 2000 Program." Slides allowing you to describe your activities to date are in the appropriate section of the presentation.

The Presentations

The following sections include short descriptions of each presentation.

A Brief Overview

This presentation is targeted to a very high level, and glosses over most of the details of Year 2000 problems and their solution. The ten-slide presentation provides a brief introduction to the How To 2000 methodology, describes what the Year 2000 problem is, where it may be found, and the steps to compliance.

General Awareness

These approximately 30 slides are aimed at a general audience. The goal is to inform your employees about the source, scope, and complexity of the Year 2000 problem; familiarize the staff with the How To 2000 approach; help everybody understand their role in reaching compliance; and broadcast the Year 2000 project points of contact.

Technical Problems and Solutions

This approximately 35-slide presentation provides additional detail about the types of problems generally encountered, and introduces solution sets. This presentation is targeted at the senior technical staff working on your Year 2000 project.

Detailed Management Briefing

The 60-slide Detailed Management Briefing is targeted at supporting managers. This presentation will help them understand the Year 2000 problem in general and your Year 2000 problem in particular. It describes the nine phases of *How To 2000* in detail.

Trade Show

The Trade Show slides describe the nine phases of *How To 2000* at a very high level, with few words and many pictures. This presentation was created as an attention device for table-top trade shows.

Senior Management Briefing

An overview of the How To 2000 approach from a senior management perspective, describing management involvement, budget points, and soliciting support for the organization's Year 2000 effort.

Triage Briefing

A briefing template used to present the results of the Inventory phase. The briefing presents Inventory statistics, business and technical analysis results, and a proposed plan of action for Detailed Assessment. This briefing culminates in the solicitation of management support for the Detailed Assessment plan.

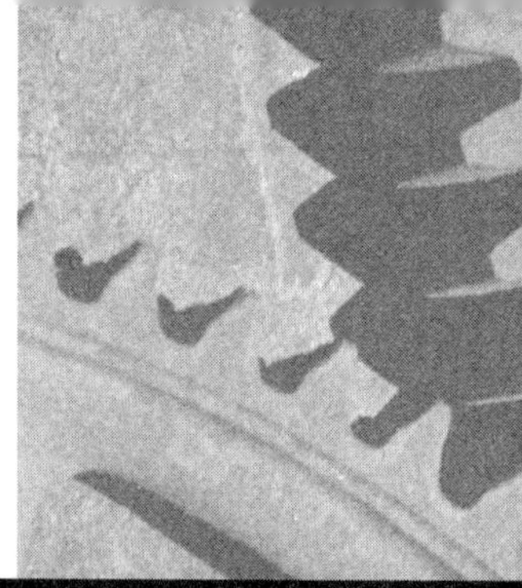

APPENDIX E

Applicability of Tools

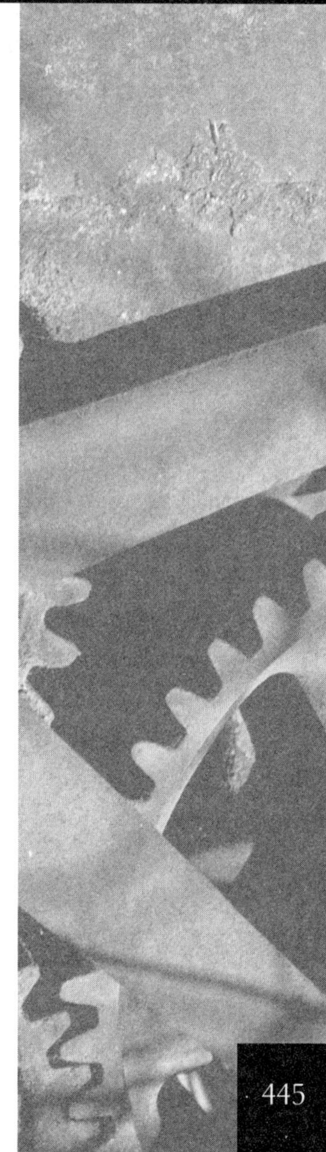

The availability of automated tools to help your organization solve its Year 2000 problem is improving.

The list of target systems and environments, as well as the sophistication of the available tools, is increasing as existing tools are expanded and integrated together. (See the How To 2000 CD-ROM for a hyperlink list of tool vendors.)

Before you procure Year 2000 tools, your organization must understand how automated tools can help solve your Year 2000 problems.

This appendix provides an overview of the types of tools available, explains when you must make a procurement decision, and describes when the tool should be available for use.

Keep in mind that you need some level of training to operate all of these tools. Commercial Year 2000 tool vendors typically offer several days of classroom instruction on the setup and use of the more sophisticated integrated tool suites. In addition, no tool is a "silver bullet." You should expect incremental gains in productivity if your organization uses the tools described in this appendix. However, you need to analyze the cost of the tool, along with the increment in maintenance and training costs against the expected increase in productivity.

Also keep in mind that most of these tools require the source code to operate (see "Executable Manipulation" later in this appendix for an exception). Even with the best tools, you must track the Year 2000 compliance status and capabil-

ity of each critical vendor-supplied product, assuming that the vendor can supply a Year 2000 compliant version.

Tool Capabilities

As the software development industry matures, tools that make development and maintenance easier, more productive, more complete, and more error free are becoming available. Automated tools generally support the following functions:

- Data repository
- Software inventory
- Code scanner
- Code parser
- Code editor
- Reverse engineering
- Configuration management
- Executable manipulation
- Debugger
- Script playback
- Date simulator
- Interface simulator
- Data conversion
- Cost-of-work estimating

Each of these tools can ease the transition to a compliant system. They can support greater uniformity, consistency, and thoroughness in applying, testing, and tracking solutions, hence reducing the number of risk items.

Tool Implementation Platform

There are two ways to implement Year 2000 support tools:

- Native, host-based conversion system
- Dedicated conversion system

Each approach has distinct advantages and disadvantages. Native mode tools operate within the environment to be corrected. Dedicated conversion systems operate in a different environment and are generally dedicated to software Year 2000 occurrence detection and correction.

A few of the tools described next run independently from the development and production platforms. For example, configuration management systems may be implemented on any platform. The configuration items under control are simply treated as data, and, if necessary, transported to the development system for modification. For such tools, the platform on which they are implemented is not generally a critical decision factor.

The native versus dedicated implementation platform approaches have complementary advantages and disadvantages.

Native System

Your organization will gain the following advantages when you procure Year 2000 correction tools to run on the target system.

Because you are correcting the software Year 2000 problems on your software development system, you generally do not need to move the source code from one system to another. You can often use your existing configuration management (CM) and quality assurance (QA) procedures, and your existing staff knows all there is to know about the development system. You probably already have adequate software development support tools, and no further procurement is necessary.

However, you may significantly affect the resources available to other projects that use the software development system. If your organization has several (or many) different production and software development systems, you may have to procure a set of tools dedicated to each system. Your existing system may not support modern graphical user interfaces (GUIs), which will make it harder for your staff to learn how to use the tools, and possibly limit productivity in other ways. With the native approach, your choices for conversion support tools will be limited to the tools available for your platform, possibly excluding better products that are only available on incompatible systems.

Pros

- No code transportation
- Staff familiar with system
- Able to use existing tools
- Smoothly integrates with existing CM and QA procedures

Cons

- Affects hardware use
- Diverse systems require multiple on-platform solutions
- Best possible computer-human interface may not be available for system
- Best possible tools may not be available for system

Dedicated Conversion System

With a dedicated system, you set up a virtual "conversion factory." You download software from each development system onto the dedicated machine for conversion. If you choose a dedicated conversion system, there will be minimal impact on the resources of your existing systems. The staff responsible for the conversions will only have to learn one set of detection and correction tools. You will not have to buy tools for each different system, and you can procure the best-in-class tool set that will apply to all your conversion efforts.

On the other hand, you will have additional burdens as you transport the software to the dedicated system and copy the updated code back to the native system. The CM becomes a bit more difficult because of the multiple storage locations, and some simple steps, such as compilations of the updated code, cannot be performed until the software is transported back to the native system.

Pros

- Reduces resource impact on existing system
- Reduces training requirements
- Opens procurement to best-in-class without regard to target system

Cons

- Requires transportation of code to conversion system
- Requires additional hardware
- Complicates configuration management
- Basic checks, such as compilations, require transportation back to original system

Tool Class Descriptions

The available tools can be classified by the type of function they perform. Some helpful tools have been created specifically to address Year 2000 problems, others were created to support general software development, and may be applied to Year 2000 conversions.

Data Repository

A *data repository* is a tailored database that will contain all the information gathered during Inventory, Detailed Assessment, and Correction. See Appendix G, "Year 2000 Repository," for a description of the types of data and structures that should be held in a data repository.

The data repository will help your organization keep track of each inventory item. As Detailed Assessment progresses, a properly implemented data repository will track each date-dependent occurrence within your system.

Your organization can write its own data repository tools using COTS database packages such as Oracle, DB2, Informix, or Access. The functionality needed is fairly simple and easy to implement and may already exist within the existing configuration management processes. However, more and more Year 2000 correction tools use proprietary data repositories to keep track of date-dependent occurrences during scanning and editing. Proprietary Year 2000 data repositories have the advantage of being integrated with the functions offered by a specific set of tools, but they have the disadvantage of possibly not fulfilling all the requirements of a true, end-to-end data repository.

Any COTS data repository you procure should have import and export capability, and be able to support SQL queries. With these capabilities your organization can generate any needed reports, and can extend the capabilities of the repository with tools from other vendors or via custom applications.

You should use a data repository to keep track of low-level date-dependent occurrences and, where possible, use existing configuration management procedures to keep track of higher-level information obtained during Inventory. Then you can use the import capability to make your data repository the repository of all available system information.

Software Inventory

Software inventory tools support the generation of system inventory by searching for code, JCL, databases, control files, and other data that may require attention. Inventory tools are typically dedicated to a particular platform, and are generally integrated with other Year 2000 tools.

Inventory tools will help your organization find things your staff may not have been aware of. By systematically searching your computer, the tool should find everything on the system. Inventory tools may be most useful in diverse, distributed environments such as an enterprise client/server network, or for performing an audit of an inventory generated by other means.

You should use inventory tools when the environment is too distributed for easy maintenance of each node, or when there are other reasons for low confidence in the inventory.

Pros

- Can find "lost" software or other data
- Are generally very thorough
- Are good for audit support

Con

- Can generate too much data to be interpreted

Code Scanner

Automated code scanners examine code for any of a set of user-specified keywords. Code scanners are generally simple search engines that look through the list of files, provided by the operator, for a list of keywords, phrases, or other user-specified patterns. The tools will generally produce a report identifying the file and the location within the file of each occurrence found. When the code scanner is integrated with a data repository, the code scanner will generally examine inventoried files, and then update the data repository with detailed keyword occurrence information.

Code scanners are most useful when performing detailed assessment of software where date dependencies follow a known pattern. For example, if all usage of date information was via data stored into one of a set of variables whose names began with "DATE_" or "YEAR_," a scanner would be very adept at locating each code fragment using the identified variables. Because code scanners are not language specific, they can be used to scan obscure and obsolete languages.

Your computer probably already contains simple code scanners. For example, on IBM MVS systems, the PANVALET tool set contains a scanning tool called PANSCAN. On UNIX systems, the grep, awk, and sed commands allow users to perform sophisticated pattern matching. In addition, most modern editors and word processing software allow the operators to perform similar, though more limited, functions.

Commercial code scanners are generally integrated within a suite of tools containing a data repository, scanners, and editors. In addition to locating each occurrence of the specified strings, the scanner usually allows the operator to review and possibly update the code fragment.

If a code scanner can address your set of problems, you should use tools that exist on your systems today. However, if scanning is just one of many approaches necessary to correct your Year 2000 problems, you should use more sophisticated correction tools, most of which include a scanning function.

Pros

- Cheap to buy, and you may already own
- Easy to use
- Functions implemented on a variety of systems
- Language independent

Cons

- Dumb—only searches for specified strings
- Dumb—only searches in specified locations
- Often not integrated with other Year 2000 tools
- Better functionality in code parsers

Code Parser

Code parsers are similar to code scanners, but they can understand how data (specifically date data) are used; and can trace variable usage through assignments, calculations, and sometimes even renames or storage overlap usage. Code parsers often are integrated with a data repository and can interactively offer the operator a chance to update the date usage instances found.

Code parsers are good choices for software environments where date usage standards did not (or do not) exist or where the standards changed over the years. Although code parsers are good at finding nonstandard usage of dates, they are generally made for a specific language. You may have to buy several, potentially from different vendors, to address diverse software environments. Not all languages are supported by code parsers.

Pros

- Traces date usage through variable name changes
- Often well integrated with other Year 2000 tools

Cons

- Language/system specific
- May not support objects such as CLISTs or parameters

Code Editor

Year 2000 code editors are usually integrated with data repositories, and allow an operator to skip from one inventoried date occurrence to another. The software usually allows the operator to examine the code around the date occurrence and to insert a standard correction, perform a manual update, skip the occurrence, or flag the occurrence for later attention.

An integrated code editor is central to allowing the repair team to examine each date occurrence and select from a few standard corrections, or implement a manual correction. It is important for a manual review of each update to ensure that the update is in context with the surrounding code.

Code editors offer a variety of ways to review date occurrences and insert standard code fragment updates. Some work on PCs or workstations, and others on mainframes. Your organization should decide on an approach regarding the use of code editors that work on the machine being updated, or that require transporting your code to a common system. For example, it may be advantageous to procure a more capable editor that runs on a PC and transport the code from the various company mainframes, workstations, minis, and so on, rather than to purchase code editors for each system.

Pros

- Often integrated with other Year 2000 tools
- Good editors let you change code in a specific way from a selection of possible updates
- Your organization probably already owns simple code editors for each development platform

Cons

- None really (code editors are needed functionality)
- Will not work with card decks
- Will not help if the source code is missing or does not match the executable

Reverse Engineering

Reverse engineering tools create database models or CASE models by analyzing existing source code. These models can then be used to introduce business rule,

data, or interface updates to the system, at the model level. Finally, the code can be regenerated from the model, with the specified updates incorporated.

Reverse engineering tools promise powerful software development, maintenance, and documentation support. Unfortunately, at this time, there is still debate about the relative productivity of code analyzers versus manual modification. The problem is that the technology for code analyzers is not yet up to the task of creating the models, from existing code, without significant human intervention. In addition, the code generators often require human intervention to produce code that meets performance goals.

This book conditionally recommends using reverse engineering and CASE tools, particularly for pilot and familiarization projects. Your organization must evaluate the ability of the available tools to analyze your system and support your environment and the availability of appropriate human resources before deciding to switch from standard software development techniques to CASE techniques. Unless your organization has significant experience with CASE tools, implementing such a shift on high-risk, mission critical systems is *not* recommended.

Pros

- Partially analyzes code to create business models of your system
- Enforces good software development practices
- Supports business process re-engineering (BPR) and other re-hosting activities by supporting code generation in any of several languages and database packages

Cons

- Partially analyzes code to create business models of your system, requiring significant human intervention to complete the model
- Requires a change in the way your software development staff operates
- Requires very specialized experience and in-depth knowledge of the CASE tool
- May not support obscure languages

Configuration Management

Configuration management tools support the management and coordination of changes to a set of software units. CM software typically tracks each modification to a unit, along with the reason for the set of changes. CM tools support the generation of particular versions of a software unit, producing the requested version from the database of changes kept within the tool. CM tools enforce serialization of changes being made by multiple individuals, or coordinate multiple updates from different sources.

In the more general case, configuration management tools support maintenance of configuration information for any type of data. The data being managed could be software source code, application data, hardware versions, and so on.

If your organization has any sizable software development, you probably already have not only configuration management tools, but CM staff to enforce and manage CM procedures. However, your existing tools may or may not integrate well with integrated Year 2000 tool sets. You must evaluate the trade-off between the Year 2000 tool set's ability to work with your existing CM operations and the CM capabilities most integrated Year 2000 tool sets provide.

Pros

- Required to manage upgrades from a software development team
- Supports reversion to back levels of software (in support of Fallback)
- Existing tools may work with Year 2000 tool sets

Cons

- CM tools may dictate modification to existing procedures
- CM tools may not work with Year 2000 tool sets

Executable Manipulation

Executable manipulation tools are minimally helpful when you don't have the source code to go with an executable that you need to modify. When the source code is missing, your organization should seriously consider replacing the executable; however, executable manipulation tools can offer you an alternative.

Disassemblers will produce assembly code from executables. The assembly produced will generally not have any labels, variable names, or comments, making the code difficult to work with. With enough effort, your staff can understand and modify the assembly code, making it Year 2000 compliant.

Executable patch tools can be used to make small modifications to an executable without using the source code or executable generation tools, such as a linker. The technical staff must have a detailed understanding of the executable, including patch insertion points, the location of existing patches, and data area usage.

You should carefully evaluate the risk of using such tools, and search far and wide for alternatives.

Pros

- Can work, even without the source code
- Patch tools can help where the source code, compiler, or link tools are not available

Cons

- Very difficult to work with
- Requires skills not generally available since the 1970s

Debugger

A debugger helps you test code by allowing you to set and examine variables and memory locations, stop code execution at predefined points, step through the code one line or unit at a time, and so on. Debuggers can operate in batch, online, and fully interactive environments. Debugging tools are not generally Year 2000 specific but are occasionally integrated with Year 2000 tool sets.

The need for a debugger is specific to the procedures of your organization's maintenance staff and the types of corrections implemented. If your organization implements a large number of custom corrections and needs additional insight into the execution of the unit during unit testing, a debugger will assist the tester with problem analysis and detection.

Pro

- May make unit testing significantly more efficient

Con

- May require operator training

Script Playback

Scripting software allows you to set up specific tests — including specific keystrokes, mouse entries, data, environments, and so on — and to reexecute those tests in a consistent, repeatable manner. Scripting software is good for performing and repeating regression tests to ensure that system modifications do not adversely affect unrelated system functions. Script playback software is not generally integrated with other Year 2000 tools.

The decision about whether to use script software should be part of Test Planning. The organization responsible for testing may already have such software.

Pros

- Supports repeatable tests
- Simplifies regression testing
- Allows simulation of a large amount of manual input

Cons

- Can be difficult to configure
- Test scripts are difficult to maintain
- Script playback tools are specific to a particular platform

Date Simulator

A date simulator allows you to specify the date to be returned to the software that is retrieving the date from operating system resources. This helps you validate

updated systems. However, because a large proportion of Year 2000 failures are in the data and interfaces, a date simulator may not validate a significant portion of the updates. You should use a date simulator for both prime Year 2000 tests of dates and for regression tests with the understanding that a date simulator is only a support tool, not a complete solution.

During Test Planning, the testing organization will determine whether there is a need for a date simulator. The decision will be based on the following:

- The requirement of the software under test to retrieve noncurrent dates from the operating system in order to thoroughly test the software
- The inability to manually change the operating system's maintained date due to license expiration or processor sharing issues

Date simulators work well, given their limited scope. You should buy such tools if they will save you testing time and money, or if there is no other way to test some of your updates.

Pros

- Supports simulation of an interface that is otherwise difficult to simulate (the operating system/software interface)
- Supports testing of COTS products

Cons

- Only minimally supports tests of interfaces or date data updates where retrieval of the current date is not part of the function
- Products are targeted to specific systems

Interface Simulator

Interface simulators support interface testing by sending scripted data to your system or by answering system outputs with scripted data. Interface simulators come in a variety of configurations, from resident software that simulates the system input and output, to complete, external packages that are wired to your system in the same way that the simulated interface connects to your system.

You can use interface simulators to test the interface between partitions being updated and existing partitions, and/or between your updated system and external organizations. In addition, by creating a standard set of interface scripts, the developers responsible for updating any connection to the common interface can test against an agreed upon standard. The approach works within an organization, and with electronic partners.

It is extremely helpful to use interface simulators if your system has any significant or mission-critical interfaces that must be updated to be Year 2000 compliant. The requirements for the interface simulation will be identified during Test Planning. Your test organization may already support such functionality.

Pro

- Supports thorough testing of interfaces in production environment

Cons

- Can be difficult to configure
- Multiple interfaces may require multiple simulators

Data Conversion

Data conversion software converts your data from one format, storage media, or encoding to another. COTS tools support data conversions to a limited degree. For example, most COTS database packages include software to convert from other database package vendor formats into a native format and conversion from one record layout into another.

Your organization probably already has the COTS data converters. For example, if you use Oracle, you have the Oracle data loaders and converters. However, some data conversion requirements will not be supported by the COTS packages. For example, if your solution to the storage of a 2-byte year field was to encode the four-digit year using a home-grown encoding scheme, your organization will have to write custom conversion software to read the existing data and create the new database.

COTS packages that release new versions of their software to be Year 2000 compliant should be equipped to convert their data from the old version to the

new version. Double-check that the vendors do provide this support and that they stipulate what is involved. It would be a critical mistake to receive a COTS upgrade during the last few months before 2000 and discover that you cannot convert the data in time.

Pros

- Required to convert data from one format/encoding to another
- COTS products support most data conversion requirements
- You may already own the data converters

Cons

- None

Cost-of-Work Estimating

Cost-of-work estimating tools support the generation of labor hour estimates. Year 2000–specific tools tailor their estimates to some of the standard phases of a Year 2000 project, and, with information on your project, will provide labor hour estimates for assessment, resolution, and testing work.

These tools are useful as a starting point for your rough-order-of-magnitude estimates. The tools typically require significant information on the size of your project, the platform implemented, the implementation language, the use of detection and correction tools, and the experience level of your staff. Although these tools are helpful, they are no substitute for experience. Once your project managers understand the scope of a Year 2000 effort, they will probably generate more accurate estimates than an automated tool.

Pros

- Relatively inexpensive tool supports labor hour estimation.
- The tool itself is the rational for estimates. "It's a software tool; it must be accurate."

- Entry of supporting information about your organization and development methods forces your staff to think about potential inefficiencies in your procedures.

Cons

- Estimates may vary widely depending on the accuracy of supporting information.
- The tool may foster unjustified reliance on the results based on the visual quality of the output.

Phase/Tool Requirements

As you can tell from the descriptions of the types of tools available, different types of tools will help your Year 2000 project during different phases. The following table specifies when the requirement for each type of tool must be identified, and when the tool should be applied to the project.

Tool Type	*Requirement Identified*	*Tool Applied*
Data repository	Planning and Awareness	All phases
Software inventory	Planning and Awareness	Detailed Assessment
Code scanner	Detailed Assessment	Detailed Assessment
Code parser	Detailed Assessment	Detailed Assessment
Code editor	Detailed Assessment	Resolution
Reverse engineering	Detailed Assessment	Resolution
Configuration management	Planning and Awareness	All phases
Executable manipulation	Detailed Assessment	Resolution
Debugger	Detailed Assessment	Resolution
Script playback	Test Planning	Test Execution
Date simulator	Test Planning	Test Execution
Interface simulator	Test Planning	Test Execution

continued

TOOL TYPE	REQUIREMENT IDENTIFIED	TOOL APPLIED
Data conversion	Detailed Assessment	Test and Deployment
Cost-of-work estimating	Planning and Awareness	Detailed Assessment, Resolution, Test Planning

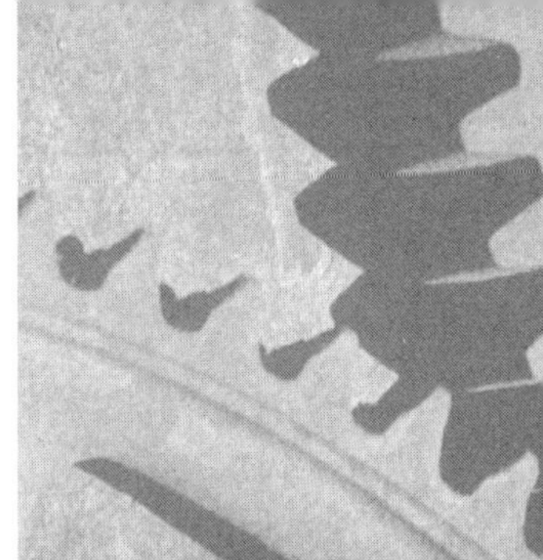

APPENDIX F

Key Tasks Outline

This appendix provides project tracking, configuration management, and quality assurance personnel with a guide and quick reference to their roles in the Year 2000 project. It identifies the tasks within each Year 2000 phase that apply to those roles, and summarizes the related activity to be performed. These staff members should review the applicable section of this appendix when they are assigned to the project to get an overview of what is expected of them. They should also review the activities identified as each phase is begun.

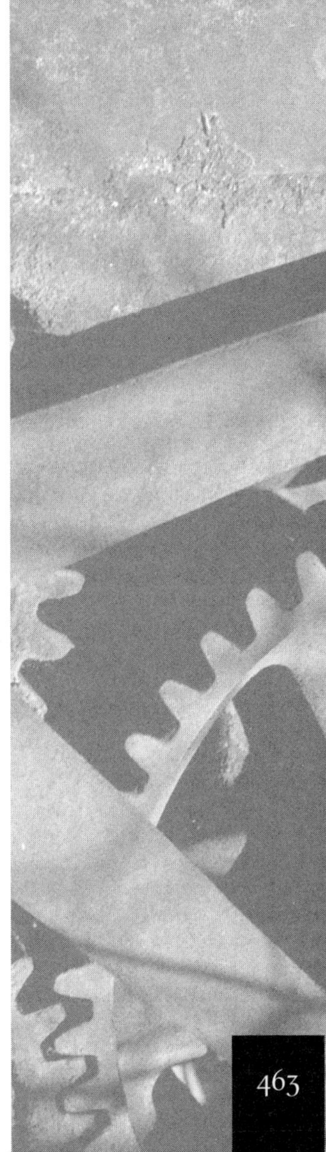

Project Tracking

The tables that follow list the How To 2000 tasks within each phase that contribute to effective project tracking. These tables will help your task management organization understand where project planning decisions are made, and where appropriate tracking and status points can be measured.

Planning and Awareness Tasks

Deliverable	*Task*	*Activity*
Initial Project Plan (1.7)	Develop Project Schedule/ Budget and Progress Tracking Plan (1.7.5)	Plan includes tracking, assessment, and recovery mechanisms used • In all subsequent phases to monitor project conformance with schedule • To specify data to be tracked • To specify project tracking and reporting requirements, including frequency and tracked events and data • To specify management feedback plans, including when to raise problems, and what kinds of recommendations should be made to management • To specify tracking data review and critical path analysis requirements • To specify degree of conformance to schedule required before corrective action is required • To specify types of corrective actions to consider
	Present and Approve Initial Project Plan (1.7.6)	Forum used to gain management approval for tracking and recovery plans.
Inventory and Triage Phase Plans (1.8)	Tailor Methodology for Inventory and Triage (1.8.1)	When tailoring the tasks and deliverables, consider the tracking and reporting requirements appropriate to your organization. Include appropriate tracking and reporting tasks and deliverables.

DELIVERABLE	TASK	ACTIVITY
	Identify Inventory and Triage Resource Requirements (1.8.2)	Develop recovery plans that may be required to correct progress deficiencies and slippages. Several recovery plans should be established. Each plan should address increasing slippages with escalating resources.
	Develop Schedule/Budget for Inventory and Triage (1.8.3)	Schedule includes progress measurement points and assessment meetings.
	Present and Approve Inventory and Triage Schedule/Budget (1.8.4)	Forum used to gain management approval for Inventory and Triage tracking, assessment, and recovery plans.

Inventory Tasks

DELIVERABLE	TASK	ACTIVITY
Inventory Phase Startup (2.1)	Establish Inventory Tracking (2.1.2)	Establish the procedures used to track progress, effort, sizing, resource usage, and risk reduction. Specify the metrics criteria beyond which your organization will initiate the implementation of a recovery plan when slippage occurs.
	Brief Staff Members on Inventory Plan (2.1.3)	Brief team members on progress reporting and assessment requirements.
	Establish Inventory Work Environment (2.1.6)	Establish progress tracking tools.

Triage Tasks

Deliverable	*Task*	*Activity*
Triage Phase Startup (3.1)	Ensure Adequacy of Triage Environment (3.1.1)	Review and confirm progress tracking and assessment requirements.
	Establish Triage Tracking (3.1.2)	Establish the procedures used to track progress, effort, sizing, resource usage, and risk reduction. Specify the measurement criteria used to initiate the implementation of a recovery plan.
Detailed Assessment Plan (3.3)	Tailor the Methodology for Detailed Assessment (3.3.1)	When tailoring the tasks and deliverables, consider the tracking and reporting requirements appropriate to your organization. Include appropriate tracking and reporting tasks and deliverables.
	Estimate Assessment Resources by System (3.3.2)	Establish the resource reallocation criteria used when deciding to reallocate resources due to deficient progress.
	Develop Schedule and Budget for Detailed Assessment (3.3.6)	The schedule developed under this task will provide input to progress tracking, and will include milestones and other measurement points. The schedule will also define the timing of progress assessment meetings.
	Present and Approve Detailed Assessment Schedule/Budget (3.3.7)	Forum to inform management of detailed progress tracking, reporting, and assessment requirements, and to gain management approval.

Detailed Assessment Tasks

Deliverable	*Task*	*Activity*
Detailed Assessment Phase Startup (4.1)	Brief Detailed Assessment Plan (4.1.4)	Brief team members of progress reporting and assessment requirements.
	Establish Detailed Assessment Tracking (4.1.7)	Identify detailed progress measurements, assessment criteria, and resource reallocation plans.
System Resolution Plan (4.4)	Develop Electronic Partner Compliance Plan (4.4.1)	Identify detailed progress measurements, assessment criteria, and resource reallocation plans.
	Develop Standard Practices for Resolution (4.4.2)	Identify detailed progress measurements, assessment criteria, and resource reallocation plans.
	Develop System Resolution Plans by System (4.4.3)	Identify detailed progress measurements, assessment criteria, and resource reallocation plans.
	Develop Interface/Bridge Plans (4.4.4)	Identify detailed progress measurements, assessment criteria, and resource reallocation plans.
	Develop Data Conversion Plans (4.4.5)	Identify detailed progress measurements, assessment criteria, and resource reallocation plans.
	Develop Resolution Training Plan (4.4.7)	Identify detailed progress measurements, assessment criteria, and resource reallocation plans.
Correction Cycle Project Plan (4.5)	Update System Technical and Business Risk Assessments (4.5.2)	As part of risk assessment, you should undertake a review of past conformance to plan to gain an understanding of the accuracy of the existing plans. Where appropriate, you should increase progress measurements and assessments to reduce risk.

continued

DELIVERABLE	TASK	ACTIVITY
	Consolidate System Resolution Plans (4.5.4)	Review detailed progress measurements, assessment criteria, and resource reallocation plans, and make adjustments as required by the changing requirements and resource allocations.
	Estimate Correction Cycle Resources by System (4.5.5)	Generate recovery plans to provide additional resources if required to maintain progress at anticipated levels.
	Identify Staff Requirements for Correction Cycle (4.5.6)	Generate recovery plans to provide additional resources if required to maintain progress at anticipated levels.
	Develop Procurement Plan for Correction Cycle (4.5.7)	Identify detailed progress measurements, assessment criteria, and resource reallocation plans.
	Develop Schedule and Budget for Correction Cycle (4.5.8)	Finalize all detailed progress measurements, assessment criteria, and resource reallocation plans, and specify periodic progress reviews.
	Present and Approve Plans, Schedule, and Budget for Correction Cycle (4.5.9)	Present detailed progress and recovery requirements.

Resolution Tasks

DELIVERABLE	TASK	ACTIVITY
Resolution Phase Startup (5.1)	Establish Cost and Scheduling Tracking Mechanisms (5.1.10)	Finalize all detailed progress measurements, assessment criteria, and resource reallocation plans, and specify periodic progress reviews for Resolution phase.

Deliverable	*Task*	*Activity*
System Retirement (5.2)	Prepare Phase-out Plans (5.2.1)	Finalize all detailed progress measurements, assessment criteria, and resource reallocation plans, and specify periodic progress reviews.
	Review and Approve Phase-out Plans (5.2.2)	Gain management approval for detailed progress tracking, assessment, and recovery plans.

Test Planning Tasks

Deliverable	*Task*	*Activity*
Test Planning and Execution Phase Startup (6.1)	Tailor Methodology for Testing (6.1.1)	When tailoring the tasks and deliverables, consider the tracking and reporting requirements appropriate to your organization. Include appropriate tracking and reporting tasks and deliverables.
	Acquire Human Resources for Testing (6.1.3)	Generate recovery plans to provide additional resources if required to maintain progress at anticipated levels.
	Establish Test Phases Tracking (6.1.6)	Finalize all detailed progress measurements, assessment criteria, and resource reallocation plans, and specify periodic progress reviews for all system test activities.
	Present and Approve Formal Test Plan (6.1.7)	Gain management approval for tracking, progress assessment, and correction plans.

Test Execution Tasks

Deliverable	*Task*	*Activity*
Test Kickoff Briefing (7.2)	Prepare Formal Test Execution Briefing (7.2.1)	Include progress tracking, measurement, and assessment requirements and potential recovery plans.

Deployment Tasks

Deliverable	*Task*	*Activity*
Deployment Phase Startup (8.1)	Establish and Brief Deployment Team (8.1.1)	Include progress tracking, measurement, and assessment requirements. Discuss potential recovery plans.
Data Conversion Plan (8.2)	Develop Conversion Plan (8.2.3)	Include specific progress tracking and measurement points, and resource reallocation criteria.
Deployment Plan (8.3)	Develop Customer Service Plan (8.3.6)	Include specific progress tracking goals for updated customer service capability.
	Develop User Training Plan (8.3.7)	Include training progress tracking and measurement requirements.
	Identify Notification Requirements (8.3.8)	Include notification progress tracking and measurement requirements.
	Develop Deployment Plan (8.3.9)	Include specific deployment progress tracking and measurement points, and resource reallocation criteria.
	Present and Approve Deployment Plan (8.3.10)	Obtain approval for tracking, monitoring, assessment, and resource reallocation plans.

Fallout Tasks

DELIVERABLE	TASK	ACTIVITY
QA and CM Procedures Report (9.1)	Review QA Procedures (9.1.1)	Support review of QA department productivity and department ability to meet performance goals.
	Improve QA Procedures (9.1.2)	Assist in the identification and implementation of improved productivity, effort, sizing, resource utilization and risk reduction measurements, tracking, and assessment.
	Review CM Procedures (9.1.3)	Support review of CM department productivity and department ability to meet performance goals.
	Improve CM Procedures (9.1.4)	Assist in the identification and implementation of improved productivity, effort, sizing, resource utilization and risk reduction measurements, tracking, and assessment.
Lessons Learned (9.6)	Revise Year 2000 Methods (9.6.2)	Incorporate the lessons learned from progress tracking, reporting, assessment, and resource allocation into the plans for other ongoing Year 2000 work.

CONFIGURATION MANAGEMENT

The following tables list the How To 2000 tasks within each phase that contribute to effective configuration management. These tables will help your configuration management organization understand where configuration management decisions are made and implemented.

Planning and Awareness Tasks

DELIVERABLE	TASK NAME	ACTIVITY
Management Awareness Briefings (1.1)	Identify Isolated Business Units (1.1.2)	Become familiar with overall organization structure. Determine effective means of communications.
Enterprise Schematic (1.3)	Develop an Enterprise Schematic (1.3.1)	Establish baseline, controlled, Enterprise Schematic. Use this schematic to help plan the Year 2000 repository.
Initial Project Plan (1.7)	Review Existing Configuration Management Plan and Apply to Year 2000 Project (1.7.3)	Evaluate existing CM plan(s) and define a tailored Year 2000 CM plan.

Inventory Tasks

DELIVERABLE	TASK NAME	ACTIVITY
Inventory Phase Startup (2.1)	Define Detailed Technical Requirements for Inventory Tools (2.1.4)	Provide input on what CM characteristics the Inventory tools should have.
	Establish Repository and CM Environment (2.1.7)	Design and construct the Year 2000 repository and establish control methods.
Internal Tool Inventory (2.2)	Create and Circulate Internal Tool Questionnaire (2.2.2)	Log internal tool questionnaire.
	Analyze Questionnaire (2.2.3)	Log results.
	Capture Internal Tool List (2.2.4)	Log internal tool list.
System Inventory (2.5)	Develop System Survey (2.5.1)	Ensure that the Year 2000 repository is consistent with the survey elements.
	Capture System Inventory (2.5.3)	Ensure that established data collection methods and repository updating procedures are adhered to.

Deliverable	Task Name	Activity
	Verify System Inventory (2.5.4)	Ensure that established repository change control methods are used.
	Baseline System Inventory (2.5.5)	Establish the system inventory baseline, using the Year 2000 CM procedures.
	Establish Change Control (2.5.6)	Control all changes, using the Year 2000 CM procedures.
Inventory Schematic (2.6)	Develop Inventory Schematic (2.6.1)	Place the Inventory Schematic under CM control.

Triage Tasks

Deliverable	Task Name	Activity
Business Risks and Priorities (3.2)	Capture Business Priorities (3.2.5)	Establish business priorities baseline, and control all changes, using the Year 2000 CM procedures.

Detailed Assessment Tasks

Deliverable	Task Name	Activity
Detailed Assessment Phase Startup (4.1)	Acquire Tools for Detailed Assessment (4.1.1)	Maintain a control list of the tools being used for Detailed Assessment, and monitor and record any changes.
	Develop Detailed Assessment Tools (4.1.2)	Ensure that developed tools meet established baseline requirements and that they are placed under CM control.

continued

DELIVERABLE	TASK NAME	ACTIVITY
	Brief Detailed Assessment Plan (4.1.4)	Help prepare for and give the Detailed Assessment Plan briefing.
	Ensure Capture of Assessment Data in Year 2000 Repository (4.1.6)	Ensure that all changes to be controlled are being submitted to CM and logged in the Year 2000 repository. Make any necessary revisions to the repository structure and/or CM process.
	Establish Detailed Assessment Tracking (4.1.7)	Establish Detailed Assessment tracking information baseline, and update related CM files (for example, Project Plan).
System Assessment (4.2)	Assess Custom Software (4.2.1)	Ensure that collected information is submitted to CM, and update the custom software repository.
	Assess Custom Hardware and Embedded Systems (4.2.2)	Ensure that collected information is submitted to CM, and update the custom hardware and embedded systems repository.
	Assess COTS Systems (4.2.3)	Ensure that collected information is submitted to CM, and update the COTS systems repository. CM will ensure that vendor software meets baseline requirements. If not, ensure that correct change control methods are used.
	Assess Electronic Partners (4.2.4)	Ensure that collected information is submitted to CM, and update the electronic partners repository.
Draft Assessment Solutions (4.3)	Categorize Findings by Problem Type (4.3.1)	Ensure that collected information is submitted to CM, and that established change control methods are used.
	Define System Partitions (4.3.2)	Ensure that collected information is submitted to CM, and CM will ensure that established change control methods are used.

Deliverable	*Task Name*	*Activity*
	Select Resolution Tools by System (4.3.4)	Maintain a control list of the Resolution tools, and monitor and record any changes.
System Resolution Plan (4.4)	Develop Electronic Partner Compliance Plan (4.4.1)	Provide guidance as to CM requirements and ensure that plans meet project standards.
	Develop Standard Practices for Resolution (4.4.2)	Ensure that established change control methods are incorporated into these standard practices.
	Develop System Resolution Plans by System (4.4.3)	Ensure that established change control methods are incorporated into system resolution plans.
	Develop Interface/Bridge Plans (4.4.4)	Ensure that established change control methods are incorporated into interface/bridge plans.
	Develop Data Conversion Plans (4.4.5)	Ensure that established change control methods are incorporated into data conversion plans.
Correction Cycle Project Plan (4.5)	Present and Approve Plans, Schedule, and Budget for Correction Cycle (4.5.9)	Ensure that CM has recorded all revisions made to the various plans.

Resolution Tasks

Deliverable	*Task Name*	*Activity*
Resolution Phase Startup (5.1)	Conduct Resolution Kickoff (5.1.7)	Contribute explanation of established CM policies and procedures.
	Ensure Capture of Resolution Data in Year 2000 Repository (5.1.8)	Ensure that all applicable resolution data are submitted to CM and that the defined change control processes are followed.

continued

DELIVERABLE	TASK NAME	ACTIVITY
System Retirement (5.2)	Prepare Phase-out Plans (5.2.1)	Ensure that phase-out plans incorporate the defined CM change control processes.
System Repair or Replacement (5.3)	Notify Affected Parties of Repair/Replace Responsibilities (5.3.1)	Ensure that all affected parties are aware of the CM change control process.
	Develop Repair Tools (5.3.4)	Ensure that all developed repair tools are placed under CM and that established check-in/checkout and change control methods are used.
	Develop Bridge Code (5.3.6)	Ensure that all developed bridge code is placed under CM and that established check-in/checkout and change control methods are used.
	Develop Data Conversion Code (5.3.7)	Ensure that all developed data conversion code is placed under CM and that established check-in/checkout change control methods are used.
Unit Testing (5.4)	Capture Development Test Baselines (5.4.3)	Ensure that all development test baseline data are placed under CM and that the specified change control processes are followed.

Test Planning Tasks

DELIVERABLE	TASK NAME	ACTIVITY
Test Planning and Execution Phase Startup (6.1)	Define Strategy for Formal Testing (6.1.2)	Provide guidance as to the CM processes that will need to be followed.
Test Facility Environment Report (6.2)	Identify Test Environment Requirements (6.2.1)	Provide guidance as to the CM processes that will need to be followed.

Deliverable	Task Name	Activity
	Identify Existing Test Environments (6.2.2)	Provide guidance as to the CM processes that will need to be followed.
	Identify Alternative Test Locations (6.2.3)	Provide guidance as to the CM processes that will need to be followed.
Test Support Tool Requirements (6.3)	Present and Approve Test Support Tool Requirements (6.3.4)	Ensure that CM control over all test tools has been incorporated into these requirements.
Electronic Partnership Test Plan (6.4)	Present and Approve Electronic Partnership Test Plans (6.4.2)	Ensure that the electronic partnership test plans are placed under CM and that change control procedures are followed.
Partition Test Description and Data (6.5)	Present and Approve Partition Test and Data Descriptions (6.5.6)	Ensure that the partition test and data descriptions are placed under CM and that change control procedures are followed.
Integration Test Description and Data (6.6)	Present and Approve Integration Test and Data Descriptions (6.6.3)	Ensure that the integration test and data descriptions are placed under CM and that change control procedures are followed.

Test Execution Tasks

Deliverable	Task Name	Activity
Formal Dry Run Report (7.1)	Perform the Dry Run (7.1.1)	Ensure that all results from the formal dry run are captured and controlled by CM.
Test Execution Report (7.3)	Set Up the Test Environment (7.3.1)	Ensure that the correct test environment (that is, software, data files) is used.
	Execute the Test Procedures (7.3.3)	Ensure that all results from the formal test are captured and controlled by CM.

Deployment Tasks

Deliverable	*Task Name*	*Activity*
Deployment Phase Startup (8.1)	Establish and Brief Deployment Team (8.1.1)	Ensure that all deployment team members understand the established change control methods.
Deployment Plan (8.3)	Define Go/No-Go (Rollback) Criteria and Metrics (8.3.1)	Ensure that change control methods are defined for collecting the data.
	Determine Critical Performance Indicators and Metrics (8.3.2)	Ensure that change control methods are defined for collecting the data.
	Develop Deployment Plan (8.3.9)	Place Deployment plan under CM.
Data Conversion (8.5)	Back Up Preconversion Data Structures (8.5.1)	Place Preconversion data structures and metrics under CM.
	Develop Configuration Management of Conversion Routines (8.5.2)	Place all preconversion custom and COTS software under CM.
	Convert Data (8.5.3)	Place converted data under CM and ensure that established change control methods are used.
	Generate Post-Conversion Accuracy Metrics (8.5.4)	Ensure that change control methods are defined for collecting the data.
	Baseline and Back Up Converted Data Structures (8.5.6)	Place validated, converted data under CM, establish a baseline, and ensure that established change control methods are used.
Deployment Execution (8.6)	Baseline and Back Up Pre-Deployment Environment (8.6.3)	Place pre-Deployment under CM, establish a baseline, and ensure that established change control methods are used.
Deployment Validation (8.7)	Generate Post-Deployment Critical Performance Indicators (8.7.1)	Log post-Deployment critical performance indicators.

DELIVERABLE	TASK NAME	ACTIVITY
Rollback (8.8)	Execute Rollback Plan (8.8.1)	Provide baseline for rollback and confirm that it has been put in place as appropriate.

Fallout Tasks

DELIVERABLE	TASK NAME	ACTIVITY
QA and CM Procedures Report (9.1)	Review CM Procedures (9.1.3)	Evaluate the CM process used to determine potential areas of improvement.
	Improve CM Procedures (9.1.4)	Suggest improvements based on discoveries during this project.
Bridge Control Report (9.3)	Coordinate Interface Updates (9.3.2)	Place new and changed interface environments under CM, and ensure that established change control methods are used.
Inventory Maintenance Report (9.4)	Update Inventory Continuously (9.4.1)	Ensure that established change control methods are used.
Systems Reevaluation Report (9.5)	Execute Correction Cycle Tasks (9.5.4)	Ensure that all revised correction plan data are placed under CM, and that established change control methods are used.
Lessons Learned (9.6)	Revise Year 2000 Methods (9.6.2)	Revise Year 2000 Project CM methods to reflect lessons learned.

Quality Assurance

The following tables list the How To 2000 tasks within each phase that contribute to effective quality assurance. These tables will help your quality assurance organization understand where quality assurance tasks apply to the overall project plan.

Planning and Awareness Tasks

Deliverable	Task	Activity
Management Awareness Briefings (1.1)	Investigate Year 2000 Problem (1.1.1)	Assist in risk assessment related to not fully solving the Year 2000 problem in an orderly and timely manner.
	Develop Management Awareness Briefings (1.1.3)	Identify QA issues that should be addressed in these briefings.
Compliance Definition (1.2)	Define Compliance for Your Organization (1.2.1)	Review the compliance statement from a QA perspective.
	Define Year 2000 Project Objectives for Your Organization (1.2.2)	Review the project objectives from a QA perspective.
Organization Awareness Program (1.4)	Distribute Year 2000 Project Establishment Notification (1.4.1)	Ensure that notification plans are sufficiently comprehensive.
Initial Project Plan (1.7)	Review Existing Quality Assurance Plan and Apply to Year 2000 Project (1.7.4)	Evaluate existing QA plan(s) and define a tailored Year 2000 QA plan.
Inventory and Triage Phase Plans (1.8)	Tailor Methodology for Inventory and Triage (1.8.1)	Provide tailoring guidance on QA issues.

Inventory Tasks

Deliverable	*Task*	*Activity*
Inventory Phase Startup (2.1)	Establish Repository and CM Environment (2.1.7)	Verify that the defined CM process has been put in place.
System Inventory (2.5)	Verify System Inventory (2.5.4)	Participate in the System Inventory verification process.
	Baseline System Inventory (2.5.5)	Verify that all System Inventory data has been baselined in CM.
Inventory Schematic (2.6)	Develop Inventory Schematic (2.6.1)	Participate in the verification of the Inventory Schematic.

Triage Tasks

Deliverable	*Task*	*Activity*
Business Risks and Priorities (3.2)	Assess Business Risk (3.2.3)	Evaluate risk assessment to ensure that all areas have been addressed and that the approved approaches have been followed.
	Capture Business Priorities (3.2.5)	Verify that each system has been assigned a priority and that these priorities have been added to the Year 2000 repository.
Detailed Assessment Plan (3.3)	Tailor the Methodology for Detailed Assessment (3.3.1)	Tailor the QA areas related to Detailed Assessment and ensure that the other tailoring does not remove any crucial tasks.

Detailed Assessment Tasks

Deliverable	*Task*	*Activity*
Detailed Assessment Phase Startup (4.1)	Brief Detailed Assessment Plan (4.1.4)	Participate in preparing for and giving the Detailed Assessment Plan briefing.
System Assessment (4.2)	Assess Custom Software (4.2.1)	Verify that all custom software has been reviewed.
	Assess Custom Hardware and Embedded Systems (4.2.2)	Verify that all hardware has been reviewed.
	Assess Electronic Partners (4.2.4)	Verify that all electronic partners have been solicited and have provided a response.
	Assess COTS Systems (4.2.3)	Verify that vendors have been solicited and have provided a response.
Draft Assessment Solutions (4.3)	Categorize Findings by Problem Type (4.3.1)	Verify that all errors have been categorized.
	Define System Partitions (4.3.2)	Verify that all applications and/or systems have been included in some partition.
	Prepare Solution Sets by System (4.3.3)	Verify that solution sets for all applications and/or systems have been identified.
System Resolution Plan (4.4)	Develop Electronic Partner Compliance Plan (4.4.1)	Ensure that plans conform to best practices guidelines.
	Develop Standard Practices for Resolution (4.4.2)	Evaluate standard practices to ensure that they will lead to your definition of Year 2000 compliance.
	Develop System Resolution Plans by System (4.4.3)	Evaluate the plans to ensure that they conform to the related project standards.
	Develop Interface/Bridge Plans (4.4.4)	Evaluate the plans to ensure that they conform to the related project standards.

DELIVERABLE	TASK	ACTIVITY
	Develop Data Conversion Plans (4.4.5)	Evaluate the plans to ensure that they conform to the related project standards.
	Identify Business Process Plan (4.4.6)	Evaluate the plan to ensure that it covers all business areas.
	Develop Resolution Training Plan (4.4.7)	Evaluate the plans to ensure that they conform to the related project standards.
Correction Cycle Project Plan (4.5)	Tailor Methodology for Correction Cycle (4.5.1)	Tailor the QA areas related to the correction cycle and ensure that other tailoring does not remove any crucial tasks.
	Develop Procurement Plan for Correction Cycle (4.5.7)	Evaluate the plan to ensure that it conforms to the related project standards.

Resolution Tasks

DELIVERABLE	TASK	ACTIVITY
Resolution Phase Startup (5.1)	Conduct Resolution Kickoff (5.1.7)	Provide a clear overview of QA's role during the Resolution phase.
	Ensure Implementation of Quality Assurance Process (5.1.9)	Revise the definition of the QA process and its responsibilities to reflect lessons learned up to this point on the project.
System Repair or Placement (5.3)	Notify Affected Parties of Repair/Replace Responsibilities (5.3.1)	Ensure that notifications include all affected parties and that they provide clear impact statements.
	Repair Systems (5.3.5)	Ensure that the defined processes are followed, especially CM change controls.
Unit Testing (5.4)	Develop Developer Unit/ System Test Plans (5.4.1)	Review plans to ensure that they cover all needed test conditions.

continued

DELIVERABLE	TASK	ACTIVITY
	Prepare Test Data (5.4.2)	Ensure that all test data has been placed under CM control.
	Capture Development Test Baselines (5.4.3)	Ensure that the full baseline has been placed under CM control.
	Execute Unit Tests (5.4.4)	Audit task activities for compliance to plans, standards, and procedures, and track deviations.
	Execute Developer System Test (5.4.5)	Audit task activities for compliance to plans, standards, and procedures, and track deviations.
Documentation (5.5)	Modify Business Process Documents (5.5.1)	Review modified process documents to ensure that required changes have been made.
	Modify User/System Documentation (5.5.2)	Review modified user/system documents to ensure that required changes have been made.
	Modify System Training Materials (5.5.3)	Review modified materials to ensure that they address the applicable Year 2000 changes.

Test Planning Tasks

DELIVERABLE	TASK	ACTIVITY
Test Planning and Execution Startup (6.1)	Tailor Methodology for Testing (6.1.1)	Review the test methodology for compliance to standards and procedures and for test deviation tracking.
	Present and Approve Formal Test Plan (6.1.7)	Review plan to ensure that it addresses all required test conditions.

DELIVERABLE	TASK	ACTIVITY
Test Facility Environment Report (6.2)	Present and Approve Test Facility Environment Report (6.2.4)	Review the report for conformance to environment requirements and documentation standards.
Test Support Tool Requirements (6.3)	Present and Approve Test Support Tool Requirements (6.3.4)	Review the report for conformance to tool requirements and documentation standards.
Electronic Partnership Test Plan (6.4)	Prepare Electronic Partnership Test Plans (6.4.1)	Review plans to ensure that they address all required test conditions.
Partition Test Description and Data (6.5)	Present and Approve Partition Test and Data Descriptions (6.5.6)	Review plans to ensure that they address all required test conditions.
Integration Test Description and Data (6.6)	Present and Approve Integration Test and Data Descriptions (6.6.3)	Review plans to ensure that they address all required test conditions.

Test Execution Tasks

DELIVERABLE	TASK	ACTIVITY
Test Execution Report (7.3)	Execute the Test Procedures (7.3.3)	Observe the Test Execution and ensure that the procedures are followed, all test results are collected, and all problems recorded.
	Prepare the Test Documentation and Report (7.3.4)	Ensure that the test report is complete and correct.
Electronic Partnership Recertification Report (7.4)	Execute the Test Procedures (7.4.3)	Observe the Test Execution and ensure that the procedures are followed, all test results are collected, and all problems recorded.

continued

Deliverable	*Task*	*Activity*
	Prepare the Test Documentation and Report (7.4.4)	Ensure that the test report is complete and correct.

Deployment Tasks

Deliverable	*Task*	*Activity*
Deployment Phase Startup (8.1)	Establish and Brief Deployment Team (8.1.1)	Provide QA input for Deployment team.
Deployment Plan (8.3)	Define Go/No-Go (Rollback) Criteria and Metrics (8.3.1)	Participate in the definition of the go/no-go criteria.
	Develop Deployment Plan (8.3.9)	Verify that the Deployment plan adequately includes QA control points.
	Present and Approve Deployment Plan (8.3.10)	Provide briefing material related to QA's Deployment role.
Data Conversion (8.5)	Validate Data Conversion (8.5.5)	Observe and verify the results of the conversion process. Document and report any problems.
Deployment Execution (8.6)	Determine Deployment Readiness (8.6.2)	Help determine Deployment readiness.
	Deploy Systems (8.6.4)	Observe Deployment process, confirm that procedures are followed, and record any problems.
Deployment Validation (8.7)	Generate Post-Deployment Critical Performance Indicators (8.7.1)	Ensure that all related Deployment results are incorporated.
	Validate Deployment (8.7.2)	Assist in the Deployment validation and establish a baseline.
	Make Go/No-Go Decision (8.7.3)	Participate in the go/no-go decision.

Deliverable	*Task*	*Activity*
Rollback (8.8)	Execute Rollback Plan (8.8.1)	Make sure that the planned process is followed.
	Validate Restored Environment (8.8.2)	Help validate that the system was properly restored.

Fallout Tasks

Deliverable	*Task*	*Activity*
QA and CM Procedures Report (9.1)	Review QA Procedures (9.1.1)	Evaluate the QA process used to determine potential areas of improvement.
	Improve QA Procedures (9.1.2)	Suggest improvements based on discoveries made during this project.
Customer Service Report (9.2)	Review Problem Reports (9.2.2)	Review problem reports to verify that they are clear and complete, that they have been categorized, and that they are tracked.
	Distribute Problem Reports (9.2.3)	Ensure that all applicable people receive the problem reports.
Bridge Control Report (9.3)	Coordinate Interface Updates (9.3.2)	Review the revised interfaces to ensure that they meet their requirements.
Lessons Learned (9.6)	Revise Year 2000 Methods (9.6.2)	Revise the Year 2000 project's QA methods to reflect lessons learned.

APPENDIX

Year 2000 Repository

G

The Year 2000 repository is a key tool, used in conjunction with your project tracking utility, to manage your Year 2000 compliance effort. In its basic form, the Year 2000 repository is a configuration management utility. This book recommends enhancing your existing configuration management system to track the critical Year 2000 information suggested in this appendix. Tracking Year 2000 elements in parallel with your regular configuration and system release processes will simplify the tracking task and the ultimate merger of data when compliance is achieved.

It is important that your organization share a single centralized Year 2000 repository. Most large organizations can use economies of scale by centrally tracking COTS vendor and third-party compliance. In addition, senior management can quickly check the pulse of corporate Year 2000 efforts. The status of Year 2000 efforts may be critical to support investor and customer demands.

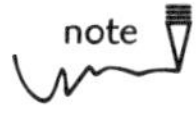

Each business area should have access to the central repository.

You should maintain the repository in a configuration utility supported by a relational database. This database architecture greatly simplifies reporting progress metrics and its supporting data.

The elements listed in the tables that follow are How To 2000 core repository suggestions. The suggestions encom-

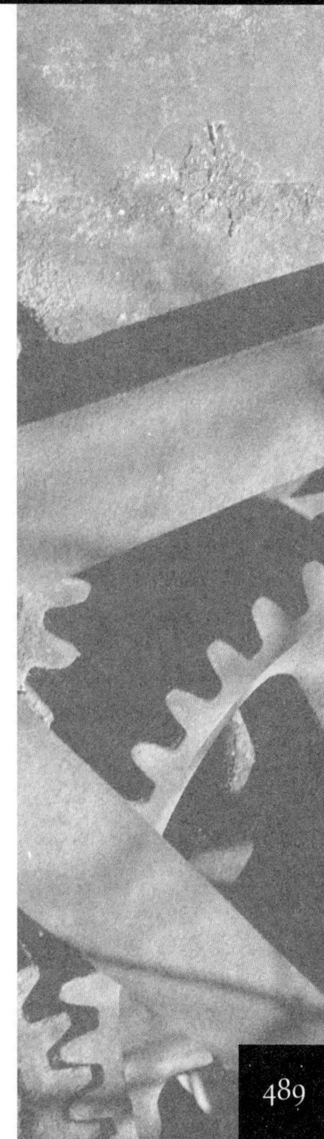

pass a thorough implementation of a data repository. However, because each situation is unique, your organization should tailor the requirements of your data repository to match the needs of your enterprise. You should review each data item to determine whether it is really needed, and ensure that gathering the information does not place an undue burden on the organization. The analysis should also determine whether additional items, not specified in the following table, would be required, or helpful to your Year 2000 project. Once implemented, the functional requirements of the data repository should apply to the entire enterprise.

The entities are

- Hardware platforms
- General application systems information
- Commercial off the shelf (COTS) systems
- Contact information for vendors, contractors, and third-party interfaces
- Module-level information
- Data structures
- Third-party interfaces

The entities have their attributes or characteristics arranged in order of the nine How To 2000 phases.

The following notations are used within the tables:

- C marks the phase of an attribute creation.
- U marks a phase of possible attribute update.
- PK means the primary key of the entity, the field or fields that uniquely describe a single row from another row. Place a constraining index on the primary key to certify uniqueness.
- FK means the foreign key, the field or fields that point or link to a row in another table. Index foreign keys to support queries or searches.
- 1 through 5 are simple scalar values representing from low (1) to high (5). Blank or null represents unknown value. A zero (0) represents none.

Hardware Platforms

This repository element occurs once for each computer host platform or other hardware components (including all hardware possibly affected by noncompliance —phone switches, controllers, security systems, and so on).

Element Description	Planning and Awareness	Inventory	Triage	Detailed Assessment	Resolution	Test Execution	Deployment	Fallout
PK: Hardware name	C							
Hardware location	C							
Hardware use or type (host, server, phone system, security, and so on)	C							
Isolated business unit	C							
Person responsible for platform (hardware administrator)	C							
Notes	C	U	U	U	U	U	U	U
FK: Hardware vendor name		C						
Hardware serial number		C						
Hardware model /version		C						
Compliant model version/ release				C				
Date compliant version available (*mm/dd/yyyy*)				C	U			
Associated software compliance required? (Y/N)				C				
Estimated cost of compliance				C	U			
Component replacement necessary? (Y/N)				C				
Will compliance implementation affect user training? (Y/N)				C	U			
Person responsible for resolution				C	U			
Year 2000 compliance rating (1-5)				C	U	U	U	
Last test anomaly date (*mm/dd/yyyy*)						C		
Date user accepted (*mm/dd/yyyy*)						C		
Date Deployment complete (*mm/dd/yyyy*)							C	

General Application Systems Information

This repository element occurs once for each system or subsystem on each platform.

ELEMENT DESCRIPTION	PLANNING AND AWARENESS	INVENTORY	TRIAGE	DETAILED ASSESSMENT	RESOLUTION	TEST EXECUTION	DEPLOYMENT	FALLOUT
PK, FK: Hardware name (host platform)		C		U				
PK: System (or subsystem) acronym		C						
Version/release number of system		C					U	
System name or description		C						
Isolated business unit owning the system		C	U					
Supported business areas (possible multiple occurrences)		C	U	U				
Future plans for utilization (enhancement, replacement, and so on)		C	U					
Organization responsible for system support		C						
Contact for system support (contact information)		C						
Contact level of expertise with system (1-5)		C		U				
Current documentation level (1-5)		C		U				
Location of documentation		C		U				
Configuration management process used on system		C						
Purpose or functions of system		C		U				
Operating system required by system		C		U				
Primary database architecture		C		U				
Primary language		C		U				
Lines of code		C		U				
Current system date format(s) (possible multiple occurrences)		C	U	U				
System naming standard impacts compliance? (Y/N)		C		U	U			
Survey completed by (contact information)		C						
Technical rate Year 2000 problems (1-5)		C		U	U			
Expected technical severity (1-5)		C		U	U			
Probable failure date (*mm/dd/yyyy*)		C		U	U			
Year 2000 compliance status (1-5)		C	U	U	U	U	U	
Notes		C	U	U	U	U	U	U

Element Description	Planning and Awareness	Inventory	Triage	Detailed Assessment	Resolution	Test Execution	Deployment	Fallout
Probability of Year 2000 business impact (estimated % or 1-5)			C	U				
Expected business severity (1-5)			C	U				
Business probable failure date (*mm/dd/yyyy*)			C	U				
Number of expected users Year 2000			C	U	U			
Days to replace in the event of failure (ROM)			C	U				
System failure impact to business (text)			C	U				
Owning organization priority (1-5)			C	U				
Estimated cost to fix			C	U	U			
Date system must come compliant (*mm/dd/yyyy*)			C	U	U	U		
Priority to fix (1-5)			C	U	U			
Retire system? (Y/N)			C					
Triage decision (Detailed Assessment)? (Y/N)			C					
Access (security) information/limitations				C				
Number of current users				C	U			
Number of internal interfaces				C				
Number of commercial off the shelf packages employed by system				C	U			
Number of third-party interfaces				C	U			
Will compliance affect user training? (Y/N)				C				
Partition name				C	U			
Scheduled date for Resolution (*mm/dd/yyyy*)				C	U	U		
Person responsible for Resolution				C	U	U		
Date user accepted (*mm/dd/yyyy*)						C		
Test anomaly date (*mm/dd/yyyy*)						C		
Date Deployment complete (*mm/dd/yyyy*)							C	
Actual cost of compliance							C	

Commercial Off the Shelf Systems (COTS)

This repository element occurs once for each COTS package on each platform (including operating systems, utilities, sorts, data structures, and so on).

Element Description	Planning and Awareness	Inventory	Triage	Detailed Assessment	Resolution	Test Execution	Deployment	Fallout
PK, FK: Hardware name (host platform)		C		U				
PK: Product name or acronym		C						
Current product version/release		C						
Product use (operating system, sort, data structure, report writer, and so on)		C	U	U				
System description		C						
Isolated business unit owning the system		C	U					
Supported business areas (possible multiple occurrences)		C	U	U				
Future plans for utilization (enhancement, replacement, and so on)		C	U					
FK: Vendor name		C						
Current documentation level (1-5)		C		U				
Location of documentation		C		U				
Purpose or functions of system		C		U				
Operating system required by system		C		U				
Primary database architecture		C		U				
Current system date format(s) (possible multiple occurrences)		C	U	U				
System naming standard impacts compliance? (Y/N)		C		U	U			
Survey completed by (contact information)		C						
Date of license agreement *(mm/dd/yyyy)*		C						
Maintenance agreement covers compliance? (Y/N)		C		U				
Technical rate Year 2000 problems (1-5)		C		U	U			
Expected technical severity (1-5)		C		U	U			
Probable failure date *(mm/dd/yyyy)*		C		U	U			
Customized in-house? (Y/N)		C		U				
Year 2000 compliance status (1-5)		C	U	U	U	U	U	
Notes		C	U	U	U	U	U	U

Element Description	Planning and Awareness	Inventory	Triage	Detailed Assessment	Resolution	Test Execution	Deployment	Fallout
Probability of Year 2000 business impact (estimated % or 1-5)			C	U				
Expected business severity (1-5)			C	U				
Business probable failure date (*mm/dd/yyyy*)			C	U				
Number of expected users Year 2000			C	U	U			
Days to replace in the event of failure (ROM)			C	U				
System failure impact to business (text)			C	U				
Owning organization priority (1-5)			C	U				
Estimated cost to fix			C	U	U			
Date system must come compliant (*mm/dd/yyyy*)			C	U	U	U		
Priority to fix (1-5)			C	U	U			
Retire system? (Y/N)			C					
Triage decision (Detailed Assessment)? (Y/N)			C					
Access (security) information/limitations				C				
Number of current users				C	U			
Number of third-party interfaces				C	U			
Compliant version/release				C	U			
Date compliant version available (*mm/dd/yyyy*)				C	U			
Contract/license location				C				
License agreement summary				C				

Element Description	Planning and Awareness	Inventory	Triage	Detailed Assessment	Resolution	Test Execution	Deployment	Fallout
Date of contract/license (*mm/dd/yyyy*)				C				
Contract/license restrictions				C				
Contract term				C				
Will compliance affect user training? (Y/N)				C				
Partition name				C	U			
Scheduled date for Resolution (*mm/dd/yyyy*)				C	U	U		
Person responsible for Resolution				C	U	U		
Date user accepted (*mm/dd/yyyy*)						C		
Test anomaly date (*mm/dd/yyyy*)						C		
Date Deployment complete (*mm/dd/yyyy*)							C	
Actual cost of compliance							C	

Contact Information for Vendors, Contractors, and Third-Party Interfaces

This repository element occurs once for each product vendor, third-party electronic partner, or company used as outsourcer.

Element Description	Planning and Awareness	Inventory	Triage	Detailed Assessment	Resolution	Test Execution	Deployment	Fallout
PK: Vendor name or contractor company		C						
Type of vendor: product vendor, third-party interface, or service contractor (P/T/S)		C						
Notes		C	U	U	U	U	U	U
Type of contract (contract code)		C						
Web site (URL) of vendor or contractor company				C				
Address of vendor or contractor company				C				
Contact at vendor or contractor company				C				
Phone of contact at vendor or contractor company				C				
E-mail address of contact at vendor or contractor company				C				
Vendor Year 2000 awareness (1-5)				C				

Module-Level Information

This repository element occurs once for each application program, module, parameter file, copybook, procedure, macro, bridge, and so on.

ELEMENT DESCRIPTION	PLANNING AND AWARENESS	INVENTORY	TRIAGE	DETAILED ASSESSMENT	RESOLUTION	TEST EXECUTION	DEPLOYMENT	FALLOUT
PK, FK: Hardware name (host platform)				C				
PK: Path, PDS, or directory name				C				
PK: Module name				C				
FK: System (or subsystem) acronym				C				
Type of module (program, parm, copybook, and so on)				C				
Language type (COBOL, C, Fortran, SQL, and so forth)				C				
Naming standard affecting compliance				C				
Source available? (Y/N)				C	U			
Duplicate modules? (Y/N)				C	U			
Archived module? (Y/N)				C	U			
Number of lines				C				
Compiler/assemble/link editor compliant? (Y/N)				C	U	U		
Object code match? (Y/N)				C	U			
Detailed Assessment priority				C	U			
FK: Name of contractor company				C				
Name of contractor (if contractor developed)				C				
Turnover contact				C				
Number of Year 2000 problems found by category				C	U	U		
Year 2000 solution sets selected				C	U	U		
Development tools to use for Resolution				C	U			
Selected for Resolution? (Y/N)				C	U			
Notes				C	U	U	U	U
Name of person responsible for Resolution					C			
Date of Resolution initiation (*mm/dd/yyyy*)					C			
Date of Resolution completion (*mm/dd/yyyy*)					C			
Will compliance affect user training? (Y/N)					C	U		

Element Description	Planning and Awareness	Inventory	Triage	Detailed Assessment	Resolution	Test Execution	Deployment	Fallout
Person responsible for implementation					C			
Date user accepted (*mm/dd/yyyy*)						C		
Test anomaly date (*mm/dd/yyyy*)						C		
Date Deployment complete (*mm/dd/yyyy*)							C	
Actual cost of compliance							C	

Data Structure

This repository element occurs once for each data structure on a hardware platform.

Element Description	Planning and Awareness	Inventory	Triage	Detailed Assessment	Resolution	Test Execution	Deployment	Fallout
PK, FK: Hardware name (host platform)				C				
PK: Path, PDS, or directory name				C				
PK: File name				C				
FK: System (or subsystem) acronym				C				
Data structure type (flat file, DB2, IDMS, Oracle, Sybase, and so on)				C				
Number of rows or records				C	U			
Naming standard affects compliance				C				
Data structure version/release (if applicable)				C				
Frequency updated (day, month, week, quarter, *ad hoc*)				C	U			
Number of active versions or GDGs (Group Data Generation)				C	U			
Number of inactive versions or GDGs				C	U			
Number of Year 2000 problems found by category				C	U	U		
Year 2000 solution sets selected				C	U	U		
Development tools to use for Resolution				C	U			
Selected for Resolution? (Y/N)				C				
Notes					C	U	U	U
Name of person responsible for Resolution					C			
Date of Resolution initiation (*mm/dd/yyyy*)					C			
Date of Resolution completion (*mm/dd/yyyy*)					C			
Will compliance affect user training? (Y/N)					C			
Person responsible for implementation					C			
Date user accepted (*mm/dd/yyyy*)						C		
Test anomaly date (*mm/dd/yyyy*)						C		
Date Deployment complete (*mm/dd/yyyy*)							C	

Third-Party Interfaces

This repository element occurs once for each external third-party interface (external is defined as those interfaces that your interface manager does not directly control or influence).

Element Description	Planning and Awareness	Inventory	Triage	Detailed Assessment	Resolution	Test Execution	Deployment	Fallout
PK: Name of third-party interface		C		U				
FK: System (or subsystem) acronym		C						
FK: Name of third-party organization		C						
Notes		C	U	U	U	U	U	U
FK: Interface's hardware name (host platform)				C				
FK: Interface's path, PDS, or directory name				C				
FK: Interface's module name				C				
Name of interface standard (ACH, EDI, and so on)				C				
Interface frequency				C	U			
Interface medium (tape, disk, CD, electronic transfer interface device, and so on)				C	U			
Originating party compliant? (Y/N)				C	U	U	U	U
Receiving party compliant? (Y/N)				C	U	U	U	U
Bridge required? (Y/N)				C	U	U		
FK: Bridge's hardware name (host platform)				C				
FK: Bridge's path, PDS, or directory name				C				
FK: Bridge's module name (track bridge status through module)				C				
Planned bridge retirement date (*mm/dd/yyyy*)					C	U	U	U

APPENDIX

H

Integrated Project Plan

The How To 2000 Project Plan is a Microsoft Project format plan that lists each task and deliverable specified in *How To 2000*. You can download the How To 2000 Project Plan from the CD-ROM and tailor it to your Year 2000 project.

Microsoft Project

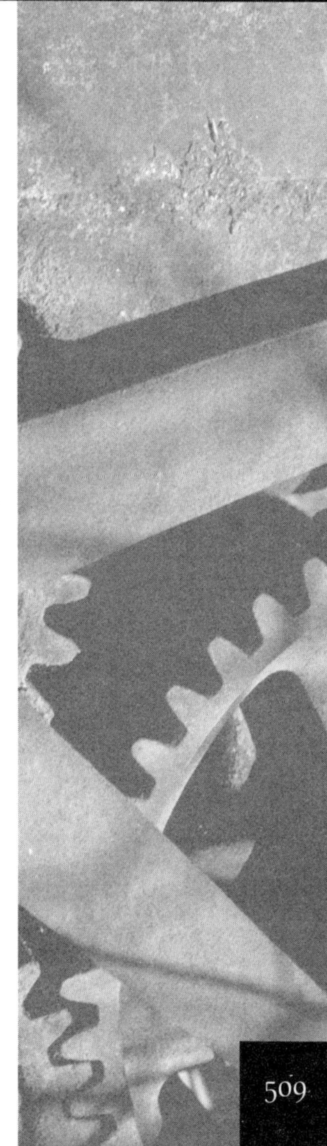

The following discussions assume some familiarity with project control software in general, and Microsoft Project in particular. The How To 2000 Integrated Project Plan was created using Version 4.0 of Microsoft Project, which requires your system to meet or exceed this configuration:

- Microsoft Windows 3.1 or later (Windows for Workgroups 3.11, 95, NT)
- 486/33
- 8MB Memory
- 12MB disk space (to install MS Project)
- 600KB disk space (to install the How To 2000 Project Plan)

Although you may use MS Project to open the file directly from the CD, it is preferable to copy the project file from the CD directly to your hard drive. This will require

approximately 600KB of free space. The How To 2000 Project Plan is in the file HOWTO2K.MPP. Use your preferred method to copy the file from the CD to the appropriate directory on your hard drive or network, start MS Project, and load the file.

The How To 2000 Project Plan lists each task and deliverable as specified in the How To 2000 methodology. The How To 2000 Project Plan specifies the WBS (work breakdown structure), the task name, predecessors, and resources for each task. The GANTT view shows each task and the relation between a task and its predecessors. Using MS Project, you can customize the tasks by adding tasks specific to your project, deleting tasks not required by your project, assigning resources specific to your project, and specifying task durations appropriate for the amount of work required by your project.

MS Project will help you with planning, tracking, and resource allocation. Planning and tracking is easier because MS Project automatically maintains task start and end dates based on the completion of the preceding tasks and the task duration you specify. Once you have tailored the How To 2000 Project Plan to your project, you can see when each task will start and finish.

You can use MS Project to track your Year 2000 project by entering actual start and end dates as each task starts or completes. MS Project will automatically adjust following activities, and report percent complete for each deliverable. If you activate the Schedule Baseline function, you can track deviations from the baseline schedule in both the task tables and the GANTT charts.

MS Project allows you to specify resource allocation by tailoring the human resources assigned to each task. In the How To 2000 Project Plan, resources are specified by job category; however, you can tailor the resources by specifying specific individuals assigned to the project. MS Project will report resource overutilization, and can automatically adjust the schedule to level the resources. MS Project can produce resource charts, graphs, and reports which help track project cost. You can assign a cost per hour for each resource and track actual and projected costs for the entire project.

FIELDS

MS Project allows you to enter dozens of different types of project management data. The How To 2000 Project Plan supplied the following fields in the GANTT Chart view:

- **WBS**: The WBS is a unique identifier of the particular task, deliverable, or phase. The How To 2000 Project Plan uses a work breakdown structure (WBS) type numbering scheme (that is, *X.Y.Z*, where *X* is the phase number, *Y* is the deliverable number, and *Z* is the task number). The WBS IDs in the How To 2000 Project Plan correspond to the number associated with each task in *How To 2000.*
- **Task**: The task is a brief title or description of the task, deliverable, or phase. The task name in the How To 2000 Project Plan corresponds to the name in the *How To 2000* book.
- **Duration**: The duration is intended to represent the number of calendar work days that a task will take to complete. In the How To 2000 Project Plan, all task durations have been set to 1 day. The intent of the How To 2000 Project Plan included with the CD is to provide a template to be used to tailor the plan to your needs. When you customize the project, you need to allocate a realistic duration for each task. Be sure to use the guidelines for phase duration specified in the beginning of each phase description in the *How To 2000* book.
- **Start**: This is an arbitrary start date assigned to each task after MS Project aligns tasks in order (as specified by "Predecessors"). In this template, the assumed project start date is January 1, 1997. Task start dates will be updated automatically by MS Project as you correct the project start date and customize the project by adding or deleting tasks and assigning valid task durations. You can override calculated start dates by entering a firm start date. MS Project tracks planned, actual, and baseline dates.
- **Finish**: This is the date each task is planned to complete, calculated by the start date and the duration (as described earlier).
- **Predecessors**: For each task, the predecessors specify which tasks the current task has a dependency on. The dependency could be Start to Finish (no suffix), Start to Start (SS), Finish to Finish (FF), or offset by a specified

number of days (for example, +5d). Most dependencies in the How To 2000 Project Plan are Start to Finish. Please note that where C depends on B, and B depends on A, we tried to refrain from specifying both B and A as predecessors of C, unless C also had a direct dependency on A.

- **Resources**: The How To 2000 Project Plan specifies job categories in the resources for each task. The specified resources correspond with those specified for each task in the *How To 2000* book. Although MS Project does offer the capability, no attempt was made to specify resource count or resource duration allocations.
- **Who**: A numeric identification of each job category assigned to the task. The Who and Resources fields specify the same data—Who as a number, Resources as a job category.

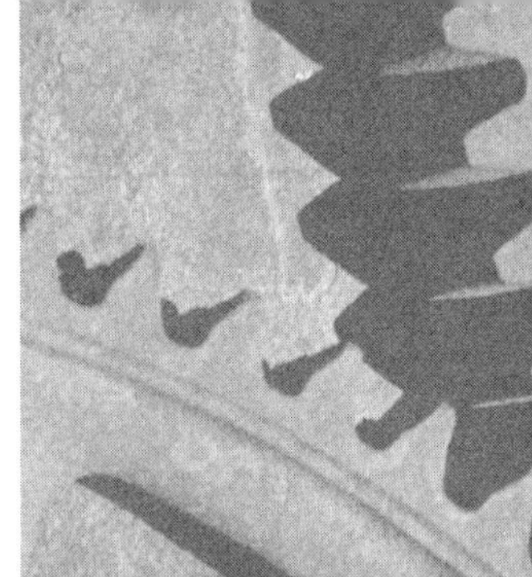

APPENDIX

How To 2000 Risk Management

I

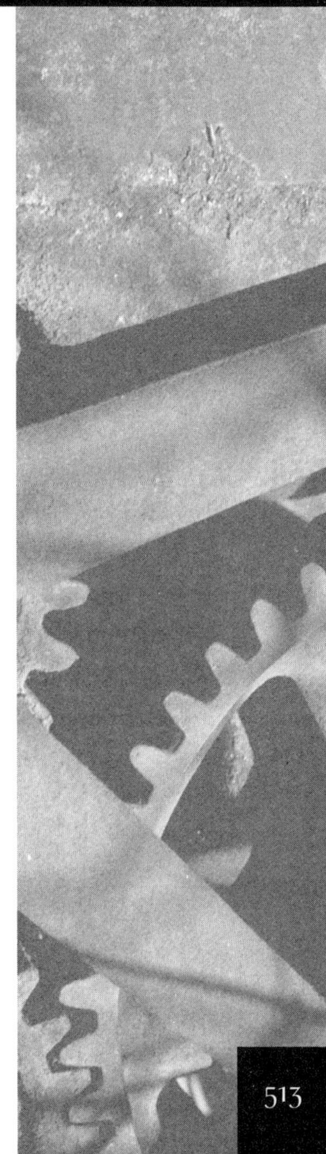

A Year 2000 project is an exercise in risk management. The primary objective of a Year 2000 project manager is to foresee potential difficulties, or risks, resulting from Year 2000 problems and to take steps to avoid these difficulties. To support this objective, this book incorporates a comprehensive approach to the identification, mitigation, and management of Year 2000 risks. This appendix discusses *How To 2000*'s three-pronged approach to risk: an approach that looks at risk from a technical, business, and project standpoint.

Managers in many fields—whether defense contracting, software development, or manufacturing—are becoming increasingly aware of the importance of risk management. Of course, risk management is nothing new. Throughout history, managers have found it useful to anticipate potential calamities (or near calamities), and then take steps to forestall the realization of those calamities. This process of anticipation and circumvention has been formalized in the process of risk management.

As the awareness of the importance of effective risk management has grown, businesses and scholars have created myriad risk management methodologies. These methodologies usually define the essential elements of risk and the procedures that should be used to manage risk. Of course, there is a certain amount of variation among these methodologies. The definition of "risk" differs from one methodology to another, as do the procedures for successful

risk management. This appendix discusses *How To 2000*'s specific approach to and definition of risk management

Risk Definition

This book adopts its definition of risk from William D. Rowe's *An Anatomy of Risk* (John Wiley and Sons, 1977). Rowe characterizes this concept as "the potential for realization of unwanted, negative consequences of an event." An important element of this definition is the notion of *potential*. Risk is associated with an occurrence that *may* happen, but *may not*. Because of the uncertainty associated with a risk situation, probabilistic concepts and tools are often associated with risk.

note

Risk is commonly calculated by determining the probability that a potential negative event will actually occur and factoring that probability by the magnitude of the consequences of that event. Note that risk incorporates two distinct factors: a potential event and the consequences of that event. Due to the probabilistic nature of risk, risk and risk factors are most frequently expressed on a 0 - 1 scale. For example, risk managers would say that the risk associated with a potential event is .2 (relatively low) or .8 (relatively high). The two risk factors are multiplied to determine the risk associated with a given event.

AN EXAMPLE OF MEASURING RISK

If the probability that a hurricane will occur is .2 and the magnitude of the consequences associated with that hurricane can be rated as .99, the risk associated with that hurricane is .198 (.2 x .99 = .198).

In some instances, it may be difficult to assign numeric values to risk factors. There may not be enough information to derive credible numeric values. In these cases, *How To 2000* recommends using Likert scale values. A typical Likert scale includes values such as "Very High," "High," "Medium," "Low," and "Very Low." These values are assigned to various risk factors and risk is determined by blending the values. In the hurricane example, the probability that the hurricane will occur was 20%, a "Low" chance of the hurricane striking. This was factored by a "Very High" rating of the consequences of the hurricane striking. *How To 2000*'s use of the Likert scale arrives at a "Medium" assessment of the overall risk associated with that event.

The Risk Process

How To 2000's approach to risk management relies heavily on the risk methodology developed by Barry W. Boehm (*Software Risk Management: A Tutorial*, IEEE Computer Society Press, 1989). Boehm developed a methodology of risk management that complements his larger Spiral Model of software development. This model has proven to be very influential in both government and industry.

Boehm's risk management process includes two major phases:

- **Risk assessment**: Risk identification, risk analysis, and risk prioritization
- **Risk control**: Risk management planning, risk resolution, and risk monitoring

His approach follows a simple, logical six-step progression.

A SIX-STEP RISK MANAGEMENT PROCESS

1. Identify the potential negative events, or risks, that loom on the horizon.
2. Estimate the two factors that characterize each risk:
   - The probability that each event will occur
   - The magnitude of the consequences of that event

   Use these factors to calculate a numeric or Likert scale value for each risk.
3. Decide which risks are the most important and the least important to your business.
4. Plan what to do to mitigate these risks.
5. Mitigate.
6. Monitor each risk as the project progresses. You may need to reassess these risks periodically.

This book incorporates these six activities in its risk management methodology. The next section identifies the three major types of risks that you will be dealing with throughout your Year 2000 project.

Risk Components of Your Year 2000 Project

In your Year 2000 project, you will be dealing with three types of risk—technical risk, business risk, and project risk. The first two types of risk concern the individual systems that incorporate Year 2000 problems, and the third type of risk concerns the Year 2000 endeavor itself. These three types of risk are defined as follows:

- Technical risk is the risk associated with the technical operation of an individual system (that is, the probability that the system will fail factored by the technical consequences of that failure). To assess technical risk, you must determine which systems are subject to potential operational failure, or may cause the failure of other systems, due to Year 2000–related problems. Also, you must determine the technical consequences, or costs, of the realization of such an operational failure. These determinations will allow you to calculate the technical risk associated with each system.

- Business risk is the risk associated with the successful fulfillment of your business objectives—that is, the probability that a system's Year 2000-related failure will adversely affect your ability to meet business objectives factored by the business consequences of that adverse effect. To assess business risk, you must determine which systems have a probability of Year 2000 failure that consequently will have an impact on your business. In addition, you must determine the magnitude of that impact. These determinations will allow you to measure the business risk associated with each system.
- Project risk is the risk associated with the successful completion of your Year 2000 project—that is, the probability that negative events will occur during the Year 2000 project factored by the consequences of each occurrence. To assess project risk, you must identify events that threaten the successful completion of the Year 2000 project, determine the probability that these negative events will occur, and estimate the magnitude of the impact of each event. You should review project risk and plan mitigating activities at the start of each phase.

Your Year 2000 project is primarily concerned with the mitigation of business risk. Technical risk and project risk gain importance because of their ultimate impact on your business. At the end of the Introduction, there is a Project Benchmark chart citing where business, technical, and project risks should be addressed in your compliance project. The following sections include additional information about the management of each of these types of risk.

Technical Risk

Throughout your Year 2000 project, you will gather information about every system in your organization. The information regarding a specific system will include an assessment of the probability that the system's technical operation will be negatively impacted by one or more Year 2000 problems, as well as an assessment of the magnitude of that impact. These assessments will stem from the expert opinions of information system professionals who have detailed knowledge of the capabilities of each system. The recipients of your system survey will provide the information you need to calculate technical risk.

Technical risk information about each system will be accumulated during the Inventory phase. The determination of technical risk will provide critical input

to the prioritization of your organization's systems that will take place during the Triage phase.

Business Risk

During the Triage phase, you will specify the order in which your organization's systems will be made Year 2000 compliant. More importantly, you will decide which systems will be fixed, and which ones will not. You will base these decisions on analysis of both the technical and business risks associated with each system, although business risk considerations will generally remain more important than technical risk considerations. In fact, your Year 2000 project is primarily concerned with the mitigation of business risk, the probability that the business objectives of your organization will be negatively impacted by a Year 2000–related failure of a given system factored by the magnitude of that impact.

Note that the business risk associated with a certain system may be "Low" even though the technical risk associated with that system is "High." For example, if a given software application incorporates multiple date fields, all of which are not Year 2000 compliant, and the system analyst has determined that these date fields will cause complete system failure in the Year 2000, the technical risk associated with that system would be "High." However, suppose this software application is scheduled to be dropped from use in the near future, and you have already planned to duplicate the functionality that this system provides. In this case, the failure of this system would have minimal impact on your business—that is, the business risk associated with this system would be "Low."

Project Risk

During your Year 2000 project, you will often turn your attention to project risk. Each time you do, you will attempt to:

- Identify the potential negative events that you may face while completing your Year 2000 tasks.
- Assess the probability that each negative event will actually occur.
- Assess the impact of each occurrence.
- Using the assessments of the two risk factors, calculate the risk related to each potential event.

- Identify a method (or methods) of mitigating each risk.
- Identify a method (or methods) of monitoring each risk.

At the outset of the Year 2000 endeavor, you need to consider the overall project risk. What are the potential negative events that you will encounter throughout the entire course of the project? For example, one potential negative event is the failure to obtain adequate personnel resources to accomplish Year 2000 tasks. Based on organizational constraints, you must estimate the probability that this potential event will become a reality. Also, what would be the impact of this failure? How can you track this risk? What can you do to ensure that this potential problem is never realized, or, at the very least, has a less severe impact? This initial assessment includes predicting risks for your entire Year 2000 project. It is the single most important project risk determination of your project. This initial assessment provides the foundation for additional assessments of project risk that take place as you initiate each *How To 2000* phase. Because of the importance of this assessment, the Planning and Awareness phase includes a task that covers this initial project risk determination.

Samples of project risks could include

- Failing to convince senior staff of the importance of the Year 2000 project
- Failing to obtain project funding
- Failing to identify adequate resources to accomplish Year 2000 tasks
- Spending too much time in Planning and Awareness and Inventory
- Starting too late to bring key business systems into compliance

Project risk will be revisited in each *How To 2000* phase. Sections entitled "Phase Risk" contain tables that list a variety of candidate risks. The specific risks you will face will depend upon the characteristics of your organization and your Year 2000 project. It is up to you to review the information in these tables and determine the relevance of the listed risks to your Year 2000 project.

Conclusion

The information about technical risks and business risks that you consider during the Year 2000 project will enable you to make better judgments about the optimal completion of Year 2000 tasks. Periodically appraising project risk will help you anticipate and forestall possible negative events in the course of the Year 2000 project. As always, it is better to foresee and manage risks than to wait until they come to fruition.

APPENDIX

Steps To Prepare Your PC for the Year 2000

J

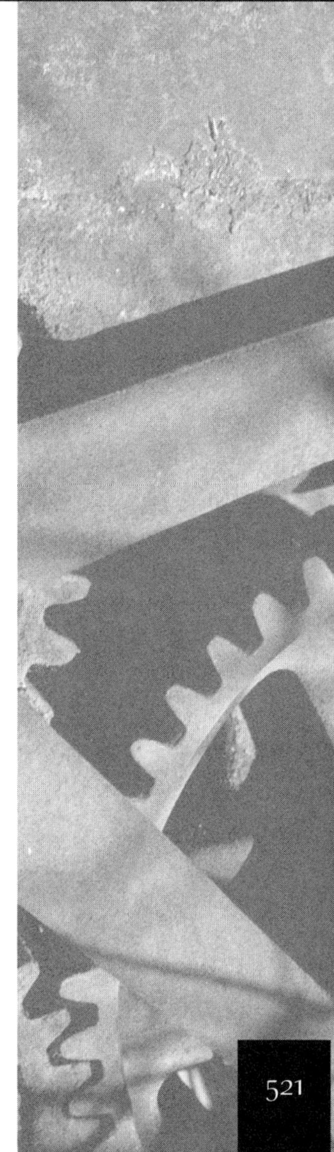

People's workstations are the most widespread and diverse platform to prepare for Year 2000. This appendix covers some of the essential detailed steps for determining whether your Intel-based personal computer (PC) and applications are going to cross smoothly into the next millennium. You should modify this document to cover the standard suite of applications in your business, thoroughly test it, and then disseminate it quickly throughout your business.

This appendix is structured differently than the other appendices in this book because of the large number of applications and operating systems on this platform. It is divided into major areas and then further divided into sections covering each item or application. The major sections cover

- J1: BIOS Firmware Compliance Tests
- J2: Fix Windows Compliance (Windows 3.1*x*, 95, and NT)
- J3: Fix Software Applications Compliance, which covers MS Office (Windows 3.1*x*, 95, and 97), as well as other software applications
- J4: Nonstandard and User-Developed Software Compliance

You do not need to read this appendix from beginning to end. It's best to proceed as follows: First, execute the BIOS tests. Second, skip to the appropriate Windows environment

and make your changes. Third, skip to the appropriate standard Office applications. (Note that different versions of the same application are in different sections and require different modifications.) Finally, read the section about nonstandard applications.

Task J1: BIOS Firmware Compliance Tests

Software necessary to start up your computer is embedded into your hardware. The first tests will determine whether this essential part of your hardware is Year 2000 ready.

There may be a number of side effects that could cause problems even if your system rolls over correctly to the Year 2000. If you have any software (licensed, leased, or demo) that has a time limit, this test could trigger the software to expire and be permanently disabled. This single failure could lead to other failures resulting in a more catastrophic problem such as a nonaccessible machine. There could be other problems like dated security certificates becoming invalid, archive files disappearing, your calendar ignoring or removing important appointments, and so on.

Perform your tests on a test machine if possible. If you are not sure whether you have software with a time limit, you have two options:

1. First boot directly to DOS only from a floppy disk that does not contain a config.sys or autoexec.bat file.
2. Back up your system before executing these tests.

Regardless, it's a good idea to check you have current backups.

Test J1A: Computer Transitions Automatically to Year 2000

1. Go to the DOS prompt.

2. Type **DATE 12-31-1999** at the DOS prompt. (Yes, it should handle 1999!) Press Enter.
3. Type **TIME 23:59:30** at the DOS prompt. Press Enter.
4. Wait for one minute.
5. Type **DATE**, press Enter, and observe whether the date is Sat 01-01-2000.
6. Press Enter again.
7. If the PC fails this test, the computer should *not* be running during the 12-31-1999 transition.
8. Reboot your PC. Either turn the power off and on again, or press the Ctrl, Alt, and Delete keys simultaneously.
9. Type **DATE**, press Enter, and observe whether the date is Sat 01-01-2000.
10. Press Enter again.

If the PC fails this test also, the computer should *not* be running during the 12-31-1999 transition.

Test J1B: If Computer Fails Test J1A, Test for Manual Set DATE

1. Type **DATE 01-01-2000**. Press Enter.
2. Type **DATE**, press Enter, and observe whether the date is Sat 01-01-2000.
3. Press Enter again.
4. Reboot your PC.
5. Type **DATE**, press Enter, and observe whether the date is Sat 01-01-2000.
6. Press Enter again.

If your computer passes these two tests, it should be off during the 12-31-1999 transition.

Manually set the correct date and time upon first boot up of Year 2000.

Test J1C: Leap Year Test

1. Type **DATE 02-29-2000**, and press Enter.
2. Type **DATE**, press Enter, and observe whether the date is Tues. 02-29-2000.

3. Type **DATE 03-01-2000**, and press Enter.
4. Type **DATE**, press Enter, and observe whether the date is Wed 03-01-2000.

   If your computer fails test J1B or J1C, your options are

- Upgrade the BIOS chip. The preferred method is to reload the BIOS instructions; this is possible if you have a "flash BIOS" type. The second method is swapping the chip to an upgraded compliant version from the same manufacturer.
- Upgrade to a new computer.
- Upgrade to Windows NT (Version 3.5.1 or better), which employs a boot routine that self-corrects BIOS settings.

Task J2: Fix Windows Compliance

Applications will continue to use dates that are Year 2000 compliant even if you do not make these changes. However, you risk miscommunication of date-related information until you make these changes. For this reason, it is a good idea to make these changes to these applications, and to their active documents and databases. You should also segregate inactive and unconverted documents, back them up, and remove them from the hard drive.

Making these changes may affect the final display and/or printed output. Preview the screens and reports after completing the changes to each document.

J2A: Windows 3.1*x* Version

1. Open Control Panel by double-clicking the icon.
2. Within Control Panel, open International by double-clicking the icon.
3. Click the Change Button within the Date Format box.
4. Check the Century Box within Short Date Format.
5. Within the Long Date Format pull-down, select a four-digit year.

J2B: Windows 95 Version

1. Open Control Panel and select Regional Settings.
2. Select the Date tab.
3. Change Short Date Style to display all four digits of a year. You can type directly into the pull-down box to create your custom date format. For example, MMM/dd/yyyy would look like Aug/02/1997.
4. If Long Date does not already have four digits, change it also.

J2C: Windows NT Version

1. Open Control Panel and select Regional Settings.
2. Select the Date tab.
3. Change Short Date Style to display all four digits of a year. You can type directly into the pull-down box to create your custom date format. For example, MMM/dd/yyyy would look like Aug/02/1997.
4. If Long Date does not already have four digits, change it also.

Task J3: Fix Software Applications Compliance

You must have changed the generic Windows environment before making the changes described here.

J3A: MS Office Windows 3.1*x* Version

The following activities will fix the versions of Microsoft Word, Excel, PowerPoint, Project, and Access commonly associated with Windows 3.1*x*. Note that these versions could also be installed on a Windows 95 platform.

Activity J3A1: Microsoft Word Version 6.0x General

There are no generic changes to make.

Activity J3A2: Microsoft Word Documents

1. Open each MS Word document.
2. You have to fix header or footers if 19 was hard coded in front of the date.
3. Pull down the File menu and select Page Setup.
4. Select the Header/Footer tab.
5. Select Custom Header or Custom Footer if 19&[Date] appears in either the header or footer.
6. Delete the 19.

Activity J3A3: Microsoft Excel Version 5.0x General

1. Open MS Excel or an MS Excel document.
2. Pull down the Tools menu and select Options.
3. Select Tab Module General.
4. Within the International box, pull-down Language/Country and select English/Custom.

Activity J3A4: Microsoft Excel Documents

1. Open each MS Excel document.
2. Select a Date field, column, or row on the spreadsheet.
3. Pull down the Format menu and select Cell.
4. Select the Number tab.
5. Choose Date under Category.
6. Select or create a date format that contains a four-digit year. For example, you can type **yyyy/mm/dd** in the Code field as a valid date format.
7. You have to fix headers or footers if 19&[Date] was hard coded.

7a. Pull down the File menu and select Page Setup.

7b. Select the Header/Footer tab.

7c. Select Custom Header or Custom Footer if 19&[Date] appears in either the header or footer.

7d. Delete the 19.

8. You have to fix formulas or macros that have century evaluated as 19.

Activity J3A5: Microsoft PowerPoint Version 4.0x General

There are no generic changes to make.

Activity J3A6: Microsoft PowerPoint Documents

Date fields are usually found on the master slide. Instructions follow for that scenario.

1. Open each PowerPoint document.
2. Pull down the View menu, select Master, and then select Slide Master.
3. Select (highlight) the date field.
4. Pull down the Insert menu and select Date/Time.
5. Select a date field with four digits.

Activity J3A7: Microsoft Project Version 4.0x General

1. Open MS Project or an MS Project document.
2. Pull down the Tools menu and select Options.
3. Select Tab View.
4. Pull down Date Format and select a format with a four-digit year.
5. Select Tab Module General.
6. Within the International box, pull down Language/Country and select English/Custom.

Activity J3A8: Microsoft Project Documents (Optional)

1. Open each MS Project document.
2. Pull down the Format menu and select Layout.
3. Pull down Date Format for Bars.
4. Select a date format that contains a four-digit year.

Activity J3A9: Microsoft Access Version 2.0x General

There are no generic changes to make.

Activity J3A10: Microsoft Access Databases

You should back up each database before proceeding.

1. Open each MS Access document.
2. Select the Table tab.
3. For each Table:

3a. Select Design.

3b. Review the Data Type column; look for DATE fields.

3c. Modify Medium Date to Short Date (Yes. Short shows four digits; Medium does not!)

4. Select the Query tab.
5. For each Query:

5a. Select Design.

5b. Review column Criteria, and look for prompt text that displays the date format.

5c. Modify the prompt text to show the Short Date format (yyyy/mm/dd).

6. Select the Form tab.
7. For each Form:

7a. Select Design.

7b. Pull down the View menu and select Properties.

7c. Select and review each date field on the form; look for Format of Medium Date.

7d. Modify Format to Short Date.

8. Select the Report tab.
9. For each Report:

9a. Select Design.

9b. Pull down the View menu and select Properties.

9c. Select and review each date field on the report; look for Format of Medium Date.

9d. Modify Format to Short Date.

Macros and modules are beyond the scope of this book. Call a programmer if you need help with these items.

J3B: MS Office 95

The following activities will fix the versions of Microsoft Word, Excel, PowerPoint, Project, and Access commonly associated with Windows 95 and the Office 95 suite. Note that these versions could also be installed on a Windows NT platform.

Activity J3B1: Microsoft Word General

There are no generic changes to make.

note **We have not found a way to fix the default date format.**

Activity J3B2: Microsoft Word Documents

You can fix the format for any embedded dates, including those in header/footers.

1. Open each MS Word document.
2. Select (highlight) the date field.
3. Pull down the Insert menu and select Date and Time.
4. Select a date format with four digits.
5. Pull down the View menu and select Header and Footer.
6. Select (highlight) the date field.
7. Pull down the Insert menu and select Date and Time.
8. Select a date format with four digits.

Activity J3B3: Microsoft Excel General

There are no generic changes to make.

Activity J3B4: Microsoft Excel Documents

1. Open each MS Excel document.
2. Select a Date field, column, or row on the spreadsheet.
3. Pull down menu item Format and select Cell.
4. Select Number tab.
5. Select Custom under Category.

6. Select or create a date format that contains a four-digit year. For example, you can type **yyyy/mm/dd** in the Code field as a valid date format.
7. You have to fix Header or Footers if 19&[Date] was hard coded.

7a. Pull down the File menu and select Page Setup.

7b. Select the Header/Footer tab.

7c. Select Custom Header or Custom Footer if 19&[Date] appears in either the header or footer.

7d. Delete the 19.

8. You have to fix formulas or macros that have a century evaluated as 19.

Activity J3B5: Microsoft PowerPoint General

There are no generic changes to make.

Activity J3B6: Microsoft PowerPoint Documents

Date fields are usually found on the master slide. Instructions follow for that scenario.

1. Open each MS PowerPoint document.
2. Pull down the View menu, select Master, and then select Slide Master.
3. Select (highlight) the date field.
4. Pull down the Insert menu and select Date/Time.
5. Select a date field with four digits.

Activity J3B7: Microsoft Project General

1. Open MS Project or an MS Project document.
2. Pull down the Tools menu and select Options.
3. Select Tab View.
4. Pull down Date Format and select a format with a four-digit year.

Activity J3B8: Microsoft Project Documents (Optional)

1. Open each MS Project document.
2. Pull down the Format menu and select Layout.

3. Pull down Date Format for Bars.
4. Select a date format that contains a four-digit year.

Activity J3B9: Microsoft Access General

There are no generic changes to make.

Activity J3B10: Microsoft Access Databases

You should back up each database before proceeding.

1. Open each MS Access document.
2. Select the Table tab.
3. For each Table:

3a. Select Design.

3b. Review Data Type column; look for DATE fields.

3c. Modify Medium Date to Short Date (Yes. Short shows four digits; Medium does not!)

4. Select the Query tab.
5. For each Query:

5a. Select Design.

5b. Review column Criteria; look for prompt text that displays the date format.

5c. Modify the prompt text to show the Short Date format (yyyy/mm/dd).

6. Select the Form tab.
7. For each Form:

7a. Select Design.

7b. Pull down the View menu and select Properties.

7c. Select and review each date field on the form; look for Format of Medium Date.

7d. Modify Format to Short Date.

8. Select the Report tab.
9. For each Report:

9a. Select Design.

9b. Pull down the View menu and select Properties.

9c. Select and review each date field on the report; look for Format of Medium Date.

9d. Modify Format to Short Date.

Macros and modules are beyond the scope of this document. Call a programmer if you need help with these items.

J3C: MS Office 97

The following activities will fix the versions of Microsoft Word, Excel, PowerPoint, and Access commonly associated with Windows 95/NT and the Office 97 suite.

Activity J3C1: Microsoft Word General

1. Open a new document.
2. Pull down the Insert menu and select Date and Time.
3. Click the Default button.
4. Click the Yes button to indicate that you want to change the default to match your compliant format.
5. Click the OK button.
6. Close this document without saving it.

The default Date for your headers and footers will now be correct!

Activity J3C2: Microsoft Word Documents

You can fix the format for any embedded dates.

1. Open each MS Word document.
2. Select (highlight) the date field.
3. Pull down Insert and select DATE-TIME.
4. Select a date format with four digits.

Activity J3C3: Microsoft Excel General

There are no generic changes to make.

Activity J3C4: Microsoft Excel Documents

1. Open each MS Excel document.
2. Select a Date field, column, or row on the spreadsheet.
3. Pull down the Format menu and select Cell.
4. Select the Number tab.
5. Select Custom under Category.
6. Select or create a date format that contains a four-digit year. For example, you can type **yyyy/mm/dd** in the Code field as a valid date format.
7. You have to fix headers or footers if 19&[Date] was hard coded.

7a. Pull down the File menu and select Page Setup.

7b. Select the Header/Footer tab.

7c. Select Custom Header or Custom Footer if 19&[Date] appears in either the header or footer.

7d. Delete the 19.

8. You have to fix formulas or macros that have century evaluated as 19.

Activity J3C5: Microsoft PowerPoint General

There are no generic changes to make.

Activity J3C6: Microsoft PowerPoint Documents

Date fields are usually found on the master slide. Instructions follow for that scenario.

1. Open each MS PowerPoint document.
2. Pull down the View menu, select Master, and then select Slide Master.
3. Select (highlight) the date field.
4. Pull down the Insert item and select Date and Time.
5. Select a date field with four digits.

Activity J3C7: Microsoft Access General

There are no generic changes to make.

Activity J3C8: Microsoft Access Databases

You should back up each database before proceeding.

1. Open each MS Access document.
2. Select the Table tab.
3. For each Table:

3a. Select Design.

3b. Review Data Type column; look for DATE fields.

3c. Modify Medium Date to Short Date. (Yes. Short shows four digits; Medium does not!)

4. Select the Query tab.
5. For each Query:

5a. Select Design.

5b. Review column Criteria; look for prompt text that displays a date format.

5c. Modify the prompt text to show the Short Date format (yyyy/mm/dd).

6. Select the Form tab.
7. For each Form:

7a. Select Design.

7b. Pull down the View menu and select Properties.

7c. Select and review each date field on the form; look for Format of Medium Date.

7d. Modify Format to Short Date.

8. Select the Report tab.
9. For each Report:

9a. Select Design.

9b. Pull down the View menu and select Properties.

9c. Select and review each date field on the report; look for Format of Medium Date.

9d. Modify Format to Short Date.

Macros and modules are beyond the scope of this book. Call a programmer if you need help with these items.

J3D: Other Software Applications

Besides the standard suite of applications, other company-approved software could be installed on your machine. Please check the following software items.

Activity J3D1: Netscape Version 3.0 and Web Usage in General

There are no generic changes to make.

Assuring that your World Wide Web browsers (Netscape, MS Explorer, and so on) are Year 2000 compliant only addresses part of your exposure to Web-based problems. The additional issues, described next, need to be handled procedurally within your organization.

Dynamically Run Downloads

Web browsers routinely download and run programs dynamically as part of Web page functionality. Typically, these programs are treated as plug-ins or self-executing applications (for example, Java applets, JavaScript, C-based programs) by your Web browsers. Although some Web-based languages have attempted to address century date handling, no universal standard has been applied to either the applications, languages, or technical architectures. You may experience Year 2000 date-related problems from these "downloaded" programs. You cannot control or standardize date handling for the entire World Wide Web. This book recommends that you identify and correct issues supported by your staff and set standards of intranet-based applications. In addition, you should identify business uses of the World Wide Web that may be affected and find alternatives to meet those business needs in case a failure occurs outside the scope of your control.

Downloading Programs

You may experience Year 2000-related issues from Web-based downloads. These utilities, demos, databases, and other executables infrequently offer guarantees against Year 2000 anomalies. Set standards in your organization for allowable use of Web-based downloads. Pay particular attention to macros and utilities that could provide short-term problem resolution but cause long-term issues.

Activity J3D2: Other Company Standard Software

1. Expand this document pertaining to your environment and applications used.

Task J4: Nonstandard and User-Developed Software Compliance

These questions will help you and your users determine the viability of other software packages and systems not covered by the preceding tasks.

Activity J4A: Is the Software Still Being Used?

If not, back it up then remove it from the PC.

Activity J4B: Is the Software Really Necessary for the Timely Performance of My Job?

If not, back it up then remove it from the PC.

Activity J4C: Is There Another Method That Is Year 2000 Compliant or Company Standard?

If so, now is the time to determine the best method to make the conversion.

Activity J4D: Is It Business Critical?

- Can I justify the expense of fixing, testing, fixing, upgrading, and deploying a Year 2000–compliant version?
- Can I justify the associated risks involved?
- Can I determine a contingency plan if it fails before it can be fixed?

Please report nonstandard business critical applications that require attention.

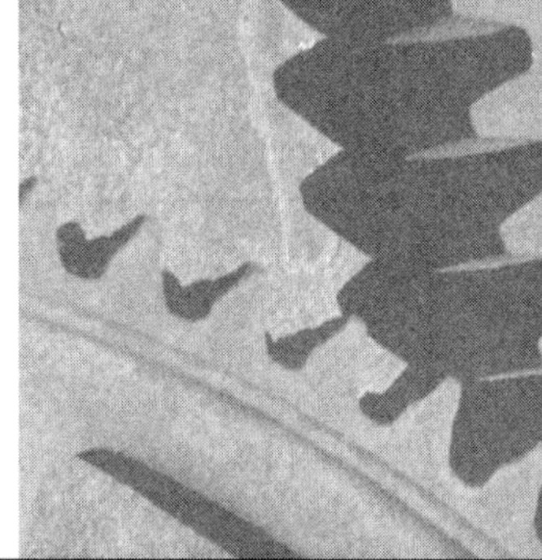

APPENDIX K

What's on the CD-ROM?

The compact disc (CD-ROM) that accompanies *How To 2000* contains a variety of electronic files that can help you "jump start" some of your crucial tasks. This appendix describes the contents of the CD-ROM.

The CD-ROM contains the following folders:

- \Acrobat
- \Book
- \Present
- \ProjPlan
- \Repos
- \Web

The contents of each folder are discussed below.

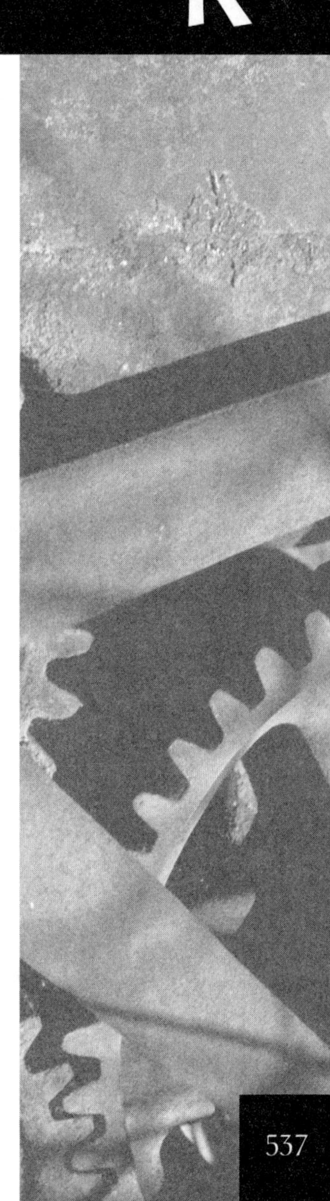

Acrobat: Acrobat Reader

The `Acrobat` folder contains the Adobe Acrobat Reader software. Acrobat Reader is a helpful program that will enable you to view the electronic version of this book in the same page format as the actual book.

To install and run Adobe Acrobat Reader and view the electronic version of this book, follow these steps:

1. Start Windows Explorer (if you're using Windows 95), Windows NT Explorer (if you're using Windows NT), or File Manager (if you're using Windows 3.1), and then open the `Windows 95` folder or `Windows 3.1` folder (if you're using Windows 3.1) on the CD-ROM.
2. In the `Windows 95` folder, double-click `ar32e301.exe` and follow the instructions presented onscreen for installing Adobe Acrobat Reader. (In the `Windows 3.1` folder, double-click `ar16e301.exe` and follow the instructions.)

Book: Electronic Version of *How To 2000*

The `Book` folder contains an electronic version of the *How To 2000* book. To view the electronic version of the book with the Adobe Acrobat Reader, follow these steps:

1. Start Windows Explorer (if you're using Windows 95), Windows NT Explorer (if you're using Windows NT), or File Manager (if you're using Windows 3.1) and open the `Book` folder on the CD-ROM.
2. In the `Book` folder, double-click the chapter or appendix file you want to view. All documents in this folder end with a `.pdf` extension.

Note: To copy the electronic version of the book onto your hard drive, select the `Book` folder in Windows Explorer or File Manager and copy and paste the file into a folder on your hard drive.

ProjPlan: The How To 2000 Project Plan

The `ProjPlan` folder contains a detailed schedule template for completing Year 2000 Project deliverables and tasks. The Project Plan includes task, deliverables, and milestones. See Appendix H for more information on the Project Plan. The file name is `howto2k.mpp`. To access this file you need Microsoft Project version 4.0.

The How To 2000 Project Plan (the ProjPlan Directory)

Here's how to access the How To 2000 Project Plan:

1. Launch Microsoft Project.
2. From the File menu, choose Open.
3. From the File Open dialog box, double-click the drive letter that corresponds to your CD-ROM drive.
4. From the folders shown, double-click `ProjPlan`.
5. Double-click the file named `howto2k.mpp`.
6. The File Open dialog box will be replaced by the main application window as the Year 2000 Project Plan is displayed.

Repos: Year 2000 Project Repository Template

The `Repos` folder contains a template for each of the tables that are included in a typical Year 2000 Project repository. The file name is `howto2k.mdb`. To access this file you need Microsoft Access.

The Year 2000 Repository file includes the following tables:

Table Name	*Table Contents*
COTS	Commercial-off-the-shelf systems
Data	Data structures
Hardware	Hardware platforms
Interfaces	Third-party interfaces
Modules	Module-level information
Systems	General systems information
Vendors	Contact information for vendors, contractors, and third-party interfaces

Year 2000 Project Repository Template (the Repos Directory)

Here's how to access the Year 2000 Project Repository Template:

1. Launch Microsoft Access.
2. From the File menu, choose Open.
3. From the File Open dialog box, double-click the drive letter that corresponds to your CD-ROM drive.
4. From the folders shown, double-click `Repos`.
5. Double-click the file named `howto2k.mdb`.
6. The File Open dialog box will be replaced by the main database window that contains the titles of the tables and forms that comprise the Year 2000 Project repository.
7. From the database window, click the Tables button.
8. The table names are listed. Click the Design button at the top of the window to display a description of a specific table.

Present: Year 2000 Project Presentations

The `Present` folder includes seven files containing electronic slides that support a variety of Year 2000 Project presentations. You need Microsoft PowerPoint version 4.0 to access the presentation files listed in the following table.

File	*Name of Presentation*	*Contents of Presentation*
`y2overvw.ppt`	A Brief Overview	Brief, very high-level view of the Year 2000 problem and *How To 2000*
`y2aware.ppt`	General Awareness	More detailed look at the Year 2000 problem, *How To 2000*, and recommended team responsibilities
`y2prbsol.ppt`	Technical Problems and Solutions	A look at specific Year 2000 problems and corresponding solutions

FILE	NAME OF PRESENTATION	CONTENTS OF PRESENTATION
`y2mgmtbr.ppt`	Detailed Management Briefing	A briefing for mid-level managers that summarizes the problem, risks, goals, and tasks of a typical Year 2000 project
`y2trade.ppt`	Trade Show	Variable time frame; a high-graphic, low-text overview of *How To 2000* for use at trade shows and other marketing events
`y2senior.ppt`	Senior Management Briefing	A short and to-the-point summary of Year 2000 project activities and budget milestones
`y2triage.ppt`	Triage Briefing	A summary of information obtained during the Inventory phase and support for planning Detailed Assessment phase tasks

Year 2000 Project Presentations (the Present Directory)

Here's how to access the Year 2000 Project Presentations:

1. Launch Microsoft PowerPoint.
2. From the File menu, choose Open.
3. From the File Open dialog box, double-click the drive letter that corresponds to your CD-ROM drive.
4. From the folders shown, double-click Present.
5. Double-click a specific file name.
6. The Open File dialog box will be replaced by the main application window as a specific presentation is displayed.

Web: World Wide Web Bookmarks for Year 2000 Information

The `Web` folder contains a Web page that includes bookmarks (electronic links) to over 300 Web sites dealing with Year 2000 topics. The file name is `howto2k.htm`. You can access the file with any Internet browser (for example, Netscape, Windows Internet Explorer, and so on).

World Wide Web Bookmarks for Year 2000 Information (the Web Directory)

Here's how to access the Web Bookmarks for Year 2000 Information:

1. Launch your browser.
2. From the File menu, choose Open.
3. From the File Open dialog box, double-click the drive letter that corresponds to your CD-ROM drive.
4. From the directories shown, double-click `Web`.
5. Double-click the file named `howto2k.htm`.
6. The File Open dialog box will be replaced by the How To 2000 Web page with electronic bookmarks.
7. Click a specific bookmark to access Year 2000 information described in the bookmark text.

Read This Before Using the CD-ROM

By opening the CD-ROM packaging, you agree to be bound by the following: The software, templates, databases, project plans, and material on this CD-ROM are copyrighted and all copyrights are reserved by Raytheon E-Systems, the publisher, and its licensers. You are licensed to use this material and software on a single computer. You may copy the material or software for backup and archival purposes only. Making copies of this material for any other purpose is a violation of United States copyright laws. THIS SOFTWARE AND MATERIAL ARE SOLD AS

IS, WITHOUT WARRANTY OF ANY KIND, EITHER EXPRESSED OF IMPLIED, INCLUDING BUT NOT LIMITED TO THE IMPLIED WARRANTIES OF MERCHANTABILITY AND FITNESS FOR A PARTICULAR PURPOSE. Neither Raytheon E-Systems, the publisher, nor their dealers and distributors nor its licensers assume any liability for any alleged or actual damages arising from the use of this material or software. (Some states do not allow exclusion of implied warranties, so the exclusion may not apply to you.) The entire contents of this disc and the compilation of materials and software are copyrighted and protected by the United States copyright laws. Any individual programs on the disc are copyrighted by the authors and owners of each program. Each program has its own use permissions and limitations. To use each program, you must follow the individual requirements and restrictions detailed for each. Do not use a program if you do not agree to follow its licensing agreement.

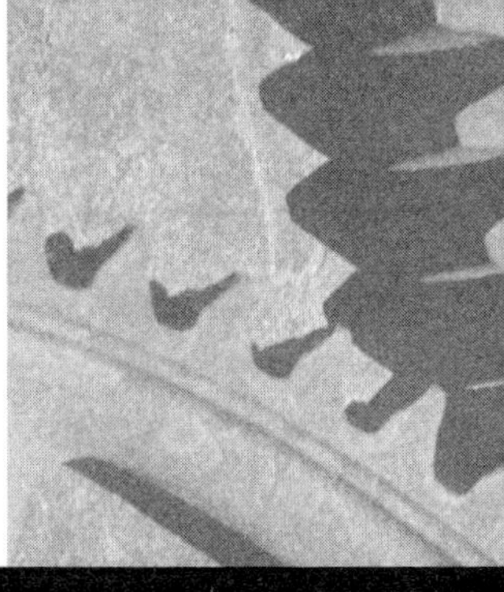

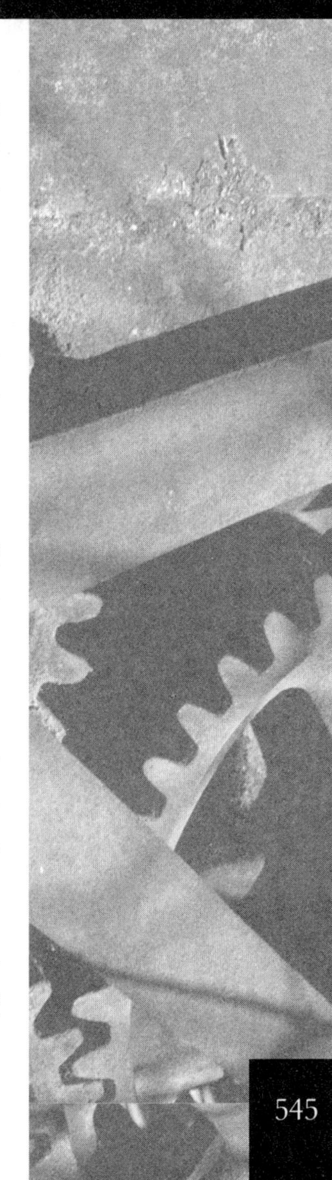

acceptance test procedure

The step-by-step written instructions with expected results for the tests that are necessary to demonstrate the capability of a system to the satisfaction of the user, customer, or business partner.

anomaly

Any deviation from requirements, expected or desired behavior, or performance of the software (from IEEE STD 1074-1991).

application or system partitioning

The process of defining individual systems among a group of systems and ensuring that each system has clearly discernable boundaries.

assessment strategy

Systematic approach for the identification of individual Year 2000 problems in a specific system that will yield a rough-order-of-magnitude estimate of Year 2000 impact on a system.

attribute

Any detail that serves to qualify, identify, classify, quantify, or express the state of an entity. A property or characteristic of one or more entries.

awareness strategy

Systematic approach to the promotion of Year 2000 awareness within your organization.

baseline

1. An inventory of objects (that is, program elements, documentation, and so on) and their relationships captured at a given moment in time.
2. Configuration identification at a preselected point in time.
3. A specification or product that has been formally reviewed and agreed upon that, thereafter, serves as the basis for further development and can be changed only through formal change control procedures (IEEE-STD-60).

baseline inventory

Initial inventory of system data.

benchmark

A standard against which measurements or comparisons can be made (IEEE-STD-610).

bridge

A permanent or temporary module whose purpose is to convert data on one side of an interface so that it is compatible with what is expected on the other side of the interface. For the Year 2000 project, bridges provide the needed conversions when only one side of an interface is Year 2000 compliant or when the updated interfaces implement conflicting Year 2000 solutions.

CASE

Computer-Aided Systems (or Software) Engineering is the combination of graphical, dictionary, generator, project management, and other software tools to assist the computer development staff in engineering and maintaining high-quality systems for their end users, within the framework of a structured method.

change request (CR)

A method for users to report system problems and to request resolution of those problems or desired system enhancements.

code editors

Software tools that allow users to modify source code or other text files. Year 2000 code editors are usually integrated with data repositories, and allow you to skip from one inventoried date occurrence to another. You can examine the code around the date occurrence and insert a standard correction, perform a manual update, skip the occurrence, or flag the occurrence for later attention.

code parsers

Code parsers are similar to code scanners, except that parsers are designed to understand how data (specifically date data) are used, and can trace variable usage through assignments, calculations, and sometimes even renames or storage overlap usage. Code parsers often are integrated with a data repository and can interactively let you offer the operator a chance to update the date usage instances found. *See* Appendix E, "Applicability of Tools," for more information about code parsers.

code scanners

Tools that examine code for any of a set of user-specified keywords. Code scanners are generally simple search engines that look through the list of files provided by the operator for a list of keywords, phrases, or other user-specified patterns. The tools generally produce a report identifying the file and the location within the file of each occurrence found. When the code scanner is integrated with a data repository, the code scanner generally examines inventoried files, and then updates the data repository with detailed keyword occurrence information. *See* Appendix E, "Applicability of Tools," for more information about code scanners.

compliance

1. A functional definition: Year 2000–compliant systems:

- Accept, process, calculate, sort, store, display, and report dates using the correct century and year
- Interface with other Year 2000–compliant systems
- Automatically cross into the Year 2000 without date-related failures
- Do not cause premature expiration of security systems, licenses, or files due to Year 2000 crossover
- Treat the Year 2000 as a leap year

Note: Some organizations require full two-digit to four-digit system and data conversions. In this case, the following applies: A system is completely compliant if all century dates are expressed in four-digit format. A system is partially compliant if some or all century dates are expressed in a format that does not incorporate four digits.

2. The federal definition: Federal Acquisition Regulation (FAR), Part 39.002, published in Federal Acquisition Circular (FAC) 90-45. "Year 2000 compliant means information technology that accurately processes date/time data (including, but not limited to, calculating, comparing, and sequencing) from, into, and between the twentieth and twenty-first centuries, and the years 1999 and 2000 and leap year calculations. Furthermore, Year 2000–compliant information technology, when used in combination with other information technology, shall accurately process date/time data if the other information technology properly exchanges date/time data with it."
3. Standards:

- ANSI X3.30-1985 (R1991):
  - For Calendar Date and Ordinal Date for Information Interchange
  - ANSI X3L8 standard X3-30, Nov-1996 'ccyymmdd'
  - IRS adopted
- National Institute of Standards and Technology (NIST):
  - FIPS 4-1 Federal Standard number 6 'yyyymmdd'
  - Working on Julian as 'yyyyddd'
- ANSI X3.51-1994 Information Systems:
  - For Universal Time, Local Time Differentials, and United States Time Zone References for Information Interchange
- ISO 8601:1988 Data elements and interchange formats:
  - Information interchange—Representation of dates and times

concept of operations

A system description that incorporates a high-level view of the functionality of a specific system within its operational environment.

configuration control board (CCB)

A group of people that meet to review, discuss, and approve/disapprove proposed changes to systems under their control.

configuration item

Any component of an automated system placed under change control. A software component, hardware component, system requirements specification, system design specification, system support document, or any other artifact of an automated system that has been placed under formal configuration management. Configuration item information that is stored in support of system management needs generally includes data items such as production date, version number, person making modifications, and so on.

configuration management (CM)

A discipline applying technical and administrative direction and surveillance to identify and document functional and physical characteristics of a hardware configuration item or computer software configuration item; control changes to those characteristics; record and report change processing and implementation status; and verify compliance with specified requirements (IEEE-STD-610).

configuration management (CM) tools

Software tools that support the management and coordination of changes to a selected set of automated system components. CM software tools typically store information regarding each modification of various system components. CM tools also identify the generation of various versions of system components. *See* Appendix E, "Applicability of Tools," for more information about configuration management tools.

consolidated software development record (C-SDR)

A document that consolidates descriptive information concerning the development or maintenance of a software system, including the Software Project Plan, the Software Requirements Specification, the Software Design Specification, the Software Test Plans, and so on.

Correction stage

Second of two How To 2000 stages; includes the Resolution, Test Planning, Test Execution, Deployment, and Fallout phases.

cost-of-work estimating tools

Software tools, spreadsheets, or methodologies that predict how much work will be needed to ensure the compliance of systems included in a Year 2000 project. *See* Appendix E, "Applicability of Tools," for more information about cost estimating tools.

COTS

Commercial Off The Shelf. An item that is purchased from an outside vendor and that is not customized, or is only minimally customized.

critical design review (CDR)

A formal review of the design of a specific system for the purpose of determining completeness and accuracy. Conducted when the detailed design is essentially complete. Ensures that all requirements have been accurately depicted in the completed system design.

custom systems

Automated systems built to provide one or more functions unique to an organization. Usually "one of a kind" systems built internally within an organization. Viewed as the opposite of a COTS system.

D&O insurance

Directors and Officers liability insurance. *See* Appendix C for a discussion of Year 2000 liability.

data approach

Long-term compliance approach in which files, programs, and control language constructs using a two-digit date format (*yy*) are converted into a four-digit format (*yyyy*). More time-consuming and expensive than logic approach. Also referred to as field expansion.

data conversion tools

Software tools that convert stored data from one format, storage media, or encoding to another. COTS tools support data conversions to a limited degree. For example, most COTS database packages include software to convert from other database package vendor formats into a native format and conversion from one record layout into another.

data dictionary

1. A comprehensive description of the data elements incorporated within a specific database.
2. A database for holding definitions of the tables, columns, and views that pertain to a specific database.

data flow diagram (DFD)

A graphical approach for describing the information flow characteristics within a system. Used in conjunction with the structured software design approach originally developed by Edward Yourdon and supplemented by Tom DeMarco.

data repository

A database created to store and track all system information gathered during your Year 2000 project. *See* Appendix G, "Year 2000 Repository," for a description of the types of data to be held in a data repository, and Appendix E, "Applicability of Tools," for more information about data repositories.

data structure diagram

A diagram representing data relationships.

database administrator (DBA)

The individual responsible for the functional integrity of a database system. Tasks include ensuring the quality of data and controlling user access to the database.

date simulator

A date simulator allows you to specify the date to be returned to the software that is retrieving the date from operating system resources. This will help you validate updated systems. However, because a large proportion of Year 2000 failures are in

the data and interfaces, a date simulator may not validate a significant portion of the updates. A date simulator should be used for both prime Year 2000 tests of dates and for regression tests.

debuggers

Software tools that facilitate the identification of errors in software system source code. These tools allow software developers to examine variables and memory locations, stop code execution at predefined points, step through the code one line or unit at a time, and so on. Debuggers can operate in batch, online, and fully interactive environments. Debugging tools are not generally Year 2000 specific but are occasionally integrated with Year 2000 tool sets. *See* Appendix E, "Applicability of Tools," for more information about debuggers.

deliverable

A specific, defined, and measurable result of work that is required to be created and usually delivered to an organization or repository. Deliverables include items such as hardware and software configuration items, design specifications, requirements specifications, product data files, plans, and documentation. *See also* work product.

Deployment (phase 8)

Period in which efforts focus on placing Year 2000 compliant systems into production.

Detailed Assessment (phase 4)

Period in which efforts focus on: (a) identification of individual Year 2000 problems within specific systems, and (b) identification of appropriate solutions to those problems.

Detection stage

The first of two How To 2000 stages (the other is correction). The Detection stage includes four phases: Planning and Awareness, Inventory, Triage, and Detailed Assessment.

draft

An unapproved, unsigned, and unreleased version, usually of a document.

electronic partner

An external organization that interacts electronically with one or more of your organization's automated systems. Typically, data is exchanged by fixed, predefined, and formatted messages or files.

embedded system

Computer programs, instructions, or functions implemented and integrated as part of a hardware system. Includes programs or instructions that are stored permanently in programmable, read-only memory (PROM), and constitute a fundamental part of system hardware. *See also* EPROM, PROM.

Enterprise Schematic

A diagram or table identifying each major automated entity, and the electronic or data interface between each automated entity.

entity

A person, place, or thing of interest to the user community about which the system is to maintain, correlate, and display information.

entity relationship diagram (ERD)

A diagram that pictorially represents entities, the vital business relationships between them, and the attributes used to describe them. The process of creating this diagram is called entity modeling.

EPROM

Erasable programmable read-only memory. A hardware component that stores software to control the hardware, and is capable of being reprogrammed. These components may have embedded date logic as a resident function. *See also* embedded systems, firmware, and PROM.

executable manipulation tools

Software tools that allow software developers to modify an object or executable file, as opposed to modifying and recompiling a source code file. Executable manipulation tools are minimally helpful when you do not have the source code that corresponds to the executable that must be modified. *See* executable manipu-

lation, disassemblers, and executable manipulation, patch, for a definition of two executable manipulation tools. *See* Appendix E, "Applicability of Tools," for more information about executable manipulation tools.

executable manipulation, disassemblers

Software tools that will produce assembly code from executables. The assembly code produced will generally not have labels, variable names, or comments, making it difficult to manipulate. Nevertheless, with enough effort, your staff can understand and modify the assembly code, making it Year 2000 compliant.

executable manipulation, patch

Software tools that can be used to make small modifications to an executable without requiring the source code or executable generation tools, such as a linker. The technical staff must possess a detailed understanding of the executable, including patch insertion points and data area usage.

Fallout (phase 9)

Period in which efforts focus on: (a) supporting the continued operation of the deployed system and handling errors, (b) addressing customer service issues, arising from newly deployed systems, (c) managing and remove bridges and patches implemented as part of the correction cycle, and (d) revisiting any lessons learned on system deployments to simplify future deployments.

firmware

Computer programs, instructions, or functions implemented in hardware. Such programs or instructions—stored permanently in programmable, read-only memory—constitute a fundamental part of system hardware. *See also* embedded system, EPROM, PROM.

function

1. A specific purpose of an entity or its characteristic action (IEEE STD 1074-1991).
2. A set of related actions, undertaken by individuals or tools that are specifically assigned or fitted for their roles, to accomplish a set purpose or end (CMU/SEI-93-TR-25).

impact assessment

The analysis of potential results of a particular action (or inaction).

implementation strategy

The overall approach to providing a Year 2000–compliant system. An implementation strategy provides general guidelines for an implementation approach taking into account cost, schedule, risk, quality, and production requirements.

information services (IS)

The unit within an organization whose goal is to achieve integrated planning and implementation of data processing, network, and telecommunication systems developed for administrative support.

Initial Project Plan

The first comprehensive plan for the conduct of the Year 2000 project, created during the Planning and Awareness phase.

Integrated Project Plan

A proposed schedule for the conduct of a Year 2000 project, including a comprehensive list of tasks and a timetable for completion of each task. The How To 2000 Integrated Project Plan is provided on CD-ROM with the methodology.

integration testing

Testing of two or more previously tested and accepted entities (for example, partitions, group of integrated partitions, subsystems, and so on) to show that they work as required when combined into a single entity.

interface

1. A connection between two automated systems.
2. The hardware and software needed to enable one device to communicate with another.

interface simulators

Software tools that will send scripted data to your system or respond to system outputs with scripted data. Interface simulators come in a variety of configura-

tions, from resident software that simulates the system input and output to complete, external packages that are wired to your system in the same way that the simulated interface connects to your system. *See* Appendix E, "Applicability of Tools," for more information about interface simulators.

Inventory (phase 2)

The process of identifying each automated system within an organization and collecting system information relevant to Year 2000 project activities.

isolated business unit

An organizational unit whose interfaces with other units are limited due to budgetary, organizational, functional, physical, or security boundaries.

leap year

Years that include 366 rather than 365 days. In the Gregorian calendar, those years are divisible by 4, but exclude centesimal years not divisible by 400 (for example, the Year 2000 is divisible by 400 and will be a leap year; the year 2100 is not divisible by 400 and will not be a leap year).

life cycle

A set of standardized activities, organized by specific phases, by which system development or maintenance is accomplished.

logic approach

A compliance approach involving retention of a two-digit year format (*yy*) and modification of date processing logic to correctly interpret dates following Dec. 31, 1999. Typically allows up to a 100-year date span to be processed by a system. Also referred to as procedural approach, field interpretation, and windowing. *See also* Appendix B, "Solution Sets."

management information systems (MIS)

Software systems designed to support the information needs of managers within a given organization. Can include such systems as payroll, personnel, and inventory control.

milestone

A designated point in time on a project schedule that coincides with the completion of a set of tasks required to produce a project deliverable. Evaluating milestone completion provides a measurement of the progress of the project.

parallel test

A test of the new system and new processes in conjunction with the execution of the old system and old processes. Differences and similarities between the two environments can then be examined. A validation of a new system and/or processes by running the updated system against live data and interfaces and running along with (in parallel with) the existing production system. Results of the new system can then be compared to the results of the existing, known system to reveal errors or validate the update.

partition

A system with clearly defined boundaries that is treated as a unit for the purpose of assessment, resolution, testing, and deployment within the Year 2000 process. An individual partition is an arbitrarily sized set of hardware and software components defined by a set of functional, technical, and/or business criteria appropriate to Year 2000 project needs.

Planning and Awareness (phase 1)

Period in which efforts focus on promoting Year 2000 awareness at all levels across the organization and creating plans (that is, budgets and schedules) for the completion of Year 2000 project tasks. Includes identifying points of contact; gathering information throughout the organization, industry, and so on; and establishing communication channels and processes to be used throughout Year 2000 resolution efforts.

problem report

Form used to report mainframe and microcomputer application software, network, and hardware problems.

program element

1. A uniquely named software item invoked during execution. Some examples of program elements include source code, subroutines, scripts, parameter data files, procedures, and screens.
2. A subelement of code, which can only be used by one program, that is controlled under the program element. (It should be so documented in the code also.) If a subelement (for example, copybooks) cannot be used or reused by different programs, it is a separate program element.

Project Management Plan

Defines the organization's overall strategy for the successful completion of Year 2000 project tasks. Addresses Year 2000 goals and supporting objectives. Includes certification and accreditation processes, cost/benefit analyses, performance measures, management approaches, responsibilities, configuration management, and more.

PROM

Programmable read-only memory. A hardware component containing control information that is not capable of being reprogrammed after being initially loaded. These components may have embedded date logic as a resident function. *See also* embedded systems, EPROM, and firmware.

prototyping

A technique for demonstrating a partial or total implementation of a developing system in order to evaluate the system. Prototyping is often used to determine or refine system requirements.

redevelopment

The modification of a system, either on its existing platform, or on a new platform (such as client/server) to improve some factor of the system's performance, such as its processing time, human machine interface, or maintainability.

repair

Modifying a system to meet Year 2000 compliance requirements.

replacement

Insertion of a different (presumably new) automated system in place of an existing system. In Year 2000 projects, replacement generally refers to replacing an existing COTS product with a functionally similar but Year 2000–compliant product.

Resolution (phase 5)

Period in which efforts focus on the repair, replacement, or retirement of systems in your organization that incorporate Year 2000 problems.

resolution strategy

Systematic approach designed to ensure the efficient completion of repair, replacement, and retirement tasks that take place within the Resolution phase.

reverse engineering tools

Software tools that facilitate the re-creation of software system components that fail to correspond to existing related components. Year 2000 developers may have to reverse engineer software components that are out of date, or that simply cannot be located. These components can include system requirements, system designs, source code modules, and so on. *See* Appendix E, "Applicability of Tools," for more information about reverse engineering tools.

rough order of magnitude (ROM)

A quick estimate, usually given after minimal research. Also called a "ballpark figure." (ROM also refers to "read-only memory.")

script playback tools

Software tools that allow you to define specific tests that can be executed repeatedly, as necessary. Scripting software is often used for performing and repeating regression tests to ensure that system modifications do not adversely affect unrelated system functions. *See* Appendix E, "Applicability of Tools," for more information about script playback tools.

Software Engineering Institute (SEI)

A software engineering research organization that operates under the auspices of Carnegie Mellon University and is largely funded by the U.S. Department of Defense.

software inventory tools

Software tools that support the generation of system inventory. Inventory tools typically seek and identify such system components as source code modules, JCL, databases, control files, and so on. *See* Appendix E, "Applicability of Tools," for more information about software inventory tools.

software quality assurance (SQA)

The process of ensuring that the software development process yields products of acceptable quality. Largely a process of control and auditing. SQA's role in software development is to ensure by audit that the software process adheres to designated standards.

software requirements review (SRR)

A formal review of a developing system's functional and nonfunctional requirements in order to evaluate the completeness and accuracy of the requirements set.

straw man

A rough cut or first draft—so named because everybody gets a chance to poke, punch, and knock it down.

system

By necessity, a very general and "context sensitive" term. The *IEEE Standard Glossary of Software Engineering Terminology* defines system as "a collection of components organized to accomplish a specific function or set of functions." It also defines a subsystem as "a secondary or subordinate system within a larger system." MIL-STD-498 (5 Dec. 1994) tries to deal with the potential ambiguity as follows:

1. A network of interdependent components that work together to try to accomplish the aim of the system (W. Edwards Demming).

2. A collection of components organized to accomplish a specific function or set of functions (IEEE-STD-610).

task

Activities undertaken to complete a How To 2000 deliverable. How To 2000 incorporates a hierarchical work breakdown structure: work is broken down by phase, then by deliverable, and finally by task.

Test Execution (phase 7)

Period in which efforts focus on executing and documenting the formal acceptance testing of those systems included in the Year 2000 project.

Test Planning (phase 6)

Period in which efforts focus on planning and getting ready for the formal testing of those systems included in the Year 2000 project.

test strategy

The high-level approach to designing and carrying out system tests. The test strategy will provide the high-level approach to testing, accommodating requirements such as schedule, availability of interfaces, availability of resources, system risk and customer requirements.

testing phase

Period in which efforts are focused on testing, certification, and accreditation of systems for Year 2000 compliance.

third party

An organization that is not a primary member of a business relationship but is in a relationship with one of the primary members in a way that can affect the primary business relationship. For example, Company X provides developed software to Company Y (primary relationship). Company X obtains software from Company T (third party) that is necessary for them to support Company Y. Therefore, noncompliance of Company T will affect Company Y even though there is not a direct business relationship between them.

Triage (phase 3)

The phase in which your organization makes critical decisions about the inclusion of specific systems in your Year 2000 project. These decisions are based on reviews of the technical risks and business risks associated with each automated system. Systems critical to the business are assigned a place in the Detailed Assessment Plan, are assessed, and, if necessary, corrected later. Noncritical systems are not included in Year 2000 efforts or are the focus of delayed efforts. Some organizations revisit Triage decisions throughout their Year 2000 project.

unit

A single item or a collection of items that performs a particular function. A software unit is typically a single module or program and can include called libraries or programs. The unit definition will vary depending on whether the system is written in Ada, C, COBOL, or another language.

unit testing

Developer-level testing. Tests each program unit.

URL

Uniform resource locator. The address for an Internet Web site, generally beginning: http://. For example, the *How To 2000* Web site URL is `http://www.howto2000.com/`.

user interface

The component of a system that allows the user to communicate with the system. A software system's graphical user interface (GUI) includes the graphically designed screens that appear on a monitor and allow users to input information, receive information, and control the functionality of the system.

validation

1. The process of evaluating software during, or at the end of, the development process to determine whether it satisfies the specified requirements (IEEE-STD-610).
2. The process of questioning whether the right product is being built.

verification

1. The process of evaluating software to determine whether the products of a given development phase satisfy the conditions imposed at the start of that phase (IEEE-STD-610).
2. The process of questioning whether the product is being built correctly.

walkthrough

A technical review of a new or modified program or system design, code, or unit test. The review is conducted by such interested parties as programmers, system analysts, users, and/or auditors. Program walkthroughs are conducted by peer programmers to detect program errors. A walkthrough is a situation in which people play "devil's advocate" in reviewing another person's or team's effort.

work product

A specific, defined, and measurable result of work that is required to be created and usually delivered to an organization or repository. Work products include items such as hardware and software configuration items, design specifications, requirements, product data files, plans, and documentation. *See also* deliverable.

Year 2000 repository

Collection of all Year 2000 project information, including deliverables, system information, and project management information.

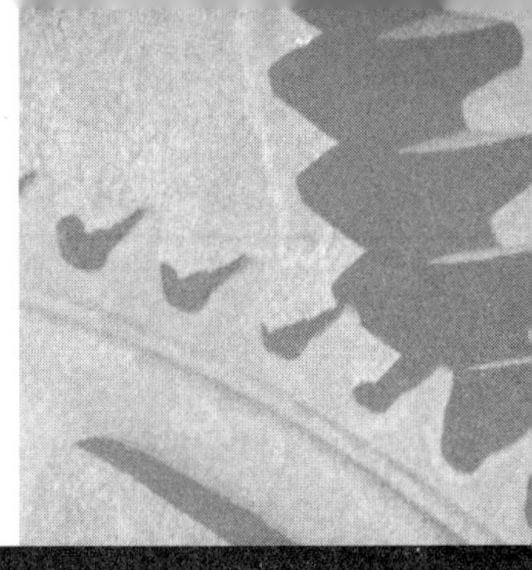

Index

A

B

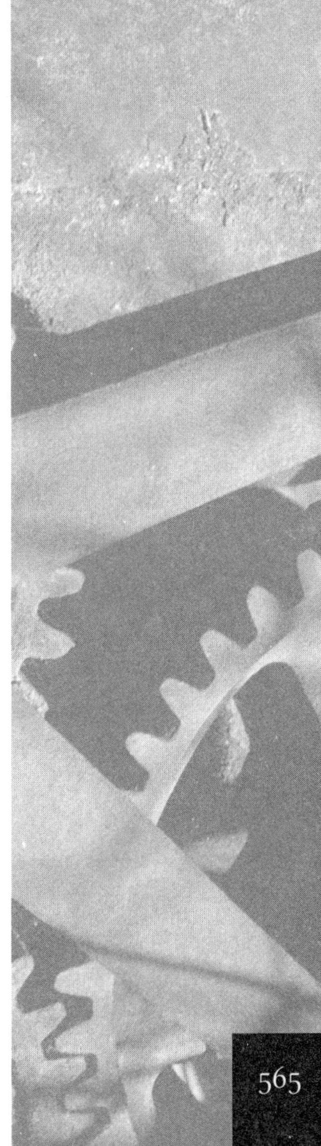

C

(continued)

D

(continued)

E

M

N

O

P

(continued)

Q

R

S

(continued)

T

(continued)

(continued)

U

V

(continued)

W

Y

IDG BOOKS WORLDWIDE, INC. END-USER LICENSE AGREEMENT

Read This. You should carefully read these terms and conditions before opening the software packet(s) included with this book ("Book"). This is a license agreement ("Agreement") between you and IDG Books Worldwide, Inc. ("IDGB"). By opening the accompanying software packet(s), you acknowledge that you have read and accept the following terms and conditions. If you do not agree and do not want to be bound by such terms and conditions, promptly return the Book and the unopened software packet(s) to the place you obtained them for a full refund.

1. **License Grant.** IDGB grants to you (either an individual or entity) a nonexclusive license to use one copy of the enclosed software program(s) (collectively, the "Software") solely for your own personal or business purposes on a single computer (whether a standard computer or a workstation component of a multiuser network). The Software is in use on a computer when it is loaded into temporary memory (i.e., RAM) or installed into permanent memory (e.g., hard disk, CD-ROM, or other storage device). IDGB reserves all rights not expressly granted herein.
2. **Ownership.** IDGB is the owner of all right, title, and interest, including copyright, in and to the compilation of the Software recorded on the disk(s)/CD-ROM. Copyright to the individual programs on the disk(s)/CD-ROM is owned by the author or other authorized copyright owner of each program. Ownership of the Software and all proprietary rights relating thereto remain with IDGB and its licensors.
3. **Restrictions on Use and Transfer.**

   (a) You may only (i) make one copy of the Software for backup or archival purposes, or (ii) transfer the Software to a single hard disk, provided that you keep the original for backup or archival purposes. You may not (i) rent or lease the Software, (ii) copy or reproduce the Software through a LAN or other network system or through any computer subscriber system or bulletin-board system, or (iii) modify, adapt, or create derivative works based on the Software.

   (b) You may not reverse engineer, decompile, or disassemble the Software. You may transfer the Software and user documentation on

a permanent basis, provided that the transferee agrees to accept the terms and conditions of this Agreement and you retain no copies. If the Software is an update or has been updated, any transfer must include the most recent update and all prior versions.

4. **Restrictions on Use of Individual Programs.** You must follow the individual requirements and restrictions detailed for each individual program in Appendix K "What's on the CD-ROM?" These limitations are contained in the individual license agreements recorded on the disk(s)/CD-ROM. These restrictions may include a requirement that after using the program for the period of time specified in its text, the user must pay a registration fee or discontinue use. By opening the Software packet(s), you will be agreeing to abide by the licenses and restrictions for these individual programs. None of the material on this disk(s) or listed in this Book may ever be distributed, in original or modified form, for commercial purposes.

5. **Limited Warranty.**

(a) IDGB warrants that the Software and disk(s)/CD-ROM are free from defects in materials and workmanship under normal use for a period of sixty (60) days from the date of purchase of this Book. If IDGB receives notification within the warranty period of defects in materials or workmanship, IDGB will replace the defective disk(s)/CD-ROM.

(b) IDGB AND THE AUTHOR OF THE BOOK DISCLAIM ALL OTHER WARRANTIES, EXPRESS OR IMPLIED, INCLUDING WITHOUT LIMITATION IMPLIED WARRANTIES OF MERCHANTABILITY AND FITNESS FOR A PARTICULAR PURPOSE, WITH RESPECT TO THE SOFTWARE, THE PROGRAMS, THE SOURCE CODE CONTAINED THEREIN, AND/OR THE TECHNIQUES DESCRIBED IN THIS BOOK. IDGB DOES NOT WARRANT THAT THE FUNCTIONS CONTAINED IN THE SOFTWARE WILL MEET YOUR REQUIREMENTS OR THAT THE OPERATION OF THE SOFTWARE WILL BE ERROR FREE.

(c) This limited warranty gives you specific legal rights, and you may have other rights which vary from jurisdiction to jurisdiction.

6. **Remedies.**

   (a) IDGB's entire liability and your exclusive remedy for defects in materials and workmanship shall be limited to replacement of the Software, which may be returned to IDGB with a copy of your receipt at the following address: Disk Fulfillment Department, Attn: How To 2000, IDG Books Worldwide, Inc., 7260 Shadeland Station, Ste. 100, Indianapolis, IN 46256, or call 1-800-762-2974. Please allow 3-4 weeks for delivery. This Limited Warranty is void if failure of the Software has resulted from accident, abuse, or misapplication. Any replacement Software will be warranted for the remainder of the original warranty period or thirty (30) days, whichever is longer.

   (b) In no event shall IDGB or the author be liable for any damages whatsoever (including without limitation damages for loss of business profits, business interruption, loss of business information, or any other pecuniary loss) arising from the use of or inability to use the Book or the Software, even if IDGB has been advised of the possibility of such damages.

   (c) Because some jurisdictions do not allow the exclusion or limitation of liability for consequential or incidental damages, the above limitation or exclusion may not apply to you.

7. **U.S. Government Restricted Rights.** Use, duplication, or disclosure of the Software by the U.S. Government is subject to restrictions stated in paragraph (c) (1) (ii) of the Rights in Technical Data and Computer Software clause of DFARS 252.227-7013, and in subparagraphs (a) through (d) of the Commercial Computer—Restricted Rights clause at FAR 52.227-19, and in similar clauses in the NASA FAR supplement, when applicable.

8. **General.** This Agreement constitutes the entire understanding of the parties and revokes and supersedes all prior agreements, oral or written, between them and may not be modified or amended except in a writing signed by both parties hereto which specifically refers to this Agreement. This Agreement shall take precedence over any other documents that may be in conflict herewith. If any one or more provisions contained in this Agreement are held by any court or tribunal to be invalid, illegal, or otherwise unenforceable, each and every other provision shall remain in full force and effect.

CD-ROM Installation Instructions

The following instructions guide you through the steps of installing Adobe Acrobat Reader and viewing the electronic version of the *How To 2000* book.

Installing Adobe Acrobat Reader

The Adobe Acrobat Reader is a helpful program that will enable you to view the electronic version of this book in the same page format as the actual book.

To install and run Adobe Acrobat Reader and view the electronic version of this book, follow these steps:

1. Start Windows Explorer (if you're using Windows 95), Windows NT Explorer (if you're using Windows NT), or File Manager (if you're using Windows 3.1), and then open the `Acrobat` folder on the CD-ROM.
2. Open either the `Windows95` folder (if you're using Windows 95 or Windows NT) or `Windows31` folder (if you're using Windows 3.1).
3. Double-click `ar32e301.exe` (for Windows 95 or Windows NT) or `ae16e301` (for Windows 3.1) and follow the instructions presented onscreen for installing Adobe Acrobat Reader.

Viewing the Adobe Acrobat Version of *How To 2000*

To view the electronic version of the book after you have installed Adobe Acrobat Reader, follow these steps:

1. Start Windows Explorer (if you're using Windows 95), Windows NT Explorer (if you're using Windows NT), or File Manager (if you're using Windows 3.1), and open the `Book` folder on the CD-ROM.
2. In the `Book` folder, double-click the chapter or appendix file you want to view. All documents in this folder end with a `.pdf` extension.

Note: To copy the electronic version of the book onto your hard drive, select the `Book` folder in Windows Explorer and copy and paste the file into a folder on your hard drive.

Please see Appendix K, "What's on the CD-ROM?," for instructions on installing other useful files you'll find on the disc that accompanies this book.